The firstwriter.com
Writers' Handbook
2020

The firstwriter.com

Writers' Handbook

2020

EDITOR
J. PAUL DYSON

Published in 2019 by JP&A Dyson
27 Old Gloucester Street, London WC1N 3AX, United Kingdom
Copyright JP&A Dyson

https://www.jpandadyson.com
https://www.firstwriter.com

ISBN 978-1-909935-28-0

Registered with the IP Rights Office
Copyright Registration Service
Ref: 3145762129

Foreword

The firstwriter.com Writers' Handbook returns for its 2020 edition with over 1,300 listings of literary agents, publishers, and magazines, updated in firstwriter.com's online databases between 2017 and 2019, including revised and updated listings from the previous edition and over 30% new entries.

Previous editions of this handbook have been bought by writers across the United States, Canada, and Europe; and ranked in the United Kingdom as the number one bestselling writing and publishing directory on Amazon. The 2020 edition continues this international outlook, giving writers all over the English-speaking world access to the global publishing markets.

The handbook also provides free online access to the entire current firstwriter.com databases, including over 2,400 magazines, over 2,500 literary agents and agencies, over 2,000 book publishers that don't charge fees, and constantly updated listings of current writing competitions, with typically more than 50 added each month.

For details on how to claim your free access please see the back of this book.

Included in the subscription

A subscription to the full website is not only free with this book, but comes packed with all the following features:

Advanced search features

- Save searches and save time – set up to 15 search parameters specific to your work, save them, and then access the search results with a single click whenever you log in. You can even save multiple different searches if you have different types of work you are looking to place.
- Add personal notes to listings, visible only to you and fully searchable – helping you to organise your actions.
- Set reminders on listings to notify you when to submit your work, when to follow up, when to expect a reply, or any other custom action.
- Track which listings you've viewed and when, to help you organise your search – any listings which have changed since you last viewed them will be highlighted for your attention.

Daily email updates

As a subscriber you will be able to take advantage of our email alert service, meaning you can specify your particular interests and we'll send you automatic email updates when we change or add a listing that matches them. So if you're interested in agents dealing in romantic fiction

---

in the United States you can have us send you emails with the latest updates about them – keeping you up to date without even having to log in.

User feedback

Our agent, publisher, and magazine databases all include a user feedback feature that allows our subscribers to leave feedback on each listing – giving you not only the chance to have your say about the markets you contact, but giving a unique authors' perspective on the listings.

Save on copyright protection fees

If you're sending your work away to publishers, competitions, or literary agents, it's vital that you first protect your copyright. As a subscriber to firstwriter.com you can do this through our site and save 10% on the copyright registration fees normally payable for protecting your work internationally through the Intellectual Property Rights Office (https://www.Copyright RegistrationService.com).

Monthly newsletter

When you subscribe to firstwriter.com you also receive our monthly email newsletter – described by one publishing company as "the best in the business" – including articles, news, and interviews for writers. And the best part is that you can continue to receive the newsletter even after you stop your paid subscription – at no cost!

For details on how to claim your free access please see the back of this book.

Contents

Publishers

Free Access

Glossary of Terms

This section explains common terms used in this handbook, and in the publishing industry more generally.

Academic

Listings in this book will be marked as targeting the academic market only if they publish material of an academic nature; e.g. academic theses, scientific papers, etc. The term is not used to indicate publications that publish general material aimed at people who happen to be in academia, or who are described as academic by virtue of being educated.

Adult

In publishing, "adult" simply refers to books that are aimed at adults, as opposed to books that are aimed at children, or young adults, etc. It is not a euphemism for pornographic or erotic content. Nor does it necessarily refer to content which is unsuitable for children; it is just not targeted at them. In this book, most ordinary mainstream publishers will be described as "adult", unless their books are specifically targeted at other groups (such as children, professionals, etc.).

Advance

Advances are up-front payments made by traditional publishers to authors, which are off-set against future royalties.

Agented

An *agented* submission is one which is submitted by a literary agent. If a publisher accepts only *agented* submissions then you will need a literary agent to submit the work on your behalf.

Author bio

A brief description of you and your life – normally in relation to your writing activity, but if intended for publication (particularly in magazines) may be broader in scope. May be similar to *Curriculum Vitae* (CV) or résumé, depending on context.

Bio

See *Author bio*.

Curriculum Vitae

A brief description of you, your qualifications, and accomplishments – normally in this context in relation to writing (any previous publications, or awards, etc.), but in the case of nonfiction proposals may also include relevant experience that qualifies you to write on the subject. Commonly abbreviated to "CV". May also be referred to as a résumé. May be similar to *Author bio*, depending on context.

CV

See *Curriculum Vitae*.

International Reply Coupon

When submitting material overseas you may be required to enclose *International Reply Coupons*, which will enable the recipient to send a response and/or return your material at your cost. Not applicable/available in all countries, so check with your local Post Office for more information.

IRC
See *International Reply Coupon.*

Manuscript
Your complete piece of work – be it a novel, short story, or article, etc. – will be referred to as your manuscript. Commonly abbreviated to "ms" (singular) or "mss" (plural).

MS
See *Manuscript.*

MSS
See *Manuscript.*

Professional
Listings in this book will be marked as targeting the professional market if they publish material serving a particular profession: e.g. legal journals, medical journals, etc. The term is not used to indicate publications that publish general material aimed at a notional "professional class".

Proposal
A proposal is normally requested for nonfiction projects (where the book may not yet have been completed, or even begun). Proposals can consist of a number of components, such as an outline, table of contents, CV, marketing information, etc. but the exact requirements will vary from one publisher to another.

Query
Many agents and publishers will prefer to receive a query in the first instance, rather than your full *manuscript*. A query will typically consist of a cover letter accompanied by a *synopsis* and/or sample chapter(s). Specific requirements will vary, however, so always check on a case by case basis.

Recommendation
If an agent is only accepting approaches by recommendation this means that they will only consider your work if it comes with a recommendation from an established professional in the industry, or an existing client.

RoW
Rest of world.

SAE
See *Stamped Addressed Envelope.* Can also be referred to as SASE.

SASE
Self-Addressed Stamped Envelope. Variation of SAE. See *Stamped Addressed Envelope.*

Simultaneous submission
A simultaneous submission is one which is sent to more than one market at the same time. Normally you will be sending your work to numerous different magazines, agents, and publishers at the same time, but some demand the right to consider it exclusively – i.e. they don't accept simultaneous submissions.

Stamped Addressed Envelope
Commonly abbreviated to "SAE". Can also be referred to as Self-Addressed Stamped Envelope, or SASE. When supplying an SAE, ensure that the envelope and postage is adequate for a reply or the return of your material, as required. If you are submitting overseas, remember that postage from your own country will not be accepted, and you may need to provide an *International Reply Coupon.*

Synopsis
A short outline of your story. This should cover all the main characters and events, including the ending. It is not the kind of "teaser" found on a book's back cover. The length of synopsis required can vary, but is generally between one and three pages.

TOC
Table of Contents. These are often requested as part of nonfiction proposals.

Unagented
An unagented submission is one which is not submitted through a literary agent. If a publisher accepts unagented submissions then you can approach them directly.

Unsolicited mss

A manuscript which has not been requested. Many agents and publishers will not accept unsolicited mss, but this does not necessarily mean they are closed to approaches – many will prefer to receive a short *query* in the first instance. If they like the idea, they will request the full work, which will then be a solicited manuscript.

Youth

The term "Youth" in this book is used to indicate the Young Adult market.

*Claim your free access to **www.firstwriter.com**: See p.383*

The Writer's Roadmap

With most objectives in life, people recognise that there is a path to follow. Whether it is career progression, developing a relationship, or chasing your dreams, we normally understand that there are foundations to lay and baby steps to take before we'll be ready for the main event.

But for some reason, with writing (perhaps because so much of the journey of a writer happens in private, behind closed doors), people often overlook the process involved. They often have a plan of action which runs something like this:

1.   Write novel.

2.   Get novel published.

This is a bit like having a plan for success in tennis which runs:

1.   Buy tennis racket.

2.   Win Wimbledon.

It misses out all the practice that is going to be required; the competing in the minor competitions and the learning of the craft that will be needed in order to succeed in the major events; the time that will need to be spent gaining reputation and experience.

In this roadmap we'll be laying out what we think is the best path to follow to try and give yourself the best shot of success in the world of writing. You don't necessarily have to jump through all the hoops, and there will always be people who, like Pop Idol or reality TV contestants, get a lucky break that propels them to stardom without laying any of the foundations laid out below, but the aim here is to limit your reliance on luck and maximise your ability to shape your destiny yourself.

1: Write short material

Writers will very often start off by writing a novel. We would advise strongly against this. It's like leaving school one day and applying for a job as a CEO of an international corporation the next. Novels are the big league. They are expensive to produce, market, and distribute. They require significant investment and pose a significant financial risk to publishers. They are not a good place for new writers to try and cut their teeth. If you've already written your novel that's great – it's great experience and you'll have learned a lot – but we'd recommend shelving it for now (you can always come back to it later) and getting stuck into writing some short form material, such as poetry and short fiction.

This is what novelist George R. R. Martin, author of *A Game of Thrones*, has to say on the subject:

> "I would also suggest that any aspiring writer begin with short stories. These days, I meet far too many young writers who try to start off with a novel right off, or a trilogy, or even a nine-book series. That's like starting in at rock climbing by tackling Mt Everest. Short stories help you learn your craft."

You will find that writing short material will improve your writing no end. Writing short fiction allows you to play with lots of different stories and characters very quickly. Because you will probably only spend a few days on any given story you will quickly gain a lot of experience with plotting stories and will learn a lot about what works, what doesn't work, and what you personally are good at. When you write a novel, by contrast, you may spend years on a single story and one set of characters, making this learning process much slower.

Your writing will also be improved by the need to stick to a word limit. Writers who start their career by writing a novel often produce huge epics, the word counts of which they wear as a badge of honour, as if they demonstrate their commitment to and enthusiasm for writing. What they actually demonstrate is a naivety about the realities of getting published. The odds are already stacked against new writers getting a novel published, because of the cost and financial risk of publishing a novel. The bigger the novel, the more it will cost to print, warehouse, and distribute. Publishers will not look at a large word count and be impressed – they will be terrified. The longer the novel, the less chance it has of getting published.

A lengthy first novel also suggests that the writer has yet to learn one of the most critical skills a writer must possess to succeed: brevity. By writing short stories that fit the limits imposed by competitions and magazines you will learn this critical skill. You will learn to remove unnecessary words and passages, and you will find that your writing becomes leaner, more engaging, and more exciting as a result. Lengthy first novels are often rambling and sometimes boring – but once you've been forced to learn how to "trim the fat" by writing short stories, the good habits you've got into will transfer across when you start writing long form works, allowing you to write novels that are pacier and better to read. They will stand a better chance of publication not just because they are shorter and cheaper to produce, but they are also likely to be better written.

2: Get a professional critique

It's a good idea to get some professional feedback on your work at some point, and it's probably better to do this sooner, rather than later. There's no point spending a long time doing something that doesn't quite work if a little advice early on could have got you on the right track sooner. It's also a lot cheaper to get a short story critiqued than a whole novel, and if you can learn the necessary lessons now it will both minimise the cost and maximise the benefit of the advice.

Should you protect the copyright of short works before showing them to anyone?

This is a matter of personal preference. We'd suggest that it certainly isn't as important to register short works as full novels, as your short works are unlikely to be of much financial value to you. Having said that, films do sometimes get made which are based on short stories, in which case you'd want to have all your rights in order. If you do choose to register your short works this can be done for a relatively small amount online at https://www.copyrightregistrationservice.com/register.

3: Submit to competitions and magazines, and build a list of writing credits

Once you have got some short works that you are happy with you can start submitting them to competitions and small magazines. You can search for competitions at https://www.firstwriter.com/competitions and magazines at https://www.firstwriter.com/magazines. Prize money may not be huge, and you probably won't be paid for having your work appear in the kind of small literary magazines you will probably be approaching at first, but the objective here is to build up a list of writing credits to give you more credibility when approaching agents and publishers. You'll be much more likely to grab their attention if you can reel off a list of places where you have already been published, or prizes you have won.

4: Finish your novel and protect your copyright

Okay – so you've built up a list of writing credits, and you've decided it's time to either write a novel, or go back to the one you had already started (in which case you'll probably find yourself cutting out large chunks and making it a lot shorter!). Once you've got your novel to the point where you're happy to start submitting it for publication you should get it registered for copyright. Unlike the registration of short works, which we think is a matter of personal preference, we'd definitely recommend registering a novel, and doing so before you show it to anybody. That *includes* family and friends. Don't worry that you might want to change it – as long as you don't rewrite it to the point where it's not recognisable it will still be protected – the important thing is to get it registered without delay. You can protect it online at https://www.copyrightregistrationservice.com/register.

If you've already shown it to other people then just register it as soon as you can. Proving a claim to copyright is all about proving you had a copy of the work before anyone else, so time is of the essence.

5: Editing

These days, agents and publishers increasingly seem to expect manuscripts to have been professionally edited before being submitted to them – and no, getting your husband / wife / friend / relative to do it doesn't count. Ideally, you should have the whole manuscript professionally edited, but this can be expensive. Since most agents and publishers aren't going to want to see the whole manuscript in the first instance you can probably get away with just having the first three chapters edited. It may also be worth having your query letter and synopsis edited at the same time.

6: Submit to literary agents

There will be many publishers out there who will accept your submission directly, and on the face of it that might seem like a good idea, since you won't have to pay an agent 15% of your earnings.

However, all the biggest publishers are generally closed to direct submissions from authors, meaning that if you want the chance of getting a top publisher you're going to need a literary agent. You'll also probably find that their 15% fee is more than offset by the higher earnings you'll be likely to achieve.

To search for literary agents go to https://www.firstwriter.com/Agents. Start by being as specific in your search as possible. So if you've written a historical romance select "Fiction", "Romance", and "Historical". Once you've approached all the agents that specifically mention all three elements broaden your search to just "Fiction" and "Romance". As long as the new results don't specifically say they don't handle historical romance, these are still valid markets to approach. Finally, search for just "Fiction", as there are many agents who are willing to consider all kinds of fiction but don't specifically mention romance or historical.

Don't limit your approaches to just agents in your own country. With more and more agents accepting electronic queries it's now as easy to approach agents in other countries as in your own, and if you're ignoring either London or New York (the two main centres of English language publishing) you're cutting your chances of success in two.

7: Submit directly to publishers

Once you're certain that you've exhausted all potential agents for your work, you can start looking for publishers to submit your work directly to. You can search for publishers at https://www.firstwriter.com/publishers. Apply the same filtering as when you were searching for agents: start specific and gradually broaden, until you've exchausted all possibilities.

8: Self-publishing

In the past, once you got to the point where you'd submitted to all the publishers and agents who might be interested in your book, it would be time to pack away the manuscript in the attic, chalk it up to experience, and start writing another. However, these days writers have the option to take their book directly to market by publishing it themselves.

Before you decide to switch to self-publishing you must be sure that you've exhausted all traditional publishing possibilities – because once you've self-published your book you're unlikely to be able to submit it to agents and publishers. It will probably take a few years of exploring the world of traditional publishing to reach this point, but if you do then you've nothing to lose by giving self-publishing a shot. See our guide to self-publishing for details on how to proceed.

Why Choose Traditional Publishing

When **firstwriter.com** first started, back in 2001, there were only two games in town when it came to getting your book published: traditional publishing, and vanity publishing – and which you should pick was a no-brainer. Vanity publishing was little more than a scam that would leave you with an empty bank account and a house full of unsold books. If you were serious about being a writer, you had to follow the traditional publishing path.

Since then, there has been a self-publishing revolution, with new technologies and new printing methods giving writers a genuine opportunity to get their books into the market by themselves. So, is there still a reason for writers to choose traditional publishing?

The benefits of traditional publishing

Despite the allure and apparent ease of self-publishing, the traditional path still offers you the best chance of making a success of being a writer. There are rare cases where self-published writers make staggering fortunes and become internationally renowned on the back of their self-published books, but these cases are few and far between, and a tiny drop in the rapidly expanding ocean of self-published works. The vast majority of successful books – and the vast majority of successful writers – have their homes firmly in the established publishing houses. Even those self-published authors who find success usually end up moving to a traditional publisher in the end.

This is because the traditional publishers have the systems, the market presence, and the financial clout to *make* a book a bestseller. While successful self-published authors often owe their success in no small part to a decent dose of luck (a social media comment that goes viral; the right mention on the right media outlet at the right time), traditional publishers are in the business of engineering that success. They might not always succeed, but they have the marketing budgets and the distribution channels in place to give themselves, and the book they are promoting, the best possible chance.

And it's not just the marketing and the distribution. Getting signed with a traditional publisher brings a whole team of people with a wealth of expertise that will all work towards the success of the book. It will provide you with an editor who may have experience of working on previous bestsellers, who will not only help you get rid of mistakes in your work but may also help you refine it into a better book. They will help make sure that the quality of your content is good enough to make it in the marketplace.

The publishers will source a professional cover designer who will make your book look the part on the shelves and on the pages of the bookselling websites. They will have accountants who will handle the technicalities of tax regimes both home and abroad. They will have overseas contacts for establishing foreign publishing rights; translations; etc. They may even have contacts in the film industry, should there be a prospect of a movie adaptation. They will have experts working on every aspect of your book, right down to the printing and the warehousing and the shipping of the physical products. They will have people to manage the ebook conversion and the electronic distribution. As an author, you don't need to worry about any of this.

This means you get more time to simply be a writer. You may have to go on book tours, but even these will be organised for you by PR experts, who will also be handling all the press releases, etc.

And then there's the advances. Advances are up-front payments made by traditional publishers to authors, which are off-set against future royalties. So, an author might receive a $5,000 advance before their book is published. When the royalties start coming in, the publisher keeps the first $5,000 to off-set the advance. The good news for the author is that if the book flops and doesn't make $5,000 in royalties they still get to keep the full advance. In an uncertain profession, the security of an advance can be invaluable for an author – and of course it's not something available to self-published authors.

The drawbacks of traditional publishing

The main downside of traditional publishing is just that it's so hard to get into. If you choose to self-publish then – provided you have enough perseverance, the right help and advice, and perhaps a little bit of money – you are guaranteed to succeed and see your book in print and for sale. With traditional publishing, the cold hard fact is that most people who try will not succeed.

And for many of those people who fail it may not even be their fault. That aspect of traditional publishing which can bring so many benefits as compared to self-publishing – that of being part of a team – can also be part of its biggest drawback. It means that you have to get other people to buy into your book. It means that you have to rely on other people being competent enough to spot a bestseller. Many failed to spot the potential of the Harry Potter books. How many potential bestsellers never make it into print just because none of the professionals at the publishers' gates manage to recognise their potential?

So if you choose traditional publishing your destiny is not in your own hands – and for some writers the lack of exclusive control can also be a problem. Sometimes writers get defensive when editors try to tinker with their work, or annoyed when cover artists don't realise their vision the way they expect. But this is hardly a fair criticism of traditional publishing, as most writers (particularly when they are starting out) will benefit from advice from experienced professionals in the field, and will often only be shooting themselves in the foot if they insist on ignoring it.

The final main drawback with traditional publishing is that less of the sale price of each copy makes it to the writer. A typical royalty contract will give the writer 15%. With a self-published book, the author can expect to receive much more. So, all other things being equal, the self-published route can be more profitable – but, of course, all things are not equal. If self-publishing means lower sales (as is likely), then you will probably make less money overall. Remember, it's better to have 15% of something than 50% of nothing.

Conclusion

In conclusion, our advice to writers would be to aim for traditional publishing first. It might be a long shot, but if it works then you stand a much better chance of being successful. If you don't manage to get signed by an agent or a publisher then you still have the option of self-publishing, but make sure you don't get tempted to resort to self-publishing too soon – most agents and publishers won't consider self-published works, so this is a one-way street. Once you've self-published your work, you probably won't be able to change your mind and go back to the traditional publishers with your book unless it becomes a huge hit without them. It's therefore important that you exhaust all your traditional publishing options before making the leap to self-publishing. Be prepared for this to take perhaps a few years (lots of agents and publishers can take six months just to respond), and make sure you've submitted to everyone you can on *both* sides of the Atlantic (publishing is a global game these days, and you need to concentrate on the two main centres of English-language publishing (New York and London) equally) before you make the decision to self-publish instead.

Formatting Your Manuscript

Before submitting a manuscript to an agent, magazine, or publisher, it's important that you get the formatting right. There are industry norms covering everything from the size of your margins to the font you choose – get them wrong and you'll be marking yourself out as an amateur. Get them right, and agents and editors will be far more likely to take you seriously.

Fonts

Don't be tempted to "make your book stand out" by using fancy fonts. It *will* stand out, but not for any reason you'd want. Your entire manuscript should be in a monospaced font like Courier (not a proportional font, like Times Roman) at 12 points. (A monospaced font is one where each character takes up the same amount of space; a proportional font is where the letter "i" takes up less space than the letter "m".)

This goes for your text, your headings, your title, your name – everything. Your objective is to produce a manuscript that looks like it has been produced on a simple typewriter.

Italics / bold

Your job as the author is to indicate words that require emphasis, not to pick particular styles of font. This will be determined by the house style of the publisher in question. You indicate emphasis by underlining text; the publisher will decide whether they will use bold or italic to achieve this emphasis – you shouldn't use either in your text.

Margins

You should have a one inch (2.5 centimetre) margin around your entire page: top, bottom, left, and right.

Spacing

In terms of line spacing, your entire manuscript should be double spaced. Your word processor should provide an option for this, so you don't have to insert blank lines manually.

While line spacing should be double, spaces after punctuation should be single. If you're in the habit of putting two spaces after full stops this is the time to get out of that habit, and remove them from your manuscript. You're just creating extra work for the editor who will have to strip them all out.

Do not put blank lines between paragraphs. Start every paragraph (even those at the start of chapters) with an indent equivalent to five spaces. If you want a scene break then create a line with the "#" character centred in the middle. You don't need blank lines above or below this line.

Word count

You will need to provide an estimated word count on the front page of your manuscript. Tempting as it will be to simply use the word processor's word counting function to tell you exactly how many words there are in your manuscript, this is not what you should do. Instead, you should work out the maximum number of characters on a line, divide this number by six, and then multiply by the total number of lines in your manuscript.

Once you have got your estimated word count you need to round it to an approximate value. How you round will depend on the overall length of your manuscript:

- up to 1,500 words: round to the nearest 100;
- 1,500–10,000 words: round to the nearest 500;
- 10,000–25,000 words: round to the nearest 1,000;
- Over 25,000 words: round to the nearest 5,000.

The reason an agent or editor will need to know your word count is so that they can estimate how many pages it will make. Since actual pages include varying amounts of white space due to breaks in paragraphs, sections of speech, etc. the formula above will actually provide a better idea of how many pages will be required than an exact word count would.

And – perhaps more importantly – providing an exact word count will highlight you immediately as an amateur.

Layout of the front page

On the first page of the manuscript, place your name, address, and any other relevant contact details (such as phone number, email address, etc.) in the top left-hand corner. In the top right-hand corner write your approximate word count.

If you have registered your work for copyright protection, place the reference number two single lines (one double line) beneath your contact details. Since your manuscript will only be seen by agents or editors, not the public, this should be done as discreetly as possible, and you should refrain from using any official seal you may have been granted permissions to use. (For information on registering for copyright protection see "Protecting Your Copyright", below.)

Place your title halfway down the front page. Your title should be centred and would normally be in capital letters. You can make it bold or underlined if you want, but it should be the same size as the rest of the text.

From your title, go down two single lines (or one double line) and insert your byline. This should be centred and start with the word "By", followed by the name you are writing under. This can be your name or a pen name, but should be the name you want the work published under. However, make sure that the name in the top left-hand corner is your real, legal name.

From your byline, go down four single lines (or two double lines) and begin your manuscript.

Layout of the text

Print on only one side of the paper, even if your printer can print on both sides.

In the top right-hand corner of all pages except the first should be your running head. This should be comprised of the surname used in your byline; a keyword from your title, and the page number, e.g. "Myname / Mynovel Page 5".

Text should be left-aligned, *not* justified. This means that you should have a ragged right-hand edge to the text, with lines ending at different points. Make sure you don't have any sort of hyphenation function switched on in your word processor: if a word is too long to fit on a line it should be taken over to the next.

Start each new chapter a third of the way down the page with the centred chapter number / title, underlined. Drop down four single lines (two double lines) to the main text.

At the end of the manuscript you do not need to indicate the ending in any way: you don't need to write "The End", or "Ends", etc. The only exception to this is if your manuscript happens to end at the bottom of a page, in which case you can handwrite the word "End" at the bottom of the last page, after you have printed it out.

Protecting Your Copyright

Protecting your copyright is by no means a requirement before submitting your work, but you may feel that it is a prudent step that you would like to take before allowing strangers to see your material.

These days, you can register your work for copyright protection quickly and easily online. The Intellectual Property Rights Office operates a website called the "Copyright Registration Service" which allows you to do this:

- *https://www.CopyrightRegistrationService.com*

This website can be used for material created in any nation signed up to the Berne Convention. This includes the United States, United Kingdom, Canada, Australia, Ireland, New Zealand, and most other countries. There are around 180 countries in the world, and over 160 of them are part of the Berne Convention.

Provided you created your work in one of the Berne Convention nations, your work should be protected by copyright in all other Berne Convention nations. You can therefore protect your copyright around most of the world with a single registration, and because the process is entirely online you can have your work protected in a matter of minutes, without having to print and post a copy of your manuscript.

What is copyright?

Copyright is a form of intellectual property (often referred to as "IP"). Other forms of intellectual property include trade marks, designs, and patents. These categories refer to different kinds of ideas which may not exist in a physical form that can be owned as property in the traditional sense, but may nonetheless have value to the people who created them. These forms of intellectual property can be owned in the same way that physical property is owned, but – as with physical property – they can be subject to dispute and proper documentation is required to prove ownership.

The different types of intellectual property divide into these categories as follows:

- **Copyright:** copyright protects creative output such as books, poems, pictures, drawings, music, films, etc. Any work which can be recorded in some way can be protected by copyright, as long as it is original and of sufficient length. Copyright does not cover short phrases or names.

- **Trade marks:** trade marks cover words and/or images which distinguish the goods or services of one trader from another. Unlike copyright, trade marks can cover names and short phrases.

- **Designs:** designs cover the overall visual appearance of a product, such as its shape, etc.

- **Patents:** patents protect the technical or functional aspects of designs or inventions.

The specifics of the legal protection surrounding these various forms of intellectual property will vary from nation to nation, but there are also generally international conventions to which a lot if not most of the nations of the world subscribe. The information provided below outlines the common situation in many countries but you should be aware that this may not reflect the exact situation in every territory.

The two types of intellectual property most relevant to writers are copyright and trade marks. If a writer has written a novel, a short story, a poem, a script, or any other piece of writing then the contents themselves can be protected by copyright. The title, however, cannot be protected by copyright as it is a name. An author may therefore feel that they wish to consider protecting the title of their work by registering it as a trade mark, if they feel that it is particularly important and/or more valuable in itself than the cost of registering a trade mark.

If a writer wants to register the copyright for their work, or register the title of their work as a trade mark, there are generally registration fees to be paid. Despite the fact that copyright covers long works that could be hundreds of thousands of words long, while trade marks cover single words and short phrases, the cost for registering a trade mark is likely to be many times higher than that for registering a work for copyright protection. This is because trade marks must be unique and are checked against existing trade marks for potential conflicts. While works to be registered for copyright must also not infringe existing works, it is not practical to check the huge volume of new works to be registered for copyright against the even larger volume of all previously copyrighted works. Copyright registration therefore tends to simply archive the work in question as proof of the date at which the person registering the work was in possession of it.

In the case of both copyright and trade marks the law generally provides some protection even without any kind of registration, but registration provides the owner of the intellectual property with greater and more enforceable protection. In the case of copyright, the creator of a work usually automatically owns the copyright as soon as the work is recorded in some way (i.e. by writing it down or recording it electronically, etc.), however these rights can be difficult to prove if disputed, and therefore many countries (such as the United States) also offer an internal country-specific means of registering works. Some countries, like the United Kingdom, do not offer any such means of registration, however an international registration is available through the Intellectual Property Rights Office's Copyright Registration Service, and can be used regardless of any country-specific provisions. This can help protect copyright in all of the nations which are signatories of the Berne Convention.

In the case of trade marks, the symbol "™" can be applied to any mark which is being used as a trade mark, however greater protection is provided if this mark is registered, in which case the symbol "®" can be applied to the mark. It is often illegal to apply the "®" symbol to a trade mark which has not been registered. There are also options for international registrations of trade marks, which are administered by the World Intellectual Property Organization, however applications cannot be made to the WIPO directly – applications must be made through the relevant office of the applicant's country.

Copyright law and its history

The modern concept of copyright can be traced back to 1710 and the "Statute of Anne", which applied to England, Scotland, and Wales. Prior to this Act, governments had granted monopoly rights to publishers to produce works, but the 1710 Act was the first time that a right of ownership was acknowledged for the actual creator of a work.

From the outset, the attempt to protect the creator's rights was beset with problems due to the local nature of the laws, which applied in Britain only. This meant that lots of copyrighted works were reproduced without the permission of the author in Ireland, America, and in European countries. This not only hindered the ability of the London publishers to sell their legitimate copies of their books in these territories, but the unauthorised reproductions would also find their way into Britain, harming the home market as well.

A natural progression for copyright law was therefore its internationalisation, beginning in 1846 with a reciprocal agreement between Britain and Prussia, and culminating in a series of international treaties, the principal of which is the Berne Convention, which applies to over 160 countries.

Traditionally in the United Kingdom and the United States there has been a requirement to register a work with an official body in order to be able to claim copyright over it (Stationers Hall and the US Library of Congress respectively), however this has been changed by the Berne Convention, which requires signatory countries to grant copyright as an automatic right: i.e. the creator of a work immediately owns its copyright by virtue of creating it and recording it in some physical way (for instance by writing it down or making a recording of it, etc.). The United Kingdom and the United States have both been slow to fully adopt this approach. Though the United Kingdom signed the Berne Convention in 1887, it took 100 years for it to be fully implemented by the Copyright Designs and Patents Act 1988. The United States did not even sign the convention until 1989.

In the United States the US Library of Congress continues to provide archiving services for the purposes of copyright protection, but these are now optional. US citizens no longer need to register their work in order to be able to claim copyright over it. It is necessary, however, to be able to prove when the person who created it did so, and this is essentially the purpose of the registration today. In the United Kingdom, Stationers Hall has ceased to exist, and there is no longer any state-run means of registering the copyright to unpublished works, leaving the only available options as independent and/or international solutions such as the copyright registration service provided by the IP Rights Office.

Registering your work for copyright protection

Registering your work for copyright protection can help you protect your rights in relation to your work. Generally (particularly if you live in a Berne Convention country, as most people do) registration will not be compulsory in order to have rights over your work. Any time you create a unique original work you will in theory own the copyright over it, however you will need to be able to prove when you created it, which is the purpose of registering your work for copyright protection. There are other ways in which you might attempt to prove this, but registration provides better evidence than most other forms.

There are a range of different options for protecting your copyright that vary depending on where you live and the kind of coverage you want. Some countries, like the United States, provide internal means of registering the copyright of unpublished works, however the scope of these will tend to be restricted to the country in question. Other countries, like the United

Kingdom, do not offer any specific government-sponsored system for registering the copyright of unpublished works. An international option is provided by the Intellectual Property Rights Office, which is not affiliated to any particular government or country. As long as you live in a Berne Convention country you should be able to benefit from using their Copyright Registration Service. You can register your work with the Intellectual Property Rights Office regardless of whether or not there are any specific arrangements in your home country (you may even choose to register with both to offer your work greater protection). Registration with the Intellectual Property Rights Office should provide you with protection throughout the area covered by the Berne Convention, which is most of the world.

Registering your work for copyright protection through the Intellectual Property Rights Office is an online process that can be completed in a few minutes, provided you have your file in an accepted format and your file isn't too large (if your file is too large and cannot be reduced you may have to split it and take out two or more registrations covering it). There is a registration fee to pay ($45 / £25 / €40 at the time of writing) per file for registration, however if you are a subscriber to **firstwriter.com** you can benefit from a 10% discount when you start the registration process on our site.

When registering your work, you will need to give some consideration to what your work actually consists of. This is a straightforward question if your work is a novel, or a screenplay, but if it is a collection of poetry or short stories then the issue is more difficult. Should you register your collection as one file, or register each poem separately, which would be more expensive? Usually, you can answer this question by asking yourself what you propose to do with your collection. Do you intend to submit it to publishers as a collection only? Or do you intend to send the constituent parts separately to individual magazines? If the former is the case, then register the collection as a single work under the title of the collection. If the latter is the case then this could be unwise, as your copyright registration certificate will give the name of the collection only – which will not match the names of the individual poems or stories. If you can afford to, you should therefore register them separately. If you have so many poems and / or stories to register that you cannot afford to register them all separately, then registering them as a collection will be better than nothing.

Proper use of the copyright symbol

The first thing to note is that for copyright there is only one form of the symbol (©), unlike trade marks, where there is a symbol for registered trade marks (®) and a symbol for unregistered trade marks (™).

To qualify for use of the registered trade mark symbol (®) you must register your trade mark with the appropriate authority in your country, whereas the trade mark symbol (™) can be applied to any symbol you are using as a trade mark. Use of the copyright symbol is more similar to use of the trade mark symbol, as work does not need to be registered in order to use it.

You can place the copyright symbol on any original piece of work you have created. The normal format would be to include alongside the copyright symbol the year of first publication and the name of the copyright holder, however there are no particular legal requirements regarding this. While it has historically been a requirement in some jurisdictions to include a copyright notice on a work in order to be able to claim copyright over it, the Berne Convention does not allow such restrictions, and so any country signed up to the convention no longer has this requirement. However, in some jurisdictions failure to include such a notice can affect the damages you may be able to claim if anyone infringes your copyright.

A similar situation exists in relation to the phrase "All Rights Reserved". This phrase was a requirement in order to claim international copyright protection in countries signed up to the 1910 Buenos Aires Convention. However, since all countries signed up to the Buenos Aires Convention are now also signed up to the Berne Convention (which grants automatic copyright) this phrase has become superfluous. The phrase continues to be used frequently but is unlikely to have any legal consequences.

The Berne Convention

The Berne Convention covers 162 of the approximately 190 countries in the world, including most major nations. Countries which are signed up to the convention are compelled to offer the same protection to works created in other signatory nations as they would to works created in their own. Nations not signed up to the Berne Convention may have their own arrangements regarding copyright protection.

You can check if your country is signed up to the Berne Convention at the following website:

- *https://www.CopyrightRegistrationService.com*

The status of your country should be shown automatically on the right side of the screen. If not, you can select your country manually from the drop-down menu near the top right of the page.

Should You Self-Publish?

Over recent years there has been an explosion in self-published books, as it has become easier and easier to publish your book yourself. This poses writers with a new quandary: continue to pursue publication through the traditional means, or jump into the world of self-publishing? As the rejections from traditional publishers pile up it can be tempting to reach for the control and certainty of self-publishing. Should you give into the temptation, or stick to your guns?

Isn't it just vanity publishing?

Modern self-publishing is quite different from the vanity publishing of times gone by. A vanity publisher would often pose or at least seek to appear to be a traditional publisher, inviting submissions and issuing congratulatory letters of acceptance to everyone who submitted – only slowly revealing the large fees the author would have to pay to cover the cost of printing the books.

Once the books were printed, the vanity publisher would deliver them to the author then cut and run. The author would be left with a big hole in their pocket and a mountain of boxes of books that they would be unlikely to ever sell a fraction of.

Modern self-publishing, on the other hand, is provided not by shady dealers but by some of the biggest companies involved in the publishing industry, including Penguin and Amazon. It doesn't have the large fees that vanity publishing did (depending on the path you choose and your own knowledge and technical ability it can cost almost nothing to get your book published); it *does* offer a viable means of selling your books (they can appear on the biggest bookselling websites around the world); and it *doesn't* leave you with a house full of unwanted books, because modern technology means that a copy of your book only gets printed when it's actually ordered.

That isn't to say that there aren't still shady characters out there trying to take advantage of authors' vanity by charging them enormous fees for publishing a book that stands very little chance of success, but it does mean that self-publishing – done right – can be a viable and cost effective way of an author taking their book to market.

The benefits of self-publishing

The main benefit of self-publishing, of course, is that the author gets control of whether their book is published or not. There is no need to spend years submitting to countless agents and publishers, building up countless heartbreaking rejection letters, and possibly accepting in the end that your dreams of publication will never come true – you can make them come true.

And this need not be pure vanity on the author's part. Almost every successful book – even such massive hits as *Harry Potter* – usually build up a string of rejections before someone finally accepts them. The professionals that authors rely on when going through the traditional publishing process – the literary agents and the editors – are often, it seems, just not that good at spotting what the public are going to buy. How many potential bestsellers might languish forever in the slush pile, just because agents and editors fail to spot them? What if your book is one of them? The traditional publishing process forces you to rely on the good judgment of others, but the self-publishing process enables you to sidestep that barrier and take your book directly to the public, so that readers can decide for themselves.

Self-publishing also allows you to keep control in other areas. You won't have an editor trying to change your text, and you'll have complete control over what kind of cover your book receives.

Finally, with no publisher or team of editors and accountants taking their slice, you'll probably get to keep a lot more of the retail price of every book you sell. So if you can sell the same amount of books as if you were traditionally published, you'll stand to make a lot more money.

The drawbacks of self-publishing

While self-publishing can guarantee that your book will be available for sale, it cannot guarantee that it will actually sell. Your self-published book will probably have a much lower chance of achieving significant sales than if it had been published traditionally, because it will lack the support that a mainstream publisher could bring. You will have no marketing support, no established position in the marketplace, and no PR – unless you do it yourself. You will have to arrange your own book tours; you will have to do your own sales pitches; you will have to set your own pricing structure; and you will have to manage your own accounts and tax affairs. If you're selling through Amazon or Smashwords or Apple (and if you're not, then why did you bother self-publishing in the first place?) you're going to need to fill in the relevant forms with the IRS (the US tax office) – whether you're a US citizen or not. If you're not a US citizen then you'll have to register with the IRS and complete the necessary tax forms, and potentially other forms for claiming treaty benefits so that you don't get taxed twice (in the US and your home country). And then of course you'll also have to register for tax purposes in your home nation and complete your own tax return there (though you would also have to do this as a traditionally published author).

It can all get very complicated, very confusing, and very lonely. Instead of being able to just be a writer you can find yourself writing less and less and becoming more and more embroiled in the business of publishing a book.

And while it's great to have control over your text and your cover, you'd be ill advised to ignore the value that professionals such as editors and cover designers can bring. It's tempting to think that you don't need an editor – that you've checked the book and had a friend or family member check it too, so it's probably fine – but a professional editor brings a totally different mindset to the process and will check things that won't have even occurred to you and your reader. Without a professional editor, you will almost certainly end up publishing a book which is full of embarrassing mistakes, and trust me – there is no feeling quite as deflating as opening up the first copy of your freshly printed book to see an obvious error jump out – or, even worse, to have it pointed out in an Amazon review, for all to see.

The cover is also incredibly important. Whether for sale on the shelf or on a website, the cover is normally the first point of contact your potential reader has with your book, and will cause them to form immediate opinions about it. A good cover can help a book sell well, but a bad one can kill its chances – and all too often self-published books have amateurish covers that will have readers flicking past them without a second glance.

Finally, the financial benefits of self-publishing can often be illusory. For starters, getting a higher proportion of the retail price is pretty irrelevant if you don't sell any copies. Fifty per cent of nothing is still nothing. Far better to have 15% of something. And then there's the advances. Advances are up-front payments made by traditional publishers to authors, which are off-set against future royalties. So, an author might receive a $5,000 advance before their book is published. When the royalties start coming in, the publisher keeps the first $5,000 to off-set the advance. The good news for the author is that if the book flops and doesn't make $5,000 in royalties they still get to keep the full advance. In an uncertain profession, the security of an advance can be invaluable for an author – and of course it's not something available to self-published authors.

Conclusion

Self-publishing can seem like a tempting shortcut to publication, but in reality it has its own challenges and difficulties. For the moment at least, traditional publishing still offers you the best shot of not only financial success, but also quality of life as a writer. With other people to handle all the other elements of publishing, you get to concentrate on doing what you love.

So we think that writers should always aim for traditional publishing first. It might be a long shot, but if it works then you stand a much better chance of being successful. If you don't manage to get signed by an agent or a publisher then you still have the option of self-publishing, but make sure you don't get tempted to resort to self-publishing too soon – most agents and publishers won't consider self-published works, so this is a one-way street. Once you've self-published your work, you probably won't be able to change your mind and go back to the traditional publishers with your book unless it becomes a huge hit without them. It's therefore important that you exhaust all your traditional publishing options before making the leap to self-publishing. Be prepared for this to take perhaps a few years (lots of agents and publishers can take six months just to respond), and make sure you've submitted to everyone you can on *both* sides of the Atlantic (publishing is a global game these days, and you need to concentrate on the two main centres of English-language publishing (New York and London) equally) before you make the decision to self-publish instead.

However, once you have exhausted all options for traditional publishing, modern self-publishing does offer a genuine alternative path to success, and there are a growing number of self-published authors who have managed to sell millions of copies of their books. If you don't think traditional publishing is going to be an option, we definitely think you should give self-publishing a shot.

For directions on your path through the traditional publishing process see our Writers' Roadmap, above.

If you're sure you've already exhausted all your options for traditional publishing then see below for our quick guide to the self-publishing process.

The Self-Publishing Process

Thinking about self-publishing your book? Make sure you go through all these steps first – and in the right order! Do them the wrong way round and you could find yourself wasting time and/or money.

1. Be sure you want to self-publish

You need to be 100% sure that you want to self-publish, because after you've done it there is no going back. Publishers and literary agents will not normally consider books that have been self-published, so if you wanted to get your book to print the old fashioned way you should stop now and rethink. Make absolutely sure that you've exhausted every possible opportunity for traditional publishing before you head down the self-publishing path.

For more information, see "Why choose traditional publishing?" and "Should you self-publish?", above.

2. Protect your copyright

Authors often wonder about what stage in the process they should protect their copyright – often thinking that it's best to leave it till the end so that there are no more changes to make to the book after it is registered.

However, this isn't the case. The key thing is to protect your work before you let other people see it – or, if you've already let other people see it, as soon as possible thereafter.

Don't worry about making small changes to your work after registering it – as long as the work is still recognisable as the same piece of work it will still be protected. Obviously, if you completely change everything you've written then you're going to need another registration, as it will effectively be a different book, but if you've just edited it and made minor alterations this won't affect your protection.

You can register you copyright online at https://www.copyrightregistrationservice.com.

3. Get your work edited

Editing is a vital step often overlooked by authors who self-publish. The result can often be an amateurish book littered with embarrassing mistakes. Any professionally published book will go through an editing process, and it's important that the same applies to your self-published book. It's also important to complete the editing process before beginning the layout, or you could find yourself having to start the layout again from scratch.

4. Choose your self-publishing path

Before you can go any further you are going to need to choose a size for your book, and in order to do that you are going to need to choose a self-publishing path.

There are various different ways of getting self-published, but in general these range from the expensive hands off approach, where you pay a company to do the hard work for you, to the cheap DIY approach, where you do as much as you can yourself.

At the top end, the hands off approach can cost you thousands. At the bottom end, the DIY approach allows you to publish your book for almost nothing.

5. Finalise your layout / typesetting

Before you can finalise your layout (often referred to in the industry as "typesetting") you need to be sure that you've finalised your content – which means having your full work professionally edited and all the necessary changes made. If you decide to make changes after this point it will be difficult and potentially costly, and will require you to go through many of the following steps all over again.

You also need to have selected your path to publication, so that you know what page sizes are available to you, and what page margins you are going to need to apply. If you create a layout that doesn't meet printing requirements (for instance, includes text too close to the edge of the page) then you will have to start the typesetting process all over again.

6. Organise your ISBN

Your book needs to have an ISBN. If you are using a self-publishing service then they may provide you with one of their own, but it is likely to come with restrictions, and the international record for your book will show your self-publishing service as the publisher.

You can acquire your own ISBNs directly from the ISBN issuer, but they do not sell them individually, so you will end up spending quite a lot of money buying more ISBNs than you need. You will, however, have control of the ISBN, and you will be shown as the publisher.

Alternatively, you can purchase a single ISBN at a lower price from an ISBN retailer. This should give you control over the ISBN, however the record for the book will show the ISBN retailer as the publisher, which you may not consider to be ideal.

Whatever you choose, you need to arrange your ISBN no later than this point, because it needs to appear in the preliminary pages (prelims) of your book.

7. Compile your prelims

Your prelims may include a variety of pages, but should always include a title page, a half title page, and an imprint/copyright page. You might then also include other elements, such as a foreword, table of contents, etc. You can only compile your table of contents at this stage, because you need to know your ISBN (this will be included on the copyright/imprint page) and the page numbers for your table of contents. You therefore need to make sure that you are happy with the typesetting and have no further changes to make before compiling your prelims.

8. Create your final press proof

Depending on the self-publishing path you have chosen, you may be able to use a Word file as your final document. However, you need to be careful. In order to print your book it will have to be converted into a press-ready PDF at some point. If a self-publishing service is doing this for you then you will probably find that they own the PDF file that is created, meaning you don't have control over your own press files. Some services will impose hefty charges (hundreds or even more than a thousand dollars) to release these press files.

It might also be the case that you won't get to see the final PDF, and therefore won't get chance to check it for any errors introduced by the conversion process. If it's an automated system, it may also be difficult to control the output you get from it.

We'd suggest that it's best to produce your own PDF files if possible. To do this you will need a copy of Adobe Acrobat Professional, and you will need to be familiar with the correct settings for creating print ready PDFs. Be careful to embed all fonts and make sure that all images are at 300 DPI.

9. Create your cover

Only once your press proof is finalised can you complete your cover design. That's because your cover includes not only the front cover and the back cover, but also (critically) the spine – and the width of the spine will vary according to the number of pages in your final press proof. In order to complete your cover design you therefore need to know your page size, your page count (including all prelims), and your ISBN, as this will appear on the back cover. You also need to get a barcode for your ISBN.

10. Produce your book

Once your cover and press proof are ready you can go through whichever self-publishing path you have chosen to create your book. With some pathways the production of a print proof can be an optional extra that is only available at an extra cost – but we'd recommend standing that cost and getting a print version of your book to check. You never know exactly how it's going to come out until you have a physical copy in your hand.

If you're happy with the proof you can clear your book for release. You don't need to do anything to get it on online retailers like Amazon – they will automatically pick up the ISBN and add your book to their websites themselves.

11. Create an ebook version

In the modern day, having an ebook version of your book is imperative. Ebooks account for a significant proportion of all book sales and are a particularly effective vehicle for unknown and self-published authors.

There are various different file formats used by the different platforms, but .epub is emerging as a standard, and having your book in .epub format should enable you to access all the platforms with a single file.

12. Distribute your ebook

Unlike with print books, you will need to act yourself to get your ebooks into sales channels. At a minimum, you need to ensure that you get your ebook available for sale through Amazon, Apple, and Google Play.

US Magazines

For the most up-to-date listings of these and hundreds of other magazines, visit https://www.firstwriter.com/magazines

*To claim your **free** access to the site, please see the back of this book.*

aaduna

144 Genesee Street Suite 102-259
Auburn, New York 13021
Email: submissionsmanager@aaduna.org
Website: http://www.aaduna.org

Publishes: Fiction; Nonfiction; Poetry;
Markets: Adult; *Treatments:* Literary

Publishes fiction, poetry, and nonfiction.
Submissions must be sent both by post and by email. See website for full guidelines.

AARP Bulletin

601 E Street, NW
Washington DC 20049
Tel: +1 (877) 434-7598
Email: member@aarp.org
Website: http://www.aarp.org

Publishes: Articles; Essays; News;
Nonfiction; *Areas:* Health; Lifestyle;
Politics; *Markets:* Adult

Publishes material relating to health, social
security, and consumer protection. No
unsolicited mss.

Abramelin

Email: nessaralindaran@aol.com
Website: http://thegiantgilamonsters.com/
abramelin

Publishes: Poetry; *Markets:* Adult;
Treatments: Literary

Editors: Vanessa Kittle

Publishes modern, literary poetry. Send
submissions by email, but no attachments.
See website for full guidelines.

The Account

Email: poetryprosethought@gmail.com
Website: http://theaccountmagazine.com

Publishes: Essays; Fiction; Nonfiction;
Poetry; *Areas:* Short Stories; *Markets:* Adult;
Treatments: Literary

Editors: Tyler Mills, Editor-in-Chief;
Christina Stoddard, Managing Editor/
Publicist; Brianna Noll, Poetry Editor;
Jennifer Hawe, Nonfiction Editor; M. Milks,
Fiction Editor

Accepts poetry, fiction, and creative
nonfiction, between May 1 and September 1,
annually, and between November 15 and
February 1. Send 3-5 poems, essays up to
6,000 words, or fiction between 1,000 and
6,000 words, through online submission
system. Each piece of work must be
accompanied by an account between 150 and
500 words, giving voice to the artist's
approach.

Adelaide Literary Magazine

1340 Stratford Avenue, Suite 3K
Bronx, NY 10472
Tel: +35 918 635 457

Email: info@adelaidemagazine.org
Website: http://www.adelaidemagazine.org

Publishes: Articles; Essays; Fiction; Interviews; News; Nonfiction; Poetry; Reviews; *Areas:* Arts; Criticism; Culture; Literature; Media; Short Stories; *Markets:* Academic; Adult; Professional; *Treatments:* Contemporary; Literary

Editors: Stevan V. Nikolic, Adelaide Franco Nikolic

An independent international quarterly publication, based in New York and Lisbon. Founded in 2015, the magazine's aim is to publish quality poetry, fiction, nonfiction, artwork, and photography, as well as interviews, articles, and book reviews, written in English and Portuguese. Most of our content comes from unsolicited submissions.

We publish print, digital, and online editions of our magazine four times a year, in Fall (September), Winter (December), Spring (March), and Summer (June). The online edition is updated continuously. There are no charges for reading the magazine online.

Adornment

Website: http://www.
jewelryandrelatedarts.com

Publishes: Nonfiction; *Areas:* Antiques; *Markets:* Adult; Professional

Quarterly electronic magazine delivered to association members. Publishes material for collectors of and professionals involved with jewellery.

The Adroit Journal

Email: editors@theadroitjournal.org
Website: http://www.theadroitjournal.org

Publishes: Fiction; Poetry; *Areas:* Short Stories; *Markets:* Adult; *Treatments:* Literary

Submit up to three pieces of prose up to 3,000 words each, or up to six poems of any length, during open submission periods. Currently closed to submissions until October 1, 2018.

Advisor Today

2901 Telestar Court
Falls Church, VA 22042
Tel: +1 (703) 770-8204
Email: amseka@naifa.org
Website: https://www.advisortoday.com

Publishes: Articles; Features; News; Nonfiction; *Areas:* Business; Finance; *Markets:* Professional

Editors: Ayo Mseka

Magazine for insurance and financial planning advisors.

After Happy Hour Review

4750 Centre Avenue
Apt 60
Pittsburgh, PA 15213
Email: hourafterhappyhour@gmail.com
Website: https://afterhappyhourreview.com/

Publishes: Fiction; Nonfiction; Poetry; *Markets:* Adult; *Treatments:* Contemporary; Dark; Experimental; Light; Literary; Mainstream; Progressive; Traditional

Editors: Mike Good, Jason Peck

An online journal. We gravitate towards work that is quirky, accessible, and unconventional. An ideal piece might cover a subject few people write about or cover familiar subjects from an unexpected angle.

Agricultural History

Kennesaw State University
Dept. of History and Philosophy
402 Bartow Ave.
Kennesaw, GA 30144
Email: aghistory@kennesaw.edu
Website: http://www.aghistorysociety.org/journal/

Publishes: Articles; Nonfiction; *Areas:* Historical; Nature; *Markets:* Academic

Editors: Albert Way

Publishes articles on all aspects of the history of agriculture and rural life with no geographical or temporal limits. Submit via online submission system. See website for full guidelines.

Air Force Times

Sightline Media Group
1919 Gallows Road, 4th Floor
Vienna, VA 22182
Email: mtan@militarytimes.com
Website: https://www.airforcetimes.com

Publishes: Articles; News; Nonfiction;
Areas: Military; *Markets:* Professional

Editors: Michelle Tan

Magazine for those serving in the Air Force, and their families.

Alabama Heritage

Box 870342
Tuscaloosa, AL 35487-0342
Tel: +1 (205) 348-7467
Fax: +1 (205) 348-7473
Email: alabama.heritage@ua.edu
Website: http://www.alabamaheritage.com

Publishes: Articles; Features; Nonfiction;
Areas: Culture; Historical; *Markets:* Adult

Publishes stories of the history and culture of Alabama and the South.

Aliterate

Email: editor@aliterate.org
Website: https://www.aliterate.org

Publishes: Fiction; *Areas:* Fantasy; Horror; Romance; Sci-Fi; Short Stories; Thrillers; Westerns; *Markets:* Adult; *Treatments:* Contemporary; Literary

Editors: R.S. Mason

Closed to submissions, but plans to re-open before 2019. Check website for current status.

Biannual print journal dedicated to "literary genre fiction". Accepts stories between 2,500 and 8,000 words. No poetry, erotica, inspirational fiction, polemics, nonfiction, gore, fanfic, or young adult fiction. Accepts submissions by email only.

All Animals

Email: allanimals@humanesociety.org
Website: http://www.humanesociety.org

Publishes: Articles; News; Nonfiction;
Areas: Nature; *Markets:* Adult

Publishes material relating to animal welfare and the humane movement, including profiles of people on the front lines, tips for pet owners and wildlife watchers, tales of rescue and rehab, actions readers can take, and more.

Alternative Therapies in Health and Medicine

1400 Corporate Center Curve Suite 130
Eagan MN 55121
Tel: +1 (877) 904-7951
Fax: +1 (651) 344-0774
Email: athmsubmissions@
innovisionhm.com
Website: http://www.alternative-therapies.com

Publishes: Articles; Nonfiction; *Areas:* Health; Medicine; *Markets:* Academic; Professional

Editors: Craig Gustafson

International scientific forum for the dissemination of peer-reviewed information indexed in the National Library of Medicine to healthcare professionals regarding the use of complementary and alternative therapies in promoting health and healing.

America's Pharmacist

National Community Pharmacists Association
100 Daingerfield Road
Alexandria, VA 22314
Tel: +1 (703) 683-8200
Fax: +1 (703) 683-3619
Website: http://www.ncpanet.org/newsroom/america's-pharmacist

Publishes: Articles; News; Nonfiction;
Areas: Business; Health; *Markets:* Professional

Magazine aimed at independent community pharmacists, publishing articles on business, management, and the latest legal and regulatory information.

American Baby

Meredith Corporation
125 Park Avenue, 6th Floor
New York, NY 10017
Website: http://www.americanbaby.com

Publishes: Articles; Nonfiction; *Areas:* Health; Medicine; *Markets:* Adult

Magazine for new and expectant parents.

American History

1919 Gallows Road, Suite 400
Vienna, VA 22182
Email: americanhistory@historynet.com
Website: http://www.historynet.com

Publishes: Articles; Features; Nonfiction; *Areas:* Historical; *Markets:* Adult

Magazine of American history for a general readership. Send stories or ideas by post or by email. See website for full guidelines.

The American Poetry Review

1906 Rittenhouse Square, 3rd Floor
Philadelphia, PA 19103
Email: escanlon@aprweb.org
Website: https://aprweb.org

Publishes: Essays; Interviews; Nonfiction; Poetry; Reviews; *Areas:* Literature; *Markets:* Adult; *Treatments:* Contemporary; Literary

Editors: Elizabeth Scanlon

Publishes poetry and literary prose. No previously published material. Send up to five poems or a piece of prose via online submission system ($3 charge) or by post with SASE. Accepts simultaneous submissions if notice of acceptance elsewhere is given. Six month response time.

American Quarter Horse Journal

American Quarter Horse Association
1600 Quarter Horse Drive
Amarillo, TX 79104
Tel: +1 (806) 376-4811
Website: https://www.aqha.com

Publishes: Articles; Nonfiction; *Areas:* Business; How-to; Lifestyle; Nature; *Markets:* Adult

Magazine covering horse ownership, horse breeding, and Western lifestyle. Send query with published clips.

American Snowmobiler

Email: editor@amsnow.com
Website: http://www.amsnow.com

Publishes: Articles; Nonfiction; *Areas:* Hobbies; How-to; Leisure; Technology; Travel; *Markets:* Adult

Magazine publishing material relating to snowmobiles, their use and modification, etc. Send query or complete ms by email. See website for full guidelines.

AntiqueWeek

PO Box 90
27 North Jefferson Street
Knightstown, IN 46148-0090
Tel: +1 (765) 345-5133
Email: cswaim@antiqueweek.com
Website: http://www.antiqueweek.com

Publishes: Articles; Nonfiction; *Areas:* Antiques; *Markets:* Adult; Professional

Editors: Connie Swaim

Publishes articles on antiques for collectors, dealers, and auctioneers.

Aphelion: The Webzine of Science Fiction and Fantasy

Alpharetta, GA
Email: editor@aphelion-webzine.com
Website: http://www.aphelion-webzine.com

Publishes: Essays; Features; Fiction; Interviews; Nonfiction; Poetry; Reviews; *Areas:* Adventure; Fantasy; Gothic; Horror; Humour; Literature; Sci-Fi; Short Stories; Suspense; Thrillers; *Markets:* Family; Professional; *Treatments:* Commercial; Contemporary; Cynical; Dark; Experimental; In-depth; Light; Literary; Mainstream; Niche; Popular; Positive; Progressive; Satirical; Serious; Traditional

Editors: Dan Hollifield, Nate Kailhofer, Curtis Manges, Iain Muir, Rob Wynne

Published since 1997. Free Science Fiction, Fantasy, and Horror Webzine which offers original fiction by new and established writers published on the first Sunday of every month except January. There is a double issue in December. The magazine includes poetry, short stories, serials and novellas, flash fiction, and reviews of interest to science fiction, fantasy, and horror fans. New writers are encouraged to submit their work to the webzine, and feedback to the authors is encouraged through the forum.

APICS Magazine

8430 West Bryn Mawr Avenue, Suite 1000
Chicago, IL 60631
Email: editorial@apics.org
Website: http://www.apics.org

Publishes: Articles; Nonfiction; *Areas:* Business; *Markets:* Professional

Publishes articles on supply chain management.

Architectural Record

350 5th Ave, Suite 6000
New York, NY 10118
Tel: +1 (646) 849-7100
Fax: +1 (646) 849-7148
Email: mcguiganc@bnpmedia.com
Website: https://www.
architecturalrecord.com

Publishes: Articles; Nonfiction; *Areas:* Architecture; Design; *Markets:* Professional

Magazine for architects and designers.

Arizona Wildlife Views

Arizona Game and Fish Department
5000 W. Carefree Highway
Phoenix, AZ 85086-5000
Tel: +1 (623) 236-7216
Email: hrayment@azgfd.gov
Website: https://www.azgfd.com/media/
magazine/

Publishes: Articles; Nonfiction; *Areas:* How-to; Leisure; Nature; *Markets:* Adult

Editors: Heidi Rayment

Publishes articles on the wildlife and outdoors or Arizona, including general interest, how-to, photo features, popularized technical material on Arizona wildlife and wildlife management, habitat issues, outdoor recreation (involving wildlife, boating, fishing, hunting, bird watching, animal observation, off-highway vehicle use, etc.), and historical articles about wildlife and wildlife management. No "me and Joe" articles, anthropomorphism of wildlife or opinionated pieces not based on confirmable facts.

Arkansas Review

Department of English and Philosophy
PO Box 1890
State University, AR 72467
Tel: +1 (870) 972-3043
Fax: +1 (870) 972-3045
Email: arkansasreview@astate.edu
Website: http://arkreview.org

Publishes: Articles; Essays; Fiction; Nonfiction; Poetry; *Areas:* Anthropology; Arts; Culture; Historical; Literature; Music; Politics; Short Stories; Sociology; *Markets:* Academic; Adult

Editors: Marcus Tribbett

Publishes articles in various disciplines focusing on the seven-state Mississippi River Delta, aimed at a general academic audience. Also publishes creative work including poetry, essays, fiction, and artwork that evoke or respond to the culture or nature of the delta. Academic articles should be submitted by post or by email. Creative material should be submitted through online system. Allow 3-12 months for response.

Arthritis Today

1355 Peachtree St NE, 6th Floor
Atlanta, GA 30309
Tel: +1 (404) 872-7100
Website: https://www.arthritis.org

Publishes: Articles; News; Nonfiction; *Areas:* Health; Medicine; *Markets:* Adult

Consumer health magazine aimed at sufferers of arthritis.

Assaracus

Email: info@siblingrivalrypress.com
Website: https://siblingrivalrypress.com/
assaracus/

Publishes: Poetry; *Markets:* Adult;
Treatments: Literary

Journal of gay poetry. While contributors
should self-identify as gay, poems need not
have a gay theme. See website for calls for
submissions.

Athletic Business
22 E. Mifflin St., Suite 910
Madison, WI 53703
Email: editors@athleticbusiness.com
Website: https://www.athleticbusiness.com

Publishes: Articles; Nonfiction; *Areas:*
Health; Leisure; Sport; *Markets:*
Professional

Magazine for Athletic, Fitness and
Recreation Professionals.

Aviation History
1919 Gallows Road, Ste 400
Vienna, VA 22182
Email: aviationhistory@historynet.com
Website: http://www.historynet.com/
aviation-history

Publishes: Articles; Features; Nonfiction;
Areas: Historical; Military; Travel; *Markets:*
Adult

Publishes articles on the history of military
and civil aviation.

The Awakenings Review
The Awakenings Project
PO Box 177
Wheaton, IL 60187
Email: ar@awakeningsproject.org
Website: http://awakeningsproject.org

Publishes: Essays; Fiction; Nonfiction;
Poetry; *Areas:* Short Stories; *Markets:* Adult;
Treatments: Literary

Publishes poetry, short stories, and essays by
people who have had a personal experience
with mental illness.

Backcountry Magazine
60 Main Street, PO Box 190
Jeffersonville, VT 05464
Tel: +1 (802) 644-6606

Email: tyler@backcountrymagazine.com
Website: https://backcountrymagazine.com

Publishes: Articles; Nonfiction; *Areas:*
Adventure; Hobbies; Leisure; Sport;
Markets: Adult

Magazine of skiing and snowboarding. Send
query by email.

Bacopa Literary Review
Website: https://writersalliance.org/bacopa-
literary-review/

Publishes: Fiction; Nonfiction; Poetry;
Markets: Adult; *Treatments:* Literary

Annual print journal publishing short stories,
creative nonfiction, poetry, and prose poetry.
Accepts submissions only through annual
contest that runs from March 18 to May 17
annually.

Barking Sycamores
Email: barkingsycamores@gmail.com
Website: https://barkingsycamores.
wordpress.com

Publishes: Fiction; Nonfiction; Poetry;
Reviews; *Areas:* Short Stories; *Markets:*
Adult; *Treatments:* Literary

Editors: N.I. Nicholson; V.E. Maday

A literary journal entirely edited and
operated by transgender queer
neurodivergent people of colour. Publishes
poetry, artwork, short fiction, creative
nonfiction, and hybrid genre work by
emerging and established neurodivergent
writers. Also book reviews. Submit up to
five poems; up to five short stories up to
1,000 words each; creative nonfiction up to
8,500 words; or book reviews up to 1,000
words, via online submission system.

Barren Magazine
Email: info@barrenmagazine.com
Website: https://barrenmagazine.com

Publishes: Fiction; Nonfiction; Poetry;
Areas: Photography; Short Stories; *Markets:*
Adult; *Treatments:* Literary

Editors: Jason D. Ramsey

An Alt.Lit Introspective.

A literary publication that features fiction, poetry, creative nonfiction, and photography for hard truths, long stares, and gritty lenses. We revel in the shadow-spaces that make up the human condition, and aim to find antitheses to that which defines us: light in darkness; beauty in ugliness; peace in disarray. We invite you to explore it with us.

Bartender

PO Box 157
Spring Lake, NJ 07762
Tel: +1 (732) 449-4499
Email: barmag2@gmail.com
Website: https://bartender.com

Publishes: Articles; Features; News; Nonfiction; *Areas:* Business; Leisure; *Markets:* Professional

Editors: Jackie Foley

Magazine for establishments which mix drinks on site.

BedTimes

501 Wythe Street
Alexandria, VA 22314
Tel: +1 (703) 683-8371
Fax: +1 (703) 683-4503
Email: mbest@sleepproducts.org
Website: https://bedtimesmagazine.com

Publishes: Articles; News; Nonfiction; *Areas:* Business; *Markets:* Professional

Editors: Mary Best

Publishes news, trends and issues of interest to mattress manufacturers and their suppliers, as well as more general business stories. Send queries, CV, and writing samples by email.

Bella Grace New Generation

Stampington & Company
22992 Mill Creek Drive, Suite B
Laguna Hills, CA 92653
Tel: +1 (949) 380-7318
Fax: +1 (949) 380-9355
Email: bellagrace@stampington.com
Website: https://stampington.com

Publishes: Articles; Nonfiction; *Areas:* Women's Interests; *Markets:* Youth; *Treatments:* Positive

Inspirational magazine for young women aged 12-19, devoted to "discovering magic in the ordinary". Interested in hearing from writers and photographers who fall within the target age range; young women aged 12 to 19 interested in being part of a special focus group where they will help generate ideas for content as well as provide feedback on potential topics, designs, and stories; parents of young women in this age range willing to share what kinds of content they would like their daughters to read; and parents who can write thoughtful, reflective articles geared toward young women in this age group.

Bellingham Review

MS-9053
Western Washington University
Bellingham, WA 98225
Tel: +1 (360) 650-4863
Email: bellingham.review@wwu.edu
Website: http://bhreview.org

Publishes: Essays; Fiction; Nonfiction; Poetry; *Areas:* Short Stories; *Markets:* Adult; *Treatments:* Literary

Editors: Bailey Cunningham

Send submissions of prose up to 6,000 words, or up to three poems, via online submission system only. Submit material between September 15 and December 1 only. Simultaneous submissions accepted provided immediate notification is given of acceptance elsewhere.

Better Than Starbucks

7711 Ashwood Lane
Lake Worth, FL 33467
Tel: +1 (561) 719-8627
Email: betterthanstarbucks2@gmail.com
Website: http://www.betterthanstarbucks.org

Publishes: Fiction; Interviews; Poetry; *Areas:* Short Stories; Translations; *Markets:* Adult; Youth; *Treatments:* Contemporary; Literary; Popular; Traditional

Editors: Vera Ignatowitsch

Monthly online literary magazine. Founded 1995, renamed 1998, revived in May 2016. While based in US, The editors are based in the US and three other countries.

The journal publishes original poetry, poetry reviews and interviews with established poets or translators. As of August 2017, the publication has seven poetry sections, each with its own page editor. Each of the various page editors also occasionally contribute an interview, as well as helping select the featured poem and nominees for various awards. There is also both a fiction section as well as nonfiction, and the publisher's monthly column on things poetic and sometimes not so poetic.

At this point, the publication is strictly online (older issues are archived on site).

Big Fiction

Email: info@bigfictionmagazine.com
Website: https://www.
bigfictionmagazine.org

Publishes: Fiction; *Areas:* Short Stories; *Markets:* Adult; *Treatments:* Literary

Closed to submissions until January 1, 2019

Literary magazine devoted to longer short fiction, between 7,500 and 30,000 words. Accepts submissions online via competition ($20 entry fee).

BizTimes Milwaukee

126 N. Jefferson St., Suite 403
Milwaukee, WI 53202
Tel: +1 (414) 336-7120
Fax: +1 (414) 277-8191
Website: https://www.biztimes.com

Publishes: Articles; News; Nonfiction; *Areas:* Business; *Markets:* Professional

Publishes news and analysis for business leaders in southeastern Wisconsin.

Blue Collar Review

PO 11417
Norfolk, VA 23517

Email: red-ink@earthlink.net
Website: http://www.partisanpress.org

Publishes: Essays; Fiction; Poetry; Reviews; *Areas:* Short Stories; *Markets:* Adult; *Treatments:* Literary

Magazine that aims to "expand and promote a progressive working class vision of culture that inspires us and that moves us forward as a class". Submit up to five poems or short stories, essays, or reviews up to 1,000 words by post with SASE for response.

Body

Website: https://bodyliterature.com

Publishes: Essays; Fiction; Interviews; Nonfiction; Poetry; *Areas:* Criticism; Literature; Short Stories; Translations; *Markets:* Adult; *Treatments:* Literary

Online journal publishing poetry, fiction, and nonfiction (including personal essays, criticism and art interviews). Submit up to five poems or prose up to 10 pages through online submission system. Accepts simultaneous submissions.

BoxOffice Magazine

63 Copps Hill Road
Ridgefield, CT 06877
Tel: +1 (203) 438-8389
Email: ken@boxoffice.com
Website: https://pro.boxoffice.com

Publishes: Articles; News; Nonfiction; *Areas:* Business; Entertainment; Film; Media; *Markets:* Professional

Editors: Kenneth James Bacon

Magazine for professionals in the film industry.

Briar Cliff Review

3303 Rebecca Street
Sioux City, IA 51104-2100
Email: currans@briarcliff.edu
Website: http://www.bcreview.org

Publishes: Essays; Fiction; Nonfiction; Poetry; *Areas:* Short Stories; *Markets:* Adult; *Treatments:* Literary

Editors: Tricia Currans-Sheehan

Publishes poetry, fiction, nonfiction and Siouxland essays. Submit online for $3 fee or by post with SASE. See website for full details.

Cadaverous Magazine

Email: cadaverousmagazine@gmail.com
Website: https://cadaverousmagazine.wixsite.com/litmag

Publishes: Fiction; Poetry; *Areas:* Horror; *Markets:* Academic; Adult; Youth; *Treatments:* Dark; Literary

Editors: Alexa Findlay

A not-for-profit online supernatural horror (global) literary magazine. We feature: poetry, prose, fiction, flash fiction, art and photography. We accept submissions from writers and artists of all ages from all across the globe. They must be at least 13 years old.

Cahoodaloodaling

Email: cahoodaloodaling@gmail.com
Website: http://cahoodaloodaling.com

Publishes: Articles; Essays; Fiction; Interviews; Nonfiction; Poetry; Reviews; *Markets:* Adult; *Treatments:* Literary

Editors: Raquel Thorne

Themed quarterly journal, publishing poetry, fiction, and articles and essays that are either about writing and publishing, or match the current submission call. See website for upcoming themes, and to submit via online submission system. If you would like your book reviewing, query by email with a brief sample.

California Quarterly

PO Box 7126
Orange, CA 92863
Email: apc@californiastatepoetrysociety.org
Website: https://www.californiastatepoetrysociety.org

Publishes: Poetry; *Areas:* Translations; *Markets:* Adult; *Treatments:* Literary

We are open to poets anywhere, any style or theme The only criterion is quality. Prefer poems of one page (40 lines) but two pages (80 lines) maximum. Submit no more than 6 poems. Include SASE or email address for response.

The Caribbean Writer

University of the Virgin Islands
RR 1, Box 10,000
Kingshill, St Croix USVI 00850
Tel: +1 (340) 692-4152
Fax: +1 (340) 692-4122
Email: submit@TheCaribbeanWriter.com
Website: http://TheCaribbeanWriter.com

Publishes: Essays; Fiction; Interviews; Nonfiction; Poetry; Reviews; Scripts; *Areas:* Drama; Short Stories; Translations; *Markets:* Adult; *Treatments:* Literary

Editors: Alscess Lewis-Brown

An international magazine with a regional focus. Explores the diverse and multi-ethnic culture in poetry, short fiction, personal essays, creative nonfiction, and short plays.

Catster

535 Connecticut Avenue
Norwalk, CT 06854-1713
Email: catstermag@belvoir.com
Website: http://www.catster.com

Publishes: Articles; Features; Nonfiction; *Areas:* Health; How-to; Lifestyle; Nature; *Markets:* Adult

Magazine covering the subjects of cats and cat ownership. No completed articles. Send query by email with details of your background and a link to writing samples online. Response only if interested.

Charleston Magazine

PO Box 1794
Mount Pleasant, SC 29465-1794
Tel: +1 (888) 242-7624
Email: dshankland@charlestonmag.com
Website: http://charlestonmag.com

Publishes: Articles; News; Nonfiction; *Areas:* Arts; Culture; Current Affairs; Gardening; Leisure; Lifestyle; Travel; *Markets:* Adult

Editors: Darcy Shankland

Magazine covering the city of Charleston and surrounding areas.

Charleston Style and Design Magazine

Email: editor@ charlestonstyleanddesign.com
Website: https://www. charlestonstyleanddesign.com

Publishes: Articles; Nonfiction; *Areas:* Antiques; Architecture; Arts; Beauty and Fashion; Design; Health; Lifestyle; Travel; *Markets:* Adult

Editors: Mary Love

Design and lifestyle magazine for the Lowcountry, covering architects, designers and builders, home projects, lifestyle trends, restaurants, wines, fashions, art galleries, and travel destinations. Experienced writers should send their resume and writing samples by email, with "writer" in the subject line.

CHEST

2595 Patriot Boulevard
Glenview, IL 60026
Tel: +1 (224) 521-9800
Fax: +1 (224) 521-9801
Email: poetrychest@aol.com
Website: https://journal.chestnet.org

Publishes: Articles; News; Nonfiction; Poetry; *Areas:* Medicine; *Markets:* Professional

Medical journal for chest physicians. Also publishes poetry up to 350 words relating to the concerns of healthcare providers. Send submissions by email. See website for full details.

The Christian Science Monitor

210 Massachusetts Avenue
Boston, MA 02115
Tel: +1 (617) 450-2300
Website: https://www.csmonitor.com

Publishes: Articles; Essays; News; Nonfiction; *Areas:* Culture; Current Affairs;

Finance; Literature; Nature; Religious; Science; *Markets:* Adult

Editors: Mark Sappenfield

Accepts new writers' work on spec only. Approach via contact forms on website.

Christianity & Literature

Department of English
Azusa Pacific University
901 E. Alosta Avenue
Azusa, CA 91702-7000
Email: cal@apu.edu
Website: https://www. christianityandliterature.com/journal

Publishes: Articles; Essays; Nonfiction; Poetry; Reviews; *Areas:* Literature; Religious; *Markets:* Academic; Adult

Editors: Mark Eaton

Journal devoted to the scholarly exploration of how literature engages Christian thought, experience, and practice. Submit articles and essays via online submission system. Send poems by post only. Book reviews by invitation only. See website for full details.

Cirque

Email: cirquejournal@gmail.com
Website: http://www.cirquejournal.com

Publishes: Essays; Fiction; Nonfiction; Poetry; Scripts; *Areas:* Drama; Short Stories; Translations; *Markets:* Adult; *Treatments:* Literary

Editors: Sandra Kleven

Publishes short stories, poems, creative nonfiction, translations, and plays by writers born in, or resident for at least five years in, the North Pacific Rim (Alaska, Washington, Oregon, Idaho, Montana, Hawaii, Yukon Territory, Alberta, British Columbia and Chukotka). Submit via online submission system.

Classical Singer

PO Box 1710
Draper, UT 84020
Email: support@csmusic.net
Website: https://csmusic.net

Publishes: Articles; News; Nonfiction; *Areas:* Music; *Markets:* Professional

Magazine for professional classical singers.

Clubhouse Magazine
Focus on the Family
8605 Explorer Drive
Colorado Springs, CO 80920
Tel: +1 (800) 232-6459
Website: https://www.
clubhousemagazine.com

Publishes: Essays; Fiction; Interviews; Nonfiction; *Areas:* Fantasy; Historical; Humour; Religious; Sci-Fi; Short Stories; *Markets:* Children's

Editors: Rachel Pfeiffer (Assistant Editor)

Magazine for boys and girls aged 8-12 providing wholesome, educational material with Scriptural or moral insight. Avoid bible stories, poems, and strictly informational pieces. See website for full guidelines.

Conjunctions
21 East 10th St., #3E
New York, NY 10003
Email: conjunctions@bard.edu
Website: http://www.conjunctions.com

Publishes: Fiction; Nonfiction; Poetry; *Areas:* Short Stories; *Markets:* Adult; *Treatments:* Literary

Editors: Bradford Morrow

Publishes short and long form fiction, poetry, and creative nonfiction. No academic essays or book reviews. Do not query or send samples – submit complete ms by post with SASE. If submitting from outside the US, submissions may be sent by email. See website for full guidelines.

Construction Equipment Guide
470 Maryland Drive
Fort Washington, PA 19034
Tel: +1 (800) 523-2200
Email: cmongeau@cegltd.com
Website: https://www.
constructionequipmentguide.com

Publishes: News; Nonfiction; *Areas:* Business; Technology; *Markets:* Professional

Editors: Craig Mongeau; Christine Allen

Covers the United States with four regional newspapers offering construction industry news and information, and new and used construction equipment for sale.

Coping with Cancer Magazine
PO Box 682268
Franklin, TN 37068-2268
Tel: +1 (615) 790-2400
Email: info@copingmag.com
Website: https://www.copingmag.com

Publishes: Articles; Nonfiction; Poetry; *Areas:* Health; Medicine; *Markets:* Adult; *Treatments:* Positive

Publishes articles, poems, reflections, and professional advice relating to cancer. See website for full submission guidelines.

Copper Nickel
Email: wayne.miller@ucdenver.edu
Website: http://copper-nickel.org

Publishes: Essays; Fiction; Nonfiction; Poetry; *Areas:* Short Stories; Translations; *Markets:* Adult; *Treatments:* Literary

Editors: Wayne Miller (Managing Editor); Brian Barker (Poetry Editor); Nicky Beer (Poetry Editor); Joanna Luloff (Fiction and Nonfiction Editor); Teague Bohlen (Fiction Editor)

Submit four to six poems, or one story or one essay at a time. Wait at least six months between submissions. Submit via online submission system.

Creative Knitting
Website: https://www.
creativeknittingmagazine.com

Publishes: Nonfiction; *Areas:* Crafts; Design; Hobbies; *Markets:* Adult

Knitting magazine, featuring clear instructions for classic and current trends in knitting design.

Curve

Email: editor@curvemag.com
Website: http://www.curvemag.com

Publishes: Articles; News; Nonfiction; *Areas:* Culture; Entertainment; Film; Lifestyle; Literature; TV; *Markets:* Adult

Editors: Merryn Johns

Magazine of lesbian culture, entertainment, and lifestyle.

The Daily Tea

Media40
1000 Germantown Pike, Suite F2
Plymouth Meeting, PA 19462
Tel: +1 (484) 688-0299
Email: alexis@thedailytea.com
Website: http://thedailytea.com

Publishes: Articles; Essays; Features; Interviews; Nonfiction; *Areas:* Historical; How-to; Humour; Travel; *Markets:* Adult

Magazine publishing material relating to tea. Send query with proposal or complete ms.

DairyBusiness

1350C W Southport Road Suite 297
Indianapolis, IN 46217
Tel: +1 (317) 721-4694
Email: WebContact@DairyBusiness.com
Website: https://www.dairybusiness.com

Publishes: Articles; Interviews; Nonfiction; *Areas:* Business; Nature; *Markets:* Professional

Magazine covering the large-herd commercial dairy industry.

DargonZine

Email: editor@dargonzine.org
Website: http://dargonzine.org

Publishes: Fiction; *Areas:* Fantasy; Short Stories; *Markets:* Adult

Electronic magazine publishing fantasy fiction based in a shared world, where authors write in a common milieu, sharing settings, mythos, and characters. To submit, writers need to join (free until a year after first publication) and work with a mentor to produce a piece of work that will fit the shared world.

december Magazine

PO Box 16130
St. Louis, MO 63130
Tel: +1 (314) 956-9210
Email: jenniferg@decembermag.org
Website: http://decembermag.org

Publishes: Essays; Fiction; Nonfiction; Poetry; *Areas:* Arts; Autobiography; Biography; Culture; Entertainment; Humour; Literature; Short Stories; Women's Interests; *Markets:* Adult; *Treatments:* Experimental; Literary; Progressive; Satirical

Editors: Jennifer Goldring

An independent non-profit literary journal that is published twice a year. We publish poetry, fiction, creative nonfiction, and art. We accept submissions from October 1 to May 15 through our submission portal online. We charge a small administrative fee ($2.50) to help cover our cost for the submission manager. You may also submit for free via USPS. Our complete submission guidelines are on our website. We do not read full manuscripts. We read short stories and essays of any length and we will read up to 5 poems at a time.

Deracine

Email: deracinemagazine@gmail.com
Website: http://deracinemagazine. wordpress.com

Publishes: Fiction; Poetry; *Areas:* Gothic; Literature; *Markets:* Adult; Professional; Youth; *Treatments:* Contemporary; Cynical; Dark; Experimental; In-depth; Literary; Serious

Editors: Victoria Elghasen and Michelle Baleka

A literary magazine featuring dark, psychological fiction, poetry, and art. Started in 2017, we are a nonprofit publication. Our goal is to share literature that raises awareness of and expresses psychological issues and feelings of displacement through the literary gothic. We're open to a variety of styles, including writing that is minimalistic or that has elements of fantasy or horror, so long as it fits within our theme.

Descant

c/o TCU Department of English
Box 297270
2850 S. University Dr.
Fort Worth, TX 76129
Email: descant@tcu.edu
Website: https://descant.tcu.edu

Publishes: Fiction; Poetry; *Areas:* Short Stories; *Markets:* Adult; *Treatments:* Literary

Submit one story up to 5,000 words, or up to five poems via online submission system, or by post with SASE. Closed to submissions in April, May, June, July, and August. See website for full guidelines.

Digital Engineering

111 Speen Street, Ste 200
Framingham MA 01701
Tel: +1 (508) 663-1500
Email: de-editors@digitaleng.news
Website: http://www.digitaleng.news

Publishes: Articles; News; Nonfiction; *Areas:* Design; Technology; *Markets:* Professional

Magazine covering the use of computers and other digital technology for design / engineering.

Downstate Story

1825 Maple Ridge
Peoria, IL 61614
Tel: +1 (309) 688-1409
Email: chopkins7@prodigy.net
Website: https://www.downstatestory.com

Publishes: Fiction; *Areas:* Short Stories; *Markets:* Adult; *Treatments:* Literary

Editors: Elaine Hopkins

A regional magazine featuring mostly writers from Illinois and the Midwest. As of 2012, online only.

Ecotone

Department of Creative Writing
University of North Carolina Wilmington
601 South College Road
Wilmington, NC 28403-5938
Email: info@ecotonejournal.com
Website: https://ecotonemagazine.org

Publishes: Fiction; Nonfiction; Poetry; *Markets:* Adult; *Treatments:* Literary

Editors: David Gessner

Publishes work from a wide range of voices. Particularly interested in hearing from writers historically underrepresented in literary publishing and in place-based contexts: people of colour, Indigenous people, people with disabilities, gender-nonconforming people, LGBTQIA+, women, and others. Check website for specific reading periods and submit prose up to 30 double-spaced pages or 3-5 poems by post with SAE or using online system ($3 charge). No hard copy submissions from outside the US.

Edison Literary Review

13 Waverly Drive East
Edison, NJ 08817
Website: http://edisonliteraryreview.org

Publishes: Poetry; *Markets:* Adult; *Treatments:* Literary

Submit 3-5 poems. Poems under 40 lines stand a better chance of acceptance. Will accept submissions by post with SASE, but prefers submissions via form on website.

Electronic Musician

NewBay Media, LLC
28 East 28th Street, 12th floor
New York, NY 10016
Email: gino@ginorobair.com
Website: https://www.emusician.com

Publishes: Articles; News; Nonfiction; Reviews; *Areas:* Business; Music; Technology; *Markets:* Adult

Editors: Gino Robair

Magazine covering all aspects of music production: performance, recording, and technology. Includes product news and reviews on the latest equipment and services, tips and techniques, gear reviews, and insights from top artists.

Ellery Queen Mystery Magazine

Tel: +1 (212) 686-7188 x 675
Email: elleryqueenmm@dellmagazines.com
Website: http://www.
elleryqueenmysterymagazine.com

Publishes: Fiction; *Areas:* Crime; Mystery; Short Stories; *Markets:* Adult

Mystery magazine, publishing every kind of mystery short story: psychological suspense; deductive puzzle; private eye case; realistic to imaginative; hard-boiled to "cozies". However, no explicit sex or violence, or true crime. Always seeking original detective stories, and especially happy to review first stories by authors who have never before published fiction professionally (submit to the "Department of First Stories). No need to send query – unsolicited MSS welcome. Submit through online system (see website for details). Accepts postal submissions only from those with a prior publishing history with the magazine.

Empty Mirror

Email: mirror@emptymirrorbooks.com
Website: http://www.emptymirrorbooks.com

Publishes: Articles; Essays; Features; Interviews; Nonfiction; Poetry; Reviews; *Areas:* Arts; Criticism; Culture; Literature; Music; *Markets:* Adult; *Treatments:* Experimental; In-depth; Literary

Editors: Denise Enck

We accept features, articles, criticism and essays on literary or art-related topics, for instance, essays about authors or artists, styles or periods, places, movements, or some aspect of writing or art. Scholarly papers are sometimes accepted. Book reviews and interviews are welcome.

We occasionally accept previously published nonfiction.

For personal essays, we especially like to some connection to art or literature or to cultural or societal issues.

Special interests include art and literature outside the mainstream, the Beat Generation, Surrealism, and countercultural movements.

We also publish poetry and are very open to experimental poetry and visual poetry.

Emrys Journal

The Emrys Foundation
201 West Stone Avenue, Suite D
Greenville, SC 29609
Email: info@emrys.org
Website: http://www.emrys.org

Publishes: Fiction; Nonfiction; Poetry; *Areas:* Short Stories; *Markets:* Adult; *Treatments:* Literary

Editors: Katherine Burgess

Literary journal publishing fiction, poetry, and creative nonfiction. Submit up to three poems or prose up to 5,000 words between August 1 and November 1 annually, via online submission system. No postal submissions. $250 awarded to one piece selected from each category.

Enchanted Living

Email: submissions@faeriemag.com
Website: https://enchantedlivingmag.com

Publishes: Articles; Fiction; Nonfiction; Poetry; *Areas:* Arts; Beauty and Fashion; Crafts; Design; Fantasy; Nature; Travel; *Markets:* Adult

A quarterly print magazine that celebrates all things enchanted. Publishes photography, recipes, original fiction and poetry, travel pieces, artist profiles, home decor, otherworldly beauty tips, craft tutorials, and more. Send submissions by email. See website for specific email address for poetry.

Enchanted Tales Literary Magazine

Email: enchantedtaleslitmag@gmail.com
Website: http://enchantedtalesliterarymagazine.weebly.com

Publishes: Fiction; Poetry; *Areas:* Fantasy; Romance; Short Stories; *Markets:* Academic; *Treatments:* Literary

Editors: Alexa Findlay

A not-for-profit online global literary magazine. Our mission is to create a space for writers and artists to share their passion and love for fairy tales as much as we do. We are dedicated to publishing new fairy tales as well as re-told classic fairy tales.

The Engravers Journal

P.O. Box 318
Brighton, MI 48116-0318
Tel: +1 (810) 229-5725
Fax: +1 (810) 229-8320
Email: editor@engraversjournal.com
Website: http://www.engraversjournal.com

Publishes: Articles; Nonfiction; *Areas:* Business; How-to; Technology; *Markets:* Professional

Magazine offering practical advice and trade-oriented articles for the recognition and personalisation industry.

Essence

241 37th Street, 4th floor
Brooklyn, NY 11232
Email: toletters@essence.com
Website: http://www.essence.com

Publishes: Articles; Nonfiction; *Areas:* Beauty and Fashion; Culture; Entertainment; Health; Lifestyle; Politics; *Markets:* Adult

Magazine of black culture.

The Evansville Review

University of Evansville Creative Writing Department
Room 416A, Olmsted Administration Hall
1800 Lincoln Avenue
Evansville, IN 47722
Tel: +1 (812) 488-2963
Email: evvreview@evansville.edu
Website: https://www.evansville.edu/majors/creativewriting/evansvilleReview.cfm

Publishes: Fiction; Interviews; Nonfiction; Poetry; Scripts; *Areas:* Drama; Short Stories; *Markets:* Adult; *Treatments:* Experimental; Literary; Traditional

Publishes poetry, fiction, nonfiction, plays, and interviews by a wide range of authors, from emerging writers to Nobel Prize recipients. Accepts submissions between September 1 and October 31 annually, through online submission system.

failbetter.com

2022 Grove Avenue
Richmond, VA 23220
Email: editor@failbetter.com
Website: http://failbetter.com

Publishes: Fiction; Poetry; *Areas:* Short Stories; *Markets:* Adult; *Treatments:* Literary

Online literary journal. Publishes poetry, short stories, self-contained novel excerpts, and novellas. Send one piece of prose or between 4 and 6 poems at a time via online submission system.

Feminist Studies

4137 Susquehannna Hall
4200 Lehigh Road
University of Maryland
College Park, MD 20742
Tel: +1 (301) 405-7415
Fax: +1 (301) 405-8395
Email: info@feministstudies.org
Website: http://www.feministstudies.org

Publishes: Essays; Fiction; Nonfiction; Poetry; *Areas:* Criticism; Short Stories; Women's Interests; *Markets:* Academic; Adult

Feminist journal publishing research and criticism, creative writing, art, essays, and other forms of writing and visual expression. See website for submission guidelines and specific submission email addresses.

The Fifth Di...

Email: thefifthdi@yahoo.com
Website: http://www.
nomadicdeliriumpress.com/fifth.htm

Publishes: Fiction; *Areas:* Fantasy; Sci-Fi;
Short Stories; *Markets:* Adult

Publishes science fiction and fantasy stories
up to 10,000 words. No horror or poetry.
Flash fiction is unlikely to find favour unless
exceptional. Send submissions by email as
RTF attachments. No Word files. See
website for full guidelines.

Five:2:One

Website: http://five2onemagazine.com

Publishes: Essays; Fiction; Nonfiction;
Poetry; *Areas:* Short Stories; *Markets:* Adult;
Treatments: Experimental; Literary

Publishes fiction of 1,000 words or more;
visual / experimental / written poetry of 120
words or more; and nonfiction / essays /
manifestos of 1,000 words or more. Submit
online through website.

Flint Hills Review

Dept. of English, Modern Languages, and
Journalism
Emporia State University
1 Kellogg Circle
Emporia, KS 66801
Email: bluestem@emporia.edu
Website: http://www.emporia.edu/fhr

Publishes: Fiction; Nonfiction; Poetry;
Scripts; *Areas:* Drama; Short Stories;
Markets: Adult; *Treatments:* Literary

Annual literary magazine, publishing poetry,
short stories, short plays, and creative
nonfiction. Send 3-6 poems, short fiction
2,000-5,000 words (or one or two short
pieces of flash fiction between 500 and 1,500
words), play scripts up to 10 minutes, or
creative nonfiction between 2,000 and 5,000
words. Accepts work both by post and by
email. See website for full details.

Florida Monthly

999 Douglas Avenue, Suite 3301
Altamonte Springs, FL 32714
Tel: +1 (407) 816-9596
Fax: +1 (407) 816-9373
Email: editorial@floridamagazine.com
Website: https://www.floridamagazine.com

Publishes: Articles; Features; Interviews;
News; Nonfiction; Reviews; *Areas:*
Business; Finance; Health; Historical;
Lifestyle; Sport; Travel; *Markets:* Adult

General interest magazine covering Florida.
Send query with published clips.

Flyway: Journal of Writing & Environment

Email: flywayjournal@gmail.com
Website: https://flyway.org

Publishes: Essays; Fiction; Nonfiction;
Poetry; *Areas:* Nature; Short Stories;
Markets: Adult; *Treatments:* Literary

Online journal publishing poetry, fiction,
nonfiction, and visual art that explores the
many complicated facets of the word
"environment". Submit online between
August 15 and May 1 each year.

Fogged Clarity

Email: submissions@foggedclarity.com
Website: http://foggedclarity.com

Publishes: Essays; Fiction; Nonfiction;
Poetry; Reviews; *Markets:* Adult;
Treatments: Literary

Online journal publishing poetry, fiction,
essays, reviews and visual art. Send up to
five poems, or up to two pieces of prose up
to 8,000 words, or one review between 300
and 1,000 words.

Fourteen Hills

Fourteen Hills Press
Department of Creative Writing
San Francisco State University
1600 Holloway Avenue
San Francisco, CA 94137
Email: hills@sfsu.edu
Website: http://www.14hills.net

Publishes: Fiction; Nonfiction; Poetry;
Areas: Short Stories; *Markets:* Adult;
Treatments: Literary

Publishes poetry, fiction, and creative nonfiction. Submit 1-3 poems (up to 7 pages max); or one short story or novel excerpt, or piece of creative nonfiction (up to 20 pages or 6,000 words). Submit via website using online submission system ($2 charge for non-subscribers). Accepts submissions between September 1 and December 1, and between March 1 and June 1, annually.

The Fourth River

Email: 4thriver@gmail.com
Website: https://www.thefourthriver.com

Publishes: Fiction; Nonfiction; Poetry; *Areas:* Short Stories; *Markets:* Adult; *Treatments:* Literary

Print and digital literary magazine publishing creative writing that explores the relationship between humans and their environments, whether natural or man-made. Submit 3-5 poems or prose up to 7,000 words between July 1 and December 1, via online submission system. No submissions by email.

Alternatively, submit one poem or up to 500 words of fiction or nonfiction for online publication at any time of the year.

Fugue

Email: fugue@uidaho.edu
Website: http://www.fuguejournal.com

Publishes: Essays; Fiction; Nonfiction; Poetry; *Areas:* Short Stories; *Markets:* Adult; *Treatments:* Literary

Editors: Caitlin Hill, Editor-in-Chief; Steven Pfau, Managing Editor

Submit up to 5 poems, up to two short shorts, one story, or one essay per submission. Accepts submissions online only, between September 1 and May 1. Submission service charges $3 per submission.

Gallows Hill

Email: josh@gallowshillmagazine.com
Website: https://gallowshillmagazine.com

Publishes: Fiction; Interviews; News; Nonfiction; Poetry; Reviews; *Areas:* Horror; *Markets:* Adult; *Treatments:* Dark

Print and online horror magazine publishing fiction up to 12,000 words (online) or 6,000 words (print), dark poetry, and nonfiction, including creative nonfiction, stranger-than-fiction, real life horror, movie and book reviews, and horror community reviews. Submit through online submission system.

Garbled Transmissions

Email: editor@garbledtransmission.com
Website: http://garbledtransmission.com

Publishes: Fiction; News; Nonfiction; Reviews; *Areas:* Fantasy; Film; Sci-Fi; *Markets:* Adult; *Treatments:* Dark

Editors: James Robert Payne

Online magazine publishing science fiction and fantasy short stories between 500 and 15,000 words, and book, movie, and comic book reviews and news, slanted towards the science fiction and fantasy genres, between 500 and 3,000 words. Submit by email as .doc or OpenOffice documents. Responds in a month to all serious enquiries. Accepts simultaneous submissions, but no multiple submissions.

A Gathering of the Tribes

PO Box 20693
Tompkins Square Station
New York, NY 10009
Tel: +1 (212) 777-2038
Email: gatheringofthetribes@gmail.com
Website: http://www.tribes.org

Publishes: Essays; Fiction; Interviews; Nonfiction; Poetry; *Areas:* Arts; Short Stories; *Markets:* Adult; *Treatments:* Literary

Magazine focusing on excellence in the arts from a diverse perspective.

Gertrude

Email: EditorGertrudePress@gmail.com
Website: http://www.gertrudepress.org

Publishes: Essays; Fiction; Interviews; Nonfiction; Poetry; Reviews; *Markets:* Adult; *Treatments:* Literary

Editors: Tammy

Closed to fiction submissions as at May 2018. Check website for current status.

Online LGBTQA journal publishing fiction, poetry, and creative nonfiction. Subject matter need not be LGBTQA-specific, and writers from all backgrounds are welcomed. Submit fiction or creative nonfiction up to 3,000 words, or up to five poems (no line limit, but under 40 lines preferred), via online submission system. For book reviews and interviews, email editor with proposal. See website for full guidelines.

The Gettysburg Review
Gettysburg College
300 N. Washington Street
Gettysburg, PA 17325-1491
Tel: +1 (717) 337-6770
Email: mdrew@gettysburg.edu
Website: http://www.gettysburgreview.com

Publishes: Essays; Fiction; Poetry; Reviews; *Areas:* Short Stories; *Markets:* Adult; *Treatments:* Literary

Editors: Mark Drew, Editor

Send submission by post with SASE for return, or through online submission system (small admin charge). Accepts submissions from September 1 to May 31 only: submissions received between June 1 and August 31 are returned unread. For poetry, submit up to five poems. Accepts both short poetry and longer narrative verse. Fiction is usually short stories, but will consider longer pieces for serialisation. No length limit. Accepts essays on any subject, so long as treated in a literary fashion. Simultaneous submissions accepted if immediate notification of acceptance elsewhere is given. No previously published material or submissions by fax or email.

Grasslimb
PO Box 420816
San Diego, CA 92142

Email: editor@grasslimb.com
Website: http://www.grasslimb.com

Publishes: Fiction; Nonfiction; Poetry; Reviews; *Areas:* Short Stories; *Markets:* Adult; *Treatments:* Literary

Editors: Valerie Polichar

Submit 4-6 poems, or prose up to 2,500 words, by email or by post. No submissions via links/downloads. See website for full details.

Green Hills Literary Lantern
Dept of English and Linguistics
Truman State University
Kirksville, MO 63501
Email: adavis@truman.edu
Website: http://ghll.truman.edu

Publishes: Fiction; Poetry; *Areas:* Short Stories; *Markets:* Adult; *Treatments:* Literary

Editors: Adam Brooke Davis; Joe Benevento

Online, open-access journal. Submit 3-7 poems, a short story or excerpt from a novel (15-18 double-spaced pages), or up to three short shorts, by email as a .doc, .rtf, or .txt attachment; or by post with SASE if return is required. See website for full details.

Green Mountains Review (GMR)
Johnson, VT 05656
Email: gmr@jsc.edu
Website: http://greenmountainsreview.com

Publishes: Essays; Fiction; Interviews; Nonfiction; Poetry; Reviews; *Areas:* Short Stories; *Markets:* Adult; *Treatments:* Literary

Editors: Jessica Hendry Nelson

Literary magazine publishing poetry, fiction, creative nonfiction, literary essays, interviews, and book reviews by both well-known writers and promising newcomers. Submit up to 5 poems, or prose up to 25 pages, via online submission system ($3 charge per submission).

Guernica

447 Broadway, 2nd Floor
New York, NY 10013
Email: editors@guernicamag.com
Website: https://www.guernicamag.com

Publishes: Essays; Fiction; Interviews;
News; Nonfiction; Poetry; Reviews; *Areas:*
Arts; Autobiography; Politics; Short Stories;
Translations; *Markets:* Adult; *Treatments:*
Literary

Editors: Hillary Brenhouse; Rachel Riederer

Non-profit online magazine focused on the
intersection of arts and politics. Prefers work
with a diverse international outlook – or, if
it's American, from an underrepresented or
alternative perspective. No stories about
American tourists in other countries. Submit
fiction between 1,200 and 4,500 words; up to
five poems of any length (translations
welcome); news, reviews, Q&A, and
commentary up to 2,500 words; or memoirs,
essays, reportage, or interviews between
2,500 and 7,500 words. Submit via online
form on website only.

Gulf Coast: A Journal of Literature and Fine Arts

4800 Calhoun Road
Houston, TX 77204-3013
Email: gulfcoastmc@gmail.com
Website: http://www.gulfcoastmag.org

Publishes: Essays; Fiction; Interviews;
Nonfiction; Poetry; Reviews; *Markets:*
Adult; *Treatments:* Literary

Editors: Luisa Muradyan Tannahill

Submit up to five poems, or fiction or essays
up to 7,000 words, by post or via online
submission manager. For other material,
send query by email to address on website.
$2.50 submission fee. Accepts material
September 1 to March 1, annually.

Gulf Stream Magazine

FIU English Dept. AC 1 338
3000 NE 151 St.
North Miami, FL 33181
Email: gulfstreamlitmag@gmail.com
Website: https://gulfstreamlitmag.com

Publishes: Fiction; Interviews; Nonfiction;
Poetry; Reviews; *Markets:* Adult;
Treatments: Literary

Editors: Ariel Francisco

A print magazine until 2008, now publishes
two online issues a year. Publishes fiction up
to 5,000 words; nonfiction; poetry; artwork;
and graphic narratives. Submit via online
submission system or by post. No
submissions by email. Reading periods run
from September 1 to November 1, and
January 15 to April 1. No work by current or
former students of the university.

Haibun Today

Email: ray@raysweb.net
Website: http://haibuntoday.com

Publishes: Articles; Interviews; Nonfiction;
Poetry; Reviews; *Areas:* Literature; *Markets:*
Adult; *Treatments:* Literary

Editors: Ray Rasmussen; Melissa Allen;
Rich Youmans; Terri French; Tish Davis;
Tim Gardiner; Patricia Prime

Online magazine publishing haibun, tanka
prose, and nonfiction, including articles,
interviews, reviews, and commentary. See
website for specific email addresses to use
for specific times / genres and full
submission guidelines.

Haight Ashbury Literary Journal

558 Joost Avenue
San Francisco, CA 94127
Email: haljeditor@gmail.com
Website: https://haightashburyliteraryjournal.
wordpress.com

Publishes: Fiction; Poetry; *Areas:* Short
Stories; *Markets:* Adult; *Treatments:*
Literary

Publishes poetry and fiction – often by
people who have been marginalised,
oppressed, or abused. Submit up to 6 poems
and/or 1-3 short stories or one long story.
Submit by post with SASE. Email
submissions from overseas authors only.

Hanging Loose

231 Wyckoff Street
Brooklyn, NY 11217
Tel: +1 (317) 529-4738
Fax: +1 (347) 227-8215
Email: print225@aol.com
Website: http://hangingloosepress.com

Publishes: Fiction; Poetry; *Markets:* Adult;
Treatments: Literary

Send up to six poems or one story at a time.
Potential contributors should familiarise
themselves with the magazine before
submitting. Includes regular section of High
School writers. Send submissions by post
with SASE. Allow up to three months for a
response.

Hawai'i Pacific Review

Website: https://hawaiipacificreview.org

Publishes: Essays; Fiction; Nonfiction;
Poetry; *Markets:* Adult; *Treatments:*
Experimental; Literary

Editors: Tyler McMahon

Literary journal founded in 1987, publishing
online only as of 2013. Publishes poetry and
prose by authors from Hawai'i, the
mainland, and around the world, on a rolling
basis. Accepts poetry, short fiction, and
personal essays. Encourages experimental
narrative techniques and poetic styles. Send
up to three poems or fiction or nonfiction up
to 4,000 words, via online submission
system.

Hawai'i Review

Hemenway Hall 107
2445 Campus Road
Honolulu, HI 96822
Tel: +1 (808) 956-3030
Fax: +1 (808) 956-3083
Email: managing@hawaiireview.org
Website: http://hawaiireview.org

Publishes: Essays; Fiction; Nonfiction;
Poetry; Scripts; *Areas:* Arts; Autobiography;
Fantasy; Music; Science; Sci-Fi; Short
Stories; Translations; *Markets:* Adult;
Treatments: Literary

Editors: LynleyShimat Lys; Sashily Kling;
Marley Aiu; Tina Togafau

Accepts Prose (Fiction, Creative Nonfiction,
Lyric Essay); Poetry; Theatre and Drama;
Visual and Performing Arts; Hybrid and
Multimedia Work; Translation, Creative
Translation, and Multilingual Work; and
Educational Materials. Submit through
online submission system.

Hayden's Ferry Review

Box 870302
Arizona State University
Tempe, AZ 85287
Email: hfr@asu.edu
Website: http://www.haydensferryreview.org

Publishes: Essays; Fiction; Nonfiction;
Poetry; *Areas:* Short Stories; *Markets:* Adult;
Treatments: Literary

Submit up to six poems or one essay or piece
of fiction per submission only, via online
submission system. See website.

The Helix

Email: helixmagazine@gmail.com
Website: https://helixmagazine.org

Publishes: Essays; Fiction; Nonfiction;
Poetry; Scripts; *Areas:* Drama; Short Stories;
Markets: Adult; *Treatments:* Literary

Editors: Victoria-Lynn Bell

Publishes fiction, creative nonfiction, poetry,
plays, and art. Submit up to four pieces of
prose up to 3,000 words each, or up to four
poems.

HelloHorror

Email: submissions@hellohorror.com
Website: http://www.hellohorror.com

Publishes: Fiction; Nonfiction; Poetry;
Areas: Horror; Psychology; Short Stories;
Markets: Adult

Online magazine, publishing fiction, short
stories, micros, flash fiction, nonfiction, and
poetry, in the horror genre. Aims to offer
something new within the genre, with a
focus on the psychological aspects of horror.
See website for full submission guidelines.

Hennen's Observer

Email: moderator@hennensobserver.com
Website: https://www.hennensobserver.com

Publishes: Articles; Fiction; Nonfiction;
Poetry; *Areas:* Arts; Entertainment; Short
Stories; *Markets:* Adult; *Treatments:*
Literary

Literary magazine and website that supports
artists taking their first steps in the world of
publishing. Join online community for free in
order to submit work. Selected works from
those submitted to the online community will
be chosen for print publication and receive
payment. Also runs competitions.

Hoot

Email: info@hootreview.com
Website: http://www.hootreview.com

Publishes: Fiction; Nonfiction; Poetry;
Reviews; *Areas:* Autobiography; *Markets:*
Adult; *Treatments:* Literary

Publishes a postcard each month featuring
one piece of fiction or nonfiction up to 150
words, or one poem, up to 10 lines. Publishes
four pieces in each online issue. Accepts
fiction, nonfiction, memoir, poetry, and book
reviews year-round. Graphic fiction /
nonfiction also welcome, but it must fit on a
postcard. Submit via online submission
system.

Ibbetson Street

25 School Street
Somerville, MA 02143
Tel: +1 (617) 628-2313
Email: tapestryofvoices@yahoo.com
Website: http://ibbetsonpress.com

Publishes: Poetry; *Markets:* Adult;
Treatments: Literary

Editors: Harris Gardner; Lawrence
Kessenich; Emily Pineau

Publishes poetry that is not too abstract.
Looks for simplicity and economy of words.
Send 3-5 poems with author bio in the body
of an email with "Poetry Submission" in the
subject line. No attachments.

Iconoclast

1675 Amazon Road
Mohegan Lake, NY 10547-1804
Website: http://www.
iconoclastliterarymagazine.com

Publishes: Fiction; Poetry; *Areas:* Short
Stories; *Markets:* Adult; *Treatments:*
Literary

Editors: Phil Wagner

Publishes poetry and prose from authors
interested in the creation, sharing, and
transmission of ideas, imaginings, and
experiences. Send prose up to 3,500 words or
poetry up to two pages with SASE. See
website for full guidelines.

Idaho Review

Boise State University
1910 University Drive
Boise, Idaho 83725
Email: mwieland@boisestate.edu
Website: http://idahoreview.org

Publishes: Fiction; Poetry; *Areas:* Short
Stories; *Markets:* Adult; *Treatments:*
Literary

**Closed to submissions until September
2019.**

Annual literary journal publishing poetry and
fiction. No specific limit for fiction, but most
of the stories accepted are under 25 double-
spaced pages. For poetry, submit up to five
poems. Reading period runs from September
to March (see website for specific dates for
this year). Accepts submissions by post with
SASE, but prefers submissions through
online submission system ($3 fee).

Indefinite Space

PO Box 40101
Pasadena, CA 91114
Email: indefinitespace@yahoo.com
Website: http://www.indefinitespace.net

Publishes: Poetry; *Markets:* Adult;
Treatments: Experimental; Literary

Literary journal publishing innovative,
imagistic, philosophical, and experimental

poetry, drawings, collage, photography and paintings. Reads year round.

Indiana Review

Indiana University
Ballantine Hall 529
1020 E. Kirkwood Avenue
Indiana University
Bloomington, IN 47405-7103
Tel: +1 (812) 855-3439
Email: inreview@indiana.edu
Website: http://www.indiana.edu/~inreview

Publishes: Essays; Fiction; Nonfiction; Reviews; *Areas:* Short Stories; Translations; *Markets:* Adult; *Treatments:* Literary

Editors: Tessa Yang

Send fiction or nonfiction up 8,000 words or 3-6 poems per submission, during specific submission windows only (see website for details). No submissions by post or by email – all submissions must be made through online submission manager ($3 fee). See website for full guidelines, and to submit.

Infinite Rust

Texas Southern University
Department of English – MLK 107
3100 Cleburne Street
Houston, TX 77004
Email: editor@infiniterust.com
Website: http://www.infiniterust.com

Publishes: Articles; Essays; Features; Fiction; Interviews; Nonfiction; Poetry; *Areas:* Arts; Autobiography; Biography; Criticism; Culture; Current Affairs; Historical; Lifestyle; Literature; Music; Philosophy; Photography; Politics; Short Stories; Sociology; Spiritual; Travel; Women's Interests; *Markets:* Academic; Adult; Professional; *Treatments:* Contemporary; Experimental; Literary; Niche; Progressive; Satirical

Editors: Marjorie Ward; Dr. Michael Sollars

University-affiliated quarterly online literary arts journal showcasing creative work. We publish short fiction, poetry, creative nonfiction, and essays, as well as art and photography. The goal of our publication is to assemble a variety of literary and artistic

styles as well as a broad range of voices, perspectives, and life experiences.

We accept unsolicited submissions year-round, however the submission deadline for our Spring 2019 issue is February 28, 2019. We are interested in unexpected new perspectives, originality of language, creative vision, and high-quality content. Send us your best work, we are excited to read it.

Please include a brief author bio of no more than 100 words. Limit submissions to no more than 2,500 words of prose, five poems, or five artworks or photographic images. Works previously published elsewhere cannot be submitted. Simultaneous and multiple submissions are fine. Please notify if work gets accepted for publication elsewhere. Contributors retain all rights to their work. We do not charge a submission fee.

Please visit our website to view our current issue and to submit your work.

InJoy Magazine

2302 Noblewood Road
Edgewater, MD 21037
Tel: +1 (660) 281-4488
Email: cjsmith@injoymagazine.com
Website: http://www.injoymagazine.com

Publishes: Articles; Features; Fiction; Poetry; Reviews; *Areas:* Arts; Beauty and Fashion; Culture; Entertainment; Hobbies; How-to; Humour; Romance; Short Stories; Spiritual; Women's Interests; *Markets:* Family; *Treatments:* Positive

Editors: Crystal Smith

Provides a collaborative platform for art, encouragement and enjoying life. Our target audience is Women in all walks of life seeking to connect with others, share stories and laugh.

The Iowa Review

The University of Iowa
308 English-Philosophy Building
Iowa City, IA 52242
Tel: +1 (319) 335-0462

---

*Access more listings online at **www.firstwriter.com***

Fax: +1 (319) 335-2535
Email: iowa-review@uiowa.edu
Website: http://www.iowareview.org

Publishes: Essays; Fiction; Poetry; Reviews;
Areas: Short Stories; Translations; *Markets:*
Adult; *Treatments:* Literary

Editors: Harilaos Stecopoulos

Publishes poetry, fiction, and nonfiction.
Submit in September, October, and
November only, via online submission
system ($4 charge for non-subscribers) or by
post with SASE. Accepts prose up to 25
pages and poetry up to 8 pages (query by
email if your poem is longer). Do not mix
genres in a single envelope. Work must be
unpublished. Simultaneous submissions
accepted if immediate notification of
acceptance elsewhere is given.

J Journal
Department of English
John Jay College of Criminal Justice
524 West 59th Street, 7th Floor
New York, NY 10019
Email: submissionsjjournal@gmail.com
Website: http://jjournal2.jjay.cuny.edu/
jjournal/

Publishes: Essays; Fiction; Nonfiction;
Poetry; *Areas:* Crime; Legal; Short Stories;
Markets: Adult; *Treatments:* Literary

Publishes fiction, creative nonfiction (1st
person narrative, personal essay, memoir)
and poetry that examines questions of
justice, either obliquely or directly
addressing crime and the criminal justice
system. Unlikely to publish genre fiction.
Send up to three poems or prose up to 6,000
words.

Josephine Quarterly
Website: https://www.
josephinequarterly.com

Publishes: Poetry; *Markets:* Adult;
Treatments: Literary

Online poetry journal. Submit up to five
poems of any length via online submission
system.

Kaimana: Literary Arts Hawai'i
Email: reimersa001@hawaii.rr.com
Website: http://www.hawaii.edu/hlac/
kaimana.htm

Publishes: Fiction; Poetry; *Areas:* Short
Stories; *Markets:* Adult; *Treatments:*
Literary

Publishes poetry and fiction, with a
particular (but not exclusive) interest in work
which makes reference to the Pacific / Asia /
Polynesia / Hawai'i. Send complete ms with
SASE. No submissions by email.

Kairos
Email: submissions.kairos@gmail.com
Website: http://kairoslit.com

Publishes: Articles; Fiction; Nonfiction;
Poetry; *Areas:* Short Stories; *Markets:* Adult;
Treatments: Literary

Publishes poetry, fiction, creative nonfiction,
and opinion / editorial pieces. Submit up to
five poems or prose up to 10,000 words.

La Galería
Email: submissions@lagaleriamag.com
Website: http://www.lagaleriamag.com

Publishes: Articles; Fiction; Nonfiction;
Poetry; *Areas:* Culture; *Markets:* Adult

Publishes articles and creative writing that
highlight issues and topics that are of interest
to the Dominican Diaspora. See website for
full submission guidelines.

Lake Relo
2820 Bagnell Dam Boulevard, #1B
Lake Ozark, MO 65049
Tel: +1 (573) 365-2323
Fax: +1 (573) 365-2351
Email: SPublishingCO@msn.com
Website: http://www.
relocatingtothelakeoftheozarks.com

Publishes: Articles; Features; Nonfiction;
Areas: Entertainment; Lifestyle; Travel;
Markets: Adult

Magazine for people relocating to the Lake
Ozark area.

Little Rose Magazine

460 N 50 E
Apt 460
Orem, UT 84057
Email: littlerosemagazine@gmail.com
Website: https://littlerosemagazine.
weebly.com/

Publishes: Articles; Essays; Fiction;
Interviews; Nonfiction; Poetry; *Areas:* Arts;
Autobiography; Culture; Current Affairs;
Entertainment; Lifestyle; Literature;
Photography; Politics; Psychology;
Religious; Self-Help; Short Stories;
Sociology; Spiritual; Technology; *Markets:*
Academic; Adult; Family; Professional;
Youth; *Treatments:* Contemporary;
Experimental; Literary; Progressive; Serious;
Traditional

Editors: Kendra Nuttall

A Utah-based online magazine of literature
and art, aiming to confront issues of identity,
such as gender, race, class, religion,
intersectionality, internet identity, and
culture. We want to give artists and authors a
space to reveal everything about the human
experience – the good, bad, ugly, and
everything in between.

Long Life Magazine

Cryonics Institute
24355 Sorrentino Court
Clinton Township, MI 48035
Tel: +1 (586) 791-5961
Email: info@cryonics.org
Website: http://www.cryonics.org/resources/
long-life-magazine

Publishes: Articles; Essays; Fiction;
Nonfiction; Poetry; *Areas:* Science; Short
Stories; Technology; *Markets:* Adult;
Treatments: Positive

Magazine on the subject of cryonics,
publishing articles and essays covering the
various aspects and challenges of being
frozen and then re-animated. Welcomes
poetry and occasionally accepts fiction,
provided cryonics are central. No horror or
stories portraying a dismal future.

Louisiana Literature

SLU Box 10792
Hammond, LA 70402
Email: lalit@selu.edu
Website: http://www.louisianaliterature.org

Publishes: Fiction; Nonfiction; Poetry;
Areas: Short Stories; *Markets:* Adult;
Treatments: Literary

Editors: Dr Jack Bedell

Literary journal publishing fiction, poetry,
and creative nonfiction. Submit via online
system available at the website.

The Lyric

PO Box 110
Jericho, VT 05465
Email: themuse@thelyricmagazine.com
Website: https://thelyricmagazine.com

Publishes: Poetry; *Markets:* Adult;
Treatments: Literary; Traditional

Editors: Jean Mellichamp Milliken

Publishes rhymed verse in traditional forms,
with an occasional piece of blank or free
verse. Poems must be original, unpublished,
and not under consideration elsewhere. Send
submissions by post with SASE if return
required (not necessary if email response is
sufficient). No submissions by email unless
from outside the US.

The MacGuffin

Schoolcraft College
18600 Haggerty Road
Livonia, MI 48152
Tel: +1 (734) 462-5327
Email: macguffin@schoolcraft.edu
Website: https://schoolcraft.edu/macguffin

Publishes: Fiction; Nonfiction; Poetry;
Areas: Short Stories; *Markets:* Adult;
Treatments: Experimental; Literary;
Traditional

Publishes fiction, creative nonfiction, and
poetry. Send complete MS by post with
return postage, or by email as a Word
document attachment. Submissions in the
body of the email will not be accepted.
Submit up to five poems or up to two stories.

Midway Journal

Email: editors@midwayjournal.com
Website: http://midwayjournal.com

Publishes: Fiction; Nonfiction; Poetry;
Markets: Adult; *Treatments:* Literary

Editors: Ralph Pennel (Fiction Editor); Paige
Riehl (Poetry Editor); Christopher Lowe
(Nonfiction Editor)

Accepts submissions of fiction, poetry, and
creative nonfiction via online submission
system between January 1 and May 1 each
year. Seeks aesthetically ambitious work that
invokes the colliding and converging
energies of the fairgrounds. See website for
full guidelines.

Nailpolish Stories

Email: ncmonaghan@gmail.com
Website: https://nailpolishstories.
wordpress.com

Publishes: Fiction; *Markets:* Adult

Editors: Nicole Monaghan

Online literary journal publishing stories
exactly 25 words long. All stories must use a
nail polish colour as the title. Submit by
email.

The Oakland Arts Review

Email: ouartsreview@oakland.edu
Website: https://oaklandartsreview.com

Publishes: Fiction; Nonfiction; Poetry;
Scripts; *Areas:* Drama; Short Stories;
Markets: Adult; *Treatments:* Literary

Literary journal publishing work by
undergraduates around the world. Publishes
fiction between 10 and 15 double spaced
pages; creative nonfiction between 7 and 10
double spaced pages; comics of high literary
quality; screenwriting; and both free verse
and formal poetry (submit 3-5 poems).
Submit through online submission system
via website.

Old Red Kimono

Georgia Highlands College
3175 Cedartown Hwy SE
Rome, GA 30161

Email: napplega@highlands.edu
Website: https://www2.highlands.edu/site/
ork

Publishes: Fiction; Poetry; *Areas:* Short
Stories; *Markets:* Adult; *Treatments:*
Literary

Editors: Steven Godfrey

Annual student-edited literary magazine.
Send 3-5 poems or short stories up to 1,500
words by post or by email. Submissions from
contributors outside the university are
considered between October and February
each year.

Overtime

PO Box 250382
Plano, TX 75025-0382
Email: overtime@workerswritejournal.com
Website: http://www.
workerswritejournal.com/overtime.htm

Publishes: Fiction; *Areas:* Short Stories;
Markets: Adult; *Treatments:* Literary

Editors: David LaBounty

A series of one-story chapbooks, publishing
stories between 5,000 and 10,000 words,
where work is a central theme.

Pacifica Literary Review

Seattle, WA
Email: pacificalitreview@gmail.com
Website: http://www.pacificareview.com

Publishes: Fiction; Nonfiction; Poetry;
Markets: Adult; *Treatments:* Literary

Editors: Matt Muth

Accepts poetry, fiction, and creative
nonfiction. Prose should be under 5,000
words. Flash fiction up to 1,000 words. Will
consider novel excerpts, but must work as
stand alone entities. For poetry and flash
fiction submit a maximum of three pieces at
a time. Send submissions through online
submission system. See website for full
guidelines.

Phase 2 Magazine

Email: submissions@darkfuturesfiction.net
Website: http://www.darkfuturesfiction.net

Publishes: Fiction; Nonfiction; Poetry; Reviews; *Areas:* Sci-Fi; *Markets:* Adult

Science fiction magazine publishing fiction up to 1,500 words; reviews up to 800 words; and poetry up to 19 lines. See website for full guidelines.

Pirene's Fountain
Email: pirenesfountain@gmail.com
Website: http://pirenesfountain.com

Publishes: Poetry; *Markets:* Adult; *Treatments:* Literary

Send between three and eight previously unpublished poems in the body of an email with a brief bio, between May 1 and August 1 annually.

Poetica Magazine
5215 Colley Avenue #138
Norfolk, VA 23508
Email: poeticapublishing@aol.com
Website: http://www.poeticamagazine.com

Publishes: Poetry; *Markets:* Adult; *Treatments:* Contemporary; Literary

Editors: Michal (Mitak) Mahgereftch

Publishes contemporary Jewish poetry. Submit via online submission manager.

The Progressive Populist
PO Box 819
Manchaca, Texas 78652
Tel: +1 (512) 828-7245
Email: populist@usa.net
Website: http://www.populist.com

Publishes: Articles; Essays; News; Nonfiction; *Areas:* Business; Finance; Lifestyle; Politics; *Markets:* Adult

Editors: Jim Cullen

Fortnightly newspaper reporting on issues of interest to workers, small-business owners and family farmers and ranchers.

Publishers Weekly
Email: jmilliot@publishersweekly.com
Website: https://www.publishersweekly.com

Publishes: Articles; Features; News; Nonfiction; Reviews; *Areas:* Business; Literature; *Markets:* Professional

Editors: Jim Milliot

Weekly news magazine aimed at publishers, booksellers, librarians, literary agents, authors and the media, providing news and feature articles relating to the book industry, but best known for its pre-publication book reviews.

Qu
Email: qulitmag@queens.edu
Website: http://www.qulitmag.com

Publishes: Essays; Fiction; Nonfiction; Poetry; Scripts; *Markets:* Adult; *Treatments:* Literary

Submit prose up to 8,000 words or up to three poems via online submission system. $2 fee. Does not accept international submissions.

Qualified Remodeler
Tel: +1 (847) 920-5996
Email: Patrick@SOLAbrands.com
Website: http://www.qualifiedremodeler.com

Publishes: Articles; News; Nonfiction; *Areas:* Business; Design; How-to; Technology; *Markets:* Professional

Editors: Patrick O'Toole

Magazine aimed at residential remodelling contractors. Particularly interested in business management issues. Send query with published clips.

R.kv.r.y. Quarterly Literary Journal
Email: r.kv.r.y.editor@gmail.com
Website: http://rkvryquarterly.com

Publishes: Essays; Fiction; Nonfiction; Poetry; *Areas:* Short Stories; *Markets:* Adult; *Treatments:* Literary

Literary journal publishing works relating to acts, processes, or instances of recovery. Submit up to 3,000 words for prose, up to 1,000 words for flash fiction, or up to three poems, via online submission system. Closed to submissions during the summer months.

Reason

5737 Mesmer Avenue
Los Angeles, CA 90230
Tel: +1 (310) 391-2245
Fax: +1 (310) 390-8986
Email: submissions@reason.com
Website: http://reason.com

Publishes: Articles; Essays; News; Nonfiction; Reviews; *Areas:* Culture; Current Affairs; Finance; Politics; Science; *Markets:* Adult

Editors: Brian Doherty, Associate Editor

Publishes articles and essays on politics, economics, culture, and science, from a broad-minded libertarian perspective. Accepts unsolicited MSS but prefers queries in writing either by post with SASE or by email.

Relevant

55 West Church St. Suite #211
Orlando, FL 32801
Email: submissions@
relevantmediagroup.com
Website: https://relevantmagazine.com

Publishes: Articles; Nonfiction; *Areas:* Culture; Lifestyle; Religious; *Markets:* Adult

Christian lifestyle magazine aimed at adults in their 20s and 30s, covering faith, culture, and "intentional living".

Reptiles

Email: reptiles@chewy.com
Website: http://www.reptilesmagazine.com

Publishes: Articles; Nonfiction; *Areas:* Hobbies; Nature; *Markets:* Adult

Magazine publishing material relating to reptiles and amphibians. Send query by email.

Ripcord.

Email: ndowney@ripcordmagazine.org
Website: https://www.ripcordmagazine.org

Publishes: Essays; Fiction; Poetry; *Areas:* Short Stories; *Markets:* Adult; *Treatments:* Experimental; Literary; Progressive

Editors: Noelle Downey

An online multimedia literary magazine where we celebrate stories in all their forms, no matter how bizarre or unconventional those forms may be. We want to create a platform that embraces diverse, exciting, and inventive narratives. Whether it's a poem, a short story, a photo set, a performance piece, or something even weirder, if it's quality and has a narrative we can sink our teeth into, it's for us. We help tell the stories that would otherwise be lost, and yours could be next. Send us something that helps us see the world in a new way.

River Heron Review

PO Box 543
New Hope, PA 18953
Email: riverheronreview@gmail.com
Website: http://www.riverheronreview.com

Publishes: Poetry; *Markets:* Adult; *Treatments:* Contemporary; Experimental; Literary; Satirical; Serious; Traditional

Editors: Robbin Farr, Judith Lagana

Established to support the arts through the sharing of poetry in our online journal, at readings, workshops and by making public the transformative power of poetic expression.

We hope to contribute to the expansion of a community of poets, to establish a creative outlet that does not discriminate by age, race, or sexual orientation in order to offer voice to all and to represent poetry in its many forms, styles, perspectives, and intentions.

River Hills Traveler

212 E Main Street
Neosho, MO 64850
Tel: +1 (417) 451-3798
Fax: +1 (417) 451-3798
Email: jimmy@riverhillstraveler.com
Website: http://www.riverhillstraveler.com

Publishes: Articles; Nonfiction; *Areas:* Hobbies; Nature; Sport; *Markets:* Adult

Editors: Jimmy Sexton

Magazine covering outdoor sports and nature in the southeast quarter of Missouri, the east and central Ozarks. Send query by email with writing samples.

The Road Not Taken: The Journal of Formal Poetry

Email: TheRoadNotTakenJournal@gmail.com
Website: http://www.journalformalpoetry.com

Publishes: Poetry; *Markets:* Adult; *Treatments:* Literary

Editors: Kathryn Jacobs; Rachel Jacobs

Publishes metrical poetry in modern English. See website for previous issues and full guidelines. Submit 3-5 poems by email during specific reading periods (August 15 – October 15; January 15 – March 15; and April 1 – June 15).

Romantic Homes

17890 Sky Park Circle, Suite 250
Irvine, CA 92614
Email: mdombrowski@engagedmediainc.com
Website: https://www.romantichomes.com

Publishes: Articles; Nonfiction; *Areas:* Design; How-to; *Markets:* Adult

Editors: Margie Monin Dombrowski

Publishes elegant inspiration for everyday life, including decorating ideas and entertaining advice.

Rural Builder

PO Box 420235
Palm Coast, FL 32142-0235
Email: sharon.thatcher@fwmedia.com
Website: http://www.ruralbuilder.com

Publishes: Features; News; Nonfiction; *Areas:* Architecture; Business; Design; How-to; *Markets:* Professional

Magazine for builders and suppliers of primarily low-rise agricultural and small retail and municipal structures in cities with populations under 250,000.

Sacramento Magazine

5750 New King Drive, Suite 100
Troy, MI 48098
Tel: +1 (866) 660-6247
Email: darlena@sacmag.com
Website: http://www.sacmag.com

Publishes: Articles; Nonfiction; *Areas:* Arts; Culture; Health; Lifestyle; Travel; *Markets:* Adult

Editors: Darlena Belushin McKay

Magazine covering culture, events, and entertainment in and around Sacramento.

San Diego Home / Garden Lifestyles

4577 Viewridge Avenue
San Diego, CA 92123
Tel: +1 (858) 571-0529
Email: ditler@sdhg.net
Website: https://www.sandiegohomegarden.com

Publishes: Articles; Features; Nonfiction; *Areas:* Arts; Culture; Design; Gardening; Lifestyle; *Markets:* Adult

Editors: Eva Ditler

Lifestyle magazine for residents of San Diego city and county.

Saveur

PO Box 6364
Harlan, IA 51593
Tel: +1 (515) 237-3697
Email: edit@saveur.com
Website: https://www.saveur.com

Publishes: Articles; Features; Nonfiction; *Areas:* Cookery; Culture; Travel; *Markets:* Adult

Welcomes pitches from writers who want to tell amazing stories about food and travel. Queries should include a brief summary of the proposed article and proposed timescale, along with any links to past work. Response only if interested.

Scale Auto

Kalmbach Publishing Co.
21027 Crossroads Circle
Waukesha, WI 53187-1612
Email: msavage@kalmbach.com
Website: http://www.scaleautomag.com

Publishes: Articles; Nonfiction; Reviews;
Areas: Hobbies; How-to; *Markets:* Adult

Editors: Mark Savage

Magazine for model car enthusiasts. See
website for full submission guidelines.

Scientific American

1 New York Plaza, Suite 4500
New York, NY 10004
Email: editors@sciam.com
Website: https://www.
scientificamerican.com

Publishes: Articles; Nonfiction; *Areas:*
Health; Psychology; Science; Technology;
Markets: Adult

Welcomes ideas for articles on recent
scientific discoveries, technical innovations
and overviews of ongoing research. Send
proposals by email or by post. See website
for full details.

Scifaikuest

Email: gatrix65@yahoo.com
Website: https://www.
albanlakepublishing.com/scifaikuest

Publishes: Articles; Nonfiction; Poetry;
Areas: Horror; Sci-Fi; *Markets:* Adult;
Treatments: Literary

Print and online magazine publishing science
fiction and horror poetry in forms such as
scifaiku, haibun, senryu, and tanka. Also
publishes articles. See website for full
submission guidelines.

Screem

41 Mayer Street
Wilkes Barre, PA 18702
Email: Screemagazine@msn.com
Website: http://screemmag.com

Publishes: Articles; News; Nonfiction;
Areas: Horror; *Markets:* Adult

Magazine publishing articles relating to
Horror. Query in first instance.

Seshat Literary Magazine

Email: seshatlitmag@gmail.com
Website: http://seshatlitmag.wordpress.com

Publishes: Fiction; Nonfiction; Poetry;
Areas: Adventure; Fantasy; Historical;
Literature; Mystery; Nature; Romance; Sci-
Fi; Short Stories; *Markets:* Adult; Family;
Youth; *Treatments:* Contemporary; Literary

Editors: Maribel C. Pagan

This literary journal is dedicated to mostly
young writers who are homeschooled or
have been homeschooled in the past.
However, all ages (13+) are encouraged to
submit to this journal. Literary fiction,
speculative fiction, creative non-fiction, and
poetry, are all welcome here.

Sinister Wisdom

2333 McIntosh Road
Dover, FL 33527
Tel: +1 (813) 502-5549
Email: julic@sinisterwisdom.org
Website: http://www.sinisterwisdom.org

Publishes: Essays; Fiction; Nonfiction;
Poetry; *Areas:* Arts; Culture; Short Stories;
Women's Interests; *Markets:* Adult

Editors: Julie R. Enszer

Multicultural lesbian literary and art journal.
Material may be in any style or form, or
combination of forms. Submit five poems,
two short stories or essays, OR one longer
piece of up to 5,000 words, via online
submission system.

Smart Retailer

PO Box 5000
N7528 Aanstad Road
Iola, WI 54945-5000
Tel: +1 (800) 331-0038
Fax: +1 (715) 445-4053
Email: danb@jonespublishing.com
Website: http://smart-retailer.com

Publishes: Articles; Interviews; News;
Nonfiction; *Areas:* Business; Finance; How-
to; Legal; *Markets:* Professional

Editors: Dan Brownell

Trade magazine for independent gift retailers. Send complete ms by email with CV and published clips.

SnoWest
360 B Street
Idaho Falls, ID 83402
Tel: +1 (208) 524-7000
Fax: +1 (208) 522-5241
Website: https://www.snowest.com

Publishes: Articles; Features; Nonfiction; *Areas:* Leisure; Sport; *Markets:* Adult

Snowmobiling magazine. Send query with published clips.

Somerset Home
22992 Mill Creek Drive
Laguna Hills, CA 92653
Email: somersethome@stampington.com
Website: https://stampington.com/somerset-home

Publishes: Articles; Nonfiction; *Areas:* Design; *Markets:* Adult

Home decor magazine.

Southern Theatre
3309 Northampton Drive
Greensboro, NC 27408-5224
Tel: +1 (336) 292-6041
Fax: +1 (336) 294-3292
Email: deanna@setc.org
Website: https://www.setc.org/publications-resources/southern-theatre/

Publishes: Articles; Nonfiction; *Areas:* Theatre; *Markets:* Adult

Editors: Deanna Thompson

Theatre magazine focusing on the 10 Southeastern states of the US. Submit by post or email.

Specialty Fabrics Review
1801 County Road B W
Roseville, MN 55113-4061
Tel: +1 (651) 222-2508

Email: generalinfo@ifai.com
Website: https://specialtyfabricsreview.com

Publishes: Articles; Nonfiction; *Areas:* Business; Design; *Markets:* Professional

Magazine covering the industrial textiles industry.

Spirituality & Health
Tel: +1 (844) 375-3755
Email: editors@spiritualityhealth.com
Website: https://spiritualityhealth.com

Publishes: Articles; Features; Interviews; Nonfiction; Reviews; *Areas:* Health; Lifestyle; Spiritual; *Markets:* Adult

Magazine that aims to help people improve their lives both physically and spiritually. Send submissions by email. No attachments. Response not guaranteed. See website for full guidelines.

Spitball
536 Lassing Way
Walton, KY 41094
Email: spitball5@hotmail.com
Website: http://www.spitballmag.com

Publishes: Fiction; Poetry; Reviews; *Areas:* Short Stories; Sport; *Markets:* Adult; *Treatments:* Literary

Literary baseball magazine, publishing poems, fiction, prose, art, and book reviews relating to baseball. Potential contributors must publish a sample copy ($6) before submitting. See website for full guidelines.

Sports Afield
P.O. Box 271305
Fort Collins, CO 80527
Email: editorinchief@sportsafield.com
Website: http://sportsafield.com

Publishes: Articles; Nonfiction; *Areas:* Adventure; Nature; Sport; *Markets:* Adult

Hunting adventure magazine. Publishes articles on high-end hunting and shooting, and coverage of guns, optics, clothing, and other equipment. Send complete ms by email only. See website for full guidelines.

St Anthony Messenger

28 West Liberty Street
Cincinnati, OH 45202
Tel: +1 (513) 241-5615
Email: MagazineEditors@
FranciscanMedia.org
Website: http://www.americancatholic.org

Publishes: Articles; Fiction; Interviews;
Nonfiction; Poetry; *Areas:* How-to; Humour;
Lifestyle; Religious; Short Stories; *Markets:*
Adult; Family; *Treatments:* Mainstream

Catholic magazine publishing fiction, poetry,
and nonfiction relating to the Catholic faith.
Send query (nonfiction) or submissions
(fiction and poetry) by email only. See
website for full guidelines.

Stanford Magazine

Email: stanford.magazine@stanford.edu
Website: https://stanfordmag.org

Publishes: Articles; Essays; Features;
Nonfiction; *Markets:* Academic; Adult

University alumni magazine.

State Journal

324 Hewes Avenue PO Box 2000
Clarksburg, WV 26301
Tel: +1 (800) 982-6034
Email: news@theet.com
Website: http://www.theet.com/statejournal/

Publishes: Articles; News; Nonfiction;
Areas: Business; *Markets:* Professional

Magazine aimed at the West Virginia
business community.

Stone World

2401 W. Big Beaver Rd., Suite 700
Troy, MI 48084-3333
Tel: +1 (248) 362-3700
Fax: +1 (248) 362-0317
Email: info@stoneworld.com
Website: http://www.stoneworld.com

Publishes: Articles; News; Nonfiction;
Areas: Architecture; Design; Technology;
Markets: Professional

Editors: Jennifer Richinelli

Magazine for professionals working with
natural building stone.

Stormwater

Forester Media Inc.
PO Box 3100
Santa Barbara, CA 93130
Email: asantiago@forester.net
Website: http://foresternetwork.com/
magazines/stormwater/

Publishes: Articles; Features; Interviews;
News; Nonfiction; *Areas:* Architecture;
Business; Design; *Markets:* Professional

Magazine aimed at professionals concerned
with storm water management. Send query
by email.

StoryNews

Email: jess@storynews.net
Website: https://www.storynews.net

Publishes: Essays; Nonfiction; *Areas:* Arts;
Culture; Current Affairs; Literature; Media;
Politics; *Markets:* Adult

Editors: Jess Millman

An online literary journal committed to
showcasing the human stories behind
headlines. We're seeking nonfiction writing
as well as visual, audio, and multimedia art
that tells a true story in response to news
articles, capturing something unique, special,
and personal about the way you see the
world.

Our mission isn't to convert folks to new
political ideologies, but to give people of all
backgrounds insights into each other's
worldviews for the sake of understanding
and more open dialogues, both personally
and globally. All stories are welcome – so
long as they are honest, thoughtful,
vulnerable, and free of hate speech or
bigotry.

Our full submission guidelines are accessible
on our website.

Strategic Finance

Email: aschulman@imanet.org
Website: https://sfmagazine.com

Publishes: Articles; Nonfiction; *Areas:* Finance; *Markets:* Professional

Publishes articles that help financial professionals perform their jobs more effectively, advance their careers, grow personally and professionally, and make their organisations more profitable.

Studio One

Murray Hall 170, College of St. Benedict
37 South College Avenue
St Joseph, MN 56374
Email: studio1@csbsju.edu
Website: https://digitalcommons.csbsju.edu/studio_one/

Publishes: Essays; Fiction; Nonfiction; Poetry; *Areas:* Short Stories; *Markets:* Adult; *Treatments:* Literary

Literary and visual arts magazine published each spring. Founded in 1976 as a print publication. Online only since 2012. Prefers email submissions, but will accept submissions by post. See website for full guidelines.

SuCasa

Bella Media, LLC
4100 Wolcott Avenue. NE, Suite B
Albuquerque, NM 87109
Tel: +1 (505) 344-1783
Fax: +1 (505) 345-3795
Email: amygross@sucasamagazine.com
Website: http://www.sucasamagazine.com

Publishes: Articles; Nonfiction; *Areas:* Architecture; Design; *Markets:* Adult; *Treatments:* Contemporary

Editors: Amy Gross

Magazine on contemporary home building in the South West. Send query with published clips.

Successful Meetings

100 Lighting Way
Secaucus, NJ 07094-3626
Tel: +1 (201) 902-1978
Email: ledelstein@ntmllc.com
Website: http://www.successfulmeetings.com

Publishes: Articles; *Areas:* Business; *Markets:* Professional

Editors: Loren Edelstein

Magazine for multi-tasking meeting planners.

Sunshine Artist

N7528 Aanstad Road
PO Box 5000
Iola, WI 54945
Tel: +1 (800) 597-2573
Email: editor@sunshineartist.com
Website: http://www.sunshineartist.com

Publishes: Nonfiction; Reviews; *Areas:* Arts; Crafts; *Markets:* Professional

Editors: Stephanie Hintz

Publishes reviews of fine art fairs, festivals, events, and small craft shows around the country, for professionals making a living through art shows.

Surface

601 West 26th St. Suite 1507
New York, NY 10001
Tel: +1 (212) 229-1500
Email: editorial@surfacemag.com
Website: https://www.surfacemag.com

Publishes: Articles; *Areas:* Architecture; Arts; Culture; Design; *Markets:* Adult; *Treatments:* Contemporary

American magazine of global contemporary design. Covers architecture, art, design, fashion, and travel, with a focus on how these fields shape and are shaped by contemporary culture.

Susquehanna Life

217 Market Street
Lewisburg, PA 17837
Tel: +1 (800) 232-1670
Fax: +1 (570) 524-7796
Email: susquehannalife@gmail.com
Website: http://www.susquehannalife.com

Publishes: Articles; Nonfiction; *Areas:* Arts; Beauty and Fashion; Business; Entertainment; Gardening; Health; Lifestyle; Nature; Travel; *Markets:* Adult

Lifestyle magazine covering central Pennsylvania.

Tagvverk

Email: tagvverk@gmail.com
Website: http://tagvverk.info

Publishes: Essays; Fiction; Nonfiction; Poetry; Reviews; *Areas:* Criticism; *Markets:* Adult; *Treatments:* Literary

Editors: Barrett White; Miriam Karraker

Online magazine publishing poetry, fiction, essays, reviews, criticisms, visual poems and multimedia projects. Send submissions by email.

Tallahassee Magazine

Rowland Publishing, Inc.
1932 Miccosukee Road
Tallahassee, FL 32308
Tel: +1 (850) 878-0554
Email: info@rowlandpublishing.com
Website: http://www.
tallahasseemagazine.com

Publishes: Articles; Features; Interviews; Nonfiction; *Areas:* Business; Entertainment; Historical; Lifestyle; Sport; Travel; *Markets:* Adult

Publishes material for visitors to and residents of Florida's capital city. Send query with published clips.

TD Magazine

Tel: +1 (703) 299-8723
Email: submissions@td.org
Website: https://www.td.org/td-magazine

Publishes: Articles; Features; Nonfiction; *Areas:* Business; *Markets:* Professional

Magazine for talent development professionals. No unsolicited mss. Send query with outline up to 100 words.

Tech Directions

251 Jackson Plaza, Suite A
Ann Arbor, MI 48103-1955
Tel: +1 (734) 975-2800
Fax: +1 (734) 975-2787

Email: vanessa@techdirections.com
Website: http://www.techdirections.com

Publishes: Articles; Nonfiction; *Areas:* Science; Technology; *Markets:* Professional

Editors: Vanessa Revelli

Publishes articles about what is going on in the career-technical and STEM education fields; ideas teachers can use in the classroom; and anything that can help prepare students for a career. See website for submission guidelines.

Texas Co-op Power

1122 Colorado Street, 24th Floor
Austin, TX 78701
Email: info@texascooppower.com
Website: http://www.texascooppower.com

Publishes: Articles; Nonfiction; *Areas:* Technology; *Markets:* Adult

Magazine which aims to improve the quality of life of electric co-operative member-customers in Texas in an informative and engaging format. Potential contributors should familiarise themselves with the magazine, then submit query by email.

Texas Monthly

PO Box 1569
Austin, TX 78767-1569
Tel: +1 (512) 320-6900
Fax: +1 (512) 476-9007
Email: news@texasmonthly.com
Website: https://www.texasmonthly.com

Publishes: Articles; News; *Areas:* Culture; Film; Lifestyle; Music; Politics; Travel; TV; *Markets:* Adult

Monthly magazine covering Texas.

Thick With Conviction

Email: twczine@gmail.com
Website: http://twczine.blogspot.com

Publishes: Poetry; *Markets:* Adult; *Treatments:* Literary

Editors: Arielle LaBrea

Online magazine publishing poems that are unique or thought provoking. No religious poems, nature poems, greeting card styled poems or teenage angst. Send submissions in the body of an email with bio up to 75 words and author photo.

30 North

Website: https://30northliterarymagazine.com

Publishes: Fiction; Nonfiction; Poetry; *Markets:* Adult; *Treatments:* Literary

Publishes previously unpublished poetry, fiction, creative non-fiction, and art by undergraduate writers and artists. Submit via online submission system.

This Is Bill Gorton

Hacienda Publishing
300 State Street
PO Box 92951
Southlake, TX 76092
Tel: +1 (936) 468-5759
Email: thisisbillgorton@gmail.com
Website: http://thisisbillgorton.org

Publishes: Fiction; Nonfiction; *Areas:* Short Stories; *Markets:* Adult; *Treatments:* Literary

Editors: Andrew Brininstool; Joshua Hines

Accepts fiction and nonfiction of any length. Submit via online submission system.

This Old House

262 Harbor Drive
Stamford, CT 06902
Tel: +1 (475) 209-8665
Email: contact@thisoldhouse.com
Website: https://www.thisoldhouse.com

Publishes: Articles; Features; Nonfiction; *Areas:* Design; How-to; *Markets:* Adult

Home improvement magazine. Send query with published clips.

TimberWest

PO Box 610
Edmonds, WA 98020
Tel: +1 (425) 778-3388
Fax: +1 (425) 771-3623
Email: timberwest@forestnet.com

Website: http://forestnet.com/TimberWest.php

Publishes: Articles; Interviews; Nonfiction; *Areas:* Business; Historical; *Markets:* Professional

Magazine covering the logging industry in the Northwest. No material that puts a negative slant on the industry.

Tin House Magazine

Email: alana@tinhouse.com
Website: http://www.tinhouse.com

Publishes: Essays; Fiction; Nonfiction; Poetry; *Areas:* Short Stories; *Markets:* Adult; *Treatments:* Literary

Editors: Alana Csaposs

Closed to submissions as at April 2019. Check website for current status.

Publishes unpublished fiction, nonfiction, and poetry through daily blog. Submit via online submission system.

Tobacco International

Lockwood Publications, Inc.
3743 Crescent Street, 2nd Floor
Long Island City, NY 11101
Tel: +1 (212) 391-2060
Fax: +1 (212) 827-0945
Email: editor@tobaccointernational.com
Website: http://www.tobaccointernational.com

Publishes: Articles; News; Nonfiction; *Areas:* Business; *Markets:* Professional

Magazine publishing material relating to the tobacco industry.

Trailer Life Magazine

2750 Park View Ct., Suite 240
Oxnard, CA, 93036
Tel: +1 (800) 765-1912
Email: info@trailerlife.com
Website: http://www.trailerlife.com

Publishes: Articles; Features; News; Nonfiction; *Areas:* Hobbies; Leisure; Technology; Travel; *Markets:* Adult

Magazine written for, and by, mature and discerning RVers. No unsolicited submissions, or queries by email. Send queries by post only.

TravelWorld International Magazine

3579 Foothill Boulevard, #744
Pasadena, CA 91107
Tel: +1 (626) 376-9754
Fax: +1 (626) 628-1854
Website: http://www.
travelworldmagazine.com

Publishes: Articles; Nonfiction; *Areas:* Travel; *Markets:* Adult

Editors: Dennis A. Britton

Travel magazine. Contributors must be members of NATJA.

Tropical Fish Hobbyist Magazine

Email: associateeditor@tfh.com
Website: http://www.tfhmagazine.com

Publishes: Articles; Nonfiction; *Areas:* Hobbies; Nature; *Markets:* Adult

Publishes articles of interest to keepers of tropical fish. Articles are normally between 10,000 and 20,000 words. See website for full submission guidelines.

The 2River View

University City, MO 63130
Email: Belong@2river.org
Website: http://www.2river.org

Publishes: Poetry; *Markets:* Adult; *Treatments:* Literary

Editors: Richard Long

Considers unpublished poems only. Submit via online submission system. See website for more details.

UCity Review

Email: editors@ucityreview.com
Website: http://www.ucityreview.com

Publishes: Poetry; *Markets:* Adult; *Treatments:* Literary

Online magazine accepting submissions of poetry year-round. Submit up to six poems in .doc or .docx format, by email.

Underground Construction

Oildom Publishing Company of Texas, Inc.
1160 Dairy Ashford Road, Suite 610
Houston, TX 77079
Tel: +1 (281) 558-6930
Email: rcarpenter@oildom.com
Website: https://ucononline.com

Publishes: Articles; News; Nonfiction; *Areas:* Business; Design; How-to; *Markets:* Professional

Publishes material for industries involved in the construction and maintenance of underground pipelines. Send query with published clips in first instance.

Unfit Magazine

Eugene, OR 97401
Email: contact@unfitmag.com
Website: http://unfitmag.com

Publishes: Fiction; *Areas:* Sci-Fi; *Markets:* Adult; Youth; *Treatments:* Commercial; Contemporary; Experimental; Mainstream; Niche; Popular; Satirical

Editors: Daniel Scott White

This magazine is about fiction that isn't fit for "them". What do I mean by "them"? Who in particular are "they"? They are the government. They are your parents. They are your teachers. They are everywhere.

US Glass Magazine

Key Communications Inc.
20 PGA Drive, Suite 201
Stafford, VA 22554
Tel: +1 (540) 720-5584
Fax: +1 (540) 720-5687
Email: info@usglassmag.com
Website: http://www.usglassmag.com

Publishes: Articles; Nonfiction; *Areas:* Architecture; Business; *Markets:* Professional

Editors: Ellen Rogers

Magazine aimed at companies involved in the architectural class industry. Send query with published clips.

Vagabond City

Email: vagabondcityliterary@gmail.com
Website: https://vagabondcitylit.com

Publishes: Essays; Interviews; Nonfiction; Poetry; Reviews; *Markets:* Adult; *Treatments:* Literary

Electronic magazine featuring poetry, art, creative nonfiction, essays, interviews, and reviews by marginalised creators. Submit up to five pieces at a time in the body of an email. No attachments. See website for full guidelines.

Vegetable Growers News Magazine

Great American Media Services
PO Box 128
Sparta, Michigan 49345
Tel: +1 (616) 887-9008
Fax: +1 (616) 887-2666
Email: vgnedit@vegetablegrowersnews.com
Website: http://vegetablegrowersnews.com

Publishes: Articles; Interviews; News; Nonfiction; Reviews; *Areas:* Nature; *Markets:* Professional

Magazine for professional vegetable growers. Send query with published clips and author CV.

VFW (Veterans of Foreign Wars) Magazine

406 West 34th Street
Kansas City, MO 64111
Tel: +1 (816) 756-3390
Email: magazine@vfw.org
Website: http://www.vfwmagazine.org

Publishes: Articles; News; Nonfiction; *Areas:* Current Affairs; Historical; Military; *Markets:* Adult

Magazine aimed at veterans of US overseas conflicts. Send query by email with

published clips. No poetry, fiction, op-eds, reprints or book reviews.

Vogue Patterns

The McCall Pattern Company
Attn: Customer Service
120 Broadway, 34th floor
New York, New York 10271
Email: editor@voguepatterns.com
Website: https://voguepatterns.mccall.com

Publishes: Articles; Nonfiction; *Areas:* Crafts; Hobbies; How-to; *Markets:* Adult

Publishes sewing articles and patterns.

Waccamaw

Website: http://waccamawjournal.com

Publishes: Essays; Fiction; Nonfiction; Poetry; *Markets:* Adult; *Treatments:* Literary

Online literary journal publishing poems, stories, and essays. Submit prose up to 6,000 words or 3-5 poems between January 15 and February 15 or August 1 and August 31 annually. Submit via online submission system only.

Walls & Ceilings

2401 West Big Beaver Road, Suite 700
Troy, MI 48084-3333
Tel: +1 (248) 362-3700
Fax: +1 (248) 362-5103
Email: wyattj@bnpmedia.com
Website: http://www.wconline.com

Publishes: Nonfiction; *Areas:* Architecture; Design; How-to; *Markets:* Professional

Editors: John Wyatt

Magazine aimed at interior and exterior wall and ceiling contractors, architects, manufacturers, suppliers and distributors. Send query or complete ms.

Water Well Journal

National Ground Water Association
Attn: Water Well Journal
601 Dempsey Road
Westerville, OH 43081-8978
Email: tplumley@ngwa.org
Website: http://waterwelljournal.com

Publishes: Articles; Features; Interviews;
Nonfiction; *Areas:* Business; How-to;
Technology; *Markets:* Professional

Editors: Thad Plumley

Magazine serving the water well drilling
industry. Send query with published clips.

Welding Design & Fabrication
1300 E. 9th St.
Cleveland, OH 44114-1503
Tel: +1 (216) 696-7000
Fax: +1 (216) 931-9524
Email: Robert.brooks@penton.com
Website: http://weldingdesign.com

Publishes: Articles; News; Nonfiction;
Areas: Business; How-to; Technology;
Markets: Professional

Magazine for welders, and those involved in
the welding industry.

Western & Eastern Treasures
PO Box 647
Pacific Grove, CA 93950-0647
Tel: +1 (831) 920-2426
Email: editor@wetreasures.com
Website: http://www.wetreasures.com

Publishes: Articles; Nonfiction; *Areas:*
Hobbies; Leisure; Sport; *Markets:* Adult

Magazine for metal detectorists, covering
every aspect of the hobby. Articles must be
between 1,500 and 2,500 words and must be
accompanied by digital photos of at least 300
dpi.

Western Outdoor News
Email: pat@wonews.com
Website: http://www.wonews.com

Publishes: Articles; Nonfiction; *Areas:*
Hobbies; Leisure; Sport; *Markets:* Adult

Editors: Pat McDonell

Magazine serving the interests of fishermen
and hunters living in and around California.
Submit articles via website or by email. See
website for full details.

Westview
Southwestern Oklahoma State University
100 Campus Drive
Weatherford, OK 73096
Email: westview@swosu.edu
Website: https://dc.swosu.edu/westview/

Publishes: Fiction; Nonfiction; Poetry;
Areas: Short Stories; *Markets:* Adult

Editors: Amanda Smith

Publishes unpublished short fiction, poetry,
prose poems, creative nonfiction, and
artwork. Accepts submissions year-round
and supports emerging writers and artists.
Electronic submissions only.

The Wholesaler
6201 West Howard Street, Suite 201
Niles, IL 60714
Email: danielle@tmbpublishing.com
Website: http://www.thewholesaler.com

Publishes: Articles; News; Nonfiction;
Areas: Business; How-to; *Markets:*
Professional

Editors: Danielle Galian

Publishes news, trends, developments and
management how-to for wholesalers and
distributors in the plumbing, heating, air
conditioning and industrial piping
marketplace.

Willow and Sage
22992 Mill Creek, Suite B
Laguna Hills, CA 92653
Email: willowandsage@stampington.com
Website: https://stampington.com/willow-
and-sage

Publishes: Articles; Nonfiction; *Areas:*
Crafts; How-to; *Markets:* Adult

Publishes recipes, uses, and packaging ideas
for homemade bath and body products. Send
submissions by post or email.

Window Fashion Vision
4756 Banning Avenue, Suite 206
St. Paul, MN 55110
Tel: +1 (651) 330-0574
Fax: +1 (651) 756-8141

Email: susan@wf-vision.com
Website: https://www.wf-vision.com

Publishes: Articles; Interviews; Nonfiction; *Areas:* Design; How-to; *Markets:* Professional

Editors: Susan Schultz

Magazine serving the window fashions industry. Send query or complete ms.

Wire Rope News & Sling Technology

VS Enterprises
PO Box 871
Clark, New Jersey 07067-0871
Email: info@wireropenews.com
Website: http://www.wireropenews.com

Publishes: Articles; Interviews; News; Nonfiction; *Areas:* Business; Technology; *Markets:* Professional

Publishes articles of interest to those in the wire rope industry. Send ideas by email or by post.

Wisconsin Natural Resources Magazine

P.O. Box 7921
Madison, WI 53707-7921
Tel: +1 (608) 266-2625
Email: kathryn.kahler@wisconsin.gov
Website: http://dnr.wi.gov/wnrmag/

Publishes: Articles; Essays; Features; Nonfiction; *Areas:* How-to; Leisure; Nature; *Markets:* Adult

Editors: Kathryn Kahler, Acting Editor

Publishes features on Wisconsin resources, environmental issues, observation and research, and outdoor activities. Contact editor with ideas before starting a story. See website for full guidelines.

Women's Health Magazine

400 South 10th Street
Emmaus, PA 18098
Tel: +1 (800) 324-1731
Email: whsubmissions@rodale.com
Website: http://www.womenshealthmag.com

Publishes: Articles; Nonfiction; *Areas:* Health; Women's Interests; *Markets:* Adult

Women's health magazine for women who want to reach a healthy, attractive weight.

WoodmenLife Magazine

Woodmen Tower
1700 Farnam Street
Omaha, NE 68102
Tel: +1 (402) 342-1890
Fax: +1 (402) 271-7269
Email: service@woodmen.com
Website: https://www.woodmenlife.org

Publishes: Articles; News; Nonfiction; *Markets:* Adult

Magazine for members of non-profit insurance company.

World War II

1919 Gallows Road, Suite 400
Vienna, VA 22182
Email: worldwar2@historynet.com
Website: http://www.historynet.com

Publishes: Articles; Features; Nonfiction; *Areas:* Historical; Military; *Markets:* Adult

Publishes material relating to the second world war. No unsolicited mss. Send query by post or by email in first instance.

Xavier Review

Email: radamo@xula.edu
Website: http://www.xavierreview.com

Publishes: Essays; Fiction; Interviews; Nonfiction; Poetry; Reviews; *Areas:* Criticism; Religious; Short Stories; Spiritual; *Markets:* Adult; *Treatments:* Literary

Editors: Ralph Adamo

Publishes poetry, fiction, essays, reviews, and interviews. Prefers email submissions with attachments to postal submissions. Send 3-6 poems, or one piece of prose.

The Yale Review

Yale University
PO Box 208243
New Haven, CT 06520-8243

Tel: +1 (203) 432-0499
Fax: +1 (203) 432-0510
Website: https://yalereview.yale.edu

Publishes: Essays; Fiction; Nonfiction;
Poetry; *Areas:* Arts; Literature; Politics;
Markets: Adult; *Treatments:* Literary

Editors: Meghan O'Rourke

Currently closed to submissions.

Accepts submissions during specific reading
periods only. See website for current status.

The Yalobusha Review

Email: yreditors@gmail.com
Website: https://yr.olemiss.edu

Publishes: Fiction; Poetry; *Areas:* Literature;
Short Stories; *Markets:* Adult; *Treatments:*
Literary

Editors: Helene Achanzar; Lara Avery;
Andy Sia; Linda Masi; Nicholas Sabo

Submit 3-5 poems, one short story up to
5,000 words, or up to three shorter stories up
to 1,000 words each. Accepts a certain
number of free entries per month. Once the
limit has been reached writers can wait till
the next month, or make payment to submit.

Yemassee

Department of English
University of South Carolina
Columbia, SC 29208
Email: editor@yemasseejournal.org
Website: http://yemasseejournal.org

Publishes: Essays; Fiction; Nonfiction;
Poetry; Reviews; *Areas:* Short Stories;
Markets: Adult; *Treatments:* Literary

Editors: Sarah Benal; Trezlen Drake;
Andrew Green; Dylan Nutter; Hannah Ford;
Victoria Romero

Publishes poetry, fiction, and nonfiction.
Submit 3-5 poems or pieces of flash fiction
up to 1,000 words, or a longer short story up
to 5,000 words, via online submission
system. See website for full guidelines. $3
submission fee. Not accepting nonfiction
submissions as at August 2018.

Yes! Magazine

PO Box 10818
Bainbridge Island, WA 98110
Email: editors@yesmagazine.org
Website: http://www.yesmagazine.org

Publishes: Articles; Nonfiction; *Areas:*
Current Affairs; Nature; Politics; *Markets:*
Adult; *Treatments:* Positive

Magazine reframing the biggest problems of
our time in terms of their solutions.

Zetetic: A Record of Unusual Inquiry

Website: http://zeteticrecord.org

Publishes: Fiction; Nonfiction; Poetry;
Areas: Short Stories; *Markets:* Adult;
Treatments: Literary

Online magazine publishing fiction,
nonfiction, and poetry. Accepts prose
between 100 and 2,500 words, or up to three
poems between three and 100 lines.

Zoetrope: All-Story

916 Kearny Street
San Francisco, CA 94133
Tel: +1 (415) 788-7500
Email: info@all-story.com
Website: http://www.all-story.com

Publishes: Fiction; Scripts; *Areas:* Short
Stories; *Markets:* Adult; *Treatments:*
Literary

**Closed to submissions from June 1, 2018,
to May 31, 2019.**

Send short stories or one act-plays up to
7,000 words only, with SASE. No excerpts
from larger works, screenplays, treatments,
poetry, multiple submissions (no more than
one story or play at a time), or submissions
by email. No submissions between June 1
and August 31.

Zoning Practice

American Planning Association
205 North Michigan Avenue, Suite 1200
Chicago, IL 60601-5927
Tel: +1 (312) 431-9100
Fax: +1 (312) 786-6700

Email: zoningpractice@planning.org
Website: https://www.planning.org/
zoningpractice

Publishes: Articles; Features; Nonfiction;
Areas: Architecture; Politics; *Markets:*
Professional

Professional magazine covering planning
and land use.

UK Magazines

For the most up-to-date listings of these and hundreds of other magazines, visit https://www.firstwriter.com/magazines

*To claim your **free** access to the site, please see the back of this book.*

Accountancy Age

Tel: +44 (0) 20 8080 9388
Email: beth.mcloughlin@contentive.com
Website: https://www.accountancyage.com

Publishes: Articles; Features; News; Nonfiction; *Areas:* Business; Finance; *Markets:* Professional

Editors: Beth McLoughlin

Weekly magazine publishing articles on accountancy, business, and the financial world.

Acumen

6 The Mount
Higher Furzeham
Brixham
South Devon
TQ5 8QY
Tel: +44 (0) 1803 851098
Email: patriciaoxley6@gmail.com
Website: http://www.acumen-poetry.co.uk

Publishes: Articles; Features; Nonfiction; Poetry; *Areas:* Criticism; Literature; *Markets:* Adult; *Treatments:* Literary

Editors: Patricia Oxley

Magazine publishing poetry, articles, and features connected to poetry. Send submissions with SAE and author details on each page, or submit by email as Word attachment. See website for full submission guidelines.

Aeroplane

Key Publishing Ltd
PO BOX 100
Stamford
PE9 1XQ
Tel: +44 (0) 1780 755131
Fax: +44 (0) 1780 751323
Email: ben.dunnell@keypublishing.com
Website: http://www.aeroplanemonthly.com

Publishes: Features; News; Nonfiction; *Areas:* Historical; Technology; *Markets:* Adult

Editors: Ben Dunnell

Publishes news and features relating to historic aviation and aircraft preservation, up to the 1960s. Send query by post or email. Features must be illustrated with good quality photographs.

Aesthetica: A Review of Contemporary Artists

PO Box 371
York
YO23 1WL
Tel: +44 (0) 1904 629137
Email: info@aestheticamagazine.com
Website: http://www.aestheticamagazine.com

Publishes: Articles; Essays; Features;
Interviews; News; Nonfiction; Reviews;
Areas: Arts; Culture; Current Affairs;
Drama; Film; Humour; Literature; Music;
Theatre; Women's Interests; *Markets:* Adult;
Treatments: Literary

Editors: Cherie Federico

I am the founder and editor of a literary and
arts magazine that I actually began with my
MA fee money (I eventually paid the fees
and received my MA). I started the magazine
because I believe that there are too many
closed doors in the literary and art world. I
believe in making the arts accessible and
available for all. My convictions are deep
because I believe that in this modern, some
say, post-modern world that we live in it is
important to remember the essentials about
being human. There are too many reality TV
shows that mock existence. As a culture we
are slipping away from the arts. Writing has
too many stigmas attached and people
believe that there are too many rules. My aim
was to bring a magazine to life that would
challenge some of these notions and make a
difference.

This writing and artistic platform is
spreading across the UK and making it to
places like Israel, Italy, Ireland, New
Zealand, Australia, America, Canada,
Bulgaria, and Switzerland. We started in
York and are now selling at Borders in York,
Leeds, Brighton, Islington, and Oxford Street
as well as in some local York bookshops and
direct either from the website or by post.

I believe that art and literature is something
that is found within all of us. We need to
believe in ourselves and see the beauty of the
moment to take this concept further. With
my literary magazine I have created a space
for new ideas and fresh opinions. I believe in
creativity, diversity, and equality.

Agenda
Harts Cottage
Stonehurst Lane
Five Ashes
Mayfield
East Sussex
TN20 6LL
Tel: +44 (0) 1825 831994

Email: submissions@agendapoetry.co.uk
Website: http://www.agendapoetry.co.uk

Publishes: Essays; Poetry; Reviews; *Areas:*
Criticism; Literature; *Markets:* Adult;
Treatments: Literary

Editors: Patricia McCarthy

Publishes poems, critical essays, and
reviews. Send up to five poems or up to two
essays / reviews with email address, age, and
short bio. No previously published material.
Submit by email only, with each piece in a
separate Word attachment. Accepts work
only during specific submission windows –
see website for current status.

AIR International
PO BOX 100
Stamford
PE9 1XQ
Tel: +44 (0) 1780 755131
Fax: +44 (0) 1780 751323
Email: airint@keypublishing.com
Website: http://www.airinternational.com

Publishes: Articles; Features; News;
Nonfiction; *Areas:* Design; Military;
Technology; *Markets:* Adult

Editors: Mark Ayton

Aviation magazine covering military and
civilian aircraft. Happy to receive
contributions.

Amateur Gardening
Westover House
West Quay Road
Poole
BH15 1JG
Tel: +44 (0) 1202 440840
Fax: +44 (0) 1202 440860
Email: amateurgardening@timeinc.com
Website: http://www.amateurgardening.com

Publishes: Articles; Features; News;
Nonfiction; *Areas:* Gardening; *Markets:*
Adult

Editors: Garry Coward-Williams

Publishes news items, articles, and features
relating to gardening.

Amazing! Magazine

Amazing Publishing Limited
4 Old Park Lane
Mayfair
London
W1K 1QW
Tel: +44 (0) 20 3633 2531
Email: hello@amazing.org.uk
Website: https://amazing.org.uk

Publishes: Nonfiction; *Markets:* Children's

Editors: Yousuf Aslam

Monthly printed magazine for children aged 6-12 that makes learning fun. Each issue covers maths, english, science, history, geography, and more. Inside are articles, facts, stories, debates, activities, puzzles, and jokes.

Ambit

Staithe House
Main Road
Brancaster Staithe
Norfolk
PE31 8BP
Tel: +44 (0) 7715 233221
Email: contact@ambitmagazine.co.uk
Website: http://ambitmagazine.co.uk

Publishes: Fiction; Poetry; *Areas:* Arts; Short Stories; *Markets:* Adult; *Treatments:* Literary

An international magazine. Potential contributors are advised to read a copy before submitting work. Send up to 5 poems, a story up to 5,000 words, or flash fiction up to 1,000 words. Submit via online portal, or by post if unable to use online portal. No submissions by email. Accepts submission only during specific submission windows – see website for details.

Amethyst Review

Email: Sarah.Poet@gmail.com
Website: https://amethystmagazine.org

Publishes: Fiction; Nonfiction; Poetry; *Areas:* Religious; Short Stories; Spiritual; *Markets:* Adult

Editors: Sarah Law

Publishes work that engages in some way with spirituality or the sacred. Submit up to five poems (of any length) and / or prose pieces of up to 2,000 words. Simultaneous submissions if notification of acceptance elsewhere is provided. No previously published work. Send submissions by email with author bio of around 50 words. See website for full guidelines.

Architectural Design

Email: architecturaldesign@wiley.com
Website: http://wileyactual.com/architect-design/

Publishes: Articles; Nonfiction; *Areas:* Architecture; Design; *Markets:* Professional

Editors: Helen Castle

Prestigious magazine of architecture and design.

Arena Fantasy

Arena Fantasy Magazine
12 Edward Stone Rise
Chipping Norton
Oxfordshire
OX7 5EP
Tel: +44 (0) 7528 924361
Email: arenafantasymagazine@gmail.com
Website: https://arenafantasymagazine.carrd.co

Publishes: Articles; Fiction; Nonfiction; *Areas:* Fantasy; *Markets:* Adult; Youth; *Treatments:* Commercial; Literary; Mainstream; Traditional

Editors: Andy Hesford

Fantasy ezine that publishes every quarter. We specialise in fantasy stories as well as articles that help authors old and new. There are also competitions and a myriad of tools that will help you grow as an author.

Submissions – Prose and Artwork
Query via email initially. Your query should contain your Name, Pseudonym email address and contact details. Please give us a brief overview of your piece and a brief bio of anything you have published before if we like your work we will let you know and invite you to submit your piece.

Areté

8 New College Lane
Oxford
OX1 3BN
Email: craigraine@aretemagazine.co.uk
Website: https://www.aretemagazine.co.uk

Publishes: Fiction; Poetry; Reviews; *Areas:*
Drama; Short Stories; *Markets:* Adult

Editors: Craig Raine

Arts magazine publishing fiction, poetry,
reportage, and reviews. Previous contributors
have included TS Eliot, William Golding,
Harold Pinter, Ian McEwan, Martin Amis,
Simon Armitage, Rosemary Hill, Ralph
Fiennes, and many more.

Send hard copy only. Unsolicited MSS
should be accompanied by an SAE or email
address for response. No International Reply
Coupons, and no submissions by email.

Art + Framing Today

2 Wye House
6 Enterprise Way
London
SW18 1FZ
Tel: +44 (0) 20 7381 6616
Email: Lynn@fineart.co.uk
Website: https://www.fineart.co.uk/
art_and_framing_today.aspx

Publishes: Articles; Features; Interviews;
Nonfiction; *Areas:* Arts; Business; *Markets:*
Professional

Editors: Lynn Jones

Trade journal for the art, framing and
printing industries.

Art Quarterly

Art Fund
2 Granary Square
King's Cross
London
N1C 4BH
Tel: +44 (0) 20 7225 4856
Email: artquarterly@artfund.org
Website: https://www.artfund.org/about-us/
art-quarterly

Publishes: Articles; Features; Nonfiction;
Areas: Arts; *Markets:* Adult

Arts magazine publishing features on artists,
galleries and museums.

ARTEMISpoetry

3 Springfield Close
East Preston
West Sussex
BN16 2SZ
Email: editor@poetrypf.co.uk
Website: http://www.secondlightlive.co.uk/
artemis.shtml

Publishes: Poetry; *Markets:* Adult;
Treatments: Literary

Editors: Dilys Wood; Kathy Miles; Lyn
Moir

For poems by women. Submit up to four
poems, up to 200 lines total, by post only.
Poems must be unpublished and not out for
submission elsewhere. See website for full
guidelines.

Artists & Illustrators

The Chelsea Magazine Company
Jubilee House
2 Jubilee Place
London
SW3 3TQ
Email: info@artistsandillustrators.co.uk
Website: https://www.
artistsandillustrators.co.uk

Publishes: Articles; Nonfiction; *Areas:* Arts;
How-to; *Markets:* Adult; Professional

Publishes articles for both amateur and
professional artists.

Auto Express

31-32 Alfred Place
London
WC1E 7DP
Tel: +44 (0) 20 3890 3890
Email: steve_fowler@dennis.co.uk
Website: http://www.autoexpress.co.uk

Publishes: Articles; Features; News;
Nonfiction; Reviews; *Areas:* How-to; Men's
Interests; Technology; Travel; *Markets:*
Adult

Editors: Steve Fowler

Publishes motoring news, features, test drives, etc. Welcomes news items and fillers up to 100 words and leads up to 300 words, but no submissions of complete features. Send ideas for features in first instance.

Banipal

1 Gough Square
London
EC4A 3DE
Email: editor@banipal.co.uk
Website: http://www.banipal.co.uk

Publishes: Features; Fiction; Poetry; Reviews; *Areas:* Short Stories; Translations; *Markets:* Adult

Editors: Margaret Obank

Contemporary Arab authors in English translations. Publishes new and established writers, and diverse material including translations, poetry, short stories, novel excerpts, profiles, interviews, appreciations, book reviews, reports of literary festivals, conferences, and prizes. Welcomes submissions by post, but queries only by email. Unsolicited email submissions with attachments will be automatically deleted. Response in 3-6 months.

Bare Fiction Magazine

177 Copthorne Road
Shrewsbury
Shropshire
SY3 8NA
Email: info@barefiction.co.uk
Website: https://www.barefictionmagazine.co.uk

Publishes: Essays; Fiction; Interviews; Nonfiction; Poetry; Reviews; Scripts; *Areas:* Drama; Literature; Short Stories; Theatre; *Markets:* Adult; *Treatments:* Literary

Closed to submissions as at March 2019. Check website for current status.

Publishes poetry, fiction and plays, literary review, interviews and commentary. Does not accept submissions at all times – check website for current status and sign up to newsletter to be notified when submissions next open.

BBC Countryfile Magazine

14th Floor
Tower House
Fairfax Street
Bristol
BS1 3BN
Tel: +44 (0) 1173 147399
Email: editor@countryfile.com
Website: http://www.countryfile.com

Publishes: Articles; Features; Nonfiction; *Areas:* Nature; *Markets:* Adult

Editors: Fergus Collins; Joe Pontin (Features Editor)

Magazine on British countryside and rural life. Send queries with ideas by email. No unsolicited mss.

BBC Focus

Immediate Media, 9th floor
Tower House
Fairfax Street
Bristol
BS1 3BN
Tel: +44 (0) 1173 008755
Email: editorialenquiries@sciencefocus.com
Website: https://www.sciencefocus.com

Publishes: Articles; News; Nonfiction; *Areas:* Science; Technology; *Markets:* Adult

Publishes news and articles on science and technology. Accepts queries from previously published science writers only.

BBC Wildlife Magazine

4th Floor
Tower House
Fairfax St
Bristol
BS1 3BN
Tel: +44 (0) 1173 147366
Email: wildlifemagazine@immediate.co.uk
Website: http://www.discoverwildlife.com

Publishes: Articles; Features; News; Nonfiction; *Areas:* Nature; *Markets:* Adult

Editors: Ben Hoare

Magazine publishing news, articles, and features covering the natural world.

Birdwatch

Warners Group Publications
The Maltings
West Street
Bourne
Lincolnshire
PE10 9PH
Tel: +44 (0) 20 8881 0550
Website: http://www.birdwatch.co.uk

Publishes: Articles; Features; News; Nonfiction; *Areas:* Nature; *Markets:* Adult

Editors: Dominic Mitchell

Magazine of birds and birdwatching, publishing articles, news, and features.

Black Static

TTA Press
5 Martins Lane
Witcham
Ely
Cambs
CB6 2LB
Website: http://ttapress.com

Publishes: Fiction; *Areas:* Fantasy; Horror; Short Stories; *Markets:* Adult; *Treatments:* Dark

Editors: Andy Cox

Publishes short stories of horror and dark fantasy. See website for full guidelines and online submission system.

Blithe Spirit

Email: ed.blithespirit@gmail.com
Website: http://britishhaikusociety.org.uk

Publishes: Poetry; *Markets:* Adult

Editors: Caroline Skanne

Primarily a membership magazine featuring haiku and related forms, however members do not enjoy an automatic right to publication – quality is key. Non-members may appear as featured writers. All work must be original. Submissions should be sent by email with a covering note. Alternatively, send by post with SAE or IRCs for reply.

Boat International

First Floor
41-47 Hartfield Road
London
SW19 3RQ
Tel: +44 (0) 20 8545 9330
Fax: +44 (0) 20 8545 9333
Email: stewart.campbell@
boatinternationalmedia.com
Website: https://www.boatinternational.com

Publishes: Articles; News; Nonfiction; *Areas:* Design; Lifestyle; Technology; Travel; *Markets:* Adult

Editors: Stewart Campbell

Magazine celebrating superyachts and the life that comes with them.

British Medical Journal (BMJ)

BMA House
Tavistock Square
London
WC1H 9JP
Tel: +44 (0) 20 7387 4410
Fax: +44 (0) 20 7383 6418
Email: papersadmin@bmj.com
Website: https://www.bmj.com

Publishes: Articles; Features; News; Nonfiction; *Areas:* Medicine; *Markets:* Professional

Editors: Fiona Godlee

Leading medical journal for healthcare professionals. Papers can be submitted using online submission system available via website.

Brittle Star

Diversity House
72 Nottingham Road
Arnold
Nottingham
NG5 6LF
Website: http://www.brittlestar.org.uk

Publishes: Fiction; Nonfiction; Poetry; Reviews; *Areas:* Short Stories; *Markets:* Adult

Publishes original and unpublished poetry and short stories. Send 1-4 poems or 1-2 stories of up to 2,000 words each. Include short bio of up to 40 words. No simultaneous submissions. Also reviews of first, full poetry collections and single-author short fiction collections.

Broadcast

Media Business Insight
Zetland House
5-25 Scrutton Street
London
EC2A 4HJ
Tel: +44 (0) 20 8102 0900
Email: chris.curtis@broadcastnow.co.uk
Website: https://www.broadcastnow.co.uk

Publishes: Features; News; Nonfiction; *Areas:* Business; Entertainment; Technology; TV; *Markets:* Adult; Professional

Editors: Chris Curtis

Publishes news and features relating to broadcasting.

Building Design

Email: bdonline@ubm.com
Website: https://www.bdonline.co.uk

Publishes: Articles; Features; News; Nonfiction; *Areas:* Architecture; Design; *Markets:* Professional

Editors: Thomas Lane

Publishes news, comment, and reviews of interest to architects.

Bunbury Magazine

Email: submissions@bunburymagazine.com
Website: https://bunburymagazine.com

Publishes: Articles; Fiction; Nonfiction; Poetry; Reviews; *Areas:* Short Stories; *Markets:* Adult; *Treatments:* Literary

Online literary magazine. Publishes anything from poetry to artwork, flash fiction to graphic story, life writing to photography, plus reviews and articles. Send submissions by email. See website for full guidelines, and for current issue theme.

The Burlington Magazine

14-16 Duke's Road
London
WC1H 9SZ
Tel: +44 (0) 20 7388 1228
Email: mhall@burlington.org.uk
Website: http://www.burlington.org.uk

Publishes: Articles; Nonfiction; Reviews; *Areas:* Arts; Historical; *Markets:* Adult

Editors: Michael Hall

Monthly magazine devoted to the fine and decorative arts. Publishes concise articles based on original research, presenting new works, art-historical discoveries and fresh interpretations.

The Burnt Candle

Hamilton House
Nottingham
NG5 1AE
Email: theburntcandle@compsncalls.com
Website: https://www.compsncalls.com/burntcandle.html

Publishes: Fiction; Poetry; *Areas:* Crime; Drama; Erotic; Fantasy; Literature; Mystery; Romance; Short Stories; Suspense; Thrillers; *Markets:* Adult; *Treatments:* Dark; Literary; Mainstream; Popular; Serious

Editors: Judith Darcey-Blake

Magazine looking for original, well-written, powerful and emotional stories. Also open for poetry. New and up-and-coming writers are just as welcome as established writers.

Candis

Newhall Publications Ltd
Newhall Lane
Hoylake
Wirral
CH47 4BQ
Tel: +44 (0) 1516 323232
Email: info@newhallpublishing.com
Website: https://www.candis.co.uk

Publishes: Features; Nonfiction; *Areas:* Cookery; Health; Lifestyle; Travel; *Markets:* Adult

Publishes features on food, health, travel, and charity.

Cat World

PO Box 2258
Pulborough
West Sussex
RH20 9BA
Tel: +44 (0) 1903 884988
Email: support@ashdown.co.uk
Website: http://www.catworld.co.uk

Publishes: Articles; Features; News;
Nonfiction; *Areas:* Humour; Nature;
Markets: Adult

Publishes articles about cats and cat
ownership.

Catholic Pictorial

Media House
Mann Island
Liverpool
L3 1DG
Tel: +44 (0) 1512 362191
Fax: +44 (0) 1512 362216
Email: catherine@merseymirror.com
Website: http://www.catholicpic.co.uk

Publishes: Features; News; Nonfiction;
Areas: Religious; *Markets:* Adult

Publishes news and photo features of relating
to Catholicism and Merseyside.

Catholic Universe

The Universe Media Group Ltd
Guardian Print Centre
Parkway
Longbridge Road
Trafford Park
M17 1SN
Tel: +44 (0) 1619 085301
Website: http://www.
thecatholicuniverse.com

Publishes: Articles; Features; News;
Nonfiction; *Areas:* Religious; *Markets:*
Adult

Catholic Sunday newspaper. Launched in
1860 and based in Manchester.

Chat

TI Media
161 Marsh Wall
London
London
E14 9AP
Tel: +44 (0) 20 3148 5000
Email: chat_magazine@ti-media.com
Website: https://www.ti-media.com

Publishes: Articles; Features; Nonfiction;
Areas: Humour; Lifestyle; Women's
Interests; *Markets:* Adult

General interest women's magazine.
Approach in writing with ideas only after
becoming familiar with the magazine and the
kind of material it publishes. No fiction.

Climber

Email: climbereditorial@gmail.com
Website: https://www.climber.co.uk

Publishes: Articles; Nonfiction; *Areas:*
Sport; *Markets:* Adult

Monthly climbing magazine for experienced
climbers, boulderers, mountaineers, and
those who are just starting out. Query editor
by email in first instance.

Coin News

No 40, Southernhay East
Exeter
Devon
EX1 1PE
Tel: +44 (0) 1404 46972
Email: info@tokenpublishing.com
Website: https://www.tokenpublishing.com

Publishes: Articles; News; Nonfiction;
Areas: Hobbies; *Markets:* Adult

Magazine covering coin collecting.

Cotswold Life

Archant House
Oriel Road
Cheltenham
Gloucestershire
GL50 1BB
Tel: +44 (0) 1242 216050
Email: mike.lowe@archant.co.uk
Website: http://www.cotswoldlife.co.uk

Publishes: Articles; Nonfiction; *Areas:*
Gardening; Leisure; Lifestyle; Nature;
Travel; *Markets:* Adult

Editors: Mike Lowe

Publishes articles relating to the Cotswolds.

Country Life
Pinehurst 2
Pinehurst Road
Farnborough Business Park
Farnborough
Hants
GU14 7BF
Tel: +44 (0) 1252 555062
Email: mark.hedges@ti-media.com
Website: https://www.countrylife.co.uk

Publishes: Articles; News; Nonfiction;
Areas: Architecture; Arts; Current Affairs;
Lifestyle; Nature; Sport; *Markets:* Adult

Editors: Mark Hedges

Magazine covering all aspects of country
living. Looks for strong, well informed
material rather than material by amateur
enthusiasts.

Criminal Law & Justice Weekly (Incorporating Justice of the Peace)
Lexis House
30 Farringdon Street
London
EC4A 4HH
Tel: +44 (0) 20 7400 2828
Email: diana.rose@lexisnexis.co.uk
Website: http://www.
criminallawandjustice.co.uk

Publishes: Articles; Nonfiction; *Areas:*
Legal; *Markets:* Professional

Editors: Diana Rose

Weekly magazine covering key
developments in criminal law, plus practice
and procedure across the whole criminal
court system. Includes licensing and the
coroners' court. Send complete ms or précis
by email. See website for full details.

Critical Quarterly
Newbury
Crediton
Devon

EX17 5HA
Email: CQpoetry@gmail.com
Website: http://onlinelibrary.wiley.com/
journal/10.1111/(ISSN)1467-8705

Publishes: Essays; Fiction; Nonfiction;
Poetry; *Areas:* Criticism; Culture; Literature;
Short Stories; *Markets:* Adult; *Treatments:*
Literary

Editors: Clare Bucknell; Colin MacCabe

Publishes literary criticism, cultural studies,
poetry and fiction. Send submissions by
email. See website for separate email address
for submissions of criticism.

Crystal Magazine
3 Bowness Avenue
Prenton
Birkenhead
CH43 0SD
Tel: +44 (0) 1516 089736
Email: christinecrystal@hotmail.com
Website: http://www.christinecrystal.
blogspot.com

Publishes: Articles; Fiction; Nonfiction;
Poetry; *Areas:* Adventure; Fantasy; Horror;
Humour; Literature; Mystery; Nature;
Romance; Sci-Fi; Short Stories; Suspense;
Thrillers; Travel; Westerns; *Markets:* Adult;
Treatments: Light; Literary; Mainstream;
Popular; Traditional

For subscribers only. If you're not a
subscriber please don't send any work.

An A4, spiral-bound bi-monthly. Forty pages
of poems, stories and articles with colour
images. Most genres and themes covered.
Also includes the very popular
'Wordsmithing', a look into the lives of
writers and writing. The magazine usually
contains pages and pages of Readers'
Letters. Subscribers' News provides an
opportunity to share writing achievements.

Cumbria
Country Publications Limited
The Gatehouse
Skipton Castle
Skipton
BD23 1AL
Tel: +44 (0) 1756 701381

Fax: +44 (0) 1756 701326
Email: johnm@dalesman.co.uk
Website: http://www.cumbriamagazine.co.uk

Publishes: Articles; Nonfiction; *Areas:*
Nature; Travel; *Markets:* Adult

Editors: John Manning

Regional magazine focusing on the nature of
and walks in the Lake District.

Custom PC

Dennis Publishing Ltd
PO Box 843
HAYWARDS HEATH
RH16 9NY
Tel: +44 (0) 330 333 9493
Email: subscriptions@custompc.co.uk
Website: http://www.custompc.co.uk

Publishes: Articles; Nonfiction; *Areas:*
Technology; *Markets:* Adult

Editors: Ben Hardwidge

PC modding and overclocking magazine for
people who are passionate about PC
technology and hardware.

Dancing Times

36 Battersea Square
London
SW11 3RA
Tel: +44 (0) 20 7250 3006
Email: editorial@dancing-times.co.uk
Website: https://www.dancing-times.co.uk

Publishes: Articles; Features; News;
Nonfiction; Reviews; *Areas:* Music;
Markets: Adult

Monthly magazine of dance, publishing
features, news, and review.

The Dark Horse

3A Blantyre Mill Road
Bothwell
South Lanarkshire
G71 8DD
Website: http://thedarkhorsemagazine.com

Publishes: Poetry; *Markets:* Adult;
Treatments: Literary

Editors: Gerry Cambridge

International literary magazine committed to
British, Irish and American poetry. Send
submissions by post only, to UK or US
editorial addresses. No simultaneous
submissions. See website for full guidelines.

The Dawntreader

24 Forest Houses
Halwill
Beaworthy
Devon
EX21 5UU
Email: dawnidp@gmail.com
Website: https://www.indigodreams.co.uk/
the-dawntreader

Publishes: Articles; Fiction; Nonfiction;
Poetry; *Areas:* Nature; Short Stories;
Spiritual; *Markets:* Adult; *Treatments:*
Literary

Editors: Ronnie Goodyer

A quarterly publication specialising in myth,
legend; in the landscape, nature; spirituality
and love; the mystic, the environment.
Welcomes poetry up to 40 lines, and prose,
articles, and local legends up to 1,000 words.

Descent

Wild Places Publishing
PO Box 100
Abergavenny
NP7 9WY
Tel: +44 (0) 1873 737707
Email: descent@wildplaces.co.uk
Website: https://www.wildplaces.co.uk

Publishes: Articles; Features; News;
Nonfiction; Reviews; *Areas:* Historical;
Hobbies; Technology; *Markets:* Adult

Editors: Chris Howes

Magazine publishing material for mine
enthusiasts and cavers, including news items,
equipment reviews, historical and modern
expeditions, etc.

Director

3-7 Herbal Hill
London
EC1R 5EJ
Email: director-ed@iod.com

Website: https://www.director.co.uk

Publishes: Articles; Features; News; Nonfiction; *Areas:* Business; *Markets:* Professional

Magazine for entrepreneurs and business leaders.

Diver Magazine
Suite B, 74 Oldfield Road
Hampton
Middlesex
TW12 2HR
Tel: +44 (0) 20 8941 8152
Email: nigel@divermag.co.uk
Website: https://divernet.com/contact/

Publishes: Articles; News; *Areas:* Hobbies; Sport; Technology; Travel; *Markets:* Adult

Magazine covering every aspect of recreational scuba diving, especially in the realms of gear testing and surveys, diving holiday destinations, and advances in technology and techniques.

Dorset Life
7, The Leanne
Sandford Lane
Wareham
Dorset
BH20 4DY
Tel: +44 (0) 1929 551264
Email: editor@dorsetlife.co.uk
Website: https://www.dorsetlife.co.uk

Publishes: Articles; Nonfiction; *Markets:* Adult

Editors: Joël Lacey

County magazine for Dorset.

Dream Catcher
Stairwell Books
161 Lowther Street
York
YO31 7LZ
Tel: +44 (0) 1904 733767
Email: dreamcatchersubmissions@gmail.com
Website: http://www.dreamcatchermagazine.co.uk

Publishes: Fiction; Interviews; Nonfiction; Poetry; Reviews; *Areas:* Short Stories; Translations; *Markets:* Adult; *Treatments:* Literary

Editors: Wendy Pratt

Send submissions by post, following guidelines on website. No electronic submissions, except from overseas contributors.

Eastern Art Report
EAPGROUP
PO Box 13666
London
SW14 8WF
Email: ear@eapgroup.com
Website: http://easternartreport.net

Publishes: Articles; News; Nonfiction; *Areas:* Arts; Culture; *Markets:* Adult

International magazine focused on the arts of Asia and Africa and the arts practiced by the people of Asian and African origin in North America, Europe and elsewhere. Increasingly, Australia, New Zealand the Pacific region are covered in articles and news. Send query by email or through online contact form.

Economica
Email: economica@lse.ac.uk
Website: https://onlinelibrary.wiley.com/journal/14680335

Publishes: Articles; Nonfiction; *Areas:* Business; Finance; *Markets:* Academic

Editors: Nava Ashraf; Oriana Bandiera; Tim Besley; Francesco Caselli; Maitreesh Ghatak; Stephen Machin; Ian Martin; Gianmarco Ottaviano

Academic journal or economics. See website for submission guidelines.

The Engineer
Centaur Communications Ltd
Wells Point
79 Wells Street
London
W1T 3QN
Tel: +44 (0) 20 7970 4437

Email: jon.excell@centaurmedia.com
Website: https://www.theengineer.co.uk

Publishes: Articles; Features; News;
Nonfiction; *Areas:* Technology; *Markets:*
Adult; Professional

Editors: Jon Excell

Publishes news and features on the latest
technology and engineering innovations.

Envoi

Meirion House
Glan yr afon
Tanygrisiau
Blaenau Ffestiniog
LL41 3SU
Tel: +44 (0) 1766 832112
Email: envoi@cinnamonpress.com
Website: https://www.cinnamonpress.com/
index.php/about-cinnamon-press/about-envoi

Publishes: Articles; Nonfiction; Poetry;
Reviews; *Areas:* Literature; Translations;
Markets: Adult; *Treatments:* Literary

Editors: Dr Jan Fortune-Wood

Magazine of poems, poetry sequences,
reviews, and competitions, now more than
50 years old. Occasional poetry related
articles and poetry in translation. Submit up
to four poems up to 40 lines each or one or
two longer poems by email only (in the body
of the email; attachments will not be read).
No submissions by post.

What others say:

"Probably the best poetry magazine currently
available" – The Writers' College

"Without a grant and obviously well read,
this poetry magazine excels itself." – Ore

"The policy of giving poets space to show
their skills is the right one." – Haiku
Quarterly

"Good quality, lots of bounce, poems,
comps, reviews, reader comeback" – iota

"If you haven't tried it yet, do so, you'll get
your money's worth." – New Hope
International

EQy Magazine (Scottish Equestrian Year)

Wyvex Media
Fettes Park
496 Ferry Road
Edinburgh
EH5 2DL
Tel: +44 (0) 1315 511000
Email: heddy@eqymagazine.co.uk
Website: https://www.eqymagazine.co.uk

Publishes: Nonfiction; *Areas:* Nature;
Markets: Adult

Luxury magazine published once a year,
covering Scottish equestrianism.

Erotic Review

Email: editorial@ermagazine.org
Website: http://eroticreviewmagazine.com

Publishes: Articles; Features; Fiction;
Nonfiction; Reviews; *Areas:* Erotic;
Lifestyle; Short Stories; *Markets:* Adult

Editors: Jamie Maclean (Fiction)

Literary lifestyle publication about sex and
sexuality aimed at sophisticated, intelligent
and mature readers. Print version has been
retired and is now online only. Publishes
features, articles, short stories, and reviews.
See website for full submission guidelines.

Essex Life

Portman House
120 Princes Street
Ipswich
IP1 1RS
Tel: +44 (0) 7834 101686
Email: julian.read@archant.co.uk
Website: http://www.essexlifemag.co.uk

Publishes: Articles; Nonfiction; *Areas:* Arts;
Cookery; Culture; Design; Entertainment;
Gardening; Leisure; Lifestyle; Nature;
Markets: Adult

Magazine publishing material relating to
Essex.

Families First

Mothers' Union Publishing
Mary Sumner House

24 Tufton Street
London
SW1P 3RB
Tel: +44 (0) 20 7222 5533
Fax: +44 (0) 20 7227 9737
Email: mu@mothersunion.org
Website: https://www.mothersunion.org/
FamiliesFirst

Publishes: Articles; Features; Nonfiction;
Areas: Lifestyle; Religious; *Markets:* Adult

Editors: Catherine Butcher

Publishes features on family life, social
issues, marriage, Christian faith, etc. No
fiction or poetry.

Family Office Magazine
FOE Limited
27 Old Gloucester Street
London
WC1N 3AX
Tel: +44(0) 20 7193 8870
Email: contact@familyofficeelite.com
Website: http://www.familyofficemag.com

Publishes: Articles; *Areas:* Business;
Finance; Leisure; *Markets:* Professional;
Treatments: Mainstream

Editors: Ty Murphy

Caters for the ultra-wealthy Family Office
sector. The publication is widely read by the
world's leading experts from many of the
World's leading institutions from the Family
Office and the wealth sector. Many of these
institutions are regular advertisers and
sponsors while others are contributors who
provide insightful interviews and
contributions for the magazine.

Some of these institutions include Deloitte,
Manulife Asset Management, Caplin &
Drysdale, City Bank, BNY Mellon, PWC,
Ernst & Young, BMO Private Bank, ING
Private Bank, TSG Europe, Piraeus Bank,
Global Family Offices, Trusted Family,
Family Office Institute. Fuchs & AssociÃ©s
Finance, Credit Suisse, Northwood Family
Office, Lugen Family Office, Guernsey
Finance, Family Office Association, FOSS
Family Office Services Switzerland,
Luxembourg For Family Office and many
others. Family Office Elite also has

publishing agreements in place with some
these institutions including Deloitte which
contribute expert articles in every issue.

Luxury brands include Heirloom, Tesla Cars,
Heathrow Airport VIP , Luxury Channel,
Ghurka Luggage, British Polo Day, 1066
Pianos, Holland & Holland, Burgess Yachts,
DOMOS Fine Art, Signature Golf Events,
Global Fine Arts Awards, Concierge-
Aviation, Timeless Art Gallery,
Charterworld, Alpha-Centauri Hydroplanes,
Zimbali Costal Resorts, Chivas Luggage,
Caprice Products, Polo & Tweed, Blenheim
Palace, and more. Non – Profit Adverts
include the Universal Film & Festival
Organisation and Amnesty.

The Fenland Reed
Email: thefenlandreed@gmail.com
Website: https://www.thefenlandreed.co.uk

Publishes: Fiction; Poetry; *Areas:* Short
Stories; *Markets:* Adult; *Treatments:*
Literary

Editors: Jonathan Totman and Mary
Livingstone

Closed to submissions as at March 2019.
Check website for current status.

East Anglian literary magazine published
biannually, with one themed and one non-
themed issue each year. Publishes poetry and
short stories. See website for full guidelines
and any current theme.

The Field
Time Inc. (UK) Ltd
Pinehurst II, Pinehurst Road
Farnborough Business Park, Farnborough
Hampshire
GU14 7BF
Tel: +44 (0) 1252 555220
Email: field.secretary@timeinc.com
Website: http://www.thefield.co.uk

Publishes: Articles; Features; Nonfiction;
Areas: Nature; *Markets:* Adult

Editors: Jonathan Young

Publishes material relating to the countryside, including shooting, food and drink, fishing, country houses, gundogs, etc.

Flash: The International Short-Short Story Magazine

Department of English
University of Chester
Parkgate Road
Chester
CH1 4BJ
Email: flash.magazine@chester.ac.uk
Website: http://www.chester.ac.uk/flash.magazine

Publishes: Fiction; *Areas:* Short Stories; *Markets:* Adult; *Treatments:* Literary

Editors: Dr Peter Blair; Dr Ashley Chantler

Publishes flash fiction up to 360 words, including the title. Send up to four pieces per issue. Attach submissions to a single email. See website for full submission guidelines.

Fly Fishing & Fly Tying Magazine

Locus Centre
The Square
Aberfeldy
Perthshire
PH15 2DD
Tel: +44 (0) 1887 829868
Fax: +44 (0) 1887 829856
Email: MarkB.ffft@btinternet.com
Website: http://flyfishing-and-flytying.co.uk

Publishes: Articles; Nonfiction; Reviews; *Areas:* Nature; Sport; *Markets:* Adult

Editors: Mark Bowler

Magazine publishing articles and reviews relating to fly fishing and fly tying.

Fortean Times: The Journal of Strange Phenomena

Dennis Publishing
31-32 Alfred Place
London
WC1E 7DP
Email: drsutton@forteantimes.com
Website: http://subscribe.forteantimes.com

Publishes: Articles; Features; News; Nonfiction; Reviews; *Markets:* Adult

Editors: David Sutton

Publishes accounts of strange phenomena, experiences, curiosities, mysteries, prodigies, and portents. No fiction or poetry.

Gibbons Stamp Monthly

399 Strand
London
WC2R 0LX
Tel: +44 (0) 1425 472363
Website: http://www.gibbonsstampmonthly.com

Publishes: Articles; Features; News; Nonfiction; *Areas:* Hobbies; *Markets:* Adult

Magazine publishing features and news relating to stamps.

Golf Monthly

Pinehurst 2
Pinehurst Road
Farnborough Business Park
Farnborough
Hampshire
GU14 7BF
Tel: +44 (0) 1252 555197
Email: golfmonthly@timeinc.com
Website: http://www.golf-monthly.co.uk

Publishes: Articles; Features; Nonfiction; *Areas:* Sport; *Markets:* Adult

Editors: Michael Harris

Golfing magazine. Publishes profiles on players, and general features and columns. Welcomes unsolicited MSS but approach in writing with ideas first. No instruction material from external contributors.

Good Housekeeping

72 Broadwick Street
London
W1F 9EP
Tel: +44 (0) 20 7439 5000
Fax: +44 (0) 20 7437 6886
Email: goodh.mail@hearst.co.uk
Website: http://www.goodhousekeeping.co.uk

Publishes: Features; Nonfiction; *Areas:* Cookery; Health; Lifestyle; Women's Interests; *Markets:* Adult

Editors: Lindsay Nicholson

Monthly glossy women's magazine publishing material on health, lifestyle, cookery, etc.

Granta

12 Addison Avenue
Holland Park
London
W11 4QR
Tel: +44 (0) 20 7605 1360
Fax: +44 (0) 20 7605 1361
Email: editorial@granta.com
Website: http://www.granta.com

Publishes: Fiction; Nonfiction; Poetry; *Areas:* Short Stories; *Markets:* Adult; *Treatments:* Contemporary; Literary

Editors: Sigrid Rausing

Submit one story or essay, or up to three poems, via online submission system. £3 charge for prose submissions. No specific length limits for prose, but most pieces are between 3,000 and 6,000 words. Unlikely to read anything over 10,000 words.

Grazia

Media House
Peterborough Business Park
Lynch Wood
Peterborough
PE2 6EA
Tel: +44 (0) 1858 438884
Email: graziadaily@graziamagazine.co.uk
Website: https://graziadaily.co.uk

Publishes: Articles; Features; News; Nonfiction; *Areas:* Beauty and Fashion; Lifestyle; Women's Interests; *Markets:* Adult

Weekly glossy women's magazine published for more than 50 years in Italy, now brought to the UK market. Publishes articles and news aimed at women aged between 25 and 45.

The Great Outdoors (TGO)

Kelsey Media Ltd
Cudham Tithe Barn
Berry's Hill
Cudham
Kent
TN16 3AG
Tel: +44 (0) 1959 541444
Email: carey.davies@kelsey.co.uk
Website: https://www.tgomagazine.co.uk

Publishes: Articles; Features; News; Nonfiction; *Areas:* Hobbies; Leisure; Sport; Travel; *Markets:* Adult

Editors: Carey Davies

Magazine publishing features and news articles on outdoor pursuits, including walking and back-packing, etc. Query editor by email in first instance.

Harper's Bazaar

The National Magazine Company Ltd
72 Broadwick Street
London
W1F 9EP
Tel: +44 (0) 20 7439 5000
Email: Justine.picardie@hearst.co.uk
Website: http://www.harpersbazaar.co.uk

Publishes: Articles; Features; News; Nonfiction; *Areas:* Arts; Beauty and Fashion; Business; Film; Health; Lifestyle; Theatre; Travel; Women's Interests; *Markets:* Adult

Editors: Justine Picardie

Women's glossy magazine aimed at discerning, style-conscious, intelligent 30+ women who are cultured, well-travelled and independent.

Hello!

Wellington House
69-71 Upper Ground
London
SE1 9PQ
Tel: +44 (0) 20 7667 8721
Email: holly.nesbitt-larking@ hellomagazine.com
Website: https://www.hellomagazine.com

Publishes: Articles; Features; Interviews; News; Nonfiction; *Areas:* Beauty and Fashion; Culture; Lifestyle; Women's Interests; *Markets:* Adult

Editors: Holly Nesbitt-Larking

Magazine of celebrity and lifestyle.

History Today

2nd Floor, 9 Staple Inn
London
WC1V 7QH
Tel: +44 (0) 20 3219 7810
Email: p.lay@historytoday.com
Website: http://www.historytoday.com

Publishes: Articles; Features; Nonfiction; *Areas:* Historical; *Markets:* Adult

Historical magazine publishing short articles (600-1,000 words); mid-length articles (1,300-2,200 words) and feature articles (3,500 to 4,000 words). Send query by email with proposal and details of your career / academic background. See website for full guidelines.

Horse and Rider

DJ Murphy Publishers Ltd
Marlborough House
Headley Road
Grayshott, Surrey
GU26 6LG
Tel: +44 (0) 1428 601020
Email: editor@djmurphy.co.uk
Website: http://www.horseandrideruk.com

Publishes: Articles; Features; News; Nonfiction; *Areas:* How-to; Leisure; *Markets:* Adult

Editors: Louise Kittle

Magazine on horses, including news, instructional features, etc. Aimed mainly at horse-owners.

House & Garden

Email: houseandgarden@condenast.co.uk
Website: http://www.houseandgarden.co.uk

Publishes: Articles; Nonfiction; *Areas:* Architecture; Cookery; Design; Gardening; Lifestyle; Travel; *Markets:* Adult

Editors: Hatta Byng

Publishes articles on gardens, architecture, home decor, recipes, travel, and lifestyle.

Improve Your Coarse Fishing

Media House
Peterborough Business Park
Peterborough
PE2 6EA
Tel: +44 (0) 1733 395102
Email: ben.miles@bauermedia.co.uk
Website: https://www.anglingtimes.co.uk/magazines/improve-your-coarse-fishing/

Publishes: Articles; Features; News; *Areas:* Leisure; Sport; *Markets:* Adult

Editors: Ben Miles

Magazine on coarse fishing.

The Independent Publishing Magazine

Email: mickrooney@theindependentpublishingmagazine.com
Website: http://www.theindependentpublishingmagazine.com

Publishes: Articles; News; Nonfiction; *Areas:* Media; *Markets:* Adult

Editors: Mick Rooney

Magazine covering the self-publishing industry specifically and the wider publishing industry generally.

Ink Sweat and Tears

Email: inksweatandtearssubmissions@gmail.com
Website: http://www.inksweatandtears.co.uk

Publishes: Poetry; Reviews; *Markets:* Adult; *Treatments:* Literary

Editors: Helen Ivory

UK-based webzine publishing poetry, prose, prose-poetry, word and image pieces, and poetry reviews. Send 4-6 pieces by email only. Accepts unsolicited reviews of poetry and short story collections. See website for full guidelines.

Insurance Age

Infopro Digital
Haymarket House
28-29 Haymarket
London
SW1Y 4RX
Tel: +44 (0) 20 7316 9458
Fax: +44 (0) 20 7681 3401
Email: sian.barton@infopro-digital.com
Website: https://www.insuranceage.co.uk

Publishes: Articles; Features; News;
Nonfiction; *Areas:* Business; Finance;
Markets: Professional

Editors: Sian Barton

Publishes news and features on the insurance
industry.

The Interpreter's House

37A Spencer Street
Holywood
County Down
Northern Ireland
BT18 9DN
Email: interpretershousesubmissions@
gmail.com
Website: http://www.
theinterpretershouse.com

Publishes: Fiction; Poetry; *Areas:* Short
Stories; *Markets:* Adult; *Treatments:*
Literary

Editors: Georgi Gill

Send up to five poems or up to two short
stories by email in a single Word attachment,
or by post with SAE. Accepts work in
October, February, and June.

Interzone

TTA Press
5 Martins Lane
Witcham
Ely
Cambs
CB6 2LB
Website: http://ttapress.com

Publishes: Fiction; *Areas:* Fantasy; Sci-Fi;
Short Stories; *Markets:* Adult

Editors: Andy Cox

Publishes science fiction and fantasy short
stories up to about 10,000 words. No
simultaneous submissions, multiple
submissions or reprints. See website for full
guidelines and online submission system.

Investors Chronicle

Email: john.hughman@ft.com
Website: https://www.
investorschronicle.co.uk

Publishes: Articles; News; Nonfiction;
Areas: Business; Finance; *Markets:*
Professional

Editors: John Hughman

Magazine for investors.

Irish Pages

129 Ormeau Road
Belfast
BT7 1SH
Tel: +44 (0) 2890 434800
Email: editor@irishpages.org
Website: http://www.irishpages.org

Publishes: Essays; Fiction; Nonfiction;
Poetry; Reviews; *Areas:* Autobiography;
Historical; Nature; Science; Short Stories;
Translations; *Markets:* Adult; *Treatments:*
Literary

Editors: Chris Agee

Non-partisan and non-sectarian literary
journal publishing writing from the island of
Ireland and elsewhere in equal measure.
Publishes work in English, and in the Irish
Language or Ulster Scots with English
translations or glosses. Welcomes
submissions throughout the year by post only
with stamps, coupons or cash for return
postage (no self-addressed envelope is
needed). See website for more details.

Jewish Chronicle

28 St. Albans Lane
London
NW11 7QE
Tel: +44 (0) 20 7415 1500
Email: editorial@thejc.com
Website: https://www.thejc.com

Publishes: News; Nonfiction; *Areas:* Arts; Cookery; Lifestyle; Politics; Religious; Travel; *Markets:* Adult

Weekly paper publishing material of Jewish interest. No fiction.

Jewish Quarterly

28 St Albans Lane
London
NW11 7QE
Email: Community@JewishQuarterly.org
Website: http://www.jewishquarterly.org

Publishes: Essays; Fiction; News; Nonfiction; Poetry; *Areas:* Arts; Culture; Current Affairs; Film; Historical; Literature; Music; Philosophy; Politics; Religious; Short Stories; *Markets:* Adult; *Treatments:* Contemporary; Literary

Says of itself it "leads the field in Jewish writing, covering a wide spectrum of subjects including art, criticism, fiction, film, history, Judaism, literature, poetry, philosophy, politics, theatre, the Shoah, Zionism and much more".

Leisure Painter

The Artists' Publishing Company Ltd.
Caxton House
63-65 High Street
Tenterden
Kent TN30 6BD
Tel: +44 (0) 1580 763315
Website: http://www.painters-online.co.uk

Publishes: Articles; Features; Nonfiction; *Areas:* Arts; Hobbies; How-to; *Markets:* Adult

Editors: Ingrid Lyon

Magazine offering artistic inspiration, guidance, tuition and encouragement for beginners and amateur artists. Includes features and step-by-step painting and drawing demonstrations.

LGC (Local Government Chronicle)

EMAP Publishing Limited
Telephone House
69 – 77 Paul Street
London
EC2A 4NQ
Tel: +44 (0) 20 3953 2774
Email: lgcnews@emap.com
Website: https://www.lgcplus.com

Publishes: Articles; News; Nonfiction; *Areas:* Business; Politics; Sociology; *Markets:* Professional

Editors: Nick Golding

Magazine aimed at managers in local government.

Life and Work

121 George Street
Edinburgh
EH2 4YN
Tel: +44 (0) 1312 255722
Email: magazine@lifeandwork.org
Website: https://www.lifeandwork.org

Publishes: Articles; Features; News; Nonfiction; *Areas:* Religious; *Markets:* Adult

Magazine of the Church of Scotland.

Lighthouse

Email: submissions@lighthouse.gatehousepress.com
Website: http://www.gatehousepress.com/lighthouse/

Publishes: Fiction; Poetry; *Areas:* Short Stories; *Markets:* Adult; *Treatments:* Contemporary; Literary

Magazine of contemporary fiction and poetry, aimed at a UK audience. Submit up to six poems or up to one piece of fiction by email as attachments. No previously published material or simultaneous submissions. See website for full guidelines.

The Linguist

Chartered Institute of Linguists (CIOL)
7th Floor
167 Fleet Street
London
EC4A 2EA
Tel: +44 (0) 20 7940 3100
Website: https://www.ciol.org.uk/the-linguist

Publishes: Articles; News; Nonfiction; *Areas:* Science; *Markets:* Professional

Magazine for language professionals.

Litro Magazine
1-15 Cremer Street
Studio 213
E2 8HD
Tel: +44 (0) 20 3371 9971
Email: editor@litro.co.uk
Website: http://www.litro.co.uk

Publishes: Features; Fiction; Interviews; Nonfiction; Poetry; Reviews; *Areas:* Arts; Autobiography; Culture; Lifestyle; Literature; Politics; Short Stories; Translations; Travel; *Markets:* Adult; *Treatments:* Literary

Free print publication and online platform publishing short fiction, flash/micro fiction, nonfiction (memoir, literary journalism, travel narratives, etc), and original artwork in the print magazine, and short fiction, essays, reviews, and features on the online platform. Publishes poetry and novel extracts in the print magazine but does not accept unsolicited submissions in these areas. Does not publish poetry online. See website for full guidelines and to submit.

The London Magazine
11 Queen's Gate
London
SW7 5EL
Tel: +44 (0) 20 7584 5977
Email: info@thelondonmagazine.org
Website: http://thelondonmagazine.org

Publishes: Articles; Essays; Features; Fiction; Nonfiction; Poetry; Reviews; *Areas:* Arts; Autobiography; Criticism; Literature; Short Stories; *Markets:* Adult; *Treatments:* Literary

Send submissions through online submission system. Does not normally publish science fiction or fantasy writing, or erotica. Will consider postal submissions, but prefers submissions electronically. See website for full guidelines and to access online submission system.

London Review of Books
28 Little Russell Street
London
WC1A 2HN
Tel: +44 (0) 20 7209 1101
Fax: +44 (0) 20 7209 1151
Email: edit@lrb.co.uk
Website: http://www.lrb.co.uk

Publishes: Articles; Essays; Nonfiction; Poetry; Reviews; *Areas:* Arts; Culture; Film; Literature; Politics; Science; *Markets:* Adult; *Treatments:* Literary

Editors: Mary-Kay Wilmers

Contact editor in writing in first instance, including SAE. Publishes mainly reviews, essays, and articles, but also publishes poetry.

Magma
23 Pine Walk
Carshalton
SM5 4ES
Email: info@magmapoetry.com
Website: http://www.magmapoetry.com

Publishes: Nonfiction; Poetry; Reviews; *Areas:* Literature; *Markets:* Adult; *Treatments:* Literary

Editors: Laurie Smith

Prefers submissions through online submission system. Postal submissions accepted from the UK only, and must include SAE. No submissions by email. Accepts poems and artwork. Poems are considered for one issue only – they are not held over from one issue to the next. Seeks poems that give a direct sense of what it is to live today – honest about feelings, alert about world, sometimes funny, always well crafted. Also publishes reviews of books and pamphlets of poetry. See website for details.

Management Today
Bridge House
69 London Road
Twickenham
TW1 3SP
Tel: +44 (0) 20 8267 4967
Email: adam.gale@haymarket.com

Website: https://www.
managementtoday.co.uk

Publishes: Articles; Features; Nonfiction;
Areas: Business; *Markets:* Professional

Editors: Adam Gale

Publishes features and articles on general
business and management topics. Send query
with brief synopsis by email only.

Maritime Journal
Spinnaker House
Waterside Gardens
Fareham
Hampshire
PO16 8SD
Tel: +44 (0) 1329 825335
Fax: +44 (0) 1329 550192
Email: editor@maritimejournal.com
Website: http://www.maritimejournal.com

Publishes: Articles; News; Nonfiction;
Areas: Business; Travel; *Markets:*
Professional

Magazine providing insight for the European
commercial marine business.

Men's Health
Hearst UK
30 Panton Street
Leicester Square
London
SW1Y 4AJ
Website: https://www.menshealth.com/uk

Publishes: Articles; Nonfiction; *Areas:*
Health; Lifestyle; Medicine; Men's Interests;
Markets: Adult

Publishes articles related to the health of
men, including such topics as fitness, stress,
sex, nutrition, and health in general.

Modern Poetry in Translation
The Queens College
Oxford
OX1 4AW
Tel: +44 (0) 1865 244701
Email: editor@mptmagazine.com
Website: http://
modernpoetryintranslation.com

Publishes: Essays; Nonfiction; Poetry;
Areas: Literature; Translations; *Markets:*
Adult

Editors: Clare Pollard

Respected poetry series originally founded
by prominent poets in the sixties. New Series
continues their editorial policy: translation of
good poets by translators who are often
themselves poets, fluent in the foreign
language, and sometimes working with the
original poet. See website for submission
guidelines.

Mojo
Bauer Media
Endeavour House
189 Shaftesbury Avenue
London
WC2H 8JG
Tel: +44 (0) 20 7208 3443
Email: MOJO@bauermedia.co.uk
Website: http://www.mojo4music.com

Publishes: Articles; Interviews; News;
Nonfiction; Reviews; *Areas:* Music;
Markets: Adult; *Treatments:* Serious

Rock music magazine publishing news,
reviews, and interviews.

Moneywise
First Floor, Standon House
21 Mansell Street
London
E1 8AA
Email: editorial@moneywise.co.uk
Website: http://www.moneywise.co.uk

Publishes: Articles; News; Nonfiction;
Areas: Business; Finance; *Markets:* Adult

Helps people learn how to make the most of
their money, helping them to identify the
right investment products, and avoid the
unnecessary costs associated with some
financial products.

Motor Boat & Yachting
Email: mby@ti-media.com
Website: http://www.mby.com

Publishes: Features; News; Nonfiction;
Areas: How-to; Technology; Travel;
Markets: Adult

Editors: Hugo Andreae

Magazine publishing news and features
related to motor boats and motor cruising.

Motorcycle News (MCN)
Media House
Lynch Wood
Peterborough
PE2 6EA
Tel: +44 (0) 1858 438884
Email: andy.calton@motorcyclenews.com
Website: https://www.motorcyclenews.com

Publishes: Articles; Features; Nonfiction;
Areas: Leisure; Technology; Travel;
Markets: Adult

Editors: Andy Calton

Magazine for motorbike enthusiasts.

The Motorship
Mercator Media Ltd
Spinnaker House
Waterside Gardens
Fareham
Hampshire
PO16 8SD
Tel: +44 (0) 1329 825335
Fax: +44 (0) 1329 550192
Email: editor@motorship.com
Website: http://www.motorship.com

Publishes: Articles; News; Nonfiction;
Areas: Business; Technology; Travel;
Markets: Professional

Magazine aimed at marine technology
professionals.

Mslexia
PO Box 656
Newcastle upon Tyne
NE99 1PZ
Tel: +44 (0) 1912 048860
Email: postbag@mslexia.co.uk
Website: http://www.mslexia.co.uk

Publishes: Articles; Essays; Features;
Fiction; Interviews; News; Nonfiction;

Poetry; Reference; Reviews; *Areas:*
Autobiography; Short Stories; Women's
Interests; *Markets:* Adult

By women, for women who write, who want
to write, who teach creative writing or who
have an interest in women's literature and
creativity. It is a mixture of original work,
features, news, views, advice and listings.
The UK's only magazine devoted to women
writers and their writing.

See website for themes of upcoming issues /
competitions.

Publishes features, columns, reviews, flash
fiction, and literature listings. Some themes
are open to subscribers only. Submit via
online submission system on website.

Music Week
NewBay Media Europe Ltd
Emerson Studios
4th Floor
4-8 Emerson Street
London
SE1 9DU
Tel: +44 (0) 20 7226 7246
Email: msutherland@nbmedia.com
Website: http://www.musicweek.com

Publishes: Articles; News; Nonfiction;
Areas: Business; Music; *Markets:* Adult;
Professional

Editors: Mark Sutherland

Weekly magazine covering the music
business, including production, marketing,
and retailing.

Nature
The Macmillan Building
4-6 Crinan Street
London
N1 9XW
Tel: +44 (0) 20 7833 4000
Fax: +44 (0) 20 7843 4596
Email: nature@nature.com
Website: http://www.nature.com

Publishes: Articles; News; Nonfiction;
Areas: Science; *Markets:* Academic; Adult;
Professional

Editors: Philip Campbell

Journal covering all aspects of science. Scope for freelance writers with specialist knowledge.

New Scientist
110 High Holborn
London
WC1V 6EU
Email: richard.webb@newscientist.com
Website: http://www.newscientist.com

Publishes: Articles; Features; News; Nonfiction; Reviews; *Areas:* Science; Technology; *Markets:* Adult; Professional

Editors: Richard Webb

Weekly science magazine. No unsolicited MSS but accepts pitches by email. See website for more details and specific contact details and focus areas for the different editors. Reviews are commissioned.

New Statesman
John Carpenter House
7 Carmelite Street
Blackfriars
London
EC4Y 0BS
Tel: +44 (0) 20 7936 6400
Fax: +44 (0) 20 7305 7304
Email: editorial@newstatesman.co.uk
Website: http://www.newstatesman.com

Publishes: Articles; Features; News; Nonfiction; Poetry; Reviews; *Areas:* Arts; Current Affairs; Politics; *Markets:* Adult

Editors: Jason Cowley

Weekly political magazine. For nonfiction, send initial pitch by email to address provided on website. No fiction, but welcomes poems up to 30 lines, on any subject and in any style (do not need to be political). Send up to 4 poems by email in the body of the email or as a single Word attachment, to the specific poetry email address provided on the website.

New Welsh Reader
PO Box 170
Aberystwyth
SY23 1WZ
Tel: +44 (0) 1970 628410
Email: submissions@newwelshreview.com
Website: http://www.newwelshreview.com

Publishes: Features; Fiction; Nonfiction; Poetry; Reviews; *Areas:* Short Stories; *Markets:* Adult; *Treatments:* Literary

Editors: Gwen Davies

Focus is on Welsh writing in English, but has an outlook which is deliberately diverse, encompassing broader UK and international contexts. For feature articles, send 300-word query by email. Submit fiction or up to 6 poems by email only. Postal submissions will be returned unopened. Full details available on website.

Note: Not accepting fiction submissions as at May 2018 due to high volume of submissions. See website for current status.

Nine Muses Poetry
Email: ninemusespoetry@talktalk.net
Website: https://ninemusespoetry.com

Publishes: Poetry; *Markets:* Adult; *Treatments:* Literary

Editors: Annest Gwilym

A webzine featuring all forms of poetry by new, emerging and established poets, showcasing the best of contemporary poetry.

The North
The Poetry Business
Campo House
54 Campo Lane
Sheffield
S1 2EG
Tel: +44 (0) 1144 384074
Email: office@poetrybusiness.co.uk
Website: http://www.poetrybusiness.co.uk

Publishes: Articles; Poetry; Reviews; *Areas:* Autobiography; Criticism; Literature; *Markets:* Adult; *Treatments:* Contemporary; Literary

Editors: Peter Sansom; Ann Sansom

Send up to 6 poems with SASE / return postage. We publish the best of contemporary poetry. No "genre" or derivative poetry. Submitters should be aware of, should preferably have read, the magazine before submitting. See our website for notes on submitting poems. No submissions by email.

Also publishes critical articles and reviews of contemporary poetry. Submit ideas/synopses only in first instance.

Nursing Times

EMAP Publishing Company
7th Floor, Vantage London
Great West Road
Brentford
TW8 9AG
Tel: +44 (0) 20 3953 2707
Fax: +44 (0) 20 7874 0505
Email: jenni.middleton@emap.com
Website: http://www.nursingtimes.net

Publishes: Articles; Nonfiction; *Areas:* Health; Medicine; *Markets:* Professional; *Treatments:* Contemporary

Editors: Jenni Middleton

Magazine aimed at nurses, covering all aspects of health care and nursing.

The Oldie

65 Newman Street
London
W1T 3EG
Tel: +44 (0) 20 7436 8801
Email: editorial@theoldie.co.uk
Website: http://www.theoldie.co.uk

Publishes: Articles; Features; *Areas:* Humour; *Markets:* Adult

Editors: Richard Ingrams

Prefers to receive completed articles by email (see website for specific email address). No commissions based on ideas. Publishes cartoons, letters, articles, and features on a range of topics, with a humorous slant, aimed at the older reader. No poetry.

Olive

Vineyard House
44 Brook Green
Hammersmith
London
W6 7BT
Tel: +44 (0) 020 7150 5000
Email: oliveweb@immediate.co.uk
Website: http://www.olivemagazine.com

Publishes: Articles; Features; Nonfiction; *Areas:* Cookery; *Markets:* Adult

Monthly food magazine. Welcomes unsolicited queries but responds only when interested.

Orbis International Literary Journal

17 Greenhow Avenue
West Kirby
Wirral
CH48 5EL
Email: carolebaldock@hotmail.com
Website: http://www.orbisjournal.com

Publishes: Articles; Essays; Features; Fiction; News; Nonfiction; Poetry; Reviews; *Areas:* Arts; Humour; Short Stories; Women's Interests; *Markets:* Adult; *Treatments:* Literary

Editors: Carole Baldock

One of the longest running UK magazines; established 1969

And one of the most highly regarded; Peter Finch, Chief Executive of the Welsh Academi includes this magazine in his Top 10 publications (The Poetry Business).

Around one third of the poems in each issue are from Overseas (and around one fifth of subscribers):read, enjoy, inwardly digest; and improve your chances of being published abroad.

One of the few magazines which is also a useful resource. Includes news items, competition listings and magazine reviews.

One of the few magazines to provide contributors with proofs and editorial critique.

Readers' Award: £50 for the piece receiving the most votes, plus £50 between four runners-up.

Oxford Poetry

Magdalen College
Oxford
OX1 4AU
Email: editors@oxfordpoetry.co.uk
Website: http://www.oxfordpoetry.co.uk

Publishes: Essays; Interviews; Nonfiction; Poetry; Reviews; *Areas:* Translations; *Markets:* Adult; *Treatments:* Literary

Closed to submissions as at July 2018. Check website for current status.

Publishes poems, interviews, reviews, and essays. Accepts unpublished poems on any theme and of any length. Send up to four poems by email. See website for full details.

Park Home and Holiday Caravan

Kelsey Publishing
Cudham Tithe Barn
Berry's Hill
Cudham
Kent
TN16 3AG
Tel: +44 (0) 1959 541444
Email: phhc.ed@kelsey.co.uk
Website: https://www.
parkhomemagazine.co.uk

Publishes: Articles; Features; News; Nonfiction; *Areas:* Hobbies; How-to; Lifestyle; Travel; *Markets:* Adult

Editors: Alex Melvin

Magazine for those owning holiday caravans or living in residential park homes.

People Management

Email: pmeditorial@haymarket.com
Website: http://www.
peoplemanagement.co.uk

Publishes: Articles; Features; Nonfiction; *Areas:* Business; How-to; Legal; *Markets:* Professional

Editors: Robert Jeffery

Human resources magazine, publishing articles and features on all aspects of managing and developing people at work.

The People's Friend

Albert Square
Dundee
DD1 1DD
Tel: +44 (0) 1382 223131
Email: peoplesfriend@dcthomson.co.uk
Website: http://www.thepeoplesfriend.co.uk

Publishes: Articles; Features; Fiction; Nonfiction; Poetry; *Areas:* Adventure; Cookery; Crafts; Crime; Hobbies; Mystery; Nature; Romance; Short Stories; Thrillers; Travel; Women's Interests; *Markets:* Adult; Family; *Treatments:* Traditional

Publishes complete short stories (1,200-3,000 words (4,000 for specials)) and serials, focusing on character development rather than complex plots, plus 10,000-word crime thrillers. Also considers nonfiction from nature to nostalgia and from holidays to hobbies, and poetry. Guidelines available on website.

People's Friend Pocket Novels

DC Thomson & Co. Ltd
2 Albert Square
Dundee
DD1 9QJ
Tel: +44 (0) 1382 223131
Email: tsteel@dcthomson.co.uk
Website: http://www.thepeoplesfriend.co.uk

Publishes: Fiction; *Areas:* Romance; *Markets:* Adult; Family

Editors: Tracey Steel

Publishes romance and family fiction between 40,000 and 42,000 words, aimed at adults aged over 30. Send query by post or by email (preferred) with synopsis and first two chapters in first instance. See website for more information.

Picture Postcard Monthly

6 Carmarthen Avenue
Drayton
Portsmouth

Hampshire
PO6 2AQ
Tel: +44 (0) 2392 423527
Email: info@picturepostcardmagazine.co.uk
Website: http://www.
picturepostcardmagazine.co.uk

Publishes: Articles; Features; News;
Nonfiction; Reference; *Areas:* Arts;
Hobbies; Photography; *Markets:* Adult

Editors: Mark Wingham

Magazine for postcard collectors, publishing
news, views, stories and feature articles.

Planet
PO Box 44
Aberystwyth
Ceredigion
SY23 3ZZ
Tel: +44 (0) 1970 611255
Email: submissions@planetmagazine.org.uk
Website: http://www.planetmagazine.org.uk

Publishes: Articles; Features; Fiction;
Nonfiction; Poetry; Reviews; *Areas:* Arts;
Current Affairs; Literature; Music; Politics;
Short Stories; Theatre; *Markets:* Adult;
Treatments: Literary

Editors: Emily Trahair

Publishes mostly commissioned material, but
will accept ideas for articles and reviews,
and unsolicited submissions of fiction and
poetry. Submit one piece of short fiction
between 1,500 and 2,500 words, or 4-6
poems at a time. A range of styles and
themes are accepted, but postal submissions
will not be considered unless adequate return
postage is provided. If you have an idea for a
relevant article send a query with brief
synopsis.

PN Review
4th Floor, Alliance House
30 Cross Street
Manchester
M2 7AQ
Tel: +44 (0) 161 834 8730
Fax: +44 (0) 161 832 0084
Email: PNRsubmissions@carcanet.co.uk
Website: http://www.pnreview.co.uk

Publishes: Articles; Features; Interviews;
News; Poetry; Reviews; *Areas:* Translations;
Markets: Adult

Editors: Michael Schmidt

Send query with synopsis and sample pages,
after having familiarised yourself with the
magazine. Accepts prose up to 15 double-
spaced pages or 4 poems / 5 pages of poetry.

Bimonthly magazine of poetry and poetry
criticism. Includes editorial, letters, news,
articles, interviews, features, poems,
translations, and a substantial book review
section. No short stories, children's prose /
poetry, or non-poetry related work
(academic, biography etc.). Accepts
electronic submissions from individual
subscribers only – otherwise only hard copy
submissions are considered.

Poetry London
Goldsmiths, University of London
New Cross
London
SE14 6NW
Tel: +44 (0) 20 8228 5707
Email: admin@poetrylondon.co.uk
Website: http://www.poetrylondon.co.uk

Publishes: Features; Nonfiction; Poetry;
Reviews; *Areas:* Translations; *Markets:*
Adult; *Treatments:* Contemporary; Literary

Editors: Ahren Warner; Martha Kapos

Send up to six poems with SASE or adequate
return postage. Considers poems by both
new and established poets. Also publishes
book reviews. No submissions by email.

The Poetry Review
The Poetry Society
22 Betterton Street
London
WC2H 9BX
Tel: +44 (0) 20 7420 9880
Fax: +44 (0) 20 7240 4818
Email: poetryreview@poetrysociety.org.uk
Website: http://www.poetrysociety.org.uk

Publishes: Essays; Nonfiction; Poetry;
Reviews; *Areas:* Translations; *Markets:*
Adult; *Treatments:* Literary

Describes itself as "one of the liveliest and most influential literary magazines in the world", and has been associated with the rise of the New Generation of British poets – Carol Ann Duffy, Simon Armitage, Glyn Maxwell, Don Paterson... though its scope extends beyond the UK, with special issues focusing on poetries from around the world. Poets from the UK must submit by post; those from elsewhere in the world may submit using online system. See website for details. Send up to 6 unpublished poems, or literary translations of poems.

Poetry Wales

57 Nolton Street
Bridgend
CF31 3AE
Tel: +44 (0) 1656 663018
Email: info@poetrywales.co.uk
Website: http://poetrywales.co.uk

Publishes: Essays; Nonfiction; Poetry; Reviews; *Markets:* Adult; *Treatments:* Literary

Editors: Nia Davies

Closed to submissions as at September 2018. Check website for current status.

Publishes poetry, features, and reviews from Wales and beyond. Submit via online submission system.

The Police Journal

SAGE Publications Ltd
1 Oliver's Yard
55 City Road
London
EC1Y 1SP
Tel: +44 (0) 20 7324 8500
Fax: +44 (0) 20 7324 8600
Email: authorqueries@sagepub.co.uk
Website: https://uk.sagepub.com/en-gb/eur/the-police-journal/journal202314

Publishes: Articles; Nonfiction; *Areas:* Crime; Legal; *Markets:* Professional

Editors: Colin Rogers

Publishes articles aimed at police forces around the world. Submit using online submission manager only.

The Pool

Email: hello@thepoolltd.com
Website: https://www.the-pool.com

Publishes: Articles; News; Nonfiction; *Areas:* Arts; Beauty and Fashion; Culture; Health; Lifestyle; Women's Interests; *Markets:* Adult

Online platform for news and comment aimed at women. Send proposals by email.

Prac Crit

Email: editors@praccrit.com
Website: http://www.praccrit.com

Publishes: Essays; Interviews; Nonfiction; Poetry; *Areas:* Criticism; Literature; *Markets:* Adult; *Treatments:* Contemporary; Literary

Publishes close analysis of poems; essays; interviews; and reflections from poets. Most articles are commissioned, but will accept proposals for essays or interviews. No direct submissions of poetry.

The Practising Midwife

Medical Education Solutions Ltd
Monks Ridge
Burrows Lane
Gomshall
GU5 9QE
Tel: +44 (0) 20 8313 9617
Email: laurayeates@virginmedia.com
Website: http://www.practisingmidwife.co.uk

Publishes: Articles; News; Nonfiction; *Areas:* Health; Medicine; Women's Interests; *Markets:* Professional

Editors: Laura Yeates

Publishes accessible, authoritative and readable information for midwives, students and other professionals in the maternity services.

Press Gazette

40 Hatton Garden
London
EC1N 8EV
Tel: +44 (0) 20 7936 6433

Email: pged@pressgazette.co.uk
Website: http://www.pressgazette.co.uk

Publishes: Articles; Features; News;
Nonfiction; *Areas:* Current Affairs; Media;
Markets: Professional

Editors: Freddy Mayhew

Publishes news, features, and analysis related
to all areas of journalism: print,
broadcasting, online; national, regional,
magazines, etc. Pitch stories by phone or by
email.

Prole
Prolebooks
15 Maes-y-Dre
Abergele
Conwy
LL22 7HW
Email: submissionspoetry@
prolebooks.co.uk
Website: http://www.prolebooks.co.uk

Publishes: Fiction; Nonfiction; Poetry;
Areas: Short Stories; *Markets:* Adult;
Treatments: Literary

Publishes accessible literature of high
quality, including poetry, short fiction, and
creative nonfiction. Seeks to appeal to a wide
audience and avoid literary elitism (obscure
references and highly stylised structures and
forms are unlikely to find favour). No
previously published material or
simultaneous submissions. Submit one piece
of prose or up to five poems (or three longer
poems) in the body of an email, with your
name, contact details, word count and third
person author bio up to 100 words. See
website for appropriate email addresses for
prose and poetry submissions, and full
submission guidelines. No attachments.

Prospect
Email: editorial@prospect-magazine.co.uk
Website: https://prospectmagazine.co.uk

Publishes: Essays; Features; Nonfiction;
Reviews; *Areas:* Arts; Culture; Current
Affairs; Literature; Politics; *Markets:* Adult

Editors: Tom Clark

Intelligent magazine of current affairs and
cultural debate. No news features. Almost all
articles are commissioned from regular
writers, but will consider unsolicited
nonfiction submissions if suitable for the
magazine, but no unsolicited fiction
submissions. Does not publish any poetry.
No postal submissions or telephone pitches.
Submit by email only.

Psychologies
KELSEY Media Ltd
Cudham Tithe Barn
Berry's Hill
Cudham
Kent
TN16 3AG
Email: suzy.greaves@psychologies.co.uk
Website: https://www.psychologies.co.uk

Publishes: Articles; Nonfiction; *Areas:*
Beauty and Fashion; Cookery; Culture;
Health; Lifestyle; Travel; Women's
Interests; *Markets:* Adult

Editors: Suzy Greaves

Grown up women's lifestyle magazine,
seeking to enrich women's emotional lives.
Covers self, relationships, family, work,
beauty and wellbeing, culture, travel, food
and more.

Pulse
Cogora Limited
140 London Wall
London
EC2Y 5DN
Tel: +44 (0) 20 7214 0567
Email: jaimiekaffash@cogora.com
Website: http://www.pulsetoday.co.uk

Publishes: Articles; Nonfiction; *Areas:*
Medicine; *Markets:* Professional

Editors: Jaimie Kaffash

Magazine aimed at GPs.

Pushing Out the Boat
Email: submission-queries@
pushingouttheboat.co.uk
Website: https://www.
pushingouttheboat.co.uk

Publishes: Fiction; Poetry; Scripts; *Areas:* Arts; Short Stories; *Markets:* Adult; *Treatments:* Literary

Closed to submissions as at October 2018. Check website for current status.

Magazine of prose, poetry and visual arts, based in North-East Scotland. Welcomes work in English, Doric or Scots. Submit via online submission system during open reading periods. See website for details.

Radio Times
Vineyard House
44 Brook Green
London
W6 7BT
Tel: +44 (0) 20 7150 5800
Fax: +44 (0) 20 8433 3160
Email: feedback@radiotimes.com
Website: http://www.radiotimes.com

Publishes: Articles; Interviews; News; Nonfiction; *Areas:* Entertainment; Radio; TV; *Markets:* Adult

Articles and interviews relating to UK TV and radio. All articles are commissioned. Willing to consider synopses and ideas, but no unsolicited mss.

The Railway Magazine
Mortons Media Group Ltd
Morton Way
Horncastle
Lincolnshire
LN9 6JR
Tel: +44 (0) 1507 529589
Email: cmilner@mortons.co.uk
Website: https://www.
railwaymagazine.co.uk

Publishes: Articles; News; Nonfiction; *Areas:* Historical; Technology; Travel; *Markets:* Adult

Editors: Chris Milner

Magazine for the railway community, covering all aspects from steam through to modern rail developments.

Reach
IDP
24 Forest Houses
Halwill
Beaworthy
Devon
EX21 5UU
Email: publishing@indigodreams.co.uk
Website: http://www.indigodreams.co.uk/reach-poetry/4563791643

Publishes: Poetry; *Markets:* Adult; *Treatments:* Literary

Editors: Ronnie Goodyer

Publishes quality poetry from both experienced and new poets. Formal or free verse, haiku... everything is considered. Subscribers can comment on and vote for poetry from the previous issue, the winner receiving £50, plus regular in-house anthologies and competitions. Receives no external funding and depends entirely on subscriptions. Submit up to two poems by email. No simultaneous submissions.

Record Collector Magazine
The Perfume Factory
Room 101, Diamond Publishing Ltd
140 Wales Farm Road
London
W3 6UG
Tel: +44 (0) 870 732 8080
Email: ian.mccann@metropolis.co.uk
Website: http://www.
recordcollectormag.com

Publishes: Articles; Features; Nonfiction; *Areas:* Hobbies; Music; *Markets:* Adult

Editors: Ian McCann

Magazine on record collecting. Most material is commissioned, but will consider unsolicited mss and welcomes ideas for articles and features.

Report
Association of Teachers and Lecturers
7 Northumberland Street
London
WC2N 5RD
Tel: +44 (0) 20 7930 6441

Fax: +44 (0) 20 7930 1359
Website: http://www.atl.org.uk

Publishes: Articles; Nonfiction; *Markets:*
Professional

Magazine for teachers and lecturers
publishing articles of practical interest to the
target audience.

Restaurant Magazine
William Reed Business Media Ltd
Broadfield Park
Crawley
RH11 9RT
Tel: +44 (0) 1293 610342
Email: Stefan.chomka@wrbm.com
Website: http://www.
restaurantmagazine.co.uk

Publishes: Articles; Features; News;
Nonfiction; *Areas:* Business; Cookery;
Markets: Professional

Editors: Stefan Chomka

Magazine publishing articles, features, and
news for the restaurant trade.

The Rialto
PO Box 309
Aylsham
Norwich
NR11 6LN
Email: info@therialto.co.uk
Website: https://www.therialto.co.uk

Publishes: Articles; Nonfiction; Poetry;
Reviews; *Markets:* Adult; *Treatments:*
Literary

Editors: Michael Mackmin

Send up to six poems with SASE or adequate
return postage, or submit through online
submission system. No submissions by
email. Reviews and articles commissioned.

Running
Kelsey Media
Cudham Tithe Barn
Berry's Hill
Cudham
Kent
TN16 3AG

Email: rf.ed@kelsey.co.uk
Website: https://www.runnersradar.com

Publishes: Articles; Nonfiction; *Areas:*
Health; Hobbies; Leisure; Sport; *Markets:*
Adult

Magazine for runners, including advice on
health, fitness, and injury.

RUSI Journal
Royal United Services Institute
Whitehall
London
SW1A 2ET
Tel: +44 (0) 20 7747 2615
Email: publications@rusi.org
Website: https://rusi.org

Publishes: Articles; Nonfiction; Reviews;
Areas: Historical; Military; Technology;
Markets: Professional

Editors: Emma De Angelis

Journal publishing articles, book reviews,
and letters to the editor, relating to defence,
international security, military history, etc.
See website for submission guidelines.

Sarasvati
24 Forest Houses
Halwill
Beaworthy
Devon
EX21 5UU
Email: dawnidp@gmail.com
Website: http://www.indigodreams.co.uk/
sarasvati/

Publishes: Fiction; Poetry; *Areas:* Short
Stories; *Markets:* Adult

Editors: Dawn Bauling

Showcases poetry and prose. Each
contributor will have three to four A5 pages
available to their work. Submit up to five
poems, or prose up to 1,000 words.

The Savage Kick
Murder Slim Press
22 Bridge Meadow
Hemsby
Norfolk

NR29 4NE
Email: murderslimpress@gmail.com
Website: http://www.murderslim.com/
TheSavageKick.html

Publishes: Articles; Fiction; Interviews;
Nonfiction; *Areas:* Crime; Literature;
Military; Westerns; *Markets:* Adult;
Treatments: Niche

Accepts only three or four stories per year.
Publishes work dealing with any
passionately held emotion and/or alternative
viewpoints. Sleazy tales are encouraged.
Prefers real-life stories. No genre fiction or
poetry. See website for full submission
guidelines. Also accepts articles and
interviews relating to authors on the reading
list provided on the website.

Scintilla

Email: subscriptions@
vaughanassociation.org
Website: http://www.vaughanassociation.org

Publishes: Articles; Essays; Fiction;
Nonfiction; Poetry; *Areas:* Drama; Health;
Nature; Science; Spiritual; *Markets:* Adult;
Treatments: Literary

Editors: Joseph Sterrett; Damian Walford
Davies; Dr. Kevin Mills; Erik Ankerberg

An international, peer-reviewed journal of
literary criticism, prose, and new poetry in
the metaphysical tradition. Submit using
online submission form.

The Scots Magazine

D.C. Thomson & Co. Ltd
1 Albert Square
Dundee
DD1 1DD
Tel: +44 (0) 1382 223131
Email: mail@scotsmagazine.com
Website: http://www.scotsmagazine.com

Publishes: Articles; Nonfiction; Reviews;
Areas: Historical; Leisure; Lifestyle;
Literature; Music; Nature; *Markets:* Adult

Editors: John Methven

Scottish interest magazine publishing
material covering history, folklore, wildlife,

outdoor pursuits, Scottish personalities, etc.
Send initial query by post or by email.

The Sewing Directory

11a Tedders Close
Hemyock
Cullompton
EX15 3XD
Tel: +44 (0) 1823 680588
Email: fiona@thesewingdirectory.net
Website: http://www.
thesewingdirectory.co.uk

Publishes: Articles; Features; Nonfiction;
Areas: Crafts; Hobbies; *Markets:* Adult

Editors: Fiona Pullen

Online sewing directory, publishing articles
on sewing and sewing projects.

Sewing World

Email: sw@mytimemedia.com
Website: https://www.
sewingworldmagazine.com

Publishes: Articles; Features; Interviews;
News; Nonfiction; *Areas:* Crafts; Hobbies;
Markets: Adult

Sewing magazine, publishing inspirational
projects, sewing techniques, interviews and
features as well as all the latest news,
products and fabrics. Submit projects and
articles by email.

SFX

Future Publishing Limited Quay House
The Ambury
Bath
BA1 1UA
Email: sfx@futurenet.com
Website: http://www.gamesradar.com/sfx/

Publishes: Articles; News; Nonfiction;
Areas: Fantasy; Film; Hobbies; Sci-Fi; TV;
Markets: Adult; Youth

Magazine covering science fiction and
fantasy TV, films, comics, and games.

Shooter Literary Magazine

Email: submissions.shooterlitmag@
gmail.com
Website: https://shooterlitmag.com

Publishes: Essays; Fiction; Nonfiction;
Poetry; *Markets:* Adult; *Treatments:* Literary

Publishes literary fiction, poetry, creative
nonfiction and narrative journalism relating
to specific themes for each issue. Send one
piece of prose between 2,000 and 7,500
words or up to three poems per issue, by
email. See website for current theme and full
submission guidelines.

Shout Magazine

2 Albert Square
Dundee
DD1 1DD
Tel: +44 (0) 1382 223131
Email: shout@dcthomson.co.uk
Website: https://www.shoutmag.co.uk

Publishes: Articles; Essays; Features;
Nonfiction; *Areas:* Beauty and Fashion;
Entertainment; Lifestyle; Music; Women's
Interests; *Markets:* Youth; *Treatments:*
Popular

Magazine for girls covering pop music,
soaps, hunks, beauty and fashion, etc.

Skald

2 Greenfield Terrace
Hill St
Menai Bridge
Anglesey
LL59 5AY
Email: submissions@skald.co.uk
Website: http://www.skald.co.uk

Fiction; Poetry; Short Stories

Editors: Zoe Skoulding

Predominantly a poetry magazine, though
short prose is sometimes included. Work
may be submitted in English or Welsh.
Although based in Wales, this is an outward-
looking magazine which publishes
interesting writing from further afield. Visual
poetry is welcome, as is any artwork which
is easily reproducible in black and white. It
need not be illustration to accompany text.

Ski+board

Tel: +44 (0) 20 8410 2010
Email: harriet.johnston@skiclub.co.uk
Website: https://www.skiclub.co.uk

Publishes: Articles; Features; News;
Nonfiction; Reviews; *Areas:* Sport; Travel;
Markets: Adult

Editors: Harriet Johnston (Deputy Editor)

Magazine publishing articles, reviews,
features and news relating to skiing and
snowboarding.

Slimming World

Clover Nook Road
Alfreton
Derbyshire
DE55 4SW
Email: editorial@slimming-world.co.uk
Website: http://www.slimmingworld.co.uk/
magazine/latest-issue.aspx

Publishes: Articles; Features; Nonfiction;
Areas: Health; How-to; *Markets:* Adult

Magazine covering slimming, healthy eating,
and fitness.

SlingInk Magazine

The Old Lighthouse
83 High St
Belmont
Bolton
BL7 8AJ
Email: balloon@slingink.co.uk
Website: http://www.slingink.co.uk

Publishes: Articles; Fiction; *Areas:* Short
Stories; *Markets:* Adult; *Treatments:*
Literary

Editors: Rob Moss

Online community's regular fiction
magazine, including articles on writing
fiction and a myriad of different styles of
short story written by the community
members.

Songwriting & Composing Magazine

Westland House
2 Penlee Close

Praa Sands
Penzance
Cornwall
TR20 9SR
Tel: +44 (0) 1736 761112
Email: gisc@btconnect.com
Website: http://songwriters-guild.co.uk/
magazine.htm

Publishes: Articles; Nonfiction; *Areas:*
Business; Music; *Markets:* Professional

Magazine free for guild members, publishing
articles of interest to professional composers
and songwriters.

South
PO Box 4228
Bracknell
RG42 9PX
Email: south@southpoetry.org
Website: http://www.southpoetry.org

Publishes: Poetry; *Markets:* Adult

Editors: Anne Peterson; Peter Keeble;
Chrissie Williams

Submit up to three poems by post (two
copies of each), along with submission form
available on website. No previously
published poems (including poems that have
appeared on the internet). Submissions are
not returned. See website for full details. No
translations or submissions by email.

Spear's Magazine
Tel: +44 (0) 20 7936 6445
Email: alec.marsh@spearswms.com
Website: http://www.spearswms.com

Publishes: Articles; News; Nonfiction;
Areas: Business; Finance; Lifestyle;
Markets: Adult

Editors: Alec Marsh

Wealth management and luxury lifestyle
magazine.

The Spectator
The Spectator (1828) Ltd
22 Old Queen Street
London
SW1H 9HP

Tel: +44 (0) 20 7961 0200
Email: editor@spectator.co.uk
Website: http://www.spectator.co.uk

Publishes: Articles; Features; *Areas:* Arts;
Current Affairs; Literature; Politics;
Markets: Adult

Editors: Fraser Nelson

Magazine of politics, literature, and arts.

The Stage
Stage House
47 Bermondsey Street
London
SE1 3XT
Tel: +44 (0) 20 7403 1818
Email: alistair@thestage.co.uk
Website: http://www.thestage.co.uk

Publishes: Articles; Features; News;
Nonfiction; *Areas:* Theatre; *Markets:*
Professional

Editors: Alistair Smith

Query with ideas in first instance. Publishes
material relating to the theatre: tabloid-style
articles up to 800 words, profiles up to 1,200
words, and news items up to 300 words.

Surrey Life
C/O Archant
28 Teville Road
Worthing
West Sussex
BN11 1UG
Tel: +44 (0) 1903 703730
Email: editor@surreylife.co.uk
Website: http://www.surreylife.co.uk

Publishes: Articles; Nonfiction; *Areas:* Arts;
Cookery; Gardening; Lifestyle; Travel;
Markets: Adult

Editors: Rebecca Younger

Magazine publishing articles on Surrey,
covering such topics as home, gardens,
popular destinations, history, food and drink,
people, education, style, and motoring.

Swimming Times Magazine
Sport Park
3 Oakwood Drive

Loughborough
Leicestershire
LE11 3QF
Tel: +44 (0) 1509 632230
Fax: +44 (0) 1509 618701
Email: swimmingtimes@swimming.org
Website: http://www.swimming.org/
swimengland/subscribe-to-swimming-times-
magazine/

Publishes: Articles; Features; Interviews;
Nonfiction; *Areas:* Sport; *Markets:* Adult

Editors: P. Hassall

Magazine featuring coaching tips, teaching
articles and club stories plus interviews and
features from across the swimming
community.

Take a Break's Take a Puzzle

Academic House
24-28 Oval Road
London
NW1 7DT
Email: puzzlesfeedback@bauer.co.uk
Website: https://www.
puzzlemagazines.co.uk/puzzle-magazines/
take-a-puzzle

Publishes: Nonfiction; *Areas:* Hobbies;
Markets: Adult

Magazine of puzzles. Welcomes ideas.

Tears in the Fence

Portman Lodge
Durweston
Blandford Forum
Dorset
DT11 0QA
Tel: +44 (0) 7824 618708
Email: tearsinthefence@gmail.com
Website: http://tearsinthefence.com

Publishes: Essays; Fiction; Interviews;
Nonfiction; Poetry; Reviews; *Areas:* Short
Stories; Translations; *Markets:* Adult;
Treatments: Literary

Editors: David Caddy

International literary magazine publishing
poetry, fiction, prose poems, essays,
translations, interviews and reviews.
Publishes fiction as short as 100 words or as
long as 3,500. Maximum 6 poems per poet
per issue. No simultaneous submissions or
previously published material. Send
submissions by post or by email as an
attachment and in the body of the email.

Teen Breathe

GMC Publications Ltd
86 High Street
Lewes
BN7 1XU
Tel: +44 (0) 1273 477374
Email: hello@teenbreathe.co.uk
Website: https://www.teenbreathe.co.uk

Publishes: Articles; Nonfiction; *Areas:*
Health; Lifestyle; *Markets:* Youth

Magazine for young people who want to find
time for themselves. Focuses on Wellbeing,
Mindfulness, Creativity and Escaping.
Experienced writers should send ideas with
examples of previous work. New writers
should submit complete articles. Submit
using forms on website.

TES (The Times Educational Supplement)

26 Red Lion Square
London
WC1R 4HQ
Tel: +44 (0) 20 3194 3000
Email: help@tesglobal.com
Website: https://www.tes.com

Publishes: Articles; Features; News;
Nonfiction; Reviews; *Markets:* Academic;
Adult

Weekly supplement of educational news and
resources. Most material is commissioned,
but accepts queries outlining ideas by email.

The Lady

39-40 Bedford Street
London
WC2E 9ER
Tel: +44 (0) 20 7379 4717
Email: editors@lady.co.uk
Website: http://www.lady.co.uk

Publishes: Articles; Features; Nonfiction;
Areas: Arts; Beauty and Fashion; Cookery;

Finance; Gardening; Health; Historical; Travel; Women's Interests; *Markets:* Adult

England's longest-running weekly magazine for women.

This England
The Lypiatts
Lansdown Road
Cheltenham
Gloucestershire
GL50 2JA
Tel: +44 (0) 1242 225780
Email: thisengland@dcthomson.co.uk
Website: https://www.thisengland.co.uk

Publishes: Articles; Features; Nonfiction; Poetry; *Areas:* Crafts; Culture; Historical; Nature; *Markets:* Adult

Magazine celebrating English culture, history, people, nature, traditions, customs, legends, etc. Generally rural. Publishes articles between 250 and 2,000 words and poems 12-24 lines.

Times Higher Education
TES Global Limited
26 Red Lion Square
London
WC1R 4HQ
Tel: +44 (0) 20 3194 3300
Email: john.gill@timeshighereducation.com
Website: https://www.
timeshighereducation.com

Publishes: Articles; Nonfiction; *Markets:* Academic; Adult

Magazine publishing articles on higher education.

The Times Literary Supplement (TLS)
1 London Bridge Street
London
SE1 9GF
Tel: +44 (0) 20 7782 5000
Email: letters@the-tls.co.uk
Website: http://www.the-tls.co.uk

Publishes: Articles; Features; News; Nonfiction; Poetry; Reviews; *Areas:* Arts;

Film; Historical; Literature; Philosophy; Science; Theatre; *Markets:* Adult

Editors: Stig Abell

Publishes coverage of the latest and most important publications, as well as current theatre, opera, exhibitions and film. Also publishes letters to the editor and poetry. Send books for review by post. For poetry, submit up to six poems with SASE. Letters to the Editor may be sent by post or by email to the address provided on the website.

Trail
Bauer Consumer Media Limited
Media House
Peterborough Business Park
Peterborough
PE2 6EA
Email: simon.ingram@lfto.com
Website: http://www.livefortheoutdoors.com

Publishes: Articles; Features; Nonfiction; *Areas:* Hobbies; Leisure; Travel; *Markets:* Adult

Editors: Simon Ingram

Monthly walking magazine, covering hillwalking, mountain climbing, gear, historic walks, and gentle strolls in the countryside.

Trout & Salmon
Media House
Peterborough Business Park
Peterborough
PE2 6EA
Tel: +44 (0) 1733 468000
Email: troutandsalmon@bauermedia.co.uk
Website: https://www.troutandsalmon.com

Publishes: Articles; Nonfiction; *Areas:* Hobbies; Leisure; Sport; *Markets:* Adult

Editors: Andrew Flitcroft

Magazine publishing articles on the fishing of salmon and trout.

Trucking
Kelsey Media Ltd
Cudham Tithe Barn
Berry's Hill

Cudham
Kent TN16 3AG
Tel: +44 (0) 1959 541444
Email: trucking.ed@kelsey.co.uk
Website: https://truckingmag.co.uk

Publishes: Articles; Features; News;
Nonfiction; *Areas:* Business; Travel;
Markets: Professional

Magazine for owners, drivers, and operators
of road haulage vehicles.

Vanity Fair
Conde Nast Publications
Vogue House
1-2 Hanover Square
London
W1S 1JU
Email: letters@vf.com
Website: http://www.vanityfair.com

Publishes: Articles; Nonfiction; *Areas:*
Beauty and Fashion; Culture; Current
Affairs; Entertainment; Media; Politics;
Markets: Adult; *Treatments:* Popular

Magazine of glamour, popular culture,
current affairs, fashion, and politics.

Vegetarian Living
Select Publisher Services
PO Box 6337
Bournemouth
BH1 9EH
Tel: +44 (0) 1202 586848
Email: editorial@vegmag.co.uk
Website: http://www.vegetarianliving.co.uk

Publishes: Articles; Features; Nonfiction;
Areas: Cookery; Health; *Markets:* Adult

Magazine for those interested in vegetarian
and vegan cooking.

Viz
Dennis Publishing Ltd
31-32 Alfred Place
London
WC1E 7DP
Email: viz@viz.co.uk
Website: http://www.viz.co.uk

Publishes: Articles; Fiction; *Areas:* Humour;
Markets: Adult

Magazine of adult humour, including
cartoons, spoof articles, etc.

Wasafiri
c/o School of English and Drama
Queen Mary, University of London
Mile End Road
London
E1 4NS
Tel: +44 (0) 20 7882 2686
Email: wasafiri@qmul.ac.uk
Website: http://www.wasafiri.org

Publishes: Articles; Essays; Fiction;
Interviews; Nonfiction; Poetry; Reviews;
Areas: Criticism; Culture; Literature; Short
Stories; *Markets:* Academic; Adult;
Treatments: Literary

Editors: Susheila Nasta

The indispensable journal of contemporary
African, Asian Black British, Caribbean and
transnational literatures.

In over fifteen years of publishing, this
magazine has changed the face of
contemporary writing in Britain. As a literary
magazine primarily concerned with new and
postcolonial writers, it continues to stress the
diversity and range of black and diasporic
writers world-wide. It remains committed to
its original aims: to create a definitive forum
for the voices of new writers and to open up
lively spaces for serious critical discussion
not available elsewhere. It is Britain's only
international magazine for Black British,
African, Asian and Caribbean literatures. Get
the whole picture, get the magazine at the
core of contemporary international literature
today.

Submit via online submissions portal only
(see website).

Weight Watchers Magazine
PO Box 326
Sittingbourne
Email: weightwatchers@
servicehelpline.co.uk
Website: https://www.weightwatchers.co.uk

Publishes: Articles; Features; News;
Nonfiction; *Areas:* Beauty and Fashion;
Cookery; Health; *Markets:* Adult

Magazine covering slimming, health, beauty, etc.

What's on TV
Time Inc. (UK) Ltd
161 Marsh Wall
London
E14 9AP
Email: michelle.briant@timeinc.com
Website: https://www.whatsontv.co.uk

Publishes: Articles; Features; Nonfiction; *Areas:* Entertainment; Media; TV; *Markets:* Adult

Magazine publishing articles on TV programmes, soaps, celebrities, etc.

The White Review
A.104 Fuel Tank
8-12 Creekside
London
SE8 3DX
Email: submissions@thewhitereview.org
Website: http://www.thewhitereview.org

Publishes: Essays; Fiction; Nonfiction; Poetry; Reviews; *Areas:* Arts; Culture; Literature; Short Stories; *Markets:* Adult; *Treatments:* Literary; Serious

Print and online arts and literature magazine. Publishes cultural analysis, reviews, and new fiction and poetry. Accepts nonfiction year-round but only accepts poetry and fiction in specific submission windows. Prose submissions should be a minimum of 1,500 words. See website for guidelines and submit by email.

Woman
Time Inc. UK
Blue Fin Building
110 Southwark Street
London
SE1 0SU
Tel: +44 (0) 20 3148 5000
Email: woman@timeinc.com
Website: http://www.womanmagazine.co.uk

Publishes: Articles; Features; News; Nonfiction; *Areas:* Entertainment; Lifestyle; Women's Interests; *Markets:* Adult

Magazine for women, publishing celebrity and real-life features up to 1,000 words.

Woman's Weekly
Time Inc (UK)
161 Marsh Wall
London
E14 9AP
Email: womansweeklypostbag@timeinc.com
Website: http://www.womansweekly.com

Publishes: Features; Fiction; News; Nonfiction; *Areas:* Beauty and Fashion; Cookery; Crafts; Gardening; Health; Short Stories; Travel; Women's Interests; *Markets:* Adult; *Treatments:* Contemporary

Editors: Diane Kenwood; Sue Pilkington (Features); Gaynor Davies (Fiction)

Publishes features of interest to women over forty, plus fiction between 1,000 and 2,000 words and serials in four or five parts of 3,400 words each. Only uses experienced journalists for nonfiction. No submissions by email. Submit by post with SAE.

Woman's Weekly Fiction Special
Time Inc (UK)
161 Marsh Wall
London
E14 9AP
Email: womansweeklypostbag@timeinc.com
Website: https://www.womansweekly.com

Publishes: Fiction; *Areas:* Short Stories; Women's Interests; *Markets:* Adult

Editors: Gaynor Davies

Publishes short stories for women between 1,000 and 8,000 words. Send stories by post with SAE – no correspondence by email.

Women Together
SWI
42 Heriot Row
Edinburgh
EH3 6ES
Email: magazine@theswi.org.uk
Website: https://www.theswi.org.uk

Publishes: Articles; Features; Nonfiction; *Areas:* Cookery; Crafts; Health; Hobbies; Lifestyle; Literature; Travel; Women's Interests; *Markets:* Adult

Looking for features on a wide range of subjects including crafts, food and drink, women's issues, travel, health, lifestyle and general interest. Send articles / features between 600 and 1,200 words by post or by email.

The World of Interiors
Vogue House
Hanover Square
London
W1S 1JU
Tel: +44 (0) 20 7499 9080
Email: augusta.pownall@condenast.co.uk
Website: http://www.worldofinteriors.co.uk

Publishes: Articles; Features; Nonfiction; *Areas:* Design; *Markets:* Adult

Magazine publishing material related to interiors. All material commissioned. Send query with photos and article synopsis / ideas.

Yorkshire Life
PO Box 163
Ripon
HG4 9AG
Tel: +44 (0) 1928 240668
Email: esther.leach@yorkshirelife.co.uk
Website: http://www.yorkshirelife.co.uk

Publishes: Articles; Nonfiction; *Areas:* Arts; Entertainment; Historical; Lifestyle; Travel; *Markets:* Adult

Magazine covering the people, places, history, arts, food and events of Yorkshire.

You & Your Wedding
Immediate Media Company
Vineyard House
44 Brook Green
London
W6 7BT
Tel: +44 (0) 20 7439 5000
Fax: +44 (0) 20 7439 2985
Email: yywwebeditor@immediate.co.uk
Website: http://www.
youandyourwedding.co.uk

Publishes: Articles; Features; Nonfiction; Reviews; *Areas:* Beauty and Fashion; Travel; *Markets:* Adult

Magazine publishing material relating to weddings and honeymoons.

Your Horse
Media House
Peterborough Business Park
Lynch Wood
Peterborough
PE2 6EA
Tel: +44 (0) 1733 395051
Email: getinvolved@yourhorse.co.uk
Website: http://www.yourhorse.co.uk

Publishes: Articles; Nonfiction; *Areas:* Hobbies; How-to; Nature; Travel; *Markets:* Adult

Magazine of horse ownership and riding. Most material produced in-house but willing to consider appropriate articles.

Canadian Magazines

For the most up-to-date listings of these and hundreds of other magazines, visit https://www.firstwriter.com/magazines

To claim your *free* access to the site, please see the back of this book.

The Antigonish Review
PO Box 5000
Antigonish
Nova Scotia
B2G 2W5
Tel: +1 (902) 867-3962
Fax: +1 (902) 867-5563
Email: tar@stfx.ca
Website: http://www.antigonishreview.com

Publishes: Articles; Essays; Fiction; Interviews; Nonfiction; Poetry; Reviews; *Areas:* Arts; Autobiography; Culture; Historical; Literature; Short Stories; Sport; Travel; *Markets:* Adult; *Treatments:* Literary

Submit via online portal only. Submit no more than 6-8 poems (preferably 3-4) and submit no more till a response is received. Considers poetry on any subject written from any point of view and in any form. For fiction, send only one story at a time. Also considers critical articles and essays that are fresh, vigorous, and free from jargon. Welcomes creative nonfiction. No email submissions, postal submissions, or simultaneous submissions.

Business London
PO Box 7400
London, ON
N5Y 4X3
Email: sajones@postmedia.com
Website: http://www.businesslondon.ca

Publishes: Articles; Nonfiction; *Areas:* Business; Health; Politics; Sport; Travel; *Markets:* Professional

Editors: Sarah Jones

Business magazine for southwestern Ontario.

Canadian Yachting
538 Elizabeth Street
Midland
Ontario
L4R 2A3
Email: elissacampbell@kerrwil.com
Website: http://www.kerrwil.com

Publishes: Articles; News; Nonfiction; *Areas:* Technology; Travel; *Markets:* Adult

Describes itself as the premier boating magazine in Canada.

Event
PO Box 2503
New Westminster, BC
V3L 5B2
Tel: +1 (604) 527-5293
Email: event@douglascollege.ca
Website: http://event.douglas.bc.ca

Publishes: Fiction; Nonfiction; Poetry; Reviews; *Markets:* Adult; *Treatments:* Literary

Closed to submissions until August 1, 2019.

Send one story or up to eight poems via online submission system only. Occasional unsolicited reviews published – query before submitting.

FellowScript

c/o Box 463
Glendon, Alberta
Tel: +1 (780) 646-3068
Email: fellowscripteditor2@gmail.com
Website: https://inscribe.org/fellowscript/

Publishes: Articles; Nonfiction; Poetry; Reviews; *Areas:* Hobbies; Religious; *Markets:* Adult

Editors: Nina Morey

Magazine for Christian writers. Includes articles and book and market reviews of interest to writers, and also poetry. See website for full guidelines.

The Fiddlehead

The Fiddlehead
Campus House
11 Garland Court
University of New Brunswick
PO Box 4400
Fredericton NB
E3B 5A3
Tel: +1 (506) 453-3501
Email: fiddlehd@unb.ca
Website: https://thefiddlehead.ca

Publishes: Fiction; Nonfiction; Poetry; Reviews; *Areas:* Short Stories; *Markets:* Adult; *Treatments:* Experimental; Literary

Publishes poetry, fiction, and creative nonfiction in a variety of styles, including experimental genres. Also publishes excerpts from longer works, and reviews. Submit up to six poems, or a piece of fiction up to 6,000 words. All submissions must be original and unpublished. Prefers submissions through online submission system (Jan 1 to April 30 and Sep 15 to November 30 only), but will accept submissions by post. See website for full details.

Filling Station

filling Station Publications Society
Box 22135

Bankers Hall RPO
Calgary AB T2P 4J5
Email: mgmt@fillingstation.ca
Website: http://www.fillingstation.ca

Publishes: Articles; Fiction; Interviews; Nonfiction; Poetry; Reviews; *Areas:* Arts; Criticism; Literature; Short Stories; *Markets:* Adult; *Treatments:* Literary

Publishes previously unpublished poetry, fiction, creative nonfiction, and critical nonfiction (about literature and occasionally about visual art). Submit up to 10 pages of fiction; up to 6 pages of poetry; or up to two piece of nonfiction, via online submission system. See website for full details.

S/tick

Email: editor@dontdiepress.org
Website: https://www.dontdiepress.org/stickmag/

Publishes: Fiction; Poetry; *Areas:* Short Stories; Women's Interests; *Markets:* Adult; *Treatments:* Literary

Editors: Sarah-Jean Krahn

Online magazine publishing feminist prose and poetry. Send up to five poems or up to 2,000 words of prose by email. See website for full guidelines.

The Starlit Path

1105 Mill hill
Laval, QC, H7W 1P7
Tel: N/A
Fax: N/A
Email: judie@stardragonpress.com
Website: http://starlitpathmagazine.com

Publishes: Articles; Essays; Features; Fiction; Interviews; Nonfiction; Poetry; Reference; Reviews; *Areas:* Entertainment; Fantasy; Historical; How-to; New Age; Religious; Sci-Fi; Short Stories; Spiritual; *Markets:* Adult; Family; Professional; *Treatments:* Contemporary; Experimental; Positive; Traditional

Editors: Judie Troyansky

A new Online New Age magazine to become a resource for people wanting to research a variety of topics. I'm looking for articles and artwork geared towards those looking for information on all types of new age and spiritual topics.

First edition March 20, 2018

Seeking articles, interviews, inspiration, reviews, fiction, poetry, artwork and photography centred around many New Age topics: Spiritual practices, Tarot, gods and goddesses, How-to, chakras, kabbalah, reiki, healing, mindset work, guides, paganism, wicca, mysticism, plants as medicine, paranormal and psychic phenomenon, etc. See our complete guidelines.

The Temz Review
London, ON
Email: thetemzreview@gmail.com
Website: https://www.thetemzreview.com

Publishes: Fiction; Nonfiction; Poetry; Reviews; *Markets:* Adult; *Treatments:* Literary

Quarterly online magazine. Submit one piece of fiction or creative nonfiction (or more than one if under 1,000 words) or 1-8 poems via online submission system. For reviews, send query by email.

Toronto Life
111 Queen St. E., Suite 320
Toronto, Ont. M5C 1S2
Email: editorial@torontolife.com
Website: http://torontolife.com

Publishes: Articles; News; Nonfiction; *Areas:* Lifestyle; *Markets:* Adult

Editors: Sarah Fulford

Local lifestyle magazine for Toronto. Send queries and unsolicited mss by email.

Windspeaker
13245 – 146 Street
Edmonton, Alberta, T5L 4S8
Tel: +1 (780) 455-2700
Fax: +1 (780) 455-7639
Email: dsteel@ammsa.com
Website: http://www.ammsa.com/publications/windspeaker

Publishes: Articles; Features; News; Nonfiction; Reviews; *Areas:* Arts; Culture; Entertainment; Lifestyle; Politics; Sport; *Markets:* Adult

Editors: Debora Steel

Publishes news, sports, arts, entertainment, reviews and features of interest to Aboriginal people. Accepts unsolicited mss, but prefers query by email in first instance. See website for full guidelines.

Irish Magazines

Crannog Magazine

Email: submissions@crannogmagazine.com
Website: http://www.crannogmagazine.com

Publishes: Fiction; Poetry; *Areas:* Literature; Short Stories; *Markets:* Adult; *Treatments:* Literary; Mainstream

Editors: Sandra Bunting, Tony O'Dwyer, Ger Burke, Jarlath Fahy

A literary magazine publishing fiction and poetry only. No reviews or nonfiction. Published twice yearly in March and September. Accepts submissions in June and November. Authors who have been previously published in the magazine are recommended to purchase a copy of the current issue (or take out a subscription); for authors who have not been previously published in the magazine this is a requirement. Send up to one story or up to three poems by email only. No postal submissions.

Cyphers

3 Selskar Terrace
Ranelagh
Dublin 6
Email: letters@cyphers.ie
Website: http://www.cyphers.ie

Publishes: Fiction; Poetry; *Areas:* Short Stories; Translations; *Markets:* Adult; *Treatments:* Literary

Publishes poetry and fiction in English and Irish, from Ireland and around the world. Translations are welcome. No unsolicited critical articles. Submissions by post only. Attachments sent by email will be deleted. See website for full guidelines.

The Dublin Review

PO Box 7948
Dublin 1
Email: enquiry@thedublinreview.com
Website: https://thedublinreview.com

Publishes: Essays; Fiction; Nonfiction; *Areas:* Criticism; Literature; Short Stories; *Markets:* Adult; *Treatments:* Literary

Publishes essays, criticism, reportage, and fiction for a general, intelligent readership. No poetry. Accepts submissions by post with email address for response, but prefers submissions by via form on website. Physical material is not returned, so do not include return postage. No response without email address.

The Furrow

St Patrick's College
Maynooth
Co. Kildare
Tel: 01-7083741
Fax: 01-7083908
Email: editor.furrow@spcm.ie
Website: https://thefurrow.ie

Publishes: Articles; *Areas:* Religious; *Markets:* Adult

Editors: PÃ¡draig Corkery

A monthly journal for the contemporary Church, providing a forum for discussion of challenges facing the Church today and of the resources available to meet them.

Ireland's Own
Channing House
Rowe Street
Wexford
Tel: 053 9140140
Email: info@irelandsown.ie
Website: https://irelandsown.ie

Publishes: Articles; Features; Fiction; Nonfiction; *Areas:* Short Stories; *Markets:* Adult; Children's; Family; Youth; *Treatments:* Literary; Traditional

Editors: Sean Nolan

Magazine publishing stories and articles of Irish interest for the whole family, plus puzzles and games.

Irish Journal of Medical Science
RAMI Office
Setanta House
2nd Floor
Setanta Place
Dublin 2
Tel: +353 1 633 4820
Email: helenmoore@rcpi.ie
Website: http://www.springer.com/medicine/internal/journal/11845

Publishes: Articles; News; Nonfiction; *Areas:* Medicine; *Markets:* Academic; Professional

Editors: William P. Tormey; Helen Moore

Quarterly medical science journal providing a forum for the exchange of scientific information, and promoting academic discussion.

Irish Medical Times
Tel: +353 (0) 1 817
Email: editor@imt.ie
Website: https://www.imt.ie

Publishes: Articles; News; Nonfiction; *Areas:* Medicine; *Markets:* Professional

Editors: Lloyd Mudiwa

Newspaper for medical professionals.

The Moth
Ardan Grange
Milltown
Belturbet
Co. Cavan
Tel: 353 (0) 87 2657251
Email: editor@themothmagazine.com
Website: http://www.themothmagazine.com

Publishes: Fiction; Poetry; *Areas:* Short Stories; *Markets:* Adult; *Treatments:* Literary

Editors: Rebecca O'Connor

Submit up to six poems or up to two short stories by post or by email. See website for full submission guidelines.

Poetry Ireland Review
11 Parnell Square East
Dublin 1
D01 ND60
Tel: +353 (0)1 6789815
Fax: +353 (0)1 6789782
Email: info@poetryireland.ie
Website: http://www.poetryireland.ie

Publishes: Articles; Nonfiction; Poetry; Reviews; *Areas:* Literature; *Markets:* Adult

Editors: Eavan Boland

Send up to 6 poems with SASE / IRCs or email address for response. Poetry is accepted from around the world, but must be previously unpublished. No sexism or racism. No submissions by email. Articles and reviews are generally commissioned, however proposals are welcome. No unsolicited reviews or articles.

Woman's Way

Rosemount House
Dundrum Road
Dundrum
Dublin 14
Tel: +353 (0) 1 240 5318
Email: atoner@harmonia.ie
Website: http://womansway.ie

Publishes: Articles; Features; Interviews; Nonfiction; *Areas:* Beauty and Fashion; Entertainment; Lifestyle; Media; Women's Interests; *Markets:* Adult

Magazine for women aged 35-65. Describes itself as "Irelands best read and only Irish Woman's Weekly" [sic].

Australasian Magazines

For the most up-to-date listings of these and hundreds of other magazines, visit https://www.firstwriter.com/magazines

*To claim your **free** access to the site, please see the back of this book.*

Idiom 23

PO Box 172
Central Queensland University
554-700 Yaamba Road
Rockhampton QLD 4702
Email: idiom@cqu.edu.au
Website: https://www.cqu.edu.au/about-us/
structure/schools/ea/idiom-23-literary-
magazine

Publishes: Essays; Fiction; Nonfiction;
Poetry; *Areas:* Short Stories; *Markets:* Adult;
Treatments: Literary

Editors: Dr Nicole Anae

Annual literary magazine publishing fiction
and nonfiction up to 3,000 words, and poems
up to one page. See website for full
submission guidelines and to submit via
online submission system.

Island

PO Box 4703
Hobart TAS 7000
Tel: +61 (0) 3 6234 1462
Email: admin@islandmag.com
Website: http://www.islandmag.com

Publishes: Articles; Essays; Fiction; Poetry;
Areas: Short Stories; *Markets:* Adult

**Closed to submissions as at January 2018.
Check website for current status.**

Welcomes submissions of nonfiction, fiction

and poetry during specific reading periods.
See website for details and to submit using
online submission system.

Landfall

Otago University Press
PO Box 56
Dunedin 9054
Tel: +64 (0) 3 479 4155
Email: landfall.press@otago.ac.nz
Website: http://www.otago.ac.nz/press/
landfall

Publishes: Essays; Fiction; Nonfiction;
Poetry; *Areas:* Arts; Biography; Criticism;
Markets: Adult; *Treatments:* Literary

Open to work by New Zealand and Pacific
writers or by writers whose work has a
connection to the region in subject matter or
location. Work from Australian writers is
occasionally included as a special feature.
Send up to five poems or up to two pieces of
prose per issue. Preferred length is 3,000
words, but longer pieces will be considered.

SisterShip Magazine

59 Bellemount Lane
Email: editor@sistershipmagazine.com
Website: https://www.
sistershipmagazine.com

Publishes: Articles; Essays; Features;
Interviews; News; Nonfiction; Reference;
Reviews; *Areas:* Adventure; Arts;

Autobiography; Biography; Business; Cookery; Crafts; Culture; Current Affairs; Drama; Entertainment; Health; Historical; Hobbies; How-to; Humour; Legal; Leisure; Lifestyle; Literature; Nature; Photography; Science; Self-Help; Sport; Travel; Women's Interests; *Markets:* Adult; *Treatments:* Commercial; Contemporary; In-depth; Light; Literary; Mainstream; Niche; Popular; Positive; Progressive; Satirical

Editors: Jackie Parry and Shelley Wright

First launched thirty years ago, this magazine has been taken out of drydock, refitted, and is now ready to set sail!

Our team have been busy in the "shipyard" for over twelve months, but now it's time to share our work and ideas with you. Just like going to sea, it's all about taking the plunge and casting off, if you wait until everything is perfect you'll never leave the marina! We are about to untie the lines.

We are an international magazine; written by women for women on the water.

We are THE first boating magazine for women, our ethos is:
Belong: Share passions with like-minded people;
Encourage: Support women, assist, advise, share, trust;
Inspire: Creating ideas, thoughts, hopes, dreams;
Inform: Promote safety, topical, newsy, fresh, detail; and
Entertain: Be exciting, new, fun, rich, safe,

honest, reliable.
We'd love you to join us on our journey.

Vintage Made

ArtWear Publications Pty Ltd
PO Box 469
Ashburton VIC 3147
Tel: +61 (0) 3 9888 1853
Fax: +61 (0) 3 9807 0248
Email: thegirls@artwearpublications.com.au
Website: http://www.
artwearpublications.com.au

Publishes: Articles; Features; Nonfiction; *Areas:* Beauty and Fashion; Crafts; Design; Historical; Hobbies; How-to; *Markets:* Adult

Magazine on vintage style and design, with tutorials and dress patterns, etc. See website for full submission guidelines.

Yarn

ArtWear Publications Pty Ltd
PO Box 469
Ashburton, VIC, 3147
Tel: +61 (0) 3 9888 1853
Fax: +61 (0) 3 9807 0248
Email: thegirls@artwearpublications.com.au
Website: http://artwearpublications.com.au

Publishes: Articles; Nonfiction; *Areas:* Crafts; Design; Hobbies; *Markets:* Adult

Publishes articles on knitting and patterns. Send query by email with bio, details of any previous writing credits, contact details, and details of your proposal.

Magazines Subject Index

This section lists magazines by their subject matter, with directions to the section of the book where the full listing can be found.

You can create your own customised lists of magazines using different combinations of these subject areas, plus over a dozen other criteria, instantly online at https://www.firstwriter.com.

*To claim your **free** access to the site, please see the back of this book.*

Leisure Painter (*UK*)
Litro Magazine (*UK*)
Little Rose Magazine (*US*)
London Review of Books (*UK*)
Lothian Life (*UK*)
New Statesman (*UK*)
Niche (*US*)
Nob Hill Gazette (*US*)
NY Literary Magazine (*US*)
Orbis International Literary Journal (*UK*)
Philly Weekly (*US*)
Picture Postcard Monthly (*UK*)
The Pool (*UK*)
Prospect (*UK*)
Pushing Out the Boat (*UK*)
Sacramento Magazine (*US*)
San Diego Home / Garden Lifestyles (*US*)
Santa Barbara Magazine (*US*)
Sinister Wisdom (*US*)
SisterShip Magazine (*Aus*)
The Spectator (*UK*)
StoryNews (*US*)
Sunshine Artist (*US*)
Surrey Life (*UK*)
Susquehanna Life (*US*)
The Lady (*UK*)
The Times Literary Supplement (TLS) (*UK*)
Windspeaker (*Can*)
Yorkshire Life (*UK*)
Autobiography
The Carolina Quarterly (*US*)
Cold Mountain Review (*US*)
Confrontation Magazine (*US*)
december Magazine (*US*)
Ducts (*US*)
EarthLines Magazine (*Ire*)
Guernica (*US*)
Hawai'i Review (*US*)
Hoot (*US*)
Infinite Rust (*US*)
Irish Pages (*UK*)
Litro Magazine (*UK*)
Little Rose Magazine (*US*)
Mslexia (*UK*)
The North (*UK*)
SisterShip Magazine (*Aus*)
Beauty and Fashion
Bust (*US*)
Cambridge Magazine (*UK*)
Charleston Style and Design Magazine (*US*)
Essence (*US*)
GQ Magazine (*UK*)
Harper's Bazaar (*UK*)
InJoy Magazine (*US*)
marie claire (*UK*)
Nob Hill Gazette (*US*)
Phoenix Magazine (*US*)
The Pool (*UK*)
Psychologies (*UK*)
Self (*US*)
Shout Magazine (*UK*)
Shropshire Magazine (*UK*)
Susquehanna Life (*US*)

The Lady (*UK*)
Top Sante (*UK*)
Vanity Fair (*UK*)
Vintage Made (*Aus*)
Weight Watchers Magazine (*UK*)
Woman's Own (*UK*)
Woman's Way (*Ire*)
You & Your Wedding (*UK*)
Biography
december Magazine (*US*)
Infinite Rust (*US*)
Landfall (*Aus*)
SisterShip Magazine (*Aus*)
Business
Accountancy Age (*UK*)
Advisor Today (*US*)
America's Pharmacist (*US*)
American Quarter Horse Journal (*US*)
APICS Magazine (*US*)
Art + Framing Today (*UK*)
The Author (*UK*)
Bartender (*US*)
BedTimes (*US*)
BizTimes Milwaukee (*US*)
BoxOffice Magazine (*US*)
Broadcast (*UK*)
Business London (*Can*)
The Caterer (*UK*)
Construction Equipment Guide (*US*)
DairyBusiness (*US*)
Director (*UK*)
Electronic Musician (*US*)
The Engravers Journal (*US*)
Family Office Magazine (*UK*)
Harper's Bazaar (*UK*)
The Huffington Post (United Kingdom) (*UK*)
Irish Farmers Journal (*Ire*)
LGC (Local Government Chronicle) (*UK*)
Maritime Journal (*UK*)
Moneywise (*UK*)
The Motorship (*UK*)
Music Week (*UK*)
Niche (*US*)
OfficePro (*US*)
People Management (*UK*)
Pizza Today (*US*)
The Progressive Populist (*US*)
Properties Magazine (*US*)
Publishers Weekly (*US*)
QSR (*US*)
Qualified Remodeler (*US*)
Quill & Quire (*Can*)
Remodeling (*US*)
Restaurant Magazine (*UK*)
Retail Week (*UK*)
Rochester Business Journal (*US*)
SignCraft Publishing Co., Inc. (*US*)
SisterShip Magazine (*Aus*)
Smart Retailer (*US*)
Songwriting & Composing Magazine (*UK*)
Spear's Magazine (*UK*)
State Journal (*US*)
Stormwater (*US*)

Susquehanna Life (*US*)
Tallahassee Magazine (*US*)
TimberWest (*US*)
Tobacco International (*US*)
Trucking (*UK*)
Underground Construction (*US*)
US Glass Magazine (*US*)
Water Well Journal (*US*)
Welding Design & Fabrication (*US*)
The Wholesaler (*US*)
Wire Rope News & Sling Technology (*US*)
Cookery
Bust (*US*)
Eat In Magazine (*UK*)
Essex Life (*UK*)
Good Housekeeping (*UK*)
House & Garden (*UK*)
Kitchen Garden (*UK*)
Lothian Life (*UK*)
Nob Hill Gazette (*US*)
Olive (*UK*)
The People's Friend (*UK*)
Phoenix Magazine (*US*)
Pizza Today (*US*)
Psychologies (*UK*)
QSR (*US*)
Real Simple (*US*)
Restaurant Magazine (*UK*)
Saveur (*US*)
SisterShip Magazine (*Aus*)
Surrey Life (*UK*)
The Lady (*UK*)
Vegan Life (*UK*)
Vegetarian Living (*UK*)
Weight Watchers Magazine (*UK*)
Women Together (*UK*)
Crafts
Bust (*US*)
Creative Knitting (*US*)
The Dolls' House (*UK*)
Flora International (*UK*)
Niche (*US*)
Online Quilt Magazine (*Aus*)
The People's Friend (*UK*)
Sew Simple (*US*)
The Sewing Directory (*UK*)
Sewing World (*UK*)
SisterShip Magazine (*Aus*)
Spin Off (*US*)
The Stampers' Sampler (*US*)
Sunshine Artist (*US*)
This England (*UK*)
Vintage Made (*Aus*)
Vogue Patterns (*US*)
Willow and Sage (*US*)
Women Together (*UK*)
Yarn (*Aus*)
Crime
The Burnt Candle (*UK*)
Ellery Queen Mystery Magazine (*US*)
Into The Void Magazine (*Ire*)
The People's Friend (*UK*)
The Police Journal (*UK*)

The Savage Kick (*UK*)
ShortStorySunday.com (*UK*)
The Washington Pastime (*US*)
Criticism
Adelaide Literary Magazine (*US*)
ArtReview (*UK*)
Body (*US*)
Caveat Lector (*US*)
Chicago Review (*US*)
Empty Mirror (*US*)
Filling Station (*Can*)
Infinite Rust (*US*)
Landfall (*Aus*)
The North (*UK*)
Prac Crit (*UK*)
Wasafiri (*UK*)
Culture
Adelaide Literary Magazine (*US*)
Aesthetica: A Review of Contemporary Artists (*UK*)
Alabama Heritage (*US*)
Bust (*US*)
Callaloo (*US*)
Cambridge Magazine (*UK*)
Central and Eastern European London Review (*UK*)
Charleston Magazine (*US*)
The Christian Science Monitor (*US*)
Confrontation Magazine (*US*)
Curve (*US*)
december Magazine (*US*)
Diva (*UK*)
Eastern Art Report (*UK*)
Empty Mirror (*US*)
Essence (*US*)
Essex Life (*UK*)
Frieze (*UK*)
Geographical (*UK*)
GQ Magazine (*UK*)
H&E Naturist (*UK*)
Hot Press (*Ire*)
Infinite Rust (*US*)
InJoy Magazine (*US*)
Jewish Quarterly (*UK*)
Litro Magazine (*UK*)
Little Rose Magazine (*US*)
London Review of Books (*UK*)
The Pool (*UK*)
Prospect (*UK*)
Psychologies (*UK*)
Rain Taxi (*US*)
Reason (*US*)
Relevant (*US*)
Sacramento Magazine (*US*)
San Diego Home / Garden Lifestyles (*US*)
Saveur (*US*)
Sinister Wisdom (*US*)
SisterShip Magazine (*Aus*)
StoryNews (*US*)
This England (*UK*)
Vanity Fair (*UK*)
Wasafiri (*UK*)
Windspeaker (*Can*)

Current Affairs
Aesthetica: A Review of Contemporary Artists (*UK*)
Charleston Magazine (*US*)
The Christian Science Monitor (*US*)
The Huffington Post (United Kingdom) (*UK*)
Infinite Rust (*US*)
Into The Void Magazine (*Ire*)
Jewish Quarterly (*UK*)
Little Rose Magazine (*US*)
New Statesman (*UK*)
Philly Weekly (*US*)
Press Gazette (*UK*)
Prospect (*UK*)
Reason (*US*)
Reform (*UK*)
SisterShip Magazine (*Aus*)
The Spectator (*UK*)
StoryNews (*US*)
Vanity Fair (*UK*)
VFW (Veterans of Foreign Wars) Magazine (*US*)
Yes! Magazine (*US*)
Design
AIR International (*UK*)
Architectural Design (*UK*)
Architectural Record (*US*)
Boat International (*UK*)
Building Design (*UK*)
Charleston Style and Design Magazine (*US*)
Creative Knitting (*US*)
Digital Engineering (*US*)
Essex Life (*UK*)
House & Garden (*UK*)
Lothian Life (*UK*)
Nob Hill Gazette (*US*)
Play & Playground Magazine (*US*)
Properties Magazine (*US*)
Qualified Remodeler (*US*)
Remodeling (*US*)
Romantic Homes (*US*)
San Diego Home / Garden Lifestyles (*US*)
SelfBuild & Design (*UK*)
Stone World (*US*)
Stormwater (*US*)
Style at Home (*UK*)
SuCasa (*US*)
This Old House (*US*)
Underground Construction (*US*)
Vintage Made (*Aus*)
Walls & Ceilings (*US*)
Window Fashion Vision (*US*)
The World of Interiors (*UK*)
Yarn (*Aus*)
Drama
Aesthetica: A Review of Contemporary Artists (*UK*)
The Burnt Candle (*UK*)
The Caribbean Writer (*US*)
The Claremont Review (*Can*)
Connotation Press (*US*)
Current Accounts (*UK*)
The Evansville Review (*US*)

Flint Hills Review (*US*)
Gold Dust (*UK*)
Into The Void Magazine (*Ire*)
Scintilla (*UK*)
SisterShip Magazine (*Aus*)
The Washington Pastime (*US*)
Entertainment
BoxOffice Magazine (*US*)
Broadcast (*UK*)
Curve (*US*)
december Magazine (*US*)
Essence (*US*)
Essex Life (*UK*)
Hennen's Observer (*US*)
Hot Press (*Ire*)
The Huffington Post (United Kingdom) (*UK*)
InJoy Magazine (*US*)
Inside Soap (*UK*)
Lake Relo (*US*)
Little Rose Magazine (*US*)
The New Accelerator (*UK*)
Philly Weekly (*US*)
Radio Times (*UK*)
Shout Magazine (*UK*)
Shropshire Magazine (*UK*)
SisterShip Magazine (*Aus*)
The Starlit Path (*Can*)
Susquehanna Life (*US*)
Tallahassee Magazine (*US*)
Vanity Fair (*UK*)
The Washington Pastime (*US*)
What's on TV (*UK*)
Windspeaker (*Can*)
Woman (*UK*)
Woman's Own (*UK*)
Woman's Way (*Ire*)
Yorkshire Life (*UK*)
Erotic
The Burnt Candle (*UK*)
Bust (*US*)
Fantasy
Aliterate (*US*)
Aphelion: The Webzine of Science Fiction and Fantasy (*US*)
The Burnt Candle (*UK*)
The Dark (*US*)
Enchanted Tales Literary Magazine (*US*)
The Fifth Di... (*US*)
Garbled Transmissions (*US*)
GUD Magazine (*US*)
Hawai'i Review (*US*)
Interzone (*UK*)
Into The Void Magazine (*Ire*)
The New Accelerator (*UK*)
Orson Scott Card's InterGalactic Medicine Show (*US*)
Seshat Literary Magazine (*US*)
SFX (*UK*)
ShortStorySunday.com (*UK*)
The Starlit Path (*Can*)
The Washington Pastime (*US*)
Fiction
Adelaide Literary Magazine (*US*)

The Adroit Journal (*US*)
After Happy Hour Review (*US*)
Alebrijes (*US*)
Aliterate (*US*)
Amethyst Review (*UK*)
Aphelion: The Webzine of Science Fiction and Fantasy (*US*)
The Awakenings Review (*US*)
Barking Sycamores (*US*)
Better Than Starbucks (*US*)
Big Fiction (*US*)
Blue Collar Review (*US*)
Body (*US*)
Briar Cliff Review (*US*)
Bugle (*US*)
Bunbury Magazine (*UK*)
The Burnt Candle (*UK*)
Bust (*US*)
Cadaverous Magazine (*US*)
Cadet Quest (*US*)
The Cafe Irreal (*US*)
Cahoodaloodaling (*US*)
Callaloo (*US*)
Camas (*US*)
The Capilano Review (*Can*)
The Caribbean Writer (*US*)
The Carolina Quarterly (*US*)
The Casket of Fictional Delights (*UK*)
Caveat Lector (*US*)
The Chaffin Journal (*US*)
The Chattahoochee Review (*US*)
Chicago Quarterly Review (*US*)
Chicago Review (*US*)
Cimarron Review (*US*)
The Claremont Review (*Can*)
Cloud Rodeo (*US*)
Cloudbank (*US*)
Coal City Review (*US*)
Cold Mountain Review (*US*)
The Collagist (*US*)
Colorado Review (*US*)
Columbia: A Journal of Literature and Art (*US*)
Compose (*US*)
Conduit (*US*)
Confrontation Magazine (*US*)
Connotation Press (*US*)
Cottonwood (*US*)
Crab Creek Review (*US*)
Crucible (*US*)
The Cumberland River Review (*US*)
Current Accounts (*UK*)
The Dark (*US*)
The Dead Mule School of Southern Literature (*US*)
december Magazine (*US*)
Denver Quarterly (*US*)
Devil's Lake (*US*)
Diagram (*US*)
The Dos Passos Review (*US*)
Down in the Dirt (*US*)
Ducts (*US*)
EarthLines Magazine (*Ire*)
Ellery Queen Mystery Magazine (*US*)

Enchanted Tales Literary Magazine (*US*)
The Evansville Review (*US*)
failbetter.com (*US*)
The Fifth Di... (*US*)
Filling Station (*Can*)
Five:2:One (*US*)
Flint Hills Review (*US*)
Flyway: Journal of Writing & Environment (*US*)
Fogged Clarity (*US*)
Fourteen Hills (*US*)
Fugue (*US*)
Garbled Transmissions (*US*)
A Gathering of the Tribes (*US*)
Gertrude (*US*)
The Gettysburg Review (*US*)
Gold Dust (*UK*)
Granta (*UK*)
Grasslimb (*US*)
Green Hills Literary Lantern (*US*)
Green Mountains Review (GMR) (*US*)
The Grey Press (*Can*)
GUD Magazine (*US*)
Guernica (*US*)
Gulf Coast: A Journal of Literature and Fine Arts (*US*)
Gulf Stream Magazine (*US*)
Haight Ashbury Literary Journal (*US*)
Hanging Loose (*US*)
Hawai'i Pacific Review (*US*)
Hawai'i Review (*US*)
Hayden's Ferry Review (*US*)
HelloHorror (*US*)
Hennen's Observer (*US*)
Hoot (*US*)
Iconoclast (*US*)
Idiom 23 (*Aus*)
Indiana Review (*US*)
Infinite Rust (*US*)
InJoy Magazine (*US*)
The Interpreter's House (*UK*)
Interzone (*UK*)
Into The Void Magazine (*Ire*)
The Iowa Review (*US*)
Ireland's Own (*Ire*)
Irish Pages (*UK*)
Island (*Aus*)
Jewish Quarterly (*UK*)
Kaimana: Literary Arts Hawai'i (*US*)
Landfall (*Aus*)
Lighthouse (*UK*)
Litro Magazine (*UK*)
Little Rose Magazine (*US*)
Long Life Magazine (*US*)
Louisiana Literature (*US*)
Midway Journal (*US*)
The Moth (*Ire*)
Mslexia (*UK*)
The New Accelerator (*UK*)
New Fairy Tales (*UK*)
New Welsh Reader (*UK*)
Old Red Kimono (*US*)
Orbis International Literary Journal (*UK*)

Orson Scott Card's InterGalactic Medicine Show (*US*)
Overtime (*US*)
The People's Friend (*UK*)
People's Friend Pocket Novels (*UK*)
Prole (*UK*)
Pushing Out the Boat (*UK*)
Ripcord. (*US*)
The Savage Kick (*UK*)
Scintilla (*UK*)
Seshat Literary Magazine (*US*)
Shooter Literary Magazine (*UK*)
ShortStorySunday.com (*UK*)
Sinister Wisdom (*US*)
Skald (*UK*)
SlingInk Magazine (*UK*)
Spitball (*US*)
St Anthony Messenger (*US*)
St Petersburg Review (*US*)
Stand Magazine (*UK*)
The Starlit Path (*Can*)
Studio One (*US*)
Tears in the Fence (*UK*)
This Is Bill Gorton (*US*)
Viz (*UK*)
Wasafiri (*UK*)
The Washington Pastime (*US*)
Westview (*US*)
Yemassee (*US*)
Zoetrope: All-Story (*US*)

Film
Aesthetica: A Review of Contemporary Artists (*UK*)
BoxOffice Magazine (*US*)
Central and Eastern European London Review (*UK*)
Columbia: A Journal of Literature and Art (*US*)
Curve (*US*)
Garbled Transmissions (*US*)
Harper's Bazaar (*UK*)
Hot Press (*Ire*)
Into The Void Magazine (*Ire*)
Jewish Quarterly (*UK*)
London Review of Books (*UK*)
SFX (*UK*)
The Times Literary Supplement (TLS) (*UK*)

Finance
Accountancy Age (*UK*)
Advisor Today (*US*)
Africa Confidential (*UK*)
The Christian Science Monitor (*US*)
Family Office Magazine (*UK*)
Moneywise (*UK*)
Niche (*US*)
Nob Hill Gazette (*US*)
Phoenix Magazine (*US*)
The Progressive Populist (*US*)
Reason (*US*)
Self (*US*)
Smart Retailer (*US*)
Spear's Magazine (*UK*)
The Lady (*UK*)

Gardening
Amateur Gardening (*UK*)
Cambridge Magazine (*UK*)
Charleston Magazine (*US*)
Cotswold Life (*UK*)
Essex Life (*UK*)
House & Garden (*UK*)
Kitchen Garden (*UK*)
Lothian Life (*UK*)
Organic Life (*US*)
San Diego Home / Garden Lifestyles (*US*)
Santa Barbara Magazine (*US*)
Surrey Life (*UK*)
Susquehanna Life (*US*)
The Lady (*UK*)

Gothic
Aphelion: The Webzine of Science Fiction and Fantasy (*US*)
Into The Void Magazine (*Ire*)
ShortStorySunday.com (*UK*)
The Washington Pastime (*US*)

Health
AARP Bulletin (*US*)
Alternative Therapies in Health and Medicine (*US*)
America's Pharmacist (*US*)
American Baby (*US*)
Arthritis Today (*US*)
Athletic Business (*US*)
Business London (*Can*)
Bust (*US*)
Catster (*US*)
Charleston Style and Design Magazine (*US*)
Coach (*UK*)
Coping with Cancer Magazine (*US*)
Diabetes Balance (*UK*)
Essence (*US*)
Good Housekeeping (*UK*)
Harper's Bazaar (*UK*)
Lothian Life (*UK*)
marie claire (*UK*)
Nob Hill Gazette (*US*)
Nursing Times (*UK*)
Organic Life (*US*)
Phoenix Magazine (*US*)
PN (Paraplegia News) (*US*)
The Pool (*UK*)
The Practising Midwife (*UK*)
Psychologies (*UK*)
Running (*UK*)
Sacramento Magazine (*US*)
Scientific American (*US*)
Scintilla (*UK*)
Self (*US*)
SisterShip Magazine (*Aus*)
Ski Patrol Magazine (*US*)
Slimming World (*UK*)
Susquehanna Life (*US*)
The Lady (*UK*)
Top Sante (*UK*)
Vegan Life (*UK*)
Vegetarian Living (*UK*)
Weight Watchers Magazine (*UK*)

Women Together (*UK*)
Women's Health Magazine (*US*)
Historical
Aeroplane (*UK*)
Alabama Heritage (*US*)
American History (*US*)
Aviation History (*US*)
Bugle (*US*)
The Daily Tea (*US*)
Descent (*UK*)
GUD Magazine (*US*)
H&E Naturist (*UK*)
History Today (*UK*)
Infinite Rust (*US*)
Into The Void Magazine (*Ire*)
Irish Pages (*UK*)
Jewish Quarterly (*UK*)
Nob Hill Gazette (*US*)
Nostalgia Magazine (*US*)
Preservation in Print (*US*)
The Railway Magazine (*UK*)
RUSI Journal (*UK*)
Santa Barbara Magazine (*US*)
Scots Heritage Magazine (*UK*)
The Scots Magazine (*UK*)
Seshat Literary Magazine (*US*)
ShortStorySunday.com (*UK*)
Shropshire Magazine (*UK*)
SisterShip Magazine (*Aus*)
The Starlit Path (*Can*)
Tallahassee Magazine (*US*)
The Lady (*UK*)
This England (*UK*)
TimberWest (*US*)
The Times Literary Supplement (TLS) (*UK*)
VFW (Veterans of Foreign Wars) Magazine (*US*)
Vintage Made (*Aus*)
World War II (*US*)
Yorkshire Life (*UK*)
Hobbies
American Snowmobiler (*US*)
Angler's Mail (*UK*)
Bugle (*US*)
Cadet Quest (*US*)
Climb Magazine (*UK*)
Country Walking (*UK*)
Creative Knitting (*US*)
Custom Car (*UK*)
Descent (*UK*)
The Dolls' House (*UK*)
Engineering In Miniature (*UK*)
Everyday Practical Electronics (*UK*)
Flora International (*UK*)
InJoy Magazine (*US*)
Kitchen Garden (*UK*)
Leisure Painter (*UK*)
Online Quilt Magazine (*Aus*)
Park Home and Holiday Caravan (*UK*)
The People's Friend (*UK*)
Picture Postcard Monthly (*UK*)
Record Collector Magazine (*UK*)
Reptiles (*US*)

River Hills Traveler (*US*)
Running (*UK*)
Scale Auto (*US*)
Scouting (*US*)
Sew Simple (*US*)
The Sewing Directory (*UK*)
Sewing World (*UK*)
SFX (*UK*)
SisterShip Magazine (*Aus*)
Southern Boating (*US*)
Spin Off (*US*)
The Stampers' Sampler (*US*)
Take a Break's Take a Puzzle (*UK*)
Trail (*UK*)
Trailer Life Magazine (*US*)
Tropical Fish Hobbyist Magazine (*US*)
Trout & Salmon (*UK*)
Vintage Made (*Aus*)
Vogue Patterns (*US*)
Western & Eastern Treasures (*US*)
Western Outdoor News (*US*)
Women Together (*UK*)
Yachts & Yachting (*UK*)
Yarn (*Aus*)
Your Dog Magazine (*UK*)
Your Horse (*UK*)
Horror
Aliterate (*US*)
Aphelion: The Webzine of Science Fiction and Fantasy (*US*)
Cadaverous Magazine (*US*)
The Dark (*US*)
GUD Magazine (*US*)
HelloHorror (*US*)
Into The Void Magazine (*Ire*)
The New Accelerator (*UK*)
Scifaikuest (*US*)
Screem (*US*)
ShortStorySunday.com (*UK*)
The Washington Pastime (*US*)
How-to
American Quarter Horse Journal (*US*)
American Snowmobiler (*US*)
Arizona Wildlife Views (*US*)
Artists & Illustrators (*UK*)
The Author (*UK*)
Auto Express (*UK*)
Catster (*US*)
Compose (*US*)
Computeractive Magazine (*UK*)
The Daily Tea (*US*)
The Dolls' House (*UK*)
Eat In Magazine (*UK*)
The Engravers Journal (*US*)
Flora International (*UK*)
InJoy Magazine (*US*)
Kitchen Garden (*UK*)
Leisure Painter (*UK*)
Park Home and Holiday Caravan (*UK*)
People Management (*UK*)
Play & Playground Magazine (*US*)
Police and Security News (*US*)
Qualified Remodeler (*US*)

Remodeling (*US*)
Rider Magazine (*US*)
Romantic Homes (*US*)
Runner's World (*US*)
Scale Auto (*US*)
SelfBuild & Design (*UK*)
Sew Simple (*US*)
Shutterbug (*US*)
SignCraft Publishing Co., Inc. (*US*)
SisterShip Magazine (*Aus*)
Sky at Night Magazine (*UK*)
Slimming World (*UK*)
Smart Retailer (*US*)
Southern Boating (*US*)
St Anthony Messenger (*US*)
The Starlit Path (*Can*)
Style at Home (*UK*)
This Old House (*US*)
Underground Construction (*US*)
Vintage Made (*Aus*)
Vogue Patterns (*US*)
Walls & Ceilings (*US*)
Water Well Journal (*US*)
Welding Design & Fabrication (*US*)
The Wholesaler (*US*)
Willow and Sage (*US*)
Window Fashion Vision (*US*)
Wisconsin Natural Resources Magazine (*US*)
Yachts & Yachting (*UK*)
Your Dog Magazine (*UK*)
Your Horse (*UK*)

Humour

Aesthetica: A Review of Contemporary Artists (*UK*)
Aphelion: The Webzine of Science Fiction and Fantasy (*US*)
Bugle (*US*)
Cadet Quest (*US*)
The Daily Tea (*US*)
december Magazine (*US*)
Ducts (*US*)
GUD Magazine (*US*)
InJoy Magazine (*US*)
Into The Void Magazine (*Ire*)
The Oldie (*UK*)
Orbis International Literary Journal (*UK*)
ShortStorySunday.com (*UK*)
SisterShip Magazine (*Aus*)
St Anthony Messenger (*US*)
Viz (*UK*)
The Washington Pastime (*US*)

Legal

The Author (*UK*)
Criminal Law & Justice Weekly (Incorporating Justice of the Peace) (*UK*)
The Lawyer (*UK*)
People Management (*UK*)
Police and Security News (*US*)
The Police Journal (*UK*)
SisterShip Magazine (*Aus*)
Smart Retailer (*US*)

Leisure

American Snowmobiler (*US*)

Arizona Wildlife Views (*US*)
Athletic Business (*US*)
Bartender (*US*)
Charleston Magazine (*US*)
Climb Magazine (*UK*)
Coach (*UK*)
Cotswold Life (*UK*)
Essex Life (*UK*)
Family Office Magazine (*UK*)
Improve Your Coarse Fishing (*UK*)
Motorcycle News (MCN) (*UK*)
Play & Playground Magazine (*US*)
PN (Paraplegia News) (*US*)
Runner's World (*US*)
Running (*UK*)
The Scots Magazine (*UK*)
Scouting (*US*)
Shropshire Magazine (*UK*)
SisterShip Magazine (*Aus*)
Southern Boating (*US*)
Trail (*UK*)
Trailer Life Magazine (*US*)
Trout & Salmon (*UK*)
Vegan Life (*UK*)
Western & Eastern Treasures (*US*)
Western Outdoor News (*US*)
Wisconsin Natural Resources Magazine (*US*)
Your Dog Magazine (*UK*)

Lifestyle

AARP Bulletin (*US*)
American Quarter Horse Journal (*US*)
Boat International (*UK*)
Cambridge Magazine (*UK*)
Catster (*US*)
Charleston Magazine (*US*)
Charleston Style and Design Magazine (*US*)
Cotswold Life (*UK*)
Country Walking (*UK*)
Curve (*US*)
Diabetes Balance (*UK*)
Diva (*UK*)
Essence (*US*)
Essex Life (*UK*)
Good Housekeeping (*UK*)
GQ Magazine (*UK*)
H&E Naturist (*UK*)
Harper's Bazaar (*UK*)
Hot Press (*Ire*)
House & Garden (*UK*)
Infinite Rust (*US*)
Lake Relo (*US*)
Litro Magazine (*UK*)
Little Rose Magazine (*US*)
marie claire (*UK*)
Nob Hill Gazette (*US*)
Organic Life (*US*)
Park Home and Holiday Caravan (*UK*)
Phoenix Magazine (*US*)
PN (Paraplegia News) (*US*)
The Pool (*UK*)
The Progressive Populist (*US*)
Psychologies (*UK*)
Real Simple (*US*)

Relevant (*US*)
Sacramento Magazine (*US*)
San Diego Family Magazine (*US*)
San Diego Home / Garden Lifestyles (*US*)
Santa Barbara Magazine (*US*)
The Scots Magazine (*UK*)
Self (*US*)
Shout Magazine (*UK*)
Shropshire Magazine (*UK*)
SisterShip Magazine (*Aus*)
Southern Boating (*US*)
Spear's Magazine (*UK*)
St Anthony Messenger (*US*)
Surrey Life (*UK*)
Susquehanna Life (*US*)
Tallahassee Magazine (*US*)
Toronto Life (*Can*)
Vegan Life (*UK*)
Windspeaker (*Can*)
Woman (*UK*)
Woman's Own (*UK*)
Woman's Way (*Ire*)
Women Together (*UK*)
Yorkshire Life (*UK*)
Your Dog Magazine (*UK*)

Literature
Adelaide Literary Magazine (*US*)
Aesthetica: A Review of Contemporary Artists (*UK*)
The American Poetry Review (*US*)
Aphelion: The Webzine of Science Fiction and Fantasy (*US*)
Body (*US*)
The Burnt Candle (*UK*)
Callaloo (*US*)
Caveat Lector (*US*)
Central and Eastern European London Review (*UK*)
Chicago Review (*US*)
The Christian Science Monitor (*US*)
The Collagist (*US*)
Compose (*US*)
Connotation Press (*US*)
Curve (*US*)
december Magazine (*US*)
Empty Mirror (*US*)
Filling Station (*Can*)
Infinite Rust (*US*)
Into The Void Magazine (*Ire*)
Jewish Quarterly (*UK*)
Litro Magazine (*UK*)
Little Rose Magazine (*US*)
London Review of Books (*UK*)
Magma (*UK*)
The North (*UK*)
Poetry Ireland Review (*Ire*)
Prac Crit (*UK*)
Prospect (*UK*)
Publishers Weekly (*US*)
Quill & Quire (*Can*)
Rain Taxi (*US*)
The Savage Kick (*UK*)
The Scots Magazine (*UK*)

Seshat Literary Magazine (*US*)
ShortStorySunday.com (*UK*)
SisterShip Magazine (*Aus*)
The Spectator (*UK*)
StoryNews (*US*)
The Times Literary Supplement (TLS) (*UK*)
Wasafiri (*UK*)
The Washington Pastime (*US*)
Women Together (*UK*)

Media
Adelaide Literary Magazine (*US*)
BoxOffice Magazine (*US*)
British Journalism Review (*UK*)
Hot Press (*Ire*)
Inside Soap (*UK*)
Press Gazette (*UK*)
StoryNews (*US*)
Vanity Fair (*UK*)
What's on TV (*UK*)
Woman's Way (*Ire*)

Medicine
Alternative Therapies in Health and Medicine (*US*)
American Baby (*US*)
Arthritis Today (*US*)
CHEST (*US*)
Coping with Cancer Magazine (*US*)
Diabetes Balance (*UK*)
Irish Journal of Medical Science (*Ire*)
Irish Medical Times (*Ire*)
Nurseweek (*US*)
Nursing Times (*UK*)
Pediatric Annals (*US*)
PracticeLink Magazine (*US*)
The Practising Midwife (*UK*)
Pulse (*UK*)

Men's Interests
Auto Express (*UK*)
GQ Magazine (*UK*)

Military
Air Force Times (*US*)
AIR International (*UK*)
Aviation History (*US*)
RUSI Journal (*UK*)
The Savage Kick (*UK*)
VFW (Veterans of Foreign Wars) Magazine (*US*)
World War II (*US*)

Music
Aesthetica: A Review of Contemporary Artists (*UK*)
Bust (*US*)
Central and Eastern European London Review (*UK*)
Classical Singer (*US*)
Columbia: A Journal of Literature and Art (*US*)
Connotation Press (*US*)
Electronic Musician (*US*)
Empty Mirror (*US*)
Hawai'i Review (*US*)
Hot Press (*Ire*)
Infinite Rust (*US*)
Jewish Quarterly (*UK*)

Mojo (*UK*)
Music Week (*UK*)
Opera News (*US*)
Record Collector Magazine (*UK*)
The Scots Magazine (*UK*)
Shout Magazine (*UK*)
Songwriting & Composing Magazine (*UK*)
Tempo: A Quarterly Review of New Music (*UK*)

Mystery
The Burnt Candle (*UK*)
Ellery Queen Mystery Magazine (*US*)
GUD Magazine (*US*)
Into The Void Magazine (*Ire*)
The People's Friend (*UK*)
Seshat Literary Magazine (*US*)
ShortStorySunday.com (*UK*)
The Washington Pastime (*US*)

Nature
All Animals (*US*)
American Quarter Horse Journal (*US*)
Arizona Wildlife Views (*US*)
BBC Countryfile Magazine (*UK*)
BBC Wildlife Magazine (*UK*)
Birdwatch (*UK*)
British Birds (*UK*)
Bugle (*US*)
Camas (*US*)
Catster (*US*)
The Christian Science Monitor (*US*)
Cotswold Life (*UK*)
Country Walking (*UK*)
DairyBusiness (*US*)
EarthLines Magazine (*Ire*)
Essex Life (*UK*)
The Field (*UK*)
Flora International (*UK*)
Fly Fishing & Fly Tying Magazine (*UK*)
Flyway: Journal of Writing & Environment (*US*)
Geographical (*UK*)
Into The Void Magazine (*Ire*)
Irish Farmers Journal (*Ire*)
Irish Pages (*UK*)
Organic Life (*US*)
The People's Friend (*UK*)
Pest Management Professional (*US*)
Reptiles (*US*)
River Hills Traveler (*US*)
Scintilla (*UK*)
The Scots Magazine (*UK*)
Scouting (*US*)
Seshat Literary Magazine (*US*)
ShortStorySunday.com (*UK*)
SisterShip Magazine (*Aus*)
Susquehanna Life (*US*)
This England (*UK*)
Tropical Fish Hobbyist Magazine (*US*)
Vegetable Growers News Magazine (*US*)
Wisconsin Natural Resources Magazine (*US*)
Yes! Magazine (*US*)
Your Horse (*UK*)

New Age
ShortStorySunday.com (*UK*)

The Starlit Path (*Can*)
Nonfiction
AARP Bulletin (*US*)
Accountancy Age (*UK*)
Adelaide Literary Magazine (*US*)
Adornment (*US*)
Advisor Today (*US*)
Aeroplane (*UK*)
Aesthetica: A Review of Contemporary Artists (*UK*)
Africa Confidential (*UK*)
After Happy Hour Review (*US*)
Air Force Times (*US*)
AIR International (*UK*)
Alabama Heritage (*US*)
Alebrijes (*US*)
All Animals (*US*)
All Out Cricket (*UK*)
Alternative Therapies in Health and Medicine (*US*)
Amateur Gardening (*UK*)
Amazing! Magazine (*UK*)
America's Pharmacist (*US*)
American Baby (*US*)
American History (*US*)
The American Poetry Review (*US*)
American Quarter Horse Journal (*US*)
American Snowmobiler (*US*)
Amethyst Review (*UK*)
Angler's Mail (*UK*)
AntiqueWeek (*US*)
Aphelion: The Webzine of Science Fiction and Fantasy (*US*)
APICS Magazine (*US*)
Architectural Design (*UK*)
Architectural Record (*US*)
Arizona Wildlife Views (*US*)
Art + Framing Today (*UK*)
Arthritis Today (*US*)
Artists & Illustrators (*UK*)
ArtReview (*UK*)
Athletic Business (*US*)
The Author (*UK*)
Auto Express (*UK*)
Aviation History (*US*)
The Awakenings Review (*US*)
Barking Sycamores (*US*)
Bartender (*US*)
BBC Countryfile Magazine (*UK*)
BBC Focus (*UK*)
BBC Wildlife Magazine (*UK*)
BedTimes (*US*)
Bella Grace New Generation (*US*)
Birdwatch (*UK*)
BizTimes Milwaukee (*US*)
Boat International (*UK*)
Body (*US*)
BoxOffice Magazine (*US*)
Briar Cliff Review (*US*)
British Birds (*UK*)
British Journalism Review (*UK*)
Broadcast (*UK*)
Bugle (*US*)

Seshat Literary Magazine (*US*)
Sew Simple (*US*)
The Sewing Directory (*UK*)
Sewing World (*UK*)
SFX (*UK*)
Shooter Literary Magazine (*UK*)
Shout Magazine (*UK*)
Shropshire Magazine (*UK*)
Shutterbug (*US*)
SignCraft Publishing Co., Inc. (*US*)
Sinister Wisdom (*US*)
SisterShip Magazine (*Aus*)
Ski Patrol Magazine (*US*)
Ski+board (*UK*)
Sky at Night Magazine (*UK*)
Slimming World (*UK*)
Smart Retailer (*US*)
Snooker Scene (*UK*)
Songwriting & Composing Magazine (*UK*)
Southern Boating (*US*)
Spear's Magazine (*UK*)
Spin Off (*US*)
SQL Server Pro (*US*)
St Anthony Messenger (*US*)
St Petersburg Review (*US*)
The Stage (*UK*)
The Stampers' Sampler (*US*)
The Starlit Path (*Can*)
State Journal (*US*)
Stone World (*US*)
Stormwater (*US*)
StoryNews (*US*)
Studio One (*US*)
Style at Home (*UK*)
SuCasa (*US*)
Sunshine Artist (*US*)
Surrey Life (*UK*)
Susquehanna Life (*US*)
Swimming Times Magazine (*UK*)
Take a Break's Take a Puzzle (*UK*)
Tallahassee Magazine (*US*)
Tears in the Fence (*UK*)
Tech Directions (*US*)
Television (*UK*)
Tempo: A Quarterly Review of New Music (*UK*)
TES (The Times Educational Supplement) (*UK*)
Texas Co-op Power (*US*)
The Lady (*UK*)
This England (*UK*)
This Is Bill Gorton (*US*)
This Old House (*US*)
TimberWest (*US*)
Times Higher Education (*UK*)
The Times Literary Supplement (TLS) (*UK*)
Tobacco International (*US*)
Top Sante (*UK*)
Toronto Life (*Can*)
Trail (*UK*)
Trailer Life Magazine (*US*)
TravelWorld International Magazine (*US*)
Tropical Fish Hobbyist Magazine (*US*)
Trout & Salmon (*UK*)

Truck & Driver (*UK*)
Trucking (*UK*)
Underground Construction (*US*)
US Glass Magazine (*US*)
Vanity Fair (*UK*)
Vegan Life (*UK*)
Vegetable Growers News Magazine (*US*)
Vegetarian Living (*UK*)
VFW (Veterans of Foreign Wars) Magazine (*US*)
Vintage Made (*Aus*)
Vogue Patterns (*US*)
Walls & Ceilings (*US*)
Wanderlust Magazine (*UK*)
Wasafiri (*UK*)
The Washington Pastime (*US*)
Water Well Journal (*US*)
Weight Watchers Magazine (*UK*)
Welding Design & Fabrication (*US*)
Western & Eastern Treasures (*US*)
Western Outdoor News (*US*)
Westview (*US*)
What Car? (*UK*)
What's on TV (*UK*)
The Wholesaler (*US*)
Willow and Sage (*US*)
Window Fashion Vision (*US*)
Windspeaker (*Can*)
Wire Rope News & Sling Technology (*US*)
Wisconsin Natural Resources Magazine (*US*)
Woman (*UK*)
Woman's Own (*UK*)
Woman's Way (*Ire*)
Women Together (*UK*)
Women's Health Magazine (*US*)
WoodmenLife Magazine (*US*)
The World of Interiors (*UK*)
World War II (*US*)
Yachts & Yachting (*UK*)
Yarn (*Aus*)
Yemassee (*US*)
Yes! Magazine (*US*)
Yorkshire Life (*UK*)
You & Your Wedding (*UK*)
Your Dog Magazine (*UK*)
Your Horse (*UK*)
Zoning Practice (*US*)
Philosophy
Infinite Rust (*US*)
Into The Void Magazine (*Ire*)
Jewish Quarterly (*UK*)
ShortStorySunday.com (*UK*)
The Times Literary Supplement (TLS) (*UK*)
Photography
Infinite Rust (*US*)
Little Rose Magazine (*US*)
Picture Postcard Monthly (*UK*)
Shutterbug (*US*)
SisterShip Magazine (*Aus*)
Poetry
Abramelin (*US*)
Adelaide Literary Magazine (*US*)
The Adroit Journal (*US*)

Into The Void Magazine (*Ire*)
The Iowa Review (*US*)
Ireland's Own (*Ire*)
Irish Pages (*UK*)
Island (*Aus*)
Jewish Quarterly (*UK*)
Kaimana: Literary Arts Hawai'i (*US*)
Lighthouse (*UK*)
Litro Magazine (*UK*)
Little Rose Magazine (*US*)
Long Life Magazine (*US*)
Louisiana Literature (*US*)
The Moth (*Ire*)
Mslexia (*UK*)
The New Accelerator (*UK*)
New Fairy Tales (*UK*)
New Welsh Reader (*UK*)
Old Red Kimono (*US*)
Orbis International Literary Journal (*UK*)
Orson Scott Card's InterGalactic Medicine Show (*US*)
Overtime (*US*)
The People's Friend (*UK*)
Prole (*UK*)
Pushing Out the Boat (*UK*)
Ripcord. (*US*)
Seshat Literary Magazine (*US*)
ShortStorySunday.com (*UK*)
Sinister Wisdom (*US*)
Skald (*UK*)
SlingInk Magazine (*UK*)
Spitball (*US*)
St Anthony Messenger (*US*)
St Petersburg Review (*US*)
Stand Magazine (*UK*)
The Starlit Path (*Can*)
Studio One (*US*)
Tears in the Fence (*UK*)
This Is Bill Gorton (*US*)
Wasafiri (*UK*)
The Washington Pastime (*US*)
Westview (*US*)
Yemassee (*US*)
Zoetrope: All-Story (*US*)

Sociology
H&E Naturist (*UK*)
Infinite Rust (*US*)
Into The Void Magazine (*Ire*)
LGC (Local Government Chronicle) (*UK*)
Little Rose Magazine (*US*)
Reform (*UK*)

Spiritual
Amethyst Review (*UK*)
Infinite Rust (*US*)
InJoy Magazine (*US*)
Little Rose Magazine (*US*)
The New Accelerator (*UK*)
Reform (*UK*)
Scintilla (*UK*)
The Starlit Path (*Can*)

Sport
All Out Cricket (*UK*)
Angler's Mail (*UK*)

Athletic Business (*US*)
Business London (*Can*)
Climb Magazine (*UK*)
Climber (*UK*)
Coach (*UK*)
Fly Fishing & Fly Tying Magazine (*UK*)
Golf Monthly (*UK*)
Hot Press (*Ire*)
The Huffington Post (United Kingdom) (*UK*)
Improve Your Coarse Fishing (*UK*)
PN (Paraplegia News) (*US*)
Referee (*US*)
River Hills Traveler (*US*)
Runner's World (*US*)
Running (*UK*)
SisterShip Magazine (*Aus*)
Ski Patrol Magazine (*US*)
Ski+board (*UK*)
Snooker Scene (*UK*)
Southern Boating (*US*)
Spitball (*US*)
Swimming Times Magazine (*UK*)
Tallahassee Magazine (*US*)
Trout & Salmon (*UK*)
Western & Eastern Treasures (*US*)
Western Outdoor News (*US*)
Windspeaker (*Can*)
Yachts & Yachting (*UK*)

Suspense
Aphelion: The Webzine of Science Fiction and Fantasy (*US*)
The Burnt Candle (*UK*)
GUD Magazine (*US*)
Into The Void Magazine (*Ire*)
ShortStorySunday.com (*UK*)
The Washington Pastime (*US*)

Technology
Aeroplane (*UK*)
AIR International (*UK*)
American Snowmobiler (*US*)
Auto Express (*UK*)
BBC Focus (*UK*)
Boat International (*UK*)
Broadcast (*UK*)
Cambridge Magazine (*UK*)
Canadian Yachting (*Can*)
Computeractive Magazine (*UK*)
Construction Equipment Guide (*US*)
Custom PC (*UK*)
Descent (*UK*)
Digital Engineering (*US*)
Electronic Musician (*US*)
The Engineer (*UK*)
Engineering In Miniature (*UK*)
The Engravers Journal (*US*)
Everyday Practical Electronics (*UK*)
GQ Magazine (*UK*)
The Huffington Post (United Kingdom) (*UK*)
Little Rose Magazine (*US*)
Long Life Magazine (*US*)
Motorcycle News (MCN) (*UK*)
The Motorship (*UK*)
The New Accelerator (*UK*)

New Scientist (*UK*)
Photonics & Imaging Technology (*US*)
Play & Playground Magazine (*US*)
Popular Science (*US*)
Qualified Remodeler (*US*)
The Railway Magazine (*UK*)
Rider Magazine (*US*)
RUSI Journal (*UK*)
Scientific American (*US*)
Screen Printing (*US*)
Shutterbug (*US*)
Sky at Night Magazine (*UK*)
SQL Server Pro (*US*)
Stone World (*US*)
Tech Directions (*US*)
Television (*UK*)
Texas Co-op Power (*US*)
Trailer Life Magazine (*US*)
Water Well Journal (*US*)
Welding Design & Fabrication (*US*)
What Car? (*UK*)
Wire Rope News & Sling Technology (*US*)

Theatre
Aesthetica: A Review of Contemporary Artists (*UK*)
Central and Eastern European London Review (*UK*)
Harper's Bazaar (*UK*)
St Petersburg Review (*US*)
The Stage (*UK*)
The Times Literary Supplement (TLS) (*UK*)

Thrillers
Aliterate (*US*)
Aphelion: The Webzine of Science Fiction and Fantasy (*US*)
The Burnt Candle (*UK*)
Into The Void Magazine (*Ire*)
The New Accelerator (*UK*)
The People's Friend (*UK*)
ShortStorySunday.com (*UK*)
The Washington Pastime (*US*)

Translations
Better Than Starbucks (*US*)
Body (*US*)
California Quarterly (*US*)
The Caribbean Writer (*US*)
The Chattahoochee Review (*US*)
Columbia: A Journal of Literature and Art (*US*)
Current Accounts (*UK*)
Guernica (*US*)
Hawai'i Review (*US*)
Indiana Review (*US*)
The Iowa Review (*US*)
Irish Pages (*UK*)
Litro Magazine (*UK*)
Oxford Poetry (*UK*)
Poetry London (*UK*)
The Poetry Review (*UK*)
Stand Magazine (*UK*)
Tears in the Fence (*UK*)

Travel
American Snowmobiler (*US*)
Auto Express (*UK*)

Aviation History (*US*)
Boat International (*UK*)
Business London (*Can*)
Bust (*US*)
Canadian Yachting (*Can*)
The Carolina Quarterly (*US*)
Central and Eastern European London Review (*UK*)
Charleston Magazine (*US*)
Charleston Style and Design Magazine (*US*)
Cotswold Life (*UK*)
Country Walking (*UK*)
The Daily Tea (*US*)
EarthLines Magazine (*Ire*)
Geographical (*UK*)
Harper's Bazaar (*UK*)
House & Garden (*UK*)
Infinite Rust (*US*)
Lake Relo (*US*)
Litro Magazine (*UK*)
Lothian Life (*UK*)
marie claire (*UK*)
Maritime Journal (*UK*)
Motorcycle News (MCN) (*UK*)
The Motorship (*UK*)
Nob Hill Gazette (*US*)
Park Home and Holiday Caravan (*UK*)
The People's Friend (*UK*)
Phoenix Magazine (*US*)
Psychologies (*UK*)
The Railway Magazine (*UK*)
Recommend Magazine (*US*)
Rider Magazine (*US*)
Sacramento Magazine (*US*)
Saveur (*US*)
School Bus Fleet (*US*)
Scouting (*US*)
SisterShip Magazine (*Aus*)
Ski Patrol Magazine (*US*)
Ski+board (*UK*)
Southern Boating (*US*)
Surrey Life (*UK*)
Susquehanna Life (*US*)
Tallahassee Magazine (*US*)
The Lady (*UK*)
Trail (*UK*)
Trailer Life Magazine (*US*)
TravelWorld International Magazine (*US*)
Truck & Driver (*UK*)
Trucking (*UK*)
Vegan Life (*UK*)
Wanderlust Magazine (*UK*)
What Car? (*UK*)
Women Together (*UK*)
Yachts & Yachting (*UK*)
Yorkshire Life (*UK*)
You & Your Wedding (*UK*)
Your Horse (*UK*)

TV
Broadcast (*UK*)
Curve (*US*)
Radio Times (*UK*)
SFX (*UK*)

Television (*UK*)
What's on TV (*UK*)
Westerns
Aliterate (*US*)
Into The Void Magazine (*Ire*)
The Savage Kick (*UK*)
ShortStorySunday.com (*UK*)
The Washington Pastime (*US*)
Women's Interests
Aesthetica: A Review of Contemporary Artists (*UK*)
Bella Grace New Generation (*US*)
Bust (*US*)
december Magazine (*US*)
Diva (*UK*)
Good Housekeeping (*UK*)
Harper's Bazaar (*UK*)
Infinite Rust (*US*)
InJoy Magazine (*US*)
marie claire (*UK*)

Mslexia (*UK*)
Orbis International Literary Journal (*UK*)
The People's Friend (*UK*)
The Pool (*UK*)
The Practising Midwife (*UK*)
Psychologies (*UK*)
Real Simple (*US*)
Self (*US*)
Shout Magazine (*UK*)
Sinister Wisdom (*US*)
SisterShip Magazine (*Aus*)
Style at Home (*UK*)
The Lady (*UK*)
Top Sante (*UK*)
Woman (*UK*)
Woman's Own (*UK*)
Woman's Way (*Ire*)
Women Together (*UK*)
Women's Health Magazine (*US*)

US Literary Agents

For the most up-to-date listings of these and hundreds of other literary agents, visit https://www.firstwriter.com/Agents

To claim your **free** access to the site, please see the back of this book.

Aaron M. Priest Literary Agency

200 West 41st Street, 21st Floor, New York, NY 10036
Tel: +1 (212) 818-0344
Fax: +1 (212) 573-9417
Email: querypriest@aaronpriest.com
Website: http://www.aaronpriest.com

Handles: Fiction; Nonfiction; *Areas:* Autobiography; Biography; Crime; Culture; Current Affairs; Fantasy; Gothic; Historical; How-to; Mystery; Politics; Science; Suspense; Thrillers; Translations; Women's Interests; *Markets:* Adult; Youth; *Treatments:* Commercial; Contemporary; Literary; Popular

Send one-page query by email, describing your work and your background. No attachments, but you may paste the first chapter into the body of the email. Query one agent only. See website for specific agent interests and email addresses. No poetry, screenplays, sci-fi, or horror.

Above the Line Agency

468 N. Camden Drive, #200, Beverly Hills, CA 90210
Tel: +1 (310) 859-6115
Email: abovethelineagency@gmail.com
Website: http://www.abovethelineagency.com

Handles: Scripts; *Areas:* Film; TV; *Markets:* Adult; Children's

Send query via online web system only. Represents writers and directors; feature films, movies of the week, animation. Offers consultations at a rate of $200 per hour.

Bret Adams Ltd

448 West 44th Street, New York, NY 10036
Tel: +1 (212) 765-5630
Fax: +1 (212) 265-2212
Website: http://www.bretadamsltd.net

Handles: Scripts; *Areas:* Film; Theatre; TV; *Markets:* Adult

A full service agency representing writers, directors, designers, and actors.

Adams Literary

7845 Colony Road, C4 #215, Charlotte, NC 28226
Tel: +1 (704) 542-1440
Fax: +1 (704) 542-1450
Email: info@adamsliterary.com
Website: http://www.adamsliterary.com

Handles: Fiction; *Markets:* Children's; Youth

Temporarily closed to submissions as at July 2019. Check website for current status.

Handles books for children and young adults, from picture books to teen novels. No unsolicited MSS. Send query with complete ms via webform. See website for full submission guidelines.

Adler & Robin Books, Inc

3000 Connecticut Avenue, NW, Suite 317, Washington DC, 20008
Tel: +1 (202) 986-9275
Fax: +1 (202) 986-9485
Email: submissions@adlerrobin.com
Website: http://www.adlerrobin.com

Handles: Nonfiction; Reference; *Areas:* Autobiography; Biography; Culture; Historical; How-to; Humour; Lifestyle; Self-Help; *Markets:* Adult; Children's

Interested in biography/memoir, careers, gift books, how-to, humour, lifestyle, local history, pop culture, reference books, self-help, and children's books. Send queries by email only.

Aevitas

19 West 21st Street, Suite 501, New York, NY 10010
Tel: +1 (212) 765-6900
Website: http://aevitascreative.com

Handles: Fiction; Nonfiction; *Areas:* Arts; Autobiography; Beauty and Fashion; Biography; Business; Cookery; Culture; Design; Health; Historical; Humour; Lifestyle; Nature; New Age; Politics; Psychology; Religious; Science; Self-Help; Spiritual; Technology; *Markets:* Adult; Children's; Youth; *Treatments:* Commercial; Literary

See website for individual agent interests and query using online submission system.

The Ahearn Agency, Inc

2021 Pine Street, New Orleans, LA 70118
Tel: +1 (504) 861-8395
Fax: +1 (504) 866-6434
Email: pahearn@aol.com
Website: http://www.ahearnagency.com

Handles: Fiction; Nonfiction; *Areas:* Autobiography; Biography; Crime; Current Affairs; Health; Historical; Humour;

Lifestyle; Mystery; Nature; Romance; Short Stories; Suspense; Thrillers; Women's Interests; *Markets:* Adult; *Treatments:* Literary

Send one page query with SASE, description, length, market info, and any writing credits. Accepts email queries without attachments. Response in 2-3 months.

Specialises in women's fiction and suspense. No nonfiction, poetry, juvenile material or science fiction.

Alive Literary Agency

7680 Goddard Street, Suite 200, Colorado Springs, CO 80920
Tel: +1 (719) 260-7080
Email: Submissions@aliveliterary.com
Website: http://aliveliterary.com

Handles: Fiction; Nonfiction; *Areas:* Adventure; Autobiography; Biography; Business; Crime; Historical; How-to; Humour; Lifestyle; Mystery; Religious; Self-Help; Short Stories; Spiritual; Sport; Suspense; Thrillers; Westerns; Women's Interests; *Markets:* Adult; Children's; *Treatments:* Commercial; Literary; Mainstream; Popular

Accepts queries from referred authors only. Works primarily with well-established, best-selling, and career authors. Referred authors may submit query by email with bio, name of the client referring you, synopsis, and first three chapters. See website for full details.

Allen O'Shea Literary Agency

Tel: +1 (203) 820-5967
Email: marilyn@allenoshea.com
Website: https://www.allenoshea.com

Handles: Nonfiction; *Areas:* Business; Cookery; Crafts; Culture; Finance; Health; Historical; Lifestyle; Politics; Science; Sport; *Markets:* Adult

Works mainly with nonfiction writers. Send query by email, describing why your work is unique, your experience, your platform, and any awards or honours received for your writing. See website for full guidelines.

Ambassador Speakers Bureau & Literary Agency

1107 Battlewood Street, Franklin, TN 37069
Tel: +1 (615) 370-4700
Email: info@ambassadorspeakers.com
Website: https://www.
ambassadorspeakers.com

Handles: Fiction; Nonfiction; *Areas:*
Adventure; Autobiography; Biography;
Culture; Current Affairs; Finance; Health;
Historical; How-to; Legal; Lifestyle;
Medicine; Politics; Religious; Self-Help;
Women's Interests; *Markets:* Adult;
Treatments: Contemporary; Literary;
Mainstream

Represents select authors and writers who
are published by religious and general
market publishers in the US and Europe. No
short stories, children's books, screenplays,
or poetry. Send query by email with short
description. Submit work on invitation only.

Marcia Amsterdam Agency

41 W. 82nd St., New York, NY 10024-5613

Handles: Fiction; Scripts; *Areas:* Adventure;
Crime; Film; Historical; Horror; Humour;
Mystery; Romance; Science; Thrillers; TV;
Markets: Adult; Youth; *Treatments:*
Contemporary; Mainstream

Not taking on new clients as at June 2018.

Send query with SASE. No poetry, how-to,
books for the 8-10 age-group, or unsolicited
MSS. Response to queries usually in one
month.

The Anderson Literary Agency

Tel: +1 (917) 363-6829
Email: giles@andersonliteraryagency.com
Website: http://andersonliteraryagency.com

Handles: Nonfiction; *Areas:* Autobiography;
Biography; Crime; Religious; Science;
Markets: Adult

Particularly interested in books that help us
understand people, ideas and the possibility
of change. Send query by email.

Andrea Brown Literary Agency, Inc.

1076 Eagle Drive, Salinas, CA 93905
Email: andrea@andreabrownlit.com
Website: http://www.andreabrownlit.com

Handles: Fiction; Nonfiction; *Areas:*
Anthropology; Archaeology; Architecture;
Arts; Autobiography; Biography; Culture;
Current Affairs; Design; Drama; Fantasy;
Historical; How-to; Humour; Mystery;
Nature; Photography; Romance; Science;
Sci-Fi; Sociology; Sport; Technology;
Thrillers; Women's Interests; *Markets:*
Children's; Youth; *Treatments:* Commercial;
Contemporary; Literary

Handles children's from picture books to
young adult only. Send query by email only.
Visit website and view individual agent
profiles, then select one specific agent to
send a query to at their own specific email
address (given on website). Put the word
"Query" in the subject line and include all
material in the text of the email. No
attachments.

For picture books, include full MS. For
fiction send first ten pages. For nonfiction
submit proposal and a sample chapter. For
graphic novels, send summary and 2-3
sample page spreads in .jpg or .pdf format.
Indicated which publishers, if any, the MS
has been sent to. No queries by fax.

The Angela Rinaldi Literary Agency

PO Box 7875, Beverly Hills, CA 90212-
7875
Tel: +1 (310) 287-0356
Fax: +1 (310) 837-8143
Email: info@rinaldiliterary.com
Website: http://www.rinaldiliterary.com

Handles: Fiction; Nonfiction; *Areas:*
Autobiography; Biography; Business;
Cookery; Culture; Current Affairs; Finance;
Gothic; Health; Historical; Lifestyle;
Medicine; Mystery; Psychology; Suspense;
Thrillers; Women's Interests; *Markets:*
Adult; *Treatments:* Commercial;
Contemporary; Literary; Mainstream

Send query by email with the word "Query"
in the subject line. For fiction, paste synopsis

and first ten pages in the email. For nonfiction, include detailed cover letter and your credentials and platform, as well as any publishing history. See website for full guidelines. No humour, CIA espionage, drug thrillers, techno thrillers, category romances, science fiction, fantasy, horror / occult / paranormal, poetry, film scripts, magazine articles or religion.

Aponte Literary

Email: agents@aponteliterary.com
Website: http://aponteliterary.com

Handles: Fiction; Nonfiction; *Areas:* Fantasy; Historical; Politics; Science; Sci-Fi; Women's Interests; *Markets:* Adult; *Treatments:* Commercial; Mainstream

Handles any genre of mainstream fiction and nonfiction, but particularly women's novels, historical novels, supernatural and paranormal fiction, fantasy novels, political and science thrillers. Closed to submissions as at June 2017. See website for current situation.

Arcadia

31 Lake Place North, Danbury, CT 06810
Email: arcadialit@gmail.com

Handles: Nonfiction; *Areas:* Biography; Culture; Current Affairs; Health; Historical; Medicine; Psychology; Science; *Markets:* Adult

Agency handling biography, current affairs, health, history, medicine, popular culture, psychology, and science. No fiction.

Movable Type Management

244 Madison Avenue, Suite 334, New York, NY 10016
Tel: +1 (646) 431-6134
Email: AChromy@MovableTM.com
Website: http://www.mtmgmt.net

Handles: Fiction; Nonfiction; *Markets:* Adult; *Treatments:* Commercial

Looking for authors of high quality commercial fiction and nonfiction with archetypal themes, stories, and characters, especially if they have strong film/TV

potential. Send queries by email only. For nonfiction send query describing topic, approach, and bio. For fiction send query with first 10 pages. Include "Query" in the subject line. No attachments or approaches by post. Response only if interested.

The August Agency LLC

Email: submissions@augustagency.com
Website: http://www.augustagency.com

Handles: Fiction; Nonfiction; *Areas:* Arts; Autobiography; Biography; Business; Culture; Current Affairs; Entertainment; Finance; Historical; Media; Politics; Sociology; Technology; Women's Interests; *Markets:* Adult; Family; Literary

Accepts queries by referral or by request at a writers' conference only.

The Axelrod Agency

55 Main Street, P.O. Box 357, Chatham, NY 12037
Tel: +1 (518) 392-2100
Fax: +1 (518) 392-2944
Email: steve@axelrodagency.com
Website: http://axelrodagency.com

Handles: Fiction; *Areas:* Crime; Erotic; Mystery; Romance; Thrillers; Women's Interests; *Markets:* Adult

Send query by email only. No nonfiction, African-American, Christian, comedy, humour, comics, graphic novels, gay/lesbian, historical, horror, literary, poetry, puzzles, games, science fiction, fantasy, or westerns.

Ayesha Pande Literary

128 West 132 Street, New York, NY 10027
Tel: +1 (212) 283-5825
Email: queries@pandeliterary.com
Website: http://pandeliterary.com

Handles: Fiction; Nonfiction; *Areas:* Autobiography; Biography; Crime; Culture; Fantasy; Finance; Historical; Humour; Mystery; Romance; Sci-Fi; Thrillers; Women's Interests; *Markets:* Adult; Youth; *Treatments:* Commercial; Literary; Popular

A New York based boutique literary agency with a small and eclectic roster of clients.

Submit queries via form on website. No poetry, business books, screenplays, illustrated children's books or middle grade fiction.

Azantian Literary Agency

Email: queries@azantianlitagency.com
Website: http://www.azantianlitagency.com

Handles: Fiction; *Areas:* Fantasy; Horror; Sci-Fi; *Markets:* Adult; Children's; Youth

Currently accepting middle grade and young adult novels only. Send query via online submission system.

B.J. Robbins Literary Agency

5130 Bellaire Avenue, North Hollywood, CA 91607
Tel: +1 (818) 760-6602
Fax: +1 (818) 760-6616
Email: Robbinsliterary@gmail.com

Handles: Fiction; Nonfiction; *Areas:* Autobiography; Biography; Culture; Health; Historical; Mystery; Science; Sport; Suspense; Thrillers; Travel; *Markets:* Adult

Send query with outline / proposal and first 50 pages (fiction) or three sample chapters (nonfiction) by post with SASE or by email (no attachments). No screenplays, plays, poetry, science fiction, horror, westerns, romance, techno-thrillers, religious tracts, dating books or anything with the word "unicorn" in the title.

Barbara Hogenson Agency

165 West End Ave., Suite 19-C, New York, NY 10023
Tel: +1 (212) 874-8084
Fax: +1 (212) 362-3011
Email: Bhogenson@aol.com

Handles: Fiction; Nonfiction; Scripts; *Areas:* Theatre; *Markets:* Adult

Represents fiction, nonfiction, and stage plays. Send query by email only. No unsolicited MSS.

Barbara Braun Associates, Inc.

7 East 14th St #19F, New York, NY 10003
Email: bbasubmissions@gmail.com
Website: http://www.barbarabraunagency.com

Handles: Fiction; Nonfiction; *Areas:* Architecture; Arts; Autobiography; Beauty and Fashion; Biography; Criticism; Culture; Design; Entertainment; Film; Historical; Mystery; Photography; Politics; Psychology; Sociology; Thrillers; Women's Interests; *Markets:* Adult; *Treatments:* Commercial; Literary; Serious

Send query by email only, with "Query" in the subject line, including brief summary, word count, genre, any relevant publishing experience, and the first five pages pasted into the body of the email. No attachments. No poetry, science fiction, fantasy, horror, or screenplays. Particularly interested in stories for women, art-related fiction, historical and multicultural stories, and to a lesser extent mysteries and thrillers. Also interested in narrative nonfiction and current affairs books by journalists.

Barone Literary Agency

Email: baronelit@outlook.com
Website: http://www.baroneliteraryagency.com

Handles: Fiction; *Areas:* Erotic; Historical; Horror; Romance; Women's Interests; *Markets:* Adult; Youth

Send query online form on website. Include synopsis and first three chapters. No plays, screenplays, picture books, middle grade, science fiction, paranormal, or nonfiction.

Baror International, Inc.

P.O. Box 868, Armonk, NY 10504-0868
Email: Heather@Barorint.com
Website: http://www.barorint.com

Handles: Fiction; Nonfiction; *Areas:* Fantasy; Sci-Fi; *Markets:* Adult; Youth; *Treatments:* Commercial; Literary

Specialises in the international and domestic representation of literary works in both fiction and nonfiction, including commercial fiction, literary, science fiction, fantasy, young adult and more. Send query by post or by email with a few sample chapters. Taking on very few authors as at July 2017. Check website for current situation.

Barry Goldblatt Literary Agency, Inc.

C/O Industrious – Brooklyn, 594 Dean Street – 2nd Floor, Brooklyn, NY 11238
Email: query@bgliterary.com
Website: http://www.bgliterary.com

Handles: Fiction; *Areas:* Fantasy; Historical; Mystery; Romance; Sci-Fi; Thrillers; *Markets:* Children's; Youth; *Treatments:* Contemporary

Handles books for young people; from picture books to middle grade and young adult. Send query by email including the word "Query" in the subject line and synopsis and first five pages in the body of the email. No attachments. Emails with attachments will be ignored. See website for full details.

The Bent Agency

19 W. 21st St., #201, New York, NY 10010
Email: info@thebentagency.com
Website: http://www.thebentagency.com

Handles: Fiction; Nonfiction; *Areas:* Adventure; Autobiography; Cookery; Crime; Culture; Fantasy; Historical; Horror; Humour; Lifestyle; Mystery; Romance; Science; Sci-Fi; Sociology; Sport; Suspense; Thrillers; Women's Interests; *Markets:* Adult; Children's; Youth; *Treatments:* Commercial; Literary; Popular

Accepts email queries only. See website for agent bios and specific interests and email addresses, then query one agent only. See website for full submission guidelines.

Betsy Amster Literary Enterprises

607 Foothill Blvd #1061, La Canada Flintridge, CA 91012
Email: b.amster.assistant@gmail.com
Website: http://amsterlit.com

Handles: Fiction; Nonfiction; *Areas:* Autobiography; Biography; Cookery; Culture; Gardening; Health; Historical; Lifestyle; Medicine; Mystery; Psychology; Self-Help; Sociology; Thrillers; Travel; Women's Interests; *Markets:* Adult; *Treatments:* Literary; Popular

Send query by email only. For fiction and narrative nonfiction include the first three pages in the body of your email; for nonfiction include your proposal, again in the body of the email. See website for different email addresses for adult and children's/YA submissions. No unsolicited attachments or queries by phone or fax.

No romances, screenplays, adult poetry, westerns, adult fantasy, horror, science fiction, techno thrillers, spy capers, apocalyptic scenarios, political or religious arguments, or self-published books.

BiCoastal Talent

2600 West Olive Ave, Suite 500, Burbank, CA 91505
Tel: +1 (818) 845-0150
Email: submissions@BiCoastaltalent.com
Website: http://www.bicoastaltalent.com

Handles: Scripts; *Areas:* Film; TV; *Markets:* Adult

Accepts queries for completed screenplays only. You must have a minimum of three completed screenplays available for review. Send query only, including list of completed screenplays, title, genre, and one-paragraph synopsis of four to eight lines. No authors of self- or unpublished manuscripts, treatments, concepts or TV pilots. Unsolicited materials (scripts, manuscripts, graphics, DVDs, etc.) will not be reviewed. Response only if interested. Preference given to writers in LA.

firstwriter.com note: Website currently contains potentially contradictory statements:

"Writers of feature-length screenplays may submit queries at this time";

"NOT CURRENTLY ACCEPTING ANY SUBMISSIONS"

Bidnick & Company

Email: bidnick@comcast.net

Handles: Nonfiction; *Areas:* Cookery; *Markets:* Adult; *Treatments:* Commercial

Handles cookbooks and commercial nonfiction. Send query by email only.

Bleecker Street Associates, Inc.

217 Thompson Street, #519, New York, NY 10012
Tel: +1 (212) 677-4492
Fax: +1 (212) 388-0001
Email: bleeckerst@hotmail.com

Handles: Fiction; Nonfiction; *Areas:* Autobiography; Biography; Business; Cookery; Crime; Culture; Current Affairs; Entertainment; Erotic; Finance; Health; Historical; Horror; How-to; Humour; Lifestyle; Military; Mystery; Nature; New Age; Politics; Psychology; Religious; Romance; Science; Self-Help; Sociology; Spiritual; Sport; Technology; Thrillers; Women's Interests; *Markets:* Adult; Youth; *Treatments:* Literary

Send query with SASE for response. No poetry, plays, scripts, short stories, academic, scholarly, professional, science fiction, westerns, children's books, or phone calls, faxes, or emails.

Bob Mecoy Creative Book Services

460 West 24th Street, Suite 3E, New York, NY 10011
Tel: +1 (212) 296-1936
Fax: +1 (212) 226-1398
Email: bob.mecoy@gmail.com
Website: http://bobmecoy.com

Handles: Fiction; Nonfiction; *Areas:* Adventure; Arts; Autobiography; Biography; Business; Cookery; Crime; Current Affairs; Fantasy; Finance; Historical; Literature; Military; Mystery; Romance; Sci-Fi; Sport; Technology; *Markets:* Adult; Children's; Youth; *Treatments:* Literary; Mainstream

Send query with synopsis and sample chapters.

Bond Literary Agency

4340 E Kentucky Avenue, Suite 471, Denver, CO 80246
Tel: +1 (303) 781-9305
Email: queries@bondliteraryagency.com
Website: https://www.bondliteraryagency.com

Handles: Fiction; Nonfiction; *Areas:* Business; Crime; Fantasy; Historical; Horror; Mystery; Science; Sci-Fi; Thrillers; *Markets:* Adult; Youth; *Treatments:* Commercial; Literary

Temporarily closed to submissions as at November 2018

Agency based in Colorado, representing fiction and nonfiction for adults and young adults. No romance, poetry, children's picture books or screenplays. Send query by email with first five pages of your novel (if sending fiction) in the body of the email. For nonfiction, a proposal must be available before querying. No attachments. See website for full guidelines.

The Book Group

20 West 20th Street, Suite 601, New York, NY 10011
Tel: +1 (212) 803-3360
Email: submissions@thebookgroup.com
Website: http://www.thebookgroup.com

Handles: Fiction; Nonfiction; *Areas:* Autobiography; Biography; Cookery; Culture; Film; Historical; Lifestyle; Music; Psychology; Science; TV; *Markets:* Adult; Children's; Youth; *Treatments:* Commercial; Literary

Represents a broad range of fiction and nonfiction. No poetry or screenplays. Send query by email only with ten sample pages and the first and last name of the agent you are querying in the subject line (see website for individual agent interests). No attachments. Include all material in the body of the email. See website for full guidelines. Response only if interested.

Book Cents Literary Agency

Email: cw@bookcentsliteraryagency.com
Website: http://www.
bookcentsliteraryagency.com

Handles: Fiction; *Areas:* Fantasy; Humour;
Mystery; Romance; Suspense; Thrillers;
Women's Interests; *Markets:* Adult; Youth;
Treatments: Contemporary; Mainstream

**Closed to submissions (except by referral)
as at July 2017. Check website for current
status.**

No nonfiction, Third party submissions,
Previously published titles, Short Stories or
Novellas, Erotica, Inspirational, Historical,
Westerns, Sci-Fi/Fantasy (except young
adult fantasy), Horror/Pulp/slasher Thrillers,
Memoirs, Poetry, or Screenplays/Stageplays.

BookEnds, LLC

Email: Bookends@bookendsliterary.com
Website: http://www.bookends-inc.com

Handles: Fiction; Nonfiction; Reference;
Areas: Autobiography; Business; Culture;
Current Affairs; Erotic; Fantasy; Historical;
Horror; Lifestyle; Mystery; Romance; Sci-
Fi; Suspense; Thrillers; Women's Interests;
Markets: Adult; Children's; Youth;
Treatments: Contemporary; Literary

Send submissions through online submission
system (see website). No short fiction,
poetry, screenplays, or techno-thrillers.

Books & Such Literary Management

52 Mission Circle, Suite 122, PMB 170,
Santa Rosa, CA 95409-5370
Email: representation@booksandsuch.com
Website: http://www.booksandsuch.biz

Handles: Fiction; Nonfiction; *Areas:*
Historical; Humour; Lifestyle; Religious;
Romance; Women's Interests; *Markets:*
Adult; Children's; Youth

Send query by email only. No attachments.
Query should be up to one page detailing
your book, your market, your experience,
etc. No queries by post or phone. See
website for full details.

BookStop Literary Agency, LLC

67 Meadow View Road, Orinda, CA 94563
Tel: +1 (925) 254-2664
Fax: +1 (925) 254-2668
Email: info@bookstopliterary.com
Website: http://www.bookstopliterary.com

Handles: Fiction; Nonfiction; *Areas:*
Adventure; Fantasy; Gothic; Historical;
Mystery; Science; Thrillers; *Markets:*
Children's; Youth; *Treatments:* Literary

**Temporarily closed to submissions as at
January 2019. Check website for current
status.**

Handles fiction and nonfiction for children
and young adults. See website for full
submission guidelines.

Brandt & Hochman Literary Agents, Inc.

1501 Broadway, Suite 2310, New York, NY
10036
Tel: +1 (212) 840-5760
Fax: +1 (212) 840-5776
Email: ghochman@bromasite.com
Website: http://brandthochman.com

Handles: Fiction; Nonfiction; *Areas:* Arts;
Autobiography; Culture; Current Affairs;
Health; Historical; Lifestyle; Mystery;
Science; Thrillers; *Markets:* Adult;
Children's; Youth; *Treatments:* Commercial;
Literary; Popular

Send query by post with SASE or by email
with query letter up to two pages long,
including overview and author details and
writing credits. See website for full
submission guidelines and for details of
individual agents' interests and direct contact
details, then approach one agent specifically.
No screenplays or textbooks. Response to
email queries not guaranteed.

The Brattle Agency LLC

PO Box 380537, Cambridge, MA 02238
Tel: +1 (617) 721-5375
Email: submissions@thebrattleagency.com
Website: https://thebrattleagency.com

Handles: Fiction; Nonfiction; *Areas:* Arts; Culture; Historical; Politics; Sport; *Markets:* Academic; Adult; *Treatments:* Literary

Send query by email with cover letter, brief synopsis, and (if submitting an academic manuscript) an author CV. Responds to queries within 72 hours. Unsolicited mss will not be read or replied to, whether sent by post or email.

Not accepting fiction submissions as at September 2017. Check website for current status.

Browne & Miller Literary Associates

52 Village Place, Hinsdale, IL 60521
Tel: +1 (312) 922-3063
Email: mail@browneandmiller.com
Website: http://www.browneandmiller.com

Handles: Fiction; Nonfiction; *Markets:* Adult; *Treatments:* Commercial

Handles books for the adult commercial book markets. No young adult fiction, adult memoir, children's books, academic, short stories, poetry, original screenplays, or articles. Send query only by email. No attachments.

Don Buchwald and Associates

5900 Wilshire Boulevard, 31st floor, Los Angeles, CA 90036
Tel: +1 (323) 655-7400
Email: info@buchwald.com
Website: https://www.buchwald.com

Handles: Scripts; *Areas:* Film; Theatre; TV; *Markets:* Adult

Send query by post with SASE or by fax. No unsolicited MSS. Finds most new clients by combing the NY and LA theatre scenes, and by attending film festivals, entertainment symposiums and other industry gatherings.

Capital Talent Agency

419 South Washington Street, Alexandria, VA 22314
Tel: +1 (703) 349-1649
Email: literary.submissions@

capitaltalentagency.com
Website: http://capitaltalentagency.com

Handles: Fiction; Nonfiction; *Markets:* Adult

Represents authors in all genres of fiction and nonfiction. Send query by email only. Response in 6 weeks, if interested. See website for full guidelines.

Carol Mann Agency

55 Fifth Avenue, New York, NY 10003
Tel: +1 (212) 206-5635
Fax: +1 (212) 674-4809
Email: submissions@carolmannagency.com
Website: http://www.carolmannagency.com

Handles: Fiction; Nonfiction; *Areas:* Anthropology; Archaeology; Architecture; Arts; Autobiography; Biography; Business; Culture; Current Affairs; Design; Finance; Health; Historical; Humour; Legal; Lifestyle; Medicine; Music; Nature; Politics; Psychology; Religious; Self-Help; Sociology; Spiritual; Sport; Women's Interests; *Markets:* Adult; Youth; *Treatments:* Commercial; Literary

Send query by email only, including synopsis, brief bio, and first 25 pages, all pasted into the body of your email. No attachments. No submissions by post, or phone calls. Allow 3-4 weeks for response.

Carolyn Jenks Agency

30 Cambridge Park Drive, Cambridge, MA 02140
Tel: +1 (617) 354-5099
Email: queries@carolynjenksagency.com
Website: http://www.
carolynjenksagency.com

Handles: Fiction; Nonfiction; Scripts; *Areas:* Adventure; Autobiography; Biography; Crime; Historical; Literature; Mystery; Romance; Sci-Fi; Suspense; Theatre; Thrillers; Women's Interests; *Markets:* Adult; Youth; *Treatments:* Contemporary; Experimental; Literary; Mainstream

Send one-page query using form on website. No reading fees or expenses charged.

Chalberg & Sussman
115 West 29th St, Third Floor, New York, NY 10001
Tel: +1 (917) 261-7550
Email: rachel@chalbergsussman.com
Website: http://www.chalbergsussman.com

Handles: Fiction; Nonfiction; *Areas:* Autobiography; Culture; Fantasy; Historical; Horror; Psychology; Romance; Science; Sci-Fi; Self-Help; Suspense; Thrillers; Women's Interests; *Markets:* Adult; Children's; Youth; *Treatments:* Commercial; Dark; Literary; Popular

Send query by email. See website for specific agent interests and email addresses.

Chase Literary Agency
11 Broadway, Suite 1010, New York, NY 10004
Tel: +1 (212) 477-5100
Email: farley@chaseliterary.com
Website: http://chaseliterary.com

Handles: Fiction; Nonfiction; *Areas:* Autobiography; Culture; Historical; Humour; Military; Mystery; Nature; Science; Sport; *Markets:* Adult; *Treatments:* Commercial; Contemporary; Literary

New York agency, representing narrative nonfiction and fiction. No science fiction, romance, supernatural or young adult. Send query by email, specifically addressing an agent by name. For fiction, include the first few pages. See website for full guidelines.

The Cheney Agency
39 West 14th Street, Suite 403, New York, NY 10011
Tel: +1 (212) 277-8007
Fax: +1 (212) 614-0728
Email: submissions@cheneyagency.com
Website: http://cheneyassoc.com

Handles: Fiction; Nonfiction; *Areas:* Autobiography; Biography; Business; Culture; Current Affairs; Finance; Historical; Horror; Literature; Politics; Romance; Science; Sport; Suspense; Thrillers; Women's Interests; *Markets:* Adult; *Treatments:* Commercial; Contemporary; Literary

Send query with up to three chapters of sample material by post with SASE, or by email. Response not guaranteed.

Cherry Weiner Literary Agency
925 Oak Bluff Ct, Dacula, GA 30019-6660
Tel: +1 (732) 446-2096
Fax: +1 (732) 792-0506
Email: Cherry8486@aol.com

Handles: Fiction; Nonfiction; *Areas:* Adventure; Crime; Fantasy; Historical; Lifestyle; Mystery; Romance; Sci-Fi; Self-Help; Suspense; Thrillers; Westerns; *Markets:* Adult; *Treatments:* Mainstream

Only considers submissions by referral or personal contact at writers' conferences.

The Chudney Agency
72 North State Road, Suite 501, Briarcliff Manor, NY 10510
Tel: +1 (201) 758-8739
Fax: +1 (201) 758-8739
Email: steven@thechudneyagency.com
Website: http://www.thechudneyagency.com

Handles: Fiction; *Areas:* Historical; Humour; Mystery; *Markets:* Adult; Children's; Youth; *Treatments:* Commercial; Literary; Mainstream

Specialises in children's and young adult books, but will also consider adult fiction. Send query only in first instance. Happy to accept queries by email. Submit material upon invitation only. No fantasy, science fiction, early readers, or scripts. See website for full guidelines.

Compass Talent
6 E 32nd St, New York, NY 10016
Tel: +1 (646) 376-7718
Email: query@compasstalent.com
Website: http://www.compasstalent.com

Handles: Fiction; *Areas:* Autobiography; Cookery; Historical; Science; *Markets:* Adult; Children's; *Treatments:* Commercial; Literary

Full service literary agency representing literary and commercial fiction, children's

---

books, and a range of up-market nonfiction, including memoir, journalism, history, science and cookbooks. No unsolicited queries.

Corvisiero Literary Agency

275 Madison Avenue, at 40th, 14th Floor, New York, NY 10016
Tel: +1 (646) 992-1647
Fax: +1 (646) 217-3758
Email: info@corvisieroagency.com
Website: http://www.corvisieroagency.com

Handles: Fiction; Nonfiction; *Areas:* Adventure; Antiques; Architecture; Arts; Fantasy; Horror; Humour; Mystery; Romance; Sci-Fi; Thrillers; *Markets:* Adult; Children's; Youth; *Treatments:* Contemporary

Accepts queries from both established and emerging authors. See agent profiles on website and select specific agent to query. Send queries via online submission system only (see website for details).

Creative Media Agency

Email: paige@cmalit.com
Website: http://cmalit.com

Handles: Fiction; Nonfiction; *Areas:* Business; Historical; Lifestyle; Mystery; Psychology; Religious; Romance; Thrillers; Women's Interests; *Markets:* Adult; *Treatments:* Commercial; Contemporary

Handles fiction and nonfiction, but no children's, science fiction, or fantasy, and no academic nonfiction. Send query by email only. No submissions by post. See website for full submission guidelines.

Richard Curtis Associates, Inc.

200 East 72nd Street, Suite 28J, New York, NY 10021
Email: info@curtisagency.com
Website: http://www.curtisagency.com

Handles: Fiction; Nonfiction; *Areas:* Autobiography; Biography; Business; Fantasy; Finance; Health; Historical; Medicine; Mystery; Romance; Science; Sci-

Fi; Technology; Thrillers; Westerns; *Markets:* Adult; Children's; Youth

Send query with sample chapter via online submission form on website. No screenplays, stage scripts, playwrights, or screenwriters.

Curtis Brown Ltd

10 Astor Place, New York, NY 10003
Tel: +1 (212) 473-5400
Fax: +1 (212) 598-0917
Email: info@cbltd.com
Website: http://www.curtisbrown.com

Handles: Fiction; Nonfiction; *Markets:* Adult; Children's; Youth

Handles material for adults and children in all genres. See website for individual agent interests and submission policies. No unsolicited MSS. No scripts.

Cynthia Cannell Literary Agency

54 West 40th Street, New York, NY 10018
Tel: +1 (212) 396-9595
Email: info@cannellagency.com
Website: http://cannellagency.com

Handles: Fiction; Nonfiction; *Areas:* Autobiography; Biography; Current Affairs; Health; Religious; Self-Help; Spiritual; *Markets:* Adult; *Treatments:* Contemporary; Literary

Full-service literary agency based in New York. Represents fiction, memoir, biography, self-improvement, spirituality, and nonfiction on contemporary issues. No screenplays, children's books, illustrated books, cookbooks, romance, category mystery, or science fiction. Send query by email only, including brief description of the project, relevant biographical information, and any publishing credits. No attachments or submissions by post. Response not guaranteed.

D4EO Literary Agency

7 Indian Valley Road, Weston, CT 06883
Tel: +1 (203) 544-7180
Fax: +1 (203) 544-7160
Email: bob@d4eo.com
Website: http://www.d4eoliteraryagency.com

Handles: Fiction; Nonfiction; Reference; *Areas:* Adventure; Architecture; Arts; Biography; Business; Cookery; Crime; Current Affairs; Design; Erotic; Fantasy; Finance; Health; Historical; Horror; How-to; Humour; Lifestyle; Military; Mystery; Psychology; Romance; Science; Sci-Fi; Self-Help; Spiritual; Sport; Technology; Thrillers; Westerns; Women's Interests; *Markets:* Adult; Children's; Youth; *Treatments:* Commercial; Contemporary; Literary; Mainstream

See website for individual agent preferences and submission guidelines, then submit directly to one agent only.

Dana Newman Literary, LLC

1800 Avenue of the Stars, 12th Floor, Los Angeles, CA 90067
Email: dananewmanliterary@gmail.com
Website: https://www.dananewman.com

Handles: Fiction; Nonfiction; *Areas:* Autobiography; Biography; Business; Culture; Current Affairs; Health; Historical; Lifestyle; Psychology; Sociology; Sport; Technology; Women's Interests; *Markets:* Adult; *Treatments:* Literary

Send query by email only. Include "QUERY" in the subject line, and a one-page query letter, which identifies the category of your work, the title, the word count, and provides a brief overview of your project, credentials and previous publishing history, if any. Complete book proposals on request only.

Darhansoff & Verrill Literary Agents

133 West 72nd Street, Room 304, New York, NY 10023
Tel: +1 (917) 305-1300
Fax: +1 (917) 305-1400
Email: submissions@dvagency.com
Website: http://www.dvagency.com

Handles: Fiction; Nonfiction; *Areas:* Autobiography; Mystery; Suspense; *Markets:* Adult; Children's; Youth; *Treatments:* Literary

Particularly interested in literary fiction, narrative nonfiction, memoir, sophisticated suspense, and fiction and nonfiction for younger readers. No theatrical plays or film scripts. Send queries by email. See website for full submission guidelines.

David Black Literary Agency

335 Adams Street, Suite 2707, Brooklyn, NY 11201
Tel: +1 (718) 852-5500
Fax: +1 (718) 852-5539
Email: dblack@dblackagency.com
Website: http://www.davidblackagency.com

Handles: Fiction; Nonfiction; *Areas:* Arts; Autobiography; Biography; Business; Cookery; Crafts; Culture; Current Affairs; Entertainment; Finance; Health; Historical; How-to; Humour; Lifestyle; Music; Nature; Philosophy; Politics; Psychology; Science; Sociology; Sport; Thrillers; Travel; Women's Interests; *Markets:* Adult; Children's; Youth; *Treatments:* Commercial; Literary

See website for details of different agents, and specific interests and submission guidelines of each. Otherwise, query the agency generally by post only and allow 8 weeks for a response. See website for full details.

Liza Dawson Associates

121 West 27th Street, Suite 1201, New York, NY 10001
Tel: +1 (212) 465-9071
Fax: +1 (212) 947-0460
Email: queryliza@ LizaDawsonAssociates.com
Website: http://www. lizadawsonassociates.com

Handles: Fiction; Nonfiction; *Areas:* Autobiography; Business; Culture; Current Affairs; Fantasy; Historical; Humour; Lifestyle; Medicine; Military; Mystery; Politics; Psychology; Religious; Romance; Science; Sci-Fi; Self-Help; Sociology; Spiritual; Suspense; Theatre; Thrillers; Women's Interests; *Markets:* Academic; Adult; Children's; Youth; *Treatments:* Commercial; Literary; Mainstream; Popular

See website for specific agent interests and query appropriate agent directly. Specific agent submission guidelines and contact details are available on website.

DeFiore and Company

47 East 19th Street, 3rd Floor, New York, NY 10003
Tel: +1 (212) 925-7744
Fax: +1 (212) 925-9803
Email: submissions@defioreandco.com
Website: http://www.defioreandco.com

Handles: Fiction; Nonfiction; *Areas:* Arts; Biography; Culture; Current Affairs; Historical; Lifestyle; Literature; Medicine; Military; Music; Nature; Philosophy; Politics; Psychology; Romance; Science; Short Stories; Sociology; Technology; Thrillers; *Markets:* Adult; Children's; Youth; *Treatments:* Commercial; Literary; Mainstream

Always looking for exciting, fresh, new talent, and currently accepting queries for both fiction and nonfiction. Send query with summary, description of why you're writing the book, any specific credentials, and (for fiction) first five pages. Send by email (with all material in the body of the text; no attachments; and the word "Query" in the subject line) or post with SASE. See website for specific agent interests and methods of approach. No scripts for film, TV, or theatre.

Diana Finch Literary Agency

116 West 23rd Street, Suite 500, New York, NY 10011
Tel: +1 (917) 544-4470
Email: diana.finch@verizon.net
Website: http://dianafinchliteraryagency.blogspot.com

Handles: Fiction; Nonfiction; *Areas:* Autobiography; Business; Fantasy; Historical; Nature; Politics; Science; Sci-Fi; *Markets:* Adult; Children's; Youth; *Treatments:* Literary

Approach using online submission system – see website for link. No romance, but will consider other genres, especially science fiction and fantasy.

The Doe Coover Agency

PO Box 668, Winchester, MA 01890
Tel: +1 (781) 721-6000
Fax: +1 (781) 721-6727
Email: info@doecooveragency.com
Website: http://doecooveragency.com

Handles: Fiction; Nonfiction; Reference; *Areas:* Autobiography; Biography; Business; Cookery; Current Affairs; Finance; Gardening; Health; Historical; Humour; Music; Politics; Psychology; Science; Sociology; Sport; Technology; *Markets:* Adult; *Treatments:* Commercial; Literary; Popular

Handles nonfiction, popular reference, literary fiction and narrative nonfiction.

Don Congdon Associates, Inc.

110 William St. Suite 2202, New York, NY 10038
Tel: +1 (212) 645-1229
Fax: +1 (212) 727-2688
Email: dca@doncongdon.com
Website: http://doncongdon.com

Handles: Fiction; Nonfiction; *Areas:* Adventure; Anthropology; Archaeology; Arts; Autobiography; Biography; Cookery; Crime; Criticism; Culture; Current Affairs; Fantasy; Film; Health; Historical; Humour; Legal; Lifestyle; Literature; Medicine; Military; Music; Mystery; Nature; Politics; Psychology; Science; Sport; Suspense; Technology; Theatre; Thrillers; Travel; Women's Interests; *Markets:* Adult; Children's; Youth; *Treatments:* Commercial; Literary; Mainstream

Send query by email (no attachments) only. Include one-page synopsis, relevant background info, and first chapter, all within the body of the email if submitting by email. Include the word "Query" in the subject line. See website for full guidelines. No unsolicited MSS.

Donadio & Olson, Inc.

157 E 86th Street, #503, New York, NY 10028
Email: mail@donadio.com
Website: https://www.donadio.com

Handles: Fiction; Nonfiction; *Areas:* Arts; Biography; Culture; Historical; Literature; Nature; Science; *Markets:* Adult; Children's; Youth; *Treatments:* Commercial; Literary; Mainstream

Send query by email or by post with SAE and first 25 pages. Allow at least two months for reply.

Donaghy Literary Group
Email: stacey@donaghyliterary.com
Website: http://www.donaghyliterary.com

Handles: Fiction; *Areas:* Fantasy; Historical; Mystery; Romance; Sci-Fi; Suspense; Thrillers; Women's Interests; *Markets:* Adult; Children's; Youth

See website for individual agent interests, and submit using online submission system.

Donald Maass Literary Agency
1000 Dean Street, Suite 252, Brooklyn, NY 11238
Tel: +1 (212) 727-8383
Fax: +1 (212) 727-3271
Email: info@maassagency.com
Website: http://www.maassagency.com

Handles: Fiction; *Areas:* Crime; Fantasy; Historical; Horror; Humour; Mystery; Romance; Sci-Fi; Suspense; Thrillers; Westerns; Women's Interests; *Markets:* Adult; Youth; *Treatments:* Commercial; Dark; Literary; Mainstream

Welcomes all genres, in particular science fiction, fantasy, mystery, suspense, horror, romance, historical, literary and mainstream novels. Send query to a specific agent, by email, with "query" in the subject line. No queries by post. See website for individual agent interests and email addresses.

Doug Grad Literary Agency
156 Prospect Park West, #3L, Brooklyn, NY 11215
Tel: +1 (718) 788-6067
Email: query@dgliterary.com
Website: http://www.dgliterary.com

Handles: Nonfiction; *Areas:* Autobiography; Business; Cookery; Entertainment; Historical; Military; Music; Mystery; Romance; Science; Self-Help; Sport; Theatre; Thrillers; *Markets:* Adult

Handles narrative nonfiction, military, sports, celebrity memoir, thrillers, mysteries, historical fiction, romance, music, style, business, home improvement, cookbooks, self-help, science and theatre. Send query by email with "query" in the subject line, and synopsis and biography explaining what the book is and who you are. Do not include sample material.

Dunham Literary, Inc.
110 William Street, Suite 2202, New York, NY 10038
Tel: +1 (212) 929-0994
Fax: +1 (212) 929-0904
Email: query@dunhamlit.com
Website: http://www.dunhamlit.com

Handles: Fiction; Nonfiction; *Areas:* Autobiography; Biography; Culture; Current Affairs; Fantasy; Historical; Lifestyle; Music; Mystery; Nature; Politics; Science; Sci-Fi; Spiritual; Technology; Thrillers; Travel; Women's Interests; *Markets:* Adult; Children's; Youth; *Treatments:* Literary

Handles quality fiction and nonfiction for adults and children. Send query by email or by post with SASE. See website for full guidelines. No genre romance, Christian, erotica, Westerns, poetry, cookery, proeffesional, reference, textbooks, plays, or approaches by phone or fax. No email attachments.

Dunow, Carlson & Lerner Agency
27 West 20th Street, Suite 1107, New York, NY 10011
Tel: +1 (212) 645-7606
Email: mail@dclagency.com
Website: http://www.dclagency.com

Handles: Fiction; Nonfiction; *Areas:* Arts; Autobiography; Biography; Criticism; Culture; Current Affairs; Health; Historical; Humour; Music; Mystery; Science; Sport; Suspense; Thrillers; Women's Interests;

Markets: Adult; Children's; Youth; *Treatments:* Commercial; Literary

Prefers queries by email, but will also accept queries by post with SASE. No attachments. Does not respond to all email queries.

Dystel, Goderich & Bourret LLC

One Union Square West, Suite 904, New York, NY 10003
Tel: +1 (212) 627-9100
Fax: +1 (212) 627-9313
Email: miriam@dystel.com
Website: http://www.dystel.com

Handles: Fiction; Nonfiction; *Areas:* Adventure; Anthropology; Archaeology; Autobiography; Biography; Business; Cookery; Crime; Culture; Current Affairs; Fantasy; Finance; Health; Historical; Humour; Lifestyle; Military; Mystery; New Age; Politics; Psychology; Religious; Romance; Science; Sci-Fi; Spiritual; Suspense; Technology; Thrillers; Women's Interests; *Markets:* Adult; Children's; Youth; *Treatments:* Commercial; Contemporary; Literary; Mainstream; Popular

See website for individual agent interests and contact details and approach one agent only. Send query by email with brief synopsis and sample chapter in the body of the email. Attachments to blank emails will not be opened. Queries should be brief, devoid of gimmicks, and professionally presented, including author details and any writing credits. See website for more details.

E. J. McCarthy Agency

Mill Valley, CA
Tel: +1 (415) 383-6639
Email: ejmagency@gmail.com
Website: https://twitter.com/ejmccarthy

Handles: Nonfiction; *Areas:* Autobiography; Biography; Historical; Media; Military; Politics; Sport; *Markets:* Adult

Literary agency from former executive editor with experience at some of the world's largest publishing houses, specialising in military history, politics, history, biography, memoir, media, public policy, and sports.

Ebeling & Associates

Email: michael@ebelingagency.com
Website: http://www.ebelingagency.com

Handles: Nonfiction; *Areas:* Business; Health; New Age; Self-Help; Spiritual; *Markets:* Adult; *Treatments:* Commercial

Offers literary representation, coaching, and platform development. Handles nonfiction only. Send query by email with proposal.

Anne Edelstein Literary Agency

800 Riverside Drive #5E, New York, NY 10032
Tel: +1 (212) 414-4923
Fax: +1 (212) 414-2930
Email: info@aeliterary.com
Website: http://www.aeliterary.com

Handles: Fiction; Nonfiction; *Areas:* Autobiography; Historical; Psychology; Religious; *Markets:* Adult; *Treatments:* Commercial; Literary

Note: Note accepting approaches as at September 2017

Send query letter with SASE and for fiction a summary of your novel plus the first 25 pages, or for nonfiction an outline of your book and one or two sample chapters. No queries by email.

Einstein Literary Management

Tel: +1 (212) 221-8797
Email: submissions@einsteinliterary.com
Website: http://einsteinliterary.com

Handles: Fiction; Nonfiction; *Areas:* Autobiography; Biography; Crime; Fantasy; Historical; Mystery; Romance; Sci-Fi; Thrillers; Women's Interests; *Markets:* Adult; Children's; Youth; *Treatments:* Commercial; Literary

Send query by email with first ten double-spaced pages pasted into the body of the email. No attachments. See website for details of individual agents and their interests and include the name of specific agent you are submitting to in the subject line. No poetry, textbooks, or screenplays. No queries by post or by phone. Response only if interested.

Elaine Markson Literary Agency
450 Seventh Ave, Suite 1408, New York, NY 10123
Tel: +1 (212) 243-8480
Fax: +1 (212) 691-9014
Email: gary@marksonagency.com
Website: http://www.marksonagency.com

Handles: Fiction; Nonfiction; *Markets:* Adult; *Treatments:* Literary

New York literary agency working with co-agents in the UK, Germany, France, and Italy.

Emerald City Literary Agency
718 Griffin Avenue, #195, Enumclaw, WA 98022
Email: Mandy@EmeraldCityLiterary.com
Website: https://emeraldcityliterary.com

Handles: Fiction; Nonfiction; *Areas:* Horror; Romance; *Markets:* Adult; Children's; Youth; *Treatments:* Contemporary

See website for individual agent interests, contact details, and submission guidelines. Welcomes submissions about LGBTQ themes and diverse characters and by traditionally underrepresented authors. All queries must be sent by email – no snail mail submissions. No screenplays, poetry, short stories, adult nonfiction, or fiction for adults that does not fall into the romance genre.

Empire Literary, LLC
115 West 29th Street, 3rd Floor, New York, NY 10001
Tel: +1 (917) 213-7082
Email: Queries@empireliterary.com
Website: http://www.empireliterary.com

Handles: Fiction; Nonfiction; *Areas:* Autobiography; Culture; Health; Lifestyle; Women's Interests; *Markets:* Adult; Children's; Youth; *Treatments:* Literary; Popular

See website for specific agent guidelines and contact details, and query one agent at a

time. Response not guaranteed unless interested.

Felicia Eth Literary Representation
555 Bryant Street, Suite 350, Palo Alto, CA 94301
Email: feliciaeth.literary@gmail.com
Website: https://ethliterary.com

Handles: Fiction; Nonfiction; *Areas:* Business; Cookery; Culture; Historical; Lifestyle; Literature; Psychology; Science; Short Stories; Sport; Suspense; Travel; Women's Interests; *Markets:* Adult; Youth; *Treatments:* Literary; Popular

Send query by email or by post with SASE, including details about yourself and your project. Send sample pages upon invitation only.

Ethan Ellenberg Literary Agency
155 Suffolk Street, #2R, New York, NY 10002
Tel: +1 (212) 431-4554
Fax: +1 (212) 941-4652
Email: agent@ethanellenberg.com
Website: http://www.ethanellenberg.com

Handles: Fiction; Nonfiction; *Areas:* Adventure; Autobiography; Biography; Cookery; Crime; Culture; Current Affairs; Fantasy; Health; Historical; Mystery; New Age; Psychology; Romance; Science; Sci-Fi; Spiritual; Thrillers; Women's Interests; *Markets:* Adult; Children's; *Treatments:* Commercial; Literary

Send query by email (no attachments; paste material into the body of the email) or by post with SASE. For fiction send synopsis and first 50 pages. For nonfiction send proposal, author bio, and sample chapters. For picture books send complete MS. No poetry, short stories, scripts, or queries by fax.

We have been in business for over 17 years. We are a member of the AAR. We accept unsolicited submissions and, of course, do not charge reading fees.

Fairbank Literary Representation

P.O. Box 6, Hudson, NY 12534-0006
Tel: +1 (617) 576-0030
Email: queries@fairbankliterary.com
Website: http://www.fairbankliterary.com

Handles: Fiction; *Areas:* Autobiography; Culture; Design; Humour; Lifestyle; Mystery; Thrillers; Women's Interests; *Markets:* Adult; Children's; *Treatments:* Literary

Send query by email with the first three to five pages pasted below your query (no attachments), or by post with SASE and up to the first 10 pages. Unlikely to consider work over 120,000 words. No genre romance, sci-fi, fantasy, sports fiction, YA, screenplays, or children's works unless by an illustrator / artist. No queries by phone.

Flannery Literary

1140 Wickfield Court, Naperville, IL 60563-3300
Tel: +1 (630) 428-2682
Fax: +1 (630) 428-2683
Email: jennifer@flanneryliterary.com
Website: http://flanneryliterary.com

Handles: Fiction; Nonfiction; *Markets:* Children's; Youth

Send query by email, with the word "Query" in the subject line. Deals exclusively in children's and young adults' fiction and nonfiction, including picture books. See website for full guidelines.

Folio Literary Management, LLC

630 9th Avenue, Suite 1101, New York, NY 10036
Tel: +1 (212) 400-1494
Fax: +1 (212) 967-0977
Email: jeff@foliolit.com
Website: http://www.foliolit.com

Handles: Fiction; Nonfiction; Reference; *Areas:* Autobiography; Business; Cookery; Crime; Culture; Entertainment; Fantasy; Health; Historical; Horror; How-to; Humour; Lifestyle; Media; Military; Music; Mystery; Politics; Psychology; Religious; Romance; Science; Sci-Fi; Self-Help; Spiritual; Sport; Suspense; Technology; Thrillers; Women's Interests; *Markets:* Adult; Children's; Youth; *Treatments:* Commercial; Contemporary; Dark; Literary; Popular; Serious

Read agent bios on website and decide which agent to approach. Do not submit to multiple agents simultaneously. Each agent has different submission requirements: consult website for details. No unsolicited MSS or multiple submissions.

Fox Literary

110 W 40th St, Suite 2305, New York, NY 10018
Tel: +1 (212) 710-5907
Email: submissions@foxliterary.com
Website: http://www.foxliterary.com

Handles: Fiction; Nonfiction; *Areas:* Autobiography; Biography; Culture; Fantasy; Historical; Romance; Sci-Fi; Thrillers; *Markets:* Adult; Youth; *Treatments:* Commercial; Literary

A boutique agency which represents commercial fiction, along with select works of literary fiction and nonfiction that have broad commercial appeal.

I am actively seeking the following: young adult fiction (all genres), science fiction/fantasy, romance, historical fiction, thrillers, and graphic novels. I'm always interested in books that cross genres and reinvent popular concepts with an engaging new twist (especially when there's a historical and/or speculative element involved).

On the nonfiction side I'm interested in memoirs, biography, and smart narrative nonfiction. I particularly enjoy memoirs and other nonfiction about sex work, addiction and recovery, and pop culture.

Email a query letter and the first 5 pages of your novel IN THE BODY OF THE EMAIL.

Email will receive a faster reply than snail mail, but query letters can be sent. If you do choose to send me a hard copy submission, you must include your email address in your letter as I will respond to queries exclusively via email from now on. Do NOT include a SASE, as I will no longer be sending out paper rejections.

Please do not send unsolicited email attachments or manuscripts, as I cannot open the former or return the latter.

Note: does not represent screenplays, poetry, category Westerns, horror, Christian/inspirational, or children's picture books.

Frances Collin Literary Agent

PO Box 33, Wayne, PA 19087-0033
Tel: +1 (610) 254-0555
Fax: +1 (610) 254-5029
Email: queries@francescollin.com
Website: http://www.francescollin.com

Handles: Fiction; Nonfiction; *Areas:* Autobiography; Biography; Culture; Fantasy; Historical; Nature; Sci-Fi; Travel; Women's Interests; *Markets:* Adult; *Treatments:* Literary

Send query by email (no attachments) or by post with SASE, or IRCs if outside the US. No queries by phone or fax.

Frances Goldin Literary Agency, Inc.

214 W 29th St., Suite 410, New York, NY 10001
Email: agency@goldinlit.com
Website: http://www.goldinlit.com

Handles: Fiction; Nonfiction; Poetry; *Areas:* Arts; Autobiography; Biography; Crime; Culture; Current Affairs; Entertainment; Film; Historical; Legal; Nature; Philosophy; Politics; Science; Sociology; Sport; Technology; Thrillers; Translations; Travel; *Markets:* Adult; Children's; Youth; *Treatments:* Commercial; Literary; Progressive

Submit to one agent only. See website for specific agent interests and preferred method of approach. No screenplays, romances (or most other genre fiction), and only rarely poetry. No work that is racist, sexist, ageist, homophobic, or pornographic.

Fraser-Bub Literary, LLC

401 Park Avenue South, 10th Floor, New York, NY 10016
Tel: +1 (917) 524-6982
Email: submissions@fraserbubliterary.com
Website: http://www.fraserbubliterary.com

Handles: Fiction; Nonfiction; *Areas:* Beauty and Fashion; Cookery; Crime; Design; Health; Historical; Lifestyle; Mystery; Psychology; Romance; Self-Help; Thrillers; Women's Interests; *Markets:* Adult; Youth; *Treatments:* Popular

Closed to submissions, with the exception of referrals and conference requests. Check website for current status.

Send query by email only, with first chapter (fiction) or first ten pages (nonfiction) in the body of the email. Attachments will not be opened. No queries by phone.

Fresh Books Literary Agency

Email: matt@fresh-books.com
Website: http://www.fresh-books.com

Handles: Nonfiction; Reference; *Areas:* Business; Design; Finance; Health; How-to; Humour; Lifestyle; Photography; Science; Self-Help; Technology; *Markets:* Adult; *Treatments:* Popular

Handles narrative non-fiction, lifestyle and reference titles on subjects such as popular science, technology, health, fitness, photography, design, computing, gadgets, social media, career development, education, business, leadership, personal finance, how-to, and humour. No fiction, children's books, screenplays, or poetry. Send query by email. No attachments. Send further material upon request only.

The Friedrich Agency LLC

Email: mfriedrich@friedrichagency.com
Website: http://www.friedrichagency.com

Handles: Fiction; Nonfiction; *Markets:* Adult; *Treatments:* Commercial; Literary

See website for agent bios and individual contact details, then submit to one by email only. See website for full guidelines.

Fuse Literary

Email: querylaurie@fuseliterary.com
Website: http://www.fuseliterary.com

Handles: Fiction; Nonfiction; *Markets:*
Adult; Children's

A full-service, hybrid literary agency based
in the Silicon Valley with offices in New
York, Chicago, Dallas, North Dakota, and
Vancouver. See website for individual agent
interests and submission guidelines.

The G Agency, LLC

PO Box 374, Bronx, NY 10471
Tel: +1 (718) 664-4505
Email: gagencyquery@gmail.com

Handles: Fiction; Nonfiction; *Areas:*
Biography; Business; Culture; Finance;
Historical; Military; Mystery; Sport;
Technology; *Markets:* Adult; *Treatments:*
Commercial; Literary; Mainstream; Serious

Send queries by email only with sample
chapters or proposal. Write "QUERY" in the
subject line. No screenplays, sci-fi, or
romance. Response not guaranteed.

Gallt & Zacker Literary Agency

273 Charlton Avenue, South Orange , NJ
07079
Tel: +1 (973) 761-6358
Email: nancy@galltzacker.com
Website: http://www.galltzacker.com

Handles: Fiction; Nonfiction; *Areas:* Horror;
Romance; Women's Interests; *Markets:*
Children's; Youth; *Treatments:* Literary

Handles fiction and nonfiction for children,
young adults, and adults. See website for
submission guidelines and specific agent
interests / contact details and approach
relevant agent by email.

Gelfman Schneider / ICM Partners

850 Seventh Avenue, Suite 903, New York,
NY 10019
Email: mail@gelfmanschneider.com
Website: http://www.gelfmanschneider.com

Handles: Fiction; Nonfiction; *Areas:*
Autobiography; Culture; Current Affairs;
Historical; Mystery; Politics; Science;
Suspense; Thrillers; Women's Interests;
Markets: Adult; Youth; *Treatments:*
Commercial; Literary; Mainstream; Popular

Different agents within the agency have
different submission guidelines. See website
for full details. No screenplays, or poetry.

Georges Borchardt, Inc.

136 East 57th Street, New York, NY 10022
Tel: +1 (212) 753-5785
Email: anne@gbagency.com
Website: http://www.gbagency.com

Handles: Fiction; Nonfiction; *Areas:* Arts;
Biography; Current Affairs; Historical;
Literature; Philosophy; Politics; Religious;
Science; Short Stories; *Markets:* Adult;
Youth; *Treatments:* Commercial; Literary

New York based literary agency founded in
1967. No unsolicited MSS or screenplays.

Global Lion Intellectual Property Management, Inc.

PO BOX 669238, Pompano Beach, FL
33066
Tel: +1 (754) 222-6948
Email: queriesgloballionmgt@gmail.com
Website: http://www.
globallionmanagement.com

Handles: Fiction; Nonfiction; *Areas:*
Spiritual; *Markets:* Adult

Specialises in nonfiction, spirituality, and
generally anything that "improvement" for
the world and human race. Looks for cutting-
edge authors of both fiction and nonfiction
with global marketing and motion
picture/television production potential.
Authors must not only have a great book and
future, but also a specific game-plan of how
to use social media to grow their fan base.
Send query by email only with synopsis, up
to 20 pages if available (otherwise, chapter
synopsis), author bio, and any social media
outlets. See website for full details.

Grace Freedson's Publishing Network

7600 Jericho Turnpike, Suite 300, Woodbury, NY 11797
Tel: +1 (516) 931-7757
Fax: +1 (516) 931-7759
Email: gfreedson@gmail.com

Handles: Nonfiction; *Areas:* Autobiography; Business; Cookery; Crafts; Crime; Culture; Current Affairs; Design; Finance; Gardening; Health; Historical; Hobbies; How-to; Humour; Legal; Leisure; Lifestyle; Medicine; Military; Nature; Philosophy; Psychology; Religious; Science; Self-Help; Sport; Technology; Women's Interests; *Markets:* Adult; Children's; Youth

Literary agency and book packager. Handles nonfiction from qualified authors with credentials and platforms only. No fiction. Send query with synopsis and SASE.

The Greenhouse Literary Agency

Tel: +1 (571) 758-5615
Email: submissions@
greenhouseliterary.com
Website: http://www.greenhouseliterary.com

Handles: Fiction; *Markets:* Children's; Youth

Closed to submissions as at January 2019. Check website for current status.

Handles fiction for children and young adults only. No nonfiction, poetry, picturebooks, or illustrators. Send query by email only including plot outline up to three paragraphs, a paragraph about you and any other information relevant to you or your work, and in the case of a novel the first five pages, pasted into the body of the email.

Blanche C. Gregory Inc.

2 Tudor City Place, New York, NY 10017
Tel: +1 (212) 697-0828
Email: info@bcgliteraryagency.com
Website: http://www.bcgliteraryagency.com

Handles: Fiction; Nonfiction; *Markets:* Adult; Children's

Specialises in adult fiction and nonfiction, but will also consider children's literature. Send query describing your background with SASE and synopsis. No stage, film or TV scripts, or queries by fax or email.

Hannigan Salky Getzler (HSG) Agency

37 West 28th St, 8th floor, New York, NY 10001
Tel: +1 (646) 442-5770
Email: channigan@hsgagency.com
Website: http://hsgagency.com

Handles: Fiction; Nonfiction; *Areas:* Adventure; Autobiography; Business; Cookery; Crafts; Culture; Current Affairs; Design; Finance; Gardening; Health; Historical; Humour; Lifestyle; Mystery; Photography; Politics; Psychology; Science; Sociology; Suspense; Thrillers; Travel; Women's Interests; *Markets:* Adult; Children's; Youth; *Treatments:* Commercial; Literary; Popular

Send query by email only with first five pages pasted into the body of the email (no attachments), or the full ms for picture books. See website for agent interests and individual email addresses, and contact one agent only. No screenplays, romance fiction, science fiction, or religious fiction.

Joy Harris Literary Agency, Inc.

1501 Broadway, Suite 2310, New York, NY 10036
Tel: +1 (212) 924-6269
Fax: +1 (212) 840-5776
Email: submissions@joyharrisliterary.com
Website: http://www.joyharrisliterary.com

Handles: Fiction; Nonfiction; *Areas:* Autobiography; Biography; Culture; Historical; Humour; Media; Mystery; Short Stories; Spiritual; Suspense; Translations; Women's Interests; *Markets:* Adult; Youth; *Treatments:* Experimental; Literary; Mainstream; Satirical

Send query by email, including sample chapter or outline. No poetry, screenplays, genre fiction, self-help, or unsolicited mss. See website for full guidelines.

Helen Zimmermann Literary Agency

55 Riverwalk Place, New York, NY 07093
Email: Submit@ZimmAgency.com
Website: http://www.zimmagency.com

Handles: Fiction; Nonfiction; *Areas:*
Autobiography; Biography; Cookery;
Culture; Health; Historical; How-to;
Humour; Lifestyle; Music; Mystery; Nature;
Science; Spiritual; Sport; Suspense;
Technology; Thrillers; Women's Interests;
Markets: Adult; *Treatments:* Literary

Particularly interested in health and wellness,
relationships, popular culture, women's
issues, lifestyle, sports, and music. No
poetry, science fiction, horror, or romance.
Prefers email queries, but no attachments
unless requested. Send pitch letter – for
fiction include summary, bio, and first
chapter in the body of the email.

Herman Agency Inc.

350 Central Park West, New York, NY
10025
Tel: +1 (212) 749-4907
Email: ronnie@hermanagencyinc.com
Website: https://www.hermanagencyinc.com

Handles: Fiction; Nonfiction; *Markets:*
Children's; Youth

Represents fiction and nonfiction for
children and young adults, including picture
books and middle grade books, educational
books and supplementary materials,
children's toys, magazines, cartoons,
licensed characters, stationery, advertising,
and editorial illustrations. Not taking on any
new clients.

Hill Nadell Literary Agency

6442 Santa Monica Blvd, Suite 201, Los
Angeles, CA 90038
Tel: +1 (310) 860-9605
Fax: +1 (323) 380-5206
Email: queries@hillnadell.com
Website: http://www.hillnadell.com

Handles: Fiction; Nonfiction; *Areas:*
Autobiography; Biography; Cookery;
Culture; Current Affairs; Health; Historical;
Legal; Nature; Politics; Science; Thrillers;

Women's Interests; *Markets:* Adult; Youth;
Treatments: Literary; Mainstream

Handles current affairs, food, memoirs and
other narrative nonfiction, fiction, thrillers,
upmarket women's fiction, literary fiction,
genre fiction, graphic novels, and occasional
young adult novels. No scripts or
screenplays. Accepts queries both by post
and by email. See website for full
submission guidelines.

Holloway Literary

Raleigh, NC
Email: submissions@
hollowayliteraryagency.com
Website: https://hollowayliteraryagency.com

Handles: Fiction; Nonfiction; *Areas:*
Autobiography; Crime; Historical; Humour;
Lifestyle; Military; Mystery; Nature;
Politics; Romance; Sci-Fi; Self-Help; Short
Stories; Suspense; Thrillers; Travel;
Women's Interests; *Markets:* Adult; Youth;
Treatments: Commercial; Contemporary;
Literary; Satirical

See website for individual agent preferences
and select one to submit to. Send query by
email with first 15 pages pasted into the
body of your email. Approach only one
agent at a time.

Inklings Literary Agency, LLC

3419 Virginia Beach Blvd #183, Virginia
Beach, VA 23452
Tel: +1 (757) 802-0996
Fax: +1 (904) 758-5440
Email: query@inklingsliterary.com
Website: http://www.inklingsliterary.com

Handles: Fiction; Nonfiction; *Areas:*
Archaeology; Arts; Fantasy; Historical;
Horror; Mystery; Romance; Sci-Fi;
Sociology; Suspense; Thrillers; Women's
Interests; *Markets:* Adult; Children's; Youth;
Treatments: Commercial; Contemporary

Generally accepts submissions by email
only, with brief synopsis, brief author bio,
and first 10 pages – however closed to
submission as of July 1, 2017. Check website
for current status.

InkWell Management

521 Fifth Avenue, 26th Floor, New York,
NY 10175
Tel: +1 (212) 922-3500
Fax: +1 (212) 922-0535
Email: submissions@
inkwellmanagement.com
Website: http://www.
inkwellmanagement.com

Handles: Fiction; Nonfiction; *Areas:*
Business; Crime; Current Affairs; Finance;
Health; Historical; Humour; Medicine;
Mystery; Psychology; Self-Help; Thrillers;
Markets: Adult; *Treatments:* Contemporary;
Literary; Mainstream

Accepts submissions in all genres, but no
screenplays. Send query by email with up to
two sample chapters. No large attachments.
Response not guaranteed. Response within
two months if interested. See website for full
guidelines.

Irene Goodman Literary Agency (IGLA)

27 West 24th St., Suite 804, New York, NY
10010
Email: irene.queries@irenegoodman.com
Website: http://www.irenegoodman.com

Handles: Fiction; Nonfiction; *Areas:*
Autobiography; Beauty and Fashion;
Cookery; Culture; Design; Fantasy;
Historical; Horror; Lifestyle; Mystery;
Politics; Romance; Science; Sci-Fi;
Sociology; Suspense; Thrillers; Women's
Interests; *Markets:* Adult; Children's; Youth;
Treatments: Commercial; Contemporary;
Literary; Popular

Select specific agent to approach based on
details given on website (specific agent
email addresses on website). Send query by
email only with synopsis, bio, and first ten
pages in the body of the email. No poetry,
inspirational fiction, screenplays, or
children's picture books. Response only if
interested. See website for further details.

J. de S. Associates, Inc.

9 Shagbark Road, South Norwalk, CT 06854
Tel: +1 (203) 838-7571
Fax: +1 (203) 866-2713

Email: jdespoel@aol.com
Website: http://www.jdesassociates.com

Handles: Fiction; Nonfiction; *Markets:*
Adult; *Treatments:* Commercial; Literary

Welcomes brief queries by post and by
email, but no samples or other material
unless requested.

Jabberwocky Literary Agency

49 West 45th Street, 12th Floor North, New
York, NY 10036
Tel: +1 (917) 388-3010
Fax: +1 (917) 388-2998
Email: queryeddie@awfulagent.com
Website: http://awfulagent.com

Handles: Fiction; Nonfiction; *Areas:*
Fantasy; Historical; Science; Sci-Fi;
Markets: Adult; Children's; Youth;
Treatments: Literary

Handles a broad range of fiction and
nonfiction intended for general audiences,
but no series romance or poetry. Book-length
material only. Also considers graphic novels
and comics. Send query by post with SASE
or IRC, or by email. No queries by phone or
by fax. See website for full guidelines.

Jane Rotrosen Agency

318 East 51st Street, New York, NY 10022
Tel: +1 (212) 593-4330
Fax: +1 (212) 935-6985
Email: acirillo@janerotrosen.com
Website: http://www.janerotrosen.com

Handles: Fiction; Nonfiction; *Areas:*
Autobiography; Business; Crime; Culture;
Health; Historical; Humour; Mystery;
Psychology; Romance; Suspense; Thrillers;
Women's Interests; *Markets:* Adult; Youth;
Treatments: Commercial; Literary;
Mainstream; Popular

Send query by email to one of the agent
email addresses provided on the agency bios
page of the website, or by post with SASE,
describing your work and giving relevant
biographical details and publishing history,
along with synopsis and the first three
chapters in the case of fiction, or proposal in
the case of nonfiction. Submissions without
an SASE will be recycled without response.

Attachments to a blank email will not be opened. See website for full guidelines and individual agent details.

Janklow & Nesbit Associates

285 Madison Ave, 21st Floor, New York, NY 10017
Tel: +1 (212) 421-1700
Fax: +1 (212) 355-1403
Email: submissions@janklow.com
Website: http://www.janklowandnesbit.com

Handles: Fiction; Nonfiction; *Markets:* Adult; *Treatments:* Literary

Commercial as well as literary fiction. See website for full list of agents and address your query to a specific agent. Send query with first 10 pages by post or by email. See website for full guidelines.

The Jean V. Naggar Literary Agency

216 East 75th Street, Suite 1E, New York, NY 10021
Tel: +1 (212) 794-1082
Email: jvnla@jvnla.com
Website: http://www.jvnla.com

Handles: Fiction; Nonfiction; *Areas:* Adventure; Autobiography; Biography; Cookery; Crime; Culture; Current Affairs; Fantasy; Gothic; Health; Historical; Horror; Humour; Lifestyle; Music; Mystery; Psychology; Romance; Science; Self-Help; Sport; Suspense; Thrillers; Women's Interests; *Markets:* Adult; Children's; Youth; *Treatments:* Commercial; Dark; Literary; Mainstream; Popular

Accepts queries via online submission system only. See website for more details.

Jeanne Fredericks Literary Agency, Inc.

221 Benedict Hill Road, New Canaan, CT 06840
Tel: +1 (203) 972-3011
Fax: +1 (203) 972-3011
Email: jeanne.fredericks@gmail.com
Website: http://jeannefredericks.com

Handles: Nonfiction; Reference; *Areas:* Antiques; Arts; Biography; Business;

Cookery; Crafts; Design; Finance; Gardening; Health; Historical; How-to; Legal; Leisure; Lifestyle; Medicine; Nature; Photography; Psychology; Science; Self-Help; Sport; Travel; Women's Interests; *Markets:* Adult; *Treatments:* Popular

Send query by email (no attachments) or post with SASE. Specialises in adult nonfiction by authorities in their fields. No fiction, true crime, juvenile, textbooks, poetry, essays, screenplays, short stories, science fiction, pop culture, guides to computers and software, politics, horror, pornography, books on overly depressing or violent topics, romance, teacher's manuals, or memoirs. See website for full guidelines.

The Jeff Herman Agency, LLC

PO Box 1522, Stockbridge, MA 01262
Tel: +1 (413) 298-0077
Email: submissions@jeffherman.com
Website: http://www.jeffherman.com

Handles: Nonfiction; Reference; *Areas:* Autobiography; Business; Crime; Culture; Health; Historical; How-to; Lifestyle; Psychology; Self-Help; Spiritual; *Markets:* Academic; Adult; Professional

Send query by post with SASE, or by email. With few exceptions, handles nonfiction only, with particular interest in the genres given above. No scripts or unsolicited MSS.

The Jennifer DeChiara Literary Agency

245 Park Avenue, 39th Floor, New York, NY 10167
Tel: +1 (212) 372-8989
Email: jenndec@aol.com
Website: http://www.jdlit.com

Handles: Fiction; Nonfiction; *Areas:* Adventure; Arts; Autobiography; Biography; Cookery; Culture; Fantasy; Film; Health; Historical; Horror; How-to; Humour; Lifestyle; Literature; Mystery; Romance; Science; Self-Help; Sociology; Sport; Suspense; Theatre; Thrillers; Travel; Women's Interests; *Markets:* Adult; Children's; Youth; *Treatments:* Commercial; Contemporary; Literary; Mainstream; Popular

Send query online only. Posted submissions will be discarded. See website for full guidelines and for specific agent interests and email addresses.

JET Literary Associates, Inc.

941 Calle Mejia, #507, Santa Fe, NM 87501
Tel: +1 (505) 780-0721
Email: etp@jetliterary.com
Website: http://jetliterary.com

Handles: Fiction; Nonfiction; *Areas:* Business; Cookery; Crime; Gardening; Historical; How-to; Humour; Lifestyle; Politics; Romance; Suspense; Thrillers; *Markets:* Adult; *Treatments:* Literary

Send query by email only, including a brief description of your work and your background. Do not send attachments, sample chapters, or proposals in first instance. No poetry, plays, film scripts, science fiction, fantasy, YA or books for young children.

Joanna Pulcini Literary Management

Email: info@jplm.com
Website: http://www.jplm.com

Handles: Fiction; Nonfiction; *Markets:* Adult

Closed to submissions as at December 2017. See website for current status.

John Hawkins & Associates, Inc.

80 Maiden Lane, STE 1503, New York, NY 10038
Tel: +1 (212) 807-7040
Fax: +1 (212) 807-9555
Email: jha@jhalit.com
Website: http://www.jhalit.com

Handles: Fiction; Nonfiction; *Areas:* Autobiography; Biography; Business; Crime; Current Affairs; Fantasy; Gardening; Health; Historical; Lifestyle; Mystery; Nature; Politics; Psychology; Science; Sci-Fi; Short Stories; Technology; Thrillers; Travel; Women's Interests; *Markets:* Adult

Send query by email with details about you and your writing, and for fiction the first three chapters as a single Word attachment, or for nonfiction include proposal as a single attachment. Include the word "Query" in the subject line. See website for full guidelines.

Joëlle Delbourgo Associates, Inc.

101 Park St., Montclair, Montclair, NJ 07042
Tel: +1 (973) 773-0836
Email: joelle@delbourgo.com
Website: http://www.delbourgo.com

Handles: Fiction; Nonfiction; *Areas:* Autobiography; Cookery; Current Affairs; Historical; Humour; Lifestyle; Politics; Psychology; Science; *Markets:* Adult; *Treatments:* Popular

We are a highly selective agency, broad in our interests. No category romance, Westerns, early readers, or picture books. Send query by email to specific agent (see website for interests and email addresses). Submissions must include the word "QUERY" in the subject line. See website for full guidelines.

JYLA (Jason Yarn Literary Agency)

3544 Broadway #68, New York, NY 10031
Email: jason@jasonyarnliteraryagency.com
Website: http://www.jasonyarnliteraryagency.com

Handles: Fiction; Nonfiction; *Areas:* Adventure; Current Affairs; Fantasy; Historical; Science; Sci-Fi; Suspense; Thrillers; *Markets:* Adult; Children's; Youth; *Treatments:* Commercial; Literary

Accepts electronic submissions only. Send email with the word "Query" in the subject line, and the first ten pages of your manuscript or proposal in the body of the email. No attachments, or queries for film, TV, or stage scripts.

Karen Gantz Literary Management

Tel: +1 (212) 734-3619
Email: kgzahler@aol.com

Website: https://
karengantzliterarymanagement.com

Handles: Fiction; Nonfiction; *Areas:*
Autobiography; Cookery; Design;
Entertainment; Historical; Lifestyle; Politics;
Psychology; Religious; Sociology; Spiritual;
Markets: Adult

Considers all genres but specialises in
nonfiction. Send query and summary by
email only.

Kathi J. Paton Literary Agency
Tel: +1 (212) 265-6586
Email: kjplitbiz@optonline.net
Website: http://www.PatonLiterary.com

Handles: Fiction; Nonfiction; *Areas:*
Biography; Business; Culture; Current
Affairs; Finance; Health; Historical;
Humour; Lifestyle; Politics; Religious;
Science; Sport; Technology; *Markets:* Adult;
Treatments: Literary; Mainstream; Popular

Send query with brief description by email
only. No attachments or referrals to websites.
Specialises in adult nonfiction. No science
fiction, fantasy, horror, category romance,
juvenile, young adult or self-published
books. Response only if interested. Also
offers editorial services.

Ken Sherman & Associates
1275 N. Hayworth, Suite 103, Los Angeles,
CA 90046
Tel: +1 (310) 273-8840
Fax: +1 (310) 271-2875
Email: ken@kenshermanassociates.com
Website: http://www.
kenshermanassociates.com

Handles: Fiction; Nonfiction; Scripts; *Areas:*
Film; TV; *Markets:* Adult

Handles fiction, nonfiction, and writers for
film and TV. Query by referral only.

Kimberley Cameron & Associates
1550 Tiburon Blvd #704, Tiberon, CA
94920
Tel: +1 (415) 789-9191

Email: info@kimberleycameron.com
Website: http://www.kimberleycameron.com

Handles: Fiction; Nonfiction; *Areas:*
Autobiography; Biography; Cookery;
Culture; Current Affairs; Fantasy; Health;
Historical; Horror; Lifestyle; Mystery;
Politics; Religious; Science; Sci-Fi; Self-
Help; Spiritual; Technology; Thrillers;
Travel; Women's Interests; *Markets:* Adult;
Family; Youth; *Treatments:* Contemporary;
Literary; Mainstream

See website for specific agent interests and
submit to most suitable agent through their
online submission system.

Harvey Klinger, Inc
300 West 55th Street, Suite 11V, New York,
NY 10019
Tel: +1 (212) 581-7068
Email: queries@harveyklinger.com
Website: http://www.harveyklinger.com

Handles: Fiction; Nonfiction; *Areas:*
Adventure; Autobiography; Biography;
Business; Cookery; Crafts; Crime; Culture;
Current Affairs; Design; Fantasy; Film;
Health; Historical; Horror; How-to; Humour;
Lifestyle; Literature; Media; Medicine;
Music; Mystery; Politics; Psychology;
Romance; Science; Sci-Fi; Self-Help;
Spiritual; Sport; Suspense; Technology;
Thrillers; Travel; TV; Westerns; Women's
Interests; *Markets:* Adult; Children's; Youth;
Treatments: Commercial; Contemporary;
Literary; Mainstream; Popular

Send query by email. No submissions by
post. Do not query more than one agent at
the agency at a time. See website for
individual agent interests and email
addresses. No screenplays, or queries by
phone or fax. See website for full submission
guidelines.

Kneerim & Williams
90 Canal Street, Boston, MA 02114
Tel: +1 (617) 303-1650
Fax: +1 (617) 542-1660
Email: submissions@kwlit.com
Website: https://kwlit.com

Handles: Fiction; Nonfiction; *Areas:*
Adventure; Anthropology; Archaeology;

Autobiography; Biography; Business; Crime; Culture; Current Affairs; Finance; Health; Historical; Legal; Lifestyle; Literature; Medicine; Nature; Politics; Psychology; Religious; Science; Sociology; Sport; Technology; Women's Interests; *Markets:* Adult; *Treatments:* Commercial; Literary; Mainstream; Serious

Send query by email with synopsis, brief bio, and 10-20 pages of initial sample material in the body of the email. No attachments or queries by post or by phone. See website for full guidelines.

Linda Konner Literary Agency

10 West 15 Street, Suite 1918, New York, NY 10011
Email: ldkonner@cs.com
Website: http://www.
lindakonnerliteraryagency.com

Handles: Nonfiction; Reference; *Areas:* Biography; Business; Cookery; Culture; Entertainment; Finance; Health; How-to; Lifestyle; Psychology; Science; Self-Help; Women's Interests; *Markets:* Adult; *Treatments:* Popular

Send one to two page query by email or by post with SASE, synopsis, and author bio. Attachments from unknown senders will be deleted unread. Nonfiction only. Books must be written by or with established experts in their field. No Fiction, Memoir, Religion, Spiritual/Christian, Children's/young adult, Games/puzzles, Humour, History, Politics, or unsolicited MSS. See website for full guidelines.

Barbara S. Kouts, Literary Agent

PO Box 560, Bellport, NY 11713
Tel: +1 (631) 286-1278
Fax: +1 (631) 286-1538
Email: bkouts@aol.com

Handles: Fiction; *Areas:* Autobiography; Biography; Crime; Current Affairs; Health; Historical; Lifestyle; Mystery; Nature; Psychology; Suspense; Thrillers; Women's Interests; *Markets:* Adult; Children's; *Treatments:* Literary

Note: Not accepting submissions as at January 2017.

Send query with SASE. Postal queries only. Particularly interested in adult fiction and nonfiction and children's books.

KT Literary

9249 S. Broadway #200-543, Highlands Ranch, CO 80129
Tel: +1 (720) 344-4728
Fax: +1 (720) 344-4728
Email: contact@ktliterary.com
Website: http://ktliterary.com

Handles: Fiction; *Areas:* Erotic; Fantasy; Romance; Sci-Fi; *Markets:* Adult; Children's; Youth; *Treatments:* Contemporary; Dark

Actively seeking new clients for middle grade, young adult, and adult categories. See website for individual agent interests and contact details and query one agent at a time. See website for full details.

L. Perkins Associates

5800 Arlington Ave, Riverdale, NY 10471
Tel: +1 (718) 543-5344
Fax: +1 (718) 543-5354
Email: submissions@lperkinsagency.com
Website: http://lperkinsagency.com

Handles: Fiction; Nonfiction; *Areas:* Arts; Autobiography; Biography; Cookery; Crime; Culture; Erotic; Fantasy; Film; Historical; Horror; How-to; Humour; Music; Mystery; Psychology; Romance; Science; Sci-Fi; Theatre; Thrillers; Westerns; *Markets:* Adult; Children's; Youth; *Treatments:* Commercial; Dark; Literary; Popular

Send query by email with synopsis, bio, and first five pages of your novel / proposal in the body of the email. No email attachments and no queries by post or any other means apart from email. Pitch only one book at a time, and to only one agent. Specific agent email addresses are available at website, or use general address provided below. No screenplays, short story collections, or poetry.

Peter Lampack Agency, Inc

The Empire State Building, 350 Fifth
Avenue, Suite 5300, New York, NY 10118
Tel: +1 (212) 687-9106
Fax: +1 (212) 687-9109
Email: andrew@peterlampackagency.com
Website: https://www.
peterlampackagency.com

Handles: Fiction; Nonfiction; *Markets:*
Adult; *Treatments:* Commercial; Literary;
Mainstream

Specialises in commercial and literary fiction
as well as nonfiction by recognised experts
in a given field. Send query by email only,
with cover letter, author bio, sample chapter,
and 1-2 page synopsis. No children's books,
horror, romance, westerns, science fiction or
screenplays.

Laura Dail Literary Agency

121 West 27th Street, Suite 1201, New York,
NY 10001
Tel: +1 (212) 239-7477
Fax: +1 (212) 947-0460
Email: queries@ldlainc.com
Website: http://www.ldlainc.com

Handles: Fiction; Nonfiction; *Areas:*
Autobiography; Biography; Cookery; Crime;
Culture; Current Affairs; Fantasy; Historical;
Humour; Mystery; Psychology; Romance;
Science; Sci-Fi; Technology; Thrillers;
Women's Interests; *Markets:* Adult;
Children's; Youth; *Treatments:* Commercial;
Contemporary; Light; Literary; Serious

Send query by email only with synopsis and
first 5 to 10 pages. No screenplays, poetry,
illustrated adult books or queries or
manuscripts in Spanish.

Lawrence Jordan Literary Agency

231 Lenox Avenue, Suite One, New York,
NY 10027
Tel: +1 (212) 662-7871
Fax: +1 (212) 865-7171
Email: ljlagency@aol.com

Handles: Fiction; Nonfiction; *Areas:*
Autobiography; Biography; Mystery;
Religious; Spiritual; Suspense; Thrillers;
Markets: Adult

Send query by email only. Particularly
interested in spiritual / religion; biographies,
autobiographies and celebrity books;
mysteries, suspense, and thrillers. No poetry,
movie or stage scripts, juvenile, fantasy, or
science fiction.

Lee Sobel Literary Agency

9 Church Street, Middletown, NJ 07748
Tel: +1 (917) 553-4991
Email: LeeSobel15@gmail.com
Website: https://www.facebook.com/
leesobelliteraryagency/

Handles: Fiction; Nonfiction; *Areas:*
Autobiography; Biography; Crime; Culture;
Current Affairs; Entertainment; Erotic;
Fantasy; Film; Horror; Humour; Music;
Mystery; Sci-Fi; Suspense; Thrillers;
Markets: Adult; Youth; *Treatments:*
Commercial; Contemporary; Dark; Literary;
Mainstream; Popular; Positive; Progressive;
Satirical; Serious; Traditional

Currently selling a lot of nonfiction books
but more focused on finding commercial
novels now. Seeking ambitious epic novels
with attractive characters to lend themselves
for movie adaptations. Think big! Check out
the detailed Q&A with me on my agency
Facebook site as it will give you a lot of info
about why I might be the right agent for you.

Leigh Feldman Literary

Email: query@lfliterary.com
Website: http://www.lfliterary.com

Handles: Fiction; Nonfiction; *Areas:*
Autobiography; Historical; *Markets:* Adult;
Youth; *Treatments:* Contemporary

Particularly interested in historical fiction,
contemporary YA, literary fiction, memoir,
and narrative nonfiction. No adult and YA
paranormal, fantasy, science fiction,
romance, thrillers, mysteries, or picture
books. Send query by email with first ten
pages. Only makes personal response if
interested.

The Leshne Agency

590 West End Avenue, Suite 11D, New York, NY 10024
Email: Submissions@LeshneAgency.com
Website: http://leshneagency.com

Handles: Fiction; Nonfiction; *Areas:* Arts; Autobiography; Business; Cookery; Crafts; Culture; Film; Gardening; Health; Historical; Hobbies; Humour; Photography; Science; Self-Help; Spiritual; Sport; Technology; Travel; Women's Interests; *Markets:* Adult; Children's; Youth; *Treatments:* Commercial; Literary

Seeking new and existing authors across all genres. Particularly interested in narrative, memoir, prescriptive nonfiction (including sports, health, wellness, business, political and parenting topics), commercial fiction, young adult and middle grade books. No screenplays, scripts, poetry, or picture books. Submit online through online submissions system or by email. See website for full details.

Levine Greenberg Rostan Literary Agency

307 Seventh Ave., Suite 2407, New York, NY 10001
Tel: +1 (212) 337-0934
Fax: +1 (212) 337-0948
Email: submit@lgrliterary.com
Website: http://lgrliterary.com

Handles: Fiction; Nonfiction; *Areas:* Arts; Autobiography; Beauty and Fashion; Biography; Business; Cookery; Crafts; Crime; Culture; Finance; Gardening; Health; Historical; Hobbies; Humour; Leisure; Lifestyle; Mystery; Nature; New Age; Politics; Psychology; Religious; Romance; Science; Self-Help; Sociology; Spiritual; Sport; Suspense; Technology; Thrillers; Travel; Women's Interests; *Markets:* Adult; Children's; Youth; *Treatments:* Commercial; Literary; Mainstream; Popular

No queries by post. Send query using online form at website, or send email attaching no more than 50 pages. See website for detailed submission guidelines. No response to submissions by post.

Linda Chester & Associates

630 Fifth Avenue, Suite 2000, Rockefeller Center, New York, NY 10111
Tel: +1 (212) 218-3350
Email: submissions@lindachester.com
Website: http://www.lindachester.com

Handles: Fiction; Nonfiction; *Markets:* Adult; *Treatments:* Commercial; Literary

Send query by email only with short bio and first five pages pasted directly into the body of the email. Response within 4 weeks if interested only. No submissions by post.

The Lisa Ekus Group, LLC

57 North Street, Hatfield, MA 01038
Tel: +1 (413) 247-9325
Email: info@lisaekus.com
Website: http://www.lisaekus.com

Handles: Nonfiction; *Areas:* Cookery; *Markets:* Adult

Handles cookery books only. Submit proposal through submission system on website.

Literary Services, Inc.

PO Box 888, Barnegat, NJ 08005
Email: jwlitagent@msn.com
Website: http://literaryservicesinc.com

Handles: Fiction; Nonfiction; Reference; *Areas:* Business; Crime; Finance; Health; Historical; Lifestyle; Politics; Psychology; Science; Spiritual; Sport; Technology; *Markets:* Adult; *Treatments:* Commercial; Literary

Send one-page synopsis by email only. particularly interested in business and management; business narratives; careers; gift and reference books; health, fitness and aging; history and politics; literary nonfiction and historical fiction; mind, body, spirit; personal finance, investing and trading; personal growth and psychology; science; sports; technology and trends; true crime.

Literary Management Group, Inc.

PO Box 1686, Richmond Hill, GA 31324
Tel: +1 (615) 812-4445

Email: BruceBarbour@
LiteraryManagementGroup.com
Website: http://
literarymanagementgroup.com

Handles: Nonfiction; *Areas:* Biography;
Business; Lifestyle; Religious; Spiritual;
Markets: Adult

Handles Christian books (defined as books
which are consistent with the historical,
orthodox teachings of the Christian fathers).
Handles adult nonfiction only. No children's
or illustrated books, poetry, memoirs, YA
Fiction or text/academic books. Download
proposal from website then complete and
send with sample chapters.

Literary & Creative Artists Inc.

3543 Albemarle Street NW, Washington, DC
20008-4213
Tel: +1 (202) 362-4688
Fax: +1 (202) 362-8875
Email: lca9643@lcadc.com
Website: http://www.lcadc.com

Handles: Fiction; Nonfiction; *Areas:* Arts;
Autobiography; Biography; Business;
Cookery; Crime; Current Affairs; Drama;
Health; Historical; How-to; Legal; Lifestyle;
Medicine; Nature; Philosophy; Politics;
Religious; Spiritual; *Markets:* Adult

Send query by post with SASE, or by email
without attachments. No poetry, academic /
educational textbooks, or unsolicited MSS.
Currently only accepts projects from
established authors.

The LKG Agency

60 Riverside Blvd, #1101, New York, NY
10069
Email: query@LKGAgency.com
Website: http://lkgagency.com

Handles: Fiction; Nonfiction; *Areas:*
Autobiography; Beauty and Fashion; Design;
Entertainment; Health; Lifestyle;
Psychology; Women's Interests; *Markets:*
Adult; Children's; Youth

Specialises in nonfiction, but will also
consider middle grade and young adult
fiction. No history, spirituality, biography,
screenplays, true crime, poetry, religion,

picture books, or any other fiction besides
middle grade and young adult. See website
for full submission guidelines.

Lowenstein Associates, Inc.

115 East 23rd Street, 4th Floor, New York,
NY 10010
Tel: +1 (212) 206-1630
Email: assistant@bookhaven.com
Website: http://www.
lowensteinassociates.com

Handles: Fiction; Nonfiction; *Areas:*
Autobiography; Business; Crime; Culture;
Health; Medicine; Mystery; Psychology;
Science; Sociology; Thrillers; Women's
Interests; *Markets:* Adult; Children's; Youth;
Treatments: Commercial; Contemporary;
Literary

Send query by email with one-page query
letter and first ten pages pasted into the body
of the email (fiction) or table of contents and
(if available) proposal. See website for full
guidelines. No Westerns, textbooks,
children's picture books, or books in need of
translation.

MacGregor & Luedeke

PO Box 1316, Manzanita, OR 97130
Tel: +1 (503) 389-4803
Email: chip@macgregorliterary.com
Website: http://www.
macgregorandluedeke.com

Handles: Fiction; Nonfiction; *Areas:*
Autobiography; Biography; Business; Crime;
Culture; Current Affairs; Finance; Historical;
How-to; Humour; Lifestyle; Mystery;
Religious; Romance; Self-Help; Short
Stories; Sport; Suspense; Thrillers; Women's
Interests; *Markets:* Academic; Adult;
Treatments: Contemporary; Mainstream

Handles work in a variety of genres, but all
from a Christian perspective. Send query
with proposal / synopsis and first three
chapters (approximately 50 pages). See
website for full guidelines.

Mansion Street Literary Management

Email: jean@mansionstreet.com
Website: http://mansionstreet.com

Handles: Fiction; Nonfiction; *Areas:* Arts; Cookery; Culture; Design; Lifestyle; *Markets:* Adult; Children's; Youth; *Treatments:* Popular

Send query via online submission system. See website for full details and individual agent interests.

Marcil O'Farrell Literary, LLC and Denise Marcil Literary Agency, LLC

86 Dennis Street, Manhasset, NY 11030
Tel: +1 (212) 337-3402
Email: annemarie@
marcilofarrellagency.com
Website: https://www.
marcilofarrellagency.com

Handles: Nonfiction; *Areas:* Business; Cookery; Health; Self-Help; Spiritual; Sport; Travel; *Markets:* Adult

No fiction, memoirs, or screenplays. Send query up to 200 words by email.

Maria Carvainis Agency, Inc.

1270 Avenue of the Americas, Suite 2915, New York, NY 10020
Tel: +1 (212) 245-6365
Fax: +1 (212) 245-7196
Email: mca@mariacarvainisagency.com
Website: http://mariacarvainisagency.com

Handles: Fiction; Nonfiction; *Areas:* Adventure; Autobiography; Biography; Business; Crime; Culture; Finance; Historical; Horror; Humour; Mystery; Psychology; Romance; Science; Suspense; Technology; Thrillers; Women's Interests; *Markets:* Adult; Children's; Youth; *Treatments:* Commercial; Contemporary; Literary; Mainstream; Popular

Send query with synopsis, two sample chapters, and details of any previous writing credits, by post or by email. If sending by post and return of the material is required, include SASE; otherwise include email address for response, usually within 5-10 days. If submitting by email, all documents must be Word or PDF. No screenplays, children's picture books, science fiction, or poetry.

Marsal Lyon Literary Agency LLC

PMB 121, 665 San Rodolfo Dr. 124, Solana Beach, CA 92075
Email: Kevan@
MarsalLyonLiteraryAgency.com
Website: http://www.
marsallyonliteraryagency.com

Handles: Fiction; Nonfiction; *Areas:* Autobiography; Biography; Business; Cookery; Culture; Current Affairs; Finance; Health; Historical; Lifestyle; Music; Mystery; Politics; Psychology; Romance; Self-Help; Sport; Suspense; Thrillers; Women's Interests; *Markets:* Adult; Children's; Youth; *Treatments:* Commercial; Mainstream

Send query by email only to one agent only. See website for individual agent interests and email addresses. No submissions by post.

The Evan Marshall Agency

1 Pacio Court, Roseland, NJ 07068-1121
Tel: +1 (973) 287-6216
Email: evan@evanmarshallagency.com
Website: https://www.
evanmarshallagency.com

Handles: Fiction; Nonfiction; *Markets:* Adult; Youth

Represents all genres of adult and young-adult full-length fiction. New clients by referral only.

Martin Literary Management

Email: Sharlene@
martinliterarymanagement.com
Website: http://www.
martinliterarymanagement.com

Handles: Fiction; Nonfiction; *Areas:* Autobiography; Biography; Business; Crime; Culture; Current Affairs; Entertainment; Health; How-to; Lifestyle; Media; Religious; Self-Help; Women's Interests; *Markets:* Adult; Children's; Youth; *Treatments:* Commercial; Literary; Mainstream; Popular; Positive; Traditional

This agency has strong ties to film/TV. Interested in nonfiction that is highly commercial and that can be adapted to film.

Please review our website carefully to make sure we're a good match for your work. How to contact: Completely electronic: emails and MS Word only. No attachments on queries. Place letter in body of email. See submission requirements on website. Do not send materials unless requested. We give very serious consideration to the material requested.

No adult fiction. Principal agent handles adult nonfiction only. See website for submission guidelines and separate email address for submissions of picture books, middle grade, and young adult fiction and nonfiction.

Massie & McQuilkin

27 West 20th Street, Suite 305, New York, NY 10011
Tel: +1 (212) 352-2055
Fax: +1 (212) 352-2059
Email: info@lmqlit.com
Website: http://www.mmqlit.com

Handles: Fiction; Nonfiction; *Areas:* Autobiography; Biography; Crime; Culture; Current Affairs; Fantasy; Health; Historical; Humour; Politics; Psychology; Science; Sociology; Sport; Suspense; Thrillers; Women's Interests; *Markets:* Adult; Children's; Youth; *Treatments:* Commercial; Literary

See website for specific agent interests and contact details. Query only one agent at a time.

Max Gartenburg Literary Agency

912 North Pennsylvania Avenue, Yardley, PA 19067
Tel: +1 (215) 295-9230
Fax: +1 (215) 295-9240
Email: agdevlin@aol.com
Website: http://www.maxgartenberg.com

Handles: Fiction; Nonfiction; *Areas:* Biography; Culture; Current Affairs; Health; Lifestyle; Nature; Politics; Science; Sport; Women's Interests; *Markets:* Adult

Send query by email to a specific member of staff. See website for specific interests and contact details.

McCormick Literary

150 West 28th Street, Suite 903, New York, NY 10001
Email: queries@mccormicklit.com
Website: http://mccormicklit.com

Handles: Fiction; Nonfiction; *Areas:* Arts; Autobiography; Biography; Cookery; Culture; Historical; Humour; Lifestyle; Politics; Science; Self-Help; Sport; Women's Interests; *Markets:* Adult; Youth; *Treatments:* Commercial; Literary

Send queries by email with short bio and ten sample pages, indicating in the subject line which agent you are querying (see website for individual agent interests). No attachments. Will also consider submissions by post, but these will not be returned. Response only if interested.

Mendel Media Group, LLC

115 West 30th Street, Suite 209, New York, NY 10001
Tel: +1 (646) 239-9896
Email: scott@mendelmedia.com
Website: http://www.mendelmedia.com

Handles: Fiction; Nonfiction; *Areas:* Autobiography; Biography; Culture; Current Affairs; Entertainment; Finance; Historical; How-to; Humour; Literature; Media; Mystery; Politics; Religious; Science; Self-Help; Spiritual; Thrillers; Women's Interests; *Markets:* Adult; Children's; Youth; *Treatments:* Contemporary; Literary; Mainstream

Send query by email only. No longer accepts submissions by post. For fiction, send synopsis and first 20 pages. For nonfiction, send proposal and sample chapters. See website for full guidelines.

Meredith Bernstein Literary Agency, Inc.

2095 Broadway, Suite 505, New York, NY 10023
Tel: +1 (212) 799-1007
Fax: +1 (212) 799-1145

Email: mgoodbern@aol.com
Website: http://www.
meredithbernsteinliteraryagency.com

Handles: Fiction; Nonfiction; *Areas:*
Mystery; Romance; Thrillers; *Markets:*
Adult; Youth; *Treatments:* Literary

An eclectic agency which does not specialise
in any one particular area. Accepts queries
by post with SASE, or via form on website.
No poetry or screenplays. See website for
full guidelines.

The Ned Leavitt Agency

70 Wooster Street, Suite 4F, New York, NY
10012
Tel: +1 (212) 334-0999
Website: http://www.nedleavittagency.com

Handles: Fiction; Nonfiction; *Areas:*
Autobiography; Biography; Health; Mystery;
Sci-Fi; Short Stories; Spiritual; *Markets:*
Adult; *Treatments:* Commercial; Literary;
Mainstream

Accepts approaches by recommendation
only.

Nelson Literary Agency, LLC

1732 Wazee Street, Suite 207, Denver, CO
80202
Tel: +1 (303) 292-2805
Email: info@nelsonagency.com
Website: http://www.nelsonagency.com

Handles: Fiction; *Areas:* Fantasy; Historical;
Mystery; Romance; Sci-Fi; Thrillers;
Women's Interests; *Markets:* Adult;
Children's; Youth; *Treatments:* Commercial;
Literary; Mainstream

Handles young adult, upper-level middle
grade, "big crossover novels with one foot
squarely in genre", literary commercial
novels, upmarket women's fiction, single-
title romances (especially historicals), and
lead title or hardcover science fiction and
fantasy. No nonfiction, memoirs,
screenplays, short story collections, poetry,
children's picture books or chapter books, or
material for the Christian/inspirational
market. Submit through online submission
system. No queries by post, phone, in person,

or through Facebook. No email attachments.
See website for full submission guidelines.

Niad Management

15021 Ventura Blvd. #860, Sherman Oaks,
CA 91403
Tel: +1 (818) 774-0051
Fax: +1 (818) 774-1740
Email: info@NiadManagement.com
Website: http://www.niadmanagement.com

Handles: Fiction; Nonfiction; Scripts; *Areas:*
Adventure; Autobiography; Biography;
Crime; Culture; Drama; Film; Humour;
Mystery; Romance; Sport; Suspense;
Theatre; Thrillers; TV; *Markets:* Adult;
Youth; *Treatments:* Contemporary; Literary;
Mainstream

Manages mainly Hollywood writers, actors,
and directors, although does also handle a
very small number of books. Send query by
email. Responds only if interested.

One Track Literary Agency, Inc.

Tel: +1 (401) 595-1949
Email: tara@onetrackliterary.com
Website: http://www.onetrackliterary.com

Handles: Fiction; *Areas:* Mystery; Romance;
Thrillers; Women's Interests; *Markets:*
Adult; *Treatments:* Commercial;
Contemporary; Light; Mainstream; Niche;
Popular; Progressive; Satirical; Serious;
Traditional

A full-service boutique agency providing
hands-on guidance throughout each and
every part of the publishing pursuit. OTLA is
single-minded and fully dedicated to getting
you on the right track to launch your career
or progress to the next level. From honing
manuscripts to be their very best, to
identifying the right market for placement,
through contract advisement and negotiation,
to crafting promotional campaigns to help
grow your audience, the prime objective is to
help you achieve your goals. Currently
seeking completed works with vibrant, fresh
voices in these genres: romance, women's
fiction, mysteries, and young adult.

Peregrine Whittlesey Agency

Website: https://www.linkedin.com/in/
peregrine-whittlesey-33423830

Handles: Scripts; *Areas:* Film; Theatre; TV;
Markets: Adult

Handles mainly theatre scripts, plus a small
number of film/TV scripts by playwrights
who also write for screen.

Perry Literary, Inc.

211 South Ridge Street, Suite 2, Rye Brook,
NY 10573
Email: jperry@perryliterary.com
Website: https://www.perryliterary.com

Handles: Fiction; Nonfiction; *Areas:*
Biography; Business; Cookery; Crime;
Culture; Current Affairs; Film; Finance;
Historical; Legal; Lifestyle; Medicine;
Music; Philosophy; Politics; Psychology;
Science; Self-Help; Sociology; Sport;
Technology; Travel; TV; *Markets:* Adult;
Children's; *Treatments:* Literary

Send query by email with first ten pages in
the body of the email (or full manuscript for
picture books). No attachments. See website
for full guidelines.

Pippin Properties, Inc

110 West 40th Street, Suite 1704, New York,
NY 10016
Tel: +1 (212) 338-9310
Fax: +1 (212) 338-9579
Email: info@pippinproperties.com
Website: http://www.pippinproperties.com

Handles: Fiction; *Markets:* Adult;
Children's; Youth

Devoted primarily to picture books, middle-
grade, and young adult novels, but also
represents adult projects on occasion. Send
query by email with synopsis, first chapter,
or entire picture book manuscript in the body
of your email. No attachments. See website
for full guidelines.

Prentis Literary

PMB 496, 6830 NE Bothell Way, Suite C,
Kenmore, WA 98028
Tel: +1 (315) 790-5174

Email: info@prentisliterary.com
Website: https://www.prentisliterary.com

Handles: Fiction; Nonfiction; *Areas:*
Autobiography; Fantasy; Horror; Mystery;
Romance; Sci-Fi; Women's Interests;
Markets: Adult; Children's; Youth;
Treatments: Contemporary; Literary;
Mainstream

Agency with a historic focus on science
fiction and fantasy. Actively seeking new
authors with fresh, intelligent voices. Send
query through submission form on website.

Prospect Agency

551 Valley Rd., PMB 377, Upper Montclair,
NJ 07043
Tel: +1 (718) 788-3217
Fax: +1 (718) 360-9582
Email: esk@prospectagency.com
Website: http://www.prospectagency.com

Handles: Fiction; Nonfiction; *Areas:*
Adventure; Autobiography; Crime; Erotic;
Fantasy; Historical; Mystery; Romance;
Science; Sci-Fi; Suspense; Thrillers;
Westerns; Women's Interests; *Markets:*
Adult; Children's; Youth; *Treatments:*
Commercial; Contemporary; Literary;
Mainstream

Handles very little nonfiction. Specialises in
romance, women's fiction, literary fiction,
young adult/children's literature, and science
fiction. Send submissions via website
submission system **only** (no email queries –
**email queries are not accepted or
responded to** – or queries by post (these will
be recycled). No poetry, short stories, text
books, screenplays, or most nonfiction.

Publication Riot Group, Inc.

Email: db@priotgroup.com
Website: http://priotgroup.com

Handles: Fiction; Nonfiction; *Areas:*
Autobiography; Culture; Historical; Politics;
Science; Sociology; Thrillers; Women's
Interests; *Markets:* Adult; *Treatments:*
Literary; Mainstream

Closed to submissions as at December 2017.
Check website for current status.

The Purcell Agency, LLC

Email: TPAqueries@gmail.com
Website: http://thepurcellagency.com

Handles: Fiction; Nonfiction; *Areas:*
Culture; Romance; Sport; Women's
Interests; *Markets:* Adult; Children's; Youth

**Closed to submissions as at May 2018.
Check website for current status.**

Handles middle grade, young adult, women's
fiction, and some new adult. No science
fiction or fantasy, or picture book
manuscripts. See website for full submission
guidelines.

Queen Literary Agency, Inc.

30 East 60th Street, Suite 1004, New York,
NY 10024
Tel: +1 (212) 974-8333
Fax: +1 (212) 974-8347
Email: submissions@queenliterary.com
Website: http://www.queenliterary.com

Handles: Fiction; Nonfiction; *Areas:*
Business; Cookery; Historical; Mystery;
Psychology; Science; Sport; Thrillers;
Markets: Adult; *Treatments:* Commercial;
Literary

Founded by a former publishing executive,
most recently head of IMG
WORLDWIDE'S literary division. Handles
a wide range of nonfiction titles, with a
particular interest in business books, food
writing, science and popular psychology, as
well as books by well-known chefs, radio
and television personalities and sports
figures. Also handles commercial and
literary fiction, including historical fiction,
mysteries, and thrillers.

Rebecca Friedman Literary Agency

Email: queries@rfliterary.com
Website: https://rfliterary.com

Handles: Fiction; Nonfiction; *Areas:*
Autobiography; Cookery; Lifestyle;
Romance; Suspense; Women's Interests;
Markets: Adult; Youth; *Treatments:*
Commercial; Contemporary; Dark; Literary

See website for full submission guidelines
and specific agent interests and contact
details. Aims to respond in 6-8 weeks, but
may take longer.

Red Sofa Literary

Email: dawn@redsofaliterary.com
Website: https://redsofaliterary.com

Handles: Fiction; Nonfiction; *Areas:*
Biography; Criticism; Culture; Current
Affairs; Erotic; Fantasy; Historical; Humour;
Mystery; Politics; Romance; Science; Sci-Fi;
Sociology; Spiritual; Sport; Westerns;
Women's Interests; *Markets:* Adult;
Children's; Youth; *Treatments:*
Contemporary

Send query by email in first instance. See
website for individual agent contact details
and interests.

Rees Literary Agency

One Westinghouse Plaza, Suite A203,
Boston, MA 02136-2075
Tel: +1 (617) 227-9014
Email: lorin@reesagency.com
Website: http://www.reesagency.com

Handles: Fiction; Nonfiction; *Areas:*
Autobiography; Biography; Business;
Culture; Fantasy; Film; Historical; Horror;
Humour; Military; Mystery; Psychology;
Romance; Science; Sci-Fi; Self-Help;
Suspense; Thrillers; Westerns; Women's
Interests; *Markets:* Adult; Children's; Youth;
Treatments: Commercial; Contemporary;
Literary

See website for specific agents' interests and
submission requirements.

Regal Hoffmann & Associates LLC

143 West 29th Street, Suite 901, New York,
NY 10001
Tel: +1 (212) 684-7900
Fax: +1 (212) 684-7906
Email: submissions@rhaliterary.com
Website: http://www.rhaliterary.com

Handles: Fiction; Nonfiction; *Areas:*
Autobiography; Biography; Historical;
Science; Short Stories; Thrillers; *Markets:*

Adult; Children's; Youth; *Treatments:* Literary

Send one-page query by email or by post with SASE, outline, and author bio/qualifications. For fiction, include first ten pages or one story from a collection. No response unless interested.

Regina Ryan Publishing Enterprises

251 Central Park West, #7D, New York, NY 10024
Tel: +1 (212) 787-5589
Website: http://www.reginaryanbooks.com

Handles: Nonfiction; Reference; *Areas:* Adventure; Architecture; Autobiography; Business; Cookery; Gardening; Health; Historical; Legal; Leisure; Lifestyle; Nature; Politics; Psychology; Science; Spiritual; Sport; Travel; Women's Interests; *Markets:* Adult; *Treatments:* Popular

Send submissions through email. See website for full guidelines.

Richard Henshaw Group LLC

145 W. 28th Street, 12th Floor, New York, NY 10001
Tel: +1 (212) 414-1172
Email: submissions@henshaw.com
Website: https://richardhenshawgroup.com

Handles: Fiction; Nonfiction; Reference; *Areas:* Biography; Business; Culture; Current Affairs; Fantasy; Film; Health; Historical; Horror; How-to; Mystery; Psychology; Romance; Science; Sci-Fi; Sport; Thrillers; *Markets:* Adult; Youth; *Treatments:* Popular

Only considers works between 65,000 and 150,000 words. No children's books, screenplays, short fiction, poetry, textbooks, scholarly works, or coffee-table books. Send query up to 250 words by email only. No postal submissions.

Rita Rosenkranz Literary Agency

440 West End Ave, Suite 15D, New York, NY 10024
Tel: +1 (212) 873-6333

Email: rrosenkranz@mindspring.com
Website: http://www.ritarosenkranzliteraryagency.com

Handles: Nonfiction; Reference; *Areas:* Cookery; Health; Historical; How-to; Humour; Lifestyle; Music; Science; Spiritual; *Markets:* Adult; *Treatments:* Commercial; Niche; Popular

Send query only by post or email. Submit proposal on request only. Deals specifically in adult nonfiction. No screenplays, poetry, fiction, children's or YA books. Response within two weeks.

Riverside Literary Agency

41 Simon Keets Road, Leyden, MA 01337
Tel: +1 (413) 772-0067
Fax: +1 (413) 772-0969
Email: rivlit@sover.net
Website: http://www.riversideliteraryagency.com

Handles: Fiction; Nonfiction; *Markets:* Adult

Agency based in Leyden, Massachusetts.

The Robbins Office, Inc.

405 Park Avenue, New York, NY 10022
Tel: +1 (212) 223-0720
Fax: +1 (212) 223-2535
Email: translation@robbinsoffice.com
Website: http://robbinsoffice.com

Handles: Fiction; Nonfiction; *Markets:* Adult; *Treatments:* Commercial; Literary; Serious

Literary agency based in New York. Does not accept submissions of unsolicited material.

Rodeen Literary Management

3501 N. Southport #497, Chicago, IL 60657
Email: submissions@rodeenliterary.com
Website: http://www.rodeenliterary.com

Handles: Fiction; Nonfiction; *Markets:* Children's; Youth

Independent literary agency providing career management for experienced and aspiring authors and illustrators of children's literature. Open to submissions from writers and illustrators of all genres of children's literature including picture books, early readers, middle-grade fiction and nonfiction, graphic novels and comic books as well as young adult fiction and nonfiction. See website for full submission guidelines.

Andy Ross Agency

767 Santa Ray Avenue, Oakland, CA 94610
Tel: +1 (510) 238-8965
Email: andyrossagency@hotmail.com
Website: http://www.andyrossagency.com

Handles: Fiction; Nonfiction; *Areas:* Culture; Current Affairs; Historical; Religious; Science; *Markets:* Adult; Youth; *Treatments:* Commercial; Contemporary; Literary

We encourage queries for material in our fields of interest. No poetry, short stories, adult romance, science fiction and fantasy, adult and teen paranormal, or film scripts.

The agent has worked in the book business for 36 years, all of his working life. He was owner and general manager of Cody's Books in Berkeley, California from 1977-2006. Cody's has been recognised as one of America's great independent book stores.

During this period, the agent was the primary trade book buyer. This experience has given him a unique understanding of the retail book market, of publishing trends and, most importantly and uniquely, the hand selling of books to book buyers.

The agent is past president of the Northern California Booksellers Association, a board member and officer of the American Booksellers Association and a national spokesperson for issues concerning independent businesses. He has had significant profiles in the Wall Street Journal, Time Magazine, and the San Francisco Chronicle.

Queries by email only. See website for full guidelines.

Ross Yoon Agency

1666 Connecticut Avenue, NW, Suite 500, Washington, DC 20009
Tel: +1 (202) 328-3282
Email: submissions@rossyoon.com
Website: http://www.rossyoon.com

Handles: Nonfiction; *Areas:* Autobiography; Biography; Business; Culture; Current Affairs; Historical; Psychology; Science; *Markets:* Adult; *Treatments:* Commercial; Popular; Serious

Handles adult nonfiction only. Send query or complete book proposal by email only with proposal in body of email or as .doc or .docx attachment. No unsolicited MSS or approaches by post or phone. See website for full guidelines.

The Rudy Agency

825 Wildlife Lane, Estes Park, CO 80517
Tel: +1 (970) 577-8500
Fax: +1 (970) 577-8600
Email: mak@rudyagency.com
Website: http://www.rudyagency.com

Handles: Fiction; Nonfiction; *Areas:* Autobiography; Biography; Business; Culture; Current Affairs; Health; Historical; Lifestyle; Medicine; Military; Politics; Science; Technology; Thrillers; *Markets:* Adult; Children's

Concentrates on adult nonfiction in the areas listed above. Handles a very limited amount of fiction. See website for full guidelines, and appropriate email addresses for different types of submissions.

Sandra Dijkstra Literary Agency

PMB 515, 1155 Camino Del Mar, Del Mar, CA 92014
Tel: +1 (858) 755-3115
Fax: +1 (858) 794-2822
Email: queries@dijkstraagency.com
Website: http://www.dijkstraagency.com

Handles: Fiction; Nonfiction; *Areas:* Autobiography; Biography; Business; Cookery; Crime; Culture; Current Affairs; Design; Fantasy; Health; Historical; Humour; Lifestyle; Music; Mystery; Nature;

Philosophy; Politics; Religious; Romance; Science; Sci-Fi; Self-Help; Short Stories; Sociology; Sport; Suspense; Thrillers; Travel; Women's Interests; *Markets:* Adult; Children's; Youth; *Treatments:* Commercial; Contemporary; Literary

Check author bios on website and submit query by email to one agent only. For fiction, include a one-page synopsis, brief bio, and first 10-15 pages. For nonfiction, include overview, chapter outline, brief bio, and first 10-15 pages. All material must be in the body of the email. No attachments. See website for full submission guidelines.

Sanford J. Greenburger Associates, Inc.

15th Floor, 55 Fifth Avenue, New York, NY 10003
Tel: +1 (212) 206-5600
Fax: +1 (212) 463-8718
Email: queryHL@sjga.com
Website: http://www.greenburger.com

Handles: Fiction; Nonfiction; Reference; *Areas:* Arts; Autobiography; Biography; Business; Entertainment; Fantasy; Health; Historical; Humour; Lifestyle; Music; Mystery; Nature; Politics; Psychology; Romance; Science; Sci-Fi; Self-Help; Sociology; Sport; Thrillers; Women's Interests; *Markets:* Adult; Children's; Youth; *Treatments:* Commercial; Literary; Popular

Check website for specific agent interests, guidelines, and contact details. Most will not accept submissions by post. Aims to respond to queries within 6-8 weeks.

Scovil Galen Ghosh Literary Agency, Inc.

276 Fifth Avenue, Suite 708, New York, NY 10001
Tel: +1 (212) 679-8686
Fax: +1 (212) 679-6710
Email: russellgalen@sgglit.com
Website: http://www.sgglit.com

Handles: Fiction; Nonfiction; *Areas:* Adventure; Arts; Autobiography; Biography; Business; Cookery; Culture; Health; Historical; Nature; Politics; Psychology; Religious; Science; Sociology; Sport;

Women's Interests; *Markets:* Adult; Children's; Youth; *Treatments:* Commercial; Contemporary; Literary

Send query letter only in first instance. Prefers contact by email, but no attachments. If contacting by post include letter only, with email address for response rather than an SASE.

Sean McCarthy Literary Agency

Email: submissions@mccarthylit.com
Website: http://www.mccarthylit.com

Handles: Fiction; *Areas:* Adventure; Humour; Mystery; *Markets:* Children's; Youth

Accepts submissions across all genres and age ranges in children's books. Send query by email with a description of your book, author bio, and literary or relevant professional credits, and first three chapters (or roughly 25 pages) for novels, or complete ms if your work is a picture book. No picture books over 1,000 words. Response in 6-8 weeks.

Selectric Artists

9 Union Square #123, Southbury, CT 06488
Tel: +1 (347) 668-5426
Email: query@selectricartists.com
Website: http://www.selectricartists.com

Handles: Fiction; Nonfiction; *Areas:* Autobiography; Biography; Culture; Fantasy; Historical; Horror; Humour; Literature; Music; Sci-Fi; Short Stories; Suspense; Thrillers; *Markets:* Adult; Youth; *Treatments:* Commercial; Literary; Mainstream

Closed to submissions for summer 2019. Check back in September.

Send query by email with your manuscript attached as a .doc, .pdf, or .pages file. Put the word "query" in the subject line. No queries by phone. Response only if interested.

The Seymour Agency

475 Miner Street Road, Canton, NY 13617
Email: nicole@theseymouragency.com

Website: https://www.
theseymouragency.com

Handles: Fiction; Nonfiction; *Areas:*
Adventure; Autobiography; Cookery;
Fantasy; Historical; Horror; Humour;
Military; Mystery; Religious; Romance; Sci-
Fi; Self-Help; Spiritual; Suspense; Thrillers;
Women's Interests; *Markets:* Adult;
Children's; Youth; *Treatments:*
Contemporary

Brief email queries accepted (no
attachments), including first five pages
pasted into the bottom of your email. All
agents prefer queries by email. See website
for full submission guidelines and specific
interests of each agent.

Sheree Bykofsky Associates, Inc.

4326 Harbor Beach Boulevard, PO Box 706,
Brigantine, NJ 08203
Email: submitbee@aol.com
Website: http://www.shereebee.com

Handles: Fiction; Nonfiction; Reference;
Areas: Biography; Business; Cookery;
Culture; Current Affairs; Film; Hobbies;
Humour; Lifestyle; Mystery; Psychology;
Self-Help; Spiritual; Women's Interests;
Markets: Adult; *Treatments:* Commercial;
Literary

Send query by email only. Include one page
query, and for fiction a one page synopsis,
and first page of manuscript, all in the body
of the email. No attachments. Always
looking for a bestseller in any category, but
generally not interested in poetry, thrillers,
westerns, romances, occult, science fiction,
fantasy, children's or young adult.

Solow Literary Enterprises, Inc.

769 Center Blvd., #148, Fairfax, CA 94930
Email: info@solowliterary.com
Website: http://www.solowliterary.com

Handles: Nonfiction; *Areas:* Autobiography;
Business; Culture; Finance; Health;
Historical; Nature; Psychology; Science;
Markets: Adult

Handles nonfiction in the stated areas only.
Send single-page query by email or by post
with SASE, providing information on what
your book is about; why you think it has to
be written; and why you are the best person
to write it. Response only if interested.

Speilburg Literary Agency

Email: speilburgliterary@gmail.com
Website: https://speilburgliterary.com

Handles: Fiction; Nonfiction; *Areas:*
Culture; Fantasy; Historical; Horror;
Mystery; Romance; Science; Suspense;
Markets: Adult; Youth; *Treatments:*
Mainstream; Popular

**Closed to submissions between July 4 and
September 3, 2018.**

Send query by email with first three chapters
(fiction), or proposal, including table of
contents and sample chapter (nonfiction). No
picture books, poetry, or screenplays. See
website for full guidelines and individual
agent interests.

The Spieler Agency

27 West 20th Street, Suite 305, New York,
NY 10011
Tel: +1 (212) 757-4439, ext.1
Fax: +1 (212) 333-2019
Email: joe@TheSpielerAgency.com
Website: http://thespieleragency.com

Handles: Fiction; Nonfiction; Poetry; *Areas:*
Architecture; Autobiography; Biography;
Business; Cookery; Crime; Culture; Current
Affairs; Film; Finance; Gardening; Health;
Historical; Humour; Legal; Lifestyle; Music;
Mystery; Nature; Photography; Politics;
Science; Sociology; Spiritual; Theatre;
Thrillers; Travel; Women's Interests;
Markets: Adult; Children's; Youth;
Treatments: Literary; Popular

Consult website for details of specific
agents' interests and contact details. Send
query by email or by post with SASE.
Response not guaranteed if not interested.
No response to postal submissions without
SASE.

Stephanie Tade Literary Agency

Email: submissions@
stephanietadeagency.com
Website: http://www.
stephanietadeagency.com

Handles: Nonfiction; *Areas:* Autobiography;
Culture; Health; Philosophy; Politics;
Psychology; Spiritual; *Markets:* Adult

Send single-page query by email with
information about your proposed book, your
publishing history, and any media or online
platform you have developed. Response only
if interested.

Sterling Lord Literistic, Inc.

115 Broadway, New York, NY 10006
Tel: +1 (212) 780-6050
Fax: +1 (212) 780-6095
Email: info@sll.com
Website: http://www.sll.com

Handles: Fiction; Nonfiction; *Areas:*
Autobiography; Beauty and Fashion;
Biography; Business; Cookery; Culture;
Current Affairs; Health; Historical; Lifestyle;
Nature; Politics; Science; Self-Help;
Technology; Travel; Women's Interests;
Markets: Adult; Children's; Youth;
Treatments: Commercial; Literary; Popular

Send query with SASE, synopsis, brief
author bio, and first three chapters. Literary
value considered above all else. No response
to unsolicited email queries.

The Steve Laube Agency

24 W. Camelback Rd. A-635, Phoenix, AZ
85013
Email: krichards@stevelaube.com
Website: http://www.stevelaube.com

Handles: Fiction; Nonfiction; *Areas:*
Religious; *Markets:* Adult; Youth

Handles quality Christian fiction and
nonfiction in all genres, except poetry,
personal biographies, personal stories, end-
times literature (either fiction or nonfiction),
and children's picture books. Accepts
submissions by post or by email. See website
for extensive information on making
submissions.

The Stringer Literary Agency LLC

PO Box 111255, Naples, FL 34108
Email: mstringer@stringerlit.com
Website: http://www.stringerlit.com

Handles: Fiction; *Areas:* Autobiography;
Biography; Design; Fantasy; Historical;
Lifestyle; Mystery; Romance; Sci-Fi;
Suspense; Thrillers; Women's Interests;
Markets: Adult; Children's; Youth;
Treatments: Commercial; Contemporary;
Literary

Welcomes queries from both published and
unpublished writers. Particularly interested
in upmarket women's fiction, fantasy,
romance, and thrillers. No christian, comedy,
humour, comics, graphic novels, erotica,
poetry, puzzles, games, picture books, early
readers, middle grade, new adult, stage
plays, or screenplays. Submit query via form
on website.

The Strothman Agency

63 East 9th Street, 10X, New York, NY
10003
Email: strothmanagency@gmail.com
Website: http://www.strothmanagency.com

Handles: Fiction; Nonfiction; *Areas:*
Biography; Business; Current Affairs;
Finance; Historical; Nature; Politics;
Science; *Markets:* Adult; Children's; Youth

Not currently accepting unsolicited queries
as at June 2019, but will continue to accept
referrals. Check website for current status.

Stuart Krichevsky Literary Agency, Inc.

6 East 39th Street, Suite 500, New York, NY
10016
Tel: +1 (212) 725-5288
Fax: +1 (212) 725-5275
Email: query@skagency.com
Website: http://www.skagency.com

Handles: Fiction; Nonfiction; *Areas:*
Adventure; Autobiography; Biography;
Business; Culture; Current Affairs; Fantasy;
Historical; Nature; Politics; Science; Sci-Fi;
Technology; *Markets:* Adult; Youth;
Treatments: Commercial; Literary

Send query by email with first few pages of your manuscript (up to 10) pasted into body of the email (no attachments). See website for complete submission guidelines and appropriate submission addresses for each agent.

Susan Schulman Literary Agency LLC

454 West 44th Street, New York, NY 10036
Tel: +1 (212) 713-1633
Email: queries@schulmanagency.com
Website: https://twitter.com/SusanSchulman

Handles: Fiction; Nonfiction; Scripts; *Areas:* Adventure; Anthropology; Archaeology; Arts; Autobiography; Biography; Business; Cookery; Crafts; Crime; Culture; Current Affairs; Entertainment; Film; Finance; Health; Historical; Hobbies; How-to; Humour; Legal; Lifestyle; Literature; Medicine; Music; Mystery; Nature; Photography; Politics; Psychology; Religious; Science; Self-Help; Sociology; Spiritual; Sport; Suspense; Technology; Theatre; Thrillers; Travel; Women's Interests; *Markets:* Adult; Children's; Youth; *Treatments:* Commercial; Literary; Mainstream

Send query with synopsis and SASE by post; or with synopsis and first three chapters in the body of an email. No Christian, Erotica, Horror, Poetry, Puzzles, Games, Romance, Science-fiction, Fantasy, Western, Professional, Reference, or Screenplays.

Emma Sweeney Agency, LLC

245 East 80th Street, Suite 7E, New York, NY 10075-0506
Email: queries@emmasweeneyagency.com
Website: http://emmasweeneyagency.com

Handles: Fiction; Nonfiction; *Areas:* Autobiography; Biography; Historical; Mystery; Religious; Science; Thrillers; Women's Interests; *Markets:* Adult; *Treatments:* Literary

Send query by email with cover letter and first 10 pages of MS pasted into body of email. No attachments, unsolicited MSS, screenplays, romances, or westerns.

Thompson Literary Agency

115 West 29th St, Third Floor, New York, NY 10001
Tel: +1 (347) 281-7685
Email: submissions@thompsonliterary.com
Website: https://thompsonliterary.com

Handles: Fiction; Nonfiction; *Areas:* Arts; Autobiography; Beauty and Fashion; Biography; Cookery; Culture; Health; Historical; Music; Politics; Science; Spiritual; Sport; *Markets:* Adult; Children's; Youth; *Treatments:* Commercial; Literary; Popular

Accepts commercial and literary fiction, but specialises in nonfiction. See website for list of agent interests and address submission by email to specific agent.

Union Literary

30 Vandam Street, Suite 5A, New York, NY 10013
Tel: +1 (212) 255-2112
Email: queries@threeseaslit.com
Website: https://www.unionliterary.com

Handles: Fiction; Nonfiction; *Areas:* Autobiography; Business; Cookery; Historical; Science; Sociology; *Markets:* Adult; *Treatments:* Literary; Popular

Prefers queries by email. Include a proposal and sample chapter for nonfiction, or a synopsis and sample pages for fiction. See website for specific agent interests and contact details, and approach one agent only. No romance or science fiction. Response only if interested.

United Talent Agency (UTA)

888 Seventh Avenue, Seventh Floor, New York, NY 10106
Tel: +1 (212) 659-2600
Website: https://www.unitedtalent.com

Handles: Fiction; Nonfiction; *Areas:* Business; Historical; Science; Sci-Fi; *Markets:* Adult; *Treatments:* Literary

Multimedia agency representing recording artists, celebrities, and with a literary agency operating out of the New York and London offices. Accepts queries by referral only.

The Unter Agency

23 West 73rd Street, Suite 100, New York, NY 10023
Tel: +1 (212) 401-4068
Email: Jennifer@theunteragency.com
Website: http://www.theunteragency.com

Handles: Fiction; Nonfiction; *Areas:* Adventure; Autobiography; Biography; Cookery; Crime; Culture; Health; Nature; Politics; Travel; *Markets:* Adult; Children's; Youth

Interested in quality fiction and general nonfiction, particularly memoir, food/cooking, nature/environment, biography, pop culture, travel/adventure, true crime, politics and health/fitness. Also all types of children's literature (picture books, middle grade, and young adult). Send query letter by email or via online form on website. If no response within three months, assume rejection.

Upstart Crow Literary

244 Fifth Avenue, 11th Floor, New York, NY 10001
Email: danielle.submission@gmail.com
Website: http://www.upstartcrowliterary.com

Handles: Fiction; Nonfiction; *Areas:* Autobiography; Cookery; Current Affairs; Fantasy; Historical; Humour; Lifestyle; Mystery; Sci-Fi; *Markets:* Adult; Children's; Youth; *Treatments:* Commercial; Contemporary

Send query by email with 20 pages of your ms, in the body of an email. No attachments or hard copy submissions. See website for more details, and specific agent interests and contact details.

Veritas Literary Agency

601 Van Ness Avenue, Opera Plaza Suite E, San Francisco, CA 94102
Tel: +1 (415) 647-6964
Fax: +1 (415) 647-6965
Email: submissions@veritasliterary.com
Website: http://www.veritasliterary.com

Handles: Fiction; Nonfiction; *Areas:* Autobiography; Biography; Business; Culture; Fantasy; Historical; Nature; Science; Sci-Fi; Women's Interests;

Markets: Adult; Children's; Youth; *Treatments:* Commercial; Literary

Send query or proposal by email only. Submit further information on request only. For fiction, include cover letter listing previously published work, one-page summary and first five pages. For nonfiction, include author bio, overview, chapter-by-chapter summary, sample chapters or text, and analysis of competing titles.

Vicky Bijur Literary Agency

27 West 20th Street, Suite 1003, New York, NY 10011
Email: queries@vickybijuragency.com
Website: http://www.vickybijuragency.com

Handles: Fiction; Nonfiction; *Areas:* Autobiography; Thrillers; Women's Interests; *Markets:* Adult; *Treatments:* Commercial; Literary

Send query by email or by post with SASE. For fiction include synopsis and first ten pages (pasted into the body of the email if submitting electronically). For nonfiction include proposal and first ten pages. No attachments or queries by phone or fax. No picture books, poetry, self-help, science fiction, fantasy, horror, or romance.

Victoria Sanders & Associates LLC

440 Buck Road, Stone Ridge, NY 12484
Tel: +1 (212) 633-8811
Email: queriesvsa@gmail.com
Website: http://www.victoriasanders.com

Handles: Fiction; Nonfiction; *Areas:* Adventure; Arts; Autobiography; Biography; Crime; Culture; Current Affairs; Fantasy; Film; Historical; Humour; Legal; Literature; Music; Mystery; Politics; Psychology; Sociology; Suspense; Theatre; Thrillers; Translations; Women's Interests; *Markets:* Adult; Children's; Youth; *Treatments:* Commercial; Contemporary; Light; Literary; Mainstream; Satirical

Send one-page query describing the work and the author by email only, with the first 25 pages pasted into the body of the email. No attachments or submissions by post. Response usually between 1 and 4 weeks.

Waterside Productions, Inc
2055 Oxford Avenue, Cardiff, CA 92007
Tel: +1 (760) 632-9190
Fax: +1 (760) 632-9295
Email: admin@waterside.com
Website: http://www.waterside.com

Handles: Fiction; Nonfiction; *Areas:*
Business; Cookery; Culture; Health;
Hobbies; How-to; Lifestyle; Psychology;
Self-Help; Sociology; Spiritual; Sport;
Technology; Women's Interests; *Markets:*
Adult

Read each agent bio on website and
approach appropriate agent by email with
query letter in the body of your email, and
proposal or sample material as an attached
Word document.

Wells Arms Literary
Email: victoria@wellsarms.com
Website: https://www.wellsarms.com

Handles: Fiction; *Markets:* Children's;
Youth

Represents authors and illustrators of books
for children of all ages, including picture
books, middle grade, early readers, and
young adult. Closed to submissions as at
February 2018. Check website for current
status.

Wendy Schmalz Agency
402 Union St. #831, Hudson, NY 12534
Tel: +1 (518).672-7697
Email: wendy@schmalzagency.com
Website: http://www.schmalzagency.com

Handles: Fiction; Nonfiction; *Markets:*
Children's; Youth

Handles books for middle grade and young
adults. No science fiction, fantasy, or picture
books. Send query by email. No unsolicited
mss or sample chapters. If no response after
two weeks, assume no interest.

Wendy Sherman Associates, Inc.
138 West 25th Street, Suite 1018, New York,
NY 10001
Tel: +1 (212) 279-9027

Email: submissions@wsherman.com
Website: http://www.wsherman.com

Handles: Fiction; Nonfiction; *Areas:*
Autobiography; Biography; Cookery;
Culture; Entertainment; Health; Historical;
Lifestyle; Nature; Psychology; Self-Help;
Spiritual; Sport; Suspense; Women's
Interests; *Markets:* Adult; Youth;
Treatments: Literary

Send queries by email only, including query
letter and (for fiction) first ten pages pasted
into the body of the email, or (for nonfiction)
author bio. No unsolicited attachments. Do
not send emails to personal agent addresses
(these are deleted unread). Response only if
interested. Does not handle poetry,
screenplays, cozy mysteries, genre romance,
westerns, science fiction, horror, fantasy, or
children's picture books

Whimsy Literary Agency, LLC
49 North 8th Street, 6G, Brooklyn, NY
11249
Tel: +1 (212) 674-7162
Email: whimsynyc@aol.com
Website: http://whimsyliteraryagency.com

Handles: Nonfiction; *Areas:* Arts;
Autobiography; Biography; Business;
Cookery; Current Affairs; Design; Finance;
Health; Historical; How-to; Humour;
Lifestyle; Literature; New Age;
Photography; Psychology; Self-Help;
Spiritual; Technology; Women's Interests;
Markets: Adult

No unsolicited mss. Send query in first
instance. Response only if interested.

Wm Clark Associates
Tel: +1 (212) 675-2784
Email: general@wmclark.com
Website: http://www.wmclark.com

Handles: Fiction; Nonfiction; *Areas:*
Architecture; Arts; Autobiography;
Biography; Culture; Current Affairs; Design;
Film; Historical; Music; Philosophy;
Religious; Science; Sociology; Technology;
Theatre; Translations; *Markets:* Adult;
Treatments: Contemporary; Literary;
Mainstream

Query through online form on website only. No simultaneous submissions or screenplays.

Wordserve Literary

Email: admin@wordserveliterary.com
Website: http://www.wordserveliterary.com

Handles: Fiction; Nonfiction; *Areas:* Autobiography; Biography; Culture; Current Affairs; Fantasy; Finance; Health; Historical; Legal; Military; Psychology; Religious; Romance; Sci-Fi; Self-Help; Suspense; Thrillers; Women's Interests; *Markets:* Adult; Children's; Youth; *Treatments:* Literary; Mainstream

Represents books for the general and Christian markets. Nonfiction 40,000 – 100,000 words; fiction 60,000-120,000 words. No gift books, poetry, short stories, screenplays, graphic novels, children's picture books, science fiction or fantasy for any age. Email approaches only. See website for detailed submission guidelines. Submissions that disregard the submission guidelines may themselves be disregarded.

Writers' Representatives, LLC

116 W. 14th St., 11th Fl., New York, NY 10011-7305
Tel: +1 (212) 620-0023
Fax: +1 (212) 620-0023
Email: transom@writersreps.com
Website: http://www.writersreps.com

Handles: Fiction; Nonfiction; Poetry; Reference; *Areas:* Autobiography; Biography; Business; Cookery; Criticism; Current Affairs; Finance; Historical; Humour; Legal; Literature; Mystery; Philosophy; Politics; Science; Self-Help; Thrillers; *Markets:* Adult; *Treatments:* Literary; Serious

Send email describing your project and yourself, or send proposal, outline, CV, and sample chapters, or complete unsolicited MS, with SASE. See website for submission requirements in FAQ section. Specialises in serious and literary fiction and nonfiction. No screenplays. No science fiction or children's or young adult fiction unless it aspires to serious literature.

The Wylie Agency

250 West 57th Street, Suite 2114, New York, NY 10107
Email: mail@wylieagency.com
Website: http://www.wylieagency.com

Handles: Fiction; *Markets:* Adult

Agency with offices in New York and London. Not accepting submissions as at February 2018.

UK Literary Agents

For the most up-to-date listings of these and hundreds of other literary agents, visit https://www.firstwriter.com/Agents

To claim your free access to the site, please see the back of this book.

A for Authors

73 Hurlingham Road, Bexleyheath, Kent
DA7 5PE
Tel: +44 (0) 1322 463479
Email: enquiries@aforauthors.co.uk
Website: http://aforauthors.co.uk

Handles: Fiction; *Markets:* Adult;
Treatments: Commercial; Literary

**Closed to submissions until February 1,
2019.**

Query by email only. Include synopsis and
first three chapters (or up to 50 pages) and
short author bio. All attachments must be
Word format documents. No nonfiction,
scripts, poetry, fantasy, SF, horror, short
stories, adult illustrated books on art,
architecture, design, visual culture, or
submissions by post, hand delivery, or on
discs, memory sticks, or other electronic
devices. No longer accepting young adult or
children's or nonfiction. See website for full
details.

A & B Personal Management Ltd

PO Box 64671, London, NW3 9LH
Tel: +44 (0) 20 7794 3255
Email: b.ellmain@aandb.co.uk

Handles: Fiction; Nonfiction; Scripts; *Areas:*
Film; Theatre; TV; *Markets:* Adult

Handles full-length mss and scripts for film,
TV, and theatre. No unsolicited mss. Query
by email or by phone in first instance.

A.M. Heath & Company Limited, Author's Agents

6 Warwick Court, Holborn, London, WC1R
5DJ
Tel: +44 (0) 20 7242 2811
Email: enquiries@amheath.com
Website: http://www.amheath.com

Handles: Fiction; Nonfiction; *Areas:*
Biography; Cookery; Crime; Health;
Historical; Nature; Psychology; Sport;
Suspense; Thrillers; Travel; Women's
Interests; *Markets:* Adult; Children's; Youth;
Treatments: Commercial; Contemporary;
Literary

Handles general commercial and literary
fiction and nonfiction. Submit work with
cover letter and synopsis via online
submission system only. No paper
submissions. Aims to respond within six
weeks.

Abner Stein

Suite 137, China Works, 100 Black Prince
Road, London, SE1 7SJ
Email: caspian@abnerstein.co.uk
Website: http://www.abnerstein.co.uk

Handles: Fiction; Nonfiction; *Markets:*
Adult; Children's

Agency based in London. Handles fiction, general nonfiction, and children's.

The Agency (London) Ltd
24 Pottery Lane, Holland Park, London, W11 4LZ
Tel: +44 (0) 20 7727 1346
Email: info@theagency.co.uk
Website: http://www.theagency.co.uk

Handles: Fiction; Nonfiction; Scripts; *Areas:* Film; Humour; Radio; Theatre; TV; *Markets:* Adult; Children's; Youth

Closed to submissions of children's books as at November 2018. Check website for current status.

Represents writers and authors for film, television, radio and the theatre. Also represents directors, producers, composers, and film and television rights in books, as well as authors of children's books from picture books to teen fiction. **Handles adult fiction and nonfiction for existing clients only.** Does not consider adult fiction or nonfiction from writers who are not already clients. For script writers, only considers unsolicited material if it has been recommended by a producer, development executive or course tutor. If this is the case send CV, covering letter and details of your referee to the relevant agent, or to the email address below. Do not email more than one agent at a time. For directors, send CV, showreel and cover letter by email. For children's authors, send query by email with synopsis and first three chapters (middle grade, teen, or Young Adult) or complete ms (picture books) to address given on website.

Aitken Alexander Associates
291 Gray's Inn Road, Kings Cross, London, WC1X 8QJ
Tel: +44 (0) 20 7373 8672
Email: submissions@aitkenalexander.co.uk
Website: http://www.aitkenalexander.co.uk

Handles: Fiction; Nonfiction; *Markets:* Adult

Send query by email, with short synopsis, and first 30 pages as a Word document. See website for list of agents and their interests and indicate in the subject line which agent

you would like to query. No self-help, poetry, or picture books.

Alan Brodie Representation Ltd
Paddock Suite, The Courtyard, 55 Charterhouse Street, London, EC1M 6HA
Tel: +44 (0) 20 7253 6226
Fax: +44 (0) 20 7183 7999
Email: ABR@alanbrodie.com
Website: http://www.alanbrodie.com

Handles: Scripts; *Areas:* Film; Radio; Theatre; TV; *Markets:* Adult

Handles scripts only. No books. Approach with preliminary letter, recommendation from industry professional, and CV. Do not send a sample of work unless requested. No fiction, nonfiction, or poetry.

AMP Literary
c/o Studio Sixty Billion, The Metal Box Factory, 30 Great Guildford Street, London, SE1 0HS
Email: submissions@ampliterary.co.uk
Website: https://www.ampliterary.co.uk

Handles: Nonfiction; *Markets:* Adult; *Treatments:* Commercial

Specialises in commercial nonfiction. Particularly interested in bold female voices. Send query by email.

The Ampersand Agency Ltd
Ryman's Cottages, Little Tew, Chipping Norton, Oxfordshire OX7 4JJ
Tel: +44 (0) 1608 683677 / 683898
Fax: +44 (0) 1608 683449
Email: submissions@theampersandagency.co.uk
Website: http://www.theampersandagency.co.uk

Handles: Fiction; Nonfiction; *Areas:* Autobiography; Biography; Crime; Current Affairs; Fantasy; Historical; Horror; Science; Sci-Fi; Sport; Thrillers; Women's Interests; *Markets:* Adult; Youth; *Treatments:* Commercial; Contemporary; Literary

We handle literary and commercial fiction and nonfiction, including contemporary and historical novels, crime, thrillers, biography, women's fiction, history, current affairs, and memoirs. Send query by post or email with brief bio, outline, and first three chapters. If emailing material, send as attachments rather than pasted into the body of the email. Also accepts science fiction, fantasy, horror, and Young Adult material to separate email address listed on website. No scripts except those by existing clients, no poetry, self-help or illustrated children's books. No unpublished American writers, because in our experience British and European publishers aren't interested unless there is an American publisher on board. And we'd like to make it clear that American stamps are no use outside America!

Darley Anderson Children's
Suite LG4, New Kings House, 136-144 New Kings Road, London, SW6 4LZ
Tel: +44 (0) 20 7386 2674
Fax: +44 (0) 20 7386 5571
Email: childrens@darleyanderson.com
Website: http://www.
darleyandersonchildrens.com

Handles: Fiction; Nonfiction; *Markets:* Children's

Handles fiction and nonfiction for children. Send query by email with short synopsis, and first three consecutive chapters. For picture books, send complete text or picture book. Prefers to read material exclusively, but will accept simultaneous submissions if notice given on cover letter. No submissions by post or by fax.

Andlyn
Tel: +44 (0) 20 3290 5638
Email: submissions@andlyn.co.uk
Website: http://www.andlyn.co.uk

Handles: Fiction; Nonfiction; *Markets:* Children's; Youth

Specialises in children's/teen fiction and content. Handles picture books, middle-grade, young adult, and cross-over. Send query by email with one-page synopsis and first three chapters (fiction) or proposal and market analysis (nonfiction). Not accepting picture book submissions as at December 2018. Check website for current status.

Andrew Lownie Literary Agency Ltd
36 Great Smith Street, London, SW1P 3BU
Tel: +44 (0) 20 7222 7574
Fax: +44 (0) 20 7222 7576
Email: mail@andrewlownie.co.uk
Website: http://www.andrewlownie.co.uk

Handles: Nonfiction; *Areas:* Autobiography; Biography; Crime; Culture; Current Affairs; Finance; Health; Historical; Horror; How-to; Lifestyle; Literature; Media; Medicine; Men's Interests; Military; Music; Politics; Psychology; Romance; Science; Self-Help; Sport; Technology; Translations; *Markets:* Academic; Adult; Family; Professional; *Treatments:* Commercial; Mainstream; Popular; Serious; Traditional

This agency, founded in 1988, is now one of the UK's leading literary agencies with some two hundred nonfiction and fiction authors. It prides itself on its personal attention to its clients and specialises both in launching new writers and taking established writers to a new level of recognition.

Andrew Mann Ltd
6 Quernmore Road, London, N4 4QU
Tel: +44 (0) 20 7609 6218
Email: tina@andrewmann.co.uk
Website: http://www.andrewmann.co.uk

Handles: Fiction; *Areas:* Crime; Historical; Thrillers; *Markets:* Adult; *Treatments:* Commercial; Literary

Closed to submissions as at March 2018. Check website for current status.

Interested in literary and commercial fiction, historical, and crime/thriller. Send query by email, or by post if absolutely necessary with SAE, with brief synopsis and first three chapters or 30 pages. See website for specific email address for crime/thriller submissions. No children's, screenplays or theatre, misery memoirs, new age philosophy, nonfiction, fantasy, science fiction, poetry, short stories, vampires, or dystopian fiction. See website for full submission guidelines.

Andrew Nurnberg Associates, Ltd

20-23 Greville Street, London, EC1N 8SS
Tel: +44 (0) 20 3327 0400
Fax: +44 (0) 20 7430 0801
Email: submissions@nurnberg.co.uk
Website: http://www.andrewnurnberg.com

Handles: Fiction; Nonfiction; *Markets:* Adult; Children's

Handles adult fiction and nonfiction, and children's fiction. No poetry, children's picture books, or scripts for film, TV, radio or theatre. Send query by email with one-page synopsis and first three chapters or 50 pages as attachments. Prefers email approaches but will also accept submissions of the same material by post with SAE.

Anne Clark Literary Agency

Email: submissions@ anneclarkliteraryagency.co.uk
Website: http://www. anneclarkliteraryagency.co.uk

Handles: Fiction; Nonfiction; *Markets:* Children's; Youth

Handles fiction and picture books for children and young adults. Send query by email only with the following pasted into the body of the email (not as an attachment): for fiction, include brief synopsis and first 3,000 words; for picture books, send complete ms; for nonfiction, send short proposal and the text of three sample pages. No submissions by post. See website for full guidelines.

Antony Harwood Limited

103 Walton Street, Oxford, OX2 6EB
Tel: +44 (0) 1865 559615
Fax: +44 (0) 1865 310660
Email: mail@antonyharwood.com
Website: http://www.antonyharwood.com

Handles: Fiction; Nonfiction; *Areas:* Adventure; Anthropology; Antiques; Archaeology; Architecture; Arts; Autobiography; Beauty and Fashion; Biography; Business; Cookery; Crafts; Crime; Criticism; Culture; Current Affairs; Design; Drama; Entertainment; Erotic; Fantasy; Film; Finance; Gardening; Gothic; Health; Historical; Hobbies; Horror; How-to; Humour; Legal; Leisure; Lifestyle; Literature; Media; Medicine; Men's Interests; Military; Music; Mystery; Nature; New Age; Philosophy; Photography; Politics; Psychology; Radio; Religious; Romance; Science; Sci-Fi; Self-Help; Short Stories; Sociology; Spiritual; Sport; Suspense; Technology; Theatre; Thrillers; Translations; Travel; TV; Westerns; Women's Interests; *Markets:* Adult; Children's; Youth

Handles fiction and nonfiction in every genre and category, except for screenwriting and poetry. Send brief outline and first 50 pages by email, or by post with SASE.

Apple Tree Literary Ltd

86-90 Paul Street, London, EC2A 4NE
Tel: +44 (0) 7515 876444
Email: max@appletreeliterary.co.uk
Website: http://appletreeliterary.co.uk

Handles: Fiction; Nonfiction; *Markets:* Adult; Youth

Represents a range of authors, from journalism and academic non-fiction, to genre fiction and fiction for young adults. No poetry, self-help or lifestyle books, picture books, or romance novels. See website for full guidelines.

Artellus Limited

30 Dorset House, Gloucester Place, London, NW1 5AD
Tel: +44 (0) 20 7935 6972
Fax: +44 (0) 20 8609 0347
Email: artellussubmissions@gmail.com
Website: http://www.artellusltd.co.uk

Handles: Fiction; Nonfiction; *Areas:* Arts; Beauty and Fashion; Biography; Crime; Culture; Current Affairs; Entertainment; Fantasy; Historical; Military; Science; Sci-Fi; *Markets:* Adult; Youth; *Treatments:* Contemporary; Literary

Welcomes submissions from new fiction and nonfiction writers. Send first three chapters and synopsis in first instance, or send query by email. No film or TV scripts. If you would prefer to submit electronically send query by email in advance.

Barbara Levy Literary Agency

64 Greenhill, Hampstead High Street,
London, NW3 5TZ
Tel: +44 (0) 20 7435 9046
Email: blevysubmissions@gmail.com
Website: http://barbaralevyagency.com

Handles: Fiction; Nonfiction; *Markets:*
Adult

Send query with synopsis and first three
chapters (approximately 50 pages) by email
or by post with SAE. No poetry, plays,
original screenplays, scripts or picture books
for children.

Bath Literary Agency

5 Gloucester Road, Bath, BA1 7BH
Email: submissions@
bathliteraryagency.com
Website: http://bathliteraryagency.com

Handles: Fiction; Nonfiction; *Markets:*
Children's; Youth

Handles fiction and nonfiction for children,
from picture books to Young Adult. Send
query by email or by post with SAE for reply
and return of materials if required, along
with the first three chapters (fiction) or the
full manuscript (picture books). See website
for full details.

Bell Lomax Moreton Agency

Suite C, 131 Queensway, Petts Wood, Kent
BR5 1DG
Tel: +44 (0) 20 7930 4447
Fax: +44 (0) 1689 820061
Email: agency@bell-lomax.co.uk
Website: http://www.
belllomaxmoreton.co.uk

Handles: Fiction; Nonfiction; *Areas:*
Biography; Business; Sport; *Markets:* Adult;
Children's

Considers most fiction, nonfiction, and
children's book proposals. No poetry, short
stories, novellas, textbooks, film scripts,
stage plays, or science fiction. Send query by
email with details of any previous work,
short synopsis, and first three chapters (up to
50 pages). For children's picture books send
complete ms. Also accepts postal
submissions. See website for full guidelines.

Berlin Associates

7 Tyers Gate, London, SE1 3HX
Tel: +44 (0) 20 7836 1112
Fax: +44 (0) 20 7632 5296
Email: submissions@berlinassociates.com
Website: http://www.berlinassociates.com

Handles: Scripts; *Areas:* Film; Radio;
Theatre; TV; *Markets:* Adult

Most clients through recommendation or
invitation, but accepts queries by email with
CV, experience, and outline of work you
would like to submit.

The Blair Partnership

PO Box, 7828, London, W1A 4GE
Tel: +44 (0) 20 7504 2520
Email: submissions@
theblairpartnership.com
Website: http://www.theblairpartnership.com

Handles: Fiction; Nonfiction; *Areas:* Crime;
Historical; Horror; Mystery; Thrillers;
Women's Interests; *Markets:* Adult;
Children's; Youth; *Treatments:* Commercial;
Literary

Open to all genres of fiction and nonfiction,
but currently focused on commercial and
reading group fiction, including thrillers,
crime, mysteries, historical, horror,
women's, accessible literary, children's and
YA fiction, and nonfiction with an original
message or platform. Send query by email
with one-page synopsis and first thirty pages
(fiction), or proposal and writing sample
(nonfiction). No scripts, short stories, or
poetry.

Blake Friedmann Literary Agency Ltd

15 Highbury Place, London, N5 1QP
Tel: +44 (0) 20 7387 0842
Email: info@blakefriedmann.co.uk
Website: http://www.blakefriedmann.co.uk

Handles: Fiction; Nonfiction; Scripts; *Areas:*
Autobiography; Biography; Cookery; Crime;
Culture; Current Affairs; Fantasy; Film;
Finance; Historical; Military; Mystery;
Nature; Politics; Psychology; Radio;
Science; Sci-Fi; Sociology; Suspense;
Technology; Thrillers; Travel; TV; Women's

Interests; *Markets:* Adult; Children's; Youth; *Treatments:* Commercial; Contemporary; Literary; Popular

Send query by email to a specific agent best suited to your work. See website for full submission guidelines, details of agents, and individual agent contact details.

Media department currently only accepting submissions from writers with produced credits.

Reply not guaranteed. If no response within 8 weeks, assume rejection.

BookBlast Ltd.

PO Box 20184, London, W10 5AU
Tel: +44 (0) 20 8968 3089
Email: gen@bookblast.com
Website: https://www.bookblast.com

Handles: Fiction; Nonfiction; *Areas:* Autobiography; Culture; Travel; *Markets:* Adult

Closed to submissions as at January 2019. Check website for current status.

Handles adult fiction and nonfiction. Currently reading very selectively. Send query with one-page synopsis for fiction, or full outline for nonfiction, with first three chapters and SAE. No scripts or children's books. Film, TV, and radio rights normally sold for works by existing clients. Also offers translation consultancy service. No submissions on fax, email, or disc. Notification must be given of any other agencies previously or currently submitted to.

The Bright Literary Academy

Studio 102, 250 York Road, London, SW11 1RJ
Tel: +44 (0) 20 7326 9140
Email: literarysubmissions@brightgroupinternational.com
Website: http://brightliteraryagency.com

Handles: Fiction; *Areas:* Autobiography; Entertainment; Literature; Mystery; Sci-Fi; Self-Help; Short Stories; Thrillers; TV; Women's Interests; *Markets:* Children's;

Youth; *Treatments:* Commercial; Contemporary; Mainstream; Positive

A boutique literary agency representing the most fabulous new talent to grace the publishing industry in recent years. Born out of the success of a leading illustration agency with an outstanding global client list this agency aims to produce sensational material across all genres of children's publishing, including novelty, picture books, fiction and adult autobiographies, in order to become a one-stop-shop for publishers looking for something extra special to fit into their lists.

Prides itself on nurturing the creativity of its authors and illustrators so that they can concentrate on their craft rather than negotiate their contracts. As a creative agency we develop seeds of ideas into something extraordinary, before searching for the right publisher with which to develop them further to create incredible and unforgettable books.

We are fortunate enough to have a never-ending source of remarkable material at our fingertips and a stable of exceptional creators who are all united by one common goal – a deep passion and dedication to children's books and literature in all its shapes and forms.

Send query by email only, with synopsis and first three chapters, or whole text for picture books.

Brotherstone Creative Management

Mortimer House, 37-41 Mortimer Street, London, W1T 3JH
Tel: +44 (0) 7908 542866
Email: submissions@bcm-agency.com
Website: http://bcm-agency.com

Handles: Fiction; Nonfiction; *Markets:* Adult; *Treatments:* Commercial; Literary

Always on the search for talented new writers. Send query by email. For fiction, include the first three chapters or 50 pages and 2-page synopsis. For nonfiction, include detailed outline and sample chapter. No scripts.

C+W (Conville & Walsh)
Haymarket House, 28-29 Haymarket,
London, SW1Y 4SP
Tel: +44 (0) 20 7393 4200
Email: suc@cwagency.co.uk
Website: http://cwagency.co.uk

Handles: Fiction; Nonfiction; *Areas:*
Autobiography; Biography; Crime; Current
Affairs; Fantasy; Historical; Humour;
Leisure; Lifestyle; Men's Interests; Military;
Mystery; Psychology; Science; Sci-Fi; Sport;
Suspense; Thrillers; Travel; Women's
Interests; *Markets:* Adult; Children's; Youth;
Treatments: Commercial; Literary

See website for agent profiles and submit to
one particular agent only. Send submissions
by email as Word .doc files only. No postal
submissions. For fiction, please submit the
first three sample chapters of the completed
manuscript (or about 50 pages) with a one to
two page synopsis. For nonfiction, send 30-
page proposal. No poetry or scripts, or
picture books. See website for full
guidelines.

Caroline Davidson Literary Agency
5 Queen Anne's Gardens, London, W4 1TU
Tel: +44 (0) 20 8995 5768
Email: enquiries@cdla.co.uk
Website: https://www.cdla.co.uk

Handles: Fiction; Nonfiction; Reference;
Areas: Archaeology; Architecture; Arts;
Biography; Cookery; Culture; Design;
Gardening; Health; Historical; Lifestyle;
Medicine; Nature; Politics; Psychology;
Science; *Markets:* Adult

Send query by post only. See website for full
guidelines.

Caroline Sheldon Literary Agency
71 Hillgate Place, London, W8 7SS
Tel: +44 (0) 20 7727 9102
Email: carolinesheldon@
carolinesheldon.co.uk
Website: http://www.carolinesheldon.co.uk

Handles: Fiction; Nonfiction; *Areas:*
Autobiography; Fantasy; Historical;

Humour; Suspense; Women's Interests;
Markets: Adult; Children's; Youth;
Treatments: Commercial; Contemporary;
Literary

Send query by email only. Do not query both
agents. See website for both email addresses
and appropriate subject line to include.
Handles fiction and human-interest
nonfiction for adults, and fiction for children,
including full-length and picture books.

Casarotto Ramsay and Associates Ltd
3rd Floor, 7 Savoy Court, Strand, London,
WC2R 0EX
Tel: +44 (0) 20 7287 4450
Email: info@casarotto.co.uk
Website: https://www.casarotto.co.uk

Handles: Scripts; *Areas:* Film; Radio;
Theatre; TV; *Markets:* Adult

Handles scripts only – no books. Any
unsolicited scripts, treatments or other
reading materials will be deleted unread.

Caskie Mushens
London,
Email: jmsubmissions@caskiemushens.com
Website: http://www.caskiemushens.com

Handles: Fiction; Nonfiction; *Areas:*
Autobiography; Crime; Fantasy; Historical;
Humour; Politics; Romance; Science; Sci-Fi;
Thrillers; *Markets:* Adult; Youth;
Treatments: Commercial; Literary; Popular

Send query by email only. No physical
submissions. See website for individual
agent interests and contact details.

The Catchpole Agency
53 Cranham Street, Oxford, OX2 6DD
Tel: +44 (0) 7789 588070
Email: submissions@
thecatchpoleagency.co.uk
Website: http://www.
thecatchpoleagency.co.uk

Handles: Fiction; *Markets:* Children's

**Closed to submissions as at March 2019.
Check website for current status.**

Works on children's books with both artists and writers. Send query by email with sample pasted directly into the body of the email (the whole text of a picture book or a couple of chapters of a novel). No attachments. See website for full guidelines.

Catherine Pellegrino & Associates

148 Russell Court, Woburn Place, London, WC1H 0LR
Email: catherine@catherinepellegrino.co.uk
Website: http://catherinepellegrino.co.uk

Handles: Fiction; *Markets:* Children's; Youth; *Treatments:* Commercial; Literary

Handles children's books, from picture books to young adult. Send query by email with some background on you and the book, plus synopsis and first three chapters or approximately 50 pages, up to a natural break. See website for full details.

Cecily Ware Literary Agents

19C John Spencer Square, London, N1 2LZ
Tel: +44 (0) 20 7359 3787
Email: info@cecilyware.com
Website: http://www.cecilyware.com

Handles: Scripts; *Areas:* Drama; Film; Humour; TV; *Markets:* Adult; Children's

Handles film and TV scripts only. No books or theatre scripts. Submit complete script with covering letter, CV, and SAE. No email submissions or return of material without SAE and correct postage.

Chartwell

14 Gray's Inn Road, London, WC1X 8HN
Tel: +44 (0) 20 7293 0864
Email: hello@chartwellspeakers.com
Website: http://www.chartwellspeakers.com

Handles: Fiction; Nonfiction; *Areas:* Autobiography; Biography; Cookery; Crime; Health; Historical; Lifestyle; Mystery; Psychology; Science; Suspense; Technology; Thrillers; Women's Interests; *Markets:* Adult; Children's; Youth

Agency handling speakers and authors. Will consider all fiction and nonfiction, but particularly interested in General fiction, Mystery/suspense/thriller/crime, Women's fiction, Children's and YA (fiction); and Biography/memoir, Technology, Science, History, Personal development, Health (including popular psychology), Cookery and lifestyle (nonfiction). Send query by email only. See website for full guidelines.

Mic Cheetham Literary Agency

50 Albemarle Street, London, W1S 4BD
Tel: +44 (0) 20 7495 2002
Fax: +44 (0) 20 7399 2801
Email: simon@miccheetham.com
Website: http://www.miccheetham.com

Handles: Fiction; Nonfiction; *Areas:* Crime; Fantasy; Historical; Sci-Fi; Thrillers; *Markets:* Adult; *Treatments:* Commercial; Literary; Mainstream

Send query with SAE, first three chapters, and publishing history. Focuses on fiction, and is not elitist about genre or literary fiction, providing it combines good writing, great storytelling, intelligence, imagination, and (as a bonus) anarchic wit. Film and TV scripts handled for existing clients only. No poetry, children's, illustrated books, or unsolicited MSS. Do not send manuscripts by email. Approach in writing in the first instance (no email scripts accepted).

Christine Green Authors' Agent

PO Box 70098, London, SE15 5AU
Tel: +44 (0) 7507 764632
Email: info@christinegreen.co.uk
Website: http://www.christinegreen.co.uk

Handles: Fiction; Nonfiction; *Markets:* Adult; Youth; *Treatments:* Commercial; Literary

Focusses on fiction for adult and young adult, and also considers narrative nonfiction. No children's books, genre science-fiction/fantasy, poetry or scripts. Send query by email (preferred) or by post with SAE. No submissions by fax or CD. See website for full submission guidelines.

The Christopher Little Literary Agency

48 Walham Grove, London, SW6 1QR
Tel: +44 (0) 20 7736 4455
Fax: +44 (0) 20 7736 4490
Email: submissions@christopherlittle.net
Website: http://www.christopherlittle.net

Handles: Fiction; Nonfiction; *Markets:*
Adult; *Treatments:* Commercial; Literary

Closed to submissions as at February 2018

Handles commercial and literary full-length
fiction and nonfiction. Film scripts handled
for existing clients only (no submissions of
film scripts). Send query by email (preferred)
or by post with SAE or IRCs. Attach one-
page synopsis and three consecutive chapters
(fiction) or proposal (nonfiction). No poetry,
plays, textbooks, short stories, illustrated
children's books, science fiction, fantasy, or
submissions by email.

Clare Hulton Literary Agency

Tel: +44 (0) 7929 407589
Email: info@clarehulton.co.uk
Website: http://www.clarehulton.com

Handles: Fiction; Nonfiction; *Areas:*
Autobiography; Cookery; Culture;
Historical; Humour; Lifestyle; Music;
Philosophy; Self-Help; TV; *Markets:* Adult;
Children's; *Treatments:* Commercial;
Popular

Specialises in nonfiction, but also has a small
commercial fiction and children's list. Finds
most authors through recommendation, but
open to brief queries by email, explaining
what your book is about. No attachments. If
no response within two weeks, assume
rejection.

Coombs Moylett & Maclean Literary Agency

120 New Kings Road, London, SW6 4LZ
Tel: +44 (0) 20 8740 0454
Email: info@cmm.agency
Website: https://cmm.agency

Handles: Fiction; Nonfiction; *Areas:*
Biography; Cookery; Crime; Current Affairs;
Historical; Lifestyle; Mystery; Nature; Self-

Help; Suspense; Thrillers; Women's
Interests; *Markets:* Adult; Children's; Youth;
Treatments: Commercial; Contemporary;
Literary

Handles historical fiction, crime/
mystery/suspense and thrillers, women's
fiction from chick-lit to sagas to
contemporary and literary fiction. Also
children's and Young Adult fiction. In
nonfiction, considers history, biography,
current affairs, cookery, wellbeing, lifestyle,
self-help, nature, nutrition and lived
experiences.

Send query with synopsis and first three
chapters via online form. No submissions by
fax or by post. No poetry, plays or scripts for
film and TV. Whole books and postal
submissions will not be read.

Creative Authors Ltd

Email: write@creativeauthors.co.uk
Website: https://www.creativeauthors.co.uk

Handles: Fiction; Nonfiction; *Areas:* Arts;
Autobiography; Biography; Business;
Cookery; Crafts; Crime; Culture; Health;
Historical; Humour; Nature; Women's
Interests; *Markets:* Adult; Children's;
Treatments: Commercial; Literary

**As at April 2019, not accepting new fiction
clients. See website for current situation.**

We are a dynamic literary agency –
established to provide an attentive and
unique platform for writers and scriptwriters
and representing a growing list of clients.
We're on the lookout for fresh talent and
books with strong commercial potential. No
unsolicited MSS, but considers queries by
email. No paper submissions. Do not
telephone regarding submissions.

Curtis Brown

Haymarket House, 28/29 Haymarket,
London, SW1Y 4SP
Tel: +44 (0) 20 7393 4400
Email: info@curtisbrown.co.uk
Website: http://www.
curtisbrowncreative.co.uk

Handles: Fiction; Nonfiction; Scripts; *Areas:*
Biography; Crime; Fantasy; Film; Historical;

Radio; Science; Suspense; Theatre; Thrillers; TV; *Markets:* Adult; Children's; Youth; *Treatments:* Literary; Mainstream; Popular

Renowned and long established London agency. Handles general fiction and nonfiction, and scripts. Also represents directors, designers, and presenters. No longer accepts submissions by post or email – all submissions must be made using online submissions manager. Also offers services such as writing courses for which authors are charged.

The Darley Anderson Agency

Estelle House, 11 Eustace Road, London, SW6 1JB
Tel: +44 (0) 20 7386 2674
Email: camilla@darleyanderson.com
Website: http://www.darleyanderson.com

Handles: Fiction; *Areas:* Crime; Fantasy; Historical; Horror; Humour; Mystery; Romance; Suspense; Thrillers; Women's Interests; *Markets:* Adult; Children's; Youth; *Treatments:* Commercial; Literary

Accepts submissions by email and by post. See website for individual agent requirements, submission guidelines, and contact details. No poetry, short stories, screenplays, radio plays, or theatre scripts.

David Luxton Associates

23 Hillcourt Avenue, London, N12 8EY
Tel: +44 (0) 20 8922 3942
Email: nick@davidluxtonassociates.co.uk
Website: http://www.
davidluxtonassociates.co.uk

Handles: Nonfiction; Reference; *Areas:* Autobiography; Biography; Culture; Historical; Politics; Sport; Travel; *Markets:* Adult; *Treatments:* Popular

Specialises in nonfiction, including sports, memoir, history, popular reference and politics. No scripts or screenplays. Most clients by recommendation, but will consider email queries. See website for correct email addresses for different subjects. No submissions by post.

David Godwin Associates

2nd Floor, 40 Rosebery Avenue, Clerkenwell, London, EC1R 4RX
Tel: +44 (0) 20 7240 9992
Email: sebastiangodwin@
davidgodwinassociates.co.uk
Website: http://www.
davidgodwinassociates.com

Handles: Fiction; Nonfiction; *Markets:* Adult; *Treatments:* Literary

Handles a range of nonfiction and fiction. Send query by email with synopsis and first 30 pages. No poetry. No picture books, except for existing clients.

David Higham Associates Ltd

6th Floor, Waverley House, 7–12 Noel Street, London, W1F 8GQ
Tel: +44 (0) 20 7434 5900
Fax: +44 (0) 20 7437 1072
Email: submissions@davidhigham.co.uk
Website: http://www.davidhigham.co.uk

Handles: Fiction; Nonfiction; Scripts; *Areas:* Autobiography; Biography; Cookery; Crime; Current Affairs; Drama; Film; Historical; Humour; Nature; Theatre; Thrillers; TV; *Markets:* Adult; Children's; Youth; *Treatments:* Commercial; Literary; Serious

For adult fiction and nonfiction contact "Adult Submissions Department" by post only with SASE, covering letter, CV, and synopsis (fiction)/proposal (nonfiction) and first two or three chapters. For children's / YA fiction submit by email to the specific children's submission address given on the website, with covering letter, synopsis, CV, and first two or three chapters (or complete MS if a picture book). See website for complete guidelines. Scripts by referral only.

DHH Literary Agency Ltd

23-27 Cecil Court, London, WC2N 4EZ
Tel: +44 (0) 20 7836 7376
Email: enquiries@dhhliteraryagency.com
Website: http://www.dhhliteraryagency.com

Handles: Fiction; Nonfiction; Scripts; *Areas:* Adventure; Archaeology; Autobiography; Biography; Crime; Fantasy; Film; Historical; Sci-Fi; Theatre; Thrillers; TV; Women's

Interests; *Markets:* Adult; Children's; Youth; *Treatments:* Literary

Accepts submissions by email only. No postal submissions. See website for specific agent interests and email addresses and approach one agent only. Do not send submissions to generic "enquiries" email address.

Diamond Kahn and Woods (DKW) Literary Agency Ltd

Tel: +44 (0) 20 3514 6544
Email: info@dkwlitagency.co.uk
Website: http://dkwlitagency.co.uk

Handles: Fiction; Nonfiction; *Areas:* Adventure; Archaeology; Biography; Crime; Culture; Fantasy; Gothic; Historical; Humour; Politics; Sci-Fi; Sociology; Suspense; Thrillers; *Markets:* Adult; Children's; Youth; *Treatments:* Commercial; Contemporary; Literary

Send submissions by email. See website for specific agent interests and contact details. Do not send submissions to general agency email address.

Dinah Wiener Ltd

12 Cornwall Grove, Chiswick, London, W4 2LB
Tel: +44 (0) 20 8994 6011
Email: dinah@dwla.co.uk

Handles: Fiction; Nonfiction; *Areas:* Autobiography; Biography; Cookery; Science; *Markets:* Adult

Not taking on new clients as at October 2018.

Send preliminary query letter with SAE. No poetry, short stories, scripts, or children's books.

Eddison Pearson Ltd

West Hill House, 6 Swains Lane, London, N6 6QS
Tel: +44 (0) 20 7700 7763
Email: enquiries@eddisonpearson.com
Website: http://www.eddisonpearson.com

Handles: Fiction; Nonfiction; Poetry; *Markets:* Children's; Youth; *Treatments:* Literary

Send query by email only (or even blank email) for auto-response containing up-to-date submission guidelines and email address for submissions. No unsolicited MSS. No longer accepts submissions or enquiries by post. Send query with one to three chapters by email only to address provided in auto-response. Response in 6-10 weeks. If no response after 10 weeks, follow up by email.

Edwards Fuglewicz

49 Great Ormond Street, London, WC1N 3HZ
Tel: +44 (0) 20 7405 6725
Email: jill@efla.co.uk

Handles: Fiction; Nonfiction; *Areas:* Biography; Historical; *Markets:* Adult; *Treatments:* Commercial; Literary

Handles literary and commercial fiction, and nonfiction. No children's, science fiction, horror, or email submissions.

Elaine Steel

49 Greek Street, London, W1D 4EG
Tel: +44 (0) 1273 739022
Email: info@elainesteel.com
Website: http://www.elainesteel.com

Handles: Fiction; Nonfiction; Scripts; *Areas:* Film; Radio; TV; *Markets:* Adult

Send query by email with CV and outline, along with details of experience. No unsolicited mss.

Elise Dillsworth Agency (EDA)

Email: submissions@ elisedillsworthagency.com
Website: http://elisedillsworthagency.com

Handles: Fiction; Nonfiction; *Areas:* Autobiography; Biography; Cookery; Travel; *Markets:* Adult; *Treatments:* Commercial; Literary

Represents writers from around the world. Looking for literary and commercial fiction, and nonfiction (especially memoir, autobiography, biography, cookery and travel writing). No science fiction, fantasy, poetry, film scripts, or plays. No young adult, or children's, except for existing authors. Send query by email only (postal submissions no longer accepted). For fiction, include synopsis up to two pages and first three chapters, up to about 50 pages, as Word or PDF attachments. For nonfiction, send details of expertise / credentials, proposal, chapter outline, and writing sample of around 30 pages as a Word file attachment. See website for full guidelines. Allow eight weeks for response.

Elizabeth Roy Literary Agency

White Cottage, Greatford, Stamford, Lincolnshire PE9 4PR
Tel: +44 (0) 1778 560672
Website: http://www.elizabethroy.co.uk

Handles: Fiction; Nonfiction; *Areas:* Humour; Romance; *Markets:* Children's

Handles fiction and nonfiction for children. Particularly interested in funny fiction, gentle romance for young teens, picture book texts for pre-school children, and books with international market appeal. Send query by post with return postage, synopsis, and sample chapters. No science fiction, poetry, plays or adult books.

Emily Sweet Associates

Website: http://www.
emilysweetassociates.com

Handles: Fiction; Nonfiction; *Areas:* Biography; Cookery; Current Affairs; Historical; *Markets:* Adult; *Treatments:* Commercial; Literary

No Young Adult or children's. Query through form on website in first instance.

Eve White: Literary Agent

54 Gloucester Street, London, SW1V 4EG
Tel: +44 (0) 20 7630 1155
Email: fiction@evewhite.co.uk
Website: http://www.evewhite.co.uk

Handles: Fiction; Nonfiction; *Markets:* Adult; Children's; Youth; *Treatments:* Commercial; Literary

Important! Check and follow website submission guidelines before contacting!

DO NOT send nonfiction or children's submissions to email address listed on this page – see website for specific submission email addresses for different areas.

FICTION SUBMISSIONS ONLY to the email address on this page.

This agency requests that you go to their website for up-to-date submission procedure.

Commercial and literary fiction, nonfiction and children's fiction. Not currently accepting picture books as at October 2018 (check website for current status). No reading fee. See website for detailed submission guidelines. Submission by email only.

Faith Evans Associates

27 Park Avenue North, London, N8 7RU
Tel: +44 (0) 20 8340 9920
Email: faith@faith-evans.co.uk
Website: https://www.faith-evans.co.uk

Handles: Fiction; Nonfiction; *Markets:* Adult

Small agency with full list. Not accepting new clients as at June 2019. No phone calls, or unsolicited MSS.

Felix de Wolfe

20 Old Compton Street, London, W1D 4TW
Tel: +44 (0) 20 7242 5066
Fax: +44 (0) 20 7242 8119
Email: info@felixdewolfe.com
Website: http://www.felixdewolfe.com

Handles: Fiction; Scripts; *Areas:* Film; Radio; Theatre; TV; *Markets:* Adult

Send query letter with SAE, short synopsis, and CV by post only, unless alternative arrangements have been made with the agency in advance. Quality fiction and scripts only. No nonfiction, children's books, or unsolicited MSS.

Film Rights Ltd in association with Laurence Fitch Ltd

11 Pandora Road, London, NW6 1TS
Tel: +44 (0) 20 8001 3040
Fax: +44 (0) 20 8711 3171
Email: information@filmrights.ltd.uk
Website: http://filmrights.ltd.uk

Handles: Fiction; Scripts; *Areas:* Film;
Horror; Radio; Theatre; TV; *Markets:* Adult;
Children's

Represents films, plays, and novels, for
adults and children.

Fox & Howard Literary Agency

39 Eland Road, London, SW11 5JX
Tel: +44 (0) 20 7223 9452
Email: enquiries@foxandhoward.co.uk
Website: http://www.foxandhoward.co.uk

Handles: Nonfiction; Reference; *Areas:*
Biography; Business; Culture; Health;
Historical; Lifestyle; Psychology; Self-Help;
Spiritual; *Markets:* Adult

**Closed to submissions as at June 2019.
Please check website for current status.**

Send query with synopsis and SAE for
response. Small agency specialising in
nonfiction that works closely with its
authors. No unsolicited MSS.

Frances Kelly Agency

111 Clifton Road, Kingston upon Thames,
Surrey KT2 6PL
Tel: +44 (0) 20 8549 7830

Handles: Nonfiction; Reference; *Areas:*
Arts; Biography; Business; Cookery;
Finance; Health; Historical; Lifestyle;
Medicine; Self-Help; *Markets:* Academic;
Adult; Professional

Send query with SAE, CV, and synopsis or
brief description of work. Scripts handled for
existing clients only. No unsolicited MSS.

Fraser Ross Associates

6/2 Wellington Place, Edinburgh, Scotland
EH6 7EQ
Tel: +44 (0) 1315 532759

Email: fraserrossassociates@gmail.com
Website: http://www.fraserross.co.uk

Handles: Fiction; Nonfiction; *Markets:*
Adult; Children's; *Treatments:* Commercial;
Literary; Mainstream

Send query by email or by post, including
CV, the first three chapters and synopsis for
fiction, or a one page proposal and the
opening and a further two chapters for
nonfiction. For picture books, send complete
MS, without illustrations. No poetry,
playscripts, screenplays, or individual short
stories.

Georgina Capel Associates Ltd

29 Wardour Street, London, W1D 6PS
Tel: +44 (0) 20 7734 2414
Email: georgina@georginacapel.com
Website: http://www.georginacapel.com

Handles: Fiction; Nonfiction; *Areas:*
Biography; Film; Historical; Radio; TV;
Markets: Adult; *Treatments:* Commercial;
Literary

Handles general fiction and nonfiction. Send
query outlining writing history (for
nonfiction, what qualifies you to write your
book), with synopsis around 500 words and
first three chapters, plus SAE or email
address for reply. Submissions are not
returned. Mark envelope for the attention of
the Submissions Department. Accepts
submissions by email, but prefers them by
post. Response only if interested, normally
within 6 weeks. Film and TV scripts handled
for established clients only.

The Good Literary Agency

Email: info@thegoodliteraryagency.org
Website: https://www.
thegoodliteraryagency.org

Handles: Fiction; Nonfiction; *Markets:*
Adult; Children's; Family; Youth

Focused on discovering, developing and
launching the careers of writers of colour,
disability, working class, LGBTQ+ and
anyone who feels their story is not being told
in the mainstream. Writers must be born or
resident in Britain. No poetry, plays, or

screenplays. See website for full guidelines and to submit via online form.

Graham Maw Christie Literary Agency

37 Highbury Place, London, N5 1QP
Tel: +44 (0) 7971 268342
Email: submissions@
grahammawchristie.com
Website: http://www.
grahammawchristie.com

Handles: Nonfiction; Reference; *Areas:*
Autobiography; Business; Cookery; Crafts;
Gardening; Health; Historical; Humour;
Lifestyle; Philosophy; Science; Self-Help;
Markets: Adult; Children's

No fiction, poetry, or scripts. Send query with one-page summary, a paragraph on the contents of each chapter, your qualifications for writing it, details of your online presence, market analysis, what you could do to help promote your book, and a sample chapter or two. Prefers approaches by email.

Greene & Heaton Ltd

37 Goldhawk Road, London, W12 8QQ
Tel: +44 (0) 20 8749 0315
Email: submissions@greeneheaton.co.uk
Website: http://www.greeneheaton.co.uk

Handles: Fiction; Nonfiction; *Areas:*
Autobiography; Biography; Cookery; Crime;
Current Affairs; Fantasy; Gardening; Health;
Historical; Humour; Science; Sci-Fi;
Thrillers; Travel; Women's Interests;
Markets: Adult; Youth; *Treatments:*
Contemporary; Literary

Send query by email only, including synopsis and three chapters or approximately 50 pages. No submissions by post. No response unless interested. Handles all types of fiction and nonfiction, but no scripts or children's picture books.

The Greenhouse Literary Agency

Tel: +44 (0) 20 7841 3959
Email: submissions@
greenhouseliterary.com
Website: http://www.greenhouseliterary.com

Handles: Fiction; *Markets:* Children's;
Youth

Transatlantic agency with offices in the US and London. Handles children's and young adult fiction only. For novels, send query by email with first five pages pasted into the body of the email. For picture books (maximum 1,000 words) paste full text into the box of the email. No picture book submissions from authors who are not also illustrators. No attachments or hard copy submissions. See website for full guidelines.

Gregory & Company, Authors' Agents

6th Floor, Waverley House, 7–12 Noel Street, London, W1F 8GQ
Tel: +44 (0) 20 7610 4676
Email: maryjones@davidhigham.co.uk
Website: http://www.
gregoryandcompany.co.uk

Handles: Fiction; *Areas:* Crime; Historical;
Thrillers; *Markets:* Adult; *Treatments:*
Commercial

Particularly interested in Crime, Family Sagas, Historical Fiction, Thrillers and Upmarket Commercial Fiction. Send query with CV, one-page synopsis, future writing plans, and first ten pages, by post with SAE, or by email. No unsolicited MSS, Business Books, Children's, Young Adult Fiction, Nonfiction, Plays, Screenplays, Poetry, Science Fiction, Future Fiction, Fantasy, Self Help, Lifestyle books, Short Stories, Spiritual, New Age, Philosophy, Supernatural, Paranormal, Horror, Travel, or True Crime.

David Grossman Literary Agency Ltd

118b Holland Park Avenue, London, W11 4UA
Tel: +44 (0) 20 7221 2770
Email: david@dglal.co.uk

Handles: Fiction; Nonfiction; *Markets:*
Adult

Send preliminary letter before making a submission. No approaches or submissions by fax or email. Usually works with published fiction writers, but well-written and original work from beginners considered. No poetry, scripts, technical books for students, or unsolicited MSS.

Hardman & Swainson

S86, New Wing, Somerset House, Strand, London, WC2R 1LA
Tel: +44 (0) 20 3701 7449
Email: submissions@hardmanswainson.com
Website: http://www.hardmanswainson.com

Handles: Fiction; Nonfiction; *Areas:* Autobiography; Crime; Health; Historical; Horror; Humour; Medicine; Philosophy; Psychology; Science; Suspense; Thrillers; Women's Interests; *Markets:* Adult; Children's; Youth; *Treatments:* Commercial; Contemporary; Literary; Popular

Agency launched June 2012 by former colleagues at an established agency. Welcomes submissions of fiction and nonfiction, but no submissions by post. See website for full submission guidelines.

hhb agency ltd

62 Grafton Way, London, W1T 5DW
Tel: +44 (0) 20 7405 5525
Email: heather@hhbagency.com
Website: http://www.hhbagency.com

Handles: Fiction; Nonfiction; *Areas:* Adventure; Autobiography; Biography; Business; Cookery; Crime; Culture; Entertainment; Historical; Humour; Politics; Travel; TV; Women's Interests; *Markets:* Adult; *Treatments:* Commercial; Contemporary; Literary; Popular

Represents nonfiction writers, particularly in the areas of journalism, history and politics, travel and adventure, contemporary autobiography and biography, books about words and numbers, popular culture and quirky humour, entertainment and television, business, family memoir, food and cookery. Also handles commercial fiction. Not accepting unsolicited submissions as at October 2017.

Holroyde Cartey

Email: claire@holroydecartey.com
Website: http://www.holroydecartey.com

Handles: Fiction; Nonfiction; *Markets:* Children's

Handles fiction and nonfiction for children of all ages, including picture books. Also represents illustrators. Welcomes submissions from debut and established authors and illustrators. Send query by email only, with cover letter, synopsis, and full ms as separate Word file attachments. See website for individual agent details and interests and approach one agent only. Aims to respond to every submission, within six weeks.

Vanessa Holt Ltd

59 Crescent Road, Leigh-on-Sea, Essex SS9 2PF
Tel: +44 (0) 1702 473787
Email: v.holt791@btinternet.com

Handles: Fiction; Nonfiction; *Markets:* Adult

General fiction and nonfiction. No unsolicited mss or overseas approaches.

ILA (Intercontinental Literary Agency)

5 New Concordia Wharf, Mill Street, London, SE1 2BB
Tel: +44 (0) 20 7379 6611
Fax: +44 (0) 20 7240 4724
Email: ila@ila-agency.co.uk
Website: http://www.ila-agency.co.uk

Handles: Fiction; Nonfiction; *Areas:* Translations; *Markets:* Adult; Children's

Handles translation rights only for, among others, the authors of LAW Ltd, London; Harold Matson Co. Inc., New York; PFD, London. Submissions accepted via client agencies and publishers only – no submissions from writers seeking agents.

Independent Talent Group Ltd

40 Whitfield Street, London, W1T 2RH
Tel: +44 (0) 20 7636 6565
Website: http://www.independenttalent.com

Handles: Scripts; *Areas:* Film; Radio; Theatre; TV; *Markets:* Adult

Specialises in scripts and works in association with agencies in Los Angeles and New York. No unsolicited MSS. Materials submitted will not be returned.

InterSaga

237 St Helier Avenue, Morden, Surrey SM4 6JH
Tel: +44 (0) 7534 013597
Email: anna@intersaga.co.uk
Website: http://www.intersaga.co.uk

Handles: Fiction; Nonfiction; Poetry; Reference; Scripts; *Areas:* Adventure; Autobiography; Criticism; Drama; Fantasy; Romance; Sci-Fi; Suspense; Thrillers; Women's Interests; *Markets:* Adult; Children's; Family; Youth; *Treatments:* Commercial; Contemporary; Cynical; Dark; Experimental; In-depth; Light; Literary; Mainstream; Niche; Popular; Positive; Progressive; Satirical; Serious; Traditional

A literary agency that started in the heart of Chiswick. The managing director is a former bookseller and bookshop manager. You can read more on the website.
All genres are welcome. We look forward to hearing from you!

Isabel White Literary Agent

Tel: +44 (0) 20 3070 1602
Email: query.isabelwhite@googlemail.com
Website: http://www.isabelwhite.co.uk

Handles: Fiction; Nonfiction; *Markets:* Adult

Selective one-woman agency, not taking on new clients as at October 2018.

Jane Judd Literary Agency

18 Belitha Villas, London, N1 1PD
Tel: +44 (0) 20 7607 0273
Email: info@janejudd.com
Website: http://www.janejudd.com

Handles: Fiction; Nonfiction; *Areas:* Biography; Cookery; Film; Health; Historical; Self-Help; Sport; *Markets:* Adult; *Treatments:* Commercial; Literary

Closed to submissions as at May 2019.
Check website for current status.

For fiction, send query with synopsis, first two or three chapters, and SAE. For nonfiction send first and/or other sample chapter, synopsis, market info, chapter breakdown, and any supporting evidence or articles. You may telephone in advance to save time for both parties. Also option of submitting online using contact form on website. Particularly interested in self-help, health, biography, popular history and narrative nonfiction, general and historical fiction and literary fiction.

Jane Turnbull

Barn Cottage, Veryan, Truro TR2 5QA
Tel: +44 (0) 20 7727 9409 / +44 (0) 1872 501317
Email: jane@janeturnbull.co.uk
Website: http://www.janeturnbull.co.uk

Handles: Fiction; Nonfiction; *Areas:* Biography; Current Affairs; Entertainment; Gardening; Historical; Humour; Lifestyle; Nature; TV; *Markets:* Adult; Youth; *Treatments:* Commercial; Literary; Mainstream

Agency with offices in London and Cornwall. New clients always welcome and a few taken on every year. Will occasionally take on fiction for older children, but no science fiction, fantasy, or "misery memoirs". Send query by post to Cornwall office with short description of your book or idea. No unsolicited MSS, or queries by email.

Janet Fillingham Associates

52 Lowther Road, London, SW13 9NU
Tel: +44 (0) 20 8748 5594
Email: info@janetfillingham.com
Website: https://www.janetfillingham.com

Handles: Scripts; *Areas:* Film; Theatre; TV; *Markets:* Adult; Children's; Youth

Represents writers and directors for stage, film and TV, as well as librettists, lyricists and composers in musical theatre. Does not represent books. See website for full submission guidelines.

Jenny Brown Associates

31 Marchmont Road, Edinburgh, Scotland
EH9 1HU
Tel: +44 (0) 1312 295334
Email: submissions@
jennybrownassociates.com
Website: https://www.
jennybrownassociates.com

Handles: Fiction; Nonfiction; *Areas:*
Autobiography; Biography; Crime; Culture;
Finance; Historical; Humour; Music;
Romance; Science; Sport; Thrillers;
Women's Interests; *Markets:* Adult;
Children's; *Treatments:* Commercial;
Literary; Popular

Submissions by email only. Accepts
submissions only during specific reading
periods. See website for details.

Jill Foster Ltd (JFL)

48 Charlotte Street, London, W1T 2NS
Tel: +44 (0) 20 3137 8182
Email: agents@jflagency.com
Website: http://www.jflagency.com

Handles: Scripts; *Areas:* Drama; Film;
Humour; Radio; Theatre; TV; *Markets:*
Adult

Handles scripts only (for television, film,
theatre and radio). Considers approaches
from established writers with broadcast
experience, but only accepts submissions
from new writers during specific periods –
consult website for details.

Jo Unwin Literary Agency

West Wing, Somerset House, London,
WC2R 1LA
Tel: +44 (0) 20 7257 9599
Email: submissions@jounwin.co.uk
Website: http://www.jounwin.co.uk

Handles: Fiction; Nonfiction; *Areas:*
Anthropology; Autobiography; Humour;
Medicine; Politics; Psychology;
Translations; Women's Interests; *Markets:*
Adult; Children's; Youth; *Treatments:*
Commercial; Literary

**Closed to submissions as at July 2019.
Check website for current status.**

Handles literary fiction, commercial
women's fiction, comic writing, narrative
nonfiction, Young Adult fiction and fiction
for children aged 9+. No poetry, picture
books, or screenplays, except for existing
clients. Accepts submissions by email.
Mainly represents authors from the UK and
Ireland, and sometimes Australia and New
Zealand. Only represents US authors in very
exceptional circumstances. See website for
full guidelines.

Johnson & Alcock

Bloomsbury House, 74-77 Great Russell
Street, London, WC1B 3DA
Tel: +44 (0) 20 7251 0125
Email: michael@johnsonandalcock.co.uk
Website: http://www.
johnsonandalcock.co.uk

Handles: Fiction; Nonfiction; *Areas:* Arts;
Autobiography; Biography; Crime; Culture;
Current Affairs; Design; Fantasy; Film;
Health; Historical; Lifestyle; Music; Nature;
Psychology; Science; Sci-Fi; Self-Help;
Sport; Suspense; Thrillers; Women's
Interests; *Markets:* Adult; Children's; Youth;
Treatments: Commercial; Literary; Popular

Send query by email (response only if
interested), or by post with SASE. Include
synopsis and first three chapters
(approximately 50 pages). Email
submissions should go to specific agents. See
website for list of agents and full submission
guidelines. No poetry, screenplays,
children's books 0-7, or board or picture
books.

Jonathan Clowes Ltd

10 Iron Bridge House, Bridge Approach,
London, NW1 8BD
Tel: +44 (0) 20 7722 7674
Fax: +44 (0) 20 7722 7677
Email: cara@jonathanclowes.co.uk
Website: https://www.jonathanclowes.co.uk

Handles: Fiction; Nonfiction; Scripts; *Areas:*
Film; Radio; Theatre; TV; *Markets:* Adult;
Treatments: Commercial; Literary

Send query with synopsis and three chapters
(or equivalent sample) by email. No science
fiction, poetry, short stories, academic. Only
considers film/TV clients with previous

success in TV/film/theatre. If no response within six weeks, assume rejection.

Jonathan Pegg Literary Agency
67 Wingate Square, London, SW4 OAF
Tel: +44 (0) 20 7603 6830
Email: submissions@jonathanpegg.com
Website: http://www.jonathanpegg.com

Handles: Fiction; Nonfiction; *Areas:* Arts; Autobiography; Biography; Culture; Current Affairs; Historical; Lifestyle; Nature; Psychology; Science; Thrillers; *Markets:* Adult; *Treatments:* Commercial; Literary; Popular

Established by the agent after twelve years at Curtis Brown. The agency's main areas of interest are:

Fiction: literary fiction, thrillers and quality commercial in general
Non-Fiction: current affairs, memoir and biography, history, popular science, nature, arts and culture, lifestyle, popular psychology

Rights:
Aside from the UK market, the agency will work in association with translation, US, TV & film agents according to each client's best interests.

If you're looking for an agent:
I accept submissions by email. See website for full submission guidelines.

Judith Murdoch Literary Agency
19 Chalcot Square, London, NW1 8YA
Tel: +44 (0) 20 7722 4197
Email: jmlitag@btinternet.com
Website: http://www.judithmurdoch.co.uk

Handles: Fiction; *Areas:* Crime; Women's Interests; *Markets:* Adult; *Treatments:* Commercial; Literary; Popular

Send query by post with SAE or email address for response, brief synopsis, and and first three chapters. Provides editorial advice. No science fiction, fantasy, children's

stories, email submissions, or unsolicited MSS.

Juliet Burton Literary Agency
2 Clifton Avenue, London, W12 9DR
Tel: +44 (0) 20 8762 0148
Email: juliet.burton@julietburton.com

Handles: Fiction; Nonfiction; *Areas:* Crime; Women's Interests; *Markets:* Adult

Particularly interested in crime and women's fiction. Send query with SAE, synopsis, and two sample chapters. No poetry, plays, film scripts, children's, articles, academic material, science fiction, fantasy, or unsolicited MSS.

Michelle Kass Associates
85 Charing Cross Road, London, WC2H 0AA
Tel: +44 (0) 20 7439 1624
Email: office@michellekass.co.uk
Website: http://www.michellekass.co.uk

Handles: Fiction; Scripts; *Areas:* Film; Literature; TV; *Markets:* Adult; *Treatments:* Literary

No email submissions. Approach by telephone in first instance.

Kate Barker Literary, TV, & Film Agency
London,
Tel: +44 (0) 20 7688 1638
Email: kate@katebarker.net
Website: https://www.katebarker.net

Handles: Fiction; Nonfiction; *Areas:* Autobiography; Biography; Business; Crime; Historical; Lifestyle; Psychology; Science; Suspense; Thrillers; Women's Interests; *Markets:* Adult; *Treatments:* Commercial; Literary; Popular

No science fiction (unless literary) and no fantasy or children's. Submit via website submission form.

Kate Hordern Literary Agency

Tel: +44 (0) 117 923 9368
Email: katehordern@blueyonder.co.uk
Website: http://www.katehordern.co.uk

Handles: Fiction; Nonfiction; Reference;
Areas: Autobiography; Business; Crime;
Culture; Current Affairs; Historical; Nature;
Sociology; Thrillers; Women's Interests;
Markets: Adult; Children's; Youth;
Treatments: Commercial; Contemporary;
Literary; Popular

Send query by email only with pitch, outline
or synopsis, and first three chapters. No
submissions by post, or from authors not
resident in the UK. If no response within six
weeks, assume rejection.

Kate Nash Literary Agency

1 Swift Way, Brackley, Northants NN13
6PY
Tel: +44 (0) 844 415 7844
Email: submissions.kn@gmail.com
Website: http://www.katenashliterary.co.uk

Handles: Fiction; Nonfiction; *Markets:*
Adult; *Treatments:* Popular

Open to approaches from both new and
established authors. Represents general and
genre fiction and popular nonfiction. No
poetry, drama, or genre SFF. Send query by
email with synopsis and first chapter / 10
pages pasted into the body of the email (no
attachments).

Keane Kataria Literary Agency

Email: info@keanekataria.co.uk
Website: http://www.keanekataria.co.uk

Handles: Fiction; Nonfiction; *Areas:* Crime;
Women's Interests; *Markets:* Adult;
Treatments: Commercial

Currently accepting submissions in the
crime, domestic noir and women's fiction
genres. No science fiction, fantasy or
children's books. Send query by email only
with synopsis and first three chapters.
Attachments in PDF format only.

Ki Agency Ltd

Studio 315, Screenworks, 22 Highbury
Grove, London, N5 2ER
Tel: +44 (0) 20 3214 8287
Email: meg@ki-agency.co.uk
Website: http://www.ki-agency.co.uk

Handles: Fiction; Nonfiction; Scripts; *Areas:*
Culture; Film; Historical; Politics; Science;
Self-Help; Sport; Theatre; TV; *Markets:*
Adult; *Treatments:* Popular

Represents novelists and scriptwriters in all
media. No children's or poetry. Send
synopsis and first three chapters / first 50
pages by email. See website for individual
agent interests.

Kingsford Campbell Literary & Marketing Agents

Email: info@kingsfordcampbell.com
Website: http://kingsfordcampbell.com

Handles: Fiction; Nonfiction; *Markets:*
Adult

**Closed to submissions as at December
2018. Check website for current status.**

Actively seeking submissions from new and
established writers. Very broad tastes and
interests in both fiction and nonfiction across
genres, subjects and ages, but no poetry,
screenplays, or children's books. See website
for full submission guidelines and online
submission form.

Knight Hall Agency

Lower Ground Floor, 7 Mallow Street,
London, EC1Y 8RQ
Tel: +44 (0) 20 3397 2901
Fax: +44 (0) 871 918 6068
Email: office@knighthallagency.com
Website: http://www.knighthallagency.com

Handles: Scripts; *Areas:* Drama; Film;
Theatre; TV; *Markets:* Adult

**Note: Closed to submissions as at January
2018. Check website for current status.**

Send query by post or email (no
attachments). Only send sample if requested.
Represents playwrights, screenwriters and
writer-directors. Handles adaptation rights

for novels, but does not handle books directly.

Knight Features

Trident Business Centre, 89 Bickersteth Road, London, SW17 9SH
Tel: +44 (0) 20 7622 1467
Email: sam@knightfeatures.co.uk
Website: http://www.knightfeatures.com

Handles: Fiction; Nonfiction; *Areas:* Autobiography; Biography; Business; Health; Historical; Humour; Spiritual; Sport; *Markets:* Adult; Children's

Send query by email or by post with SAE, including CV, synopsis, and three sample chapters. Main areas of interest are: Motorsports; Business; History; Biography; Autobiography. No poetry, cookery, or science fiction. Initial contact may be made by phone or email. See website for full submission guidelines.

Kruger Cowne

Unit 7C, Chelsea Wharf, 15 Lots Road, London, sw100qj
Tel: +44 (0) 20 7352 2277
Email: oscar@krugercowne.com
Website: https://www.krugercowne.com

Handles: Fiction; Nonfiction; *Areas:* Adventure; Anthropology; Arts; Autobiography; Beauty and Fashion; Business; Crime; Culture; Current Affairs; Erotic; Gothic; Health; Historical; Hobbies; Horror; How-to; Humour; Lifestyle; Men's Interests; Military; Music; Nature; New Age; Philosophy; Psychology; Science; Self-Help; Spiritual; Sport; Suspense; Thrillers; Westerns; Women's Interests; *Markets:* Adult; Children's; Youth; *Treatments:* Commercial; Contemporary; Dark; Experimental; Literary; Mainstream; Niche; Popular; Positive; Progressive; Satirical

A talent management agency, with an extremely strong literary arm.
The majority of the works handled by the agency fall into the category of celebrity nonfiction. However, also regularly work with journalists, entrepreneurs and influencers on projects, with a speciality in polemics, and speculative works on the future.

Occasionally take on exceptional fiction authors.

LAW (Lucas Alexander Whitley)

2nd Floor, 16–17 Wardour Mews, London, W1F 8AT
Tel: +44 (0) 20 7471 7900
Fax: +44 (0) 20 7471 7910
Email: lawagencysubmissions@gmail.com
Website: http://www.lawagency.co.uk

Handles: Fiction; Nonfiction; Reference; Scripts; *Areas:* Autobiography; Beauty and Fashion; Biography; Business; Cookery; Crime; Culture; Current Affairs; Fantasy; Health; Historical; Horror; Military; Music; Nature; Philosophy; Politics; Science; Sci-Fi; Sport; Technology; Thrillers; Women's Interests; *Markets:* Adult; Children's; Youth; *Treatments:* Commercial; Literary

Send query by email only. Include short synopsis and the first three chapters or up to 30 pages (whichever is greatest). For children's picture books, submit complete ms. See website for separate email address for children's submissions. No plays, poetry, or textbooks. Film and TV scripts handled for existing clients only. Unlikely to accept submissions from overseas.

LBA Books Ltd

91 Great Russell Street, London, WC1B 3PS
Tel: +44 (0) 20 7637 1234
Fax: +44 (0) 20 7637 2111
Email: info@lbabooks.com
Website: http://www.lbabooks.com

Handles: Fiction; Nonfiction; *Areas:* Adventure; Cookery; Crime; Fantasy; Health; Historical; Lifestyle; Romance; Science; Sci-Fi; Thrillers; TV; Women's Interests; *Markets:* Adult; Children's; Youth; *Treatments:* Commercial; Literary

Send query with synopsis and first three chapters to specific agent by email only. See website for specific agents' interests and email addresses. No scripts, short stories, or poetry.

Limelight Management

10 Filmer Mews, 75 Filmer Road, London,
SW6 7JF
Tel: +44 (0) 20 7384 9950
Fax: +44 (0) 20 7384 9955
Email: mail@limelightmanagement.com
Website: http://www.
limelightmanagement.com

Handles: Fiction; Nonfiction; *Areas:* Arts;
Autobiography; Biography; Business;
Cookery; Crafts; Crime; Health; Historical;
Lifestyle; Mystery; Nature; Science; Sport;
Suspense; Thrillers; Travel; Women's
Interests; *Markets:* Adult; *Treatments:*
Commercial; Literary

Always looking for exciting new authors.
Send query by email with the word
"Submission" in the subject line and
synopsis and first three chapters as Word or
Open Document attachments. Also include
market info, and details of your professional
life and writing ambitions. Film and TV
scripts for existing clients only. See website
for full guidelines.

Linda Seifert Management

Screenworks, Room 315, 22 Highbury
Grove, Islington, London, N5 2ER
Tel: +44 (0) 20 3214 8293
Email: contact@lindaseifert.com
Website: http://www.lindaseifert.com

Handles: Scripts; *Areas:* Film; TV; *Markets:*
Adult; Children's

A London-based management company
representing screenwriters and directors for
film and television. Our outstanding client
list ranges from the highly established to the
new and exciting emerging talent of
tomorrow. Represents UK-based writers and
directors only. Not currently accepting
unsolicited submissions as at July 2018.

Lindsay Literary Agency

East Worldham House, East Worldham,
Alton GU34 3AT
Tel: +44 (0) 0142 083143
Email: info@lindsayliteraryagency.co.uk
Website: http://www.
lindsayliteraryagency.co.uk

Handles: Fiction; Nonfiction; *Markets:*
Adult; Children's; *Treatments:* Literary;
Serious

Send query by email only, including single-
page synopsis and first three chapters. For
picture books send complete ms. No
submissions by post.

Lorella Belli Literary Agency (LBLA)

54 Hartford House, 35 Tavistock Crescent,
Notting Hill, London, W11 1AY
Tel: +44 (0) 20 7727 8547
Fax: +44 (0) 870 787 4194
Email: info@lorellabelliagency.com
Website: http://www.lorellabelliagency.com

Handles: Fiction; Nonfiction; *Markets:*
Adult; *Treatments:* Literary

Send query by post or by email in first
instance. No attachments. Particularly
interested in multicultural / international
writing, and books relating to Italy, or
written in Italian; first novelists, and
journalists; successful self-published authors.
Welcomes queries from new authors and will
suggest revisions where appropriate. No
poetry, children's, original scripts, academic,
SF, or fantasy.

Louise Greenberg Books Ltd

The End House, Church Crescent, London,
N3 1BG
Tel: +44 (0) 20 8349 1179
Email: louisegreenberg@btinternet.com
Website: http://louisegreenbergbooks.co.uk

Handles: Fiction; Nonfiction; *Markets:*
Adult; *Treatments:* Literary; Serious

**Not accepting new writers as at July 2019.
Check website for current status.**

Handles full-length literary fiction and
serious nonfiction only. Only considers new
writers by recommendation.

Lutyens and Rubinstein

21 Kensington Park Road, London, W11
2EU
Tel: +44 (0) 20 7792 4855

Email: submissions@lutyensrubinstein.co.uk
Website: http://www.lutyensrubinstein.co.uk

Handles: Fiction; Nonfiction; *Areas:*
Cookery; *Markets:* Adult; Children's; Youth;
Treatments: Commercial; Literary

Send up to 5,000 words or first three
chapters by email with covering letter and
short synopsis. No film or TV scripts, or
unsolicited submissions by hand or by post.

Macnaughton Lord Representation
3 The Glass House, Royal Oak Yard,
London, SE1 3GE
Tel: +44 (0) 20 7407 9201
Email: info@mlrep.com
Website: http://www.mlrep.com

Handles: Scripts; *Areas:* Arts; Film; Theatre;
TV; *Markets:* Adult

Theatrical and literary agency representing
established names and emerging talent in
theatre, film, tv and the performing arts.
Send query by email with CV and a sample
of your work. Response not guaranteed
unless interested.

Madeleine Milburn Literary, TV & Film Agency
10 Shepherd Market, Mayfair, London, W1J
7QF
Tel: +44 (0) 20 7499 7550
Email: submissions@madeleinemilburn.com
Website: http://madeleinemilburn.co.uk

Handles: Fiction; Nonfiction; Scripts; *Areas:*
Autobiography; Crime; Fantasy; Film;
Historical; Horror; Humour; Lifestyle;
Mystery; Nature; Psychology; Romance;
Science; Sci-Fi; Self-Help; Sport; Suspense;
Thrillers; Translations; TV; Women's
Interests; *Markets:* Adult; Children's; Youth;
Treatments: Commercial; Literary

Send query by email only, with one-page
synopsis and first three chapters for fiction,
or proposal and 30-page writing sample for
nonfiction. See website for full submission
guidelines. Film and TV scripts for
established clients only.

Maggie Pearlstine Associates Ltd
31 Ashley Gardens, Ambrosden Avenue,
London, SW1P 1QE
Tel: +44 (0) 20 7828 4212
Fax: +44 (0) 20 7834 5546
Email: maggie@pearlstine.co.uk

Handles: Fiction; Nonfiction; *Areas:*
Biography; Current Affairs; Health;
Historical; *Markets:* Adult

Small, selective agency, not currently taking
on new clients.

The Marsh Agency
50 Albemarle Street, London, W1S 4BD
Tel: +44 (0) 20 7493 4361
Fax: +44 (0) 20 7495 8961
Email: english.language@marsh-agency.co.uk
Website: http://www.marsh-agency.co.uk

Handles: Fiction; Nonfiction; *Markets:*
Adult; Youth; *Treatments:* Literary

Not currently accepting unsolicited mss as at
March 2018. Most new clients come through
recommendations.

Martin Leonardis Ltd
71-75 Shelton Street, London, WC2H 9JQ
Email: submissions@martinleonardis.com
Website: http://martinleonardis.com

Handles: Fiction; Nonfiction; *Areas:*
Cookery; Lifestyle; Self-Help; *Markets:*
Adult; *Treatments:* Commercial

**Closed to submissions as at January 2019.
Check website for current status.**

For fiction, send complete ms by email with
250-word pitch. For nonfiction, send pitch
with proposal and details of your platform.
No fantasy, space-operas, horror or gothic
fiction, historical nonfiction, YA or
children's fiction, or poetry or short stories.
See website for full details.

Mary Clemmey Literary Agency

6 Dunollie Road, London, NW5 2XP
Tel: +44 (0) 20 7267 1290
Email: mcwords@googlemail.com

Handles: Fiction; Nonfiction; Scripts; *Areas:* Film; Radio; Theatre; TV; *Markets:* Adult

Send query with SAE and description of work only. Handles high-quality work with an international market. No children's books, science fiction, fantasy, or unsolicited MSS or submissions by email. Scripts handled for existing clients only. Do not submit a script or idea for a script unless you are already a client.

MBA Literary Agents Ltd

62 Grafton Way, London, W1T 5DW
Tel: +44 (0) 20 7387 2076
Email: submissions@mbalit.co.uk
Website: http://www.mbalit.co.uk

Handles: Fiction; Nonfiction; Scripts; *Areas:* Arts; Biography; Crafts; Film; Health; Historical; Lifestyle; Radio; Self-Help; Theatre; TV; *Markets:* Adult; Children's; Youth; *Treatments:* Commercial; Literary

For books, send query with CV, synopsis and first three chapters. Not currently accepting unsolicited film and television submissions. Submissions by email only, in Word, PDF or Final Draft format. No submissions by post. See website for full submission guidelines. Works in conjunction with agents in most countries.

Duncan McAra

3 Viewfield Avenue, Bishopbriggs, Glasgow, Scotland G64 2AG
Tel: +44 (0) 1417 721067
Email: duncanmcara@mac.com

Handles: Fiction; Nonfiction; *Areas:* Archaeology; Architecture; Arts; Biography; Historical; Military; Travel; *Markets:* Adult; *Treatments:* Literary

Also interested in books of Scottish interest. Send query letter with SAE in first instance.

Bill McLean Personal Management Ltd

23B Deodar Road, London, SW15 2NP
Tel: +44 (0) 20 8789 8191

Handles: Scripts; *Areas:* Film; Radio; Theatre; TV; *Markets:* Adult

Theatrical agent handling scripts for all media. No books.

The Michael Greer Literary Agency

51 Aragon Court, 8 Hotspur Street, Kennington, London SE11 6BX
Tel: +44 (0) 777 592 0885
Email: mmichaelgreer@yahoo.co.uk
Website: http://www.wix.com/mmichaelgreer/mgla

Handles: Fiction; Nonfiction; Scripts; *Areas:* Business; Lifestyle; Psychology; Sport; *Markets:* Adult; Children's; Professional; Youth; *Treatments:* Commercial; Contemporary; Literary; Mainstream; Popular; Positive

Currently, represents writing mainly in the Sports genre – be that covering certain players, or covering certain games and the philosophy of sports.

We also accept manuscripts in the Young Adult / Teen Fiction category, and in the Literary Fiction category – the latter with an emphasis on work set in a City environment.

Micheline Steinberg Associates

Suite 315, ScreenWorks, 22 Highbury Grove, London, N5 2ER
Tel: +44 (0) 20 3214 8292
Email: info@steinplays.com
Website: http://www.steinplays.com

Handles: Scripts; *Areas:* Film; Radio; Theatre; TV; *Markets:* Adult

We're a mid-size agency in which all the agents have background in theatre and related media. We work closely with writers and the industry, developing writers work, managing their careers, and negotiating all rights. We also have affiliations with book agents and agents overseas including in the USA. Send query with your CV and brief outline of your work through online form, available on website. No unsolicited submissions. Does not consider books.

Mulcahy Associates (Part of MMB Creative)

The Old Truman Brewery, 91 Brick Lane, London, E1 6QL
Tel: +44 (0) 20 3582 9370
Fax: +44 (0) 20 3582 9377
Email: talent@mmbcreative.com
Website: https://mmbcreative.com

Handles: Fiction; Nonfiction; *Areas:* Biography; Crime; Finance; Historical; Lifestyle; Sport; Thrillers; Women's Interests; *Markets:* Adult; Children's; Youth; *Treatments:* Commercial; Literary

See books pages of website to get an idea of the kind of material represented, and submit via online form.

Nick Turner Management Ltd

32 Tavistock Street, London, WC2E 7PB
Tel: +44 (0) 20 7450 3355
Email: nick@nickturnermanagement.com
Website: http://nickturnermanagement.com

Handles: Scripts; *Areas:* Drama; Film; Humour; Radio; TV; *Markets:* Adult; Children's

London-based creative talent agency representing a broad mix of writers, directors and producers working across feature-film, television drama, comedy, children's, continuing-drama and radio. No unsolicited submissions. New clients come through producer or personal recommendations only.

Northbank Talent Management

Email: info@northbanktalent.com
Website: http://www.northbanktalent.com

Handles: Fiction; Nonfiction; *Areas:* Autobiography; Business; Crime; Current Affairs; Drama; Fantasy; Health; Historical; Lifestyle; Politics; Psychology; Science; Sci-Fi; Self-Help; Suspense; Thrillers; Women's

Interests; *Markets:* Adult; Children's; Youth; *Treatments:* Commercial

Literary and talent agency based in central London. Actively seeking new clients. Send query by email with synopsis and first three chapters as Word or Open Document attachments. See website for specific email addresses to use for different types of material.

Deborah Owen Ltd

78 Narrow Street, Limehouse, London, E14 8BP
Tel: +44 (0) 20 7987 5119 / 5441

Handles: Fiction; Nonfiction

Represents only two authors worldwide. Not accepting any new authors.

Peters Fraser + Dunlop

55 New Oxford Street, London, WC1A 1BS
Tel: +44 (0) 20 7344 1000
Fax: +44 (0) 20 7836 9539
Email: info@pfd.co.uk
Website: http://www.pfd.co.uk

Handles: Fiction; Nonfiction; Scripts; *Areas:* Autobiography; Cookery; Crime; Culture; Film; Finance; Gothic; Historical; Horror; Humour; Nature; Psychology; Radio; Science; Sport; Suspense; Theatre; Thrillers; TV; Women's Interests; *Markets:* Adult; Children's; Youth; *Treatments:* Commercial; Dark; Literary; Popular

See website for individual agent interests and submission guidelines.

PEW Literary

46 Lexington Street, London, W1F 0LP
Tel: +44 (0) 20 7734 4464
Email: submissions@pewliterary.com
Website: http://www.pewliterary.com

Handles: Fiction; Nonfiction; *Areas:* Crime; Thrillers; *Markets:* Adult; *Treatments:* Literary

Send query by post or by email, with synopsis and first three chapters (or fifty pages) (fiction); or proposal (nonfiction). If submitting by email, send material in Word or PDF attachment. If submitting by post, do not include SAE as material will be recycled once read. Include email address for response. Aims to respond within six weeks.

Shelley Power Literary Agency Ltd

33 Dumbrells Court, North End, Ditchling, East Sussex BN6 8TG
Tel: +44 (0) 1273 844467
Email: sp@shelleypower.co.uk

Handles: Fiction; Nonfiction; *Markets:* Adult

Send query by email or by post with return postage. No attachments. No poetry, scripts, science fiction, fantasy, young adult, or children's books.

Puttick Literary Agency

Email: editorial@puttick.com
Website: http://www.puttick.com

Handles: Nonfiction; *Areas:* Biography; Culture; Current Affairs; Health; Historical; Philosophy; Science; Self-Help; *Markets:* Adult

Closed to submissions as at May 2017. See website for current situation.

Send query with short two or three page synopsis and CV by email (by preference), or by post with SAE. No fiction, poetry, drama, screenplays, children's books, or submissions by email (enquiries only). Enquiries only should be clearly marked in the subject line to avoid being deleted as spam. Make sure it is made clear if the material is under consideration elsewhere at the same time. Owing to the large volume of submissions we receive, we are only able to reply to those we wish to take further.

Redhammer

Website: http://redhammer.info

Handles: Fiction; Nonfiction; *Areas:* Autobiography; Crime; Entertainment; Mystery; Thrillers; *Markets:* Adult

Generally too busy to consider approaches from writers, unless they already have some experience of the publishing industry.

However does offer occasional pop-up submission opportunities. Check website for details.

Richford Becklow Literary Agency

Tel: +44 (0) 1564 739508 / + 44 (0) 7510 023823
Email: enquiries@richfordbecklow.co.uk
Website: http://www.richfordbecklow.com

Handles: Fiction; Nonfiction; *Areas:* Arts; Autobiography; Biography; Cookery; Crime; Fantasy; Gardening; Gothic; Historical; Horror; Lifestyle; Literature; Romance; Sci-Fi; Self-Help; Women's Interests; *Markets:* Adult; Youth; *Treatments:* Commercial; Contemporary; Literary; Satirical; Serious

Company founded in 2012 by an experienced agent, previously at the longest established literary agency in the world. Interested in fiction and nonfiction. See website for full submission guidelines.

Robert Dudley Agency

135A Bridge Street, Ashford, Kent TN25 5DP
Email: info@robertdudleyagency.co.uk
Website: http://www.robertdudleyagency.co.uk

Handles: Nonfiction; *Areas:* Adventure; Biography; Business; Current Affairs; Historical; Medicine; Military; Self-Help; Sport; Technology; Travel; *Markets:* Adult; *Treatments:* Popular

Specialises in nonfiction. No fiction submissions. Send submissions by email, preferably in Word format, as opposed to PDF.

Robert Smith Literary Agency Ltd

12 Bridge Wharf, 156 Caledonian Road, London, N1 9UU
Tel: +44 (0) 20 7278 2444
Fax: +44 (0) 20 7833 5680
Email: robert@robertsmithliteraryagency.com
Website: http://www.robertsmithliteraryagency.com

Handles: Nonfiction; *Areas:* Autobiography; Biography; Crime; Culture; Current Affairs; Health; Historical; Humour; Lifestyle; Military; Self-Help; *Markets:* Adult; *Treatments:* Mainstream; Popular

Send query with synopsis initially and sample chapter if available, by post or by email. No poetry, fiction, scripts, children's books, academic, or unsolicited MSS. See website for full guidelines.

Robertson Murray Literary Agency

3rd Floor, 37 Great Portland Street, London, W1W 8QH
Tel: +44 (0) 20 7580 0702
Email: info@robertsonmurray.com
Website: https://robertsonmurray.com

Handles: Fiction; Nonfiction; *Areas:* Autobiography; Biography; Cookery; Current Affairs; Historical; Humour; Lifestyle; Science; Sociology; Sport; *Markets:* Adult; Children's; Youth; *Treatments:* Commercial; Literary

No science fiction, academic books, scripts, or poetry. Submit online through form on website. No postal submissions. Currently closed to submissions of children's books as at April 2019. See website current status and for full guidelines.

Robin Jones Literary Agency

66 High Street, Dorchester on Thames, OX10 7HN
Tel: +44 (0) 1865 341486
Email: robijones@gmail.com
Website: https://twitter.com/AgentRobinJones

Handles: Fiction; Nonfiction; *Markets:* Adult; *Treatments:* Commercial; Literary

Literary agency founded in 2007 by an agent who has previously worked at four other agencies, and was the UK scout for international publishers in 11 countries. Handles commercial and literary fiction and nonfiction for adults. Welcomes Russian language fiction and nonfiction. No children's, poetry, young adult, or original scripts. Send query with synopsis and 50-page sample.

Rochelle Stevens & Co.

2 Terretts Place, Upper Street, London, N1 1QZ
Tel: +44 (0) 20 7359 3900
Email: info@rochellestevens.com
Website: http://www.rochellestevens.com

Handles: Scripts; *Areas:* Film; Radio; Theatre; TV; *Markets:* Adult

Handles script writers for film, television, theatre, and radio. No longer handles writers of fiction, nonfiction, or children's books. Submit by post only. See website for full submission guidelines.

Rocking Chair Books

2 Rudgwick Terrace, St Stephens Close, London, NW8 6BR
Tel: +44 (0) 7809 461342
Email: representme@rockingchairbooks.com
Website: http://www.rockingchairbooks.com

Handles: Fiction; Nonfiction; *Areas:* Adventure; Arts; Crime; Culture; Current Affairs; Entertainment; Historical; Horror; Lifestyle; Literature; Mystery; Nature; Romance; Thrillers; Translations; Travel; Women's Interests; *Markets:* Adult; *Treatments:* Commercial; Contemporary; Cynical; Dark; Experimental; In-depth; Light; Literary; Mainstream; Popular; Positive; Progressive; Satirical; Serious; Traditional

Founded in 2011 after the founder worked for five years as a Director at an established London literary agency. Send complete ms or a few chapters by email only. No Children's, YA or Science Fiction / Fantasy.

Rosica Colin Ltd

1 Clareville Grove Mews, London, SW7 5AH
Tel: +44 (0) 20 7370 1080

Handles: Fiction; Nonfiction; Scripts; *Areas:* Autobiography; Beauty and Fashion; Biography; Cookery; Crime; Current Affairs; Erotic; Fantasy; Film; Gardening; Health; Historical; Horror; Humour; Leisure; Lifestyle; Men's Interests; Military; Mystery; Nature; Psychology; Radio; Religious; Romance; Science; Sport; Suspense; Theatre; Thrillers; Travel; TV;

Women's Interests; *Markets:* Academic; Adult; Children's; *Treatments:* Literary

Send query with SAE, CV, synopsis, and list of other agents and publishers where MS has already been sent. Considers any full-length mss (except science fiction and poetry), but send synopsis only in initial query.

Rupert Crew Ltd

6 Windsor Road, London, N3 3SS
Tel: +44 (0) 20 8346 3000
Fax: +44 (0) 20 8346 3009
Email: info@rupertcrew.co.uk
Website: http://www.rupertcrew.co.uk

Handles: Fiction; Nonfiction; *Markets:* Adult

Closed to submissions as at April 2019. Check website for current status.

Send query with SAE, synopsis, and first two or three consecutive chapters. International representation, handling volume and subsidiary rights in fiction and nonfiction properties. No Short Stories, Science Fiction, Fantasy, Horror, Poetry or original scripts for Theatre, Television and Film. Email address for correspondence only. No response by post and no return of material with insufficient return postage.

Rupert Heath Literary Agency

50 Albemarle Street, London, W1S 4BD
Tel: +44 (0) 20 7060 3385
Email: emailagency@rupertheath.com
Website: http://www.rupertheath.com

Handles: Fiction; Nonfiction; *Areas:* Arts; Autobiography; Biography; Crime; Culture; Current Affairs; Historical; Humour; Nature; Politics; Science; Sci-Fi; Thrillers; *Markets:* Adult; *Treatments:* Commercial; Literary; Popular

Send query giving some information about yourself and the work you would like to submit. Prefers queries by email. Response only if interested.

The Ruppin Agency

London,
Email: submissions@ruppinagency.com
Website: http://www.ruppinagency.com

Handles: Fiction; Nonfiction; *Areas:* Adventure; Anthropology; Antiques; Archaeology; Architecture; Arts; Autobiography; Biography; Crime; Culture; Current Affairs; Design; Entertainment; Film; Gothic; Historical; Hobbies; Literature; Men's Interests; Military; Music; Mystery; Nature; Philosophy; Politics; Science; Short Stories; Sociology; Sport; Thrillers; Translations; Travel; TV; Women's Interests; *Markets:* Adult; *Treatments:* Commercial; Contemporary; Experimental; In-depth; Literary; Mainstream; Niche; Popular; Progressive; Serious

Literary agency set up by a former bookseller, offering writers a new perspective on finding the right publisher for their work. Keen to find writers with something to say about society today and particularly looking for storylines that showcase voices and communities that have tended to be overlooked by the publishing world, although that should deter no-one from sending their writing. No poetry, children's, young adult, graphic novels, plays and film scripts, self-help or lifestyle (including cookery, gardening, or interiors), religious or other esoteric titles, illustrated, academic, business or professional titles.

Sarah Such Literary Agency

81 Arabella Drive, London, SW15 5LL
Tel: +44 (0) 20 8876 4228
Email: info@sarah-such.com
Website: https://sarahsuchliteraryagency.tumblr.com

Handles: Fiction; Nonfiction; *Areas:* Autobiography; Biography; Culture; Historical; Humour; *Markets:* Adult; Children's; Youth; *Treatments:* Commercial; Literary; Popular

Handles literary and commercial nonfiction and fiction for adults, young adults and children. Particularly interested in debut novels, biography, memoir, history, popular culture and humour. Works mainly by recommendation, but does also accept unsolicited approaches, by email only. Send synopsis, author bio, and sample chapter as Word attachment. No unsolicited mss or queries by phone. Handles TV and film scripts for existing clients, but no radio or theatre scripts. No poetry, fantasy, self-help or short stories.

The Sayle Literary Agency
1 Petersfield, Cambridge, CB1 1BB
Tel: +44 (0) 1223 303035
Email: info@sayleliteraryagency.com
Website: http://www.
sayleliteraryagency.com

Handles: Fiction; Nonfiction; *Areas:*
Biography; Crime; Current Affairs;
Historical; Music; Science; Travel; *Markets:*
Adult; *Treatments:* Literary

**Note: Not accepting new manuscripts as at
July 2018. See website for current status.**

Send query with CV, synopsis, and three sample chapters. No text books, technical, legal, medical, children's, plays, poetry, unsolicited MSS, or approaches by email. Do not include SAE as all material submitted is recycled. If no response after three months assume rejection.

Sayle Screen Ltd
11 Jubilee Place, London, SW3 3TD
Tel: +44 (0) 20 7823 3883
Email: info@saylescreen.com
Website: http://www.saylescreen.com

Handles: Scripts; *Areas:* Film; Radio;
Theatre; TV; *Markets:* Adult

Only considers material which has been recommended by a producer, development executive or course tutor. In this case send query by email with cover letter and details of your referee to the relevant agent. Query only one agent at a time.

The Shaw Agency
8 Goodrich Road, London, SE22 9EH
Website: https://www.theshawagency.co.uk

Handles: Fiction; Nonfiction; *Markets:*
Adult; Children's; Youth; *Treatments:*
Commercial; Literary

Handles literary and commercial fiction, crime fiction, powerful and quirky nonfiction, teen and children's books. Send query by post with one-page synopsis, first 20 pages, and email address for response. See website for full guidelines.

Sheil Land Associates Ltd
52 Doughty Street, London, WC1N 2LS
Tel: +44 (0) 20 7405 9351
Fax: +44 (0) 20 7831 2127
Email: info@sheilland.co.uk
Website: http://www.sheilland.co.uk

Handles: Fiction; Nonfiction; Scripts; *Areas:*
Autobiography; Biography; Cookery; Crime;
Drama; Fantasy; Film; Gardening;
Historical; Humour; Lifestyle; Military;
Mystery; Politics; Psychology; Radio;
Romance; Science; Sci-Fi; Self-Help;
Theatre; Thrillers; Travel; TV; Women's
Interests; *Markets:* Adult; Children's; Youth;
Treatments: Commercial; Contemporary;
Literary

Send query with synopsis, CV, and first three chapters (or around 50 pages), by post addressed to "The Submissions Dept", or by email. If posting mss, do not send only copy as submissions are recycled and responses sent by email. If you require response by post, include SAE.

Jeffrey Simmons
15 Penn House, Mallory Street, London,
NW8 8SX
Tel: +44 (0) 20 7224 8917
Email: jasimmons@unicombox.co.uk

Handles: Fiction; Nonfiction; *Areas:*
Autobiography; Biography; Crime; Current
Affairs; Entertainment; Film; Historical;
Legal; Politics; Psychology; Sport; Theatre;
Markets: Adult; *Treatments:* Commercial;
Literary

Send query with brief bio, synopsis, history of any prior publication, and list of any publishers or agents to have already seen the MSS. Particularly interested in personality books of all kinds and fiction from young writers (under 40) with a future. No children's books, science fiction, fantasy, cookery, crafts, gardening, or hobbies. Film scripts handled for existing book clients only.

Sinclair-Stevenson

3 South Terrace, London, SW7 2TB
Tel: +44 (0) 20 7581 2550

Handles: Fiction; Nonfiction; *Areas:* Arts; Biography; Current Affairs; Historical; Travel; *Markets:* Adult

Send query with synopsis and SAE. No children's books, scripts, academic, science fiction, or fantasy.

Skylark Literary

19 Parkway, Weybridge, Surrey KT13 9HD
Tel: +44 (0) 20 8144 7440
Email: submissions@skylark-literary.com
Website: http://www.skylark-literary.com

Handles: Fiction; *Markets:* Children's; Youth

Handles fiction for children, from chapter books for emerging readers up to young adult / crossover titles. No picture books. Send query by email with one-page synopsis and full ms. No postal submissions.

Sophie Hicks Agency

60 Gray's Inn Road, London, WC1X 8AQ
Tel: +44 (0) 20 3735 8870
Email: info@sophiehicksagency.com
Website: http://www.sophiehicksagency.com

Handles: Fiction; Nonfiction; *Markets:* Adult; Children's; Youth

Welcomes submissions. Send query by email only with sample pages attached as Word or PDF documents. See website for full guidelines and specific submissions email addresses. No poetry or scripts for theatre, film or television, and not currently accepting illustrated books for children.

Standen Literary Agency

Email: submissions@ standenliteraryagency.com

Website: http://www. standenliteraryagency.com

Handles: Fiction; Nonfiction; *Areas:* Cookery; Lifestyle; Spiritual; *Markets:* Adult; Children's; Youth; *Treatments:* Commercial; Literary

Send one-page synopsis and first three chapters by email only. No picture books. Responds if interested only. If no response in 6 weeks assume rejection.

Susanna Lea Associates (UK)

55 Monmouth Street, London, WC2H 9DG
Tel: +44 (0) 20 7287 7757
Fax: +44 (0) 20 7287 7775
Email: london@susannalea.com
Website: http://www.susannalea.com

Handles: Fiction; Nonfiction; *Markets:* Adult

Literary agency with offices in Paris, London, and New York. Always on the lookout for exciting new talent. No poetry, plays, screen plays, science fiction, educational text books, short stories or illustrated works. No queries by fax or post. Accepts queries by email only. Include cover letter, synopsis, and first three chapters or proposal. Response not guaranteed.

The Susijn Agency

820 Harrow Road, London, NW10 5JU
Tel: +44 (0) 20 8968 7435
Email: submissions@thesusijnagency.com
Website: http://www.thesusijnagency.com

Handles: Fiction; Nonfiction; *Markets:* Adult; *Treatments:* Literary

Send query with synopsis and three sample chapters only by post or by email. Include SASE if return of material required. Response in 8-10 weeks. Specialises in selling rights worldwide and also represents non-English language authors and publishers for US, UK, and translation rights worldwide. No self-help, science-fiction, fantasy, romance, children's, illustrated, business, screenplays, or theatre plays.

SYLA – Susan Yearwood Literary Agency

2 Knebworth House, Londesborough Road, Stoke Newington, London N16 8RL
Tel: +44 (0) 20 7503 0954
Email: submissions@susanyearwood.com
Website: http://www.susanyearwood.com

Handles: Fiction; Nonfiction; *Areas:* Business; Cookery; Crime; Finance; Lifestyle; Romance; Self-Help; Thrillers; *Markets:* Adult; *Treatments:* Commercial

Send query by email, including synopsis and first thirty pages as Word or PDF attachment. No adult sci-fi / fantasy, short stories, or poetry.

The Tennyson Agency

109 Tennyson Avenue, New Malden, Surrey KT3 6NA
Tel: +44 (0) 20 8543 5939
Email: agency@tenagy.co.uk
Website: http://www.tenagy.co.uk

Handles: Scripts; *Areas:* Drama; Film; Radio; Theatre; TV; *Markets:* Adult

Mainly deals in scripts for film, TV, theatre, and radio, along with related material on an ad-hoc basis. Handles writers in the European Union only. Send query with CV and outline of work. Prefers queries by email. No nonfiction, poetry, short stories, science fiction and fantasy or children's writing, or unsolicited MSS.

Teresa Chris Literary Agency Ltd

43 Musard Road, London, W6 8NR
Tel: +44 (0) 20 7386 0633
Email: teresachris@litagency.co.uk
Website: http://www.
teresachrisliteraryagency.co.uk

Handles: Fiction; Nonfiction; *Areas:* Biography; Cookery; Crafts; Crime; Gardening; Historical; Lifestyle; Women's Interests; *Markets:* Adult; *Treatments:* Commercial; Literary

Welcomes submissions. Overseas authors may approach by email, otherwise hard copy submissions preferred. For fiction, send query with SAE, first three chapters, and one-page synopsis. For nonfiction, send overview with two sample chapters. Specialises in crime fiction and commercial women's fiction. No poetry, short stories, fantasy, science fiction, horror, children's fiction or young adult.

Tibor Jones & Associates

PO Box 74604, London, SW2 9NH
Email: enquiries@tiborjones.com
Website: http://www.tiborjones.com

Handles: Fiction; Nonfiction; *Areas:* Autobiography; Biography; Culture; Literature; Music; *Markets:* Adult; *Treatments:* Commercial; Literary

Welcomes fiction and nonfiction proposals from writers who are looking to publish something different. Send query by email giving details about you and your writing background, with one-page synopsis and first five pages of the novel/proposal.

Toby Mundy Associates Ltd

38 Berkeley Square, London, W1J 5AE
Tel: +44 (0) 20 3713 0067
Email: submissions@tma-agency.com
Website: http://tma-agency.com

Handles: Fiction; Nonfiction; *Areas:* Autobiography; Biography; Crime; Current Affairs; Historical; Politics; Science; Thrillers; *Markets:* Adult; *Treatments:* Literary

Send query by email with brief synopsis, first chapter, and a note about yourself, all pasted into the body of the email. No poetry, plays, short stories, science fiction, horror, attachments or hard copy submissions.

Lavinia Trevor Agency

29 Addison Place, London, W11 4RJ
Tel: +44 (0) 20 7603 0895
Email: info@laviniatrevor.co.uk
Website: http://www.laviniatrevor.co.uk

Handles: Fiction; Nonfiction; *Areas:* Science; *Markets:* Adult; *Treatments:* Commercial; Literary

Does not handle poetry, children's, technical, academic, fantasy, science fiction, or scripts. No unsolicited material.

Uli Rushby-Smith Literary Agency

72 Plimsoll Road, London, N4 2EE
Tel: +44 (0) 20 7354 2718
Email: uli.rushby-smith@btconnect.com

Handles: Fiction; Nonfiction; *Markets:* Adult; *Treatments:* Commercial; Literary

Send query with SAE, outline, and two or three sample chapters. Film and TV rights handled in conjunction with a sub-agent. No disks, poetry, picture books, films, or plays.

United Agents

12-26 Lexington Street, London, W1F 0LE
Tel: +44 (0) 20 3214 0800
Fax: +44 (0) 20 3214 0801
Email: info@unitedagents.co.uk
Website: http://unitedagents.co.uk

Handles: Fiction; Nonfiction; Scripts; *Areas:* Biography; Film; Radio; Theatre; TV; *Markets:* Adult; Children's; Youth

Do not approach the book department generally. Consult website and view details of each agent before selecting a specific agent to approach personally. Accepts submissions by email only. Submissions by post will not be returned or responded to.

Valerie Hoskins Associates

20 Charlotte Street, London, W1T 2NA
Tel: +44 (0) 20 7637 4490
Email: info@vhassociates.co.uk
Website: http://www.vhassociates.co.uk

Handles: Scripts; *Areas:* Film; Radio; TV; *Markets:* Adult

Always on the lookout for screenwriters with an original voice and creatives with big ideas. Query by email or by phone. Allow up to eight weeks for response to submissions.

The Viney Agency

23 Erlanger Road, Telegraph Hill, London, SE14 5TF

Tel: +44 (0) 20 7732 3331
Email: charlie@thevineyagency.com
Website: http://thevineyagency.com

Handles: Fiction; Nonfiction; *Markets:* Adult; Children's

Handles high quality nonfiction, and adult and children's fiction. See website for examples of the kinds of books represented. Send query by first or second class post.

Wade & Co Literary Agency

33 Cormorant Lodge, Thomas More Street, London, E1W 1AU
Tel: +44 (0) 20 7488 4171
Fax: +44 (0) 20 7488 4172
Email: rw@rwla.com
Website: http://www.rwla.com

Handles: Fiction; Nonfiction; *Markets:* Adult; Youth

New full-length proposals for adult and young adult fiction and nonfiction always welcome. Send query with detailed 1—6 page synopsis, brief biography, and first 10,000 words via email as Word documents (.doc) or PDF; or by post with SAE if return required. We much prefer to correspond by email. Actively seeking new writers across the literary spectrum. No poetry, children's, short stories, scripts or plays.

Watson, Little Ltd

Suite 315, ScreenWorks, 22 Highbury Grove, London, N5 2ER
Tel: +44 (0) 20 7388 7529
Email: submissions@watsonlittle.com
Website: http://www.watsonlittle.com

Handles: Fiction; Nonfiction; *Areas:* Business; Crime; Film; Historical; Humour; Leisure; Music; Psychology; Science; Self-Help; Sport; Technology; Women's Interests; *Markets:* Adult; Children's; Youth; *Treatments:* Commercial; Literary; Popular

Send query by email only with synopsis and sample material, addressed to a specific agent. See website for full guidelines and details of specific agents. No scripts, poetry, or unsolicited MSS.

Whispering Buffalo Literary Agency Ltd

97 Chesson Road, London, W14 9QS
Tel: +44 (0) 20 7565 4737
Email: info@whisperingbuffalo.com
Website: http://www.whisperingbuffalo.com

Handles: Fiction; Nonfiction; *Areas:*
Adventure; Anthropology; Arts;
Autobiography; Beauty and Fashion; Design;
Entertainment; Film; Health; Humour;
Lifestyle; Music; Nature; Politics; Romance;
Sci-Fi; Self-Help; Thrillers; *Markets:* Adult;
Children's; Youth; *Treatments:* Commercial;
Literary

Handles commercial/literary
fiction/nonfiction and children's/YA fiction
with special interest in book to film
adaptations. No TV, film, radio or theatre
scripts, or poetry or academic. Accepts
submissions by email only. For fiction, send
query with CV, synopsis, and first three
chapters. For nonfiction, send proposal and
sample chapter. Response only if interested.
Aims to respond within 6-8 weeks.

William Morris Endeavor (WME) London

100 New Oxford Street, London, WC1A
1HB
Tel: +44 (0) 20 7534 6800
Fax: +44 (0) 20 7534 6900
Email: ldnsubmissions@
wmeentertainment.com
Website: http://www.wmeentertainment.com

Handles: Fiction; Nonfiction; *Areas:*
Autobiography; Biography; Crime; Culture;
Historical; Thrillers; *Markets:* Adult; Youth;
Treatments: Commercial; Literary

London office of a worldwide theatrical and
literary agency, with offices in New York,
Beverly Hills, Nashville, Miami, and
Shanghai, as well as associates in Sydney.

The Writers' Practice

Tel: +44 (0) 7940 533243
Email: jemima@thewriterspractice.com
Website: http://www.thewriterspractice.com

Handles: Fiction; Nonfiction; *Markets:*
Adult; *Treatments:* Commercial; Literary

Send query by email with for fiction a
synopsis, brief bio, and first three chapters;
and for nonfiction a pitch, brief bio, chapter
outline, and at least one sample chapter. Also
offers consultancy services to writers.

The Wylie Agency (UK) Ltd

17 Bedford Square, London, WC2B 3JA
Tel: +44 (0) 20 7908 5900
Fax: +44 (0) 20 7908 5901
Email: mail@wylieagency.co.uk
Website: http://www.wylieagency.co.uk

Handles: Fiction; Nonfiction; *Markets:*
Adult

**Note: Not accepting unsolicited mss as at
October 2018**

Send query by post or email before
submitting. All submissions must include
adequate return postage. No scripts,
children's books, or unsolicited MSS.

Zeno Agency Ltd

Primrose Hill Business Centre, 110
Gloucester Avenue, London, NW1 8HX
Tel: +44 (0) 20 7096 0927
Email: louisebuckleyagent@gmail.com
Website: http://zenoagency.com

Handles: Fiction; Nonfiction; *Areas:*
Autobiography; Biography; Cookery; Crime;
Fantasy; Health; Historical; Horror;
Lifestyle; Nature; Sci-Fi; Sociology;
Suspense; Thrillers; Women's Interests;
Markets: Adult; Children's; Youth;
Treatments: Commercial; Literary; Popular

**Both agents are closed to queries as at
November 2018. Check website for
current status.**

London-based literary agency specialising in
Science Fiction, Fantasy, and Horror, but
expanding into other areas such as crime,
thrillers, women's fiction, and young adult
fiction. Adult fiction must be at least 75,000
words and children's fiction should be at
least 50,000 words. Send query by email
with synopsis up to two pages, and first three
chapters (or approximately 50 double-spaced
pages) as attachments in .docx or .pdf
format. No submissions by post.

Canadian Literary Agents

For the most up-to-date listings of these and hundreds of other literary agents, visit https://www.firstwriter.com/Agents

*To claim your **free** access to the site, please see the back of this book.*

K2 Literary
Toronto, Ontario
Tel: +1 (416) 910-1661
Website: https://k2literary.com

Handles: Fiction; Nonfiction; *Markets:* Adult; Children's

As at January 2018, considering submissions by referral only. See website for current status.

The Rights Factory
PO Box 499, Station C, Toronto, Ontario M6J 3P6
Website: http://therightsfactory.com

Handles: Fiction; Nonfiction; *Areas:* Adventure; Autobiography; Biography; Business; Cookery; Crime; Culture; Fantasy; Health; Historical; Lifestyle; Mystery; Politics; Romance; Science; Sci-Fi; Spiritual; Sport; Thrillers; Travel; Women's Interests; *Markets:* Adult; Children's; Youth; *Treatments:* Commercial; Contemporary; Literary; Popular

Send first three chapters (fiction), proposal (nonfiction), or complete ms (picture books) via online submission form on website.

Seventh Avenue Literary Agency
Email: info@seventhavenuelit.com
Website: http://www.seventhavenuelit.com

Handles: Nonfiction; *Markets:* Adult

Describes itself as one of Canada's largest nonfiction and personal management agencies.

Beverley Slopen Literary Agency
131 Bloor St. W., Suite 711, Toronto, M5S 1S3
Tel: +1 (416) 964-9598
Fax: +1 (416) 921-7726
Email: beverley@slopenagency.ca
Website: http://www.slopenagency.com

Handles: Fiction; Nonfiction; *Areas:* Anthropology; Biography; Crime; Historical; Self-Help; *Markets:* Adult; Children's; *Treatments:* Commercial; Literary

Send query by email with a few sample pages. No hard copy submissions. Takes on few new authors.

Handles very few children's books, and almost no romance, horror, or illustrated. No poetry.

Transatlantic Literary Agency, Inc.
2 Bloor Street East, Suite 3500, Toronto, Ontario M4W 1A8
Tel: +1 (416) 488-9214
Fax: +1 (416) 929-3174

Email: info@transatlanticagency.com
Website: http://transatlanticagency.com

Handles: Fiction; Nonfiction; *Areas:*
Adventure; Architecture; Autobiography;
Biography; Business; Cookery; Crime;
Culture; Current Affairs; Fantasy; Historical;
Hobbies; Humour; Lifestyle; Mystery;
Nature; Politics; Religious; Romance;
Science; Sci-Fi; Technology; Thrillers;
Travel; Women's Interests; *Markets:* Adult;
Children's; Youth; *Treatments:* Commercial;
Contemporary; Literary

Canadian branch of international agency
with agents in Toronto, ON; New York, NY;
Portland, OR; Vancouver, BC; and Petite
Rivière, NS. Founded in Canada in 1993.
The different agents have different interests
and different submission requirements, so
essential to consult website for individual
interests and contact details before
submitting.

Irish Literary Agents

For the most up-to-date listings of these and hundreds of other literary agents, visit https://www.firstwriter.com/Agents

*To claim your **free** access to the site, please see the back of this book.*

The Book Bureau Literary Agency

7 Duncairn Avenue, Bray, Co. Wicklow
Tel: +353 (0) 1276 4996
Fax: +353 (0) 1276 4834
Email: thebookbureau@oceanfree.net

Handles: Fiction; Nonfiction; *Areas:* Crime; Thrillers; Women's Interests; *Markets:* Adult; *Treatments:* Commercial; Literary

Handles mainly general and literary fiction, plus some nonfiction. Particularly interested in women's, crime, Irish novels, and thrillers. Send query by email (preferred) or by post with SAE, synopsis, and first three chapters. Prefers single line spacing. No poetry, children's, horror, or science fiction. Strong editorial support provided before submission to publishers.

Frank Fahy

5 Barna Village Centre, Seapoint, Galway H91 DF24
Tel: +353 (0) 86 226 9330
Email: submissions@frank-fahy.com
Website: http://www.frank-fahy.com

Handles: Fiction; *Markets:* Adult; Youth

Handles adult and young adult fiction. No picture books, poetry, or nonfiction. Send query by email with author profile, synopsis, and first three chapters by email. No hard copy submissions.

Marianne Gunn O'Connor Literary Agency

Morrison Chambers, Suite 17, 32 Nassau Street, Dublin, D02 XW77
Tel: 353 1 677 9100
Fax: 353 1 677 9101
Email: mgoclitagency@eircom.net

Handles: Fiction; Nonfiction; *Areas:* Biography; Health; *Markets:* Adult; Children's; *Treatments:* Commercial; Literary

Send query with half-page synopsis by email.

The Lisa Richards Agency

108 Upper Leeson Street, Dublin, 4
Tel: +353 1 637 5000
Fax: +353 1 667 1256
Email: info@lisarichards.ie
Website: http://www.lisarichards.ie

Handles: Fiction; Nonfiction; Scripts; *Areas:* Autobiography; Biography; Culture; Historical; Humour; Lifestyle; Self-Help; Sport; Theatre; *Markets:* Adult; Children's; *Treatments:* Commercial; Literary; Popular

Send query by email or by post with SASE, including three or four sample chapters in the case of fiction, or proposal and sample chapter for nonfiction. No horror, science fiction, screenplays, or children's picture books.

The Rights Bureau

The Old Post Office, Kilmacanogue, Co Wicklow
Email: dominic@therightsbureau.ie
Website: http://www.therightsbureau.ie

Handles: Fiction; Nonfiction; *Areas:* Autobiography; Cookery; Historical; How-to; Self-Help; *Markets:* Children's; Youth

Not taking on new clients as at October 2018. Check website for current status. Specialises in nonfiction, though also represents some children's and young adult fiction. Accepts proposals for nonfiction projects only. These should be sent hard copy by post. See website for full guidelines. Sister company provides chargeable services to writers.

Literary Agents Subject Index

This section lists literary agents by their subject matter, with directions to the section of the book where the full listing can be found.

You can create your own customised lists of literary agents using different combinations of these subject areas, plus over a dozen other criteria, instantly online at https://www.firstwriter.com.

*To claim your **free** access to the site, please see the back of this book.*

Adventure
Alive Literary Agency (*US*)
Ambassador Speakers Bureau & Literary Agency (*US*)
Marcia Amsterdam Agency (*US*)
Antony Harwood Limited (*UK*)
The Bent Agency (*US*)
Bob Mecoy Creative Book Services (*US*)
BookStop Literary Agency, LLC (*US*)
Carolyn Jenks Agency (*US*)
Cherry Weiner Literary Agency (*US*)
Corvisiero Literary Agency (*US*)
D4EO Literary Agency (*US*)
DHH Literary Agency Ltd (*UK*)
Diamond Kahn and Woods (DKW) Literary Agency Ltd (*UK*)
Don Congdon Associates, Inc. (*US*)
Dystel, Goderich & Bourret LLC (*US*)
Ethan Ellenberg Literary Agency (*US*)
Hannigan Salky Getzler (HSG) Agency (*US*)
hhb agency ltd (*UK*)
InterSaga (*UK*)
The Jean V. Naggar Literary Agency (*US*)
The Jennifer DeChiara Literary Agency (*US*)
JYLA (Jason Yarn Literary Agency) (*US*)
Harvey Klinger, Inc (*US*)
Kneerim & Williams (*US*)
Kruger Cowne (*UK*)
LBA Books Ltd (*UK*)
Maria Carvainis Agency, Inc. (*US*)
Niad Management (*US*)
Prospect Agency (*US*)
Regina Ryan Publishing Enterprises (*US*)
The Rights Factory (*Can*)
Robert Dudley Agency (*UK*)
Rocking Chair Books (*UK*)
The Ruppin Agency (*UK*)
Scovil Galen Ghosh Literary Agency, Inc. (*US*)
Sean McCarthy Literary Agency (*US*)
The Seymour Agency (*US*)
Stuart Krichevsky Literary Agency, Inc. (*US*)
Susan Schulman Literary Agency LLC (*US*)
Transatlantic Literary Agency, Inc. (*Can*)
The Unter Agency (*US*)
Victoria Sanders & Associates LLC (*US*)
Whispering Buffalo Literary Agency Ltd (*UK*)

Anthropology
Andrea Brown Literary Agency, Inc. (*US*)
Antony Harwood Limited (*UK*)
Carol Mann Agency (*US*)
Don Congdon Associates, Inc. (*US*)
Dystel, Goderich & Bourret LLC (*US*)
Jo Unwin Literary Agency (*UK*)
Kneerim & Williams (*US*)
Kruger Cowne (*UK*)
The Ruppin Agency (*UK*)
Beverley Slopen Literary Agency (*Can*)
Susan Schulman Literary Agency LLC (*US*)
Whispering Buffalo Literary Agency Ltd (*UK*)

Antiques
Antony Harwood Limited (*UK*)
Corvisiero Literary Agency (*US*)
Jeanne Fredericks Literary Agency, Inc. (*US*)
The Ruppin Agency (*UK*)

Archaeology
Andrea Brown Literary Agency, Inc. (*US*)
Antony Harwood Limited (*UK*)
Carol Mann Agency (*US*)

William Morris Endeavor (WME) London (*UK*)
Wm Clark Associates (*US*)
Wordserve Literary (*US*)
Writers' Representatives, LLC (*US*)
Zeno Agency Ltd (*UK*)

Beauty and Fashion
Aevitas (*US*)
Antony Harwood Limited (*UK*)
Artellus Limited (*UK*)
Barbara Braun Associates, Inc. (*US*)
Fraser-Bub Literary, LLC (*US*)
Irene Goodman Literary Agency (IGLA) (*US*)
Kruger Cowne (*UK*)
LAW (Lucas Alexander Whitley) (*UK*)
Levine Greenberg Rostan Literary Agency (*US*)
The LKG Agency (*US*)
Rosica Colin Ltd (*UK*)
Sterling Lord Literistic, Inc. (*US*)
Thompson Literary Agency (*US*)
Whispering Buffalo Literary Agency Ltd (*UK*)

Biography
A.M. Heath & Company Limited, Author's Agents (*UK*)
Aaron M. Priest Literary Agency (*US*)
Adler & Robin Books, Inc (*US*)
Aevitas (*US*)
The Ahearn Agency, Inc (*US*)
Alive Literary Agency (*US*)
Ambassador Speakers Bureau & Literary Agency (*US*)
The Ampersand Agency Ltd (*UK*)
The Anderson Literary Agency (*US*)
Andrea Brown Literary Agency, Inc. (*US*)
Andrew Lownie Literary Agency Ltd (*UK*)
The Angela Rinaldi Literary Agency (*US*)
Antony Harwood Limited (*UK*)
Arcadia (*US*)
Artellus Limited (*UK*)
The August Agency LLC (*US*)
Ayesha Pande Literary (*US*)
B.J. Robbins Literary Agency (*US*)
Barbara Braun Associates, Inc. (*US*)
Bell Lomax Moreton Agency (*UK*)
Betsy Amster Literary Enterprises (*US*)
Blake Friedmann Literary Agency Ltd (*UK*)
Bleecker Street Associates, Inc. (*US*)
Bob Mecoy Creative Book Services (*US*)
The Book Group (*US*)
C+W (Conville & Walsh) (*UK*)
Carol Mann Agency (*US*)
Caroline Davidson Literary Agency (*UK*)
Carolyn Jenks Agency (*US*)
Chartwell (*UK*)
The Cheney Agency (*US*)
Coombs Moylett & Maclean Literary Agency (*UK*)
Creative Authors Ltd (*UK*)
Curtis Brown (*UK*)
Richard Curtis Associates, Inc. (*US*)
Cynthia Cannell Literary Agency (*US*)
D4EO Literary Agency (*US*)
Dana Newman Literary, LLC (*US*)
David Luxton Associates (*UK*)

David Black Literary Agency (*US*)
David Higham Associates Ltd (*UK*)
DeFiore and Company (*US*)
DHH Literary Agency Ltd (*UK*)
Diamond Kahn and Woods (DKW) Literary Agency Ltd (*UK*)
Dinah Wiener Ltd (*UK*)
The Doe Coover Agency (*US*)
Don Congdon Associates, Inc. (*US*)
Donadio & Olson, Inc. (*US*)
Dunham Literary, Inc. (*US*)
Dunow, Carlson & Lerner Agency (*US*)
Dystel, Goderich & Bourret LLC (*US*)
E. J. McCarthy Agency (*US*)
Edwards Fuglewicz (*UK*)
Einstein Literary Management (*US*)
Elise Dillsworth Agency (EDA) (*UK*)
Emily Sweet Associates (*UK*)
Ethan Ellenberg Literary Agency (*US*)
Fox Literary (*US*)
Fox & Howard Literary Agency (*UK*)
Frances Collin Literary Agent (*US*)
Frances Goldin Literary Agency, Inc. (*US*)
Frances Kelly Agency (*UK*)
The G Agency, LLC (*US*)
Georges Borchardt, Inc. (*US*)
Georgina Capel Associates Ltd (*UK*)
Greene & Heaton Ltd (*UK*)
Marianne Gunn O'Connor Literary Agency (*Ire*)
Joy Harris Literary Agency, Inc. (*US*)
Helen Zimmermann Literary Agency (*US*)
hhb agency ltd (*UK*)
Hill Nadell Literary Agency (*US*)
Jane Judd Literary Agency (*UK*)
Jane Turnbull (*UK*)
The Jean V. Naggar Literary Agency (*US*)
Jeanne Fredericks Literary Agency, Inc. (*US*)
The Jennifer DeChiara Literary Agency (*US*)
Jenny Brown Associates (*UK*)
John Hawkins & Associates, Inc. (*US*)
Johnson & Alcock (*UK*)
Jonathan Pegg Literary Agency (*UK*)
Kate Barker Literary, TV, & Film Agency (*UK*)
Kathi J. Paton Literary Agency (*US*)
Kimberley Cameron & Associates (*US*)
Harvey Klinger, Inc (*US*)
Kneerim & Williams (*US*)
Knight Features (*UK*)
Linda Konner Literary Agency (*US*)
Barbara S. Kouts, Literary Agent (*US*)
L. Perkins Associates (*US*)
Laura Dail Literary Agency (*US*)
LAW (Lucas Alexander Whitley) (*UK*)
Lawrence Jordan Literary Agency (*US*)
Lee Sobel Literary Agency (*US*)
Levine Greenberg Rostan Literary Agency (*US*)
Limelight Management (*UK*)
The Lisa Richards Agency (*Ire*)
Literary Management Group, Inc. (*US*)
Literary & Creative Artists Inc. (*US*)
MacGregor & Luedeke (*US*)
Maggie Pearlstine Associates Ltd (*UK*)
Maria Carvainis Agency, Inc. (*US*)

Marsal Lyon Literary Agency LLC (*US*)
Martin Literary Management (*US*)
Massie & McQuilkin (*US*)
Max Gartenburg Literary Agency (*US*)
MBA Literary Agents Ltd (*UK*)
Duncan McAra (*UK*)
McCormick Literary (*US*)
Mendel Media Group, LLC (*US*)
Mulcahy Associates (Part of MMB Creative) (*UK*)
The Ned Leavitt Agency (*US*)
Niad Management (*US*)
Perry Literary, Inc. (*US*)
Puttick Literary Agency (*UK*)
Red Sofa Literary (*US*)
Rees Literary Agency (*US*)
Regal Hoffmann & Associates LLC (*US*)
Richard Henshaw Group LLC (*US*)
Richford Becklow Literary Agency (*UK*)
The Rights Factory (*Can*)
Robert Dudley Agency (*UK*)
Robert Smith Literary Agency Ltd (*UK*)
Robertson Murray Literary Agency (*UK*)
Rosica Colin Ltd (*UK*)
Ross Yoon Agency (*US*)
The Rudy Agency (*US*)
Rupert Heath Literary Agency (*UK*)
The Ruppin Agency (*UK*)
Sandra Dijkstra Literary Agency (*US*)
Sanford J. Greenburger Associates, Inc. (*US*)
Sarah Such Literary Agency (*UK*)
The Sayle Literary Agency (*UK*)
Scovil Galen Ghosh Literary Agency, Inc. (*US*)
Selectric Artists (*US*)
Sheil Land Associates Ltd (*UK*)
Sheree Bykofsky Associates, Inc. (*US*)
Jeffrey Simmons (*UK*)
Sinclair-Stevenson (*UK*)
Beverley Slopen Literary Agency (*Can*)
The Spieler Agency (*US*)
Sterling Lord Literistic, Inc. (*US*)
The Stringer Literary Agency LLC (*US*)
The Strothman Agency (*US*)
Stuart Krichevsky Literary Agency, Inc. (*US*)
Susan Schulman Literary Agency LLC (*US*)
Emma Sweeney Agency, LLC (*US*)
Teresa Chris Literary Agency Ltd (*UK*)
Thompson Literary Agency (*US*)
Tibor Jones & Associates (*UK*)
Toby Mundy Associates Ltd (*UK*)
Transatlantic Literary Agency, Inc. (*Can*)
United Agents (*UK*)
The Unter Agency (*US*)
Veritas Literary Agency (*US*)
Victoria Sanders & Associates LLC (*US*)
Wendy Sherman Associates, Inc. (*US*)
Whimsy Literary Agency, LLC (*US*)
William Morris Endeavor (WME) London (*UK*)
Wm Clark Associates (*US*)
Wordserve Literary (*US*)
Writers' Representatives, LLC (*US*)
Zeno Agency Ltd (*UK*)

Business
Aevitas (*US*)
Alive Literary Agency (*US*)
Allen O'Shea Literary Agency (*US*)
The Angela Rinaldi Literary Agency (*US*)
Antony Harwood Limited (*UK*)
The August Agency LLC (*US*)
Bell Lomax Moreton Agency (*UK*)
Bleecker Street Associates, Inc. (*US*)
Bob Mecoy Creative Book Services (*US*)
Bond Literary Agency (*US*)
BookEnds, LLC (*US*)
Carol Mann Agency (*US*)
The Cheney Agency (*US*)
Creative Authors Ltd (*UK*)
Creative Media Agency (*US*)
Richard Curtis Associates, Inc. (*US*)
D4EO Literary Agency (*US*)
Dana Newman Literary, LLC (*US*)
David Black Literary Agency (*US*)
Liza Dawson Associates (*US*)
Diana Finch Literary Agency (*US*)
The Doe Coover Agency (*US*)
Doug Grad Literary Agency (*US*)
Dystel, Goderich & Bourret LLC (*US*)
Ebeling & Associates (*US*)
Felicia Eth Literary Representation (*US*)
Folio Literary Management, LLC (*US*)
Fox & Howard Literary Agency (*UK*)
Frances Kelly Agency (*UK*)
Fresh Books Literary Agency (*US*)
The G Agency, LLC (*US*)
Grace Freedson's Publishing Network (*US*)
Graham Maw Christie Literary Agency (*UK*)
Hannigan Salky Getzler (HSG) Agency (*US*)
hhb agency ltd (*UK*)
InkWell Management (*US*)
Jane Rotrosen Agency (*US*)
Jeanne Fredericks Literary Agency, Inc. (*US*)
The Jeff Herman Agency, LLC (*US*)
JET Literary Associates, Inc. (*US*)
John Hawkins & Associates, Inc. (*US*)
Kate Barker Literary, TV, & Film Agency (*UK*)
Kate Hordern Literary Agency (*UK*)
Kathi J. Paton Literary Agency (*US*)
Harvey Klinger, Inc (*US*)
Kneerim & Williams (*US*)
Knight Features (*UK*)
Linda Konner Literary Agency (*US*)
Kruger Cowne (*UK*)
LAW (Lucas Alexander Whitley) (*UK*)
The Leshne Agency (*US*)
Levine Greenberg Rostan Literary Agency (*US*)
Limelight Management (*UK*)
Literary Services, Inc. (*US*)
Literary Management Group, Inc. (*US*)
Literary & Creative Artists Inc. (*US*)
Lowenstein Associates, Inc. (*US*)
MacGregor & Luedeke (*US*)
Marcil O'Farrell Literary, LLC and Denise
Marcil Literary Agency, LLC (*US*)
Maria Carvainis Agency, Inc. (*US*)
Marsal Lyon Literary Agency LLC (*US*)

Martin Literary Management (*US*)
The Michael Greer Literary Agency (*UK*)
Northbank Talent Management (*UK*)
Perry Literary, Inc. (*US*)
Queen Literary Agency, Inc. (*US*)
Rees Literary Agency (*US*)
Regina Ryan Publishing Enterprises (*US*)
Richard Henshaw Group LLC (*US*)
The Rights Factory (*Can*)
Robert Dudley Agency (*UK*)
Ross Yoon Agency (*US*)
The Rudy Agency (*US*)
Sandra Dijkstra Literary Agency (*US*)
Sanford J. Greenburger Associates, Inc. (*US*)
Scovil Galen Ghosh Literary Agency, Inc. (*US*)
Sheree Bykofsky Associates, Inc. (*US*)
Solow Literary Enterprises, Inc. (*US*)
The Spieler Agency (*US*)
Sterling Lord Literistic, Inc. (*US*)
The Strothman Agency (*US*)
Stuart Krichevsky Literary Agency, Inc. (*US*)
Susan Schulman Literary Agency LLC (*US*)
SYLA – Susan Yearwood Literary Agency (*UK*)
Transatlantic Literary Agency, Inc. (*Can*)
Union Literary (*US*)
United Talent Agency (UTA) (*US*)
Veritas Literary Agency (*US*)
Waterside Productions, Inc (*US*)
Watson, Little Ltd (*UK*)
Whimsy Literary Agency, LLC (*US*)
Writers' Representatives, LLC (*US*)
Cookery
A.M. Heath & Company Limited, Author's Agents (*UK*)
Aevitas (*US*)
Allen O'Shea Literary Agency (*US*)
The Angela Rinaldi Literary Agency (*US*)
Antony Harwood Limited (*UK*)
The Bent Agency (*US*)
Betsy Amster Literary Enterprises (*US*)
Bidnick & Company (*US*)
Blake Friedmann Literary Agency Ltd (*UK*)
Bleecker Street Associates, Inc. (*US*)
Bob Mecoy Creative Book Services (*US*)
The Book Group (*US*)
Caroline Davidson Literary Agency (*UK*)
Chartwell (*UK*)
Clare Hulton Literary Agency (*UK*)
Compass Talent (*US*)
Coombs Moylett & Maclean Literary Agency (*UK*)
Creative Authors Ltd (*UK*)
D4EO Literary Agency (*US*)
David Black Literary Agency (*US*)
David Higham Associates Ltd (*UK*)
Dinah Wiener Ltd (*UK*)
The Doe Coover Agency (*US*)
Don Congdon Associates, Inc. (*US*)
Doug Grad Literary Agency (*US*)
Dystel, Goderich & Bourret LLC (*US*)
Elise Dillsworth Agency (EDA) (*UK*)
Emily Sweet Associates (*UK*)
Felicia Eth Literary Representation (*US*)

Ethan Ellenberg Literary Agency (*US*)
Folio Literary Management, LLC (*US*)
Frances Kelly Agency (*UK*)
Fraser-Bub Literary, LLC (*US*)
Grace Freedson's Publishing Network (*US*)
Graham Maw Christie Literary Agency (*UK*)
Greene & Heaton Ltd (*UK*)
Hannigan Salky Getzler (HSG) Agency (*US*)
Helen Zimmermann Literary Agency (*US*)
hhb agency ltd (*UK*)
Hill Nadell Literary Agency (*US*)
Irene Goodman Literary Agency (IGLA) (*US*)
Jane Judd Literary Agency (*UK*)
The Jean V. Naggar Literary Agency (*US*)
Jeanne Fredericks Literary Agency, Inc. (*US*)
The Jennifer DeChiara Literary Agency (*US*)
JET Literary Associates, Inc. (*US*)
Joëlle Delbourgo Associates, Inc. (*US*)
Karen Gantz Literary Management (*US*)
Kimberley Cameron & Associates (*US*)
Harvey Klinger, Inc (*US*)
Linda Konner Literary Agency (*US*)
L. Perkins Associates (*US*)
Laura Dail Literary Agency (*US*)
LAW (Lucas Alexander Whitley) (*UK*)
LBA Books Ltd (*UK*)
The Leshne Agency (*US*)
Levine Greenberg Rostan Literary Agency (*US*)
Limelight Management (*UK*)
The Lisa Ekus Group, LLC (*US*)
Literary & Creative Artists Inc. (*US*)
Lutyens and Rubinstein (*UK*)
Mansion Street Literary Management (*US*)
Marcil O'Farrell Literary, LLC and Denise Marcil Literary Agency, LLC (*US*)
Marsal Lyon Literary Agency LLC (*US*)
Martin Leonardis Ltd (*UK*)
McCormick Literary (*US*)
Perry Literary, Inc. (*US*)
Peters Fraser + Dunlop (*UK*)
Queen Literary Agency, Inc. (*US*)
Rebecca Friedman Literary Agency (*US*)
Regina Ryan Publishing Enterprises (*US*)
Richford Becklow Literary Agency (*UK*)
The Rights Bureau (*Ire*)
The Rights Factory (*Can*)
Rita Rosenkranz Literary Agency (*US*)
Robertson Murray Literary Agency (*UK*)
Rosica Colin Ltd (*UK*)
Sandra Dijkstra Literary Agency (*US*)
Scovil Galen Ghosh Literary Agency, Inc. (*US*)
The Seymour Agency (*US*)
Sheil Land Associates Ltd (*UK*)
Sheree Bykofsky Associates, Inc. (*US*)
The Spieler Agency (*US*)
Standen Literary Agency (*UK*)
Sterling Lord Literistic, Inc. (*US*)
Susan Schulman Literary Agency LLC (*US*)
SYLA – Susan Yearwood Literary Agency (*UK*)
Teresa Chris Literary Agency Ltd (*UK*)
Thompson Literary Agency (*US*)
Transatlantic Literary Agency, Inc. (*Can*)
Union Literary (*US*)

Sheil Land Associates Ltd (*UK*)
Jeffrey Simmons (*UK*)
Beverley Slopen Literary Agency (*Can*)
The Spieler Agency (*US*)
Susan Schulman Literary Agency LLC (*US*)
SYLA – Susan Yearwood Literary Agency (*UK*)
Teresa Chris Literary Agency Ltd (*UK*)
Toby Mundy Associates Ltd (*UK*)
Transatlantic Literary Agency, Inc. (*Can*)
The Unter Agency (*US*)
Victoria Sanders & Associates LLC (*US*)
Watson, Little Ltd (*UK*)
William Morris Endeavor (WME) London (*UK*)
Zeno Agency Ltd (*UK*)

Criticism
Antony Harwood Limited (*UK*)
Barbara Braun Associates, Inc. (*US*)
Don Congdon Associates, Inc. (*US*)
Dunow, Carlson & Lerner Agency (*US*)
InterSaga (*UK*)
Red Sofa Literary (*US*)
Writers' Representatives, LLC (*US*)

Culture
Aaron M. Priest Literary Agency (*US*)
Adler & Robin Books, Inc (*US*)
Aevitas (*US*)
Allen O'Shea Literary Agency (*US*)
Ambassador Speakers Bureau & Literary
Agency (*US*)
Andrea Brown Literary Agency, Inc. (*US*)
Andrew Lownie Literary Agency Ltd (*UK*)
The Angela Rinaldi Literary Agency (*US*)
Antony Harwood Limited (*UK*)
Arcadia (*US*)
Artellus Limited (*UK*)
The August Agency LLC (*US*)
Ayesha Pande Literary (*US*)
B.J. Robbins Literary Agency (*US*)
Barbara Braun Associates, Inc. (*US*)
The Bent Agency (*US*)
Betsy Amster Literary Enterprises (*US*)
Blake Friedmann Literary Agency Ltd (*UK*)
Bleecker Street Associates, Inc. (*US*)
The Book Group (*US*)
BookBlast Ltd. (*UK*)
BookEnds, LLC (*US*)
Brandt & Hochman Literary Agents, Inc. (*US*)
The Brattle Agency LLC (*US*)
Carol Mann Agency (*US*)
Caroline Davidson Literary Agency (*UK*)
Chalberg & Sussman (*US*)
Chase Literary Agency (*US*)
The Cheney Agency (*US*)
Clare Hulton Literary Agency (*UK*)
Creative Authors Ltd (*UK*)
Dana Newman Literary, LLC (*US*)
David Luxton Associates (*UK*)
David Black Literary Agency (*US*)
Liza Dawson Associates (*US*)
DeFiore and Company (*US*)
Diamond Kahn and Woods (DKW) Literary
Agency Ltd (*UK*)
Don Congdon Associates, Inc. (*US*)

Donadio & Olson, Inc. (*US*)
Dunham Literary, Inc. (*US*)
Dunow, Carlson & Lerner Agency (*US*)
Dystel, Goderich & Bourret LLC (*US*)
Empire Literary, LLC (*US*)
Felicia Eth Literary Representation (*US*)
Ethan Ellenberg Literary Agency (*US*)
Fairbank Literary Representation (*US*)
Folio Literary Management, LLC (*US*)
Fox Literary (*US*)
Fox & Howard Literary Agency (*UK*)
Frances Collin Literary Agent (*US*)
Frances Goldin Literary Agency, Inc. (*US*)
The G Agency, LLC (*US*)
Gelfman Schneider / ICM Partners (*US*)
Grace Freedson's Publishing Network (*US*)
Hannigan Salky Getzler (HSG) Agency (*US*)
Joy Harris Literary Agency, Inc. (*US*)
Helen Zimmermann Literary Agency (*US*)
hhb agency ltd (*UK*)
Hill Nadell Literary Agency (*US*)
Irene Goodman Literary Agency (IGLA) (*US*)
Jane Rotrosen Agency (*US*)
The Jean V. Naggar Literary Agency (*US*)
The Jeff Herman Agency, LLC (*US*)
The Jennifer DeChiara Literary Agency (*US*)
Jenny Brown Associates (*UK*)
Johnson & Alcock (*UK*)
Jonathan Pegg Literary Agency (*UK*)
Kate Hordern Literary Agency (*UK*)
Kathi J. Paton Literary Agency (*US*)
Ki Agency Ltd (*UK*)
Kimberley Cameron & Associates (*US*)
Harvey Klinger, Inc (*US*)
Kneerim & Williams (*US*)
Linda Konner Literary Agency (*US*)
Kruger Cowne (*UK*)
L. Perkins Associates (*US*)
Laura Dail Literary Agency (*US*)
LAW (Lucas Alexander Whitley) (*UK*)
Lee Sobel Literary Agency (*US*)
The Leshne Agency (*US*)
Levine Greenberg Rostan Literary Agency (*US*)
The Lisa Richards Agency (*Ire*)
Lowenstein Associates, Inc. (*US*)
MacGregor & Luedeke (*US*)
Mansion Street Literary Management (*US*)
Maria Carvainis Agency, Inc. (*US*)
Marsal Lyon Literary Agency LLC (*US*)
Martin Literary Management (*US*)
Massie & McQuilkin (*US*)
Max Gartenburg Literary Agency (*US*)
McCormick Literary (*US*)
Mendel Media Group, LLC (*US*)
Niad Management (*US*)
Perry Literary, Inc. (*US*)
Peters Fraser + Dunlop (*UK*)
Publication Riot Group, Inc. (*US*)
The Purcell Agency, LLC (*US*)
Puttick Literary Agency (*UK*)
Red Sofa Literary (*US*)
Rees Literary Agency (*US*)
Richard Henshaw Group LLC (*US*)

The Rights Factory (*Can*)
Robert Smith Literary Agency Ltd (*UK*)
Rocking Chair Books (*UK*)
Andy Ross Agency (*US*)
Ross Yoon Agency (*US*)
The Rudy Agency (*US*)
Rupert Heath Literary Agency (*UK*)
The Ruppin Agency (*UK*)
Sandra Dijkstra Literary Agency (*US*)
Sarah Such Literary Agency (*UK*)
Scovil Galen Ghosh Literary Agency, Inc. (*US*)
Selectric Artists (*US*)
Sheree Bykofsky Associates, Inc. (*US*)
Solow Literary Enterprises, Inc. (*US*)
Speilburg Literary Agency (*US*)
The Spieler Agency (*US*)
Stephanie Tade Literary Agency (*US*)
Sterling Lord Literistic, Inc. (*US*)
Stuart Krichevsky Literary Agency, Inc. (*US*)
Susan Schulman Literary Agency LLC (*US*)
Thompson Literary Agency (*US*)
Tibor Jones & Associates (*UK*)
Transatlantic Literary Agency, Inc. (*Can*)
The Unter Agency (*US*)
Veritas Literary Agency (*US*)
Victoria Sanders & Associates LLC (*US*)
Waterside Productions, Inc (*US*)
Wendy Sherman Associates, Inc. (*US*)
William Morris Endeavor (WME) London (*UK*)
Wm Clark Associates (*US*)
Wordserve Literary (*US*)

Current Affairs
Aaron M. Priest Literary Agency (*US*)
The Ahearn Agency, Inc (*US*)
Ambassador Speakers Bureau & Literary
Agency (*US*)
Andrea Brown Literary Agency, Inc. (*US*)
Andrew Lownie Literary Agency Ltd (*UK*)
The Angela Rinaldi Literary Agency (*US*)
Antony Harwood Limited (*UK*)
Arcadia (*US*)
Artellus Limited (*UK*)
The August Agency LLC (*US*)
Blake Friedmann Literary Agency Ltd (*UK*)
Bleecker Street Associates, Inc. (*US*)
Bob Mecoy Creative Book Services (*US*)
BookEnds, LLC (*US*)
Brandt & Hochman Literary Agents, Inc. (*US*)
C+W (Conville & Walsh) (*UK*)
Carol Mann Agency (*US*)
The Cheney Agency (*US*)
Coombs Moylett & Maclean Literary Agency
(*UK*)
Cynthia Cannell Literary Agency (*US*)
D4EO Literary Agency (*US*)
Dana Newman, LLC (*US*)
David Black Literary Agency (*US*)
David Higham Associates Ltd (*UK*)
Liza Dawson Associates (*US*)
DeFiore and Company (*US*)
The Doe Coover Agency (*US*)
Don Congdon Associates, Inc. (*US*)

Dunham Literary, Inc. (*US*)
Dunow, Carlson & Lerner Agency (*US*)
Dystel, Goderich & Bourret LLC (*US*)
Emily Sweet Associates (*UK*)
Ethan Ellenberg Literary Agency (*US*)
Frances Goldin Literary Agency, Inc. (*US*)
Gelfman Schneider / ICM Partners (*US*)
Georges Borchardt, Inc. (*US*)
Grace Freedson's Publishing Network (*US*)
Greene & Heaton Ltd (*UK*)
Hannigan Salky Getzler (HSG) Agency (*US*)
Hill Nadell Literary Agency (*US*)
InkWell Management (*US*)
Jane Turnbull (*UK*)
The Jean V. Naggar Literary Agency (*US*)
John Hawkins & Associates, Inc. (*US*)
Johnson & Alcock (*UK*)
Jonathan Pegg Literary Agency (*UK*)
Joëlle Delbourgo Associates, Inc. (*US*)
JYLA (Jason Yarn Literary Agency) (*US*)
Kate Hordern Literary Agency (*UK*)
Kathi J. Paton Literary Agency (*US*)
Kimberley Cameron & Associates (*US*)
Harvey Klinger, Inc (*US*)
Kneerim & Williams (*US*)
Barbara S. Kouts, Literary Agent (*US*)
Kruger Cowne (*UK*)
Laura Dail Literary Agency (*US*)
LAW (Lucas Alexander Whitley) (*UK*)
Lee Sobel Literary Agency (*US*)
Literary & Creative Artists Inc. (*US*)
MacGregor & Luedeke (*US*)
Maggie Pearlstine Associates Ltd (*UK*)
Marsal Lyon Literary Agency LLC (*US*)
Martin Literary Management (*US*)
Massie & McQuilkin (*US*)
Max Gartenburg Literary Agency (*US*)
Mendel Media Group, LLC (*US*)
Northbank Talent Management (*UK*)
Perry Literary, Inc. (*US*)
Puttick Literary Agency (*UK*)
Red Sofa Literary (*US*)
Richard Henshaw Group LLC (*US*)
Robert Dudley Agency (*UK*)
Robert Smith Literary Agency Ltd (*UK*)
Robertson Murray Literary Agency (*UK*)
Rocking Chair Books (*UK*)
Rosica Colin Ltd (*UK*)
Andy Ross Agency (*US*)
Ross Yoon Agency (*US*)
The Rudy Agency (*US*)
Rupert Heath Literary Agency (*UK*)
The Ruppin Agency (*UK*)
Sandra Dijkstra Literary Agency (*US*)
The Sayle Literary Agency (*UK*)
Sheree Bykofsky Associates, Inc. (*US*)
Jeffrey Simmons (*UK*)
Sinclair-Stevenson (*UK*)
The Spieler Agency (*US*)
Sterling Lord Literistic, Inc. (*US*)
The Strothman Agency (*US*)
Stuart Krichevsky Literary Agency, Inc. (*US*)
Susan Schulman Literary Agency LLC (*US*)

Toby Mundy Associates Ltd (*UK*)
Transatlantic Literary Agency, Inc. (*Can*)
Upstart Crow Literary (*US*)
Victoria Sanders & Associates LLC (*US*)
Whimsy Literary Agency, LLC (*US*)
Wm Clark Associates (*US*)
Wordserve Literary (*US*)
Writers' Representatives, LLC (*US*)

Design
Aevitas (*US*)
Andrea Brown Literary Agency, Inc. (*US*)
Antony Harwood Limited (*UK*)
Barbara Braun Associates, Inc. (*US*)
Carol Mann Agency (*US*)
Caroline Davidson Literary Agency (*UK*)
D4EO Literary Agency (*US*)
Fairbank Literary Representation (*US*)
Fraser-Bub Literary, LLC (*US*)
Fresh Books Literary Agency (*US*)
Grace Freedson's Publishing Network (*US*)
Hannigan Salky Getzler (HSG) Agency (*US*)
Irene Goodman Literary Agency (IGLA) (*US*)
Jeanne Fredericks Literary Agency, Inc. (*US*)
Johnson & Alcock (*UK*)
Karen Gantz Literary Management (*US*)
Harvey Klinger, Inc (*US*)
The LKG Agency (*US*)
Mansion Street Literary Management (*US*)
The Ruppin Agency (*UK*)
Sandra Dijkstra Literary Agency (*US*)
The Stringer Literary Agency LLC (*US*)
Whimsy Literary Agency, LLC (*US*)
Whispering Buffalo Literary Agency Ltd (*UK*)
Wm Clark Associates (*US*)

Drama
Andrea Brown Literary Agency, Inc. (*US*)
Antony Harwood Limited (*UK*)
Cecily Ware Literary Agents (*UK*)
David Higham Associates Ltd (*UK*)
InterSaga (*UK*)
Jill Foster Ltd (JFL) (*UK*)
Knight Hall Agency (*UK*)
Literary & Creative Artists Inc. (*US*)
Niad Management (*US*)
Nick Turner Management Ltd (*UK*)
Northbank Talent Management (*UK*)
Sheil Land Associates Ltd (*UK*)
The Tennyson Agency (*UK*)

Entertainment
Antony Harwood Limited (*UK*)
Artellus Limited (*UK*)
The August Agency LLC (*US*)
Barbara Braun Associates, Inc. (*US*)
Bleecker Street Associates, Inc. (*US*)
The Bright Literary Academy (*UK*)
David Black Literary Agency (*US*)
Doug Grad Literary Agency (*US*)
Folio Literary Management, LLC (*US*)
Frances Goldin Literary Agency, Inc. (*US*)
hhb agency ltd (*UK*)
Jane Turnbull (*UK*)
Karen Gantz Literary Management (*US*)
Linda Konner Literary Agency (*US*)

Lee Sobel Literary Agency (*US*)
The LKG Agency (*US*)
Martin Literary Management (*US*)
Mendel Media Group, LLC (*US*)
Redhammer (*UK*)
Rocking Chair Books (*UK*)
The Ruppin Agency (*UK*)
Sanford J. Greenburger Associates, Inc. (*US*)
Jeffrey Simmons (*UK*)
Susan Schulman Literary Agency LLC (*US*)
Wendy Sherman Associates, Inc. (*US*)
Whispering Buffalo Literary Agency Ltd (*UK*)

Erotic
Antony Harwood Limited (*UK*)
The Axelrod Agency (*US*)
Barone Literary Agency (*US*)
Bleecker Street Associates, Inc. (*US*)
BookEnds, LLC (*US*)
D4EO Literary Agency (*US*)
Kruger Cowne (*UK*)
KT Literary (*US*)
L. Perkins Associates (*US*)
Lee Sobel Literary Agency (*US*)
Prospect Agency (*US*)
Red Sofa Literary (*US*)
Rosica Colin Ltd (*UK*)

Fantasy
Aaron M. Priest Literary Agency (*US*)
The Ampersand Agency Ltd (*UK*)
Andrea Brown Literary Agency, Inc. (*US*)
Antony Harwood Limited (*UK*)
Aponte Literary (*US*)
Artellus Limited (*UK*)
Ayesha Pande Literary (*US*)
Azantian Literary Agency (*US*)
Baror International, Inc. (*US*)
Barry Goldblatt Literary Agency, Inc. (*US*)
The Bent Agency (*US*)
Blake Friedmann Literary Agency Ltd (*UK*)
Bob Mecoy Creative Book Services (*US*)
Bond Literary Agency (*US*)
Book Cents Literary Agency (*US*)
BookEnds, LLC (*US*)
BookStop Literary Agency, LLC (*US*)
C+W (Conville & Walsh) (*UK*)
Caroline Sheldon Literary Agency (*UK*)
Caskie Mushens (*UK*)
Chalberg & Sussman (*US*)
Mic Cheetham Literary Agency (*UK*)
Cherry Weiner Literary Agency (*US*)
Corvisiero Literary Agency (*US*)
Curtis Brown (*UK*)
Richard Curtis Associates, Inc. (*US*)
D4EO Literary Agency (*US*)
The Darley Anderson Agency (*UK*)
Liza Dawson Associates (*US*)
DHH Literary Agency Ltd (*UK*)
Diamond Kahn and Woods (DKW) Literary Agency Ltd (*UK*)
Diana Finch Literary Agency (*US*)
Don Congdon Associates, Inc. (*US*)
Donaghy Literary Group (*US*)
Donald Maass Literary Agency (*US*)

Uli Rushby-Smith Literary Agency (*UK*)
Union Literary (*US*)
United Agents (*UK*)
United Talent Agency (UTA) (*US*)
The Unter Agency (*US*)
Upstart Crow Literary (*US*)
Veritas Literary Agency (*US*)
Vicky Bijur Literary Agency (*US*)
Victoria Sanders & Associates LLC (*US*)
The Viney Agency (*UK*)
Wade & Co Literary Agency (*UK*)
Waterside Productions, Inc (*US*)
Watson, Little Ltd (*UK*)
Wells Arms Literary (*US*)
Wendy Schmalz Agency (*US*)
Wendy Sherman Associates, Inc. (*US*)
Whispering Buffalo Literary Agency Ltd (*UK*)
William Morris Endeavor (WME) London (*UK*)
Wm Clark Associates (*US*)
Wordserve Literary (*US*)
The Writers' Practice (*UK*)
Writers' Representatives, LLC (*US*)
The Wylie Agency (UK) Ltd (*UK*)
The Wylie Agency (*US*)
Zeno Agency Ltd (*UK*)

Film

A & B Personal Management Ltd (*UK*)
Above the Line Agency (*US*)
Bret Adams Ltd (*US*)
The Agency (London) Ltd (*UK*)
Alan Brodie Representation Ltd (*UK*)
Marcia Amsterdam Agency (*US*)
Antony Harwood Limited (*UK*)
Barbara Braun Associates, Inc. (*US*)
Berlin Associates (*UK*)
BiCoastal Talent (*US*)
Blake Friedmann Literary Agency Ltd (*UK*)
The Book Group (*US*)
Don Buchwald and Associates (*US*)
Casarotto Ramsay and Associates Ltd (*UK*)
Cecily Ware Literary Agents (*UK*)
Curtis Brown (*UK*)
David Higham Associates Ltd (*UK*)
DHH Literary Agency Ltd (*UK*)
Don Congdon Associates, Inc. (*US*)
Elaine Steel (*UK*)
Felix de Wolfe (*UK*)
Film Rights Ltd in association with Laurence
Fitch Ltd (*UK*)
Frances Goldin Literary Agency, Inc. (*US*)
Georgina Capel Associates Ltd (*UK*)
Independent Talent Group Ltd (*UK*)
Jane Judd Literary Agency (*UK*)
Janet Fillingham Associates (*UK*)
The Jennifer DeChiara Literary Agency (*US*)
Jill Foster Ltd (JFL) (*UK*)
Johnson & Alcock (*UK*)
Jonathan Clowes Ltd (*UK*)
Michelle Kass Associates (*UK*)
Ken Sherman & Associates (*US*)
Ki Agency Ltd (*UK*)
Harvey Klinger, Inc (*US*)
Knight Hall Agency (*UK*)

L. Perkins Associates (*US*)
Lee Sobel Literary Agency (*US*)
The Leshne Agency (*US*)
Linda Seifert Management (*UK*)
Macnaughton Lord Representation (*UK*)
Madeleine Milburn Literary, TV & Film Agency
(*UK*)
Mary Clemmey Literary Agency (*UK*)
MBA Literary Agents Ltd (*UK*)
Bill McLean Personal Management Ltd (*UK*)
Micheline Steinberg Associates (*UK*)
Niad Management (*US*)
Nick Turner Management Ltd (*UK*)
Peregrine Whittlesey Agency (*US*)
Perry Literary, Inc. (*US*)
Peters Fraser + Dunlop (*UK*)
Rees Literary Agency (*US*)
Richard Henshaw Group LLC (*US*)
Rochelle Stevens & Co. (*UK*)
Rosica Colin Ltd (*UK*)
The Ruppin Agency (*UK*)
Sayle Screen Ltd (*UK*)
Sheil Land Associates Ltd (*UK*)
Sheree Bykofsky Associates, Inc. (*US*)
Jeffrey Simmons (*UK*)
The Spieler Agency (*US*)
Susan Schulman Literary Agency LLC (*US*)
The Tennyson Agency (*UK*)
United Agents (*UK*)
Valerie Hoskins Associates (*UK*)
Victoria Sanders & Associates LLC (*US*)
Watson, Little Ltd (*UK*)
Whispering Buffalo Literary Agency Ltd (*UK*)
Wm Clark Associates (*US*)

Finance

Allen O'Shea Literary Agency (*US*)
Ambassador Speakers Bureau & Literary
Agency (*US*)
Andrew Lownie Literary Agency Ltd (*UK*)
The Angela Rinaldi Literary Agency (*US*)
Antony Harwood Limited (*UK*)
The August Agency LLC (*US*)
Ayesha Pande Literary (*US*)
Blake Friedmann Literary Agency Ltd (*UK*)
Bleecker Street Associates, Inc. (*US*)
Bob Mecoy Creative Book Services (*US*)
Carol Mann Agency (*US*)
The Cheney Agency (*US*)
Richard Curtis Associates, Inc. (*US*)
D4EO Literary Agency (*US*)
David Black Literary Agency (*US*)
The Doe Coover Agency (*US*)
Dystel, Goderich & Bourret LLC (*US*)
Frances Kelly Agency (*UK*)
Fresh Books Literary Agency (*US*)
The G Agency, LLC (*US*)
Grace Freedson's Publishing Network (*US*)
Hannigan Salky Getzler (HSG) Agency (*US*)
InkWell Management (*US*)
Jeanne Fredericks Literary Agency, Inc. (*US*)
Jenny Brown Associates (*UK*)
Kathi J. Paton Literary Agency (*US*)
Kneerim & Williams (*US*)

Linda Konner Literary Agency (*US*)
Levine Greenberg Rostan Literary Agency (*US*)
Literary Services, Inc. (*US*)
MacGregor & Luedeke (*US*)
Maria Carvainis Agency, Inc. (*US*)
Marsal Lyon Literary Agency LLC (*US*)
Mendel Media Group, LLC (*US*)
Mulcahy Associates (Part of MMB Creative) (*UK*)
Perry Literary, Inc. (*US*)
Peters Fraser + Dunlop (*UK*)
Solow Literary Enterprises, Inc. (*US*)
The Spieler Agency (*US*)
The Strothman Agency (*US*)
Susan Schulman Literary Agency LLC (*US*)
SYLA – Susan Yearwood Literary Agency (*UK*)
Whimsy Literary Agency, LLC (*US*)
Wordserve Literary (*US*)
Writers' Representatives, LLC (*US*)

Gardening
Antony Harwood Limited (*UK*)
Betsy Amster Literary Enterprises (*US*)
Caroline Davidson Literary Agency (*UK*)
The Doe Coover Agency (*US*)
Grace Freedson's Publishing Network (*US*)
Graham Maw Christie Literary Agency (*UK*)
Greene & Heaton Ltd (*UK*)
Hannigan Salky Getzler (HSG) Agency (*US*)
Jane Turnbull (*UK*)
Jeanne Fredericks Literary Agency, Inc. (*US*)
JET Literary Associates, Inc. (*US*)
John Hawkins & Associates, Inc. (*US*)
The Leshne Agency (*US*)
Levine Greenberg Rostan Literary Agency (*US*)
Regina Ryan Publishing Enterprises (*US*)
Richford Becklow Literary Agency (*UK*)
Rosica Colin Ltd (*UK*)
Sheil Land Associates Ltd (*UK*)
The Spieler Agency (*US*)
Teresa Chris Literary Agency Ltd (*UK*)

Gothic
Aaron M. Priest Literary Agency (*US*)
The Angela Rinaldi Literary Agency (*US*)
Antony Harwood Limited (*UK*)
BookStop Literary Agency, LLC (*US*)
Diamond Kahn and Woods (DKW) Literary Agency Ltd (*UK*)
The Jean V. Naggar Literary Agency (*US*)
Kruger Cowne (*UK*)
Peters Fraser + Dunlop (*UK*)
Richford Becklow Literary Agency (*UK*)
The Ruppin Agency (*UK*)

Health
A.M. Heath & Company Limited, Author's Agents (*UK*)
Aevitas (*US*)
The Ahearn Agency, Inc (*US*)
Allen O'Shea Literary Agency (*US*)
Ambassador Speakers Bureau & Literary Agency (*US*)
Andrew Lownie Literary Agency Ltd (*UK*)
The Angela Rinaldi Literary Agency (*US*)
Antony Harwood Limited (*UK*)

Arcadia (*US*)
B.J. Robbins Literary Agency (*US*)
Betsy Amster Literary Enterprises (*US*)
Bleecker Street Associates, Inc. (*US*)
Brandt & Hochman Literary Agents, Inc. (*US*)
Carol Mann Agency (*US*)
Caroline Davidson Literary Agency (*UK*)
Chartwell (*UK*)
Creative Authors Ltd (*UK*)
Richard Curtis Associates, Inc. (*US*)
Cynthia Cannell Literary Agency (*US*)
D4EO Literary Agency (*US*)
Dana Newman Literary, LLC (*US*)
David Black Literary Agency (*US*)
The Doe Coover Agency (*US*)
Don Congdon Associates, Inc. (*US*)
Dunow, Carlson & Lerner Agency (*US*)
Dystel, Goderich & Bourret LLC (*US*)
Ebeling & Associates (*US*)
Empire Literary, LLC (*US*)
Ethan Ellenberg Literary Agency (*US*)
Folio Literary Management, LLC (*US*)
Fox & Howard Literary Agency (*UK*)
Frances Kelly Agency (*UK*)
Fraser-Bub Literary, LLC (*US*)
Fresh Books Literary Agency (*US*)
Grace Freedson's Publishing Network (*US*)
Graham Maw Christie Literary Agency (*UK*)
Greene & Heaton Ltd (*UK*)
Marianne Gunn O'Connor Literary Agency (*Ire*)
Hannigan Salky Getzler (HSG) Agency (*US*)
Hardman & Swainson (*UK*)
Helen Zimmermann Literary Agency (*US*)
Hill Nadell Literary Agency (*US*)
InkWell Management (*US*)
Jane Judd Literary Agency (*UK*)
Jane Rotrosen Agency (*US*)
The Jean V. Naggar Literary Agency (*US*)
Jeanne Fredericks Literary Agency, Inc. (*US*)
The Jeff Herman Agency, LLC (*US*)
The Jennifer DeChiara Literary Agency (*US*)
John Hawkins & Associates, Inc. (*US*)
Johnson & Alcock (*UK*)
Kathi J. Paton Literary Agency (*US*)
Kimberley Cameron & Associates (*US*)
Harvey Klinger, Inc (*US*)
Kneerim & Williams (*US*)
Knight Features (*UK*)
Linda Konner Literary Agency (*US*)
Barbara S. Kouts, Literary Agent (*US*)
Kruger Cowne (*UK*)
LAW (Lucas Alexander Whitley) (*UK*)
LBA Books Ltd (*UK*)
The Leshne Agency (*US*)
Levine Greenberg Rostan Literary Agency (*US*)
Limelight Management (*UK*)
Literary Services, Inc. (*US*)
Literary & Creative Artists Inc. (*US*)
The LKG Agency (*US*)
Lowenstein Associates, Inc. (*US*)
Maggie Pearlstine Associates Ltd (*UK*)
Marcil O'Farrell Literary, LLC and Denise Marcil Literary Agency, LLC (*US*)

Marsal Lyon Literary Agency LLC (*US*)
Martin Literary Management (*US*)
Massie & McQuilkin (*US*)
Max Gartenburg Literary Agency (*US*)
MBA Literary Agents Ltd (*UK*)
The Ned Leavitt Agency (*US*)
Northbank Talent Management (*UK*)
Puttick Literary Agency (*UK*)
Regina Ryan Publishing Enterprises (*US*)
Richard Henshaw Group LLC (*US*)
The Rights Factory (*Can*)
Rita Rosenkranz Literary Agency (*US*)
Robert Smith Literary Agency Ltd (*UK*)
Rosica Colin Ltd (*UK*)
The Rudy Agency (*US*)
Sandra Dijkstra Literary Agency (*US*)
Sanford J. Greenburger Associates, Inc. (*US*)
Scovil Galen Ghosh Literary Agency, Inc. (*US*)
Solow Literary Enterprises, Inc. (*US*)
The Spieler Agency (*US*)
Stephanie Tade Literary Agency (*US*)
Sterling Lord Literistic, Inc. (*US*)
Susan Schulman Literary Agency LLC (*US*)
Thompson Literary Agency (*US*)
The Unter Agency (*US*)
Waterside Productions, Inc (*US*)
Wendy Sherman Associates, Inc. (*US*)
Whimsy Literary Agency, LLC (*US*)
Whispering Buffalo Literary Agency Ltd (*UK*)
Wordserve Literary (*US*)
Zeno Agency Ltd (*UK*)

Historical
A.M. Heath & Company Limited, Author's
Agents (*UK*)
Aaron M. Priest Literary Agency (*US*)
Adler & Robin Books, Inc (*US*)
Aevitas (*US*)
The Ahearn Agency, Inc (*US*)
Alive Literary Agency (*US*)
Allen O'Shea Literary Agency (*US*)
Ambassador Speakers Bureau & Literary
Agency (*US*)
The Ampersand Agency Ltd (*UK*)
Marcia Amsterdam Agency (*US*)
Andrea Brown Literary Agency, Inc. (*US*)
Andrew Lownie Literary Agency Ltd (*UK*)
Andrew Mann Ltd (*UK*)
The Angela Rinaldi Literary Agency (*US*)
Antony Harwood Limited (*UK*)
Aponte Literary (*US*)
Arcadia (*US*)
Artellus Limited (*UK*)
The August Agency LLC (*US*)
Ayesha Pande Literary (*US*)
B.J. Robbins Literary Agency (*US*)
Barbara Braun Associates, Inc. (*US*)
Barone Literary Agency (*US*)
Barry Goldblatt Literary Agency, Inc. (*US*)
The Bent Agency (*US*)
Betsy Amster Literary Enterprises (*US*)
The Blair Partnership (*UK*)
Blake Friedmann Literary Agency Ltd (*UK*)
Bleecker Street Associates, Inc. (*US*)

Bob Mecoy Creative Book Services (*US*)
Bond Literary Agency (*US*)
The Book Group (*US*)
BookEnds, LLC (*US*)
Books & Such Literary Management (*US*)
BookStop Literary Agency, LLC (*US*)
Brandt & Hochman Literary Agents, Inc. (*US*)
The Brattle Agency LLC (*US*)
C+W (Conville & Walsh) (*UK*)
Carol Mann Agency (*US*)
Caroline Davidson Literary Agency (*UK*)
Caroline Sheldon Literary Agency (*UK*)
Carolyn Jenks Agency (*US*)
Caskie Mushens (*UK*)
Chalberg & Sussman (*US*)
Chartwell (*UK*)
Chase Literary Agency (*US*)
Mic Cheetham Literary Agency (*UK*)
The Cheney Agency (*US*)
Cherry Weiner Literary Agency (*US*)
The Chudney Agency (*US*)
Clare Hulton Literary Agency (*UK*)
Compass Talent (*US*)
Coombs Moylett & Maclean Literary Agency
(*UK*)
Creative Authors Ltd (*UK*)
Creative Media Agency (*US*)
Curtis Brown (*UK*)
Richard Curtis Associates, Inc. (*US*)
D4EO Literary Agency (*US*)
Dana Newman Literary, LLC (*US*)
The Darley Anderson Agency (*UK*)
David Luxton Associates (*UK*)
David Black Literary Agency (*US*)
David Higham Associates Ltd (*UK*)
Liza Dawson Associates (*US*)
DeFiore and Company (*US*)
DHH Literary Agency Ltd (*UK*)
Diamond Kahn and Woods (DKW) Literary
Agency Ltd (*UK*)
Diana Finch Literary Agency (*US*)
The Doe Coover Agency (*US*)
Don Congdon Associates, Inc. (*US*)
Donadio & Olson, Inc. (*US*)
Donaghy Literary Group (*US*)
Donald Maass Literary Agency (*US*)
Doug Grad Literary Agency (*US*)
Dunham Literary, Inc. (*US*)
Dunow, Carlson & Lerner Agency (*US*)
Dystel, Goderich & Bourret LLC (*US*)
E. J. McCarthy Agency (*US*)
Anne Edelstein Literary Agency (*US*)
Edwards Fuglewicz (*US*)
Einstein Literary Management (*US*)
Emily Sweet Associates (*UK*)
Felicia Eth Literary Representation (*US*)
Ethan Ellenberg Literary Agency (*US*)
Folio Literary Management, LLC (*US*)
Fox Literary (*US*)
Fox & Howard Literary Agency (*UK*)
Frances Collin Literary Agent (*US*)
Frances Goldin Literary Agency, Inc. (*US*)
Frances Kelly Agency (*UK*)

Wendy Sherman Associates, Inc. (*US*)
Whimsy Literary Agency, LLC (*US*)
William Morris Endeavor (WME) London (*UK*)
Wm Clark Associates (*US*)
Wordserve Literary (*US*)
Writers' Representatives, LLC (*US*)
Zeno Agency Ltd (*UK*)

Hobbies
Antony Harwood Limited (*UK*)
Grace Freedson's Publishing Network (*US*)
Kruger Cowne (*UK*)
The Leshne Agency (*US*)
Levine Greenberg Rostan Literary Agency (*US*)
The Ruppin Agency (*UK*)
Sheree Bykofsky Associates, Inc. (*US*)
Susan Schulman Literary Agency LLC (*US*)
Transatlantic Literary Agency, Inc. (*Can*)
Waterside Productions, Inc (*US*)

Horror
The Ampersand Agency Ltd (*UK*)
Marcia Amsterdam Agency (*US*)
Andrew Lownie Literary Agency Ltd (*UK*)
Antony Harwood Limited (*UK*)
Azantian Literary Agency (*US*)
Barone Literary Agency (*US*)
The Bent Agency (*US*)
The Blair Partnership (*UK*)
Bleecker Street Associates, Inc. (*US*)
Bond Literary Agency (*US*)
BookEnds, LLC (*US*)
Chalberg & Sussman (*US*)
The Cheney Agency (*US*)
Corvisiero Literary Agency (*US*)
D4EO Literary Agency (*US*)
The Darley Anderson Agency (*UK*)
Donald Maass Literary Agency (*US*)
Emerald City Literary Agency (*US*)
Film Rights Ltd in association with Laurence
Fitch Ltd (*UK*)
Folio Literary Management, LLC (*US*)
Gallt & Zacker Literary Agency (*US*)
Hardman & Swainson (*UK*)
Inklings Literary Agency, LLC (*US*)
Irene Goodman Literary Agency (IGLA) (*US*)
The Jean V. Naggar Literary Agency (*US*)
The Jennifer DeChiara Literary Agency (*US*)
Kimberley Cameron & Associates (*US*)
Harvey Klinger, Inc (*US*)
Kruger Cowne (*UK*)
L. Perkins Associates (*US*)
LAW (Lucas Alexander Whitley) (*UK*)
Lee Sobel Literary Agency (*US*)
Madeleine Milburn Literary, TV & Film Agency
(*UK*)
Maria Carvainis Agency, Inc. (*US*)
Peters Fraser + Dunlop (*UK*)
Prentis Literary (*US*)
Rees Literary Agency (*US*)
Richard Henshaw Group LLC (*US*)
Richford Becklow Literary Agency (*UK*)
Rocking Chair Books (*UK*)
Rosica Colin Ltd (*UK*)
Selectric Artists (*US*)

The Seymour Agency (*US*)
Speilburg Literary Agency (*US*)
Zeno Agency Ltd (*UK*)

How-to
Aaron M. Priest Literary Agency (*US*)
Adler & Robin Books, Inc (*US*)
Alive Literary Agency (*US*)
Ambassador Speakers Bureau & Literary
Agency (*US*)
Andrea Brown Literary Agency, Inc. (*US*)
Andrew Lownie Literary Agency Ltd (*UK*)
Antony Harwood Limited (*UK*)
Bleecker Street Associates, Inc. (*US*)
D4EO Literary Agency (*US*)
David Black Literary Agency (*US*)
Folio Literary Management, LLC (*US*)
Fresh Books Literary Agency (*US*)
Grace Freedson's Publishing Network (*US*)
Helen Zimmermann Literary Agency (*US*)
Jeanne Fredericks Literary Agency, Inc. (*US*)
The Jeff Herman Agency, LLC (*US*)
The Jennifer DeChiara Literary Agency (*US*)
JET Literary Associates, Inc. (*US*)
Harvey Klinger, Inc (*US*)
Linda Konner Literary Agency (*US*)
Kruger Cowne (*UK*)
L. Perkins Associates (*US*)
Literary & Creative Artists Inc. (*US*)
MacGregor & Luedeke (*US*)
Martin Literary Management (*US*)
Mendel Media Group, LLC (*US*)
Richard Henshaw Group LLC (*US*)
The Rights Bureau (*Ire*)
Rita Rosenkranz Literary Agency (*US*)
Susan Schulman Literary Agency LLC (*US*)
Waterside Productions, Inc (*US*)
Whimsy Literary Agency, LLC (*US*)

Humour
Adler & Robin Books, Inc (*US*)
Aevitas (*US*)
The Agency (London) Ltd (*UK*)
The Ahearn Agency, Inc (*US*)
Alive Literary Agency (*US*)
Marcia Amsterdam Agency (*US*)
Andrea Brown Literary Agency, Inc. (*US*)
Antony Harwood Limited (*UK*)
Ayesha Pande Literary (*US*)
The Bent Agency (*US*)
Bleecker Street Associates, Inc. (*US*)
Book Cents Literary Agency (*US*)
Books & Such Literary Management (*US*)
C+W (Conville & Walsh) (*UK*)
Carol Mann Agency (*US*)
Caroline Sheldon Literary Agency (*UK*)
Caskie Mushens (*UK*)
Cecily Ware Literary Agents (*UK*)
Chase Literary Agency (*US*)
The Chudney Agency (*US*)
Clare Hulton Literary Agency (*UK*)
Corvisiero Literary Agency (*US*)
Creative Authors Ltd (*UK*)
D4EO Literary Agency (*US*)
The Darley Anderson Agency (*UK*)

Caroline Davidson Literary Agency (*UK*)
Chartwell (*UK*)
Cherry Weiner Literary Agency (*US*)
Clare Hulton Literary Agency (*UK*)
Coombs Moylett & Maclean Literary Agency (*UK*)
Creative Media Agency (*US*)
D4EO Literary Agency (*US*)
Dana Newman Literary, LLC (*US*)
David Black Literary Agency (*US*)
Liza Dawson Associates (*US*)
DeFiore and Company (*US*)
Don Congdon Associates, Inc. (*US*)
Dunham Literary, Inc. (*US*)
Dystel, Goderich & Bourret LLC (*US*)
Empire Literary, LLC (*US*)
Felicia Eth Literary Representation (*US*)
Fairbank Literary Representation (*US*)
Folio Literary Management, LLC (*US*)
Fox & Howard Literary Agency (*UK*)
Frances Kelly Agency (*UK*)
Fraser-Bub Literary, LLC (*US*)
Fresh Books Literary Agency (*US*)
Grace Freedson's Publishing Network (*US*)
Graham Maw Christie Literary Agency (*UK*)
Hannigan Salky Getzler (HSG) Agency (*US*)
Helen Zimmermann Literary Agency (*US*)
Holloway Literary (*US*)
Irene Goodman Literary Agency (IGLA) (*US*)
Jane Turnbull (*UK*)
The Jean V. Naggar Literary Agency (*US*)
Jeanne Fredericks Literary Agency, Inc. (*US*)
The Jeff Herman Agency, LLC (*US*)
The Jennifer DeChiara Literary Agency (*US*)
JET Literary Associates, Inc. (*US*)
John Hawkins & Associates, Inc. (*US*)
Johnson & Alcock (*UK*)
Jonathan Pegg Literary Agency (*UK*)
Joëlle Delbourgo Associates, Inc. (*US*)
Karen Gantz Literary Management (*US*)
Kate Barker Literary, TV, & Film Agency (*UK*)
Kathi J. Paton Literary Agency (*US*)
Kimberley Cameron & Associates (*US*)
Harvey Klinger, Inc (*US*)
Kneerim & Williams (*US*)
Linda Konner Literary Agency (*US*)
Barbara S. Kouts, Literary Agent (*US*)
Kruger Cowne (*UK*)
LBA Books Ltd (*UK*)
Levine Greenberg Rostan Literary Agency (*US*)
Limelight Management (*UK*)
The Lisa Richards Agency (*Ire*)
Literary Services, Inc. (*US*)
Literary Management Group, Inc. (*US*)
Literary & Creative Artists Inc. (*US*)
The LKG Agency (*US*)
MacGregor & Luedeke (*US*)
Madeleine Milburn Literary, TV & Film Agency (*UK*)
Mansion Street Literary Management (*US*)
Marsal Lyon Literary Agency LLC (*US*)
Martin Leonardis Ltd (*UK*)
Martin Literary Management (*US*)

Max Gartenburg Literary Agency (*US*)
MBA Literary Agents Ltd (*UK*)
McCormick Literary (*US*)
The Michael Greer Literary Agency (*UK*)
Mulcahy Associates (Part of MMB Creative) (*UK*)
Northbank Talent Management (*UK*)
Perry Literary, Inc. (*US*)
Rebecca Friedman Literary Agency (*US*)
Regina Ryan Publishing Enterprises (*US*)
Richford Becklow Literary Agency (*UK*)
The Rights Factory (*Can*)
Rita Rosenkranz Literary Agency (*US*)
Robert Smith Literary Agency Ltd (*UK*)
Robertson Murray Literary Agency (*UK*)
Rocking Chair Books (*UK*)
Rosica Colin Ltd (*UK*)
The Rudy Agency (*US*)
Sandra Dijkstra Literary Agency (*US*)
Sanford J. Greenburger Associates, Inc. (*US*)
Sheil Land Associates Ltd (*UK*)
Sheree Bykofsky Associates, Inc. (*US*)
The Spieler Agency (*US*)
Standen Literary Agency (*UK*)
Sterling Lord Literistic, Inc. (*US*)
The Stringer Literary Agency LLC (*US*)
Susan Schulman Literary Agency LLC (*US*)
SYLA – Susan Yearwood Literary Agency (*UK*)
Teresa Chris Literary Agency Ltd (*UK*)
Transatlantic Literary Agency, Inc. (*Can*)
Upstart Crow Literary (*US*)
Waterside Productions, Inc (*US*)
Wendy Sherman Associates, Inc. (*US*)
Whimsy Literary Agency, LLC (*US*)
Whispering Buffalo Literary Agency Ltd (*UK*)
Zeno Agency Ltd (*UK*)

Literature
Andrew Lownie Literary Agency Ltd (*UK*)
Antony Harwood Limited (*UK*)
Bob Mecoy Creative Book Services (*US*)
The Bright Literary Academy (*UK*)
Carolyn Jenks Agency (*US*)
The Cheney Agency (*US*)
DeFiore and Company (*US*)
Don Congdon Associates, Inc. (*US*)
Donadio & Olson, Inc. (*US*)
Felicia Eth Literary Representation (*US*)
Georges Borchardt, Inc. (*US*)
The Jennifer DeChiara Literary Agency (*US*)
Michelle Kass Associates (*UK*)
Harvey Klinger, Inc (*US*)
Kneerim & Williams (*US*)
Mendel Media Group, LLC (*US*)
Richford Becklow Literary Agency (*UK*)
Rocking Chair Books (*UK*)
The Ruppin Agency (*UK*)
Selectric Artists (*US*)
Susan Schulman Literary Agency LLC (*US*)
Tibor Jones & Associates (*UK*)
Victoria Sanders & Associates LLC (*US*)
Whimsy Literary Agency, LLC (*US*)
Writers' Representatives, LLC (*US*)

Media
Andrew Lownie Literary Agency Ltd (*UK*)
Antony Harwood Limited (*UK*)
The August Agency LLC (*US*)
E. J. McCarthy Agency (*US*)
Folio Literary Management, LLC (*US*)
Joy Harris Literary Agency, Inc. (*US*)
Harvey Klinger, Inc (*US*)
Martin Literary Management (*US*)
Mendel Media Group, LLC (*US*)

Medicine
Ambassador Speakers Bureau & Literary
Agency (*US*)
Andrew Lownie Literary Agency Ltd (*UK*)
The Angela Rinaldi Literary Agency (*US*)
Antony Harwood Limited (*UK*)
Arcadia (*US*)
Betsy Amster Literary Enterprises (*US*)
Carol Mann Agency (*US*)
Caroline Davidson Literary Agency (*UK*)
Richard Curtis Associates, Inc. (*US*)
Liza Dawson Associates (*US*)
DeFiore and Company (*US*)
Don Congdon Associates, Inc. (*US*)
Frances Kelly Agency (*UK*)
Grace Freedson's Publishing Network (*US*)
Hardman & Swainson (*UK*)
InkWell Management (*US*)
Jeanne Fredericks Literary Agency, Inc. (*US*)
Jo Unwin Literary Agency (*UK*)
Harvey Klinger, Inc (*US*)
Kneerim & Williams (*US*)
Literary & Creative Artists Inc. (*US*)
Lowenstein Associates, Inc. (*US*)
Perry Literary, Inc. (*US*)
Robert Dudley Agency (*UK*)
The Rudy Agency (*US*)
Susan Schulman Literary Agency LLC (*US*)

Men's Interests
Andrew Lownie Literary Agency Ltd (*UK*)
Antony Harwood Limited (*UK*)
C+W (Conville & Walsh) (*UK*)
Kruger Cowne (*UK*)
Rosica Colin Ltd (*UK*)
The Ruppin Agency (*UK*)

Military
Andrew Lownie Literary Agency Ltd (*UK*)
Antony Harwood Limited (*UK*)
Artellus Limited (*UK*)
Blake Friedmann Literary Agency Ltd (*UK*)
Bleecker Street Associates, Inc. (*US*)
Bob Mecoy Creative Book Services (*US*)
C+W (Conville & Walsh) (*UK*)
Chase Literary Agency (*US*)
D4EO Literary Agency (*US*)
Liza Dawson Associates (*US*)
DeFiore and Company (*US*)
Don Congdon Associates, Inc. (*US*)
Doug Grad Literary Agency (*US*)
Dystel, Goderich & Bourret LLC (*US*)
E. J. McCarthy Agency (*US*)
Folio Literary Management, LLC (*US*)
The G Agency, LLC (*US*)

Grace Freedson's Publishing Network (*US*)
Holloway Literary (*US*)
Kruger Cowne (*UK*)
LAW (Lucas Alexander Whitley) (*UK*)
Duncan McAra (*UK*)
Rees Literary Agency (*US*)
Robert Dudley Agency (*UK*)
Robert Smith Literary Agency Ltd (*UK*)
Rosica Colin Ltd (*UK*)
The Rudy Agency (*US*)
The Ruppin Agency (*UK*)
The Seymour Agency (*US*)
Sheil Land Associates Ltd (*UK*)
Wordserve Literary (*US*)

Music
Andrew Lownie Literary Agency Ltd (*UK*)
Antony Harwood Limited (*UK*)
The Book Group (*US*)
Carol Mann Agency (*US*)
Clare Hulton Literary Agency (*UK*)
David Black Literary Agency (*US*)
DeFiore and Company (*US*)
The Doe Coover Agency (*US*)
Don Congdon Associates, Inc. (*US*)
Doug Grad Literary Agency (*US*)
Dunham Literary, Inc. (*US*)
Dunow, Carlson & Lerner Agency (*US*)
Folio Literary Management, LLC (*US*)
Helen Zimmermann Literary Agency (*US*)
The Jean V. Naggar Literary Agency (*US*)
Jenny Brown Associates (*UK*)
Johnson & Alcock (*UK*)
Harvey Klinger, Inc (*US*)
Kruger Cowne (*UK*)
L. Perkins Associates (*US*)
LAW (Lucas Alexander Whitley) (*UK*)
Lee Sobel Literary Agency (*US*)
Marsal Lyon Literary Agency LLC (*US*)
Perry Literary, Inc. (*US*)
Rita Rosenkranz Literary Agency (*US*)
The Ruppin Agency (*UK*)
Sandra Dijkstra Literary Agency (*US*)
Sanford J. Greenburger Associates, Inc. (*US*)
The Sayle Literary Agency (*UK*)
Selectric Artists (*US*)
The Spieler Agency (*US*)
Susan Schulman Literary Agency LLC (*US*)
Thompson Literary Agency (*US*)
Tibor Jones & Associates (*UK*)
Victoria Sanders & Associates LLC (*US*)
Watson, Little Ltd (*UK*)
Whispering Buffalo Literary Agency Ltd (*UK*)
Wm Clark Associates (*US*)

Mystery
Aaron M. Priest Literary Agency (*US*)
The Ahearn Agency, Inc (*US*)
Alive Literary Agency (*US*)
Marcia Amsterdam Agency (*US*)
Andrea Brown Literary Agency, Inc. (*US*)
The Angela Rinaldi Literary Agency (*US*)
Antony Harwood Limited (*UK*)
The Axelrod Agency (*US*)
Ayesha Pande Literary (*US*)

B.J. Robbins Literary Agency (*US*)
Barbara Braun Associates, Inc. (*US*)
Barry Goldblatt Literary Agency, Inc. (*US*)
The Bent Agency (*US*)
Betsy Amster Literary Enterprises (*US*)
The Blair Partnership (*UK*)
Blake Friedmann Literary Agency Ltd (*UK*)
Bleecker Street Associates, Inc. (*US*)
Bob Mecoy Creative Book Services (*US*)
Bond Literary Agency (*US*)
Book Cents Literary Agency (*US*)
BookEnds, LLC (*US*)
BookStop Literary Agency, LLC (*US*)
Brandt & Hochman Literary Agents, Inc. (*US*)
The Bright Literary Academy (*UK*)
C+W (Conville & Walsh) (*UK*)
Carolyn Jenks Agency (*US*)
Chartwell (*UK*)
Chase Literary Agency (*US*)
Cherry Weiner Literary Agency (*US*)
The Chudney Agency (*US*)
Coombs Moylett & Maclean Literary Agency (*UK*)
Corvisiero Literary Agency (*US*)
Creative Media Agency (*US*)
Richard Curtis Associates, Inc. (*US*)
D4EO Literary Agency (*US*)
Darhansoff & Verrill Literary Agents (*US*)
The Darley Anderson Agency (*UK*)
Liza Dawson Associates (*US*)
Don Congdon Associates, Inc. (*US*)
Donaghy Literary Group (*US*)
Donald Maass Literary Agency (*US*)
Doug Grad Literary Agency (*US*)
Dunham Literary, Inc. (*US*)
Dunow, Carlson & Lerner Agency (*US*)
Dystel, Goderich & Bourret LLC (*US*)
Einstein Literary Management (*US*)
Ethan Ellenberg Literary Agency (*US*)
Fairbank Literary Representation (*US*)
Folio Literary Management, LLC (*US*)
Fraser-Bub Literary, LLC (*US*)
The G Agency, LLC (*US*)
Gelfman Schneider / ICM Partners (*US*)
Hannigan Salky Getzler (HSG) Agency (*US*)
Joy Harris Literary Agency, Inc. (*US*)
Helen Zimmermann Literary Agency (*US*)
Holloway Literary (*US*)
Inklings Literary Agency, LLC (*US*)
InkWell Management (*US*)
Irene Goodman Literary Agency (IGLA) (*US*)
Jane Rotrosen Agency (*US*)
The Jean V. Naggar Literary Agency (*US*)
The Jennifer DeChiara Literary Agency (*US*)
John Hawkins & Associates, Inc. (*US*)
Kimberley Cameron & Associates (*US*)
Harvey Klinger, Inc (*US*)
Barbara S. Kouts, Literary Agent (*US*)
L. Perkins Associates (*US*)
Laura Dail Literary Agency (*US*)
Lawrence Jordan Literary Agency (*US*)
Lee Sobel Literary Agency (*US*)
Levine Greenberg Rostan Literary Agency (*US*)

Limelight Management (*UK*)
Lowenstein Associates, Inc. (*US*)
MacGregor & Luedeke (*US*)
Madeleine Milburn Literary, TV & Film Agency (*UK*)
Maria Carvainis Agency, Inc. (*US*)
Marsal Lyon Literary Agency LLC (*US*)
Mendel Media Group, LLC (*US*)
Meredith Bernstein Literary Agency, Inc. (*US*)
The Ned Leavitt Agency (*US*)
Nelson Literary Agency, LLC (*US*)
Niad Management (*US*)
One Track Literary Agency, Inc. (*US*)
Prentis Literary (*US*)
Prospect Agency (*US*)
Queen Literary Agency, Inc. (*US*)
Red Sofa Literary (*US*)
Redhammer (*UK*)
Rees Literary Agency (*US*)
Richard Henshaw Group LLC (*US*)
The Rights Factory (*Can*)
Rocking Chair Books (*UK*)
Rosica Colin Ltd (*UK*)
The Ruppin Agency (*UK*)
Sandra Dijkstra Literary Agency (*US*)
Sanford J. Greenburger Associates, Inc. (*US*)
Sean McCarthy Literary Agency (*US*)
The Seymour Agency (*US*)
Sheil Land Associates Ltd (*UK*)
Sheree Bykofsky Associates, Inc. (*US*)
Speilburg Literary Agency (*US*)
The Spieler Agency (*US*)
The Stringer Literary Agency LLC (*US*)
Susan Schulman Literary Agency LLC (*US*)
Emma Sweeney Agency, LLC (*US*)
Transatlantic Literary Agency, Inc. (*Can*)
Upstart Crow Literary (*US*)
Victoria Sanders & Associates LLC (*US*)
Writers' Representatives, LLC (*US*)

Nature
A.M. Heath & Company Limited, Author's Agents (*UK*)
Aevitas (*US*)
The Ahearn Agency, Inc (*US*)
Andrea Brown Literary Agency, Inc. (*US*)
Antony Harwood Limited (*UK*)
Blake Friedmann Literary Agency Ltd (*UK*)
Bleecker Street Associates, Inc. (*US*)
Carol Mann Agency (*US*)
Caroline Davidson Literary Agency (*UK*)
Chase Literary Agency (*US*)
Coombs Moylett & Maclean Literary Agency (*UK*)
Creative Authors Ltd (*UK*)
David Black Literary Agency (*US*)
David Higham Associates Ltd (*UK*)
DeFiore and Company (*US*)
Diana Finch Literary Agency (*US*)
Don Congdon Associates, Inc. (*US*)
Donadio & Olson, Inc. (*US*)
Dunham Literary, Inc. (*US*)
Frances Collin Literary Agent (*US*)
Frances Goldin Literary Agency, Inc. (*US*)

Grace Freedson's Publishing Network (*US*)
Helen Zimmermann Literary Agency (*US*)
Hill Nadell Literary Agency (*US*)
Holloway Literary (*US*)
Jane Turnbull (*UK*)
Jeanne Fredericks Literary Agency, Inc. (*US*)
John Hawkins & Associates, Inc. (*US*)
Johnson & Alcock (*UK*)
Jonathan Pegg Literary Agency (*UK*)
Kate Hordern Literary Agency (*UK*)
Kneerim & Williams (*US*)
Barbara S. Kouts, Literary Agent (*US*)
Kruger Cowne (*UK*)
LAW (Lucas Alexander Whitley) (*UK*)
Levine Greenberg Rostan Literary Agency (*US*)
Limelight Management (*UK*)
Literary & Creative Artists Inc. (*US*)
Madeleine Milburn Literary, TV & Film Agency (*UK*)
Max Gartenburg Literary Agency (*US*)
Peters Fraser + Dunlop (*UK*)
Regina Ryan Publishing Enterprises (*US*)
Rocking Chair Books (*UK*)
Rosica Colin Ltd (*UK*)
Rupert Heath Literary Agency (*UK*)
The Ruppin Agency (*UK*)
Sandra Dijkstra Literary Agency (*US*)
Sanford J. Greenburger Associates, Inc. (*US*)
Scovil Galen Ghosh Literary Agency, Inc. (*US*)
Solow Literary Enterprises, Inc. (*US*)
The Spieler Agency (*US*)
Sterling Lord Literistic, Inc. (*US*)
The Strothman Agency (*US*)
Stuart Krichevsky Literary Agency, Inc. (*US*)
Susan Schulman Literary Agency LLC (*US*)
Transatlantic Literary Agency, Inc. (*Can*)
The Unter Agency (*US*)
Veritas Literary Agency (*US*)
Wendy Sherman Associates, Inc. (*US*)
Whispering Buffalo Literary Agency Ltd (*UK*)
Zeno Agency Ltd (*UK*)

New Age
Aevitas (*US*)
Antony Harwood Limited (*UK*)
Bleecker Street Associates, Inc. (*US*)
Dystel, Goderich & Bourret LLC (*US*)
Ebeling & Associates (*US*)
Ethan Ellenberg Literary Agency (*US*)
Kruger Cowne (*UK*)
Levine Greenberg Rostan Literary Agency (*US*)
Whimsy Literary Agency, LLC (*US*)

Nonfiction
A & B Personal Management Ltd (*UK*)
A.M. Heath & Company Limited, Author's Agents (*UK*)
Aaron M. Priest Literary Agency (*US*)
Abner Stein (*UK*)
Adler & Robin Books, Inc (*US*)
Aevitas (*US*)
The Agency (London) Ltd (*UK*)
The Ahearn Agency, Inc (*US*)
Aitken Alexander Associates (*UK*)
Alive Literary Agency (*US*)

Allen O'Shea Literary Agency (*US*)
Ambassador Speakers Bureau & Literary Agency (*US*)
AMP Literary (*UK*)
The Ampersand Agency Ltd (*UK*)
Darley Anderson Children's (*UK*)
The Anderson Literary Agency (*US*)
Andlyn (*UK*)
Andrea Brown Literary Agency, Inc. (*US*)
Andrew Lownie Literary Agency Ltd (*UK*)
Andrew Nurnberg Associates, Ltd (*UK*)
The Angela Rinaldi Literary Agency (*US*)
Anne Clark Literary Agency (*UK*)
Antony Harwood Limited (*UK*)
Aponte Literary (*US*)
Apple Tree Literary Ltd (*UK*)
Arcadia (*US*)
Artellus Limited (*UK*)
Movable Type Management (*US*)
The August Agency LLC (*US*)
Ayesha Pande Literary (*US*)
B.J. Robbins Literary Agency (*US*)
Barbara Hogenson Agency (*US*)
Barbara Braun Associates, Inc. (*US*)
Barbara Levy Literary Agency (*UK*)
Baror International, Inc. (*US*)
Bath Literary Agency (*UK*)
Bell Lomax Moreton Agency (*UK*)
The Bent Agency (*US*)
Betsy Amster Literary Enterprises (*US*)
Bidnick & Company (*US*)
The Blair Partnership (*UK*)
Blake Friedmann Literary Agency Ltd (*UK*)
Bleecker Street Associates, Inc. (*US*)
Bob Mecoy Creative Book Services (*US*)
Bond Literary Agency (*US*)
The Book Group (*US*)
The Book Bureau Literary Agency (*Ire*)
BookBlast Ltd. (*UK*)
BookEnds, LLC (*US*)
Books & Such Literary Management (*US*)
BookStop Literary Agency, LLC (*US*)
Brandt & Hochman Literary Agents, Inc. (*US*)
The Brattle Agency LLC (*US*)
Brotherstone Creative Management (*UK*)
Browne & Miller Literary Associates (*US*)
C+W (Conville & Walsh) (*UK*)
Capital Talent Agency (*US*)
Carol Mann Agency (*US*)
Caroline Davidson Literary Agency (*UK*)
Caroline Sheldon Literary Agency (*UK*)
Carolyn Jenks Agency (*US*)
Caskie Mushens (*UK*)
Chalberg & Sussman (*US*)
Chartwell (*UK*)
Chase Literary Agency (*US*)
Mic Cheetham Literary Agency (*UK*)
The Cheney Agency (*US*)
Cherry Weiner Literary Agency (*US*)
Christine Green Authors' Agent (*UK*)
The Christopher Little Literary Agency (*UK*)
Clare Hulton Literary Agency (*UK*)

Coombs Moylett & Maclean Literary Agency (*UK*)
Corvisiero Literary Agency (*US*)
Creative Authors Ltd (*UK*)
Creative Media Agency (*US*)
Curtis Brown (*UK*)
Richard Curtis Associates, Inc. (*US*)
Curtis Brown Ltd (*US*)
Cynthia Cannell Literary Agency (*US*)
D4EO Literary Agency (*US*)
Dana Newman Literary, LLC (*US*)
Darhansoff & Verrill Literary Agents (*US*)
David Luxton Associates (*UK*)
David Black Literary Agency (*US*)
David Godwin Associates (*UK*)
David Higham Associates Ltd (*UK*)
Liza Dawson Associates (*US*)
DeFiore and Company (*US*)
DHH Literary Agency Ltd (*UK*)
Diamond Kahn and Woods (DKW) Literary Agency Ltd (*UK*)
Diana Finch Literary Agency (*US*)
Dinah Wiener Ltd (*UK*)
The Doe Coover Agency (*US*)
Don Congdon Associates, Inc. (*US*)
Donadio & Olson, Inc. (*US*)
Doug Grad Literary Agency (*US*)
Dunham Literary, Inc. (*US*)
Dunow, Carlson & Lerner Agency (*US*)
Dystel, Goderich & Bourret LLC (*US*)
E. J. McCarthy Agency (*US*)
Ebeling & Associates (*US*)
Eddison Pearson Ltd (*UK*)
Anne Edelstein Literary Agency (*US*)
Edwards Fuglewicz (*UK*)
Einstein Literary Management (*US*)
Elaine Markson Literary Agency (*US*)
Elaine Steel (*UK*)
Elise Dillsworth Agency (EDA) (*UK*)
Elizabeth Roy Literary Agency (*UK*)
Emerald City Literary Agency (*US*)
Emily Sweet Associates (*UK*)
Empire Literary, LLC (*US*)
Felicia Eth Literary Representation (*US*)
Ethan Ellenberg Literary Agency (*US*)
Eve White: Literary Agent (*UK*)
Faith Evans Associates (*UK*)
Flannery Literary (*US*)
Folio Literary Management, LLC (*US*)
Fox Literary (*US*)
Fox & Howard Literary Agency (*UK*)
Frances Collin Literary Agent (*US*)
Frances Goldin Literary Agency, Inc. (*US*)
Frances Kelly Agency (*UK*)
Fraser Ross Associates (*UK*)
Fraser-Bub Literary, LLC (*US*)
Fresh Books Literary Agency (*US*)
The Friedrich Agency LLC (*US*)
Fuse Literary (*US*)
The G Agency, LLC (*US*)
Gallt & Zacker Literary Agency (*US*)
Gelfman Schneider / ICM Partners (*US*)
Georges Borchardt, Inc. (*US*)

Georgina Capel Associates Ltd (*UK*)
Global Lion Intellectual Property Management, Inc. (*US*)
The Good Literary Agency (*UK*)
Grace Freedson's Publishing Network (*US*)
Graham Maw Christie Literary Agency (*UK*)
Greene & Heaton Ltd (*UK*)
Blanche C. Gregory Inc. (*US*)
David Grossman Literary Agency Ltd (*UK*)
Marianne Gunn O'Connor Literary Agency (*Ire*)
Hannigan Salky Getzler (HSG) Agency (*US*)
Hardman & Swainson (*UK*)
Joy Harris Literary Agency, Inc. (*US*)
Helen Zimmermann Literary Agency (*US*)
Herman Agency Inc. (*US*)
hhb agency ltd (*UK*)
Hill Nadell Literary Agency (*US*)
Holloway Literary (*US*)
Holroyde Cartey (*UK*)
Vanessa Holt Ltd (*UK*)
ILA (Intercontinental Literary Agency) (*UK*)
Inklings Literary Agency, LLC (*US*)
InkWell Management (*US*)
InterSaga (*UK*)
Irene Goodman Literary Agency (IGLA) (*US*)
Isabel White Literary Agent (*UK*)
J. de S. Associates, Inc. (*US*)
Jabberwocky Literary Agency (*US*)
Jane Judd Literary Agency (*UK*)
Jane Rotrosen Agency (*US*)
Jane Turnbull (*UK*)
Janklow & Nesbit Associates (*US*)
The Jean V. Naggar Literary Agency (*US*)
Jeanne Fredericks Literary Agency, Inc. (*US*)
The Jeff Herman Agency, LLC (*US*)
The Jennifer DeChiara Literary Agency (*US*)
Jenny Brown Associates (*UK*)
JET Literary Associates, Inc. (*US*)
Jo Unwin Literary Agency (*UK*)
Joanna Pulcini Literary Management (*US*)
John Hawkins & Associates, Inc. (*US*)
Johnson & Alcock (*UK*)
Jonathan Clowes Ltd (*UK*)
Jonathan Pegg Literary Agency (*UK*)
Joëlle Delbourgo Associates, Inc. (*US*)
Juliet Burton Literary Agency (*UK*)
JYLA (Jason Yarn Literary Agency) (*US*)
K2 Literary (*Can*)
Karen Gantz Literary Management (*US*)
Kate Barker Literary, TV, & Film Agency (*UK*)
Kate Hordern Literary Agency (*UK*)
Kate Nash Literary Agency (*UK*)
Kathi J. Paton Literary Agency (*US*)
Keane Kataria Literary Agency (*UK*)
Ken Sherman & Associates (*US*)
Ki Agency Ltd (*UK*)
Kimberley Cameron & Associates (*US*)
Kingsford Campbell Literary & Marketing Agents (*UK*)
Harvey Klinger, Inc (*US*)
Kneerim & Williams (*US*)
Knight Features (*UK*)
Linda Konner Literary Agency (*US*)

United Talent Agency (UTA) (*US*)
The Unter Agency (*US*)
Upstart Crow Literary (*US*)
Veritas Literary Agency (*US*)
Vicky Bijur Literary Agency (*US*)
Victoria Sanders & Associates LLC (*US*)
The Viney Agency (*UK*)
Wade & Co Literary Agency (*UK*)
Waterside Productions, Inc (*US*)
Watson, Little Ltd (*UK*)
Wendy Schmalz Agency (*US*)
Wendy Sherman Associates, Inc. (*US*)
Whimsy Literary Agency, LLC (*US*)
Whispering Buffalo Literary Agency Ltd (*UK*)
William Morris Endeavor (WME) London (*UK*)
Wm Clark Associates (*US*)
Wordserve Literary (*US*)
The Writers' Practice (*UK*)
Writers' Representatives, LLC (*US*)
The Wylie Agency (UK) Ltd (*UK*)
Zeno Agency Ltd (*UK*)

Philosophy
Antony Harwood Limited (*UK*)
Clare Hulton Literary Agency (*UK*)
David Black Literary Agency (*US*)
DeFiore and Company (*US*)
Frances Goldin Literary Agency, Inc. (*US*)
Georges Borchardt, Inc. (*US*)
Grace Freedson's Publishing Network (*US*)
Graham Maw Christie Literary Agency (*UK*)
Hardman & Swainson (*UK*)
Kruger Cowne (*UK*)
LAW (Lucas Alexander Whitley) (*UK*)
Literary & Creative Artists Inc. (*US*)
Perry Literary, Inc. (*US*)
Puttick Literary Agency (*UK*)
The Ruppin Agency (*UK*)
Sandra Dijkstra Literary Agency (*US*)
Stephanie Tade Literary Agency (*US*)
Wm Clark Associates (*US*)
Writers' Representatives, LLC (*US*)

Photography
Andrea Brown Literary Agency, Inc. (*US*)
Antony Harwood Limited (*UK*)
Barbara Braun Associates, Inc. (*US*)
Fresh Books Literary Agency (*US*)
Hannigan Salky Getzler (HSG) Agency (*US*)
Jeanne Fredericks Literary Agency, Inc. (*US*)
The Leshne Agency (*US*)
The Spieler Agency (*US*)
Susan Schulman Literary Agency LLC (*US*)
Whimsy Literary Agency, LLC (*US*)

Poetry
Eddison Pearson Ltd (*UK*)
Frances Goldin Literary Agency, Inc. (*US*)
InterSaga (*UK*)
The Spieler Agency (*US*)
Writers' Representatives, LLC (*US*)

Politics
Aaron M. Priest Literary Agency (*US*)
Aevitas (*US*)
Allen O'Shea Literary Agency (*US*)

Ambassador Speakers Bureau & Literary
Agency (*US*)
Andrew Lownie Literary Agency Ltd (*UK*)
Antony Harwood Limited (*UK*)
Aponte Literary (*US*)
The August Agency LLC (*US*)
Barbara Braun Associates, Inc. (*US*)
Blake Friedmann Literary Agency Ltd (*UK*)
Bleecker Street Associates, Inc. (*US*)
The Brattle Agency LLC (*US*)
Carol Mann Agency (*US*)
Caroline Davidson Literary Agency (*UK*)
Caskie Mushens (*UK*)
The Cheney Agency (*US*)
David Luxton Associates (*UK*)
David Black Literary Agency (*US*)
Liza Dawson Associates (*US*)
DeFiore and Company (*US*)
Diamond Kahn and Woods (DKW) Literary
Agency Ltd (*UK*)
Diana Finch Literary Agency (*US*)
The Doe Coover Agency (*US*)
Don Congdon Associates, Inc. (*US*)
Dunham Literary, Inc. (*US*)
Dystel, Goderich & Bourret LLC (*US*)
E. J. McCarthy Agency (*US*)
Folio Literary Management, LLC (*US*)
Frances Goldin Literary Agency, Inc. (*US*)
Gelfman Schneider / ICM Partners (*US*)
Georges Borchardt, Inc. (*US*)
Hannigan Salky Getzler (HSG) Agency (*US*)
hhb agency ltd (*UK*)
Hill Nadell Literary Agency (*US*)
Holloway Literary (*US*)
Irene Goodman Literary Agency (IGLA) (*US*)
JET Literary Associates, Inc. (*US*)
Jo Unwin Literary Agency (*UK*)
John Hawkins & Associates, Inc. (*US*)
Joëlle Delbourgo Associates, Inc. (*US*)
Karen Gantz Literary Management (*US*)
Kathi J. Paton Literary Agency (*US*)
Ki Agency Ltd (*UK*)
Kimberley Cameron & Associates (*US*)
Harvey Klinger, Inc (*US*)
Kneerim & Williams (*US*)
LAW (Lucas Alexander Whitley) (*UK*)
Levine Greenberg Rostan Literary Agency (*US*)
Literary Services, Inc. (*US*)
Literary & Creative Artists Inc. (*US*)
Marsal Lyon Literary Agency LLC (*US*)
Massie & McQuilkin (*US*)
Max Gartenburg Literary Agency (*US*)
McCormick Literary (*US*)
Mendel Media Group, LLC (*US*)
Northbank Talent Management (*UK*)
Perry Literary, Inc. (*US*)
Publication Riot Group, Inc. (*US*)
Red Sofa Literary (*US*)
Regina Ryan Publishing Enterprises (*US*)
The Rights Factory (*Can*)
The Rudy Agency (*US*)
Rupert Heath Literary Agency (*UK*)
The Ruppin Agency (*UK*)

Sandra Dijkstra Literary Agency (*US*)
Sanford J. Greenburger Associates, Inc. (*US*)
Scovil Galen Ghosh Literary Agency, Inc. (*US*)
Sheil Land Associates Ltd (*UK*)
Jeffrey Simmons (*UK*)
The Spieler Agency (*US*)
Stephanie Tade Literary Agency (*US*)
Sterling Lord Literistic, Inc. (*US*)
The Strothman Agency (*US*)
Stuart Krichevsky Literary Agency, Inc. (*US*)
Susan Schulman Literary Agency LLC (*US*)
Thompson Literary Agency (*US*)
Toby Mundy Associates Ltd (*UK*)
Transatlantic Literary Agency, Inc. (*Can*)
The Unter Agency (*US*)
Victoria Sanders & Associates LLC (*US*)
Whispering Buffalo Literary Agency Ltd (*UK*)
Writers' Representatives, LLC (*US*)

Psychology
A.M. Heath & Company Limited, Author's
Agents (*UK*)
Aevitas (*US*)
Andrew Lownie Literary Agency Ltd (*UK*)
The Angela Rinaldi Literary Agency (*US*)
Antony Harwood Limited (*UK*)
Arcadia (*US*)
Barbara Braun Associates, Inc. (*US*)
Betsy Amster Literary Enterprises (*US*)
Blake Friedmann Literary Agency Ltd (*UK*)
Bleecker Street Associates, Inc. (*US*)
The Book Group (*US*)
C+W (Conville & Walsh) (*UK*)
Carol Mann Agency (*US*)
Caroline Davidson Literary Agency (*UK*)
Chalberg & Sussman (*US*)
Chartwell (*UK*)
Creative Media Agency (*US*)
D4EO Literary Agency (*US*)
Dana Newman Literary, LLC (*US*)
David Black Literary Agency (*US*)
Liza Dawson Associates (*US*)
DeFiore and Company (*US*)
The Doe Coover Agency (*US*)
Don Congdon Associates, Inc. (*US*)
Dystel, Goderich & Bourret LLC (*US*)
Anne Edelstein Literary Agency (*US*)
Felicia Eth Literary Representation (*US*)
Ethan Ellenberg Literary Agency (*US*)
Folio Literary Management, LLC (*US*)
Fox & Howard Literary Agency (*UK*)
Fraser-Bub Literary, LLC (*US*)
Grace Freedson's Publishing Network (*US*)
Hannigan Salky Getzler (HSG) Agency (*US*)
Hardman & Swainson (*UK*)
InkWell Management (*US*)
Jane Rotrosen Agency (*US*)
The Jean V. Naggar Literary Agency (*US*)
Jeanne Fredericks Literary Agency, Inc. (*US*)
The Jeff Herman Agency, LLC (*US*)
Jo Unwin Literary Agency (*UK*)
John Hawkins & Associates, Inc. (*US*)
Johnson & Alcock (*UK*)
Jonathan Pegg Literary Agency (*UK*)

Joëlle Delbourgo Associates, Inc. (*US*)
Karen Gantz Literary Management (*US*)
Kate Barker Literary, TV, & Film Agency (*UK*)
Harvey Klinger, Inc (*US*)
Kneerim & Williams (*US*)
Linda Konner Literary Agency (*US*)
Barbara S. Kouts, Literary Agent (*US*)
Kruger Cowne (*UK*)
L. Perkins Associates (*US*)
Laura Dail Literary Agency (*US*)
Levine Greenberg Rostan Literary Agency (*US*)
Literary Services, Inc. (*US*)
The LKG Agency (*US*)
Lowenstein Associates, Inc. (*US*)
Madeleine Milburn Literary, TV & Film Agency
(*UK*)
Maria Carvainis Agency, Inc. (*US*)
Marsal Lyon Literary Agency LLC (*US*)
Massie & McQuilkin (*US*)
The Michael Greer Literary Agency (*UK*)
Northbank Talent Management (*UK*)
Perry Literary, Inc. (*US*)
Peters Fraser + Dunlop (*UK*)
Queen Literary Agency, Inc. (*US*)
Rees Literary Agency (*US*)
Regina Ryan Publishing Enterprises (*US*)
Richard Henshaw Group LLC (*US*)
Rosica Colin Ltd (*UK*)
Ross Yoon Agency (*US*)
Sanford J. Greenburger Associates, Inc. (*US*)
Scovil Galen Ghosh Literary Agency, Inc. (*US*)
Sheil Land Associates Ltd (*UK*)
Sheree Bykofsky Associates, Inc. (*US*)
Jeffrey Simmons (*UK*)
Solow Literary Enterprises, Inc. (*US*)
Stephanie Tade Literary Agency (*US*)
Susan Schulman Literary Agency LLC (*US*)
Victoria Sanders & Associates LLC (*US*)
Waterside Productions, Inc (*US*)
Watson, Little Ltd (*UK*)
Wendy Sherman Associates, Inc. (*US*)
Whimsy Literary Agency, LLC (*US*)
Wordserve Literary (*US*)

Radio
The Agency (London) Ltd (*UK*)
Alan Brodie Representation Ltd (*UK*)
Antony Harwood Limited (*UK*)
Berlin Associates (*UK*)
Blake Friedmann Literary Agency Ltd (*UK*)
Casarotto Ramsay and Associates Ltd (*UK*)
Curtis Brown (*UK*)
Elaine Steel (*UK*)
Felix de Wolfe (*UK*)
Film Rights Ltd in association with Laurence
Fitch Ltd (*UK*)
Georgina Capel Associates Ltd (*UK*)
Independent Talent Group Ltd (*UK*)
Jill Foster Ltd (JFL) (*UK*)
Jonathan Clowes Ltd (*UK*)
Mary Clemmey Literary Agency (*UK*)
MBA Literary Agents Ltd (*UK*)
Bill McLean Personal Management Ltd (*UK*)
Micheline Steinberg Associates (*UK*)

Nick Turner Management Ltd (*UK*)
Peters Fraser + Dunlop (*UK*)
Rochelle Stevens & Co. (*UK*)
Rosica Colin Ltd (*UK*)
Sayle Screen Ltd (*UK*)
Sheil Land Associates Ltd (*UK*)
The Tennyson Agency (*UK*)
United Agents (*UK*)
Valerie Hoskins Associates (*UK*)
Reference
Adler & Robin Books, Inc (*US*)
BookEnds, LLC (*US*)
Caroline Davidson Literary Agency (*UK*)
D4EO Literary Agency (*US*)
David Luxton Associates (*UK*)
The Doe Coover Agency (*US*)
Folio Literary Management, LLC (*US*)
Fox & Howard Literary Agency (*UK*)
Frances Kelly Agency (*UK*)
Fresh Books Literary Agency (*US*)
Graham Maw Christie Literary Agency (*UK*)
InterSaga (*UK*)
Jeanne Fredericks Literary Agency, Inc. (*US*)
The Jeff Herman Agency, LLC (*US*)
Kate Hordern Literary Agency (*UK*)
Linda Konner Literary Agency (*US*)
LAW (Lucas Alexander Whitley) (*UK*)
Literary Services, Inc. (*US*)
Regina Ryan Publishing Enterprises (*US*)
Richard Henshaw Group LLC (*US*)
Rita Rosenkranz Literary Agency (*US*)
Sanford J. Greenburger Associates, Inc. (*US*)
Sheree Bykofsky Associates, Inc. (*US*)
Writers' Representatives, LLC (*US*)
Religious
Aevitas (*US*)
Alive Literary Agency (*US*)
Ambassador Speakers Bureau & Literary
Agency (*US*)
The Anderson Literary Agency (*US*)
Antony Harwood Limited (*UK*)
Bleecker Street Associates, Inc. (*US*)
Books & Such Literary Management (*US*)
Carol Mann Agency (*US*)
Creative Media Agency (*US*)
Cynthia Cannell Literary Agency (*US*)
Liza Dawson Associates (*US*)
Dystel, Goderich & Bourret LLC (*US*)
Anne Edelstein Literary Agency (*US*)
Folio Literary Management, LLC (*US*)
Georges Borchardt, Inc. (*US*)
Grace Freedson's Publishing Network (*US*)
Karen Gantz Literary Management (*US*)
Kathi J. Paton Literary Agency (*US*)
Kimberley Cameron & Associates (*US*)
Kneerim & Williams (*US*)
Lawrence Jordan Literary Agency (*US*)
Levine Greenberg Rostan Literary Agency (*US*)
Literary Management Group, Inc. (*US*)
Literary & Creative Artists Inc. (*US*)
MacGregor & Luedeke (*US*)
Martin Literary Management (*US*)
Mendel Media Group, LLC (*US*)

Rosica Colin Ltd (*UK*)
Andy Ross Agency (*US*)
Sandra Dijkstra Literary Agency (*US*)
Scovil Galen Ghosh Literary Agency, Inc. (*US*)
The Seymour Agency (*US*)
The Steve Laube Agency (*US*)
Susan Schulman Literary Agency LLC (*US*)
Emma Sweeney Agency, LLC (*US*)
Transatlantic Literary Agency, Inc. (*Can*)
Wm Clark Associates (*US*)
Wordserve Literary (*US*)
Romance
The Ahearn Agency, Inc (*US*)
Marcia Amsterdam Agency (*US*)
Andrea Brown Literary Agency, Inc. (*US*)
Andrew Lownie Literary Agency Ltd (*UK*)
Antony Harwood Limited (*UK*)
The Axelrod Agency (*US*)
Ayesha Pande Literary (*US*)
Barone Literary Agency (*US*)
Barry Goldblatt Literary Agency, Inc. (*US*)
The Bent Agency (*US*)
Bleecker Street Associates, Inc. (*US*)
Bob Mecoy Creative Book Services (*US*)
Book Cents Literary Agency (*US*)
BookEnds, LLC (*US*)
Books & Such Literary Management (*US*)
Carolyn Jenks Agency (*US*)
Caskie Mushens (*UK*)
Chalberg & Sussman (*US*)
The Cheney Agency (*US*)
Cherry Weiner Literary Agency (*US*)
Corvisiero Literary Agency (*US*)
Creative Media Agency (*US*)
Richard Curtis Associates, Inc. (*US*)
D4EO Literary Agency (*US*)
The Darley Anderson Agency (*UK*)
Liza Dawson Associates (*US*)
DeFiore and Company (*US*)
Donaghy Literary Group (*US*)
Donald Maass Literary Agency (*US*)
Doug Grad Literary Agency (*US*)
Dystel, Goderich & Bourret LLC (*US*)
Einstein Literary Management (*US*)
Elizabeth Roy Literary Agency (*UK*)
Emerald City Literary Agency (*US*)
Ethan Ellenberg Literary Agency (*US*)
Folio Literary Management, LLC (*US*)
Fox Literary (*US*)
Fraser-Bub Literary, LLC (*US*)
Gallt & Zacker Literary Agency (*US*)
Holloway Literary (*US*)
Inklings Literary Agency, LLC (*US*)
InterSaga (*UK*)
Irene Goodman Literary Agency (IGLA) (*US*)
Jane Rotrosen Agency (*US*)
The Jean V. Naggar Literary Agency (*US*)
The Jennifer DeChiara Literary Agency (*US*)
Jenny Brown Associates (*UK*)
JET Literary Associates, Inc. (*US*)
Harvey Klinger, Inc (*US*)
KT Literary (*US*)
L. Perkins Associates (*US*)

Laura Dail Literary Agency (*US*)
LBA Books Ltd (*UK*)
Levine Greenberg Rostan Literary Agency (*US*)
MacGregor & Luedeke (*US*)
Madeleine Milburn Literary, TV & Film Agency (*UK*)
Maria Carvainis Agency, Inc. (*US*)
Marsal Lyon Literary Agency LLC (*US*)
Meredith Bernstein Literary Agency, Inc. (*US*)
Nelson Literary Agency, LLC (*US*)
Niad Management (*US*)
One Track Literary Agency, Inc. (*US*)
Prentis Literary (*US*)
Prospect Agency (*US*)
The Purcell Agency, LLC (*US*)
Rebecca Friedman Literary Agency (*US*)
Red Sofa Literary (*US*)
Rees Literary Agency (*US*)
Richard Henshaw Group LLC (*US*)
Richford Becklow Literary Agency (*UK*)
The Rights Factory (*Can*)
Rocking Chair Books (*UK*)
Rosica Colin Ltd (*UK*)
Sandra Dijkstra Literary Agency (*US*)
Sanford J. Greenburger Associates, Inc. (*US*)
The Seymour Agency (*US*)
Sheil Land Associates Ltd (*UK*)
Speilburg Literary Agency (*US*)
The Stringer Literary Agency LLC (*US*)
SYLA – Susan Yearwood Literary Agency (*UK*)
Transatlantic Literary Agency, Inc. (*Can*)
Whispering Buffalo Literary Agency Ltd (*UK*)
Wordserve Literary (*US*)

Science

Aaron M. Priest Literary Agency (*US*)
Aevitas (*US*)
Allen O'Shea Literary Agency (*US*)
The Ampersand Agency Ltd (*UK*)
Marcia Amsterdam Agency (*US*)
The Anderson Literary Agency (*US*)
Andrea Brown Literary Agency, Inc. (*US*)
Andrew Lownie Literary Agency Ltd (*UK*)
Antony Harwood Limited (*UK*)
Aponte Literary (*US*)
Arcadia (*US*)
Artellus Limited (*UK*)
B.J. Robbins Literary Agency (*US*)
The Bent Agency (*US*)
Blake Friedmann Literary Agency Ltd (*UK*)
Bleecker Street Associates, Inc. (*US*)
Bond Literary Agency (*US*)
The Book Group (*US*)
BookStop Literary Agency, LLC (*US*)
Brandt & Hochman Literary Agents, Inc. (*US*)
C+W (Conville & Walsh) (*UK*)
Caroline Davidson Literary Agency (*UK*)
Caskie Mushens (*UK*)
Chalberg & Sussman (*US*)
Chartwell (*UK*)
Chase Literary Agency (*US*)
The Cheney Agency (*US*)
Compass Talent (*US*)
Curtis Brown (*UK*)

Richard Curtis Associates, Inc. (*US*)
D4EO Literary Agency (*US*)
David Black Literary Agency (*US*)
Liza Dawson Associates (*US*)
DeFiore and Company (*US*)
Diana Finch Literary Agency (*US*)
Dinah Wiener Ltd (*UK*)
The Doe Coover Agency (*US*)
Don Congdon Associates, Inc. (*US*)
Donadio & Olson, Inc. (*US*)
Doug Grad Literary Agency (*US*)
Dunham Literary, Inc. (*US*)
Dunow, Carlson & Lerner Agency (*US*)
Dystel, Goderich & Bourret LLC (*US*)
Felicia Eth Literary Representation (*US*)
Ethan Ellenberg Literary Agency (*US*)
Folio Literary Management, LLC (*US*)
Frances Goldin Literary Agency, Inc. (*US*)
Fresh Books Literary Agency (*US*)
Gelfman Schneider / ICM Partners (*US*)
Georges Borchardt, Inc. (*US*)
Grace Freedson's Publishing Network (*US*)
Graham Maw Christie Literary Agency (*UK*)
Greene & Heaton Ltd (*UK*)
Hannigan Salky Getzler (HSG) Agency (*US*)
Hardman & Swainson (*UK*)
Helen Zimmermann Literary Agency (*US*)
Hill Nadell Literary Agency (*US*)
Irene Goodman Literary Agency (IGLA) (*US*)
Jabberwocky Literary Agency (*US*)
The Jean V. Naggar Literary Agency (*US*)
Jeanne Fredericks Literary Agency, Inc. (*US*)
The Jennifer DeChiara Literary Agency (*US*)
Jenny Brown Associates (*UK*)
John Hawkins & Associates, Inc. (*US*)
Johnson & Alcock (*UK*)
Jonathan Pegg Literary Agency (*UK*)
Joëlle Delbourgo Associates, Inc. (*US*)
JYLA (Jason Yarn Literary Agency) (*US*)
Kate Barker Literary, TV, & Film Agency (*UK*)
Kathi J. Paton Literary Agency (*US*)
Ki Agency Ltd (*UK*)
Kimberley Cameron & Associates (*US*)
Harvey Klinger, Inc (*US*)
Kneerim & Williams (*US*)
Linda Konner Literary Agency (*US*)
Kruger Cowne (*UK*)
L. Perkins Associates (*US*)
Laura Dail Literary Agency (*US*)
LAW (Lucas Alexander Whitley) (*UK*)
LBA Books Ltd (*UK*)
The Leshne Agency (*US*)
Levine Greenberg Rostan Literary Agency (*US*)
Limelight Management (*UK*)
Literary Services, Inc. (*US*)
Lowenstein Associates, Inc. (*US*)
Madeleine Milburn Literary, TV & Film Agency (*UK*)
Maria Carvainis Agency, Inc. (*US*)
Massie & McQuilkin (*US*)
Max Gartenburg Literary Agency (*US*)
McCormick Literary (*US*)
Mendel Media Group, LLC (*US*)

Northbank Talent Management (*UK*)
Perry Literary, Inc. (*US*)
Peters Fraser + Dunlop (*UK*)
Prospect Agency (*US*)
Publication Riot Group, Inc. (*US*)
Puttick Literary Agency (*UK*)
Queen Literary Agency, Inc. (*US*)
Red Sofa Literary (*US*)
Rees Literary Agency (*US*)
Regal Hoffmann & Associates LLC (*US*)
Regina Ryan Publishing Enterprises (*US*)
Richard Henshaw Group LLC (*US*)
The Rights Factory (*Can*)
Rita Rosenkranz Literary Agency (*US*)
Robertson Murray Literary Agency (*UK*)
Rosica Colin Ltd (*UK*)
Andy Ross Agency (*US*)
Ross Yoon Agency (*US*)
The Rudy Agency (*US*)
Rupert Heath Literary Agency (*UK*)
The Ruppin Agency (*UK*)
Sandra Dijkstra Literary Agency (*US*)
Sanford J. Greenburger Associates, Inc. (*US*)
The Sayle Literary Agency (*UK*)
Scovil Galen Ghosh Literary Agency, Inc. (*US*)
Sheil Land Associates Ltd (*UK*)
Solow Literary Enterprises, Inc. (*US*)
Speilburg Literary Agency (*US*)
The Spieler Agency (*US*)
Sterling Lord Literistic, Inc. (*US*)
The Strothman Agency (*US*)
Stuart Krichevsky Literary Agency, Inc. (*US*)
Susan Schulman Literary Agency LLC (*US*)
Emma Sweeney Agency, LLC (*US*)
Thompson Literary Agency (*US*)
Toby Mundy Associates Ltd (*UK*)
Transatlantic Literary Agency, Inc. (*Can*)
Lavinia Trevor Agency (*UK*)
Union Literary (*US*)
United Talent Agency (UTA) (*US*)
Veritas Literary Agency (*US*)
Watson, Little Ltd (*UK*)
Wm Clark Associates (*US*)
Writers' Representatives, LLC (*US*)

Sci-Fi

The Ampersand Agency Ltd (*UK*)
Andrea Brown Literary Agency, Inc. (*US*)
Antony Harwood Limited (*UK*)
Aponte Literary (*US*)
Artellus Limited (*UK*)
Ayesha Pande Literary (*US*)
Azantian Literary Agency (*US*)
Baror International, Inc. (*US*)
Barry Goldblatt Literary Agency, Inc. (*US*)
The Bent Agency (*US*)
Blake Friedmann Literary Agency Ltd (*UK*)
Bob Mecoy Creative Book Services (*US*)
Bond Literary Agency (*US*)
BookEnds, LLC (*US*)
The Bright Literary Academy (*UK*)
C+W (Conville & Walsh) (*UK*)
Carolyn Jenks Agency (*US*)
Caskie Mushens (*UK*)

Chalberg & Sussman (*US*)
Mic Cheetham Literary Agency (*UK*)
Cherry Weiner Literary Agency (*US*)
Corvisiero Literary Agency (*US*)
Richard Curtis Associates, Inc. (*US*)
D4EO Literary Agency (*US*)
Liza Dawson Associates (*US*)
DHH Literary Agency Ltd (*UK*)
Diamond Kahn and Woods (DKW) Literary Agency Ltd (*UK*)
Diana Finch Literary Agency (*US*)
Donaghy Literary Group (*US*)
Donald Maass Literary Agency (*US*)
Dunham Literary, Inc. (*US*)
Dystel, Goderich & Bourret LLC (*US*)
Einstein Literary Management (*US*)
Ethan Ellenberg Literary Agency (*US*)
Folio Literary Management, LLC (*US*)
Fox Literary (*US*)
Frances Collin Literary Agent (*US*)
Greene & Heaton Ltd (*UK*)
Holloway Literary (*US*)
Inklings Literary Agency, LLC (*US*)
InterSaga (*UK*)
Irene Goodman Literary Agency (IGLA) (*US*)
Jabberwocky Literary Agency (*US*)
John Hawkins & Associates, Inc. (*US*)
Johnson & Alcock (*UK*)
JYLA (Jason Yarn Literary Agency) (*US*)
Kimberley Cameron & Associates (*US*)
Harvey Klinger, Inc (*US*)
KT Literary (*US*)
L. Perkins Associates (*US*)
Laura Dail Literary Agency (*US*)
LAW (Lucas Alexander Whitley) (*UK*)
LBA Books Ltd (*UK*)
Lee Sobel Literary Agency (*US*)
Madeleine Milburn Literary, TV & Film Agency (*UK*)
The Ned Leavitt Agency (*US*)
Nelson Literary Agency, LLC (*US*)
Northbank Talent Management (*UK*)
Prentis Literary (*US*)
Prospect Agency (*US*)
Red Sofa Literary (*US*)
Rees Literary Agency (*US*)
Richard Henshaw Group LLC (*US*)
Richford Becklow Literary Agency (*UK*)
The Rights Factory (*Can*)
Rupert Heath Literary Agency (*UK*)
Sandra Dijkstra Literary Agency (*US*)
Sanford J. Greenburger Associates, Inc. (*US*)
Selectric Artists (*US*)
The Seymour Agency (*US*)
Sheil Land Associates Ltd (*UK*)
The Stringer Literary Agency LLC (*US*)
Stuart Krichevsky Literary Agency, Inc. (*US*)
Transatlantic Literary Agency, Inc. (*Can*)
United Talent Agency (UTA) (*US*)
Upstart Crow Literary (*US*)
Veritas Literary Agency (*US*)
Whispering Buffalo Literary Agency Ltd (*UK*)
Wordserve Literary (*US*)

Zeno Agency Ltd (*UK*)
Scripts
A & B Personal Management Ltd (*UK*)
Above the Line Agency (*US*)
Bret Adams Ltd (*US*)
The Agency (London) Ltd (*UK*)
Alan Brodie Representation Ltd (*UK*)
Marcia Amsterdam Agency (*US*)
Barbara Hogenson Agency (*US*)
Berlin Associates (*UK*)
BiCoastal Talent (*US*)
Blake Friedmann Literary Agency Ltd (*UK*)
Don Buchwald and Associates (*US*)
Carolyn Jenks Agency (*US*)
Casarotto Ramsay and Associates Ltd (*UK*)
Cecily Ware Literary Agents (*UK*)
Curtis Brown (*UK*)
David Higham Associates Ltd (*UK*)
DHH Literary Agency Ltd (*UK*)
Elaine Steel (*UK*)
Felix de Wolfe (*UK*)
Film Rights Ltd in association with Laurence
Fitch Ltd (*UK*)
Independent Talent Group Ltd (*UK*)
InterSaga (*UK*)
Janet Fillingham Associates (*UK*)
Jill Foster Ltd (JFL) (*UK*)
Jonathan Clowes Ltd (*UK*)
Michelle Kass Associates (*UK*)
Ken Sherman & Associates (*US*)
Ki Agency Ltd (*UK*)
Knight Hall Agency (*UK*)
LAW (Lucas Alexander Whitley) (*UK*)
Linda Seifert Management (*UK*)
The Lisa Richards Agency (*Ire*)
Macnaughton Lord Representation (*UK*)
Madeleine Milburn Literary, TV & Film Agency
(*UK*)
Mary Clemmey Literary Agency (*UK*)
MBA Literary Agents Ltd (*UK*)
Bill McLean Personal Management Ltd (*UK*)
The Michael Greer Literary Agency (*UK*)
Micheline Steinberg Associates (*UK*)
Niad Management (*US*)
Nick Turner Management Ltd (*UK*)
Peregrine Whittlesey Agency (*US*)
Peters Fraser + Dunlop (*UK*)
Rochelle Stevens & Co. (*UK*)
Rosica Colin Ltd (*UK*)
Sayle Screen Ltd (*UK*)
Sheil Land Associates Ltd (*UK*)
Susan Schulman Literary Agency LLC (*US*)
The Tennyson Agency (*UK*)
United Agents (*UK*)
Valerie Hoskins Associates (*UK*)
Self-Help
Adler & Robin Books, Inc (*US*)
Aevitas (*US*)
Alive Literary Agency (*US*)
Ambassador Speakers Bureau & Literary
Agency (*US*)
Andrew Lownie Literary Agency Ltd (*UK*)
Antony Harwood Limited (*UK*)

Betsy Amster Literary Enterprises (*US*)
Bleecker Street Associates, Inc. (*US*)
The Bright Literary Academy (*UK*)
Carol Mann Agency (*US*)
Chalberg & Sussman (*US*)
Cherry Weiner Literary Agency (*US*)
Clare Hulton Literary Agency (*UK*)
Coombs Moylett & Maclean Literary Agency
(*UK*)
Cynthia Cannell Literary Agency (*US*)
D4EO Literary Agency (*US*)
Liza Dawson Associates (*US*)
Doug Grad Literary Agency (*US*)
Ebeling & Associates (*US*)
Folio Literary Management, LLC (*US*)
Fox & Howard Literary Agency (*UK*)
Frances Kelly Agency (*UK*)
Fraser-Bub Literary, LLC (*US*)
Fresh Books Literary Agency (*US*)
Grace Freedson's Publishing Network (*US*)
Graham Maw Christie Literary Agency (*UK*)
Holloway Literary (*US*)
InkWell Management (*US*)
Jane Judd Literary Agency (*UK*)
The Jean V. Naggar Literary Agency (*US*)
Jeanne Fredericks Literary Agency, Inc. (*US*)
The Jeff Herman Agency, LLC (*US*)
The Jennifer DeChiara Literary Agency (*US*)
Johnson & Alcock (*UK*)
Ki Agency Ltd (*UK*)
Kimberley Cameron & Associates (*US*)
Harvey Klinger, Inc (*US*)
Linda Konner Literary Agency (*US*)
Kruger Cowne (*UK*)
The Leshne Agency (*US*)
Levine Greenberg Rostan Literary Agency (*US*)
The Lisa Richards Agency (*Ire*)
MacGregor & Luedeke (*US*)
Madeleine Milburn Literary, TV & Film Agency
(*UK*)
Marcil O'Farrell Literary, LLC and Denise
Marcil Literary Agency, LLC (*US*)
Marsal Lyon Literary Agency LLC (*US*)
Martin Leonardis Ltd (*UK*)
Martin Literary Management (*US*)
MBA Literary Agents Ltd (*UK*)
McCormick Literary (*US*)
Mendel Media Group, LLC (*US*)
Northbank Talent Management (*UK*)
Perry Literary, Inc. (*US*)
Puttick Literary Agency (*UK*)
Rees Literary Agency (*US*)
Richford Becklow Literary Agency (*UK*)
The Rights Bureau (*Ire*)
Robert Dudley Agency (*UK*)
Robert Smith Literary Agency Ltd (*UK*)
Sandra Dijkstra Literary Agency (*US*)
Sanford J. Greenburger Associates, Inc. (*US*)
The Seymour Agency (*US*)
Sheil Land Associates Ltd (*UK*)
Sheree Bykofsky Associates, Inc. (*US*)
Beverley Slopen Literary Agency (*Can*)
Sterling Lord Literistic, Inc. (*US*)

Susan Schulman Literary Agency LLC (*US*)
SYLA – Susan Yearwood Literary Agency (*UK*)
Waterside Productions, Inc (*US*)
Watson, Little Ltd (*UK*)
Wendy Sherman Associates, Inc. (*US*)
Whimsy Literary Agency, LLC (*US*)
Whispering Buffalo Literary Agency Ltd (*UK*)
Wordserve Literary (*US*)
Writers' Representatives, LLC (*US*)

Short Stories
The Ahearn Agency, Inc (*US*)
Alive Literary Agency (*US*)
Antony Harwood Limited (*UK*)
The Bright Literary Academy (*UK*)
DeFiore and Company (*US*)
Felicia Eth Literary Representation (*US*)
Georges Borchardt, Inc. (*US*)
Joy Harris Literary Agency, Inc. (*US*)
Holloway Literary (*US*)
John Hawkins & Associates, Inc. (*US*)
MacGregor & Luedeke (*US*)
The Ned Leavitt Agency (*US*)
Regal Hoffmann & Associates LLC (*US*)
The Ruppin Agency (*UK*)
Sandra Dijkstra Literary Agency (*US*)
Selectric Artists (*US*)

Sociology
Andrea Brown Literary Agency, Inc. (*US*)
Antony Harwood Limited (*UK*)
The August Agency LLC (*US*)
Barbara Braun Associates, Inc. (*US*)
The Bent Agency (*US*)
Betsy Amster Literary Enterprises (*US*)
Blake Friedmann Literary Agency Ltd (*UK*)
Bleecker Street Associates, Inc. (*US*)
Carol Mann Agency (*US*)
Dana Newman Literary, LLC (*US*)
David Black Literary Agency (*US*)
Liza Dawson Associates (*US*)
DeFiore and Company (*US*)
Diamond Kahn and Woods (DKW) Literary
Agency Ltd (*UK*)
The Doe Coover Agency (*US*)
Frances Goldin Literary Agency, Inc. (*US*)
Hannigan Salky Getzler (HSG) Agency (*US*)
Inklings Literary Agency, LLC (*US*)
Irene Goodman Literary Agency (IGLA) (*US*)
The Jennifer DeChiara Literary Agency (*US*)
Karen Gantz Literary Management (*US*)
Kate Hordern Literary Agency (*UK*)
Kneerim & Williams (*US*)
Levine Greenberg Rostan Literary Agency (*US*)
Lowenstein Associates, Inc. (*US*)
Massie & McQuilkin (*US*)
Perry Literary, Inc. (*US*)
Publication Riot Group, Inc. (*US*)
Red Sofa Literary (*US*)
Robertson Murray Literary Agency (*UK*)
The Ruppin Agency (*UK*)
Sandra Dijkstra Literary Agency (*US*)
Sanford J. Greenburger Associates, Inc. (*US*)
Scovil Galen Ghosh Literary Agency, Inc. (*US*)
The Spieler Agency (*US*)

Susan Schulman Literary Agency LLC (*US*)
Union Literary (*US*)
Victoria Sanders & Associates LLC (*US*)
Waterside Productions, Inc (*US*)
Wm Clark Associates (*US*)
Zeno Agency Ltd (*UK*)

Spiritual
Aevitas (*US*)
Alive Literary Agency (*US*)
Antony Harwood Limited (*UK*)
Bleecker Street Associates, Inc. (*US*)
Carol Mann Agency (*US*)
Cynthia Cannell Literary Agency (*US*)
D4EO Literary Agency (*US*)
Liza Dawson Associates (*US*)
Dunham Literary, Inc. (*US*)
Dystel, Goderich & Bourret LLC (*US*)
Ebeling & Associates (*US*)
Ethan Ellenberg Literary Agency (*US*)
Folio Literary Management, LLC (*US*)
Fox & Howard Literary Agency (*UK*)
Global Lion Intellectual Property Management,
Inc. (*US*)
Joy Harris Literary Agency, Inc. (*US*)
Helen Zimmermann Literary Agency (*US*)
The Jeff Herman Agency, LLC (*US*)
Karen Gantz Literary Management (*US*)
Kimberley Cameron & Associates (*US*)
Harvey Klinger, Inc (*US*)
Knight Features (*UK*)
Kruger Cowne (*UK*)
Lawrence Jordan Literary Agency (*US*)
The Leshne Agency (*US*)
Levine Greenberg Rostan Literary Agency (*US*)
Literary Services, Inc. (*US*)
Literary Management Group, Inc. (*US*)
Literary & Creative Artists Inc. (*US*)
Marcil O'Farrell Literary, LLC and Denise
Marcil Literary Agency, LLC (*US*)
Mendel Media Group, LLC (*US*)
The Ned Leavitt Agency (*US*)
Red Sofa Literary (*US*)
Regina Ryan Publishing Enterprises (*US*)
The Rights Factory (*Can*)
Rita Rosenkranz Literary Agency (*US*)
The Seymour Agency (*US*)
Sheree Bykofsky Associates, Inc. (*US*)
The Spieler Agency (*US*)
Standen Literary Agency (*UK*)
Stephanie Tade Literary Agency (*US*)
Susan Schulman Literary Agency LLC (*US*)
Thompson Literary Agency (*US*)
Waterside Productions, Inc (*US*)
Wendy Sherman Associates, Inc. (*US*)
Whimsy Literary Agency, LLC (*US*)

Sport
A.M. Heath & Company Limited, Author's
Agents (*UK*)
Alive Literary Agency (*US*)
Allen O'Shea Literary Agency (*US*)
The Ampersand Agency Ltd (*UK*)
Andrea Brown Literary Agency, Inc. (*US*)
Andrew Lownie Literary Agency Ltd (*UK*)

Antony Harwood Limited (*UK*)
B.J. Robbins Literary Agency (*US*)
Bell Lomax Moreton Agency (*UK*)
The Bent Agency (*US*)
Bleecker Street Associates, Inc. (*US*)
Bob Mecoy Creative Book Services (*US*)
The Brattle Agency LLC (*US*)
C+W (Conville & Walsh) (*UK*)
Carol Mann Agency (*US*)
Chase Literary Agency (*US*)
The Cheney Agency (*US*)
D4EO Literary Agency (*US*)
Dana Newman Literary, LLC (*US*)
David Luxton Associates (*UK*)
David Black Literary Agency (*US*)
The Doe Coover Agency (*US*)
Don Congdon Associates, Inc. (*US*)
Doug Grad Literary Agency (*US*)
Dunow, Carlson & Lerner Agency (*US*)
E. J. McCarthy Agency (*US*)
Felicia Eth Literary Representation (*US*)
Folio Literary Management, LLC (*US*)
Frances Goldin Literary Agency, Inc. (*US*)
The G Agency, LLC (*US*)
Grace Freedson's Publishing Network (*US*)
Helen Zimmermann Literary Agency (*US*)
Jane Judd Literary Agency (*UK*)
The Jean V. Naggar Literary Agency (*US*)
Jeanne Fredericks Literary Agency, Inc. (*US*)
The Jennifer DeChiara Literary Agency (*US*)
Jenny Brown Associates (*UK*)
Johnson & Alcock (*UK*)
Kathi J. Paton Literary Agency (*US*)
Ki Agency Ltd (*UK*)
Harvey Klinger, Inc (*US*)
Kneerim & Williams (*US*)
Knight Features (*UK*)
Kruger Cowne (*UK*)
LAW (Lucas Alexander Whitley) (*UK*)
The Leshne Agency (*US*)
Levine Greenberg Rostan Literary Agency (*US*)
Limelight Management (*UK*)
The Lisa Richards Agency (*Ire*)
Literary Services, Inc. (*US*)
MacGregor & Luedeke (*US*)
Madeleine Milburn Literary, TV & Film Agency (*UK*)
Marcil O'Farrell Literary, LLC and Denise Marcil Literary Agency, LLC (*US*)
Marsal Lyon Literary Agency LLC (*US*)
Massie & McQuilkin (*US*)
Max Gartenburg Literary Agency (*US*)
McCormick Literary (*US*)
The Michael Greer Literary Agency (*UK*)
Mulcahy Associates (Part of MMB Creative) (*UK*)
Niad Management (*US*)
Perry Literary, Inc. (*US*)
Peters Fraser + Dunlop (*UK*)
The Purcell Agency, LLC (*US*)
Queen Literary Agency, Inc. (*US*)
Red Sofa Literary (*US*)
Regina Ryan Publishing Enterprises (*US*)

Richard Henshaw Group LLC (*US*)
The Rights Factory (*Can*)
Robert Dudley Agency (*UK*)
Robertson Murray Literary Agency (*UK*)
Rosica Colin Ltd (*UK*)
The Ruppin Agency (*UK*)
Sandra Dijkstra Literary Agency (*US*)
Sanford J. Greenburger Associates, Inc. (*US*)
Scovil Galen Ghosh Literary Agency, Inc. (*US*)
Jeffrey Simmons (*UK*)
Susan Schulman Literary Agency LLC (*US*)
Thompson Literary Agency (*US*)
Waterside Productions, Inc (*US*)
Watson, Little Ltd (*UK*)
Wendy Sherman Associates, Inc. (*US*)
Suspense
A.M. Heath & Company Limited, Author's Agents (*UK*)
Aaron M. Priest Literary Agency (*US*)
The Ahearn Agency, Inc (*US*)
Alive Literary Agency (*US*)
The Angela Rinaldi Literary Agency (*US*)
Antony Harwood Limited (*UK*)
B.J. Robbins Literary Agency (*US*)
The Bent Agency (*US*)
Blake Friedmann Literary Agency Ltd (*UK*)
Book Cents Literary Agency (*US*)
BookEnds, LLC (*US*)
C+W (Conville & Walsh) (*UK*)
Caroline Sheldon Literary Agency (*UK*)
Carolyn Jenks Agency (*US*)
Chalberg & Sussman (*US*)
Chartwell (*UK*)
The Cheney Agency (*US*)
Cherry Weiner Literary Agency (*US*)
Coombs Moylett & Maclean Literary Agency (*UK*)
Curtis Brown (*UK*)
Darhansoff & Verrill Literary Agents (*US*)
The Darley Anderson Agency (*UK*)
Liza Dawson Associates (*US*)
Diamond Kahn and Woods (DKW) Literary Agency Ltd (*UK*)
Don Congdon Associates, Inc. (*US*)
Donaghy Literary Group (*US*)
Donald Maass Literary Agency (*US*)
Dunow, Carlson & Lerner Agency (*US*)
Dystel, Goderich & Bourret LLC (*US*)
Felicia Eth Literary Representation (*US*)
Folio Literary Management, LLC (*US*)
Gelfman Schneider / ICM Partners (*US*)
Hannigan Salky Getzler (HSG) Agency (*US*)
Hardman & Swainson (*UK*)
Joy Harris Literary Agency, Inc. (*US*)
Helen Zimmermann Literary Agency (*US*)
Holloway Literary (*US*)
Inklings Literary Agency, LLC (*US*)
InterSaga (*UK*)
Irene Goodman Literary Agency (IGLA) (*US*)
Jane Rotrosen Agency (*US*)
The Jean V. Naggar Literary Agency (*US*)
The Jennifer DeChiara Literary Agency (*US*)
JET Literary Associates, Inc. (*US*)

Johnson & Alcock (*UK*)
JYLA (Jason Yarn Literary Agency) (*US*)
Kate Barker Literary, TV, & Film Agency (*UK*)
Harvey Klinger, Inc (*US*)
Barbara S. Kouts, Literary Agent (*US*)
Kruger Cowne (*UK*)
Lawrence Jordan Literary Agency (*US*)
Lee Sobel Literary Agency (*US*)
Levine Greenberg Rostan Literary Agency (*US*)
Limelight Management (*UK*)
MacGregor & Luedeke (*US*)
Madeleine Milburn Literary, TV & Film Agency (*UK*)
Maria Carvainis Agency, Inc. (*US*)
Marsal Lyon Literary Agency LLC (*US*)
Massie & McQuilkin (*US*)
Niad Management (*US*)
Northbank Talent Management (*UK*)
Peters Fraser + Dunlop (*UK*)
Prospect Agency (*US*)
Rebecca Friedman Literary Agency (*US*)
Rees Literary Agency (*US*)
Rosica Colin Ltd (*UK*)
Sandra Dijkstra Literary Agency (*US*)
Selectric Artists (*US*)
The Seymour Agency (*US*)
Speilburg Literary Agency (*US*)
The Stringer Literary Agency LLC (*US*)
Susan Schulman Literary Agency LLC (*US*)
Victoria Sanders & Associates LLC (*US*)
Wendy Sherman Associates, Inc. (*US*)
Wordserve Literary (*US*)
Zeno Agency Ltd (*UK*)
Technology
Aevitas (*US*)
Andrea Brown Literary Agency, Inc. (*US*)
Andrew Lownie Literary Agency Ltd (*UK*)
Antony Harwood Limited (*UK*)
The August Agency LLC (*US*)
Blake Friedmann Literary Agency Ltd (*UK*)
Bleecker Street Associates, Inc. (*US*)
Bob Mecoy Creative Book Services (*US*)
Chartwell (*UK*)
Richard Curtis Associates, Inc. (*US*)
D4EO Literary Agency (*US*)
Dana Newman Literary, LLC (*US*)
DeFiore and Company (*US*)
The Doe Coover Agency (*US*)
Don Congdon Associates, Inc. (*US*)
Dunham Literary, Inc. (*US*)
Dystel, Goderich & Bourret LLC (*US*)
Folio Literary Management, LLC (*US*)
Frances Goldin Literary Agency, Inc. (*US*)
Fresh Books Literary Agency (*US*)
The G Agency, LLC (*US*)
Grace Freedson's Publishing Network (*US*)
Helen Zimmermann Literary Agency (*US*)
John Hawkins & Associates, Inc. (*US*)
Kathi J. Paton Literary Agency (*US*)
Kimberley Cameron & Associates (*US*)
Harvey Klinger, Inc (*US*)
Kneerim & Williams (*US*)
Laura Dail Literary Agency (*US*)

LAW (Lucas Alexander Whitley) (*UK*)
The Leshne Agency (*US*)
Levine Greenberg Rostan Literary Agency (*US*)
Literary Services, Inc. (*US*)
Maria Carvainis Agency, Inc. (*US*)
Perry Literary, Inc. (*US*)
Robert Dudley Agency (*UK*)
The Rudy Agency (*US*)
Sterling Lord Literistic, Inc. (*US*)
Stuart Krichevsky Literary Agency, Inc. (*US*)
Susan Schulman Literary Agency LLC (*US*)
Transatlantic Literary Agency, Inc. (*Can*)
Waterside Productions, Inc (*US*)
Watson, Little Ltd (*UK*)
Whimsy Literary Agency, LLC (*US*)
Wm Clark Associates (*US*)
Theatre
A & B Personal Management Ltd (*UK*)
Bret Adams Ltd (*US*)
The Agency (London) Ltd (*UK*)
Alan Brodie Representation Ltd (*UK*)
Antony Harwood Limited (*UK*)
Barbara Hogenson Agency (*US*)
Berlin Associates (*UK*)
Don Buchwald and Associates (*US*)
Carolyn Jenks Agency (*US*)
Casarotto Ramsay and Associates Ltd (*UK*)
Curtis Brown (*UK*)
David Higham Associates Ltd (*UK*)
Liza Dawson Associates (*US*)
DHH Literary Agency Ltd (*UK*)
Don Congdon Associates, Inc. (*US*)
Doug Grad Literary Agency (*US*)
Felix de Wolfe (*UK*)
Film Rights Ltd in association with Laurence
Fitch Ltd (*UK*)
Independent Talent Group Ltd (*UK*)
Janet Fillingham Associates (*UK*)
The Jennifer DeChiara Literary Agency (*US*)
Jill Foster Ltd (JFL) (*UK*)
Jonathan Clowes Ltd (*UK*)
Ki Agency Ltd (*UK*)
Knight Hall Agency (*UK*)
L. Perkins Associates (*US*)
The Lisa Richards Agency (*Ire*)
Macnaughton Lord Representation (*UK*)
Mary Clemmey Literary Agency (*UK*)
MBA Literary Agents Ltd (*UK*)
Bill McLean Personal Management Ltd (*UK*)
Micheline Steinberg Associates (*UK*)
Niad Management (*US*)
Peregrine Whittlesey Agency (*US*)
Peters Fraser + Dunlop (*UK*)
Rochelle Stevens & Co. (*UK*)
Rosica Colin Ltd (*UK*)
Sayle Screen Ltd (*UK*)
Sheil Land Associates Ltd (*UK*)
Jeffrey Simmons (*UK*)
The Spieler Agency (*US*)
Susan Schulman Literary Agency LLC (*US*)
The Tennyson Agency (*UK*)
United Agents (*UK*)
Victoria Sanders & Associates LLC (*US*)

Madeleine Milburn Literary, TV & Film Agency (*UK*)
Mary Clemmey Literary Agency (*UK*)
MBA Literary Agents Ltd (*UK*)
Bill McLean Personal Management Ltd (*UK*)
Micheline Steinberg Associates (*UK*)
Niad Management (*US*)
Nick Turner Management Ltd (*UK*)
Peregrine Whittlesey Agency (*US*)
Perry Literary, Inc. (*US*)
Peters Fraser + Dunlop (*UK*)
Rochelle Stevens & Co. (*UK*)
Rosica Colin Ltd (*UK*)
The Ruppin Agency (*UK*)
Sayle Screen Ltd (*UK*)
Sheil Land Associates Ltd (*UK*)
The Tennyson Agency (*UK*)
United Agents (*UK*)
Valerie Hoskins Associates (*UK*)

Westerns
Alive Literary Agency (*US*)
Antony Harwood Limited (*UK*)
Cherry Weiner Literary Agency (*US*)
Richard Curtis Associates, Inc. (*US*)
D4EO Literary Agency (*US*)
Donald Maass Literary Agency (*US*)
Harvey Klinger, Inc (*US*)
Kruger Cowne (*UK*)
L. Perkins Associates (*US*)
Prospect Agency (*US*)
Red Sofa Literary (*US*)
Rees Literary Agency (*US*)

Women's Interests
A.M. Heath & Company Limited, Author's Agents (*UK*)
Aaron M. Priest Literary Agency (*US*)
The Ahearn Agency, Inc (*US*)
Alive Literary Agency (*US*)
Ambassador Speakers Bureau & Literary Agency (*US*)
The Ampersand Agency Ltd (*UK*)
Andrea Brown Literary Agency, Inc. (*US*)
The Angela Rinaldi Literary Agency (*US*)
Antony Harwood Limited (*UK*)
Aponte Literary (*US*)
The August Agency LLC (*US*)
The Axelrod Agency (*US*)
Ayesha Pande Literary (*US*)
Barbara Braun Associates, Inc. (*US*)
Barone Literary Agency (*US*)
The Bent Agency (*US*)
Betsy Amster Literary Enterprises (*US*)
The Blair Partnership (*UK*)
Blake Friedmann Literary Agency Ltd (*UK*)
Bleecker Street Associates, Inc. (*US*)
The Book Bureau Literary Agency (*Ire*)
Book Cents Literary Agency (*US*)
BookEnds, LLC (*US*)
Books & Such Literary Management (*US*)
The Bright Literary Academy (*UK*)
C+W (Conville & Walsh) (*UK*)
Carol Mann Agency (*US*)
Caroline Sheldon Literary Agency (*UK*)

Carolyn Jenks Agency (*US*)
Chalberg & Sussman (*US*)
Chartwell (*UK*)
The Cheney Agency (*US*)
Coombs Moylett & Maclean Literary Agency (*UK*)
Creative Authors Ltd (*UK*)
Creative Media Agency (*US*)
D4EO Literary Agency (*US*)
Dana Newman Literary, LLC (*US*)
The Darley Anderson Agency (*UK*)
David Black Literary Agency (*US*)
Liza Dawson Associates (*US*)
DHH Literary Agency Ltd (*UK*)
Don Congdon Associates, Inc. (*US*)
Donaghy Literary Group (*US*)
Donald Maass Literary Agency (*US*)
Dunham Literary, Inc. (*US*)
Dunow, Carlson & Lerner Agency (*US*)
Dystel, Goderich & Bourret LLC (*US*)
Einstein Literary Management (*US*)
Empire Literary, LLC (*US*)
Felicia Eth Literary Representation (*US*)
Ethan Ellenberg Literary Agency (*US*)
Fairbank Literary Representation (*US*)
Folio Literary Management, LLC (*US*)
Frances Collin Literary Agent (*US*)
Fraser-Bub Literary, LLC (*US*)
Gallt & Zacker Literary Agency (*US*)
Gelfman Schneider / ICM Partners (*US*)
Grace Freedson's Publishing Network (*US*)
Greene & Heaton Ltd (*UK*)
Hannigan Salky Getzler (HSG) Agency (*US*)
Hardman & Swainson (*UK*)
Joy Harris Literary Agency, Inc. (*US*)
Helen Zimmermann Literary Agency (*US*)
hhb agency ltd (*UK*)
Hill Nadell Literary Agency (*US*)
Holloway Literary (*US*)
Inklings Literary Agency, LLC (*US*)
InterSaga (*UK*)
Irene Goodman Literary Agency (IGLA) (*US*)
Jane Rotrosen Agency (*US*)
The Jean V. Naggar Literary Agency (*US*)
Jeanne Fredericks Literary Agency, Inc. (*US*)
The Jennifer DeChiara Literary Agency (*US*)
Jenny Brown Associates (*UK*)
Jo Unwin Literary Agency (*UK*)
John Hawkins & Associates, Inc. (*US*)
Johnson & Alcock (*UK*)
Judith Murdoch Literary Agency (*UK*)
Juliet Burton Literary Agency (*UK*)
Kate Barker Literary, TV, & Film Agency (*UK*)
Kate Hordern Literary Agency (*UK*)
Keane Kataria Literary Agency (*UK*)
Kimberley Cameron & Associates (*US*)
Harvey Klinger, Inc (*US*)
Kneerim & Williams (*US*)
Linda Konner Literary Agency (*US*)
Barbara S. Kouts, Literary Agent (*US*)
Kruger Cowne (*UK*)
Laura Dail Literary Agency (*US*)
LAW (Lucas Alexander Whitley) (*UK*)

US Publishers

For the most up-to-date listings of these and hundreds of other publishers, visit https://www.firstwriter.com/publishers

To claim your **free** access to the site, please see the back of this book.

a...p press

Email: afterthepause@gmail.com
Website: https://afterthepause.com/a-p-press/

Publishes: Fiction; Poetry; *Areas:* Short Stories; *Markets:* Adult; *Treatments:* Experimental

Publishes poetry, flash fiction, visual poetry, experimental poetry, and any combination thereof. Manuscripts must be at least 50 pages. Send submissions by email.

ABC-CLIO / Greenwood

Acquisitions Department, ABC-CLIO/Greenwood
ABC-CLIO
PO Box 1911
Santa Barbara, CA 93116-1911
Tel: +1 (800) 368-6868
Email: acquisition_inquiries@abc-clio.com
Website: http://www.abc-clio.com

Publishes: Nonfiction; Reference; *Areas:* Arts; Biography; Business; Crime; Culture; Current Affairs; Finance; Health; Historical; Legal; Military; Nature; Politics; Psychology; Religious; Science; Sociology; Technology; Women's Interests; *Markets:* Academic; Adult

Publisher of general nonfiction and reference covering history, humanities, and general interest topics across the secondary and higher education curriculum. No fiction, poetry, or drama. Welcomes proposals in appropriate areas. See website for specific imprint / editor contact details.

Abdo Publishing Co

1920 Lookout Drive
North Mankato MN 56003
Tel: +1 (800) 800-1312
Fax: +1 (800) 862-3480
Email: fiction@abdobooks.com
Website: http://abdopublishing.com

Publishes: Fiction; Nonfiction; *Areas:* Anthropology; Arts; Biography; Cookery; Crafts; Culture; Current Affairs; Design; Entertainment; Historical; Hobbies; Medicine; Military; Politics; Religious; Science; Sociology; Sport; Technology; Travel; *Markets:* Children's

Contact: Paul Abdo

Publishes nonfiction, educational material for children up to the 12th grade, plus fiction series for children. Not accepting nonfiction submissions as at May 2017 (see website for current situation). Writers with a concept for a fiction series should send samples of manuscripts by email.

Abuzz Press

Website: https://www.abuzzpress.com

Publishes: Fiction; Nonfiction; *Areas:* Erotic; How-to; New Age; Romance; *Markets:* Adult

Publishes nonfiction, adult colouring books, how-to, new age, erotica (including erotic nonfiction and erotic romance), and exceptional fiction. No poetry, short story collections, books with colour interiors, or illegal material. Send submissions via form on website.

Academy Chicago

814 North Franklin Street
Chicago, Illinois 60610
Tel: +1 (312) 337-0747
Fax: +1 (312) 337-5110
Email: csherry@chicagoreviewpress.com
Website: http://www.chicagoreviewpress.com

Publishes: Fiction; Nonfiction; *Areas:* Autobiography; Mystery; *Markets:* Adult; *Treatments:* Contemporary; Mainstream

Contact: Cynthia Sherry

Send query by email with one-sentence description of your novel, a brief synopsis (a couple of paragraphs), word count, author bio, market info, and a few sample chapters. No mind/body/spirit, religion, diet/fitness/nutrition, family memoir, self-help, business, poetry, or photography.

Albert Whitman & Company

250 South Northwest Highway, Suite 320
Park Ridge, Illinois 60068
Tel: +1 (800) 255-7675
Fax: +1 (847) 581-0039
Email: submissions@albertwhitman.com
Website: http://www.albertwhitman.com

Publishes: Fiction; Nonfiction; *Markets:* Children's; Youth

Contact: Kathleen Tucker, Editor-in-Chief

Publishes picture books, middle-grade fiction, and young adult novels. Will consider fiction and nonfiction manuscripts for picture books for children ages 1 to 8, up to 1,000 words; fiction queries and sample pages for middle-grade novels up to 35,000 words for children up to the age of 12; and fiction queries and sample pages for young adult novels up to 70,000 words for ages 12-18. See website for full submission guidelines.

Algora Publishing

1732 1st Ave #20330
New York, NY 10128
Tel: +1 (212) 678-0232
Fax: +1 (212) 202-5488
Website: http://www.algora.com

Publishes: Nonfiction; *Areas:* Anthropology; Archaeology; Finance; Historical; Literature; Military; Music; Nature; Philosophy; Politics; Psychology; Religious; Science; Sociology; Translations; Women's Interests; *Markets:* Academic; Adult

Describes itself as an "academic-type press, publishing general nonfiction for the educated reader". Accepts proposal packages by post. An email query may optionally be sent prior to the proposal package. See website for full guidelines.

Allyn and Bacon / Merrill Education

445 Hutchinson Avenue
Columbus, OH 43235
Email: education.service@pearson.com
Website: http://www.allynbaconmerrill.com

Publishes: Nonfiction; *Markets:* Academic; Professional

Publishes books focused on the professional development of teachers, that effectively blend academic research and practical application for today's K-12 educators.

American Psychiatric Association Publishing

1000 Wilson Boulevard, Suite 1825
Arlington, VA 22209
Tel: +1 (703) 907-7871
Email: hkoch@psych.org
Website: https://www.appi.org

Publishes: Nonfiction; *Areas:* Health; Psychology; Science; *Markets:* Academic; Adult; Professional

Contact: Heidi Koch (Editorial Support Services Manager)

Publishes books, journals, and multimedia on psychiatry, mental health and behavioral science, geared toward psychiatrists, other mental health professionals, psychiatric residents, medical students and the general public.

American Psychiatric Association Publishing

800 Maine Avenue, S.W. Suite 900
Washington, DC 20024
Tel: +1 (800) 368-5777
Fax: +1 (202) 403-3094
Email: appi@psych.org
Website: https://www.appi.org

Publishes: Nonfiction; *Areas:* Health; Psychology; Science; *Markets:* Academic; Adult; Professional

Contact: Laura Roberts

Publishes books, journals, and multimedia on psychiatry, mental health, and behavioural science, aimed at psychiatrists, other mental health professionals, psychiatric residents, medical students, and the general public.

Andrews McMeel Publishing

attn: Book Submissions
1130 Walnut Street
Kansas City, MO 64106
Tel: +1 (816) 581-8921
Email: booksubmissions@amuniversal.com
Website: http://www.andrewsmcmeel.com

Publishes: Fiction; Nonfiction; Poetry; *Areas:* Cookery; Humour; Lifestyle; *Markets:* Adult; Children's

Publishes humour, inspiration, poetry, middle grade children's books, and calendars. Will consider submissions via a literary agent or direct from authors, if submission guidelines on website are adhered to.

Appalachian Mountain Club Books

5 Joy Street
Boston, MA 02108
Tel: +1 (617) 523-0636
Fax: +1 (617) 523-0722
Email: amcbooks@outdoors.org
Website: http://www.outdoors.org

Publishes: Nonfiction; *Areas:* Leisure; Nature; Travel; *Markets:* Adult

Publishes books for people interested in outdoor recreation, conservation, nature, and the outdoor world of the American north east in general.

April Gloaming

Email: inquiries.aprilgloaming@gmail.com
Website: http://www.aprilgloaming.com

Publishes: Fiction; Nonfiction; Poetry; *Markets:* Adult; *Treatments:* Literary

Nashville-based independent press that aims to capture and better understand the Southern soul, Southern writing, and the Southern holler. Send submissions of poetry, fiction, creative nonfiction, or graphic novels to the specific email addresses given on the website.

Asabi Publishing

Email: apsubmit@asabipublishing.com
Website: http://www.asabipublishing.com

Publishes: Fiction; Nonfiction; *Areas:* Autobiography; Biography; Crime; Culture; Erotic; Historical; Horror; Mystery; Thrillers; *Markets:* Adult; Children's; Youth

Check website for submission windows. Submit query by email or through form on website, with table of contents and three sample chapters. No religious or spiritual books of any kind.

Ascend Books, LLC

7221 West 79th Street, Suite 206
Overland Park, KS 66204
Tel: +1 (913) 948-5500
Email: bsnodgrass@ascendbooks.com
Website: http://ascendbooks.com

Publishes: Nonfiction; *Areas:* Entertainment; Sport; *Markets:* Adult; Children's

Contact: Bob Snodgrass

Highly specialised publishing company with a burgeoning presence in sports, entertainment and commemoration events. Send query by post with SASE if return of material required. See website for full guidelines.

Association for Supervision and Curriculum Development (ASCD)
1703 North Beauregard Street
Alexandria, VA 22311
Tel: +1 (703) 578-9600
Email: acquisitions@ascd.org
Website: http://www.ascd.org

Publishes: Nonfiction; *Markets:* Professional

Publishes books for educators. Continually searching for writers with new ideas, fresh voices, and diverse backgrounds. Submit via online submission system on website.

Augsburg Fortress
PO Box 1209
Minneapolis, MN 55440-1209
Tel: +1 (800) 328-4648
Fax: +1 (800) 722-7766
Website: https://www.augsburgfortress.org

Publishes: Fiction; Nonfiction; *Areas:* Culture; Historical; Lifestyle; Religious; *Markets:* Adult; Children's

Publishes bibles, adult nonfiction, and children's fiction for a Lutheran audience.

Aurelia Leo
3131 S. 2nd St. #223
Louisville, Kentucky 40208-1446
Email: subs@aurelialeo.com
Website: https://aurelialeo.com

Publishes: Fiction; *Areas:* Erotic; Fantasy; Gothic; Romance; Sci-Fi; Short Stories; *Markets:* Adult; Children's; Youth

Publishes comics, manuscripts, graphic novels, and anthologies. See website for submission guidelines and current calls.

Avatar Press
515 N. Century Blvd,
Rantoul, IL 61866
Fax: +1 (217) 893-9671
Email: submissions@avatarpress.net
Website: http://www.avatarpress.com

Publishes: Fiction; *Markets:* Adult; Youth

Comic book publisher. Accepts submissions from artists, but no script-only submissions at this time. See website for current status and full submission guidelines.

Baen Books
PO Box 1188
Wake Forest, NC 27588
Email: info@baen.com
Website: http://www.baen.com

Publishes: Fiction; *Areas:* Fantasy; Sci-Fi; *Markets:* Adult; *Treatments:* Contemporary

Publishes only science fiction and fantasy. Interested in science fiction with powerful plots and solid scientific and philosophical underpinnings. For fantasy, any magical system must be both rigorously coherent and integral to the plot. Work must at least strive for originality. Prefers manuscripts between 100,000 and 130,000 words. No submissions via mail or email. Full manuscripts can be submitted online, in rtf format, via an electronic submission system.

Bancroft Press
PO Box 65360
Baltimore, MD 21209-9945
Tel: +1 (410) 358-0658
Fax: +1 (410) 764-1967
Email: bruceb@bancroftpress.com
Website: https://bancroftpress.com

Publishes: Fiction; Nonfiction; *Areas:* Autobiography; Biography; Finance; Health; Historical; Humour; Lifestyle; Mystery; Sport; Thrillers; *Markets:* Adult; Youth; *Treatments:* Commercial; Literary

Contact: Bruce Bortz

Will consider any genre, but unlikely to ever publish children's fiction or poetry. Mark envelopes fiction or nonfiction and include email address for confirmation of receipt on outside of envelope. Do not use any priority mail service. Include query letter giving information on audience/marketing, plus CV and either complete MS or as many chapters as you have written (minimum 5 for nonfiction).

Baobab Press

121 California Avenue
Reno, NV 89503
Tel: +1 (775) 786-1188
Email: info@baobab.com
Website: http://baobabpress.com

Publishes: Fiction; Nonfiction; Poetry;
Areas: Short Stories; *Markets:* Adult

**Taking a break from short story
submissions as at April 2019. Aims to re-
open later in 2019. Check website for
current status.**

Constantly strives to discover, cultivate, and
nurture authors working in all genres.
Publishes Creative Nonfiction, Short-Story,
Novel, and Comic/Visual Narrative
manuscripts. (Comic/Visual Narrative
manuscripts will not be considered without
artwork.) Submit via online submission
system.

Be About It Press

Email: zinebeaboutit@gmail.com
Website: http://beaboutitpress.tumblr.com

Publishes: Fiction; Poetry; *Areas:* Short
Stories; *Markets:* Adult; *Treatments:*
Literary

Publishes zines, ebooks, chapbooks, and
other short form creative literature online
and in print. Print chapbooks by solicitation
only. Ebooks by solicitation or during an
announced contest. See website for full
details.

Beacon Hill Press of Kansas City

PO Box 419527
Kansas City, MO 64141
Tel: +1 (816) 931-1900
Fax: +1 (816) 753-4071
Email: customerservice@
beaconhillbooks.com
Website: http://beaconhillbooks.com

Publishes: Nonfiction; *Areas:* Religious;
Markets: Adult

Publishes Wesleyan Christian books, Bible
studies, and Bible commentaries. Send query
by email.

Beacon Publishing Group

New York, NY
Tel: +1 (800) 817-8480
Email: submissions@
beaconpublishinggroup.com
Website: https://www.
beaconpublishinggroup.com

Publishes: Fiction; Nonfiction; *Markets:*
Adult

A traditional publisher that specialises in
fiction and nonfiction work.

Bear Star Press

185 Hollow Oak Drive
Cohasset, CA 95973
Website: http://www.bearstarpress.com

Publishes: Poetry; *Markets:* Adult

Publishes poets living west of the central
time zone. Gives priority to work submitted
via annual poetry contest ($25 reading fee),
but will accept submissions not made
through this competition.

BearManor Media

PO Box 71426
Albany, GA 31708
Tel: +1 (580) 252-3547
Fax: +1 (800) 332-8092
Email: books@benohmart.com
Website: http://www.bearmanormedia.com

Publishes: Fiction; Nonfiction; *Areas:*
Autobiography; Biography; Film; Humour;
Radio; TV; *Markets:* Adult

Contact: Ben Ohmart

Publisher of books on the past of TV, film,
and radio. Particularly interested in books on
voice actors and supporting actors. Also
expanding ebook-only range to include such
areas as fiction, humour, etc. Send query by
email.

becker&mayer!

11120 NE 33rd Place Suite 101
Bellevue, WA 98004
Tel: +1 (425) 827-7120
Fax: +1 (425) 828-9659
Email: mike.oprins@quarto.com

Website: https://www.quartoknows.com/
BeckerMayer

Publishes: Nonfiction; *Markets:* Adult;
Children's

Contact: Mike Oprins

Publishes illustrated nonfiction for adults and
children.

Belle Lutte Press
PO Box 49858
Austin, TX 78765
Email: Inquiries@BelleLutte.com
Website: http://bellelutte.com

Publishes: Fiction; *Markets:* Adult;
Treatments: Literary

Publishes fiction. Send cover letter and up to
30 pages or three chapters of your work via
online submission system.

Bess Press
3565 Harding Avenue
Honolulu, HI 96816
Tel: +1 (808) 734-7159
Fax: +1 (808) 732-3627
Email: submission@besspress.com
Website: https://www.besspress.com

Publishes: Nonfiction; *Areas:* Culture;
Lifestyle; Travel; *Markets:* Adult; Children's

Publishes books about Hawai'i and the
Pacific. All submissions should be sent by
email. See website for full guidelines.

Beyond Words Publishing
20827 NW Cornell Road, Suite 500
Hillsboro, OR 97124
Tel: +1 (503) 531-8700
Fax: +1 (503) 531-8773
Email: info@beyondword.com
Website: http://www.beyondword.com

Publishes: Fiction; Nonfiction; *Areas:*
Health; Lifestyle; Spiritual; Women's
Interests; *Markets:* Adult; Children's; Youth

Publishes books on mind, body, and spirit;
holistic living; spiritual parenting; spiritual
lifestyles; native wisdom; and spiritual
needs. Also publishes fiction for children and
young adults. No children's picture books

(including poetry/rhyme); adult fiction, short
stories, memoirs, or poetry; cookbooks,
textbooks, or other reference books; or
illustrated coffee table or photography
books. Accepts approaches through agents
only.

BkMk Press
University of Missouri-Kansas City
5101 Rockhill Road
Kansas City, MO 64110-2499
Tel: +1 (816) 235-2558
Fax: +1 (816) 235-2611
Email: bkmk@umkc.edu
Website: http://www.newletters.org

Publishes: Fiction; Nonfiction; Poetry;
Areas: Short Stories; *Markets:* Adult;
Treatments: Literary

Send query with SASE and sample (around
ten pages for poetry; around 50 pages for
prose). Publishes collections of poetry, short
stories, and creative nonfiction essays. No
novels, mystery, western, or romance.
Novellas considered very occasionally. No
submissions by email, or in any other way
online. Accepts submissions between Feb 1
and June 30.

Black Dome Press
649 Delaware Avenue
Delmar, NY 12054
Tel: +1 (518) 439-6512
Email: blackdomep@aol.com
Website: http://www.blackdomepress.com

Publishes: Nonfiction; *Areas:* Architecture;
Arts; Biography; Culture; Historical;
Lifestyle; Nature; Science; *Markets:* Adult;
Children's

Publishes nonfiction on New York State, in
particular the Hudson River Valley and
Catskill Mountains regions.

Bloomberg BNA Books
PO Box 7814
Edison, NJ 08818-7814
Tel: +1 (800) 960-1220
Website: https://www.bna.com

Publishes: Reference; *Areas:* Legal;
Markets: Professional

Publishes reference books written by and for lawyers. Send query with outline or table of contents, CV, market info, and estimated word count.

Bloomberg Press

Professional Development
111 River Street
Hoboken, NJ 07030
Tel: +1 (201) 748-6000
Fax: +1 (201) 748-6088
Email: info@wiley.com
Website: http://www.wiley.com

Publishes: Nonfiction; Reference; *Areas:* Current Affairs; Finance; How-to; *Markets:* Professional

Publishes books on finance and public affairs for professionals. No management, strategy, leadership, professional development, entrepreneurship, personal finance, or general consumer books.

Blue Mountain Arts, Inc.

PO Box 4549
Boulder, CO 80306
Email: editorial@sps.com
Website: http://www.sps.com

Publishes: Nonfiction; Poetry; *Areas:* Lifestyle; Self-Help; *Markets:* Adult; *Treatments:* Commercial

Publishes nonfiction on personal growth, families and relationships, etc. and poetry appropriate for gift books and greetings cards. No literary poetry.

Brewers Publications

1327 Spruce Street
Boulder, CO 80302
Tel: +1 (888) 822-6273
Email: Kristi@BrewersAssociation.org
Website: https://www.brewerspublications.com

Publishes: Nonfiction; *Markets:* Adult; Professional

Contact: Kristi Switzer

Publishes books on brewing beer for professional and amateur brewers. Send

query with proposal and sample chapter. See website for full guidelines.

Bull Publishing Company

PO Box 1377
Boulder, CO 80306
Tel: +1 (800) 676-2855
Fax: +1 (303) 545-6354
Email: jim@bullpub.com
Website: http://www.bullpub.com

Publishes: Nonfiction; *Areas:* Cookery; Health; How-to; Medicine; Psychology; Self-Help; Sport; Women's Interests; *Markets:* Adult

Contact: Jim Bull

Send query with content outline or table of contents; a discussion of why you are writing the book; an overview of competing books and a concise description of what sets your book apart from the rest of the pack; and a sample chapter or two, ideally from different parts of the manuscript. Focuses on books on health, diet, nutrition, etc.

C&T Publishing

1651 Challenge Drive
Concord, CA 94520-5206
Tel: +1 (925) 677-0377
Fax: +1 (925) 677-0373
Email: support@ctpub.com
Website: http://www.ctpub.com

Publishes: Nonfiction; *Areas:* Crafts; Hobbies; *Markets:* Adult

Publishes books on sewing and related crafts.

Candlemark & Gleam

Email: eloi@candlemarkandgleam.com
Website: https://www.candlemarkandgleam.com

Publishes: Fiction; *Areas:* Fantasy; Sci-Fi; *Markets:* Adult

Publishes mainly science fiction, but also speculative fiction, broadly defined. Cross-genre/interstitial and SF/F hybrid works are fine; ones with mythic/historical echoes even better. Send query by email with one-page synopsis and 10 pages (or, for medium works (12-42K), the complete ms) as attachments. See website for full guidelines.

Career Press

65 Parker Street, Suite 7
Newburyport, MA 01950
Tel: +1 (978) 465-0504
Fax: +1 (978) 465-0243
Email: mpye@rwwbooks.com
Website: http://www.careerpress.com

Publishes: Nonfiction; Reference; *Areas:*
Business; Finance; How-to; Leisure;
Lifestyle; Self-Help; Spiritual; *Markets:*
Adult

Contact: Michael Pye, Senior Acquisitions
Editor

If available, send completed MS with SASE. Otherwise, submit outline, author bio, marketing plan, and one or two sample chapters with SASE. Publishes books of practical information and self improvement for adults, covering such topics as education, health, money matters, spiritual matters, business philosophy, etc. Author should familiarise themselves with the catalogue before submitting. No children's books, fiction, cookbooks, humour books, picture books, photography books, memoirs, gambling titles, or coffee-table publications.

Carson-Dellosa Publishing Company, Inc.

PO Box 35665
Greensboro, NC 27425-5665
Tel: +1 (336) 632-0084
Fax: +1 (336) 632-0087
Email: webhelp@carsondellosa.com
Website: http://www.carsondellosa.com

Publishes: Nonfiction; *Markets:* Academic;
Children's

Contact: Donna Walkush

Publishes teacher resource books, activity books, student workbooks, and education books for grades PK–8. Not accepting ideas or proposals as at September 2017.

The Catholic University of America Press

240 Leahy Hall
620 Michigan Avenue NE
Washington, DC 20064
Tel: +1 (202) 319-5052
Email: cua-press@cua.edu
Website: https://www.cuapress.org

Publishes: Nonfiction; *Areas:* Historical;
Literature; Philosophy; Politics; Religious;
Sociology; *Markets:* Academic; Professional

Contact: Trevor Lipscombe, Director

Publishes books disseminating scholarship in the areas of theology, philosophy, church history, and medieval studies. Send query with outline, CV, sample chapter, and publishing history.

Cedar Fort

2373 W. 700
S. Springville, UT 84663
Tel: +1 (801) 489-4084
Website: http://www.cedarfort.com

Publishes: Fiction; Nonfiction; *Areas:*
Historical; Religious; Self-Help; Short
Stories; Spiritual; *Markets:* Adult;
Children's; Youth; *Treatments:* Positive

Publishes books with strong moral or religious values that inspire readers to be better people. No memoirs, poetry, short stories, horror, erotica, young adult fiction, or middle grade fiction. See website for full submission guidelines, and to submit using online submission system.

Charlesbridge Publishing

85 Main Street
Watertown, MA 02472
Tel: +1 (617) 926-0329
Fax: +1 (800) 926-5775
Email: tradeeditorial@charlesbridge.com
Website: http://www.charlesbridge.com

Publishes: Fiction; Nonfiction; *Areas:*
Culture; Historical; Nature; Science;
Markets: Academic; Children's; Youth

Publishes research-based instructional materials for teachers and students, and award-winning picture books for children of all ages. Produces books with a strategic approach to reading, writing, maths, and science. Also publishes full-length fiction for middle grade and young adults. Send complete ms by post. Do not include SASE, as response is only given if interested. All other materials are recycled. YA novels may also be sent by email (see website for details).

Chicago Review Press

814 North Franklin Street
Chicago, Illinois 60610
Tel: +1 (312) 337-0747
Fax: +1 (312) 337-5110
Email: frontdesk@chicagoreviewpress.com
Website: http://www.chicagoreviewpress.com

Publishes: Fiction; Nonfiction; *Areas:* Autobiography; Biography; Crafts; Culture; Film; Gardening; Historical; Lifestyle; Music; Politics; Science; Sport; Travel; Women's Interests; *Markets:* Adult; Children's; Youth

Closed to fiction proposals as at January 2018. Check website for current status.

Publishes nonfiction through all imprints, and fiction through specific imprint listed above. Also publishes children's and young adult titles, but no picture books. See website for full submission guidelines.

Chronicle Books LLC

680 Second Street
San Francisco, California 94107
Tel: +1 (415) 537 4200
Email: submissions@chroniclebooks.com
Website: http://www.chroniclebooks.com

Publishes: Fiction; Nonfiction; *Areas:* Architecture; Arts; Beauty and Fashion; Cookery; Crafts; Design; Film; Health; Humour; Lifestyle; Music; Photography; Travel; TV; *Markets:* Children's; *Treatments:* Literary

Publishes nonfiction for adults, and fiction and nonfiction for children. Children submissions must be sent by post; adult submission can be sent by post or email, but email is preferred. See website for full guidelines.

Clarity Press, Inc.

2625 Piedmont Road NE, Suite 56
Atlanta, GA 30324
Tel: +1 (404) 647-6501
Email: claritypress@usa.net
Website: http://www.claritypress.com

Publishes: Nonfiction; *Areas:* Current Affairs; Finance; Historical; Legal; Military; Politics; Sociology; *Markets:* Adult

Contact: Diana G. Collier, Editorial Director

Send query letter first, with CV, table of contents and synopsis by email. No submissions by post. Publishes books on human rights issues and social justice. Visit website before querying.

Clarkson Potter

1745 Broadway
New York, NY 10019
Tel: +1 (212) 782-9000
Website: http://crownpublishing.com/archives/imprint/clarkson-potter

Publishes: Nonfiction; *Areas:* Arts; Cookery; Design; Lifestyle; *Markets:* Adult; *Treatments:* Commercial; Literary

Imprint dedicated to lifestyle, publishing books by chefs, cooks, designers, artists, and writers. Accepts approaches via literary agents only.

Coaches Choice

PO Box 1828
Monterey, CA 93942
Tel: +1 (888) 229-5745
Email: info@coaches choice.com
Website: http://www.coacheschoice.com

Publishes: Nonfiction; *Areas:* How-to; Sport; *Markets:* Adult; Professional

Publishes books for sports coaches at all levels. Send proposal package with outline, CV, and two sample chapters.

College Press Publishing

2111 N. Main Street, Suite C
Joplin, MO 64801
PO Box 1132
Joplin, MO 64802
Tel: +1 (800) 289-3300

Fax: +1 (417) 623-1929
Email: collpressjoplin@gmail.com
Website: http://collegepress.com

Publishes: Nonfiction; *Areas:* Biography; Historical; Religious; *Markets:* Adult

Publishes Bible studies, topical studies (biblically based), apologetic studies, historical biographies of Christians, Sunday/Bible School curriculum (adult electives). No poetry, game or puzzle books, books on prophecy from a premillennial or dispensational viewpoint, or any books that do not contain a Christian message. Send query by email or by post with SASE. See website for required contents.

Cornell University Press
Sage House
512 East State Street
Ithaca, New York 14850
Tel: +1 (607) 277-2239
Fax: +1 (607) 277-2374
Email: msk55@cornell.edu
Website: http://www.cornellpress.cornell.edu

Publishes: Nonfiction; *Areas:* Anthropology; Biography; Criticism; Historical; Literature; Nature; Philosophy; Politics; Science; Women's Interests; *Markets:* Academic; Adult

Contact: Mahinder Kingra

Particularly interested in anthropology, Asian studies, biological sciences, classics, history, industrial relations, literary criticism and theory, natural history, philosophy, politics and international relations, veterinary science, and women's studies. No poetry or fiction. Send proposal with table of contents, one sample chapter, author CV or resume, information about length, intended audience, plans for illustrations, and information on any other presses currently considering your proposal.

Crabtree Publishing
PMB 59051
350 Fifth Avenue, 59th Floor
New York, NY 10118
Tel: +1 (212) 496-5040
Fax: +1 (800) 355-7166
Website: http://www.crabtreebooks.com

Publishes: Nonfiction; *Areas:* Historical; Science; Sociology; *Markets:* Academic; Children's

Publishes educational books for children. No unsolicited mss -- all material is generated in-house.

Craftsman Book Co.
6058 Corte Del Cedro
Carlsbad, CA 92011
Tel: +1 (800) 829-8123
Website: http://craftsman-book.com

Publishes: Nonfiction; *Areas:* Crafts; How-to; *Markets:* Professional

Contact: Laurence Jacobs

Publishes books, software, manuals, videos, and other materials for professional builders. See website for submission details.

The Crossroad Publishing Company
831 Chestnut Ridge Road
Chestnut Ridge, NY 10977
Tel: +1 (845) 517-0180
Email: submissions@crossroadpublishing.com
Website: http://www.crossroadpublishing.com

Publishes: Nonfiction; *Areas:* Philosophy; Religious; Spiritual; Women's Interests; *Markets:* Adult

Send proposal by email, with your name, address, credentials, any endorsements supporting your work, an outline, table of contents, and at least one full chapter. For more information, see full guidelines on website.

Crossway
1300 Crescent Street
Wheaton, IL 60187
Tel: +1 (630) 682-4300
Fax: +1 (630) 682-4785
Email: info@crossway.org
Website: http://www.crossway.org

Publishes: Nonfiction; *Areas:* Religious; *Markets:* Adult

Publishes books written from an evangelical Christian perspective. Send query by email in the first instance.

The Crown Publishing Group

1745 Broadway
New York, NY 10019
Tel: +1 (212) 782-9000
Website: http://crownpublishing.com

Publishes: Fiction; Nonfiction; *Areas:* Arts; Autobiography; Biography; Business; Cookery; Historical; Humour; Politics; *Markets:* Adult

Division of large international publisher, accepting submissions via literary agent only.

CSLI Publications

Cordura Hall
Stanford University
Stanford, CA 94305
Tel: +1 (650) 723-1839
Email: pubs@csli.stanford.edu
Website: https://cslipublications.stanford.edu

Publishes: Nonfiction; *Markets:* Academic

Publishes books, lecture notes, and monographs on the study of language, information, logic, and computation. No unsolicited mss.

Cuil Press

509 Gypsy Hill Gardens
Lehighton, PA 18235
Email: admin@cuilpress.com
Website: http://www.cuilpress.com

Publishes: Fiction; *Areas:* Fantasy; Romance; Sci-Fi; *Markets:* Adult; *Treatments:* Experimental; Niche; Progressive

Contact: Jessica Burde

Publisher launched in 2017, specialising in inclusive speculative fiction and romance.

We plan to release our first book in late 2017 and are accepting manuscripts.

Cynren Press

101 Lindenwood Drive, Suite 225
Malvern, PA 19355
Tel: +1 (484) 875-3113
Email: press@cynren.com
Website: http://www.cynren.com

Publishes: Nonfiction; *Areas:* Adventure; Autobiography; Biography; Crime; Culture; Historical; Humour; Leisure; Lifestyle; Men's Interests; Mystery; Philosophy; Spiritual; Travel; Women's Interests; *Markets:* Adult; Family

Contact: Holly Monteith

We publish memoir and historical nonfiction with the aim of publishing insightful and unique perspectives on the human story.

Da Capo Press

Market Place Center, 53
State Street
Boston, MA 02109
Email: DaCapo.Info@hbgusa.com
Website: https://www.dacapopress.com

Publishes: Nonfiction; *Areas:* Arts; Culture; Historical; Music; Sport; *Markets:* Adult

Originally a music publisher in the sixties, diversified into general trade publishing in the seventies. Specialises in history, music, the performing arts, sports, and popular culture. No unsolicited mss or book proposals.

Dalkey Archive Press

3402 N Ben Wilson
Victoria, TX 77901
Email: subeditor@dalkeyarchive.com
Website: http://www.dalkeyarchive.com

Publishes: Fiction; Nonfiction; Poetry; Scripts; *Areas:* Autobiography; Biography; Criticism; Literature; *Markets:* Adult; *Treatments:* Experimental; Literary

Publishes primarily literary fiction, with an emphasis on fiction that belongs to the experimental tradition of Sterne, Joyce, Rabelais, Flann O'Brien, Beckett, Gertrude Stein, and Djuna Barnes. Occasionally publishes poetry or nonfiction. Send submissions by email. See website for full guidelines.

Dawn Publications
12402 Bitney Springs Road
Nevada City, CA 95959
Tel: +1 (530) 274-7775
Fax: +1 (530) 274-7778
Email: submission@dawnpub.com
Website: http://www.dawnpub.com

Publishes: Nonfiction; *Areas:* Nature;
Science; *Markets:* Adult; Children's

Contact: Carol Malnor

Publishes creative nonfiction manuscripts for children that relate to nature and science. Send complete MS by email or by post with SASE, with description of your work, including: audience age; previous publications (if any); your motivation; relevant background. No response to postal submissions without SASE.

Diversion Books
443 Park Ave S
New York, NY
Tel: +1 (212) 961-6390
Email: info@diversionbooks.com
Website: http://www.diversionbooks.com

Publishes: Fiction; Nonfiction; *Areas:*
Business; Crime; Culture; Fantasy;
Historical; Horror; Mystery; Sci-Fi; Sport;
Thrillers; *Markets:* Adult; Youth

Contact: Keith Wallman; Mark Weinstein;
Melanie Madden

Send proposals by email with summary and first three chapters in the body of the email. No attachments. Response not guaranteed.

DK Publishing
1450 Broadway, Suite 801
New York, NY 10018
Email: ecustomerservice@randomhouse.com
Website: http://www.dk.com

Publishes: Nonfiction; *Areas:* Culture;
Historical; Nature; Science; Travel; *Markets:*
Children's

Publishes highly visual nonfiction for children. Assumes no responsibility for unsolicited mss. Approach through an established literary agent.

Down The Shore Publishing
Attn: Acquisitions Editor
PO Box 100
West Creek, NJ 08092
Tel: +1 (609) 812-5076
Fax: +1 (609) 812-5098
Email: info@down-the-shore.com
Website: http://www.down-the-shore.com

Publishes: Fiction; Nonfiction; Poetry;
Areas: Historical; Nature; Short Stories;
Markets: Adult

Closed to submissions as at November 2017. Check website for current status.

Small regional publisher focusing on New Jersey, the Jersey Shore, the mid-Atlantic, and seashore and coastal subjects. Specialises in regional histories; pictorial, coffee table books; literary anthologies; and natural history titles appropriate to the market. Rarely publishes fiction, and does not generally publish poetry unless as part of an anthology. Willing to consider any exceptional work appropriate to the market, however. See website for more details.

Dream of Things
PO Box 872
Downers Grove, IL. 60515
Tel: +1 (847) 321-1390
Website: http://www.dreamofthings.com

Publishes: Nonfiction; *Areas:*
Autobiography; *Markets:* Adult

Publishes memoirs, essays, and anthologies. Accepts submissions during specific submission windows only. See website and/or subscribe to newsletter for details.

Eastland Press
PO Box 99749
Seattle, WA 98139
Tel: +1 (206) 931-6957
Fax: +1 (206) 283-7084
Email: info@eastlandpress.com
Website: http://www.eastlandpress.com

Publishes: Nonfiction; *Areas:* Health; Medicine; *Markets:* Professional

Publishes textbooks for practitioners of Chinese medicine, osteopathy, and other forms of bodywork.

Educe Press

Butte, MT
Email: editor@educepress.com
Website: https://educepress.com

Publishes: Fiction; Nonfiction; Poetry; *Areas:* Short Stories; *Markets:* Adult; *Treatments:* Literary

Contact: Matthew R. K. Haynes (Publisher); Carrie Seymour (Editor); Colin Cote (Editor)

Publishes literary fiction, nonfiction, and poetry. Closed to submissions as at April 2019. Check website for current status.

Elektra Press

Website: http://elektrapress.com

Publishes: Fiction; Nonfiction; *Markets:* Adult; Youth

Contact: Don Bacue

Describes itself as a conventional independent publishing house that thinks unconventionally. Willing to consider most genres of fiction and nonfiction, other than hate books and gratuitous pornography. Approach using submission form on website.

Elm Books

Laramie, WY
Email: Leila.ElmBooks@gmail.com
Website: http://www.elm-books.com

Publishes: Fiction; Nonfiction; Poetry; *Areas:* Anthropology; Culture; Historical; Mystery; Romance; Sci-Fi; Short Stories; *Markets:* Academic; Adult; Children's

Small, independent publisher and distributor based in Laramie, Wyoming. Publishes mysteries, romance, science fiction, disability literature, short story anthologies, scholarly publications in history and anthropology, and multicultural children's books. No picture books. See website for current open calls.

Encante Press, LLC

1572 Blue Lupine Lane
Victor, MT 59875
Email: Books@EncantePress.com
Website: http://encantepress.com

Publishes: Nonfiction; *Areas:* Nature; Politics; Science; Travel; *Markets:* Adult

Eco-friendly publishing company, publishing books on animals, the environment, nature, politics, science, travel, and wildlife. Closed to submissions as of June 2016. See website for current status.

Encounter Books

900 Broadway, Suite 601
New York, NY 10003
Tel: +1 (855) 203-7220
Website: https://www.encounterbooks.com

Publishes: Nonfiction; *Areas:* Autobiography; Biography; Culture; Current Affairs; Historical; Philosophy; Politics; Psychology; Religious; Science; Sociology; *Markets:* Adult

Contact: Roger Kimball

Publisher dedicated to advancing its love of liberty and the cultural achievements of the West.

Entangled Teen

Website: http://www.entangledteen.com

Publishes: Fiction; *Areas:* Fantasy; Historical; Romance; Sci-Fi; Thrillers; *Markets:* Youth; *Treatments:* Contemporary

Publishes young adult romances between 50,000 and 100,000 words, aimed at ages 16-19. Submit via website using online submission system.

Enthusiast Books

PO Box 352
Pepin, WI 54759
Tel: +1 (715) 381-9755
Email: info@iconobooks.com
Website: http://www.enthusiastbooks.com

Publishes: Nonfiction; *Areas:* Historical; Hobbies; Military; Travel; *Markets:* Adult

Publishes books for transportation enthusiasts. Send query with SASE and outline.

Entrepreneur Press

Tel: +1 (212) 464-8080
Email: justink@entrepreneur.com
Website: http://entrepreneurmedia.com/books/

Publishes: Nonfiction; *Areas:* Business; Finance; *Markets:* Adult

Contact: Justin Koenigsberger, Publisher

An independent publishing company that publishes titles focusing on starting and growing a business, personal finance, real estate and careers. Submit proposals online via online submission system.

Fahrenheit Press

Email: submissions@fahrenheit-press.com
Website: http://www.fahrenheit-press.com

Publishes: Fiction; *Areas:* Crime; Thrillers; *Markets:* Adult; *Treatments:* Commercial

Publishes crime and thriller print and ebooks. Send submissions by email.

Farcountry Press

Acquisitions
Farcountry Press
PO Box 5630
Helena, MT 59604
Tel: +1 (800) 821-3874
Email: editor@farcountrypress.com
Website: http://www.farcountrypress.com

Publishes: Nonfiction; *Areas:* Cookery; Historical; Nature; Photography; *Markets:* Adult; Children's

Publishes photography, nature, and history books for adults and children, as well as guidebooks and cookery titles. No fiction or poetry. Send query with SASE, sample chapters, and sample table of contents. See website for full submission guidelines.

Farrar, Straus & Giroux, Inc.

120 Broadway
New York, NY 10271

Tel: +1 (212) 741-6900
Email: sales@fsgbooks.com
Website: https://us.macmillan.com/fsg

Publishes: Fiction; Nonfiction; Poetry; *Markets:* Adult; Children's; Youth

Send query describing submission with first 50 pages (fiction and nonfiction), or 3-4 poems. Submissions by mail only – no queries or mss by email. No children's submissions.

Farrar, Straus and Giroux Books for Younger Readers

175 Fifth Avenue
New York, NY 10010
Email: childrens.editorial@fsgbooks.com
Website: http://us.macmillan.com/publishers/farrar-straus-giroux#FYR

Publishes: Fiction; Nonfiction; *Markets:* Children's; Youth

Publishes fiction, nonfiction, and picture books for children and teenagers. No unsolicited mss.

Fence Books

Science Library 320
University at Albany
1400 Washington Avenue
Albany, NY 12222
Tel: +1 (518) 591-8162
Email: jessp.fence@gmail.com
Website: http://www.fenceportal.org

Publishes: Fiction; Nonfiction; Poetry; *Areas:* Criticism; Literature; Short Stories; *Markets:* Adult

Contact: Jess Puglisi

Publishes poetry and fiction often received through its book contests. Has occasional open reading periods. See website for details.

First Second

175 5th Avenue
New York, NY 10010
Email: mail@firstsecondbooks.com
Website: http://firstsecondbooks.com

Publishes: Fiction; *Markets:* Children's

Contact: Mark Siegel

Publishes graphic novels for children. Not accepting submissions as at December 2017. Check website for current status.

Flashlight Press
527 Empire Blvd.
Brooklyn, NY 11225
Tel: +1 (718) 288-8300
Email: submissions@flashlightpress.com
Website: http://www.flashlightpress.com

Publishes: Fiction; *Markets:* Children's

Contact: Shari Dash Greenspan

Publishes picture books for children aged 4-8, with universal themes dealing with family/social situations, of around 1,000 words. Send queries by email including completed form from submissions page of website, and attach your manuscript. Response within three months. No submissions by post.

Florida Academic Press
PO Box 357425
Gainesville, FL 32635
Tel: +1 (352) 332-5104
Email: FAPress@gmail.com
Website: http://www.
floridaacademicpress.com

Publishes: Fiction; Nonfiction; *Areas:* Historical; Politics; Sociology; *Markets:* Academic; Adult

Publishes mainly nonfiction and scholarly books, however also publishes fiction. Particularly interested in the history and politics of the Third World (Africa, Middle East, Asia) and books on the social sciences in general. Do not send query letter. Send complete ms with SASE. See website for full guidelines.

Focal Press
Taylor & Francis Group
711 3rd Avenue
New York, NY 10017
Tel: +1 (212) 216-7800
Fax: +1 (212) 564-7854

Email: simon.jacobs@taylorandfrancis.com
Website: http://www.focalpress.com

Publishes: Nonfiction; *Areas:* Film; Media; Music; Photography; Technology; Theatre; *Markets:* Academic; Professional

Publishes media technology books for students and professionals in the fields of photography, digital imaging, graphics, animation, new media, film and digital video production, broadcast and media distribution technologies, music recording / production, mass communications, and theatre technology. Submit proposal by email.

42 Miles Press
English Department
Indiana University South Bend
1700 Mishawaka Avenue
P.O. Box 7111
South Bend, IN 46634-7111
Email: 42milespress@gmail.com
Website: https://42milespress.com

Publishes: Poetry; *Markets:* Adult; *Treatments:* Literary

Contact: David Dodd Lee

Publishes books and chapbooks of poetry. Currently only accepts submissions via its annual poetry competition, which runs from December 1 to March 15 and costs $25 to enter.

Forward Movement Publications
412 Sycamore Street
Cincinnati, OH 45202-4110
Tel: +1 (513) 721-6659
Email: editorial@forwardmovement.org
Website: http://www.forwardmovement.org

Publishes: Nonfiction; *Areas:* Biography; Religious; Spiritual; *Markets:* Adult; Children's

Publishes resources that strengthen and support discipleship and evangelism. Generally does not publish fiction or poetry, and only rarely books for children. See website for submission guidelines.

The Foundry Publishing Company

PO Box 419527
Kansas City, MO 64141
Email: customercare@
thefoundrypublishing.com
Website: https://www.
thefoundrypublishing.com

Publishes: Nonfiction; *Areas:* Religious;
Markets: Adult

Publishes Christian books. Send submissions
by post.

Four Way Books

PO Box 535, Village Station
New York, NY 10014
Tel: +1 (212) 334-5430
Email: editors@fourwaybooks.com
Website: http://www.fourwaybooks.com

Publishes: Fiction; Poetry; *Areas:* Short
Stories; *Markets:* Adult

Not-for-profit literary press publishing
poetry and short fiction by both established
and emerging writers. Submit to contests
operated by the press, or during specific
reading periods (see website for full details).
$30 processing fee.

4RV Publishing

2912 Rankin Terrace
Edmond, OK 73013
Tel: +1 (405) 225-6851
Email: President@4rvpublishingllc.com
Website: http://4rvpublishing.com

Publishes: Fiction; Nonfiction; *Areas:*
Adventure; Fantasy; Humour; Mystery;
Religious; Romance; Sci-Fi; Suspense;
Thrillers; *Markets:* Adult; Children's; Youth;
Treatments: Mainstream

Accepts most genres of fiction and
nonfiction books for all ages, including
nonfiction, mystery, romance, mainstream,
western, Christian, and science-fiction, as
well as children's books, middle grade and
young adult novels. No poetry or graphic sex
or violence. Language should not be overly
profane or vulgar. Accepts submissions by
email from the US, UK, and Australia. Not
accepting children's books as at January

2018. See website for current status and full
guidelines.

Fox and Hound Books

New York, NY 10001
Email: submissions@
foxandhoundbooks.com
Website: https://www.
foxandhoundbooks.com

Publishes: Fiction; Nonfiction; *Markets:*
Children's; Youth

A traditional publisher specialising in all
ages of children's books from toddler to
young adult.

Franciscan Media Books

28 West Liberty Street
Cincinnati, OH 45202
Tel: +1 (513) 241-5615
Email: info@franciscanmedia.org
Website: https://www.franciscanmedia.org

Publishes: Nonfiction; *Areas:* Religious;
Markets: Adult

Catholic publisher based in Ohio. Not
accepting submissions as at November 2017.
Check website for current status.

Free Spirit Publishing

6325 Sandburg Road, Suite 100
Minneapolis, MN 55427-3674
Tel: +1 (612) 338-2068
Fax: +1 (612) 337-5050
Email: help4kids@freespirit.com
Website: http://www.freespirit.com

Publishes: Fiction; Nonfiction; *Areas:* How-
to; Lifestyle; Self-Help; Sociology; *Markets:*
Academic; Adult; Children's; Youth

Publishes nonfiction books and learning
materials for children and teens, parents,
educators, counselors, and others who live
and work with young people. Also publishes
fiction relevant to the mission of providing
children and teens with the tools they need to
succeed in life, e.g.: self-esteem; conflict
resolution, etc. No general fiction or
storybooks; books with animal or mythical
characters; books with religious or New Age
content; or single biographies,

autobiographies, or memoirs. Submit by proposals by post or through online submission system. No submissions by fax or email. See website for full submission guidelines.

Garden-Door Press
Ithaca, NY
Email: gardendoorpress@gmail.com
Website: http://www.garden-doorpress.com

Publishes: Poetry; *Markets:* Adult; *Treatments:* Experimental; Literary

Micro-press based in Ithaca, New York. Publishes poetry chapbooks. Closed to submissions as at April 2019. Check website for current status.

Gemstone Publishing
1940 Greenspring Drive, Suite I-L
Timonium, MD 21093
Tel: +1 (443) 318-8467
Fax: +1 (443) 318-8411
Email: humark@gemstonepub.com
Website: https://www.gemstonepub.com

Publishes: Nonfiction; Reference; *Areas:* Hobbies; *Markets:* Adult

Publishes nonfiction and reference works such as price guides relating to comics and other collectables.

Genealogical Publishing Company
3600 Clipper Mill Road, Suite 260
Baltimore, Maryland 21211
Tel: +1 (410) 837-8271
Fax: +1 (410) 752-8492
Email: web@genealogical.com
Website: https://genealogical.com

Publishes: Nonfiction; *Areas:* Historical; Hobbies; How-to; *Markets:* Adult

Publishes books for amateur genealogists.

George Braziller, Inc.
90 Broad Street, Suite 2100
New York, NY 10007
Tel: +1 (212) 260-9256

Fax: +1 (212) 267-3165
Website: http://www.georgebraziller.com

Publishes: Fiction; Nonfiction; Poetry; *Areas:* Architecture; Arts; Biography; Literature; Short Stories; Translations; Travel; *Markets:* Adult; *Treatments:* Contemporary

Closed to submissions as at June 2018. Check website for current status.

Prefers online approaches, but will accept paper submissions by post. Include SASE if return of material is required. Does not respond to email queries unless interested.

Gertrude Press
Email: editor@gertrudepress.org
Website: https://www.gertrudepress.org

Publishes: Fiction; Nonfiction; Poetry; *Areas:* Short Stories; *Markets:* Adult; *Treatments:* Literary

Publishes work by writers identifying as LGBTQ, both in online journal form and as chapbooks. Considers work for chapbook publication through its annual contests only. See website for details.

Gibbs Smith, Publisher
PO Box 667
Layton, UT 84041
Tel: +1 (801) 544-9800
Fax: +1 (801) 544-5582
Email: debbie.uribe@gibbs-smith.com
Website: http://www.gibbs-smith.com

Publishes: Nonfiction; *Areas:* Architecture; Arts; Cookery; Crafts; Design; Humour; *Markets:* Adult; Children's

Send query by email only. Main emphasis is on interior design, architecture, children's activities, and cookbooks. Will also accept submissions of: Arts & Crafts, western humour with general appeal, general humour, gift books, and children's activity books and board books. See website for full submission guidelines. At this time not accepting fiction or poetry books.

Gold Wake Press

Email: kfmccord@gmail.com
Website: https://goldwake.com

Publishes: Fiction; Nonfiction; Poetry;
Markets: Adult

Open to manuscripts in any genre that are at
least 60 pages. Submit via website through
online submission system. Free for those
who have bought a book from the press,
otherwise there is a submission fee.

Grand Central Publishing

Website: https://www.
grandcentralpublishing.com

Publishes: Fiction; Nonfiction; *Areas:*
Beauty and Fashion; Culture; Humour;
Lifestyle; Mystery; Romance; Thrillers;
Markets: Adult

Publishes a wide variety of fiction,
nonfiction, humour, beauty, fashion,
romance, lifestyle, mystery/thrillers, and pop
culture books. Approaches from literary
agents only.

Great Potential Press, Inc.

1650 North Kolb Road, #200
Tucson, AZ 85715
Tel: +1 (520) 777-6161
Fax: +1 (520) 777-6217
Email: info@greatpotentialpress.com
Website: http://www.greatpotentialpress.com

Publishes: Nonfiction; *Markets:* Academic;
Adult; Children's

Publishes books that support the academic,
social, or emotional needs of gifted children
and adults. No fiction, poetry, or K-12
classroom materials. Approach via proposal
submission form on website.

Gryphon House, Inc.

PO Box 10
6848 Leon's Way
Lewisville, NC 27023
Tel: +1 (336) 712-3490
Fax: +1 (877) 638-7576
Email: info@ghbooks.com
Website: http://www.gryphonhouse.com

Publishes: Nonfiction; *Areas:* How-to;
Markets: Adult; Children's; Professional

Publishes books intended to help teachers
and parents enrich the lives of children from
birth to age eight. See website for proposal
submission guidelines.

Hal Leonard Performing Arts Publishing Group

33 Plymouth Street, Suite 302
Montclair, NJ 07042
Email: submissions@halleonardbooks.com
Website: https://www.halleonardbooks.com

Publishes: Nonfiction; *Areas:* Arts; Music;
Markets: Adult

Welcomes submissions pertaining to music
and the performing arts.Send proposal by
email as a Word or PDF attachment. See
website for full guidelines.

Half Mystic Press

Email: press@halfmystic.com
Website: https://www.halfmystic.com

Publishes: Fiction; Nonfiction; Poetry;
Scripts; *Areas:* Autobiography; Music; Short
Stories; *Markets:* Adult

Publishes poetry, essay, and short story
collections; drama; memoirs; novellas; full-
length novels; experimental work. See
website for full submission guidelines. $3 fee
per submission.

Hampton Roads Publishing

65 Parker Street, Suite 7
Newburyport, MA 01950
Tel: +1 (978) 465-0504
Fax: +1 (978) 465-0243
Email: submissions@rwwbooks.com
Website: http://redwheelweiser.com

Publishes: Nonfiction; *Areas:* Health;
Spiritual; *Markets:* Adult

Publishes books on metaphysics, spirituality,
and health. Send query by email with author
info and proposal. See website for full
guidelines.

Harlequin Desire

195 Broadway, 24th floor
New York, NY 10007
Tel: +1 (212) 207-7000
Email: submissions@harlequin.com
Website: https://www.harlequin.com

Publishes: Fiction; *Areas:* Romance;
Markets: Adult; *Treatments:* Contemporary

Contact: Stacy Boyd

Publishes contemporary romances up to
50,000 words, featuring strong-but-
vulnerable alpha heroes and dynamic,
successful heroines, set in a world of wealth
and glamour. See website for more details
and to submit via online submission system.

Harper Business

195 Broadway
New York, NY 10007
Tel: +1 (212) 207-7000
Website: http://www.harperbusiness.com

Publishes: Nonfiction; *Areas:* Business;
Markets: Adult; Professional

Publishes books on business. Agented
submissions only.

Harper Business

195 Broadway
New York, NY 10007
Tel: +1 (212) 207-7000
Website: http://www.harperbusiness.com

Publishes: Nonfiction; *Areas:* Business;
Markets: Adult; Professional

Publishes innovative, authoritative, and
creative business books from world-class
thinkers. Accepts approaches through literary
agents only.

HarperCollins

195 Broadway
New York, NY 10007
Tel: +1 (212) 207-7000
Website: https://www.harpercollins.com

Publishes: Fiction; Nonfiction; Reference;
Areas: Adventure; Autobiography;
Biography; Business; Cookery; Fantasy;
Finance; Gothic; Historical; Mystery;
Religious; Romance; Sci-Fi; Self-Help;
Suspense; Travel; Westerns; *Markets:* Adult;
Children's; Family; Youth; *Treatments:*
Commercial; Contemporary; Literary

One of the world's largest publishers, almost
all imprints are open to agented submissions
only. Of the two imprints that accept
approaches direct from authors the first seeks
romance, and the second seeks visionary and
transformational fiction for digital first
format. See submission section of website
for further details.

The Harvard Common Press

100 Cummings Center, Suite 253C
Beverly, MA 01915
Tel: +1 (978) 282-9590
Fax: +1 (978) 282-7765
Email: dan.rosenberg@quarto.com
Website: http://www.
harvardcommonpress.com

Publishes: Nonfiction; *Areas:* Cookery;
Lifestyle; *Markets:* Adult

Contact: Dan Rosenberg, Editorial Director

Publishes books on cookery and parenting.
See website for full guidelines.

Harvest House Publishers

PO Box 41210
Eugene, OR 97404-0322
Tel: +1 (800) 547-8979
Fax: +1 (888) 501-6012
Website: http://harvesthousepublishers.com

Publishes: Fiction; Nonfiction; *Areas:*
Cookery; Health; Historical; Humour;
Lifestyle; Men's Interests; Mystery;
Religious; Romance; Suspense; Westerns;
Women's Interests; *Markets:* Adult;
Children's; Youth; *Treatments:*
Contemporary

Publisher of Christian literature. Does not
accept submissions directly, but is a member
of an association which accepts proposals to
share with their members. See website for
full details.

Health Professions Press

Acquisitions Department
Health Professions Press
P.O. Box 10624
Baltimore , MD 21285-0624
Tel: +1 (410) 337-9585
Fax: +1 (410) 337-8539
Email: mmagnus@healthpropress.com
Website: http://www.healthpropress.com

Publishes: Nonfiction; Reference; *Areas:*
Health; How-to; Medicine; Psychology;
Self-Help; *Markets:* Academic; Adult;
Professional

Publishes health books aimed primarily at
professionals, students, and educated
consumers interested in topics related to
ageing and eldercare. See website for
submission guidelines and to download
Publication Questionnaire.

Hellgate Press

Tel: +1 (800) 795-4059
Email: harley@hellgatepress.com
Website: http://www.hellgatepress.com

Publishes: Fiction; Nonfiction; *Areas:*
Adventure; Autobiography; Historical;
Military; Travel; *Markets:* Adult; Children's;
Youth

Publishes nonfiction titles on military history
and experiences, and fast-paced Historical or
Adventure Fiction Books for Children, Teens
and Young Adults. Primarily interested in
American soldiers and their battles, but will
also consider books on other armies
(including the ancient world) and
travel/adventure books. Send query with
synopsis by email or post.

Hendrick-Long Publishing Co.

10635 Tower Oaks, Suite D
Houston, Texas 77070
Tel: +1 (281) 635-0583
Email: hendrick-long@att.net
Website: http://hendricklongpublishing.com

Publishes: Fiction; Nonfiction; *Areas:* Arts;
Biography; Cookery; Culture; Historical;
Military; Science; Westerns; *Markets:*
Children's; Youth

Contact: Michael Long; Vilma Long; Joann
Taylor Long; Caroline Ingrid Long

Publishes Texas-related fiction and
nonfiction for children and young adults.
Send query with SASE, outline, synopsis,
and two sample chapters.

Henry Holt and Company

175 Fifth Avenue
New York, NY 10010
Website: http://www.henryholt.com

Publishes: Fiction; Nonfiction; *Markets:*
Adult

No submissions. Any material submitted will
be recycled or discarded unread.

High Plains Press

PO Box 123
Glendo, WY 82213
Tel: +1 (800) 552-7819
Fax: +1 (307) 735-4590
Email: editor@highplainspress.com
Website: http://www.highplainspress.com

Publishes: Nonfiction; Poetry; *Areas:*
Autobiography; Historical; Nature; *Markets:*
Adult

Regional publisher specialising in books on
the American West. Publishes nonfiction and
one book of poetry with a strong sense of
place (the West) per year. For nonfiction
send query with 2-3 page summary and first
two chapters by post with SASE. For poetry
send sample of ten poems. No fiction or
children's material.

Hippocrene Books, Inc.

171 Madison Avenue
New York NY 10016
Tel: +1 (212) 685-4371
Fax: +1 (718) 228-6355
Email: editorial@hippocrenebooks.com
Website: https://www.hippocrenebooks.com

Publishes: Nonfiction; Reference; *Areas:*
Cookery; Historical; *Markets:* Adult

Publishes general nonfiction, particularly
foreign language reference books and ethnic
cookbooks. No fiction. Send submissions by
email.

Hobar Publications

5995 149th Street West, Suite 105
Apple Valley, MN 55124
Tel: +1 (952) 469-6699
Email: info@finneyco.com
Website: http://www.finney-hobar.com/
hobar.html

Publishes: Nonfiction; *Areas:* Crafts;
Gardening; Nature; Science; *Markets:*
Academic; Professional

Publishes career and educational materials in
the areas of agriculture, gardening, science,
and building trades.

Holiday House, Inc.

50 Broad Street #301
New York, NY 10004
Tel: +1 (212) 688-0085
Fax: +1 (212) 421-6134
Email: submissions@holidayhouse.com
Website: http://www.holidayhouse.com

Publishes: Fiction; Nonfiction; *Markets:*
Children's; Youth

Contact: Editorial Department

Independent publisher of children's books,
from picture books to young adult fiction and
nonfiction. Send complete ms by post or by
email. No need to include SASE.

Houghton Mifflin Harcourt

125 High Street
Boston, MA 02110
Tel: +1 (617) 351-5000
Email: corporate.communications@
hmhco.com
Website: http://www.hmco.com

Publishes: Fiction; Nonfiction; Reference;
Areas: Autobiography; Biography;
Historical; Literature; *Markets:* Academic;
Children's

Contact: Submissions Editor

Educational publisher publishing nonfiction
and early readers for children.

Human Kinetics

1607 N Market Street
PO Box 5076

Champaign, Illinois 61825-5076
Tel: +1 (800) 747-4457
Fax: +1 (217) 351-1549
Email: info@hkusa.com
Website: https://us.humankinetics.com

Publishes: Nonfiction; *Areas:* Health;
Leisure; Medicine; Psychology; Science;
Sport; *Markets:* Academic; Adult;
Professional

Publishes books on health, fitness, and sport,
aimed at the academic market, professionals
in the field, and the general public. Send
query with outline and sample chapters.

Ibbetson Street Press

25 School Street
Somerville, MA 02143
Tel: +1 (617) 628-2313
Email: tapestryofvoices@yahoo.com
Website: http://ibbetsonpress.com

Publishes: Poetry; *Markets:* Adult;
Treatments: Literary

Contact: Harris Gardner; Lawrence
Kessenich; Emily Pineau

Poetry press publishing a regular journal and
poetry books. Send query by email with brief
bio and 3-5 poems in the body of the email.
No attachments.

IDW Publishing

2765 Truxtun Road
San Diego, CA 92106
Email: letters@idwpublishing.com
Website: http://www.idwpublishing.com

Publishes: Fiction; *Areas:* Adventure; Sci-
Fi; *Markets:* Adult; Children's; Youth

Publisher of comic books and graphic novels
based on well known intellectual properties,
for both children and adults.

Idyll Arbor

39129 264th Ave SE
Enumclaw, WA 98022
Tel: +1 (360) 825-7797
Fax: +1 (360) 825-5670
Email: sales@idyllarbor.com
Website: http://www.idyllarbor.com

Publishes: Nonfiction; *Areas:* Health; How-to; Leisure; Medicine; Psychology; *Markets:* Adult; Professional

Publishes practical books on healthcare and therapies aimed at people or families dealing with a condition and activity directors. Will accept completed mss or queries, but prefers to receive query with outline and sample chapter by email.

Imbrifex Books

8275 South Eastern Avenue, Suite 200
Las Vegas, Nevada 89123
Tel: +1 (702) 309-0130
Email: acquisitions@imbrifex.com
Website: https://imbrifex.com

Publishes: Fiction; Nonfiction; *Areas:* Autobiography; Travel; *Markets:* Adult

Contact: Mark Sedenquist; Megan Edwards

Publishes fiction, travel and memoir. Welcomes book proposals and queries from both authors and agents. See website for full guidelines.

Indiana Historical Society Press

450 West Ohio Street
Indianapolis, IN 46202
Tel: +1 (317) 232-1882
Email: ihspress@indianahistory.org
Website: https://indianahistory.org

Publishes: Nonfiction; *Areas:* Historical; *Markets:* Adult; Children's; Family

Publishes books on the history of Indiana. Send query with SASE.

Information Today, Inc.

143 Old Marlton Pike
Medford, NJ 08055-8750

Tel: +1 (609) 654-6266
Fax: +1 (609) 654-4309
Email: custserv@infotoday.com
Website: http://www.infotoday.com

Publishes: Nonfiction; *Areas:* Technology; *Markets:* Adult

Publishes books and magazines on information technology.

Interweave Press

4868 Innovation Dr
Ft. Collins, CO 80525-5576
Tel: +1 (866) 949-1646
Email: kerry.bogert@fwcommunity.com
Website: https://www.interweave.com

Publishes: Nonfiction; *Areas:* Crafts; Hobbies; *Markets:* Adult

Contact: Kerry Bogert

Publishes books, magazines, DVDs etc. on crafts such as knitting, crocheting, spinning, weaving, needlework and jewelry.

Italica Press

99 Wall Street, Suite 650
New York, NY 10005
Tel: +1 (917) 371-0563
Email: inquiries@ItalicaPress.com
Website: http://www.italicapress.com

Publishes: Fiction; Nonfiction; Poetry; Scripts; *Areas:* Arts; Drama; Historical; Translations; Travel; *Markets:* Adult

Publishes English translations of medieval, Renaissance and early-modern texts, historical travel, English translations of modern Italian fiction, dual-language poetry, drama, and a series of studies in art and history.

Jacar Press

6617 Deerview Trl
Durham, NC 27712
Tel: +1 (919) 810-2863
Email: jacarassist@gmail.com
Website: http://jacarpress.com

Publishes: Poetry; *Markets:* Adult; *Treatments:* Literary

Publisher of full-length and chapbook collections of poetry. Accepts submissions through annual competitions only ($15 submission fee). Also publishes online magazine.

Jewish Lights Publishing

4507 Charlotte Ave, Suite 100
Nashville, TN 37209
Tel: +1 (615) 255-2665
Fax: +1 (615) 255-5081
Email: submissions@turnerpublishing.com
Website: http://jewishlights.com

Publishes: Fiction; Nonfiction; *Areas:*
Crime; Historical; Men's Interests; Mystery;
Philosophy; Religious; Sci-Fi; Spiritual;
Women's Interests; *Markets:* Adult;
Children's; Youth

Publishes work about the unity and
community of the Jewish People and the
relevance of Judaism to everyday life. Send
submissions by email.

JourneyForth

1430 Wade Hampton Boulevard
Greenville, SC 29609-5046
Tel: +1 (800) 845-5731
Email: journeyforth@bjupress.com
Website: http://www.bjupress.com

Publishes: Fiction; Nonfiction; *Areas:*
Adventure; Biography; Historical; Mystery;
Nature; Religious; Sport; Westerns; *Markets:*
Adult; Children's; Youth

Contact: Nancy Lohr

Publishes adult nonfiction and children's and
youth fiction, all from a conservative
Christian worldview.

Judson Press

1075 First Avenue
King of Prussia, PA 19406
Tel: +1 (800) 458-3766
Fax: +1 (610) 768-2107
Email: acquisitions@judsonpress.com
Website: https://www.judsonpress.com

Publishes: Nonfiction; *Areas:* Religious;
Markets: Adult

Publishes adult nonfiction for Christians.

Kaya Press

c/o USC ASE
3620 S. Vermont Ave KAP 462
Los Angeles, CA 90089

Email: acquisitions@kaya.com
Website: http://www.kaya.com

Publishes: Fiction; Nonfiction; Poetry;
Areas: Arts; Criticism; Culture; Literature;
Markets: Adult

Independent not-for-profit publisher of Asian
and Pacific Islander diasporic literature,
publishing fiction, poetry, critical essays, art,
and culture. Send complete MS by email as
Word or PDF attachment, with contact info,
description of project, why you feel this
publisher is appropriate, and list of any
previous publications / awards. See website
for full details.

Kensington Publishing Corp.

119 West 40th Street
New York, NY 10018
Tel: +1 (800) 221-2647
Email: jscognamiglio@
kensingtonbooks.com
Website: http://www.kensingtonbooks.com

Publishes: Fiction; Nonfiction; *Areas:*
Autobiography; Biography; Business; Crime;
Fantasy; Health; Historical; Lifestyle;
Military; Mystery; Romance; Sci-Fi; Self-
Help; Suspense; Thrillers; Women's
Interests; *Markets:* Adult; *Treatments:*
Commercial; Contemporary; Literary

Contact: John Scognamiglio

No children's, young adult, or poetry. Send
query only, in the body of the email. No
attachments. See website for full guidelines.

Kent State University Press

1118 Library
PO Box 5190
Kent, OH 44242
Tel: +1 (330) 672-7913
Fax: +1 (330) 672-3104
Email: ksupress@kent.edu
Website: http://www.
kentstateuniversitypress.com

Publishes: Nonfiction; *Areas:* Arts;
Biography; Criticism; Historical; Literature;
Markets: Academic

Contact: Will Underwood, Acquiring Editor

Publishes general nonfiction, but particularly scholarly works in the fields of American studies, biography, history, and literary studies.

Kirkbride Bible Company

1102 Deloss Street
Indianapolis, IN 46203
Tel: +1 (800) 428-4385
Fax: +1 (317) 633-1444
Email: info@kirkbride.com
Website: http://www.kirkbride.com

Publishes: Nonfiction; Reference; *Areas:* Religious; *Markets:* Adult

Publisher of bible reference titles.

Krause Publications

700 East State Street
Iola, WI 54990-0001
Tel: +1 (715) 445-2214
Fax: +1 (715) 445-4087
Email: info@krause.com
Website: http://www.krause.com

Publishes: Nonfiction; Reference; *Areas:* Antiques; Hobbies; How-to; Sport; *Markets:* Adult

Largest publisher of material on hobbies and collectibles in the world. Send query with outline, sample chapter, and description of how your book will make a unique contribution.

Lawrence Hill Books

Chicago Review Press
814 North Franklin Street
Chicago, Illinois 60610
Tel: +1 (312) 337-0747
Email: ytaylor@chicagoreviewpress.com
Website: http://www.
chicagoreviewpress.com

Publishes: Nonfiction; *Areas:* Politics; Women's Interests; *Markets:* Adult

Contact: Yuval Taylor

Publishes nonfiction on progressive politics, civil and human rights, feminism, and topics of interest to African Americans and other underrepresented groups. Send query by email.

Leapfrog Press

PO Box 505
Fredonia, NY 14063
Email: acquisitions@leapfrogpress.com
Website: http://www.leapfrogpress.com

Publishes: Fiction; Nonfiction; Poetry; *Areas:* Short Stories; *Markets:* Adult; Children's; Youth; *Treatments:* Literary

Publisher with an eclectic list of fiction, poetry, and nonfiction, including paperback originals of adult and middle-grade fiction and nonfiction. Closed to general submissions between January 15 and around June 15 each year, but accepts adult, young adult (YA) and middle grade (MG) novels, novellas, and short story collections through its annual fiction contest until May 1. Submit online through online submission system.

Leaping Dog Press

Email: editor@leapingdogpress.com
Website: http://www.leapingdogpress.com

Publishes: Fiction; Poetry; *Areas:* Humour; Translations; *Markets:* Adult; *Treatments:* Literary

Publishes accessible, edgy, witty, and challenging contemporary poetry, fiction, and works in translation. Not accepting submissions as at January 2019. Check website for current status.

Les Figues Press

6671 Sunset Blvd., Suite 1521
Los Angeles, CA 90028
Tel: +1 (323) 734-4732
Email: info@lesfigues.com
Website: http://www.lesfigues.com

Publishes: Fiction; Poetry; *Areas:* Short Stories; *Markets:* Adult

Publishes fiction and poetry. Accepts submissions through its annual contest only ($25 entry fee). Accepts poetry, novellas, innovative novels, anti-novels, short story collections, lyric essays, hybrids, and all forms not otherwise specified. Submit via form on website.

Less Than Three Press

PO Box 8428
Rocky Mount, NC 27804
Email: submissions@lessthanthreepress.com
Website: https://www.lessthanthreepress.com

Publishes: Fiction; *Areas:* Fantasy;
Historical; Romance; Sci-Fi; Short Stories;
Markets: Adult; *Treatments:* Contemporary

Publishes creative LGBTQIA (lesbian, gay,
bisexual/pansexual, trans, queer, intersex,
asexual/aromantic/agender) romances in any
genre. Accepts submissions of novels up to
200,000 words and short stories and novellas
of at least 10,000 words. See website for full
submission guidelines.

Lillenas Drama Resources

PO Box 419527
Kansas City, MO 64141
Tel: +1 (800) 877-0700
Fax: +1 (816) 412-8390
Email: drama@lillenas.com
Website: http://www.lillenas.com

Publishes: Scripts; *Areas:* Religious;
Markets: Adult; Children's; Family; Youth

Publishes sketches and plays. Not accepting
unsolicited submissions as at April 2018.
Check website for current status.

Little, Brown and Company

1290 Avenue of the Americas
New York, NY 10104
Website: https://www.littlebrown.com

Publishes: Fiction; Nonfiction; *Markets:*
Adult; Children's

Publishes general fiction and nonfiction for
the adult and children's markets. No
unsolicited MSS or approaches direct from
authors – will only consider approaches from
literary agents.

Lost Horse Press

105 Lost Horse Lane
Sandpoint, ID 83864
Tel: +1 (208) 255-4410
Email: losthorsepress@mindspring.com
Website: http://www.losthorsepress.org

Publishes: Fiction; Poetry; *Areas:* Short
Stories; *Markets:* Adult; *Treatments:*
Literary

Publishes collections of poetry and short
stories, submitted through their annual
competitions (reading fee applies). No
general submissions.

Loyola Press

3441 North Ashland Avenue
Chicago, IL 60657
Tel: +1 (773) 281-1818
Fax: +1 (773) 281-0152
Email: durepos@loyolapress.com
Website: http://www.loyolapress.org

Publishes: Nonfiction; *Areas:* Religious;
Spiritual; *Markets:* Adult

Contact: Joseph Durepos, Executive
Editor/Trade Acquisitions

Catholic publisher of books on Catholic
tradition, prayer, and spirituality. Send one-
page query email or by post. See website for
full guidelines.

Luna Bisonte Prods

137 Leland Avenue
Columbus OH 43214-7505
Email: bennettjohnm@gmail.com
Website: http://www.johnmbennett.net

Publishes: Poetry; *Markets:* Adult;
Treatments: Experimental

Publisher of poetry chapbooks. Avant-garde
and experimental work only. Send query
with brief bio, publishing history, and a few
sample poems.

Macmillan Publishers

175 Fifth Avenue
New York, NY 10010
Email: press.inquiries@macmillan.com
Website: https://us.macmillan.com

Publishes: Fiction; Nonfiction; *Markets:*
Adult; Children's; Youth

US office of international publisher of
hardcover, trade paperback, and paperback
books for adults, children, and teens.

Mad Gleam Press
710 Decatur Street
Brooklyn, NY 11233
Email: madgleampress@gmail.com
Website: https://www.madgleampress.com

Publishes: Fiction; Poetry; *Markets:* Adult;
Treatments: Literary

**Closed to submissions as at June 2019.
Check website for current status.**

Publishes fiction and poetry collections.
Particularly interested in collaborative /
transmedia pieces. Send submissions by
email with author bio / resume.

Martin Sisters Publishing
Email: submissions@
martinsisterspublishing.com
Website: http://www.
martinsisterspublishing.com

Publishes: Fiction; Nonfiction; *Areas:*
Fantasy; Religious; Sci-Fi; Self-Help; Short
Stories; *Markets:* Adult; Children's; Family;
Youth

Accepts queries for all genres of fiction,
including science fiction and fantasy, and
nonfiction, including self-help. Submissions
may include Christian fiction, inspirational,
collections of stories. No poetry, torrid or
any books containing extreme violence. Send
query by email with marketing plan and (for
fiction) 5-10 pages in the body of the email.
No attachments. See website for full
guidelines.

Marvel Comics
135 W. 50th Street
New York, NY 10020
Tel: +1 (212) 576-4000
Website: http://marvel.com

Publishes: Fiction; *Areas:* Adventure;
Fantasy; Horror; Humour; Sci-Fi; *Markets:*
Adult; Children's; Youth

Publisher of action comics.

MC Press
3695 W. Quail Heights Court
Boise, ID 83703-3861

Tel: +1 (208) 629-7275 Ext. 502
Email: agrubb@mcpressonline.com
Website: http://www.mcpressonline.com

Publishes: Nonfiction; *Areas:* How-to;
Technology; *Markets:* Professional

Contact: Anne Grub

Publisher of computer books (IBM
technologies) aimed at midrange IT
professionals. Send proposals by email.

McGraw-Hill Education
PO Box 182605
Columbus, OH 43218
Tel: +1 (800) 338-3987
Fax: +1 (800) 953-8691
Website: https://www.mheducation.com

Publishes: Nonfiction; *Areas:* Arts;
Business; Film; Health; Historical; Legal;
Music; Politics; Psychology; Science;
Sociology; Technology; Theatre; *Markets:*
Academic

Publishes a wide range of nonfiction
educational books.

McSweeney's Publishing
849 Valencia St.
San Francisco, CA 94110
Tel: +1 (415) 642-5609
Email: custservice@mcsweeneys.net
Website: https://www.mcsweeneys.net

Publishes: Fiction; Nonfiction; Poetry;
Areas: Arts; Cookery; Humour; *Markets:*
Adult; Children's

Accepts electronic submissions of complete
manuscripts only (except in the case of
cookbooks, which may be submitted as
complete mss or proposals). Not currently
accepting poetry submissions. See website
for full details.

Messianic Jewish Publishers
6120 Day Long Lane
Clarksville, MD 21029
Tel: +1 (410) 531-6644
Email: editor@messianicjewish.net
Website: http://www.messianicjewish.net

Publishes: Fiction; Nonfiction; *Areas:* Religious; *Markets:* Adult

Publishes books which address Jewish evangelism; the Jewish roots of Christianity; Messianic Judaism; Israel; the Jewish People. Publishes mainly nonfiction, but some fiction. See website for full submission guidelines.

Mountaineers Books

1001 SW Klickitat Way, Suite 201
Seattle, WA 98134
Tel: +1 (206) 223-6303
Fax: +1 (206) 223-6306
Email: submissions@mountaineersbooks.org
Website: https://www.mountaineers.org

Publishes: Nonfiction; *Areas:* Adventure; Leisure; Nature; Travel; *Markets:* Adult

Publishes books on adventure travel, biking, camping, climbing, conservation, environment/nature, hiking, mountaineering, mountaineering literature, natural history, outdoor adventure, paddle sports (canoeing, kayaking, SUP), safety/first aid, skiing (alpine, Nordic, boarding), snowshoeing, surfing, walking, and wilderness skills. Imprint publishes books on sustainable foods, urban and wilderness foraging, organic/sustainable gardening, wildlife gardening, urban farming, general wildlife, natural living, and general outdoor-related gift topics. No fiction, children's books, general tourist/travel guides, or guides dealing with hunting, fishing, snowmobiling, horseback riding, or organised spectator sports. Send proposal or complete ms by email. See website for full guidelines.

Native Ink Press

Email: Submissions@nativeinkpress.com
Website: http://nativeinkpress.com

Publishes: Fiction; Nonfiction; *Areas:* Autobiography; Biography; Cookery; Crafts; Gardening; Nature; Self-Help; *Markets:* Adult; Children's

Publishes nonfiction and children's fiction, including picture books, picture storybooks, easy readers, early chapter books, and middle grade novels. Accepts submissions

from US authors only. Send query by email. See website for full guidelines.

NBM Publishing

160 Broadway, Suite 700 East Wing
New York, NY 10038
Email: tnantier@nbmpub.com
Website: http://nbmpub.com

Publishes: Fiction; *Areas:* Erotic; Fantasy; Horror; Humour; Mystery; Sci-Fi; *Markets:* Adult; Youth; *Treatments:* Satirical

Contact: Terry Nantier

Publisher of graphic novels, interested in general fiction, humour, satire of fantasy and horror, erotica, and mystery. No superheroes. Accepting approaches from previously published authors only (including those with proven success in online comics). No submissions from authors outside North America, except for adult. See website for full submission guidelines.

No Starch Press, Inc.

245 8th Street
San Francisco, CA 94103
Tel: +1 (415) 863-9900
Fax: +1 (415) 863-9950
Email: editors@nostarch.com
Website: https://nostarch.com

Publishes: Nonfiction; *Areas:* Technology; *Markets:* Adult; Children's; Youth

Publishes unique books on technology, with a focus on open source, security, hacking, programming, alternative operating systems, LEGO®, science, and maths. See website for full guidelines.

NorthSouth Books

600 Third Avenue, 2nd Floor
NY, NY 10016
Tel: +1 (917) 210-5868
Email: submissionsnsb@gmail.com
Website: https://northsouth.com

Publishes: Fiction; *Markets:* Children's

Publishes picture books for children up to 1,000 words. Seeks fresh, original fiction on universal themes that would appeal to children aged 3-8. Generally does not acquire rhyming texts, as must also be translated into German. Send submissions by email as Word document or pasted directly into the body of the email. Authors do not need to include illustrations, but if the author is also an illustrator sample sketches can be included in PDF or JPEG form.

Pace Press

2006 S Mary St
Fresno, CA 93721
Tel: +1 (800) 345-4447
Email: kent@lindenpub.com
Website: https://quilldriverbooks.com/pace-press/

Publishes: Fiction; *Areas:* Fantasy; Historical; Horror; Mystery; Romance; Sci-Fi; Thrillers; Westerns; *Markets:* Adult

Send query by post or email with synopsis, author bio, and first three or four chapters / 50 pages of your manuscript. See website for full guidelines.

PassKey Publications

5348 Vegas Drive PMB 1670
Las Vegas, NV 89108
Email: support@passkeyonline.com
Website: https://www.passkeypublications.com

Publishes: Nonfiction; *Areas:* Business; Finance; *Markets:* Adult

Publishes taxation and accountancy textbooks.

Paulist Press

997 Macarthur Boulevard
Mahwah, NJ 07430
Tel: +1 (201) 825-7300
Fax: +1 (201) 825-8345
Email: submissions@paulistpress.com
Website: http://www.paulistpress.com

Publishes: Fiction; Nonfiction; *Areas:* Culture; Philosophy; Religious; Self-Help; *Markets:* Adult; Children's

Contact: Rev. Lawrence Boadt, CSP (Adult); Susan O'Keefe (Children's)

Catholic publishing house, publishing mainly religious and spiritual nonfiction for adults, as well as a small but growing number of religious fiction books for children. Send proposal by email or by post the SASE. See website for full guidelines.

Penguin Random House

1745 Broadway
New York, NY 10019
Tel: +1 (212) 366-2000
Website: https://www.penguinrandomhouse.com

Publishes: Fiction; Nonfiction; Poetry; Reference; *Areas:* Arts; Autobiography; Biography; Cookery; Entertainment; Fantasy; Historical; Humour; Mystery; Politics; Romance; Science; Sci-Fi; Suspense; Travel; *Markets:* Adult; Children's; Youth

One of the world's largest publishing houses. Accepts approaches via literary agents only.

Philosophy Documentation Center

PO Box 7147
Charlottesville, VA 22906-7147
Tel: +1 (434) 220-3300
Email: leaman@pdcnet.org
Website: https://www.pdcnet.org

Publishes: Nonfiction; Reference; *Areas:* Philosophy; *Markets:* Academic

Contact: George Leaman, Director

Publishes books, journals, and reference materials on philosophy and related fields.

Pocol Press

3911 Prosperity Avenue
Fairfax, VA 22031
Tel: +1 (703) 870-9611
Website: http://www.pocolpress.com

Publishes: Fiction; Nonfiction; *Areas:* Horror; Short Stories; *Markets:* Adult; *Treatments:* Contemporary; Literary; Mainstream

Send query with SASE, author bio, publishing credits, audience details, and synopsis. No unsolicited MSS, queries by email, or self-published books.

Princeton Architectural Press

202 Warren Street
Hudson, NY 12534
Tel: +1 (518) 671-6100
Email: submissions@papress.com
Website: http://www.papress.com

Publishes: Nonfiction; *Areas:* Architecture;
Design; *Markets:* Adult

Download submission guidelines from
website and submit by post.

Quarto Publishing Group USA

142 West 36th Street, Fourth Floor
New York, NY 10018
Tel: +1 (212) 779-4972
Fax: +1 (212) 779-6058
Website: https://www.quartoknows.com/
division/Quarto-Publishing-Group-USA/

Publishes: Nonfiction; Reference; *Areas:*
Arts; Cookery; Crafts; Current Affairs;
Design; Health; Historical; Hobbies; How-
to; Military; Music; Politics; Science; Self-
Help; Sport; Technology; Travel; *Markets:*
Adult

Nonfiction publisher with offices in the US,
UK, and Hong Kong. See website for
specific interests and guidelines for different
imprints.

Red Moon Press

P.O. Box 2461
Winchester, VA 22604-1661
Tel: +1 (540) 722-2156
Email: jim.kacian@redmoonpress.com
Website: http://www.redmoonpress.com

Publishes: Fiction; Nonfiction; Poetry;
Areas: Biography; Criticism; Literature;
Translations; *Markets:* Adult

Publishes anthologies of haiku, Haibun, and
related forms, plus relevant works of fiction,
collections of essays, translations, criticism,
etc. Send query in first instance.

Robert D. Reed Publishers

POB 1992
Bandon, OR 97411
Tel: +1 (541) 347-9882
Fax: +1 (541) 347-9883

Email: bob@rdrpublishers.com
Website: http://www.rdrpublishers.com

Publishes: Nonfiction; *Areas:*
Autobiography; Business; Finance; Health;
Historical; Humour; Lifestyle; Psychology;
Self-Help; Spiritual; *Markets:* Adult;
Children's

Publishes nonfiction by authors with a
platform to sell their books. Manuscripts
must have been professionally edited. Send
query through contact form on website. No
longer publishes fiction.

Saddle Road Press

1483 Wailuku Drive
Hilo, HI 96720
Email: info@saddleroadpress.com
Website: http://saddleroadpress.com

Publishes: Fiction; Poetry; *Areas:*
Autobiography; Short Stories; *Markets:*
Adult; *Treatments:* Literary

Small literary press publishing full-length
poetry collections, poetry chapbooks, literary
fiction, essays, memoir, and hybrid forms, in
both print and eBook editions. Currently
looking for collections of poetry and hybrid
poetry/prose, and collections of short fiction
and lyric essays. Submit through online
submission system. $20 submission fee.

Saguaro Books, LLC

16201 E. Keymar Drive
Fountain Hills, AZ 85268
Tel: +1 (602) 309-7670
Fax: +1 (480) 284-4855
Email: mjnickum@saguarobooks.com
Website: http://www.saguarobooks.com

Publishes: Fiction; *Markets:* Children's;
Youth

Contact: Mary Nickum

Publishes books for children and young
adults aged 10-18, but first-time authors over
the age of 18. Send query by email
describing your submission in first instance.
Exclusive submissions only.

Salvo Press

101 Hudson Street, 37th Floor, Suite 3705
Jersey City, NJ 07302
Tel: +1 (212) 431-5455
Email: info@salvopress.com
Website: http://salvopress.com

Publishes: Fiction; *Areas:* Mystery;
Thrillers; *Markets:* Adult; *Treatments:*
Literary

Publishes quality mysteries, thrillers, and
literary books in eBook and audiobook
formats.

Santa Monica Press

P.O. Box 850
Solana Beach, CA 92075
Tel: +1 (800) 784-9553
Email: acquisitions@santamonicapress.com
Website: http://www.santamonicapress.com

Publishes: Nonfiction; Reference; *Areas:*
Architecture; Arts; Biography; Culture;
Entertainment; Film; Historical; Humour;
Literature; Photography; Sport; Travel;
Markets: Adult

Accepts proposals from agents and directly
from authors, but post or by email. See
website for full submission guidelines.

Scholastic Library Publishing

PO Box 3765
Jefferson City, MO 65102-3765
Tel: +1 (800) 621-1115
Fax: +1 (866) 783-4361
Email: slpservice@scholastic.com
Website: http://scholasticlibrary.digital.
scholastic.com

Publishes: Fiction; Nonfiction; Reference;
Markets: Children's

Publishes children's fiction, nonfiction, and
reference.

Scribner

1230 Avenue of the Americas, 12th Floor
New York, NY 10020
Tel: +1 (212) 698-7000
Email: info@simonsays.com
Website: http://www.
simonandschusterpublishing.com/scribner/

Publishes: Fiction; Nonfiction; *Areas:*
Historical; Mystery; Philosophy;
Psychology; Religious; Science; Suspense;
Markets: Adult; *Treatments:* Literary

Accepts submissions via literary agents only.

Seaworthy Publications

6300 N Wickham Road, Unit #130-416
Melbourne, FL 32940
Tel: +1 (321) 610-3634
Fax: +1 (321) 259-6872
Email: queries@seaworthy.com
Website: http://www.seaworthy.com

Publishes: Nonfiction; *Areas:* Hobbies;
Leisure; Travel; *Markets:* Adult

Nautical book publisher specialising in
recreational boating. Send query by email
outlining your work and attaching sample
table of contents and two or three sample
chapters. See website for full submission
guidelines.

Seven Stories Press

140 Watts Street
New York, NY 10013
Tel: +1 (212) 226-8760
Fax: +1 (212) 226-1411
Email: info@sevenstories.com
Website: http://www.sevenstories.com

Publishes: Fiction; Nonfiction; *Areas:*
Autobiography; Current Affairs; Health;
Historical; Politics; Translations;
Treatments: Literary

Publishes works of the imagination and
political titles by voices of conscience. Send
query by post with two sample chapters and
46 cent SASE or postcard for reply. If you
require submission materials returned to you,
include adequate return postage. No
unsolicited mss and no email submissions.

Shipwreckt Books Publishing Company

Ruchford, MN
Email: contact@shipwrecktbooks.com
Website: http://www.shipwrecktbooks.com

Publishes: Fiction; Nonfiction; Poetry;
Areas: Autobiography; Culture; Current

Affairs; Fantasy; Gardening; Health;
Historical; Hobbies; Humour; Legal;
Leisure; Lifestyle; Medicine; Military;
Mystery; Nature; Politics; Sci-Fi; Spiritual;
Sport; Suspense; Women's Interests;
Markets: Adult; Children's; Youth;
Treatments: Literary

Publishes books and literary magazine.
Submit brief bio, synopsis, and first ten
pages (or a couple of poems) using form on
website.

Sibling Rivalry Press, LLC

PO Box 26147
Little Rock, AR 72221
Tel: +1 (870) 723-6008
Email: info@siblingrivalrypress.com
Website: https://siblingrivalrypress.com

Publishes: Poetry; *Markets:* Adult;
Treatments: Literary

Contact: Bryan Borland, Publisher; Seth
Pennington, Editor

Publishes poetry that disturbs and enraptures.
Has had award-winning success publishing
LGBTIQ authors, but is an inclusive
publishing house welcoming all authors,
regardless of sexual orientation or identity.
Open to submissions from march 1 to June 1
annually.

Silver Lake Publishing, LLC

PO Box 173
Aberdeen, WA 98520
Tel: +1 (360) 532-5758
Fax: +1 (360) 532-5728
Email: publisher@silverlakepub.com
Website: http://www.silverlakepub.com

Publishes: Nonfiction; Reference; *Areas:*
Business; Finance; How-to; Legal; Lifestyle;
Medicine; Politics; *Markets:* Adult

Publishes books that give readers tools for
making smart, aggressive decisions about
risk, security and financial matters. Send
query with synopsis, two sample chapters,
and author CV. No fiction or poetry, or
submissions by email.

Sky Pony Press

307 West 36th Street, 11th Floor
New York, NY 10018
Tel: +1 (212) 643-6816
Fax: +1 (212) 643-6819
Email: skyponysubmissions@
skyhorsepublishing.com
Website: http://skyponypress.com

Publishes: Fiction; Nonfiction; *Markets:*
Children's; Youth

Publishes picture books, chapter books,
middle grade, and YA fiction and nonfiction,
in any genre or style. Send proposal or
complete ms by email as a Word attachment.
Do not send hard copy unless requested.

Southern Illinois University Press

1915 University Press Drive
Carbondale, IL 62901-4323
Tel: +1 (618) 453-2281
Fax: +1 (618) 453-1221
Email: kageff@siu.edu
Website: http://www.siupress.com

Publishes: Fiction; Nonfiction; Poetry;
Areas: Arts; Biography; Crime; Film;
Health; Historical; Legal; Philosophy;
Photography; Politics; Theatre; Women's
Interests; *Markets:* Academic

Contact: Karl Kageff

Publishes nonfiction books for academic and
general audiences. No fiction, conference
proceedings, edited primary sources,
unrevised dissertations, or festschriften. See
website for full guidelines.

St Pauls

2187 Victory Boulevard
Staten Island, NY 10314
Tel: +1 (718) 761-0047
Fax: +1 (718) 954-9061
Email: provincialoffice@stpauls.us
Website: http://www.stpaulsusa.com

Publishes: Nonfiction; *Areas:* Biography;
Religious; Self-Help; Spiritual; *Markets:*
Adult

Publishes books for a Roman Catholic
readership.

Star Bright Books

13 Landsdowne Street
Cambridge, MA 02139
Tel: +1 (617) 354-1300
Fax: +1 (617) 354-1399
Email: info@starbrightbooks.com
Website: https://starbrightbooks.org

Publishes: Fiction; Nonfiction; *Markets:*
Children's

Publishes books that are entertaining,
meaningful and sensitive to the needs of all
children. Welcomes submissions for picture
books and longer works, both fiction and
nonfiction. See website for full submission
guidelines.

Sterling Publishing Co. Inc.

1166 Avenue of the Americas, Floor 17
New York, NY 10036
Tel: +1 (212) 532-7160
Fax: +1 (212) 213-2495
Email: editorial@sterlingpublishing.com
Website: https://www.sterlingpublishing.com

Publishes: Fiction; Nonfiction; Reference;
Areas: Arts; Crafts; Crime; Finance;
Gardening; Health; Hobbies; How-to;
Humour; Lifestyle; Literature; Music;
Mystery; Nature; New Age; Photography;
Science; Spiritual; Sport; Travel; *Markets:*
Adult; Children's; Youth

Publishes mainly adult nonfiction, reference,
and how-to, plus fiction for children. No
adult fiction. Send query with SASE, outline
of idea, sample chapter, sample illustrations
(where appropriate), and details about
yourself, including any publishing history.
No submissions by email.

Stone Bridge Press

1393 Solano Avenue, Suite C
Albany, CA 94706
Tel: +1 (510) 524-8732
Email: sbpedit@stonebridge.com
Website: http://www.stonebridge.com

Publishes: Fiction; Nonfiction; Poetry;
Reference; *Areas:* Arts; Business; Crafts;
Culture; Design; Film; Lifestyle; Literature;
Spiritual; Translations; Travel; *Markets:*
Adult; Children's

Publishes books about Asia and in particular
Japan and China. Send brief query by email
in the first instance.

Sunrise River Press

838 Lake St S
Forest Lake, MN 55025
Fax: +1 (800) 895-4585
Email: submissions@sunriseriverpress.com
Website: https://www.sunriseriverpress.com

Publishes: Nonfiction; *Areas:* Health;
Medicine; Self-Help; *Markets:* Adult;
Family; Professional

An award-winning publisher and part of a
three-company publishing house with more
than 33 years in specialty book publishing.

Since the early 1990s, this publisher has
published books exclusively for the
professional healthcare market. The
company is now transitioning its healthcare
publishing efforts to the serious end of the
consumer market, focusing on subjects such
as weight loss, nutrition, diet, food and
recipes, family health, fitness and specific
diseases such as cancer, anorexia,
Alzheimer's, autism and depression –
especially as they relate to the baby boomer
generation. We are actively seeking
proposals from potential authors on these
and related topics.

Our publishing house currently publishes
close to 30 consumer titles per calendar year
(through our two sister companies). Our
books consistently receive national and
international publicity in enthusiast
magazines.

Sunstone Press

Box 2321
Santa Fe, NM 87504-2321
Tel: +1 (800) 243-5644
Fax: +1 (505) 988-1025
Website: http://www.sunstonepress.com

Publishes: Fiction; Nonfiction; Poetry;
Reference; *Areas:* Adventure; Archaeology;
Architecture; Arts; Autobiography;
Biography; Business; Cookery; Crafts;
Crime; Fantasy; Gardening; Health;
Historical; How-to; Humour; Legal;

Military; Music; Mystery; Nature;
Photography; Politics; Religious; Romance;
Sci-Fi; Short Stories; Spiritual; Sport;
Theatre; Travel; Westerns; Women's
Interests; *Markets:* Adult; Children's; Family

Began in the 1970s with a focus on
nonfiction about the American Southwest,
but has since expanded its focus to include
mainstream themes and categories in both
fiction and nonfiction. Send query by post
only with short summary, author bio, one
sample chapter, table of contents, marketing
plan, and statement on why this is the right
publisher for your book.

Syracuse University Press

Syracuse University Press
621 Skytop Road, Suite 110
Syracuse, NY 13244-5290
Tel: +1 (315) 443-5534
Fax: +1 (315) 443-5545
Email: supress@syr.edu
Website: http://www.
syracuseuniversitypress.syr.edu

Publishes: Nonfiction; *Areas:* Anthropology;
Biography; Culture; Current Affairs;
Entertainment; Historical; Literature;
Politics; Religious; Sociology; Sport;
Translations; TV; Women's Interests;
Markets: Academic

Publishes scholarly books on international
affairs, the Middle East, women and religion,
politics, Irish studies, medieval history,
television, translations of Middle Eastern
literature, etc. Complete book proposal form
(available on website) and submit by email
with CV and preliminary table of contents.
No unsolicited mss.

Tailwinds Press

PO Box 2283, Radio City Station
New York, NY 10101-2283
Email: submissions@tailwindspress.com
Website: http://www.tailwindspress.com

Publishes: Fiction; Nonfiction; *Markets:*
Adult; *Treatments:* Literary

New York City-based independent press
specialising in high-quality literary fiction
and nonfiction. Send submissions by post or
email. See website for full guidelines.

Temple University Press

1852 North 10th Street
Philadelphia, PA 19122
Tel: +1 (215) 204-8787
Email: tempress@temple.edu
Website: http://www.temple.edu/tempress/

Publishes: Nonfiction; *Areas:* Anthropology;
Arts; Biography; Business; Crime; Culture;
Drama; Film; Finance; Health; Historical;
Legal; Leisure; Lifestyle; Literature; Media;
Nature; Photography; Politics; Psychology;
Religious; Science; Sociology; Sport;
Technology; Women's Interests; *Markets:*
Academic

Send query with brief outline, including
email address for response. Publishes
scholarly books, usually authored by
academics. Best known for publishing in the
areas of the social sciences and humanities.

Thames & Hudson Inc.

500 Fifth Avenue
New York, NY 10110
Tel: +1 (212) 354-3763
Fax: +1 (212) 398-1252
Email: bookinfo@thames.wwnorton.com
Website: https://www.
thamesandhudsonusa.com

Publishes: Nonfiction; *Areas:* Archaeology;
Architecture; Arts; Beauty and Fashion;
Biography; Culture; Design; Gardening;
Historical; Photography; Politics; Religious;
Travel; *Markets:* Adult

Send proposals up to six pages by email. No
attachments or unsolicited mss.

The Charles Press, Publishers

230 North 21st Street, Suite 312
Philadelphia, PA 19103
Tel: +1 (215) 470-5977
Email: submissions@charlespresspub.com
Website: http://www.charlespresspub.com

Publishes: Nonfiction; *Areas:* Crime;
Health; How-to; Lifestyle; Medicine;
Psychology; Religious; Sociology; *Markets:*
Adult

Send proposal outlining your book, your
purpose and rationale behind writing it, its
market, competition, ideas for marketing,

and author bio. Particularly interested in instructional (how-to) books, psychology, parenting, criminology, true crime and suicide. No fiction, poetry, children's books, short stories, science fiction, romance or humour. Consult website before submitting.

Thomas Dunne Books

St. Martin's Press
175 5th Avenue
New York, NY 10010
Email: thomasdunnebooks@stmartins.com
Website: https://us.macmillan.com/
thomasdunne

Publishes: Fiction; Nonfiction; *Areas:* Historical; Mystery; Politics; Sport; Suspense; Thrillers; Women's Interests; *Markets:* Adult; *Treatments:* Popular

Publishes popular trade fiction and nonfiction. Accepts approaches via literary agents only.

ThunderStone Books

Email: info@thunderstonebooks.com
Website: http://thunderstonebooks.com

Publishes: Fiction; Nonfiction; *Markets:* Children's

Publish children's fiction and nonfiction that has an educational aspect. Send query by email with up to first 50 pages as Word attachment.

Tor/Forge

Tom Doherty Associates, LLC
175 Fifth Avenue
New York, NY 10010
Website: https://www.torforgeblog.com

Publishes: Fiction; Nonfiction; *Areas:* Fantasy; Historical; Horror; Mystery; Sci-Fi; Suspense; Women's Interests; *Markets:* Adult; Children's

Particular emphasis on science fiction, fantasy, and horror. Open submissions policy. Send query with synopsis, first three chapters (or 40-60 pages), and SASE for response. See website for full submission guidelines.

Torah Aura Productions

2710 Supply Avenue
Los Angeles CA, 90040
Tel: +1 (800) 238-6724
Fax: +1 (323) 585-0327
Email: misrad@torahaura.com
Website: http://www.torahaura.com

Publishes: Nonfiction; *Areas:* Historical; Lifestyle; Religious; *Markets:* Academic; Children's; Youth

Contact: Jane Golub, Acquisitions

Publisher of educational materials for Jewish classrooms. No picture books.

Torrey House Press, LLC

150 S. State St. Suite 100
Salt Lake City, UT 84111
Tel: +1 (801) 209-1657
Email: mail@torreyhouse.com
Website: http://torreyhouse.com

Publishes: Fiction; Nonfiction; *Areas:* Culture; Historical; Nature; *Markets:* Adult; *Treatments:* Literary

Contact: Mark Bailey; Kirsten Johanna Allen

Closed to submissions as at June 2019. Check website for current status.

Publishes narrative nonfiction and literary fiction with a natural history, environmental, or a natural landscape theme, or about the politics and practice of sustainable living. Submit using online submission manager on website.

Triangle Square

140 Watts Street
New York, NY 10013
Tel: +1 (212) 226-8760
Fax: +1 (212) 226-1411
Email: info@sevenstories.com
Website: https://www.sevenstories.com/
imprints/triangle-square

Publishes: Fiction; Nonfiction; *Areas:* Autobiography; Biography; Health; Historical; Music; Nature; Philosophy; Politics; Religious; *Markets:* Children's; Youth

Publishes fiction and nonfiction for children and young adults, on such subjects as environmentalism, human rights, gender and feminism, etc.

Truman State University Press
100 East Normal Avenue
Kirksville, MO 63501-4221
Tel: +1 (660) 785-7336
Fax: +1 (660) 785-4480
Email: tsup@truman.edu
Website: http://tsup.truman.edu

Publishes: Nonfiction; *Areas:* Anthropology; Archaeology; Architecture; Arts; Autobiography; Biography; Criticism; Historical; Literature; Nature; Religious; Translations; Travel; *Markets:* Academic; Adult

Publishes peer-reviewed research and literature for the scholarly community and the reading public. See website for full submission guidelines.

Tumblehome Learning, Inc.
Boston, MA
Tel: +1 (781) 924-5036
Email: submissions@tumblehomelearning.com
Website: http://tumblehomelearning.com

Publishes: Fiction; *Areas:* Adventure; Science; *Markets:* Children's

Publishes books that allow kids to experience science through adventure and discovery. Submit complete ms by email.

Two Sylvias Press
PO Box 1524
Kingston, WA 98346
Email: twosylviaspress@gmail.com
Website: http://twosylviaspress.com

Publishes: Nonfiction; Poetry; *Areas:* Autobiography; *Markets:* Adult

Publishes poetry, memoirs, essays, and books on the craft of writing. Runs two poetry prizes.

Ugly Duckling Presse
The Old American Can Factory
232 Third Street, #E303 (corner Third Avenue)
Brooklyn, NY 11215
Tel: +1 (347) 948-5170
Email: office@uglyducklingpresse.org
Website: https://uglyducklingpresse.org

Publishes: Nonfiction; Poetry; *Areas:* Translations; *Markets:* Adult; *Treatments:* Experimental; Literary

Closed to submissions as at June 2019. Check website for current status.

Nonprofit publisher of poetry, translation, experimental nonfiction, performance texts, and books by artists. Check website for specific calls for submissions.

University of Alaska Press
Editorial Department
University of Alaska Press
PO Box 756240
104 Eielson Building
Fairbanks, AK 99775-6240
Tel: +1 (907) 474-5831
Fax: +1 (907) 474-5502
Email: UA-acquisitions@alaska.edu
Website: http://www.alaska.edu/uapress/

Publishes: Fiction; Nonfiction; Poetry; *Areas:* Autobiography; Biography; Culture; Historical; Nature; Politics; Science; Sport; Translations; *Markets:* Academic; Adult

Publisher based in Alaska, publishing academic and general trade books on an expanding range of subject areas, including politics and history, Native languages and cultures, science and natural history, biography and memoir, poetry, fiction and anthologies, and original translations. Send proposals by post. No unsolicited mss.

The University of Michigan Press
839 Greene Street
Ann Arbor, MI 48104-3209
Tel: +1 (734) 764-4388
Fax: +1 (734) 615-1540
Email: scottom@umich.edu
Website: http://www.press.umich.edu

Publishes: Fiction; Nonfiction; Reference; *Areas:* Anthropology; Archaeology; Arts; Autobiography; Biography; Business; Cookery; Culture; Finance; Historical; Legal; Literature; Media; Music; Nature; Philosophy; Politics; Psychology; Religious; Sociology; Sport; Theatre; Travel; Women's Interests; *Markets:* Academic

Send query with table of contents, outline of chapters, overview, and CV. Queries should include statements on the rationale of your book, similar and competing books in the field, your target audience, why you think it is right for this list, the length of MS, number of illustrations, and what your anticipated date of completion is. Send queries and proposals by email to specific editor (guidelines on website). See website for particular guidelines realting to fiction and certain series published by the press.

University of Pittsburgh Press

7500 Thomas Boulevard
Pittsburgh, PA 15260
Tel: +1 (412) 383-2456
Fax: +1 (412) 383-2466
Email: scrooms@upress.pitt.edu
Website: http://www.upress.pitt.edu

Publishes: Nonfiction; Poetry; *Areas:* Architecture; Historical; Philosophy; Science; *Markets:* Academic

Publishes books on Latin American studies, Russian and East European studies, international relations, poetry, Pittsburgh and Western Pennsylvania regional studies, environmental studies, architecture and landscape history, urban studies, composition and literacy, the history of science, and the philosophy of science. No hard sciences, memoirs, or fiction. Only considers poetry manuscripts from poets who have already published full-length collections of at least 48 pages. Poets who have not may submit to the first-book competition run by the press. See website for full guidelines.

University of Washington Press

4333 Brooklyn Avenue NE
Seattle, WA 98105

Tel: +1 (206) 543-4050
Fax: +1 (206) 543-3932
Email: uwapress@uw.edu
Website: http://www.washington.edu/uwpress/

Publishes: Nonfiction; *Areas:* Anthropology; Arts; Biography; Culture; Historical; Nature; *Markets:* Academic

Publishes scholarly books and distinguished works of regional nonfiction in the Pacific Northwest. Particularly known for Asian studies, Middle East studies, anthropology, Western history and biography, environmental studies, and natural history.

University Press of Kansas

2502 Westbrooke Circle
Lawrence, KS 66045-4444
Tel: +1 (785) 864-4154
Fax: +1 (785) 864-4586
Email: upress@ku.edu
Website: http://www.kansaspress.ku.edu

Publishes: Nonfiction; *Areas:* Historical; Legal; Military; Nature; Philosophy; Politics; *Markets:* Academic

Contact: Joyce Harrison; Kim Hogeland; David Congdon

See website for list of acquisitions editors and their interests, and send appropriate editor an email including:

1. Overview: Subject, argument, research
2. Core Contribution: what's unique, significant, exciting?
3. Comparison to other works in the field
4. Intended audience
5. Length of work (preferably in words) and number and type of illustrations
6. Annotated table of contents
7. Status of proposed work and timeline for completion
8. Bio or CV

Proposals may be sent by email but do not attach partial or complete manuscripts.

Vegetarian Alcoholic Press

Email: vegalpress@gmail.com
Website: http://www.vegetarianalcoholicpress.com

Publishes: Fiction; Poetry; *Areas:* Short Stories; *Markets:* Adult; *Treatments:* Literary

Publishes poetry and short story collections. Send submissions by email.

Venture Publishing, Inc.
1807 N. Federal Drive
Urbana, IL 61801
Tel: +1 (217) 359-5940
Fax: +1 (217) 359-5975
Email: books@sagamorepub.com
Website: http://www.sagamorepub.com

Publishes: Nonfiction; *Areas:* Leisure; Nature; Sociology; *Markets:* Adult; Professional

Publishes educational material for the park and recreation industry.

Walch Education
40 Walch Drive
PO Box 658
Portland, ME 04104-0658
Tel: +1 (207) 772-2846
Fax: +1 (207) 772-3105
Email: customerservice@walch.com
Website: http://www.walch.com

Publishes: Nonfiction; *Areas:* Arts; Science; Sociology; *Markets:* Academic

Publishes high school math curriculum and resources aligned to the Common Core and selected state and district standards.

WaterBrook & Multnomah
10807 New Allegiance Drive Suite 500
Colorado Springs, CO 80921
Tel: +1 (719) 590-4999
Fax: +1 (719) 590-8977
Email: info@waterbrookpress.com
Website: http://waterbrookmultnomah.com

Publishes: Fiction; Nonfiction; *Areas:* Adventure; Historical; Mystery; Religious; Romance; Sci-Fi; Spiritual; Suspense; *Markets:* Adult; Children's

Publishes fiction and nonfiction with a Christian perspective. Agented submissions only.

Wave Books
1938 Fairview Avenue East, Suite 201
Seattle, WA 98102
Tel: +1 (206) 676-5337
Email: info@wavepoetry.com
Website: https://www.wavepoetry.com

Publishes: Poetry; *Markets:* Adult; *Treatments:* Contemporary

Contact: Charlie Wright, Publisher

Independent poetry press based in Seattle. Accepts submissions only in response to specific calls for submissions posted on the website (see the submissions page).

Wayne State University Press
4809 Woodward Avenue
Detroit, Michigan 48201-1309
Email: annie.martin@wayne.edu
Website: https://www.wsupress.wayne.edu

Publishes: Nonfiction; *Areas:* Culture; Media; Religious; *Markets:* Academic

Actively acquiring books in African American studies, media studies, fairy-tale studies, Jewish studies, citizenship studies, and regional studies: books about the state of Michigan, the city of Detroit, and the Great Lakes region. Send query by post or by email to appropriate acquisitions editor (see website for details and individual contact details).

We Are One Body Audio Theatre
1100 Ligonier Street
Latrobe, PA 16063
Tel: +1 (844) 392-6228 ext. 5
Email: grettelyndarkey@waob.org
Website: https://waobaudiotheatre.org

Publishes: Fiction; Poetry; Scripts; *Areas:* Adventure; Crime; Drama; Fantasy; Gothic; Historical; Horror; Humour; Literature; Mystery; Religious; Romance; Sci-Fi; Short Stories; Spiritual; Suspense; Theatre; Thrillers; Westerns; *Markets:* Academic; Adult; Children's; Family; Professional; Youth; *Treatments:* Dark; Experimental; Light; Literary; Positive; Satirical

Contact: Grettelyn Darkey

Seeks to build a creative haven for writers, artists, and actors who wish to express truth, beauty, and goodness in their work. To this end, the members of the audio theatre try to create a friendly environment where all are welcome to participate as part of Christ's body, whether as contributors or as listeners.

We believe with J. R. R. Tolkien that "we have come from God, and inevitably the myths woven by us, though they [may] contain error, will also reflect a splintered fragment of the true light, the eternal truth that is with God. Indeed only by myth-making, only by becoming 'sub-creator' and inventing stories, can Man aspire to the state of perfection that he knew before the Fall." We believe that storytelling – as a creative act – is one example of how God created us in his image. By crafting stories that utilize our God-given creative energy, we believe that we join with him in bringing truth, beauty, and goodness to the earth.

In engaging in our work as sub-creators under the great Creator, we use our imaginations and the talents that we have been given to craft works of art that we hope will inspire others to create. We know that the imagination is key to our efforts, and is a great gift from God. Therefore, we strive to create inventive stories that help our listeners to engage with their imaginations, in the hope that their willingness to experience invisible things might help them to a better understanding of the invisible God.

Wesleyan University Press

215 Long Lane
Middletown, CT 06459
Tel: +1 (860) 685-7730
Fax: +1 (860) 685-7712
Email: stamminen@wesleyan.edu
Website: http://www.wesleyan.edu/wespress

Publishes: Nonfiction; Poetry; *Areas:* Culture; Film; Historical; Literature; Music; *Markets:* Academic

Publishes poetry and nonfiction in the areas of dance, music/culture, poetry, and literary studies. See website for submission guidelines.

Willow Creek Press, Inc.

PO Box 147
Minocqua, WI 54548
Tel: +1 (800) 850-9453
Fax: +1 (715) 358-2807
Email: andread@willowcreekpress.com
Website: http://www.willowcreekpress.com

Publishes: Nonfiction; Reference; *Areas:* Cookery; Gardening; How-to; Leisure; Nature; Sport; *Markets:* Adult

Send query with SASE, outline / table of contents, one or two sample chapters, author bio, and indication as to whether the proposal is simultaneously under consideration elsewhere. See website for full details. May consider but will generally not accept personal memoirs, children's books, or MSS dealing with limited regional subject matter.

World Weaver Press

Email: publisher@worldweaverpress.com
Website: http://www.worldweaverpress.com

Publishes: Fiction; *Areas:* Fantasy; Romance; Sci-Fi; Short Stories; *Markets:* Adult

Publishes speculative romance, including Paranormal Romance, Epic Fantasy, Urban Fantasy, Fairy Tale, Hard Science Fiction, Soft Science Fiction, Space Opera, Solarpunk, Steampunk, Dieselpunk, Decopunk, Fantasy Romance, Science Fiction Romance, Paranormal Mystery, and Time Travel Romance. No horror, grimdark, or dystopia. Accepts submissions in specific submission windows only (see website for details). Also publishes anthologies of short stories. See website for current opportunities.

WorthyKids / Ideals

6100 Tower Circle, Suite 210
Franklin, TN 37067
Tel: +1 (615) 932-7600
Email: idealsinfo@worthy-ideals.com
Website: https://www.idealsbooks.com

Publishes: Fiction; Nonfiction; *Areas:* Lifestyle; Religious; *Markets:* Children's

Publishes fiction and nonfiction board books, novelty books, and picture books for children aged 0-8. Subjects include inspiration/faith, patriotism, and holidays, particularly Easter and Christmas; relationships and values; and general fiction. Board book manuscripts should be no longer than 250 words. Picture book manuscripts should be no longer than 800 words. Submit complete ms by post only – no queries or proposals or submissions by email. See website for full submission guidelines.

Yellow Flag Press

Website: https://www.yellowflagpress.com

Publishes: Poetry; *Markets:* Adult; *Treatments:* Literary

Contact: J. Bruce Fuller

Publishes trade paperback books as well as handmade chapbooks and broadsides in limited edition printings. Free open reading period in April, but submissions can be made at other times of the year with a $5 discounted sample chapbook purchase.

YMAA Publication Center, Inc.
PO Box 480
Wolfeboro, NH 03894
Tel: +1 (603) 569-7988
Fax: +1 (603) 569-1889
Website: https://ymaa.com

Publishes: Nonfiction; *Areas:* Health; Medicine; Philosophy; Spiritual; Sport; *Markets:* Adult

Publishes books on martial arts, Eastern philosophy, Chinese medicine, etc.

Zumaya Publications
3209 S. Interstate 35 #1086
Austin, TX 78741
Email: acquisitions@zumayapublications.com
Website: http://www.zumayapublications.com

Publishes: Fiction; Nonfiction; *Areas:* Autobiography; Crime; Fantasy; Gothic; Historical; Horror; Mystery; Romance; Sci-Fi; Short Stories; Thrillers; Westerns; *Markets:* Adult; Children's; Youth; *Treatments:* Mainstream; Niche

Contact: Adrienne Rose

Publishes adult fiction of at least 50,000 words, and juvenile fiction of at least 40,000 words. Send queries by email only, with sample as an attachment, with a brief synopsis up to 1,000 words at its start. See website for full submission guidelines.

UK Publishers

For the most up-to-date listings of these and hundreds of other publishers, visit https://www.firstwriter.com/publishers

*To claim your **free** access to the site, please see the back of this book.*

Ian Allan Publishing Ltd

12 Ethel Street
Birmingham
B2 4BG
Email: enquiries@ianallandirect.co.uk
Website: https://www.ianallanpublishing.com

Publishes: Nonfiction; Reference; *Areas:* Historical; Hobbies; Military; Travel; *Markets:* Adult

Former publisher of nonfiction and reference books relating to transport, now publishes Masonic books and magazine.

Allison & Busby Ltd

12 Fitzroy Mews
London
W1T 6DW
Tel: +44 (0) 20 7580 1080
Fax: +44 (0) 20 7580 1180
Email: susie@allisonandbusby.com
Website: http://www.allisonandbusby.com

Publishes: Fiction; Nonfiction; *Areas:* Autobiography; Biography; Crime; Culture; Fantasy; Historical; Military; Mystery; Sci-Fi; Self-Help; Short Stories; Thrillers; Travel; Women's Interests; *Markets:* Adult; Youth; *Treatments:* Contemporary; Literary

Contact: Susie Dunlop, Publishing Director

Accepts approaches via a literary agent only. No unsolicited MSS or queries from authors.

In field of nonfiction publishes guides for writers. No horror, romance, spirituality, short stories, self-help, poetry or plays.

Alma Books Ltd

3 Castle Yard
Richmond
TW10 6TF
Tel: +44 (0) 20 8940 6917
Fax: +44 (0) 20 8948 5599
Email: info@almabooks.com
Website: http://www.almabooks.com

Publishes: Fiction; Nonfiction; *Areas:* Historical; Literature; *Markets:* Adult; *Treatments:* Contemporary; Literary

Publishes literary fiction and a small number of nonfiction titles with a strong literary or historical connotation. No novellas, short stories, children's books, poetry, academic works, science fiction, horror, or fantasy. Accepts unsolicited MSS by post with synopsis, two sample chapters, and SAE if return of material required. No submissions by email, or submissions from outside the UK. Submissions received from outside the UK will not receive a response.

Alma Classics

3 Castle Yard
Richmond
TW10 6TF
Tel: +44 (0) 20 8940 6917

Fax: +44 (0) 20 8948 5599
Email: info@almabooks.com
Website: http://www.almaclassics.com

Publishes: Fiction; Poetry; Scripts; *Areas:*
Arts; Autobiography; Biography; Literature;
Sociology; Translations; *Markets:* Adult;
Treatments: Literary

Publishes classic European literature.
Welcomes suggestions and ideas for the list,
as well as proposals from translators. Send
proposals by email.

Amber Books Ltd

United House
North Road
London
N7 9DP
Tel: +44 (0) 20 7520 7600
Email: editorial@amberbooks.co.uk
Website: https://www.amberbooks.co.uk

Publishes: Nonfiction; Reference; *Areas:*
Historical; Military; *Markets:* Adult

Publishes illustrated nonfiction in a wide
range of subject areas, particularly military.
No fiction, biography or poetry. Send query
with synopsis, contents lists, author CV, and
one or two sample chapters by post or by
email. Do not send SASE or IRCs or cash.
Response not guaranteed.

Andersen Press Ltd

20 Vauxhall Bridge Road
London
SW1V 2SA
Tel: +44 (0) 20 7840 8701
Email: andersoneditorial@
penguinrandomhouse.co.uk
Website: http://www.andersenpress.co.uk

Publishes: Fiction; *Markets:* Children's

Publishes picture books and longer
children's fiction up to 75,000 words.
Publishes rhyming stories, but no poetry,
adult fiction, nonfiction, or short story
collections. Send query with complete ms for
picture books, or synopsis and first three
chapters by post only, with SAE if return of
work required. See website for full
guidelines.

Anness Publishing Ltd

Algores Way
Wisbech
Cambridgeshire
PE13 2TQ
Email: info@anness.com
Website: http://www.aquamarinebooks.com

Publishes: Nonfiction; Poetry; Reference;
Areas: Arts; Cookery; Crafts; Design;
Gardening; Health; Historical; Hobbies;
Leisure; Lifestyle; Military; Music; Nature;
New Age; Photography; Religious; Science;
Spiritual; Sport; Travel; *Markets:* Adult;
Children's

Describes itself as one of the largest
independent book publishers in the UK.

Appletree Press Ltd

Roycroft House
164 Malone Road
Belfast
BT9 5LL
Tel: +44 (0) 28 90 243074
Fax: +44 (0) 28 90 246756
Email: editorial@appletree.ie
Website: http://www.appletree.ie

Publishes: Nonfiction; *Markets:* Adult

Send query with synopsis, descriptive
chapter list, and two or three chapters by
email. Publishes small-format gift books and
general nonfiction books of Irish and
Scottish interest. No unsolicited MSS.

Arc Publications

Nanholme Mill
Shaw Wood Road
Todmorden
Lancs
OL14 6DA
Tel: +44 (0) 1706 812338
Email: info@arcpublications.co.uk
Website: http://www.arcpublications.co.uk/
submissions

Publishes: Poetry; *Areas:* Music;
Translations; *Markets:* Adult; *Treatments:*
Contemporary

Send 16-24 poems by email as a Word / PDF
attachment, maximum one poem per page,
during December or June only. Submissions

from outside the UK and Ireland should be sent to specific address for international submissions, available on website. Cover letter should include short bio and details of the contemporary poets you read. See website for full guidelines.

Aureus Publishing Limited

Email: info@aureus.co.uk
Website: http://www.aureus.co.uk

Publishes: Nonfiction; *Areas:* Biography; Music; Sport; *Markets:* Academic; Adult

Publishes books on music, sport, biography and education.

Aurora Metro Press

67 Grove Avenue
Twickenham
TW1 4HX
Tel: +44 (0) 20 3261 0000
Email: submissions@aurorametro.com
Website: http://www.aurorametro.com

Publishes: Fiction; Nonfiction; Scripts; *Areas:* Arts; Biography; Cookery; Culture; Drama; Film; Humour; Literature; Music; Short Stories; Theatre; Translations; Women's Interests; *Markets:* Adult; Children's; Youth

Contact: Neil Gregory (Submissions Manager)

Publishes fiction, plays/theatre texts, and both general and specialist nonfiction books across theatre, film, music, literature, and popular culture. Send synopsis and complete ms by email only. For play submissions, if a production is scheduled then the full script must be sent at least 6 weeks before opening night.

The Authority Guides

SRA Books
Unit 3, Spike Island
133 Cumberland Road
Bristol
BS1 6UX
Tel: +44 (0) 1789 761345
Website: http://authorityguides.co.uk

Publishes: Nonfiction; *Areas:* Business; *Markets:* Professional

Publishes pocket-sized business books for entrepreneurs and business professionals.

Award Publications Limited

The Old Riding School
The Welbeck Estate
Worksop
Nottinghamshire
S80 3LR
Tel: +44 (0) 1909 478170
Fax: +44 (0) 1909 484632
Email: info@awardpublications.co.uk
Website: http://www.
awardpublications.co.uk

Publishes: Fiction; Nonfiction; Reference; *Markets:* Children's

Publishes children's fiction, nonfiction, and reference.

BakerSteele Publishing

P O Box 203
West Malling
ME19 6TQ
Email: mail@bakersteele.co.uk
Website: http://www.bakersteele.com

Publishes: Fiction; *Areas:* Crime; Historical; Military; *Markets:* Adult; Youth

Contact: Duncan Robinson

Ebook publishing only, preferably previously published works or new works. Fiction only. Will accept short story collections around a theme. Submissions by email ONLY, consisting of first three chapters ONLY withstood of whole book. May refer author to an editor of the manuscript needs help, at author's expense. Prefer authors without agents.

Barrington Stoke

18 Walker Street
Edinburgh
EH3 7LP
Tel: +44 (0) 131 225 4113
Fax: +44 (0) 131 225 4140
Email: info@barringtonstoke.co.uk
Website: http://www.barringtonstoke.co.uk

Publishes: Fiction; Nonfiction; Reference; *Markets:* Children's; Professional

Commissions books via literary agents only. No unsolicited material. Publishes books for "reluctant, dyslexic, disenchanted and under-confident" readers and their teachers.

Beercott Books
77 Welsh Road West
Southam
Warwickshire
Email: info@beercottbooks.co.uk
Website: https://beercottbooks.co.uk

Publishes: Reference; Scripts; *Areas:* Crafts; Theatre; *Markets:* Family; Professional

Contact: Simon Lucas

Small independent publisher specialising in craft and theatre related publications.

Bernard Babani (publishing) Ltd
The Grampians
Shepherds Bush Road
London
W6 7NF
Email: enquiries@babanibooks.com
Website: http://www.babanibooks.com

Publishes: Nonfiction; *Areas:* Technology; *Markets:* Adult

Publishes books on robotics, computing, and electronics. Always interested in hearing from potential authors. Send query by email with synopsis and details of your qualifications for writing on the topic.

Birlinn Ltd
West Newington House
10 Newington Road
Edinburgh
EH9 1QS
Tel: +44 (0) 131 668 4371
Fax: +44 (0) 131 668 4466
Email: info@birlinn.co.uk
Website: http://www.birlinn.co.uk

Publishes: Fiction; Nonfiction; Poetry; Reference; *Areas:* Adventure; Architecture; Arts; Autobiography; Biography; Culture; Current Affairs; Finance; Historical;

Humour; Legal; Medicine; Military; Nature; Politics; Sociology; Sport; Travel; *Markets:* Adult; Children's

Focuses on Scottish material: local, military, and Highland history; humour, adventure; reference, guidebooks, and folklore. Not currently accepting romantic fiction, science fiction, or short stories. Send query by post with SAE, synopsis, three sample chapters, and explanation of why you have chosen this publisher. No submissions by fax, email, or on disk. See website for full details.

Black & White Publishing Ltd
Nautical House
104 Commercial Street
Edinburgh
EH6 6NF
Tel: +44 (0) 01316 254500
Email: mail@blackandwhitepublishing.com
Website: http://www.
blackandwhitepublishing.com

Publishes: Fiction; Nonfiction; *Areas:* Autobiography; Biography; Cookery; Crime; Historical; Humour; Lifestyle; Psychology; Romance; Sport; Thrillers; Women's Interests; *Markets:* Academic; Adult; Children's; Youth; *Treatments:* Commercial; Contemporary; Literary

Contact: Campbell Brown; Alison McBride

Publisher of general fiction and nonfiction. See website for an idea of the kind of books normally published, and to submit via online submission system. No poetry, short stories, or work in languages other than English.

Black Ace Books
PO Box 7547
Perth
PH2 1AU
Tel: +44 (0) 1821 642822
Fax: +44 (0) 1821 642101
Website: http://blackace.co.uk

Publishes: Fiction; Nonfiction; *Areas:* Biography; Historical; Philosophy; Psychology; Short Stories; *Markets:* Adult

Not accepting submissions as at May 2019. Check website for current status.

Publishes Scottish and general fiction, as well as the areas of nonfiction given above. No Children's, poetry, religion, DIY, or cookery.

Black Coffey Publishing

23 Cromwell rd
Warley
Brentwood
Essex
CM14 5DT
Email: Paul@blackcoffeypublishing.com
Website: http://www.
blackcoffeypublishing.com

Publishes: Fiction; *Areas:* Adventure; Crime; Drama; Fantasy; Humour; Mystery; Sci-Fi; Short Stories; Suspense; Thrillers; Westerns; *Markets:* Adult; Family; Youth; *Treatments:* Commercial; Contemporary; Popular; Progressive; Satirical

Contact: Paul Coffey

Not accepting submissions as at January 2019. Check website for current status.

Specialist digital publisher actively looking for short stories in our 2012 release schedule. We scheduled to publish humorous short story collections on:

+ 'Office life'
+ 'Growing up in the 1970s'
+ 'Leaving home for the first time'

Submisions can be made via our website.

John Blake Publishing

Tel: +44 (0) 20 3770 8888
Email: hello@blake.co.uk
Website: https://johnblakebooks.com

Publishes: Fiction; Nonfiction; *Areas:* Autobiography; Biography; Business; Cookery; Crime; Entertainment; Film; Health; Historical; Humour; Legal; Military; Music; Nature; Politics; Science; Self-Help; Sport; Travel; TV; *Markets:* Adult; *Treatments:* Commercial; Mainstream; Popular

Send query by email with synopsis and no more than three sample chapters. No submissions by post.

Blink Publishing

2.08 The Plaza
535 Kings Road
London
SW10 0SZ
Tel: +44 (0) 20 3770 8888
Email: info@blinkpublishing.co.uk
Website: http://www.blinkpublishing.co.uk

Publishes: Nonfiction; *Areas:* Autobiography; Cookery; Crime; Culture; Historical; Humour; Lifestyle; Military; Music; Sport; Travel; *Markets:* Adult; *Treatments:* Popular

Publishes illustrated and non-illustrated adult nonfiction. No fiction. Send queries by email with one-page synopsis and first three chapters.

Bloodaxe Books Ltd

Eastburn
South Park
Hexham
Northumberland
NE46 1BS
Tel: +44 (0) 01434 611581
Email: editor@bloodaxebooks.com
Website: http://www.bloodaxebooks.com

Publishes: Poetry; *Markets:* Adult

Contact: Neil Astley, Managing/Editorial Director

Submit poetry only if you have a track record of publication in magazines. If so, send sample of up to a dozen poems with SAE, or email address for response if outside the UK. No submissions by email or on disk. Poems from the UK sent without return postage will be recycled unread; submissions by email will be deleted unread. No longer accepting poets who have already published a full-length collection with another publisher. See website for full details.

Bloomsbury Spark

Email: BloomsburySparkUK@
bloomsbury.com
Website: http://www.bloomsbury.com/spark

Publishes: Fiction; *Areas:* Historical; Mystery; Romance; Sci-Fi; Thrillers;

Markets: Children's; Youth; *Treatments:* Contemporary

Global, digital imprint from a major international publisher. Publishes ebooks for teen, young adult, and new adult readers. Willing to consider all genres, including romance, contemporary, dystopian, paranormal, sci-fi, mystery, and thrillers. Accepts unsolicited mss between 25,000 and 60,000 words. Submit by email (see website for specific email addresses for different geographic locations) along with query and author bio. See website for full details.

Blue Guides Limited

Winchester House
Dean Gate Avenue
Taunton
Somerset
TA1 2UH
Email: editorial@blueguides.com
Website: http://blueguides.com

Publishes: Nonfiction; *Areas:* Culture; Travel; *Markets:* Adult

Publishes travel guides. Always on the lookout for new authors. Contact by email in first instance, giving an indication of your areas of interest.

Blue Trident Books

34 New House
Hatton Garden
London
EC1N 8JY
Email: btbeditors@gmail.com
Website: https://bluetridentbooks.yolasite.com/

Publishes: Fiction; *Areas:* Adventure; Drama; Fantasy; Historical; Humour; Mystery; Romance; Sci-Fi; Suspense; Thrillers; *Markets:* Adult; Children's; Youth; *Treatments:* Commercial; Contemporary; Light; Literary; Mainstream; Popular; Positive; Traditional

Contact: Melanie Amann

We are an independent publisher based in Salisbury, South West of England. We specialise in a wide range of quality fiction including Children's, YA and Adult novels.

Our commitment to help our authors achieve success extends to both new and previously published authors.

As an independent publisher, we strive to publish only the best quality works. We constantly seek new and original voices, providing exclusive attention to our authors with a bespoke marketing strategy for each piece of work. Our commitment is to give each publication its every chance for success. With our passion for high-quality books, our dedicated team and personalised approach, we believe that we will forge a long lasting relationship with our authors.

Whether you are a first time author, or an existing author looking for a more personalised service, we would love to consider your work for publication. To see our information, guidelines and to submit your work to us, please visit the website.

Bodleian Library Publishing

Broad Street
Oxford
OX1 3BG
Tel: +44 (0) 1865 283850
Email: publishing@bodleian.ox.ac.uk
Website: https://www.bodleianshop.co.uk/bodleianlibrarypublishing

Publishes: Nonfiction; *Areas:* Arts; Historical; Literature; *Markets:* Academic; Adult

Publishes books relating to the library collections only.

bookouture

23 Sussex Road
Uxbridge
UB10 8PN
Email: oliver@bookouture.com
Website: http://www.bookouture.com

Publishes: Fiction; Nonfiction; *Areas:* Crime; Historical; Psychology; Romance; Suspense; Thrillers; Women's Interests; *Markets:* Adult; *Treatments:* Commercial; Contemporary

Contact: Oliver Rhodes

Publishes commercial fiction and some text-lead nonfiction.

For most authors outside the bestseller lists, traditional publishers simply aren't adding enough value to justify low royalty rates. And because authors aren't all experts in editing, design, or marketing, self-publishing doesn't get the most out of their books or time. Digital publishing offers incredible opportunities to connect with readers all over the world – but finding the help you need to make the most of them can be tricky.

That's why we bring both big publisher experience and small team creativity. We genuinely understand and invest in brands – developing long-term strategies, marketing plans and websites for each of our authors.

And we work with the most brilliant editorial, design and marketing professionals in the business to make sure that everything we do is perfectly tailored to you and ridiculously good.

Combine all of that with an incredible 45% royalty rate we think we're simply the perfect combination of high returns and inspirational publishing.

Nicholas Brealey Publishing

Hodder & Stoughton Ltd.
Carmelite House
50 Victoria Embankment
London
EC4Y 0DZ
Tel: +44 (0) 20 3122 6777
Email: educationenquiries@hodder.co.uk
Website: https://www.hodder.co.uk

Publishes: Nonfiction; *Areas:* Business; Culture; Finance; Psychology; Self-Help; Travel; *Markets:* Adult; Professional

Not accepting submissions as at March 2018.

Bristol University Press

1-9 Old Park Hill
Bristol
BS2 8BB
Tel: +44 (0) 1179 545940
Email: pp-info@bristol.ac.uk
Website: http://bristoluniversitypress.co.uk

Publishes: Nonfiction; *Areas:* Business; Current Affairs; Finance; Legal; Nature; Politics; Sociology; *Markets:* Academic

Publishes scholarship and education in the social sciences. Send query with proposal by email.

Candy Jar Books

Mackintosh House
136 Newport Road
Cardiff
CF24 1DJ
Tel: +44 (0) 29 2115 7202
Email: shaun@candyjarbooks.co.uk
Website: http://www.candyjarbooks.co.uk

Publishes: Fiction; Nonfiction; *Areas:* Biography; Fantasy; Historical; Military; Sci-Fi; TV; *Markets:* Adult; Children's; Youth

Contact: Shaun Russell (Head of Publishing)

Award-winning independent book publisher, publishing a wide variety of books, from nonfiction, general fiction and children's, through to a range of cult TV books. Submit by post or using online submission form. No children's picture books. See website for full guidelines.

Canongate Books

14 High Street
Edinburgh
EH1 1TE
Tel: +44 (0) 1315 575111
Email: support@canongate.co.uk
Website: http://www.canongate.net

Publishes: Fiction; Nonfiction; *Areas:* Autobiography; Biography; Culture; Historical; Humour; Politics; Science; Translations; Travel; *Markets:* Adult; *Treatments:* Literary

Publisher of a wide range of literary fiction and nonfiction, with a traditionally Scottish slant but becoming increasingly international. Publishes fiction in translation under its international imprint. No children's books, poetry, or drama. Send synopsis with three sample chapters and info about yourself. No submissions by fax, email or on disk.

Canopus Publishing Ltd
15 Nelson Parade
Bedminster
Bristol
BS3 4HY
Tel: +44 (0) 7970 153217
Email: robin@canopusbooks.com
Website: http://www.canopusbooks.com

Publishes: Nonfiction; *Areas:* Science;
Technology; *Markets:* Academic; Adult;
Treatments: Popular

Contact: Robin Rees

Welcomes book proposals for both academic
and popular branches of aerospace and
astronomy. Send query by email with author
bio, two-page summary outlining concept,
coverage, and readership level. See website
for more details.

Carcanet Press Ltd
4th Floor
Alliance House
Cross Street
Manchester
M2 7AP
Tel: +44 (0) 161 834 8730
Fax: +44 (0) 161 832 0084
Email: info@carcanet.co.uk
Website: http://www.carcanet.co.uk

Publishes: Nonfiction; Poetry; *Areas:*
Biography; Literature; Translations;
Markets: Academic; Adult; *Treatments:*
Literary

Award-winning small press, publishing
mainly poetry and academic material.
Authors should familiarise themselves with
the publisher's list, then, if appropriate,
submit 6-10 pages of poetry or translations,
with SAE. For other projects, send a full
synopsis and covering letter, with sample
pages, having first ascertained from the
website that the kind of book proposed is
suitable. No phone calls. No short stories,
childrens prose/poetry or non-poetry related
titles.

Carlton Publishing Group
20 Mortimer Street
London
W1T 3JW

Tel: +44 (0) 20 7612 0400
Fax: +44 (0) 20 7612 0401
Email: submissions@carltonbooks.co.uk
Website: http://www.carltonbooks.co.uk

Publishes: Nonfiction; Reference; *Areas:*
Architecture; Arts; Beauty and Fashion;
Biography; Culture; Design; Entertainment;
Film; Historical; Humour; Music; Sport;
Markets: Adult; Children's; *Treatments:*
Commercial; Mainstream; Popular

Publishes illustrated reference, sport,
entertainment and children's books.
Synopses and ideas for suitable books are
welcomed, but no unsolicited MSS,
academic, fiction, or poetry. Send query by
email only with short synopsis, author bio,
market info, and up to two chapters up to a
maximum of 20 pages. See website for full
guidelines.

Cengage Learning
Cheriton House
North Way
Andover
SP10 5BE
Tel: +44 (0)1264 332424
Fax: +44 (0)1264 342745
Email: EMEAHEPublishing@cengage.com
Website: http://www.cengage.co.uk

Publishes: Nonfiction; *Markets:* Academic

Welcomes unsolicited material aimed at
students. Send query by email in first
instance. See website for full guidelines.

Chapman Publishing
4 Broughton Place
Edinburgh
EH1 3RX
Tel: +44 (0) 131 557 2207
Email: chapman-pub@blueyonder.co.uk
Website: http://www.chapman-pub.co.uk

Publishes: Fiction; Poetry; Scripts; *Areas:*
Drama; Short Stories; *Markets:* Adult;
Treatments: Literary

Contact: Joy Hendry

**Note: No new books being undertaken as
at April 2017. Check website for current
status.**

Publishes one or two books of short stories, drama, and (mainly) poetry by established and rising Scottish writers per year. No novels. Only considers writers who have previously been published in the press's magazine (see entry in magazines database). Only publishes plays that have been previously performed. No unsolicited MSS.

Cicerone Press

2 Police Square
Milnthorpe
Cumbria
LA7 7PY
Tel: +44 (0) 1539 562069
Email: info@cicerone.co.uk
Website: http://www.cicerone.co.uk

Publishes: Nonfiction; Reference; *Areas:* Hobbies; Leisure; Travel; *Markets:* Adult

Considers synopses and ideas. Publishes guidebooks for outdoor enthusiasts. No poetry, fiction, or unsolicited MSS.

James Clarke & Co.

PO Box 60
Cambridge
CB1 2NT
Tel: +44 (0) 1223 366951
Fax: +44 (0) 1223 366951
Email: publishing@jamesclarke.co.uk
Website: http://www.jamesclarke.co

Publishes: Nonfiction; Reference; *Areas:* Religious; *Markets:* Academic

Publishes nonfiction and reference for the academic market on mainly theological subject matter. Download new book proposal form from website and return by post, fax, or email. See website for full guidelines.

Classical Comics Limited

PO Box 177
Ludlow
SY8 9DL
Tel: +44 (0) 845 812 3000
Fax: +44 (0) 845 812 3005
Email: info@classicalcomics.com
Website: http://www.classicalcomics.com

Publishes: Fiction; *Areas:* Literature; *Markets:* Children's

Contact: Gary Bryant (Managing Director); Jo Wheeler (Creative Director)

Publishes graphic novel adaptations of classical literature.

Co & Bear Productions

63 Edith Grove
London
SW10 0LB
Email: info@cobear.co.uk
Website: http://www.scriptumeditions.co.uk

Publishes: Nonfiction; *Areas:* Arts; Beauty and Fashion; Design; Lifestyle; Nature; Photography; *Markets:* Adult

Publishes illustrated books on interior design, lifestyle, fashion and photography, botanical art, natural history and exploration.

Colin Smythe Ltd

38 Mill Lane
Gerrards Cross
Buckinghamshire
SL9 8BA
Tel: +44 (0) 1753 886000
Fax: +44 (0) 1753 886469
Email: info@colinsmythe.co.uk
Website: http://www.colinsmythe.co.uk

Publishes: Fiction; Nonfiction; Poetry; Scripts; *Areas:* Biography; Criticism; Drama; Fantasy; Historical; Hobbies; Literature; Sci-Fi; Theatre; *Markets:* Adult

Contact: Colin Smythe

Publishes fiction, nonfiction, drama, and poetry. Particular interest in Irish literature. No unsolicited MSS.

Colourpoint Educational

Colourpoint House
Jubilee Business Park
21 Jubilee Road
Newtownards
Northern Ireland
BT23 4YH
Tel: +44 (0) 28 9182 0505
Email: wesley@colourpoint.co.uk
Website: http://www.colourpoint.co.uk

Publishes: Nonfiction; *Areas:* Business; Design; Health; Historical; Legal; Politics;

Religious; Science; Technology; *Markets:* Academic

Contact: Dr Wesley Johnston

Provides textbooks, ebooks and digital resources for Northern Ireland students at Key Stage 3 level, and the CCEA revised specification at GCSE and AS/A2/A-level.

Comma Press
Studio 510a, 5th Floor
Hope Mill
113 Pollard Street
Manchester
M4 7JA
Tel: +44 (0) 7792 564747
Email: info@commapress.co.uk
Website: http://commapress.co.uk

Publishes: Fiction; *Areas:* Short Stories; *Markets:* Adult

Short story publisher aiming to put the short story at the heart of contemporary narrative culture. Stories should be between 1,500 and 8,000 words. No micro-fiction or novellas. See website for full submission guidelines.

Council for British Archaeology (CBA) Publishing
Council for British Archaeology
Beatrice de Cardi House
66 Bootham
York
YO30 7BZ
Tel: +44 (0) 1904 671417
Fax: +44 (0) 1904 671384
Email: webenquiry@archaeologyUK.org
Website: http://new.archaeologyuk.org/

Publishes: Nonfiction; *Areas:* Archaeology; *Markets:* Academic

Publisher of academic books on archaeology. Query by telephone in first instance.

Countryside Books
35 Kingfisher Court
Hambridge Road
Newbury
Berkshire
RG14 5SJ

Tel: +44 (0) 1635 43816
Fax: +44 (0) 1635 551004
Email: info@countrysidebooks.co.uk
Website: http://www.countrysidebooks.co.uk

Publishes: Nonfiction; *Areas:* Architecture; Historical; Leisure; Lifestyle; Military; Photography; Travel; *Markets:* Adult

Publishes nonfiction only, mostly regional books relating to specific English counties. Covers topics such as local history, walks, photography, dialect, genealogy, military and aviation, and some transport; but not interested in natural history books or personal memories. No fiction or poetry.

Cressrelles Publishing Co. Ltd
10 Station Road Industrial Estate
Colwall
Malvern
WR13 6RN
Tel: +44 (0) 1684 540154
Fax: +44 (0) 1684 540154
Email: simon@cressrelles.co.uk
Website: http://www.cressrelles.co.uk

Publishes: Nonfiction; Scripts; *Areas:* Drama; *Markets:* Academic; Adult

Contact: Simon Smith

Welcomes submissions. Publishes plays, theatre and drama textbooks, and local interest books. Accepts scripts by post or by email.

Crown House Publishing
Submissions
Crown Buildings
Bancyfelin
Carmarthen
SA33 5ND
Tel: +44 (0) 1267 211345
Fax: +44 (0) 1267 211882
Email: submissions@crownhouse.co.uk
Website: http://www.crownhouse.co.uk

Publishes: Nonfiction; *Areas:* Business; Health; Humour; Psychology; Self-Help; Spiritual; *Markets:* Academic; Adult; Children's; *Treatments:* Popular

Publishes books on Mind Body Spirit; Business Training and Development; Education

Psychotherapy; Personal Growth; and Health and Wellbeing. Send email up to 300 words only describing your ideas in the first instance.

Crux Publishing

Email: hello@cruxpublishing.co.uk
Website: http://cruxpublishing.co.uk

Publishes: Fiction; Nonfiction; *Markets:* Adult

Founded to help authors publish (or republish) nonfiction works of the highest quality. Will also consider fiction if truly unique. Pursues a digital-first approach. See website for submission guidelines and more information.

David Fickling Books

31 Beaumont Street
Oxford
OX1 2NP
Tel: +44 (0) 1865 339000
Website: http://www.
davidficklingbooks.com

Publishes: Fiction; Poetry; *Markets:* Children's; Youth

Publishes picture books, fiction for children and young adults, and poetry. Generally accepts submissions through literary agents only, except during specific open submission competitions. See website for details.

DB Publishing

29 Clarence Road
Attenborough
Nottingham
NG9 5HY
Tel: +44 (0) 1332 384235
Fax: +44 (0) 1332 292755
Email: submissions@jmdmedia.co.uk
Website: http://www.dbpublishing.co.uk

Publishes: Fiction; Nonfiction; *Areas:* Autobiography; Biography; Crime; Health; Historical; Sociology; Sport; Travel; *Markets:* Adult

Contact: Steve Caron

Considers all types of books, but focuses on local interest, sport, biography,

autobiography and social history. Approach by email or phone – no submissions by post. See website for full guidelines.

De Montfort Literature

20-22 Wenlock Road
London
N1 7GU
Tel: +44 (0) 20 7205 2881
Email: info@demontfortliterature.com
Website: https://www.
demontfortliterature.com

Publishes: Fiction; *Markets:* Adult; Children's; Youth

Publisher founded by a hedge fund that successfully used data to predict (amongst other things) the bottom of the market in 2002, the 2008 crash, and Brexit. Now seeks to apply the same scientific approach to a new model of publishing based on predicting an author's chances of success. Where they find likely candidates, they will invest in the author by paying them an annual salary to become a full-time novelist. Applicants do not need to have already written a novel. The application process includes a psychometric test, an opportunity to discuss ideas, and a final interview. See website for full details.

Dedalus Ltd

Langford Lodge
St Judith's Lane
Sawtry
PE28 5XE
Tel: +44 (0) 1487 832382
Fax: +44 (0) 1487 832382
Email: info@dedalusbooks.com
Website: http://www.dedalusbooks.com

Publishes: Fiction; *Areas:* Literature; Translations; *Markets:* Adult; *Treatments:* Contemporary; Literary

Send query letter describing yourself along with SAE, synopsis, three sample chapters, and explanation of why you think this publisher in particular is right for you – essential to be familiar with and have read other books on this publisher's list before submitting, as most material received is entirely inappropriate. Welcomes submissions of suitable original fiction and is particularly interested in intellectually clever and unusual fiction, however undertakes only between one and three new projects a year. No email or disk submissions, or collections of short stories by unknown authors. Novels should be over 40,000 words – ideally over 50,000. Most books are translations.

Discovery Walking Guides Ltd

Email: ask.discovery@ntlworld.com
Website: http://www.dwgwalking.co.uk

Publishes: Nonfiction; *Areas:* Travel; *Markets:* Adult

Publishes walking guidebooks and maps. Welcomes proposals for new projects. Send query by email. No attachments.

Dodo Ink

Email: sam@dodoink.com
Website: http://www.dodoink.com

Publishes: Fiction; *Markets:* Adult; *Treatments:* Literary

Contact: Sam Mills

Independent UK publisher aiming to publish three novels per year, in paperback and digital formats. Publishes risk-taking, imaginative novels, that don't fall into easy marketing categories. Closed to submissions as at June 2017.

Dovecote Press

Stanbridge
Wimborne Minster
Dorset
BH21 4JD
Tel: +44 (0) 1258 840549
Email: online@dovecotepress.com
Website: http://www.dovecotepress.com

Publishes: Nonfiction; *Areas:* Architecture; Biography; Historical; Nature; *Markets:* Adult

Contact: David Burnett

Publishes books on architecture, local history, and natural history.

Dref Wen

28 Church Road
Whitchurch
Cardiff
CF14 2EA
Tel: +44 (0) 2920 617860
Fax: +44 (0) 2920 610507
Email: post@drefwen.com
Website: http://www.drefwen.com

Publishes: Fiction; Nonfiction; *Areas:* Autobiography; Travel; *Markets:* Academic; Adult; Children's

Publishes bilingual and Welsh language books for children, as well as Welsh and English educational books for those learning Welsh. Also moving into adult publishing, in particular autobiographies of Welsh personalities.

Duckworth Publishers

30 Calvin Street
London
E1 6NW
Tel: +44 (0) 20 7490 7300
Email: info@duckworth-publishers.co.uk
Website: http://www.ducknet.co.uk

Publishes: Fiction; Nonfiction; *Areas:* Arts; Autobiography; Biography; Crime; Criticism; Current Affairs; Design; Drama; Film; Finance; Historical; Horror; Humour; Literature; Music; Nature; Philosophy; Photography; Politics; Religious; Science; Sci-Fi; Sociology; Sport; Theatre; Thrillers; Translations; Travel; *Markets:* Adult; Children's; *Treatments:* Commercial; Literary

Britain's oldest active independent trade publisher. Publishes nonfiction; literary fiction; horrors and thrillers; and children's books. Advises writers to seek representation by a literary agent, but will accept proposals directly by email. Include full synopsis, author CV, and three sample chapters. See website for full guidelines.

Dunedin Academic Press Ltd

Hudson House
8 Albany Street
Edinburgh
EH1 3QB

LONDON OFICE:
352 Cromwell Tower,
Barbican,
London
EC2Y 8NB
Tel: +44 (0) 1314 732397
Fax: +44 (0) 1250 770088
Email: mail@dunedinacademicpress.co.uk
Website: http://www.
dunedinacademicpress.co.uk

Publishes: Nonfiction; *Areas:* Anthropology;
Biography; Current Affairs; Finance; Health;
Historical; Legal; Medicine; Music; Nature;
Philosophy; Religious; Science; Sociology;
Markets: Academic; Professional

Publishes academic works, mainly at levels
from first year undergraduate to postgraduate
and research levels.

Edinburgh University Press
The Tun – Holyrood Road
12 (2f) Jackson's Entry
Edinburgh
EH8 8PJ
Tel: +44 (0) 1316 504218
Fax: +44 (0) 1316 503286
Email: editorial@cup.ed.ac.uk
Website: http://www.euppublishing.com

Publishes: Nonfiction; Reference; *Areas:*
Archaeology; Architecture; Culture; Film;
Historical; Legal; Literature; Media;
Philosophy; Politics; Religious; Science;
Sociology; *Markets:* Academic

Publishes academic and scholarly nonfiction
and reference across the humanities and
social sciences.

The Emma Press Ltd
Email: queries@theemmapress.com
Website: http://theemmapress.com

Publishes: Fiction; Poetry; *Areas:* Short
Stories; *Markets:* Adult; Children's

Contact: Emma Wright

Publishes themed anthologies of poetry and
short stories. See website for themes of
current calls for submissions.

Encyclopedia Britannica (UK) Ltd
2nd Floor, Unity Wharf
Mill Street
London
SE1 2BH
Tel: +44 (0) 20 7500 7800
Fax: +44 (0) 20 7500 7878
Email: enquiries@britannica.co.uk
Website: https://britannica.co.uk

Publishes: Nonfiction; Reference; *Markets:*
Academic; Adult; Family

Global digital educational publisher,
publishing information and instructional
products used in schools, universities,
homes, libraries and workplaces throughout
the world.

Enitharmon Press
10 Bury Place
London
WC1A 2JL
Tel: +44 (0) 20 7430 0844
Email: info@enitharmon.co.uk
Website: http://www.enitharmon.co.uk

Publishes: Fiction; Poetry; *Areas:* Arts;
Criticism; Photography; *Markets:* Adult;
Treatments: Literary

One of Britain's leading literary publishers,
specialising in poetry and in high-quality
artists' books and original prints. It is
divided into two companies: the press, which
publishes poetry and general literature in
small-format volumes and anthologies, and
the editions, which produces de luxe artists'
books in the tradition of the livre d'artiste.
No unsolicited mss.

Everything With Words
Email: info@everythingwithwords.com
Website: http://www.
everythingwithwords.com

Publishes: Fiction; *Markets:* Children's;
Youth

Publisher of fiction for children aged 7 to
young adult. Completed works should be at
least 25,000 words for younger children, or
40,000 words for children aged ten and over.
Open to submissions from both authors and

illustrators, but no previously self-published works. Send query by email with brief summary, author bio, and three chapters or first 50 pages. See website for full guidelines.

Exley Publications

16 Chalk Hill
Watford
WD19 4BG
Tel: +44 (0) 1923 474480
Website: https://www.helenexley.com

Publishes: Nonfiction; *Markets:* Adult; *Treatments:* Popular

Publishes gift books.

Faber & Faber Ltd

Bloomsbury House
74-77 Great Russell Street
London
WC1B 3DA
Tel: +44 (0) 20 7927 3800
Fax: +44 (0) 20 7927 3801
Website: http://www.faber.co.uk

Publishes: Fiction; Nonfiction; Poetry; Scripts; *Areas:* Biography; Drama; Film; Music; Politics; Theatre; *Markets:* Adult; Children's

Originally published poetry and plays but has expanded into other areas. Has published some of the most prominent writers of the twentieth century, including several poet laureates. No longer accepting unsolicited MSS in any areas other than poetry. Submit 6 poems in first instance, with adequate return postage. Submissions of material other than poetry will neither be read nor returned. No submissions by email, fax, or on disk.

Faculty of 1000 Ltd

Middlesex House,
34-42 Cleveland Street,
London W1T 4LB
Email: info@f1000.com
Website: https://f1000.com

Publishes: Nonfiction; *Areas:* Science; *Markets:* Academic

Aims to transform the way science is communicated, by providing innovative solutions to rethink how research is shared, used and reused.

Findhorn Press Ltd

Delft Cottage
Dyke
Forres
IV36 2TF
Tel: +44 (0) 1309 690582
Email: submissions@findhornpress.com
Website: http://www.findhornpress.com

Publishes: Nonfiction; *Areas:* Health; New Age; Spiritual; *Markets:* Adult

Publishes books on mind, body, spirit, New Age and healing. Approach by email only. Send 1-2 page synopsis, word count, number of illustrations, table of contents, page describing intended readership, brief personal bio including any previous publications, and details on ways you can help promote your book. See website for more information.

Firefly

D.20
Cardiff Metropolitan University
Cyncoed Road
Cyncoed
Cardiff
CF23 6XD
Tel: +44 (0) 2920 218611
Email: janet.thomas@fireflypress.co.uk
Website: http://fireflypress.co.uk

Publishes: Fiction; *Markets:* Children's; Youth

Contact: Janet Thomas

Closed to submissions as at May 2019. Check website for current status.

Publishes fiction and nonfiction for children and young adults aged 5-19. Open to email or postal queries to nonfiction. Open to fiction submissions for September only. Not currently publishing any picture books or colour illustrated book for any age group.

Fisherton Press

Email: general@fishertonpress.co.uk
Website: http://fishertonpress.co.uk

Publishes: Fiction; *Markets:* Children's

Contact: Eleanor Levenson

**Closed to submissions as at April 2018.
Check website for current status.**

Aims to publish books for children that
adults will also enjoy reading, whether for
the first time or the hundredth. Send query
with ideas or fully written or illustrated texts
with short bio, by email.

Fitzrovia Press Limited

42 Monington Road
Glastonbury
Somerset
BA6 8HF
Tel: +44 (0) 20 7380 0749
Email: rprime@fitzroviapress.co.uk
Website: http://www.fitzroviapress.com

Publishes: Fiction; Nonfiction; *Areas:*
Philosophy; Spiritual; *Markets:* Adult

Contact: Ranchor Prime

Publishes fiction and nonfiction on
Hinduism, spirituality, and Eastern
philosophy. No unsolicited mss. Send query
with outline and sample chapter.

Flame Tree Publishing

6 Melbray Mews
London
SW6 3NS
Tel: +44 (0) 20 7751 9650
Fax: +44 (0) 20 7751 9651
Email: info@flametreepublishing.com
Website: http://www.
flametreepublishing.com

Publishes: Nonfiction; *Areas:* Cookery;
Culture; Lifestyle; Music; *Markets:* Adult;
Treatments: Popular

Publihses practical cookbooks, music,
popular culture and lifestyle books. Very
rarely accepts unsolicited mss or book
proposals.

Fleming Publications

134 Renfrew Street
Glasgow
G3 6ST
Email: info@ettadunn.com
Website: http://www.
flemingpublications.com

Publishes: Fiction; Nonfiction; Poetry;
Areas: Biography; Historical; Photography;
Self-Help; *Markets:* Adult

Contact: Etta Dunn

Publishes nonfiction, fiction, and poetry for
"mindful individuals".

Floris Books

2a Robertson Avenue
Edinburgh
EH11 1PZ
Tel: +44 (0) 1313 372372
Email: floris@florisbooks.co.uk
Website: http://www.florisbooks.co.uk

Publishes: Fiction; Nonfiction; *Areas:*
Architecture; Arts; Biography; Crafts;
Health; Historical; Literature; Philosophy;
Religious; Science; Self-Help; Sociology;
Spiritual; *Markets:* Adult; Children's; Youth

Publishes a wide range of books including
adult nonfiction, picture books and
children's novels. No poetry or verse, fiction
for people over the age of 14, or
autobiography, unless it specifically relates
to a relevant nonfiction subject area. No
submissions by email. Send by post or via
online form. See website for full details of
areas covered and submission guidelines.

Footprint Handbooks

5 Riverside Court
Lower Bristol Road
Bath
BA2 3DZ
Tel: +44 (0) 1225 469141
Email: contactus@
morriscontentalliance.com
Website: http://www.
footprinttravelguides.com

Publishes: Nonfiction; Reference; *Areas:*
Travel; *Markets:* Adult

Publishes travel guides written by a small team of experts. See careers section of website for any opportunities.

George Ronald Publisher
3 Rosecroft Lane
Welwyn
Herts
AL6 0UB
Tel: +44 (0) 1438 716062
Email: sales@grbooks.com
Website: http://grbooks.com

Publishes: Nonfiction; *Areas:* Religious; *Markets:* Adult

Religious publisher, concentrating solely on books of interest to Bahá'ís. Send email for copy of submission guidelines.

Galley Beggar Press
Email: submissions@galleybeggar.co.uk
Website: http://galleybeggar.co.uk

Publishes: Fiction; Nonfiction; *Areas:* Short Stories; *Markets:* Adult; *Treatments:* Literary

Publishes adult literary fiction and narrative nonfiction only. Open to submissions by email during specific submission windows. See website for full details.

Garnet Publishing
8 Southern Court
South Street
Reading
RG1 4QS
Tel: +44 (0) 118 959 7847
Fax: +44 (0) 118 959 0508
Email: info@garnetpublishing.co.uk
Website: http://www.garnetpublishing.co.uk

Publishes: Fiction; Nonfiction; *Areas:* Anthropology; Archaeology; Architecture; Arts; Autobiography; Biography; Cookery; Culture; Current Affairs; Historical; Literature; Media; Photography; Politics; Religious; Sociology; Translations; Travel; *Markets:* Academic; Adult; *Treatments:* Commercial; Literary; Mainstream; Niche

Contact: Arash Hejazi

An independent publishing company specialising in trade books, with a special interest in the Middle East. We publish in the fields of architecture, art, fiction, cookery and travel, and also in the areas of culture, heritage and history of the Middle East.

One imprint is a leading English-language publisher of academic books devoted to the Middle East Studies. Its authors are academic experts drawn from all over the world and the company has links with many major universities in the UK, the USA and Europe that have departments or faculties with Middle Eastern and Arab studies programmes.

Send query with brief cover letter, writer's bio, detailed synopsis, two sample chapters, and full contact details.

Geddes & Grosset
Gresham Publishing Company Limited
Academy Park
Building 4000
Glasgow
G51 1PR
Website: http://www.geddesandgrosset.co.uk

Publishes: Fiction; Nonfiction; Reference; *Areas:* Cookery; Health; Historical; Humour; Self-Help; Spiritual; *Markets:* Adult; Children's

Publishes dictionaries, bilingual books, English grammar and usage texts, Self-Help, Diet and Health, and Mind, Body and Spirit. Imprint focuses on Scottish titles.

Gibson Square Books Ltd
Tel: +44 (0) 20 7096 1100
Fax: +44 (0) 20 7993 2214
Email: info@gibsonsquare.com
Website: http://www.gibsonsquare.com

Publishes: Nonfiction; *Areas:* Arts; Biography; Criticism; Culture; Current Affairs; Historical; Philosophy; Politics; Psychology; Travel; Women's Interests; *Markets:* Adult

Publishes books which contribute to a general debate. Send proposals by email. See website for full guidelines.

Gingko Library

4 Molasses Row
Plantation Wharf
London
SW11 3UX
Tel: +44 (0) 20 3637 9730
Email: gingko@gingkolibrary.com
Website: http://www.gingkolibrary.com

Publishes: Nonfiction; *Areas:* Architecture;
Arts; Biography; Finance; Historical;
Literature; Music; Philosophy; Politics;
Religious; Science; Technology; *Markets:*
Academic; Adult

Welcomes proposals for new, learned books
that deal with topics pertaining to the Middle
East and North Africa, or the Islamic world
in general, whether they are academic
monographs, edited volumes, or general
interest (nonfiction) books. Send query by
email.

GL Assessment

1st Floor Vantage London
Great West Road
Brentford
TW8 9AG
Tel: +44 (0) 20 8996 3333
Fax: +44 (0) 20 8742 8767
Email: info@gl-assessment.co.uk
Website: https://www.gl-assessment.co.uk

Publishes: Nonfiction; *Markets:* Academic

Publishes educational testing and assessment
material.

Gomer Press

Llandysul Enterprise Park
Llandysul
Ceredigion
SA44 4JL
Tel: +44 (0) 1559 363092
Fax: +44 (0) 1559 363758
Email: gwasg@gomer.co.uk
Website: http://www.gomer.co.uk

Publishes: Fiction; Nonfiction; Poetry;
Reference; Scripts; *Areas:* Arts;
Autobiography; Biography; Culture; Drama;
Historical; Leisure; Literature; Music;
Nature; Religious; Sport; Theatre; Travel;
Markets: Academic; Adult; Children's;
Youth

Publishes fiction, nonfiction, plays, poetry,
language books, and educational material,
for adults and children, in English and in
Welsh. Query before making a submission.

Granta Books

12 Addison Avenue
London
W11 4QR
Tel: +44 (0) 20 7605 1360
Fax: +44 (0) 20 7605 1361
Email: info@grantabooks.com
Website: http://www.grantabooks.com

Publishes: Fiction; Nonfiction; *Areas:*
Autobiography; Biography; Criticism;
Culture; Historical; Nature; Politics;
Sociology; Travel; *Markets:* Adult;
Treatments: Literary; Serious

Publishes around 70% nonfiction / 30%
fiction. In nonfiction publishes serious
cultural, political and social history, narrative
history, or memoir. Rarely publishes
straightforward biographies. No genre
fiction. Not accepting unsolicited
submissions.

Gresham Books Ltd

The Carriage House
Ningwood Manor
Isle of Wight
PO30 4NJ
Tel: +44 (0) 1983 761389
Email: info@gresham-books.co.uk
Website: http://www.gresham-books.co.uk

Publishes: Nonfiction; *Areas:* Religious;
Markets: Academic; Adult; Children's

Contact: Paul Lewis

Publishes bespoke books for schools,
including hymn books, plus text books to
help teach British values.

Greystones Press

Email: editorial@greystonespress.com
Website: http://www.greystonespress.com

Publishes: Fiction; Nonfiction; *Areas:* Arts;
Historical; Literature; Music; Translations;
Markets: Adult; Youth

Closed to submissions as at November 2017. See website for current status.

Independent start-up publishing adult fiction and nonfiction in the areas of Art, History, Literature, Music and Mythology (including Fairy Tales and Folklore); Young Adult (teenage) fiction; and translated European fiction where there is a grant for translation in the originating country or from a UK institution. No illustrated books or memoirs. Send query by email with synopsis and first three chapters up to 10,000 words as attachments.

Grub Street Publishing

4 Rainham Close
London
SW11 6SS
Tel: +44 (0) 20 7924 3966
Fax: +44 (0) 20 7738 1008
Email: post@grubstreet.co.uk
Website: http://www.grubstreet.co.uk

Publishes: Nonfiction; Reference; *Areas:* Cookery; Historical; Military; *Markets:* Adult

Publishes books on cookery and military aviation history only. No fiction or poetry. Accepts synopses and sample material by email. See website for full submission guidelines and specific email addresses for different topics.

Halban Publishers

Tel: +44 (0) 20 7692 5541
Email: books@halbanpublishers.com
Website: http://www.halbanpublishers.com

Publishes: Fiction; Nonfiction; *Areas:* Autobiography; Biography; Criticism; Historical; Literature; Philosophy; Politics; Religious; *Markets:* Adult

Contact: Peter Halban; Martine Halban

Closed to submissions as at March 30, 2019. Check website for current status.

Independent publisher of fiction, memoirs, history, biography, and books of Jewish interest. Send query with synopsis by email only. No unsolicited MSS.

Haldane Mason Ltd

PO Box 34196
London
NW10 3YB
Tel: +44 (0) 20 8459 2131
Fax: +44 (0) 20 8728 1216
Email: sfrancis@haldanemason.com
Website: http://haldanemason.com

Publishes: Nonfiction; *Areas:* Crafts; Health; Historical; Lifestyle; Science; *Markets:* Adult; Children's; Youth

Publishes books and box-sets – mainly for children through children's imprint, but also for adults, covering such topics as alternative health, yoga, henna body art, Feng Shui, etc. Children's books include crafts, puzzles, history, science, maths, etc. Send query by email in first instance.

HarperCollins Publishers Ltd

The News Building
1 London Bridge Street
London
SE1 9GF

GLASGOW OFFICE:
103 Westerhill Road
Bishopbriggs
Glasgow
G64 2QT
Tel: +44 (0) 20 8741 7070
Fax: +44 (0) 20 8307 4440
Email: enquiries@harpercollins.co.uk
Website: http://www.harpercollins.co.uk

Publishes: Fiction; Nonfiction; Reference; *Areas:* Autobiography; Biography; Cookery; Crafts; Crime; Entertainment; Fantasy; Film; Gardening; Health; Historical; Leisure; Lifestyle; Media; Military; Science; Sci-Fi; Sport; Thrillers; *Markets:* Adult; Children's; *Treatments:* Literary

One of the UK's three largest publishers, with one of the broadest ranges of material published. All approaches must come through an agent. No unsolicited MSS.

Hart Publishing Ltd

Kemp House
Chawley Park
Cumnor Hill

Oxford
OX2 9PH
Tel: +44 (0) 1865 598648
Fax: +44 (0) 1865 727017
Email: sinead@hartpub.co.uk
Website: http://www.hartpub.co.uk

Publishes: Nonfiction; *Areas:* Legal;
Markets: Academic; Professional

Contact: Sinead Moloney; Bill Asquith

Publisher or legal books and journals for the
professional and academic markets. See
website for submission guidelines and
specific editor subject areas and contact
details.

Hawthorn Press

1 Lansdown Lane
Stroud
Gloucestershire
GL5 1BJ
Tel: +44 (0) 1453 757040
Fax: +44 (0) 1453 751138
Email: info@hawthornpress.com
Website: http://www.hawthornpress.com

Publishes: Nonfiction; *Areas:* Lifestyle;
Self-Help; *Markets:* Adult

Publisher aiming to contribute to a more
creative, peaceful and sustainable world
through its publishing. Publishes mainly
commissioned work, but will consider
approaches. Send first two chapters with
introduction, full table of contents/book plan,
brief author biography and/or CV. Allow at
least 2–4 months for response. Send
submissions by email.

Hay House Publishers

The Sixth Floor, Watson House
54 Baker Street
London
W1U 7BU
Tel: +44 (0) 20 3675 2450
Fax: +44 (0) 20 3675 2451
Email: submissions@hayhouse.co.uk
Website: http://www.hayhouse.co.uk

Publishes: Nonfiction; *Areas:* Biography;
Business; Current Affairs; Finance; Health;
Lifestyle; Medicine; Men's Interests; Nature;
Philosophy; Psychology; Religious; Self-

Help; Sociology; Spiritual; Women's
Interests; *Markets:* Adult; *Treatments:*
Positive

Describes itself as the world's leading mind
body and spirit publisher. Approach via form
on website. See website for full submission
guidelines.

Head of Zeus

Clerkenwell House
45-47 Clerkenwell Green
London
EC1R 0HT
Email: info@headofzeus.com
Website: http://www.headofzeus.com

Publishes: Fiction; Nonfiction; *Areas:*
Biography; Crime; Fantasy; Historical;
Mystery; Philosophy; Romance; Sci-Fi;
Short Stories; Sociology; Sport; Suspense;
Thrillers; *Markets:* Adult; Youth;
Treatments: Commercial; Literary

**Closed to submissions as at December
2017. Check website for current status.**

Publishes general and literary fiction, genre
fiction, and nonfiction. Submit via online
submission system.

Headline Publishing Group

Carmelite House
50 Victoria Embankment
London
EC4Y 0DZ
Tel: +44 (0) 20 3122 7222
Email: enquiries@headline.co.uk
Website: https://www.headline.co.uk

Publishes: Fiction; Nonfiction; *Areas:*
Autobiography; Biography; Cookery;
Gardening; Historical; Science; Sport; TV;
Markets: Adult; *Treatments:* Commercial;
Literary; Popular

Publishes hardback and paperback
commercial and literary fiction, as well as
popular nonfiction.

Hesperus Press Limited

28 Mortimer Street
London
W1W 7RD

Tel: +44 (0) 20 7436 0943
Email: info@hesperuspress.com
Website: http://www.hesperuspress.com

Publishes: Fiction; Nonfiction; Poetry;
Reference; *Areas:* Autobiography;
Biography; Crime; Culture; Erotic; Fantasy;
Historical; Literature; Romance; Sci-Fi;
Thrillers; Translations; Travel; *Markets:*
Adult; Children's; *Treatments:*
Contemporary; Literary; Traditional

Publishes the lesser known works of
classical authors, both in English and in
translation. No unsolicited MSS and no
submissions.

The History Press
The Mill,
Brimscombe Port
Stroud
Gloucestershire
GL5 2QG
Tel: +44 (0) 1453 883300
Fax: +44 (0) 1453 883233
Email: web@thehistorypress.co.uk
Website: http://www.thehistorypress.co.uk

Publishes: Nonfiction; *Areas:* Archaeology;
Biography; Crime; Historical; Military;
Sport; *Markets:* Adult

Publishes books on history, from local to
international. Welcomes submissions from
both new and established authors. Send
query by email. No unsolicited mss. See
website for full guidelines.

Hodder & Stoughton Ltd
Carmelite House
50 Victoria Embankment
London
EC4Y 0DZ
Tel: +44 (0) 20 3122 6777
Email: editorialwebenquiries@hodder.co.uk
Website: https://www.hodder.co.uk

Publishes: Fiction; Nonfiction; *Areas:*
Autobiography; Biography; Cookery;
Historical; Humour; Lifestyle; Spiritual;
Travel; *Markets:* Adult; *Treatments:*
Commercial; Literary

Large London-based publisher of nonfiction
and commercial and literary fiction.

Hodder Faith
Carmelite House
50 Victoria Embankment
London
EC4Y 0DZ
Tel: +44 (0) 20 3122 6777
Email: hodderfaith@hodder.co.uk
Website: http://www.hodderfaith.com

Publishes: Nonfiction; *Areas:* Religious;
Markets: Adult

Seeks to provide a platform for Christian
views to be expressed across all
denominations, races and ages.

Hodder Gibson
211 St Vincent Street
Glasgow
G2 5QY
Tel: +44 (0) 1413 334650
Email: hoddergibson@hodder.co.uk
Website: http://hoddergibson.co.uk

Publishes: Nonfiction; *Markets:* Academic

Publishes Scottish school textbooks and
learning materials. Make initial approach
through form on website.

Honno Welsh Women's Press
Honno
Unit 14, Creative Units
Aberystwyth Arts Centre
Aberystwyth
Ceredigion
SY23 3GL
Tel: +44 (0) 1970 623150
Fax: +44 (0) 1970 623150
Email: post@honno.co.uk
Website: http://www.honno.co.uk

Publishes: Fiction; Nonfiction; Poetry;
Areas: Autobiography; Crime; Fantasy; Sci-
Fi; Short Stories; Thrillers; Women's
Interests; *Markets:* Adult; Children's; Youth;
Treatments: Commercial; Literary

Contact: Caroline Oakley

Feminist Welsh publisher. Publishes work
from women born in, living in, or
significantly connected to Wales, only.
Publishes fiction, autobiographical writing
and reprints of classic titles in English and

Welsh, as well as anthologies of poetry and short stories. Particularly looking for literary fiction, crime/thriller, commercial women's fiction, science fiction and fantasy. All submissions must be sent as hard copy; no email submissions. Send query with synopsis and first 50 pages. Not currently accepting children's, novellas, poetry, or short story collections by a single author.

Hopscotch

St Jude's Church
Dulwich Road
Herne Hill
London
SE24 0PB
Tel: +44 (0) 20 7501 6736
Fax: +44 (0) 20 7738 9718
Email: hopscotch@bebc.co.uk
Website: http://www.hopscotchbooks.com

Publishes: Nonfiction; *Areas:* Historical; Science; Technology; *Markets:* Professional

Publishes teaching resources for primary school teachers.

Hot Key Books

80-81 Wimpole Street
London
W1G 9RE
Tel: +44 (0) 20 7490 3875
Email: hello@bonnierbooks.co.uk
Website: http://hotkeybooks.com

Publishes: Fiction; Nonfiction; *Markets:* Children's; Youth

Publishes fiction and nonfiction for teens and young adults. Send complete ms with full synopsis by email only. Prefers Word and PDF files. Response only if interested.

House of Lochar

Isle of Colonsay
PA61 7YR
Tel: +44 (0) 1951 200232
Fax: +44 (0) 1951 200232
Email: sales@houseoflochar.com
Website: http://www.houseoflochar.com

Publishes: Fiction; Nonfiction; *Areas:* Biography; Historical; Literature; Travel;

Markets: Adult; Children's; *Treatments:* Literary

Publishes fiction and nonfiction related to Scotland and / or Celtic themes, including history, fiction, transport, maritime, genealogy, Gaelic, and books for children. No poetry or books unrelated to Scottish or Celtic themes.

ICSA Publishing

Saffron House
6–10 Kirby Street
London
EC1N 8TS
Tel: +44 (0) 20 7580 4741
Email: publishing@icsa.co.uk
Website: https://www.icsa.org.uk/shop

Publishes: Nonfiction; Reference; *Areas:* Legal; *Markets:* Professional

Publishes books aimed at secretaries and administrators, providing guidance on legal and regulatory compliance.

Igloo Books Limited

Cottage Farm
Mears Ashby Road
Sywell
Northants
NN6 0BJ
Tel: +44 (0) 1604 741116
Fax: +44 (0) 1604 670495
Email: customerservice@igloobooks.com
Website: http://igloobooks.com

Publishes: Fiction; Nonfiction; Reference; *Areas:* Cookery; Hobbies; Lifestyle; *Markets:* Adult; Children's

Publishes nonfiction and gift and puzzle books for adults, and fiction, nonfiction, and novelty books for children.

Impress Books Limited

Innovation Centre
Rennes Drive
University of Exeter
Devon
EX4 4RN
Email: enquiries@impress-books.co.uk
Website: http://www.impress-books.co.uk

Publishes: Fiction; Nonfiction; *Areas:* Biography; Crime; Historical; Religious; *Markets:* Adult; *Treatments:* Contemporary; Literary

Interested in quality, thought-provoking titles for the enquiring general reader. Specialises in discovering and nurturing fresh voices in crime, historical and literary fiction.

Indigo Dreams Publishing

24 Forest Houses
Halwill
Beaworthy
Devon
EX21 5UU
Email: publishing@indigodreams.co.uk
Website: http://www.indigodreams.co.uk

Publishes: Poetry; *Markets:* Adult; *Treatments:* Literary

Contact: Ronnie Goodyer

Closed to submissions as at November 2018. Will re-open late 2019.

Publishes poetry collections up to 60/70 pages and poetry pamphlets up to 36 pages. See website for submission guidelines.

Infinite Ideas

36 St Giles
Oxford
OX1 3LD
Tel: +44 (0) 1865 514888
Email: richard@infideas.com
Website: http://www.infideas.com

Publishes: Nonfiction; *Areas:* Autobiography; Biography; Business; Cookery; Culture; Current Affairs; Entertainment; Gardening; Hobbies; Lifestyle; Media; Politics; Self-Help; Travel; *Markets:* Professional; *Treatments:* Commercial; Contemporary; Progressive; Traditional

Contact: Richard Burton

Set up in 2004. We were on a mission to create a publishing business like no other. In a world that is teeming with books, good and bad (mainly bad), we set out to publish books of real value to the reader. Every page has something that might change readers'

lives for the better, for ever.

160 plus books later, we like to think that we've achieved some of our ambitions. We've developed great book series.

We've worked with top brands including Marks and Spencer, Sainsbury's Champneys, Simple and Anne Summers who value our ability to produce great content in a beautiful package.

We've worked too with a number of new authors to help them get their masterpieces into the market.

We love great content, we love great books and we love great ideas.

Do feel free to get in touch to with us if you'd like to hear more. Send short synopsis by email.

InterVarsity Press (IVP)

36 Causton Street
London
SW1P 4ST
Tel: +44 (0) 20 7592 3900
Email: spck@spck.org.uk
Website: https://ivpbooks.com

Publishes: Nonfiction; *Areas:* Religious; *Markets:* Adult

Aims to produce quality, Evangelical books for the digital age. Send query through form on website.

J.A. Allen

The Stable Block
Crowood Lane
Ramsbury
Wiltshire
SN8 2HR
Tel: +44 (0) 1672 520280
Email: enquiries@crowood.com
Website: http://www.crowood.com

Publishes: Nonfiction; *Areas:* How-to; *Markets:* Adult

Contact: Lesley Gowers

Publishes books on horses and horsemanship. Send query by post, fax, or email. No unsolicited mss.

Jacaranda Books Art Music Ltd

27 Old Gloucester Street
London
WC1N 3AX
Email: office@
jacarandabooksartmusic.co.uk
Website: http://www.
jacarandabooksartmusic.co.uk

Publishes: Fiction; Nonfiction; *Areas:* Arts; Autobiography; Beauty and Fashion; Biography; Crime; Photography; Romance; *Markets:* Adult; *Treatments:* Contemporary

Contact: Valerie Brandes, Founder & Publisher

Not accepting submissions as at March 2018. Check website for current situation.

Publishes adult fiction and nonfiction, including crime, romance, illustrated books, biography, memoir, and autobiography. Particularly interested in books where the central character or theme relates to minority groups and/or has strong female protagonists. Also interested in original works from or about African, African-American, Caribbean and black British artists working in the fields of photography, fine art, fashion, and contemporary and modern art, and artists of calibre from the soul, blues, R&B and reggae traditions. Send query by email with writer CV, detailed synopsis, and two sample chapters. See website for full submission guidelines.

Jane's Information Group

Sentinel House
163 Brighton Road
Coulsdon
Surrey
CR5 2YH
Tel: +44 (0) 1344 328300
Fax: +44 (0) 20 8763 1006
Website: http://www.janes.com

Publishes: Nonfiction; Reference; *Areas:* Military; *Markets:* Adult

Publisher of magazines, books, reference works, online material, and yearbooks related to defence, aerospace, security, and transport topics.

Joffe Books Ltd

Email: submissions@joffebooks.com
Website: http://www.joffebooks.com

Publishes: Fiction; *Areas:* Crime; Mystery; Suspense; Thrillers; *Markets:* Adult

Contact: Jasper Joffe

Publishes full-length crime fiction, mysteries, and thrillers. No kids books, sci-fi, nonfiction, conspiracy theories, or erotic. Send query by email with complete ms as an attachment, a synopsis in the body of the email, and 100 words about yourself. Include "submission" in the subject line. Reply not guaranteed unless interested. See website for full guidelines.

John Murray (Publishers) Ltd

Carmelite House
50 Victoria Embankment
London
EC4Y 0DZ
Tel: +44 (0) 20 3122 6777
Website: https://www.hodder.co.uk

Publishes: Fiction; Nonfiction; *Markets:* Adult

Accepts approaches through literary agents only.

Jordan Publishing

21 St Thomas Street
Bristol
BS1 6JS
Website: http://www.lexisnexis.co.uk/
products/jordan-publishing.html

Publishes: Nonfiction; *Areas:* Legal; *Markets:* Professional

Legal publisher specialising in family law, company and commercial, insolvency, private client, civil litigation and personal injury.

Kettillonia

Sidlaw House
South Street
NEWTYLE
Angus
PH12 8UQ
Tel: +44 (0) 1828 650615
Email: james@kettillonia.co.uk
Website: http://www.kettillonia.co.uk

Publishes: Fiction; Nonfiction; Poetry;
Areas: Historical; Humour; Literature; Short
Stories; *Markets:* Adult; *Treatments:*
Literary

Contact: James Robertson

Publisher of pamphlets containing original,
adventurous, neglected and rare Scottish
writing.

Kogan Page Ltd

45 Gee Street, 2nd Floor
London
EC1V 3RS
Tel: +44 (0) 20 7278 0433
Email: kpinfo@koganpage.com
Website: https://www.koganpage.com

Publishes: Nonfiction; Reference; *Areas:*
Business; Finance; How-to; Technology;
Markets: Adult; Professional

Publisher of business management books on
training, finance, personnel, small business,
industrial relations, etc.

Lantana Publishing

Email: submissions@lantanapublishing.com
Website: http://www.lantanapublishing.com

Publishes: Fiction; Nonfiction; *Areas:*
Culture; *Markets:* Children's; *Treatments:*
Contemporary

Publishes picture books and narrative
nonfiction focused on diversity for 4 to 8
year olds up to 500 words (prefers 200-400
words). Particularly interested in
contemporary writing with modern-day
settings, especially if they feature Black,
Asian and Minority Ethnic families.
Publishes almost exclusively authors of
Black, Asian and Minority Ethnic
backgrounds.

Laurence King Publishing Ltd

361-373 City Road
London
EC1V 1LR
Tel: +44 (0) 20 7841 6900
Fax: +44 (0) 20 7841 6910
Email: commissioning@laurenceking.com
Website: http://www.laurenceking.co.uk

Publishes: Nonfiction; *Areas:* Architecture;
Arts; Beauty and Fashion; Design; Film;
Historical; Photography; *Markets:*
Academic; Adult

Publisher of books on the creative arts. Send
proposal by email.

Lawrence & Wishart

Central Books Building
Freshwater Road
Chadwell Heath
RM8 1RX
Tel: +44 (0) 20 8597 0090
Email: submissions@lwbooks.co.uk
Website: http://www.lwbooks.co.uk

Publishes: Nonfiction; *Areas:* Culture;
Current Affairs; Historical; Politics;
Markets: Adult

Contact: Katharine Harris

Independent publisher of books on current
affairs and political history and culture.
Formed through a merger in the 1930s of the
Communist Party's press and a liberal and
anti-fascist publisher.

Legend Press

107-111 Fleet Street
London
EC4A 2AB
Tel: +44 (0) 20 7936 9941
Email: submissions@legend-
paperbooks.co.uk
Website: http://www.legendpress.co.uk

Publishes: Fiction; *Areas:* Crime; Historical;
Markets: Adult; *Treatments:* Commercial;
Contemporary; Mainstream

Contact: Tom Chalmers

Publishes a diverse list of contemporary
adult novels. No children's books, poetry or
travel writing. See website for full

submission guidelines and online submission system.

LexisNexis

Lexis House
30 Farringdon Street
EC4A 4HH
Tel: +44 (0) 330 161 1234
Email: customer.services@lexisnexis.co.uk
Website: http://www.lexisnexis.co.uk

Publishes: Nonfiction; Reference; *Areas:* Legal; *Markets:* Professional

Publishes books, looseleafs, journals etc. for legal professionals.

Little Tiger Press

1 The Coda Centre
189 Munster Road
London
SW6 6AW
Tel: +44 (0) 20 7385 6333
Fax: +44 (0) 20 7385 7333
Email: info@littletiger.co.uk
Website: http://www.littletigerpress.com

Publishes: Fiction; *Markets:* Children's

Not accepting submissions as at May 2018. Check website for current status.

Accepts unsolicited MSS up to 750 words. If inside UK include SAE for response (no postage vouchers/coupons); if from outside the UK include email address for response (no material returned). See website for full guidelines. No submissions by email or on disc.

Little, Brown Book Group

Carmelite House
50 Victoria Embankment
LONDON
EC4Y 0DZ
Tel: +44 (0) 20 3122 7000
Email: info@littlebrown.co.uk
Website: http://www.littlebrown.co.uk

Publishes: Fiction; Nonfiction; *Areas:* Autobiography; Biography; Crime; Entertainment; Fantasy; Historical; How-to; Humour; Literature; Sci-Fi; Thrillers;

Markets: Adult; Youth; *Treatments:* Literary; Popular

Accepts submissions via agents only.

LOM ART

16 Lion Yard
Tremadoc Road
London
Email: lom.art@mombooks.com
Website: https://www.mombooks.com/lom/

Publishes: Nonfiction; *Markets:* Adult; Children's

Contact: Imogen Williams

Publishes illustrated nonfiction for children and adults. Send query with overview and synopsis in the body of your email, or by post with SASE.

Lonely Planet

240 Blackfriars Road
London
SE1 8NW
Tel: +44 (0) 20 3771 5100
Fax: +44 (0) 20 3771 5101
Email: recruitingcontributors@lonelyplanet.com
Website: http://www.lonelyplanet.com

Publishes: Nonfiction; *Areas:* Travel; *Markets:* Adult

Publishes international travel guides. Send query by email with speculative CV or resume.

Lost Tower Publications

Website: http://losttowerpublications.jigsy.com

Publishes: Fiction; Poetry; *Areas:* Adventure; Autobiography; Crime; Fantasy; Gothic; Horror; Leisure; Lifestyle; Mystery; Sci-Fi; Spiritual; Suspense; Thrillers; Women's Interests; *Markets:* Adult; Children's; Family; Youth; *Treatments:* Contemporary; Dark; Experimental; Niche; Positive; Progressive

Contact: Harry Yang

Formed in 2011 as part of a poetry book publishing campaign to promote poetry world wide as an attractive and entertaining art form for the twenty first century. We print 3-4 books a year collecting the best photographs and poetry from around the world, to produce high quality books for people to enjoy. Our books are available to buy worldwide either from Amazon or to order through your local bookshop.

In March 2013 we published a journey of hope through poems and photographs which have been collected from around the world. The work in this anthology has been collected from every continent of our planet and illustrates ideas of hope from many of the world religions; looks at the different forms hope can take and how hope can always be found if you look carefully into the world which surrounds you.

Luath Press Ltd

543/2 Castlehill
The Royal Mile
Edinburgh
EH1 2ND
Tel: +44 (0) 131 225 4326
Email: sales@luath.co.uk
Website: http://www.luath.co.uk

Publishes: Fiction; Nonfiction; Poetry; *Areas:* Arts; Beauty and Fashion; Biography; Crime; Current Affairs; Drama; Historical; Leisure; Lifestyle; Nature; Photography; Politics; Sociology; Sport; Thrillers; Travel; *Markets:* Adult; Children's; Youth

Contact: G.H. MacDougall, Managing Editor

Publishes a range of books, usually with a Scottish connection. Check upcoming publishing schedule on website, and – if you think your book fits – send query with SAE, synopsis up to 250 words, manuscript or sample chapters, author bio, and any other relevant material. See website for full submission guidelines. Approaches by email will not be considered.

Luna Press Publishing

149/4 Morrison Street
Edinburgh
EH3 8AG
Email: lunapress@outlook.com

Website: http://www.lunapresspublishing.com

Publishes: Fiction; *Areas:* Fantasy; Sci-Fi; Short Stories; *Markets:* Academic; Adult; *Treatments:* Dark

Publishes Science Fiction, Fantasy, and Dark Fantasy (including their sub-genres). Will consider short stories, novelettes, novellas, novels, graphic novels, academic material. See website for submission guidelines.

Note: closed to all but academic works as at May 2018 – check website for current status.

Lund Humphries Limited

Office 3, Book House
261A City Road
London
EC1V 1JX
Tel: +44 (0) 20 7440 7530
Email: lclark@lundhumphries.com
Website: http://www.lundhumphries.com

Publishes: Nonfiction; *Areas:* Architecture; Arts; Design; Historical; *Markets:* Adult

Contact: Lucy Clark

Publishes books on art, art history, and design. See website for guidelines on submitting a proposal.

Mabecron Books Ltd

3 Briston Orchard
St Mellion
Saltash
Cornwall
PL12 6RQ
Email: ronjohns@mabecronbooks.co.uk
Website: http://mabecronbooks.co.uk

Publishes: Fiction; Nonfiction; *Areas:* Cookery; *Markets:* Adult; Children's

Welcomes submissions of books with quality, style, and saleability. Favours books with a Cornish theme. Absence of a Cornish theme will not mean a book is necessarily rejected, but makes the decision more difficult. Particularly interested in children's picture books, cookery, and children's fiction. Send submissions by post only, with SAE.

Mandrake of Oxford

PO Box 250
Oxford
OX1 1AP
Email: mandrake@mandrake.uk.net
Website: http://mandrake.uk.net

Publishes: Fiction; Nonfiction; *Areas:* Arts;
Crime; Culture; Erotic; Health; Horror;
Lifestyle; Mystery; Philosophy; Sci-Fi; Self-
Help; Spiritual; *Markets:* Adult

Send query by post or by email. May also
include synopsis. See website for full
guidelines, and for examples of the kind of
material published.

Mango Books

18 Soho Square
London
W1D 3QL
Tel: +44 (0) 20 7060 4142
Email: adamwood@mangodesign.biz
Website: http://mangobooks.co.uk

Publishes: Nonfiction; *Areas:* Crime;
Historical; *Markets:* Adult

Actively seeking nonfiction books of a
historical nature, true-crime related. Send
query by email outlining your book, and
explaining what makes it different to any
already available on the same subject.

Mantra Lingua Ltd

Global House
303 Ballards Lane
London
N12 8NP
Tel: +44 (0) 20 8445 5123
Fax: +44 (0) 20 8446 7745
Email: info@mantralingua.com
Website: http://www.mantralingua.com

Publishes: Fiction; Nonfiction; *Areas:*
Translations; *Markets:* Children's

Multilingual educational publishers of
nonfiction and picture books for children up
to 12 years. 1,400 words maximum (800 for
children up to 7). All books are print
products which are sound enabled, playing
back audio narrations or music, etc. Send
submissions by email. See website for more
details.

Kevin Mayhew Publishers

Buxhall
Stowmarket
Suffolk
IP14 3BW
Tel: +44 (0) 845 3881634
Fax: +44 (0) 1449 737834
Email: submissions@kevinmayhew.com
Website: http://www.kevinmayhew.com

Publishes: Nonfiction; *Areas:* Music;
Religious; Spiritual; *Markets:* Academic;
Adult; Children's

Contact: Manuscript Submissions
Department

Publishes books relating to Christianity and
music, for adults, children, schools, etc. Send
query by email only, with first three
chapters, full contents list, sales pitch,
summary, market info, bio, and details of
any previous publications. See website for
full details.

Merlin Unwin Books

Palmers House
7 Corve Street
Ludlow
Shropshire
SY8 1DB
Tel: +44 (0) 1584 877456
Email: books@merlinunwin.co.uk
Website: http://www.merlinunwin.co.uk

Publishes: Nonfiction; *Areas:*
Autobiography; Cookery; Humour; Leisure;
Nature; Sport; *Markets:* Adult

Publishes books on the countryside and
countryside pursuits, covering such topics as
nature, fishing, shooting, etc.

Metro Publications Ltd

Po Box 6336
London
N1 6PY
Tel: +44 (0) 20 8533 7777
Fax: +44 (0) 20 8533 7777
Email: info@metropublications.com
Website: https://metropublications.com

Publishes: Nonfiction; *Areas:* Architecture;
Arts; Leisure; Travel; *Markets:* Adult

Publisher of guide books on many aspects of London life.

Michael Joseph
80 Strand
London
WC2R 0RL
Tel: +44 (0) 20 7139 3000
Website: https://www.
penguinrandomhouse.co.uk/publishers/
michael-joseph/

Publishes: Fiction; Nonfiction; *Areas:*
Autobiography; Cookery; Crime; Lifestyle;
Thrillers; Women's Interests; *Markets:*
Adult; *Treatments:* Commercial

Publishes women's fiction, crime, thrillers, cookery, memoirs and lifestyle books. Accepts submissions through literary agents only.

MIrror Books
Northern & Shell Building
10 Lower Thames Street
London
EC3R 6EN
Tel: +44 (0) 20 7293 3740
Email: submissions@mirrorbooks.co.uk
Website: https://mirrorbooks.co.uk

Publishes: Fiction; Nonfiction; *Areas:*
Autobiography; Crime; Drama; *Markets:*
Adult

Accepts submissions from new and existing authors for fiction and nonfiction. Interested in real life, memoir, crime, passion, and human drama. Approach using online form on website, email, or by post, including three draft chapters, the genre of your book, and your target market. See website for more details.

Mud Pie Books
43 Leckford Road
Oxford
OX2 6HY
Tel: +44 (0) 7985 935320
Email: info@mudpiebooks.com
Website: http://mudpiebooks.com

Publishes: Nonfiction; *Areas:* Religious;
Markets: Adult

Publishes books about Buddhism, and books for Buddhists.

Myriad Editions
New Internationalist Publications
The Old Music Hall
106-108 Cowley Rd
Oxford
OX4 1JE
Tel: +44 (0) 1865 403345
Email: submissions@myriadeditions.com
Website: https://myriadeditions.com

Publishes: Fiction; Nonfiction; *Areas:*
Autobiography; Crime; Historical; Medicine;
Politics; Thrillers; *Markets:* Adult;
Treatments: Contemporary; Literary

Publishes literary fiction: contemporary and historical; crime fiction: psychological and political thrillers with strong female characters; graphic novels: documentary comics, graphic reportage, fiction, memoir and life writing, graphic medicine; and literary or political nonfiction: feminist, literary nonfiction, memoir. No young adult fiction, children's books, horror, science fiction, fantasy, plays or poetry, or books that have been previously published or self-published (in print or as ebooks) unless you are a graphic novelist. Send query by email. See website for full guidelines.

National Museum Wales
Cathays Park
Cardiff
CF10 3NP
Tel: +44 (0) 300 111 2 333
Email: post@museumwales.ac.uk
Website: http://www.museumwales.ac.uk

Publishes: Nonfiction; *Areas:* Archaeology;
Arts; Historical; Nature; Sociology; *Markets:*
Academic; Adult; Children's

Publishes books based on the collections and research of the museum, aimed at adults, children, and schools. Publishes in both Welsh and English.

New Holland Publishers (UK) Ltd
Bentinck House
3-8 Bolsover Street

London
W1W 6AB
Tel: +44 (0) 20 3473 3220
Email: enquiries@nhpub.co.uk
Website: http://www.
newhollandpublishers.com

Publishes: Nonfiction; Reference; *Areas:*
Arts; Biography; Cookery; Crafts; Design;
Gardening; Health; Historical; How-to;
Humour; Lifestyle; Nature; Photography;
Self-Help; Spiritual; Sport; Travel; *Markets:*
Adult

International publisher of nonfiction and
reference. Send query with SAE, synopsis
and short bio of about 300 words each,
current comparison titles (and how yours is
different), proposed target market and
methods of promotion. Include first three
chapters or complete ms. See website for full
details.

New Playwrights' Network (NPN)
10 Station Road Industrial Estate
Colwall
Herefordshire
WR13 6RN
Tel: +44 (0) 1684 540154
Email: simon@cressrelles.co.uk
Website: http://www.cressrelles.co.uk

Publishes: Scripts; *Areas:* Drama; Theatre;
Markets: Adult

Contact: Simon Smith

Established in the 1970s to promote scripts
by new writers. Send scripts by email or by
post.

Nick Hern Books Ltd
The Glasshouse
49a Goldhawk Road
London
W12 8QP
Tel: +44 (0) 20 8749 4953
Fax: +44 (0) 20 8735 0250
Email: submissions@nickhernbooks.co.uk
Website: http://www.nickhernbooks.co.uk

Publishes: Nonfiction; Scripts; *Areas:* Film;
Theatre; *Markets:* Adult; Professional

Publishes plays attached to significant
professional productions in major theatres
only. No unsolicited scripts. Also publishes
books by theatre practitioners and for theatre
practitioners. No critical, analytical or
historical studies. Send proposals by email or
by post.

Northcote House Publishers Ltd
Horndon House
Horndon
Tavistock
PL19 9NQ
Tel: +44 (0) 1822 810066
Fax: +44 (0) 1822 810034
Email: admin@writersandtheirwork.co.uk
Website: http://www.northcotehouse.co.uk

Publishes: Nonfiction; *Areas:* Criticism;
Literature; *Markets:* Adult

Contact: Brian Hulme

Send proposal outlining contents, with
sample chapters. Seeks well-thought-out
approaches presented with strong marketing
arguments. See website for full guidelines
and forms.

Nourish Books
Unit 11, Shepperton House
89 Shepperton Road
London
N1 3DF
Tel: +44 (0) 20 3813 6940
Email: enquiries@watkinspublishing.com
Website: https://nourishbooks.com

Publishes: Nonfiction; *Areas:* Cookery;
Markets: Adult

Publishes books on food and drink. Send
query by email with short bio, proposal, and
sample chapter (10 pages max). See website
for full guidelines.

Michael O'Mara Books Ltd
16 Lion Yard
Tremadoc Road
London
SW4 7NQ
Tel: +44 (0) 20 7720 8643
Fax: +44 (0) 20 7627 3041

Email: enquiries@mombooks.com
Website: https://www.mombooks.com

Publishes: Nonfiction; *Areas:* Biography; Historical; Humour; *Markets:* Adult; Children's

Independent publisher dealing in general nonfiction, royal and celebrity biographies, humour, and anthologies, and books for children through its imprint (including quirky nonfiction, humour, novelty, picture, and board books). Welcomes ideas, and prefers synopses and sample text to unsolicited mss. No fiction. See website for full details.

Oberon Books
521 Caledonian Road
London
N7 9RH
Tel: +44 (0) 20 7607 3637
Fax: +44 (0) 20 7607 3629
Email: george@oberonbooks.com
Website: http://www.oberonbooks.com

Publishes: Nonfiction; Scripts; *Areas:* Drama; Theatre; *Markets:* Adult; Professional

Contact: George Spender, Senior Editor

Publishes play texts, and books on dance and theatre. Specialises in translations of European classics and contemporary plays, though also publishes edited performance versions of classics including Shakespeare. Play texts are usually published in conjunction with a production. Play scripts may be submitted by post or by email. Book proposals for trade and professional titles should include summary, table of contents, estimate word count, and sample chapter.

Oleander Press
16 Orchard Street
Cambridge
CB1 1JT
Email: editor@oleanderpress.com
Website: http://www.oleanderpress.com

Publishes: Fiction; Nonfiction; Poetry; Reference; *Areas:* Biography; Historical; Horror; Literature; Travel; *Markets:* Adult; Children's

Contact: Jon Gifford

Closed to submissions as at August 2018.

Publishes biography, Cambridge / local, children's, classic horror, language and literature, fiction, games and pastimes, modern poets, Arabia, and Libya. Looking for nonfiction – in particular children's nonfiction. Send submissions by email or by post.

Omnibus Press
14/15 Berners Street
London
W1T 3LJ
Tel: +44 (0) 20 7612 7400
Email: info@omnibuspress.com
Website: http://www.omnibuspress.com

Publishes: Nonfiction; *Areas:* Biography; Music; *Markets:* Adult

Publisher of music books, including song sheets and rock and pop biographies.

Oneworld Publications
10 Bloomsbury Street
London
WC1B 3SR
Tel: +44 (0) 20 7307 8900
Email: submissions@oneworld-publications.com
Website: http://www.oneworld-publications.com

Publishes: Fiction; Nonfiction; *Areas:* Anthropology; Arts; Biography; Business; Current Affairs; Historical; Literature; Nature; Philosophy; Politics; Psychology; Religious; Science; Self-Help; Translations; *Markets:* Adult; *Treatments:* Commercial; Literary; Popular

Not accepting fiction submissions as at August 2018, but hopes this will change in the near future. Check website for current status.

Nonfiction authors must be academics and/or experts in their field. Approaches for fiction must provide a clear and concise synopsis, outlining the novel's main themes. See website for full submission guidelines, and forms for fiction and nonfiction, which may be submitted by email.

Orenda Books

16 Carson Road
West Dulwich
London
SE21 8HU
Email: westcamel@orendabooks.co.uk
Website: http://orendabooks.co.uk

Publishes: Fiction; *Areas:* Crime; Thrillers; *Markets:* Adult; *Treatments:* Literary

Closed to submissions until February 2019. Check website for current status.

Publishes literary fiction and upmarket genre fiction only. No nonfiction, screenplays, children's books, or young adult. Send one-page synopsis and full ms (or three-chapter sample) by email.

The Orion Publishing Group Limited

Carmelite House
50 Victoria Embankment
London
EC4Y 0DZ
Tel: +44 (0) 20 3122 6444
Website: http://www.orionbooks.co.uk

Publishes: Fiction; Nonfiction; Reference; *Areas:* Adventure; Archaeology; Arts; Autobiography; Beauty and Fashion; Biography; Cookery; Culture; Current Affairs; Design; Fantasy; Gardening; Health; Historical; Lifestyle; Literature; Military; Nature; Sci-Fi; Sport; Travel; *Markets:* Adult; Children's; Youth; *Treatments:* Commercial

One of the UK's leading commercial publishers. Accepts approaches through agents only.

Osprey Publishing Ltd

Commissioning Editor
Editorial Department
Osprey Publishing
Kemp House
Chawley Park
Cumnor Hill
Oxford
OX2 9PH
Tel: +44 (0) 1865 757022
Fax: +44 (0) 1865 242009
Email: editorial@ospreypublishing.com
Website: http://www.ospreypublishing.com

Publishes: Nonfiction; *Areas:* Historical; Military; *Markets:* Adult

Publishes illustrated books on military history and aviation. Welcomes synopses and ideas for books by post or by email, but no unsolicited MSS. See website for full guidelines.

Oversteps Books

6 Halwell House
South Pool
Nr Kingsbridge
Devon
TQ7 2RX
Email: alwynmarriage@overstepsbooks.com
Website: http://www.overstepsbooks.com

Publishes: Poetry; *Markets:* Adult

Closed to submissions as at September 2018. Check website for current status.

Poetry publisher. Send email with copies of six poems that have been published in magazines or won competitions, along with details of dates or issue numbers and email addresses of the editors. Include poems and information in the body of your email. No submissions by post.

Peter Owen Publishers

Conway Hall
25 Red Lion Square
London
WC1R 4RL
Email: info@peterowen.com
Website: http://www.peterowen.com

Publishes: Fiction; Nonfiction; *Areas:* Arts; Biography; Criticism; Historical; Literature; Translations; *Markets:* Adult; *Treatments:* Literary

Contact: Antonia Owen (Editorial Director)

Publishes general nonfiction and international literary fiction. No first novels, short stories, poetry, plays, sport, spirituality, self-help, or children's or genre fiction.

Accepts query by email only, including cover letter, synopsis, and one or two sample chapters. No submissions by post. Prefers fiction to come from an agent or translator as appropriate.

P8tech

6 Woodside
Churnet View Road
Oakamoor
Staffordshire
ST10 3AE
Email: info@P8tech.com
Website: http://www.p8tech.com

Publishes: Nonfiction; *Areas:* Technology; *Markets:* Professional

Publishes IT books and ebooks for technology professionals. Current emphasis on Java and Oracle technologies. Books are heavy on the practical and full of code and screenshots.

Pan Macmillan

20 New Wharf Road
Kings Cross
London
N1 9RR
Tel: +44 (0) 20 7014 6000
Email: webqueries@macmillan.co.uk
Website: https://www.panmacmillan.com

Publishes: Fiction; Nonfiction; Poetry; *Areas:* Adventure; Biography; Crime; Fantasy; Historical; Nature; Politics; Romance; Science; Sci-Fi; Self-Help; Thrillers; *Markets:* Children's; Youth; *Treatments:* Commercial; Contemporary; Literary; Mainstream

Accepts submissions for science fiction and fantasy direct from authors. Submissions in all other areas must come via a literary agent.

PaperBooks

9 The Fairway
Northwood
Middlesex
HA6 3DZ
Email: submissions@legend-paperbooks.co.uk
Website: http://www.legend-paperbooks.co.uk

Publishes: Nonfiction; *Areas:* Autobiography; Cookery; Politics; Sociology; Travel; *Markets:* Adult

Former fiction publisher now relaunched as a nonfiction publisher. Publishes a wide range of nonfiction including cookery, memoir, travel, political and social writing. Send submissions online only, via form on website.

Parthian Books

The Old Surgery
Napier Street
Cardigan
SA43 1ED
Tel: +44 (0) 7890 968246
Email: susie@parthianbooks.com
Website: https://www.parthianbooks.co.uk

Publishes: Fiction; Nonfiction; Poetry; *Areas:* Short Stories; *Markets:* Adult; *Treatments:* Literary

Closed to poetry submissions as at June 2019. Check website for current status.

Publisher of poetry, fiction, and creative nonfiction, of Welsh origin, in the English language. Also publishes English language translations of Welsh language work. Send query with SAE, and (for fiction) a one-page synopsis and first 30 pages, or (for poetry) a sample of 15-20 poems. No email submissions, genre fiction of any kind, or children's / teenage fiction. See website for full submission guidelines.

Patrician Press

Tel: +44 (0) 7968 288651
Email: patricia@patricianpress.com
Website: https://patricianpress.com

Publishes: Fiction; Nonfiction; Poetry; *Areas:* Short Stories; *Markets:* Adult; Children's

Small and independent non-profit press, with the aim of encouraging and promoting writers of high quality fiction and poetry. Imprint publishes books for children. Contact by email only.

Pavilion Books Group Limited

43 Great Ormond Street
London
WC1N 3HZ
Tel: +44 (0) 20 7462 1500
Email: info@pavilionbooks.com
Website: http://www.pavilionbooks.com

Publishes: Fiction; Nonfiction; *Areas:* Arts;
Beauty and Fashion; Cookery; Crafts;
Culture; Design; Gardening; Historical;
Humour; Lifestyle; *Markets:* Adult;
Children's

Publishes nonfiction for adults and fiction
and nonfiction for children (including picture
books and colouring books). Send query with
SAE, outline, and sample chapter, by post.
Due to high volume of submissions, no
acknowledgement of receipt is provided.

Pavilion Publishing

Blue Sky Offices Shoreham
25 Cecil Pashley Way
Shoreham-by-Sea
West Sussex
BN43 5FF
Tel: +44 (0) 1273 434943
Email: info@pavpub.com
Website: http://www.pavpub.com

Publishes: Nonfiction; Reference; *Areas:*
Health; Sociology; *Markets:* Professional

Publishes books and resources for public,
private and voluntary workers in the health,
social care, education and community safety
sectors. Welcomes submissions from both
new and established authors, and
organisations that are developing training
materials.

Pearson UK

Edinburgh Gate
Harlow
CM20 2JE
Tel: +44 (0) 845 313 6666
Fax: +44 (0) 845 313 7777
Email: eloise.cook@pearson.com
Website: http://www.pearsoned.co.uk

Publishes: Nonfiction; *Markets:* Academic;
Professional

Contact: Eloise Cook, Publisher

World's largest publisher of educational
material, including books for primary school
pupils through to professionals. See website
for appropriate imprint to approach, and
specific submission guidelines.

Pen & Sword Books Ltd

47 Church Street
Barnsley
South Yorkshire
S70 2AS
Tel: +44 (0) 1226 734222
Fax: +44 (0) 1226 734438
Email: editorialoffice@pen-and-sword.co.uk
Website: http://www.pen-and-sword.co.uk

Publishes: Nonfiction; *Areas:* Antiques;
Archaeology; Autobiography; Biography;
Crime; Gardening; Health; Historical;
Hobbies; Lifestyle; Military; Nature;
Sociology; Sport; *Markets:* Adult

Contact: Lisa Hooson

Publishes across a number of areas including
military history, naval and maritime history,
aviation, local history, family history,
transport, discovery and exploration,
collectables and antiques, nostalgia and true
crime. In 2017, launched a new lifestyle
imprint which publishes books on areas such
as health and diet, hobbies and sport,
gardening and wildlife and space. Submit
proposal using form on website.

Penguin Random House UK

80 Strand
London
WC2R 0RL
Tel: +44 (0) 20 7010 3000
Fax: +44 (0) 20 7010 6060
Website: http://www.penguin.co.uk

Publishes: Fiction; Nonfiction; Poetry;
Reference; *Markets:* Adult; Children's

Publishes a wide range of fiction, nonfiction,
poetry, and reference, for children and
adults. No queries or unsolicited MSS, other
than through a literary agent.

Percy Publishing

Email: enquiries@percy-publishing.com
Website: https://www.percy-publishing.com

Publishes: Fiction; *Markets:* Adult

Founded in 2014 and awarded "Best Publisher" in 2016. Due to high level of submissions can now only accept submissions via a literary agent.

Periscope
8 Southern Court
South Street
Reading
Berkshire
RG1 4QS
Email: info@periscopebooks.co.uk
Website: http://www.periscopebooks.co.uk

Publishes: Fiction; Nonfiction; *Areas:* Autobiography; Biography; Crime; Current Affairs; Historical; Politics; Science; Sociology; Translations; *Markets:* Adult; *Treatments:* Literary

Send query by email with bio, synopsis, and two sample chapters.

Phaidon Press Limited
Regent's Wharf
All Saints Street
London
N1 9PA
Tel: +44 (0) 20 7843 1000
Fax: +44 (0) 20 7843 1010
Email: submissions@phaidon.com
Website: http://www.phaidon.com

Publishes: Nonfiction; *Areas:* Architecture; Arts; Beauty and Fashion; Cookery; Culture; Design; Film; Historical; Music; Photography; Travel; *Markets:* Academic; Adult; Children's

Publishes books in the areas of art, architecture, design, photography, film, fashion, contemporary culture, decorative arts, music, performing arts, cultural history, food and cookery, travel and books for children. No fiction or approaches by post. Send query by email only, with CV and short description of the project. Response only if interested.

Phoenix Yard Books
18 Deane House Studios
27 Greenwood Place

Kentish Town
London
NW5 1LB
Tel: +44 (0) 20 7239 4968
Email: hello@phoenixyardbooks.com
Website: http://www.phoenixyardbooks.com

Publishes: Fiction; Nonfiction; Poetry; *Markets:* Children's; Youth; *Treatments:* Literary

Publishes picture books, fiction, poetry, nonfiction and illustration for children aged around three to thirteen. Considers books of all genres, but leans more towards the literary and of the fiction spectrum. Particularly interested in character-based series, and fiction appealing to boys aged 6-9. Does not concentrate on young adult fiction, but will consider older fiction as part of epic series, sagas or trilogies. Accepts queries through literary agents, foreign publishers, and literary translators only.

Piccadilly Press
80-81 Wimpole Street
London
W1G 9RE
Tel: +44 (0) 20 7490 3875
Email: hello@bonnierbooks.co.uk
Website: http://www.piccadillypress.co.uk

Publishes: Fiction; Nonfiction; *Areas:* Humour; *Markets:* Children's; Youth; *Treatments:* Contemporary; Light

Send submissions by email with synopsis and full manuscript as Word or PDF attachments. No submissions by post.

Pimpernel Press
22 Marylands Road
London
W9 2DY
Tel: +44 (0) 20 7289 7100
Email: jo@pimpernelpress.com
Website: http://www.pimpernelpress.com

Publishes: Nonfiction; *Areas:* Arts; Design; Gardening; *Markets:* Adult

Publishes books on art, design, houses, and gardens. Send submissions by post.

Policy Studies Institute (PSI)

University of Westminster
35 Marylebone Road
London
NW1 5LS
Tel: +44 (0) 20 7911 7500
Fax: +44 (0) 20 7911 7501
Email: psi-admin@psi.org.uk
Website: http://www.psi.org.uk

Publishes: Nonfiction; *Areas:* Culture;
Finance; Nature; Politics; Sociology;
Markets: Academic; Adult; Professional

Has informed public policy since 1931,
through the provision, dissemination and
promotion of evidence-based research.
Currently focused on energy and climate
change; resource use and the circular
economy; mobility and transport; the role of
communities and business in delivering a
sustainable future; cities, innovation and
sustainability transitions; public behaviours,
attitudes and policy; and policy and research
evaluation.

Portobello Books Ltd

12 Addison Avenue
London
W11 4QR
Tel: +44 (0) 20 7605 1380
Fax: +44 (0) 20 7605 1361
Email: info@portobellobooks.com
Website: http://www.portobellobooks.com

Publishes: Fiction; Nonfiction; *Areas:*
Autobiography; Criticism; Culture; Current
Affairs; Historical; Translations; Travel;
Markets: Adult; *Treatments:* Literary

Contact: Submissions Editor

Publishes nonfiction and fiction in
translation. Accepts submissions through
literary agents only.

Profile Books

3 Holford Yard
Bevin Way
London
WC1X 9HD
Tel: +44 (0) 20 7841 6300
Fax: +44 (0) 20 7833 3969
Email: info@profilebooks.com
Website: https://profilebooks.com

Publishes: Nonfiction; *Areas:* Biography;
Business; Culture; Current Affairs; Finance;
Historical; Humour; Politics; Psychology;
Science; *Markets:* Adult

Award-winning small publisher noted for
author-friendly relations. Published the
number-one Christmas bestseller in 2003.
Accepts direct queries by email (up to 250
words) with first 10 pages, with QUERY and
the title of your work in the subject line. No
attachments. See website for full guidelines.

Pure Indigo Limited

Publishing Department
17 The Herons
Cottenham
Cambridge
CB24 8XX
Tel: +44 (0) 7981 395258
Email: submissions@pureindigo.co.uk
Website: http://www.pureindigo.co.uk/
publishing

Publishes: Fiction; Nonfiction; *Areas:*
Fantasy; Sci-Fi; *Markets:* Children's

Publishes books for children, including
single-player role-playing gamebooks and
books designed to support early readers.
Prefers submissions by email. See website
for guidelines.

Pushkin Press

71-75 Shelton Street
London
WC2H 9JQ
Tel: +44 (0) 20 3735 9078
Email: books@pushkinpress.com
Website: http://pushkinpress.com

Publishes: Fiction; Nonfiction; *Areas:*
Autobiography; *Markets:* Adult; Children's;
Treatments: Contemporary; Traditional

Publishes novels, essays, memoirs,
children's books, including timeless classics
and contemporary.

Quadrille Publishing Ltd

5th & 6th Floors
52-54 Southwark Street
London
SE1 1UN

Tel: +44 (0) 20 7601 7500
Email: editorial@quadrille.co.uk
Website: http://www.quadrille.co.uk

Publishes: Nonfiction; *Areas:* Beauty and
Fashion; Cookery; Crafts; Design;
Gardening; Health; Humour; *Markets:* Adult

Publishes quality illustrated nonfiction. No
fiction or books for children. Prefers to
receive submissions by email. See website
for full details.

Quarto Publishing Group UK

The Old Brewery
6 Blundell Street
London
N7 9BH
Tel: +44 (0) 20 7700 6700
Fax: +44 (0) 20 7700 8066
Email: info@quarto.com
Website: http://www.quarto.com

Publishes: Nonfiction; *Areas:* Arts; Beauty
and Fashion; Cookery; Crafts; Design;
Entertainment; Gardening; Health;
Historical; Hobbies; How-to; Lifestyle;
Sport; *Markets:* Adult; Children's

Publisher of illustrated nonfiction books for
adults and children.

Quercus Books

Carmelite House
50 Victoria Embankment
London
EC4Y 0DZ
Tel: +44 (0) 20 3122 6000
Email: enquiries@quercusbooks.co.uk
Website: https://www.quercusbooks.co.uk

Publishes: Fiction; Nonfiction; *Areas:*
Crime; Fantasy; Sci-Fi; *Markets:* Adult;
Children's

Publishes fiction and nonfiction. Accepts
submissions only via a literary agent.

Quintet Publishing

Ovest House
58 West Street
Brighton
BN1 2RA
Tel: +44 (0) 1273 716 000

Email: mark.searle@quarto.com
Website: https://www.quartoknows.com/
Quintet-Publishing

Publishes: Nonfiction; *Areas:* Cookery;
Crafts; Culture; Lifestyle; Photography;
Markets: Adult

Publishes illustrated nonfiction on a co-
edition basis with partners around the world.

Ransom Publishing Ltd

Unit 7
Brocklands Farm
West Meon
Hampshire
GU32 1JN
Tel: +44 (0) 1730 829091
Email: daisy@ransom.co.uk
Website: http://www.ransom.co.uk

Publishes: Fiction; Nonfiction; *Markets:*
Adult; Children's; Professional; Youth

Contact: Daisy Hawkins

An independent specialist publisher of high
quality, inspirational books that encourage
and help children, young adults, and adults to
develop their reading skills. Books are
intended to have content which is age
appropriate and engaging, but reading levels
that would normally be appropriate for
younger readers. Also publishes resources
for both the library and classroom. No
picture books or early years books. Will
consider unsolicited mss. Email with
synopsis and sample (up to three chapters) in
first instance, or full ms if under thousand
words.

Red Rattle Books

Email: editor@redrattlebooks.co.uk
Website: http://www.redrattlebooks.co.uk

Publishes: Fiction; Nonfiction; *Areas:*
Crime; Horror; *Markets:* Adult

**Not accepting submissions as at January
2019. Check website for current status.**

Independent, family run company,
publishing new crime, horror and nonfiction
books. Submit via website using online
submission form.

Repeater Books

Website: https://repeaterbooks.com

Publishes: Fiction; Nonfiction; Poetry;
Areas: Arts; Culture; Current Affairs;
Literature; Music; Philosophy; Politics;
Markets: Adult

Aims to publish in every sphere and genre,
"combining vigorous dissent and a pragmatic
willingness to succeed". Submit complete ms
via online submission system.

Rivers Oram Press

144 Hemingford Road
London
N1 1DE
Tel: +44 (0) 20 7607 0823
Fax: +44 (0) 20 7609 2776
Email: ro@riversoram.com
Website: http://www.riversoram.com

Publishes: Nonfiction; *Areas:* Culture;
Current Affairs; Historical; Politics;
Sociology; Women's Interests; *Markets:*
Adult

Publisher of social and political sciences,
including sexual politics, gender studies,
social history, cultural studies, and current
affairs.

Robert Hale Publishers

The Crowood Press
The Stable Block
Crowood Lane
Ramsbury
Wiltshire
SN8 2HR
Tel: +44 (0) 1672 520320
Fax: +44 (0) 1672 520280
Email: enquiries@crowood.com
Website: http://www.crowood.com

Publishes: Fiction; Nonfiction; Reference;
Areas: Arts; Biography; Crime; Design;
Health; Historical; Leisure; Lifestyle;
Nature; Romance; Spiritual; Sport;
Westerns; *Markets:* Adult; *Treatments:*
Contemporary

Contact: Editorial Department

See website for full submission guidelines.
Currently only accepting fiction submissions

for the publisher's Western series. Send
query with synopsis and complete ms
(fiction) or sample chapter (nonfiction).

Route Publishing

PO Box 167
Pontefract
WF8 4WW
Tel: +44 (0) 1977 793442
Email: info@route-online.com
Website: http://www.route-online.com

Publishes: Fiction; Nonfiction; *Areas:*
Autobiography; Biography; Culture; Film;
Music; *Markets:* Adult; *Treatments:*
Contemporary

Contact: Ian Daley; Isabel Galan

Publisher of nonfiction (particularly music
books) and occasional fiction. Only accept a
handful of titles a year. Response no
guaranteed. If submitting by post, include
SAE if return of work required.

Ruby Tuesday Books

6 Newlands Road
Tunbridge Wells
Kent
TN4 9AT
Tel: +44 (0) 1892 557767
Email: shan@rubytuesdaybooks.com
Website: http://www.rubytuesdaybooks.com

Publishes: Nonfiction; *Areas:* Nature;
Science; Technology; *Markets:* Academic;
Children's

Publisher of nonfiction books for children,
including books for schools.

Saffron Books

EAPGROUP
PO Box 13666
London
SW14 8WF
Tel: +44 (0) 20 8392 1122
Fax: +44 (0) 20 8392 1122
Email: info@eapgroup.com
Website: http://www.saffronbooks.com

Publishes: Fiction; Nonfiction; *Areas:*
Archaeology; Arts; Business; Culture;

Current Affairs; Finance; Historical; Sociology; *Markets:* Adult

Publishes books on art, archaeology and architecture, art history, current affairs and linguistics, with a particular emphasis on Asia, Africa, and the Middle East. Also publishes fiction. Welcomes proposals for books and monongraphs from new or established authors. Send query by email, post, or fax (not preferred for long documents). See website for full guidelines.

Sage Publications

1 Oliver's Yard
55 City Road
London
EC1Y 1SP
Tel: +44 (0) 20 7324 8500
Fax: +44 (0) 20 7324 8600
Email: info@sagepub.co.uk
Website: https://uk.sagepub.com

Publishes: Nonfiction; *Areas:* Anthropology; Archaeology; Arts; Business; Crime; Finance; Health; Historical; Media; Medicine; Politics; Psychology; Religious; Science; Sociology; Technology; *Markets:* Academic; Professional

Publishes academic books and journals. See website for guides for authors and making submissions, etc.

The Salariya Book Company

25 Marlborough Place
Brighton
East Sussex
BN1 1UB
Tel: +44 (0) 1273 603306
Fax: +44 (0) 1273 621619
Email: salariya@salariya.com
Website: http://www.salariya.com

Publishes: Fiction; Nonfiction; *Areas:* Adventure; Fantasy; Historical; Nature; Science; *Markets:* Children's

Not accepting submissions as at February 2019. Check website for current status.

Publishes books of fiction and nonfiction for children.

Salt Publishing Ltd

12 Norwich Road
CROMER
Norfolk
NR27 0AX
Tel: +44 (0) 1263 511011
Email: submissions@saltpublishing.com
Website: http://www.saltpublishing.com

Publishes: Fiction; Nonfiction; Poetry; *Areas:* Biography; Crime; Criticism; Gothic; Literature; Mystery; Short Stories; Thrillers; *Markets:* Adult; Children's

Currently accepting submissions of contemporary adult poetry and nonfiction by British residents. See website for full submission guidelines.

Samuel French Ltd

24-32 Stephenson Way
London
NW1 2HD
Tel: +44 (0) 20 7387 9373
Email: submissions@samuelfrench.co.uk
Website: http://www.samuelfrench-london.co.uk

Publishes: Scripts; *Areas:* Drama; *Markets:* Adult

Publishes plays only. Send submissions by email only, following the guidelines on the website.

Sandstone Press Ltd

Suite 1
Willow House
Stoneyfield Business Park
Inverness
IV2 7PA
Tel: +44 (0) 1349 865484
Email: submissions@sandstonepress.com
Website: https://sandstonepress.com

Publishes: Fiction; Nonfiction; *Areas:* Crime; Thrillers; *Markets:* Adult; *Treatments:* Literary

Accepts submissions of nonfiction from agents and authors all year. Accepts submissions of fiction from agents all year, but accepts submissions of fiction from authors during specific windows only. Check website for status regarding fiction submissions from authors. Accepts approaches via email only. See website for full guidelines.

Saqi Books

26 Westbourne Grove
London
W2 5RH
Tel: +44 (0) 20 7221 9347
Fax: +44 (0) 20 7229 7492
Email: hassan@saqibooks.com
Website: http://www.saqibooks.com

Publishes: Fiction; Nonfiction; *Areas:* Architecture; Arts; Cookery; Historical; Politics; *Markets:* Academic; Adult; *Treatments:* Literary

Publisher of books related to the Arab world and the Middle East (initially), but now also covering South and Central Asia. Also publishes European fiction. Not accepting fiction submissions as at March 2019. See website for full submission guidelines.

Sawday's

Merchants House
Wapping Road
Bristol
BS1 4RW
Tel: +44 (0) 1172 047810
Email: hello@sawdays.co.uk
Website: https://www.sawdays.co.uk

Publishes: Nonfiction; *Areas:* Nature; Travel; *Markets:* Adult

Publishes guidebooks and books on environmental topics.

Scholastic

Euston House
24 Eversholt Street
London
NW1 1DB

WITNEY:
Windrush Park
Range Road
Witney
OXON
OX29 0YD

SOUTHAM:

Westfield Road
Southam
Warwickshire
CV47 0RA
Tel: +44 (0) 1926 887799
Fax: +44 (0) 1926 883331
Email: enquiries@scholastic.co.uk
Website: https://www.scholastic.co.uk

Publishes: Fiction; Nonfiction; *Markets:* Children's

Publisher of fiction and nonfiction for children, as well as eduactional material for primary schools.

Science Museum Group

Email: wendy.burford@sciencemuseum.ac.uk
Website: https://group.sciencemuseum.org.uk

Publishes: Nonfiction; *Areas:* Science; Technology; *Markets:* Academic; Adult

Contact: Wendy Burford, Publishing Manager

Publishes books on science, technology, and engineering. Also museum guides. Send query by email.

SelfMadeHero

139 Pancras Road
London
NW1 1UN
Email: submissions@selfmadehero.com
Website: https://selfmadehero.com

Publishes: Fiction; Nonfiction; *Areas:* Biography; Crime; Horror; Sci-Fi; *Markets:* Adult

Publishes fiction and nonfiction graphic novels. Send query by email or by post with one-page synopsis and at least eight pages of sequential art (up to 5MB if sending by email). See website for full guidelines.

September Publishing

Tel: +44 (0) 20 3637 0116
Email: info@septemberpublishing.org
Website: https://www.septemberpublishing.org

Publishes: Nonfiction; *Areas:* Arts; Autobiography; Biography; Humour; Politics; Travel; *Markets:* Adult

Publishes extraordinary lives and expert insight. Welcomes submissions from both authors and agents via form on website.

Seren Books
57 Nolton Street
Bridgend
Wales
CF31 3AE
Tel: +44 (0) 1656 663018
Email: Seren@SerenBooks.com
Website: https://www.serenbooks.com

Publishes: Fiction; Nonfiction; Poetry; *Areas:* Anthropology; Arts; Biography; Criticism; Current Affairs; Drama; Historical; Music; Photography; Politics; Sport; Translations; Travel; *Markets:* Adult; Children's; *Treatments:* Literary

Contact: Mick Felton (Publisher); Amy Wack (Poetry Editor)

Publishes fiction, nonfiction, and poetry. Specialises in English-language writing from Wales and aims to bring Welsh culture, art, literature, and politics to a wider audience. Accepts nonfiction submissions by post or by email. Accepts poetry submissions by post only. Accepts fiction only from authors with whom there is an existing publishing relationship.

Serpent's Tail
3 Holford Yard
Bevin Way
London
WC1X 9HD
Tel: +44 (0) 20 7841 6300
Email: info@profilebooks.com
Website: http://www.serpentstail.com

Publishes: Fiction; Nonfiction; *Areas:* Autobiography; Biography; Crime; Culture; Current Affairs; Music; Politics; *Markets:* Adult

Accepts queries by email (up to 250 words) with sample text (10 pages or the first chapter only). See website for full submission guidelines. No poetry, Young Adult, Fantasy, Science Fiction, children's picture books, or screenplays.

Severn House Publishers
Eardley House
4 Uxbridge Street
London
W8 7SY
Tel: +44 (0) 20 3011 0525
Email: sales@severnhouse.com
Website: http://severnhouse.com

Publishes: Fiction; *Areas:* Crime; Historical; Horror; Mystery; Romance; Sci-Fi; Thrillers; *Markets:* Adult

Accepts submissions via literary agents only. Targets the UK and US fiction library markets, and considers only authors with a significant background in these markets.

Shearsman Books
50 Westons Hill Drive
Emersons Green
Bristol
BS16 7DF
Tel: +44 (0) 1179 572957
Email: editor@shearsman.com
Website: https://www.shearsman.com

Publishes: Nonfiction; Poetry; *Areas:* Autobiography; Criticism; Literature; Translations; *Markets:* Adult

Contact: Tony Frazer

Publishes poetry books of at least 60 A5 pages. Publishes mainly poetry by British, Irish, North American and Australian/New Zealand poets, plus poetry in translation from any language—although particular interest in German, Spanish and Latin American poetry.

Submit only if MS is of appropriate length and most of it has already appeared in UK or US magazines of some repute. Send selection of 6-10 pages by post with SASE or by email with material embedded in the text or as PDF attachment. No other kind of attachments accepted.

Also sometimes publishes literary criticism on poetry, and essays or memoirs by poets.

Sheldrake Press

PO Box 74852
London
SW12 2DX
Tel: +44 (0) 20 8675 1767
Fax: +44 (0) 20 8675 7736
Email: enquiries@sheldrakepress.co.uk
Website: http://www.sheldrakepress.co.uk

Publishes: Nonfiction; *Areas:* Architecture;
Cookery; Historical; Humour; Music;
Travel; *Markets:* Adult

Contact: Simon Rigge, Publisher

Publisher of illustrated nonfiction titles
covering travel, history, cookery, music,
humour, and stationery. No fiction.

Shepheard-Walwyn (Publishers) Ltd

107 Parkway House
Sheen Lane
London
SW14 8LS
Tel: +44 (0) 20 8241 5927
Email: books@shepheard-walwyn.co.uk
Website: https://shepheard-walwyn.co.uk

Publishes: Nonfiction; Poetry; *Areas:*
Biography; Finance; Historical; Philosophy;
Politics; *Markets:* Adult

Publishes mainly nonfiction, particularly the
areas listed above and also books of Scottish
interest, and gift books in calligraphy and /
or illustrated. Also some poetry.

Silvertail Books

Email: editor@silvertailbooks.com
Website: http://www.silvertailbooks.com

Publishes: Fiction; Nonfiction; *Markets:*
Adult; *Treatments:* Commercial

Welcomes submissions for commercial
fiction and nonfiction, either through an
agent or direct from authors. Submit by
email only. No postal submissions. Response
not guaranteed.

Simon & Schuster UK Limited

1st Floor
222 Gray's Inn Road
London
WC1X 8HB
Tel: +44 (0) 20 7316 1900
Fax: +44 (0) 20 7316 0332
Email: enquiries@simonandschuster.co.uk
Website: https://www.
simonandschuster.co.uk

Publishes: Fiction; Nonfiction; *Areas:*
Autobiography; Biography; Business;
Cookery; Health; Historical; Humour;
Politics; Science; Spiritual; Sport; Travel;
Markets: Adult; Children's; Youth;
Treatments: Commercial; Literary

Publisher of commercial and literary fiction
and nonfiction for adults and children,
including children's fiction and picture
books. No unsolicited MSS.

Singing Dragon

73 Collier Street
London
N1 9BE
Tel: +44 (0) 20 7833 2307
Email: hello@singingdragon.com
Website: http://singingdragon.com

Publishes: Nonfiction; *Areas:* Health;
Leisure; Medicine; Self-Help; Spiritual;
Markets: Academic; Adult; Professional

Publishes authoritative books on
complementary and alternative health, Tai
Chi, Qigong and ancient wisdom traditions
for health, wellbeing, and professional and
personal development, for parents,
professionals, academics and the general
reader. Welcomes ideas for new books. Send
query by email with CV and completed
proposal form (available on website).

Snowbooks

55 North Street
Thame
OXON
OX9 3BH
Email: emma@snowbooks.com
Website: http://www.snowbooks.com

Publishes: Fiction; Nonfiction; *Areas:*
Crafts; Crime; Fantasy; Historical; Horror;
Leisure; Sci-Fi; Sport; Thrillers; *Markets:*
Adult

Contact: Emma Barnes, Managing Director

Open to submissions of horror, science fiction, and fantasy novels over 70,000 words. Named joint Small Publisher of the Year at the 2006 British book Trade Awards. Friendly attitude towards authors and unsolicited approaches. See website for guidelines. Approach via web submission system only – postal submissions will neither be read nor returned, even if sent through an agent. £2 submission fee.

SportsBooks Limited
9 St Aubyns Place
York
YO24 1EQ
Tel: +44 (0) 1904 613475
Email: info@sportsbooks.ltd.uk
Website: http://www.sportsbooks.ltd.uk

Publishes: Nonfiction; *Areas:* Biography; Sport; *Markets:* Adult

Publishes sports nonfiction.

Springer-Verlag London Ltd
6th Floor
236 Gray's Inn Road
WC1X 8HL
Tel: +44 (0) 20 3192 2000
Website: http://www.springer.com

Publishes: Nonfiction; *Areas:* Medicine; Science; Technology; *Markets:* Academic; Professional

Publishes books professional and academic books on science, technology, and medicine, particularly computing, chemistry, biosciences, medicine, maths, and engineering. No school books, science fiction, or fiction. Also publishes a range of journals.

St Pauls Publishing
by Westminster Cathedral
Morpeth Terrace
Victoria
London
SW1P 1EP
Tel: +44 (0) 20 7828 5582
Email: editor@stpauls.org.uk
Website: http://www.stpauls.org.uk

Publishes: Nonfiction; *Areas:* Religious; *Markets:* Adult

Publisher of religious material, including books on theology, scripture, and catechetics, as well as prayer books and religious biographies.

Stonewood Press
Submissions, Stonewood Press
Diversity House
72 Nottingham Road
Arnold
Nottingham
NG5 6LF
Email: stonewoodpress@gmail.com
Website: http://www.stonewoodpress.co.uk

Publishes: Fiction; Poetry; *Areas:* Short Stories; *Markets:* Adult; *Treatments:* Contemporary

Contact: Martin Parker

Note: Current submission status is unclear. The publisher's website states it is closed to new submissions, but that submissions re-open from the start of 2017.

Independent publisher dedicated to promoting new writing, with an emphasis on contemporary short stories and poetry. Send query with biography, publishing history, and either one story and a brief outline of the others in the collection, or up to 10 poems and details of how many other poems are in the collection. Submit by post only. No children's books, creative nonfiction, novels, or drama.

Sunflower Books
Commissioning Editor
Sunflower Books
PO Box 36160
London
SW7 3WS
Email: info@sunflowerbooks.co.uk
Website: http://www.sunflowerbooks.co.uk

Publishes: Nonfiction; *Areas:* Leisure; Travel; *Markets:* Adult

Publishes walking guides only. Authors are advised to submit a proposal (hard copy by post only) before starting work on a book, as the format must match that of existing titles. No proposals by email.

Sweet Cherry Publishing

Unit 36, Vulcan House
Vulcan Road
Leicester
LE5 3EF
Email: submissions@
sweetcherrypublishing.com
Website: https://www.
sweetcherrypublishing.com

Publishes: Fiction; *Markets:* Children's

Contact: Abdul Thadha

Publishes books for children of all ages. Looking for talented new authors of children's series and collections. Send submissions by email only. No postal submissions. See website for full submission guidelines.

Tango Books Ltd

PO Box 32595
London
W4 5YD
Tel: +44 (0) 20 8996 9970
Email: info@tangobooks.co.uk
Website: https://www.tangobooks.co.uk

Publishes: Fiction; Nonfiction; *Markets:* Children's

Closed to submissions as at June 2019. Check website for current status.

Publisher of children's fiction (ages 1-8), nonfiction (ages 1-15), and novelty books, up to 1,000 words. Send query by email or by post with complete text, bio, and SAE. No poetry or verse, or texts that are very British in content or style. See website for complete guidelines.

Tate Publishing

Millbank
London
SW1P 4RG
Email: submissions@tate.org.uk
Website: https://www.tate.org.uk/publishing

Publishes: Nonfiction; *Areas:* Arts; Historical; *Markets:* Adult; Children's

Publishes exhibition-related and art-history titles, as well as books for children. Accepts proposals by post or by email. See website for guidelines.

I.B. Tauris & Co. Ltd

6 Salem Road
London
W2 4BU
Tel: +44 (0) 20 7243 1225
Fax: +44 (0) 20 7243 1226
Email: ibagherzade@ibtauris.com
Website: http://www.ibtauris.com

Publishes: Nonfiction; *Areas:* Architecture; Arts; Biography; Culture; Current Affairs; Design; Film; Historical; Media; Politics; Religious; Travel; *Markets:* Academic; Adult

Contact: Iradj Bagherzade, Publisher & Editorial Director

Publishes academic books on the latest research, student texts, and general nonfiction. No fiction, poetry, or children's. Send query with proposal outlining book's purpose and market, with synopsis, table of contents, two sample chapters, and author CV. Send proposal by email directly to appropriate editor (see website for details).

The Templar Company Limited

2.08 The Plaza
The Plaza
535 King's Road
London
SW10 0SZ
Tel: +44 (0) 20 3770 8888
Email: hello@templarco.co.uk
Website: https://www.templarco.co.uk

Publishes: Fiction; Nonfiction; *Markets:* Children's

Publishes children's fiction and picture and novelty books. Encourage anybody who wishes to have their work considered by one of their imprints to seek representation by an agent. No unsolicited mss or proposals.

Thames and Hudson Ltd
181A High Holborn
London
WC1V 7QX
Tel: +44 (0) 20 7845 5000
Email: submissions@thameshudson.co.uk
Website: http://www.thamesandhudson.com

Publishes: Nonfiction; Reference; *Areas:*
Archaeology; Architecture; Arts; Beauty and
Fashion; Biography; Crafts; Culture; Design;
Gardening; Historical; Hobbies; Lifestyle;
Literature; Nature; Philosophy; Photography;
Religious; Science; Travel; *Markets:* Adult;
Children's

Publishes illustrated nonfiction only. No
fiction. Prefers to receive submissions by
email, but will accept submissions by post.
See website for full details.

The British Museum Press
38 Russell Square
London
WC1B 3QQ
Tel: +44 (0) 20 7323 8528
Email: publicity@britishmuseum.org
Website: https://www.britishmuseum.org/
about_us/services/
the_british_museum_press.aspx

Publishes: Nonfiction; *Areas:* Archaeology;
Arts; Culture; Historical; *Markets:*
Academic; Adult; Children's; Family

Publishes books inspired by the collections
of the British Museum, covering fine and
decorative arts, history, archaeology and
world cultures.

Three Hares Publishing
Email: submissions@
threeharespublishing.com
Website: https://threeharespublishing.com

Publishes: Fiction; Nonfiction; *Areas:*
Crime; Psychology; Thrillers; *Markets:*
Adult; Children's

**Closed to submissions as at July 2019.
Check website for current status.**

Will consider all kinds of fiction and
nonfiction, except picture books. Particularly
interested in crime/psychological thrillers

and Middle Grade fiction. Send query by
email with one-page synopsis and first three
chapters. See website for full guidelines.

Tiny Owl
7 Peacock Yard
Iliffe Street
London
SE17 3LH
Email: info@tinyowl.co.uk
Website: http://tinyowl.co.uk

Publishes: Fiction; *Markets:* Children's

Publisher of books for children.

Trentham Books
Email: p.gordon-smith@ucl.ac.uk
Website: https://www.ucl.ac.uk/ucl-press

Publishes: Nonfiction; *Areas:* Design;
Science; Sociology; Technology; Women's
Interests; *Markets:* Academic

Contact: Pat Gordon-Smith

Open access publisher of edited volumes,
scholarly editions, textbooks and journals.
Welcomes proposals.

Trotman & Co. Ltd
21d Charles Street
Bath
BA1 1HX
Tel: +44 (0) 01225 584950
Email: dellao@trotman.co.uk
Website: http://www.trotman.co.uk

Publishes: Nonfiction; Reference; *Markets:*
Academic; Professional

Publishes books on careers, employment and
training resources, higher education guides,
teacher support material, etc. Send query by
email with brief summary, details of target
audience, and list of chapters / sections.

TSO (The Stationery Office)
Mandela Way
London
SE1 5SS
Tel: +44 (0) 20 7394 4200
Email: customer.services@tso.co.uk
Website: http://www.tso.co.uk

Publishes: Nonfiction; Reference; *Areas:*
Business; Current Affairs; Medicine;
Markets: Professional

One of the largest publishers by volume in
the UK, publishing more than 9,000 titles a
year in print and digital formats.

Twenty First Century Publishers Ltd

Email: tfcp@btinternet.com
Website: http://www.
twentyfirstcenturypublishers.com

Publishes: Fiction; *Areas:* Crime; Finance;
Historical; Psychology; Thrillers; *Markets:*
Adult

Publishes general fiction written thoughtfully
and with insight, plot driven original works,
and knowledgeably written financial
thrillers, in English, French, and German.
Send submissions by email, with a brief 1-2
page synopsis or overview in the body of the
email, and the full ms, or as many chapters
as you wish, in a file attachment.

UCL Press

Email: c.penfold@ucl.ac.uk
Website: https://www.ucl.ac.uk/ucl-press

Publishes: Nonfiction; *Markets:* Academic

Open access publisher of scholarly
monographs, edited volumes, scholarly
editions, textbooks and journals in all subject
areas. Welcomes proposals.

Unicorn Publishing Group

Charleston Studio
Meadow Business Centre
Ringmer, Lewes
East Sussex
BN8 5RW
Tel: +44 (0) 1273 812066
Email: lucy@unicornpublishing.org
Website: http://www.unicornpublishing.org

Publishes: Nonfiction; Reference; *Areas:*
Arts; Biography; Culture; Historical;
Military; *Markets:* Adult

Contact: Lucy Duckworth

Publishes books on the visual arts and
cultural history, military history, and
biographies and general history. Approach
by email or by post.

University of Exeter Press

Reed Hall
Streatham Drive
Exeter
EX4 4QR
Tel: +44 (0) 1392 263066
Fax: +44 (0) 1392 263064
Email: n.massen@exeterpress.co.uk
Website: http://www.exeterpress.co.uk

Publishes: Nonfiction; Reference; *Areas:*
Archaeology; Culture; Film; Historical;
Literature; Philosophy; Religious; Sociology;
Markets: Academic

Contact: Nigel Massen

Publisher of academic books. See website for
guidelines on submitting a proposal.

University of Wales Press

University Registry
King Edward VII Avenue
Cathays Park
Cardiff
CF10 3NS
Tel: +44 (0) 29 2037 6999
Email: press@press.wales.ac.uk
Website: http://www.uwp.co.uk

Publishes: Nonfiction; *Areas:* Culture;
Historical; Literature; Media; Nature;
Philosophy; Politics; Religious; Sociology;
Markets: Academic

Make contact by phone or by email at an
early stage – preferably before book is
written.

Vallentine Mitchell & Co., Limited

Catalyst House
720 Centennial Court
Centennial Park
Elstree
Herts
WD6 3SY
Tel: +44 (0) 20 8292 5637

Email: editor@vmbooks.com
Website: https://www.vmbooksuk.com

Publishes: Nonfiction; *Areas:* Culture;
Historical; Philosophy; Religious; *Markets:*
Academic; Adult

Publishes books on Jewish history, culture
and heritage, Jewish thought, Middle Eastern
history, politics and culture and the
Holocaust, for both academic and general
readerships. Offices in Hertfordshire and
Chicago, Illinois. Send proposals by email.

Verso
6 Meard Street
London
W1F 0EG
Tel: +44 (0) 20 7437 3546
Fax: +44 (0) 20 7734 0059
Email: submissions@verso.co.uk
Website: http://www.versobooks.com

Publishes: Fiction; Nonfiction; *Areas:*
Anthropology; Architecture; Arts;
Autobiography; Biography; Culture; Film;
Finance; Historical; Media; Philosophy;
Politics; Sociology; *Markets:* Academic;
Adult

"Radical" publisher of the political left.
Publishes mainly nonfiction and does not
consider unsolicited fiction submissions. For
nonfiction, send proposal up to 15 pages,
including overview, contents / chapter
outline, author background, market info, and
your timetable, by email only. No unsolicited
MSS, or hard copy submissions. If no
response within two months, assume
rejection.

W.W. Norton & Company Ltd
15 Carlisle Street
London
W1D 3BS
Tel: +44 (0) 20 7323 1579
Email: office@wwnorton.co.uk
Website: http://wwnorton.co.uk

Publishes: Fiction; Nonfiction; Poetry;
Areas: Adventure; Anthropology;
Archaeology; Architecture; Autobiography;
Biography; Business; Crafts; Crime; Current
Affairs; Design; Drama; Film; Finance;
Health; Historical; Hobbies; Humour; Legal;

Leisure; Lifestyle; Literature; Medicine;
Music; Nature; Philosophy; Politics;
Psychology; Religious; Science; Self-Help;
Sociology; Sport; Technology; Travel;
Women's Interests; *Markets:* Academic;
Adult; Professional

UK branch of a US publisher. No editorial
office in the UK – contact the main office in
New York (see separate listing).

Watkins Publishing
Unit 11, Shepperton House
89 Shepperton Road
London
N1 3DF
Tel: +44 (0) 20 3813 6940
Email: enquiries@watkinspublishing.com
Website: https://www.
watkinspublishing.com

Publishes: Nonfiction; *Areas:* Historical;
Lifestyle; Religious; Self-Help; Spiritual;
Markets: Adult

Publishes books in the field of Mind, Body
and Spirit. Not accepting submissions as at
April 2019. Check website for current status.

Welsh Academic Press
PO Box 733
Caerdydd
Cardiff
CF14 7ZY
Tel: +44 (0) 29 2021 8187
Email: post@welsh-academic-press.com
Website: http://www.welsh-academic-
press.com

Publishes: Nonfiction; *Areas:* Historical;
Politics; *Markets:* Academic

Publishes academic monographs, reference
works, text books and popular scholarly titles
in the fields of education, history, political
studies, Scandinavian and Baltic studies,
contemporary work and employment, and
medieval Wales. Complete questionnaire
available on website.

Wide-Eyed Editions
The Old Brewery
6 Blundell Street
London

N7 9BH
Tel: +44 (0) 20 7700 6700
Fax: +44 (0) 20 7700 8066
Email: QuartoExploresSubmissions@
Quartous.com
Website: https://www.quartoknows.com/
Wide-Eyed-Editions

Publishes: Nonfiction; *Areas:* Arts; Nature;
Travel; *Markets:* Children's; Family

Publishes books on the arts, natural history
and armchair travel. Send query with
proposal by email. See website for full
guidelines.

Wild Goose Publications

The Iona Community
21 Carlton Court
Glasgow
G5 9JP
Tel: +44 (0) 1414 297281
Email: admin@iona.org.uk
Website: http://www.ionabooks.com

Publishes: Nonfiction; Poetry; *Areas:*
Health; Politics; Religious; Sociology;
Spiritual; *Markets:* Adult

Publishes books on Holistic Spirituality,
Social Justice, Political and Peace Issues,
Healing – Innovative Approaches to
worship, Song and Material for Meditation
and Reflection. Send query with synopsis
and two or three sample chapters. Not a
poetry publisher, but will sometimes include
poems in its books. Samples of suitable
poems may be sent to be held on file in case
they are suitable for use in a future book.

WIT Press

Ashurst Lodge
Ashurst
Southampton
SO40 7AA
Tel: +44 (0) 23 8029 3223
Fax: +44 (0) 23 8029 2853
Email: witpress@witpress.com
Website: http://www.witpress.com

Publishes: Nonfiction; *Areas:* Architecture;
Nature; Science; Technology; *Markets:*
Academic; Adult

Contact: Professor C.A. Brebbia

Publisher of scientific and technical material
in such fields as architecture, environmental
engineering and bioengineering. Target
market is generally postgraduate and above.
No school or college texts, or material not of
a scientific or technical nature. Potential
authors should contact the Chairman by
email in the first instance (see website for
specific email address).

Yale University Press (London)

47 Bedford Square
London
WC1B 3DP
Tel: +44 (0) 20 7079 4900
Email: mark.eastment@yaleup.co.uk
Website: https://www.yalebooks.co.uk

Publishes: Nonfiction; Reference; *Areas:*
Architecture; Arts; Autobiography; Beauty
and Fashion; Biography; Business;
Criticism; Current Affairs; Finance; Health;
Historical; Legal; Literature; Medicine;
Music; Philosophy; Politics; Religious;
Science; Sociology; Technology;
Translations; *Markets:* Adult; Children's

Contact: Mark Eastment; Julian Loose;
Heather McCallum; Sophie Neve

Welcomes unsolicited MSS and synopses in
specified subject areas.

ZigZag Education

Unit 3
Greenway Business Centre
Doncaster Road
Bristol
BS10 5PY
Tel: +44 (0) 1179 503199
Fax: +44 (0) 1179 591695
Email: support@ZigZagEducation.co.uk
Website: http://www.zigzageducation.co.uk

Publishes: Nonfiction; *Areas:* Arts;
Business; Design; Drama; Finance; Health;
Historical; Legal; Leisure; Media; Music;
Philosophy; Politics; Psychology; Religious;
Science; Sociology; Sport; Technology;
Travel; *Markets:* Academic; Children's;
Professional; Youth

Educational publisher publishing
photocopiable and digital teaching resources

for schools and colleges. Register on publisher's author support website if

interested in writing or contributing to resources.

Canadian Publishers

For the most up-to-date listings of these and hundreds of other publishers, visit https://www.firstwriter.com/publishers

*To claim your **free** access to the site, please see the back of this book.*

Arsenal Pulp Press
202-211 East Georgia Street
Vancouver, BC, V6A 1Z6
Tel: +1 (604) 687-4233
Fax: +1 (604) 687-4283
Email: info@arsenalpulp.com
Website: https://arsenalpulp.com

Publishes: Fiction; Nonfiction; *Areas:* Arts; Cookery; Crafts; Culture; Health; Lifestyle; Politics; Sociology; *Markets:* Adult; Children's; Youth; *Treatments:* Literary

Publishes Cultural studies, Political/sociological studies, Regional studies and guides, in particular for British Columbia, Cookbooks, Gay and lesbian fiction and non-fiction (including young adult and children's), Visual art, Multicultural fiction and non-fiction, Literary fiction and nonfiction (no genre fiction, such as mysteries, thriller, or romance), Youth culture, Health, and books for children (especially those that emphasise diversity). Send query with synopsis, chapter by chapter outline for nonfiction, writing credentials, 50-page excerpt, and marketing analysis. Include self-addressed envelope and appropriate return postage (either Canadian postage or IRCs), or email address for response. See website for full details. No submissions by fax or email, or queries by phone.

Brick Books
PO Box 404, Toronto Station C
Toronto, ON M6J 3P5
Tel: +1 (519) 657-8579
Email: predbrick@gmail.com
Website: http://www.brickbooks.ca

Publishes: Poetry; *Markets:* Adult

Contact: Nick Thran; Cara-Lyn Morgan

Publishes poetry by Canadian citizens or landed immigrants only. Considers submissions between January 1 and April 30 only. Prospective authors are advised to familiarise themselves with other books from the publisher before sending a complete ms by post. No multiple submissions. Response in 3-4 months.

Broadview Press
PO Box 1243
Peterborough, ON
K9J 7H5
Tel: +1 (705) 743-8990
Fax: +1 (705) 743-8353
Email: customerservice@ broadviewpress.com
Website: http://www.broadviewpress.com

Publishes: Nonfiction; *Areas:* Literature; Philosophy; *Markets:* Academic

Publishes academic books on English and philosophy, aimed at undergraduates. Before sending a proposal send an email query to the appropriate editor (see website).

Caitlin Press Inc.
8100 Alderwood Road
Halfmoon Bay, BC,
V0N 1Y1
Tel: +1 (604) 885-9194
Email: vici@caitlin-press.com
Website: http://caitlin-press.com

Publishes: Fiction; Nonfiction; Poetry; *Areas:* Adventure; Arts; Autobiography; Biography; Cookery; Historical; Humour; Nature; Photography; Politics; Short Stories; Sport; Travel; Women's Interests; *Markets:* Adult; Children's

Contact: Vici Johnstone; Sarah Corsie; Holly Vestad

Publishes books on topics concerning or by writers from the British Columbia Interior and stories about and by British Columbia women. No submissions by fax or by email. See website for full guidelines.

Coteau Books
2517 Victoria Ave
Regina, SK S4P 0T2
Tel: +1 (306) 777-0170
Fax: +1 (306) 522-5152
Email: coteau@coteaubooks.com
Website: http://www.coteaubooks.com

Publishes: Fiction; Nonfiction; Poetry; Scripts; *Areas:* Autobiography; Culture; Drama; Fantasy; Historical; Humour; Literature; Media; Mystery; Short Stories; Spiritual; Sport; Travel; Women's Interests; *Markets:* Adult; Children's; Youth; *Treatments:* Literary; Mainstream

A literary press publishing novels, short fiction collections, poetry, drama, and nonfiction both creative and regional. Publishes work by Canadian citizens or permanent residents only. No multiple or simultaneous submissions, or unsolicited mss. Send query by post or by email with sample up to 20 pages.

EDGE Science Fiction and Fantasy Publishing
Acquisitions Editor
EDGE Science Fiction and Fantasy Publishing
P.O. Box 1714
Calgary, AB
T2P 2L7
Tel: +1 (403) 254-0160
Fax: +1 (403) 254-0456
Email: michelle@hadespublications.com
Website: http://www.edgewebsite.com

Publishes: Fiction; *Areas:* Fantasy; Sci-Fi; *Markets:* Adult

Currently seeking science fiction and fantasy submissions between 75,000 and 100,000 words. Occasional young adult. No horror, erotica, religious fiction, short stories, dark/gruesome fantasy, or poetry. See website for full submission guidelines.

Fairleigh Dickinson University (FDU) Press
842 Cambie Street
Vancouver, BC
V6B 2P6
Tel: +1 (604) 648-4476
Fax: +1 (604) 648-4489
Email: fdupress@fdu.edu
Website: http://www.fdupress.org

Publishes: Nonfiction; *Areas:* Arts; Biography; Film; Historical; Literature; Music; Philosophy; Religious; Sociology; Theatre; Women's Interests; *Markets:* Academic

Contact: James Gifford, Director

Publishes nonfiction books in a variety of scholarly fields. Send query by post or via form on website describing the book and the contribution it would make to the field.

Fernwood Publishing
32 Oceanvista Lane, Site 2A
Box 5
Black Point
NS B0J 1B0
Tel: +1 (902) 857-1388
Fax: +1 (902) 857-1328

Email: editorial@fernpub.ca
Website: http://www.fernwoodbooks.ca

Publishes: Nonfiction; Reference; *Areas:*
Anthropology; Archaeology; Business;
Criticism; Culture; Current Affairs; Finance;
Health; Historical; Literature; Medicine;
Nature; Philosophy; Politics; Sociology;
Sport; Translations; Women's Interests;
Markets: Academic; Adult

Contact: Errol Sharpe (Publisher); Wayne
Antony (Editor)

Social justice publisher. Publishes both for a
general and academic audience, including
reference books, for use in college and
university courses. Concentrates on social
sciences, humanities, gender studies, literary
criticism, politics, and cultural studies. Send
4-5 page proposal including tentative table of
contents; the theoretical framework of the
book, and how it relates to the subject
matter; market analysis; level (college /
university); and estimated length and
completion date. See website for full details.

Formac Publishing Company Limited

5502 Atlantic Street
Halifax, Nova Scotia
B3H 1G4
Tel: +1 (902) 421-7022 ext. 28
Email: formaceditorial@formac.ca
Website: http://www.formac.ca

Publishes: Fiction; Nonfiction; *Areas:*
Biography; Cookery; Historical; Nature;
Politics; Travel; *Markets:* Adult; Children's

Contact: Heather Thomas

Publishes adult nonfiction in the areas of
Maritime regional, travel guides, history,
biography, natural history, Maritime
Provinces politics and regional cookbooks
and cookbooks with a fresh/healthy focus.
Also classic Maritime fiction reprints. Also
publishes fiction for children. Send query
with outline, sample, and author CV. See
website for full guidelines. Response only if
interested.

Harlequin Dare

Email: CustomerService@Harlequin.com
Website: https://www.harlequin.com

Publishes: Fiction; *Areas:* Romance;
Women's Interests; *Markets:* Adult;
Treatments: Contemporary

Contact: Kathleen Scheibling

Imprint which aims to push the boundaries of
sexual explicitness while keeping the focus
on the developing romantic relationship.
Submit novels up to 50,000 words via online
submission system available on website.

Harlequin Heartwarming

22 Adelaide Street West, 41st Floor
Toronto, ON M5H 4E3
Tel: +1 (888) 432-4879
Email: submissions@harlequin.com
Website: https://www.harlequin.com

Publishes: Fiction; *Areas:* Romance;
Markets: Adult; *Treatments:* Contemporary;
Light; Positive

Contact: Kathleen Scheibling

Publishes wholesome contemporary
romances set in small towns and close-knit
communities. Interested in feel-good stories
with happy endings. No explicit or behind-
closed-doors sex, nudity, pre-marital sex,
graphic violence, religious, paranormal, or
heavy suspense. Submit via online
submission system.

Heritage House

103 – 1075 Pendergast Street
Victoria, BC, V8V 0A1
Tel: +1 (250) 360-0829 ext. 103
Email: books@heritagehouse.ca
Website: http://www.heritagehouse.ca

Publishes: Nonfiction; *Areas:* Adventure;
Anthropology; Arts; Biography; Business;
Crime; Culture; Historical; Humour;
Military; Nature; Politics; Sport; Women's
Interests; *Markets:* Adult; *Treatments:*
Contemporary

Publishes books on the heritage and
historical and contemporary culture of
Canada. Submit query by email only with

one-page synopsis and one or two sample chapters. See website for full guidelines.

Insomniac Press

520 Princess Avenue
London, ON N6B 2B8
Tel: +1 (519) 266-3556
Website: http://www.insomniacpress.com

Publishes: Fiction; Nonfiction; Poetry; Reference; *Areas:* Business; Crime; Criticism; Culture; Finance; Gardening; Health; Humour; Legal; Lifestyle; Literature; Medicine; Music; Mystery; Politics; Religious; Self-Help; Short Stories; Spiritual; Sport; Suspense; Travel; *Markets:* Adult; *Treatments:* Commercial; Experimental; Literary; Mainstream

Particularly interested in creative nonfiction on business / personal finance; gay and lesbian studies; black Canadian studies and others. No science fiction, cookbooks, romance, or children's books. Send query by email or post in first instance. Approaches by authors who have had work published elsewhere (e.g. short stories in magazines) will receive closer attention.

LexisNexis Canada

111 Gordon Baker Road, Suite 900
Toronto, ON, M2H 3R1
Tel: +1 (800) 668-6481
Email: productdevelopment@lexisnexis.ca
Website: https://www.lexisnexis.ca

Publishes: Nonfiction; Reference; *Areas:* Business; Finance; Legal; *Markets:* Professional

Publishes books for the professional legal, business, and accountancy markets. Send query by email. See website for full guidelines on submitting a proposal.

Manor House Publishing

452 Cottingham Crescent
Ancaster ON L9G 3V6
Email: mbdavie@manor-house.biz
Website: https://manor-house-publishing.com

Publishes: Fiction; Nonfiction; Poetry; *Areas:* Biography; Business; Fantasy; New

Age; Politics; Short Stories; *Markets:* Adult; Youth

Send query by email only. See website for full guidelines. Response only if interested.

Oberon Press

205–145 Spruce Street
Ottawa, Ontario
K1R 6P1
Tel: +1 (613) 238-3275
Fax: +1 (613) 238-3275
Email: oberon@sympatico.ca
Website: http://www.oberonpress.ca

Publishes: Fiction; Nonfiction; Poetry; *Markets:* Adult

No longer accepting new manuscript submissions.

Quattro Books

12 Concord Ave,
2nd Floor
Toronto, Ontario
M6H 2P1
Tel: +1 (416) 893-7979
Email: info@quattrobooks.ca
Website: http://quattrobooks.ca

Publishes: Fiction; Poetry; *Markets:* Adult; *Treatments:* Literary

Publishes novellas of literary fiction, and poetry. Accepts work from Canadian citizens residing in Canada only. Novellas should be between 20,000 and 40,000 words. No genre fiction. Not accepting poetry manuscripts as at June 2019. No electronic submissions.

TouchWood Editions

103 – 1075 Pendergast Street
Victoria, BC V8V 0A1
Tel: +1 (250) 360-0829
Fax: +1 (250) 386-0829
Email: submissions@touchwoodeditions.com
Website: http://www.touchwoodeditions.com

Publishes: Fiction; Nonfiction; *Areas:* Arts; Autobiography; Biography; Cookery; Culture; Gardening; Historical; Lifestyle; Nature; Photography; Suspense; Travel;

Markets: Adult; *Treatments:* Literary; Popular

Accepts submissions by email only. Response only if interested. Publishes Canadian authors only. See website for full guidelines.

Vehicule Press

P.O.B. 42094 BP Roy
Montreal, Quebec H2W 2T3
Tel: +1 (514) 844-6073
Fax: +1 (514) 844-7543
Email: admin@vehiculepress.com
Website: http://www.vehiculepress.com

Publishes: Fiction; Nonfiction; Poetry; *Areas:* Historical; Music; Religious; Sociology; Translations; *Markets:* Adult

Publishes poetry, literary novels, novellas, short story collections, and translations, primarily from Canadian authors. Not accepting poetry manuscripts as at April 2017. See website for current status, and full fiction submission guidelines.

ZED Press

Email: zedpresschapbook@gmail.com
Website: https://zedpresswindsor.wordpress.com

Publishes: Poetry; *Markets:* Adult; *Treatments:* Experimental; Literary

Publishes poetry chapbooks. Looks for experimental work and seeks to highlight voices that are underrepresented in literature. Accepts manuscripts up to 32 pages in length, by email. See website for full guidelines.

Irish Publishers

For the most up-to-date listings of these and hundreds of other publishers, visit https://www.firstwriter.com/publishers

*To claim your **free** access to the site, please see the back of this book.*

Cork University Press

Tel: +353 (0) 21 490 2980
Email: corkuniversitypress@ucc.ie
Website: http://www.corkuniversitypress.com

Publishes: Nonfiction; *Areas:* Architecture; Arts; Cookery; Culture; Current Affairs; Drama; Film; Historical; Legal; Literature; Music; Philosophy; Politics; Self-Help; Sociology; Sport; Travel; Women's Interests; *Markets:* Academic

Publishes distinctive and distinguished scholarship in the broad field of Irish Cultural Studies.

The Educational Company of Ireland

Ballymount Road
Walkinstown
Dublin 12
Email: amolumby@edco.ie
Website: http://www.edco.ie

Publishes: Nonfiction; *Markets:* Academic; Adult; Children's; Professional

Contact: Aoibheann Molumby

Publishes textbooks and ancillary educational materials for the Primary and Post-Primary markets. Submit proposals by post or by email. See website for full guidelines.

Four Courts Press

7 Malpas Street
Dublin
D08 YD81
Tel: 353-1-453-4668
Email: info@fourcourtspress.ie
Website: http://www.fourcourtspress.ie

Publishes: Nonfiction; *Areas:* Archaeology; Architecture; Arts; Criticism; Historical; Legal; Literature; Philosophy; Religious; *Markets:* Academic

Academic press, originally focusing on theology, now also publishing books on history, art, literature, and law. Send query by email in first instance.

The Gallery Press

Loughcrew
Oldcastle
County Meath
Tel: +353 (0) 49 8541779
Fax: +353 (0) 49 8541779
Email: gallery@indigo.ie
Website: http://www.gallerypress.com

Publishes: Fiction; Nonfiction; Poetry; Scripts; *Areas:* Theatre; *Markets:* Adult; *Treatments:* Literary

Contact: Peter Fallon

Publishes poetry, drama, and prose by Ireland's leading contemporary writers. See website for submission guidelines. No novels, historical romances, autobiographies, biographies, children's books, etc. No submissions by fax or email. Accepts work from Irish or Irish-based authors only.

Gill Books

Hume Avenue
Park West
Dublin
D12 YV96
Tel: +353 (01) 500 9500
Email: dmarsh@gill.ie
Website: http://www.gillmacmillanbooks.ie

Publishes: Fiction; Nonfiction; Reference; *Areas:* Biography; Cookery; Crafts; Crime; Current Affairs; Historical; Hobbies; Humour; Leisure; Lifestyle; Nature; Spiritual; Sport; *Markets:* Adult; Children's

Contact: Deborah Marsh, Editorial Administrator

Publishes adult nonfiction and children's fiction and nonfiction. No adult fiction, poetry, short stories or plays. Prefers proposals by email, but will also accept proposals by post. See website for full submission guidelines.

The Lilliput Press

62-63 Sitric Road
Arbour Hill
Dublin 7
Tel: +353 (01) 671 16 47
Fax: +353 (01) 671 12 33
Email: editorial@lilliputpress.ie
Website: http://www.lilliputpress.ie

Publishes: Fiction; Nonfiction; Poetry; Reference; Scripts; *Areas:* Architecture; Arts; Autobiography; Biography; Business; Cookery; Criticism; Culture; Current Affairs; Drama; Historical; Literature; Music; Nature; Philosophy; Photography; Politics; Sociology; Sport; Travel; *Markets:* Adult; *Treatments:* Literary; Popular

Contact: Submissions Editor

Publishes books broadly focused on Irish themes. Send query by post with one-page synopsis and complete ms or three sample chapters. Include SASE if response required.

No submissions by email. See website for full guidelines.

New Island

16 Priory Office Park
Stillorgan
County Dublin
Tel: + 353 1 278 42 25
Email: editor@newisland.ie
Website: http://www.newisland.ie

Publishes: Fiction; Nonfiction; Poetry; Scripts; *Areas:* Autobiography; Biography; Cookery; Crime; Criticism; Current Affairs; Drama; Historical; Humour; Literature; Politics; Short Stories; Sociology; Travel; Women's Interests; *Markets:* Adult; *Treatments:* Literary; Popular

Contact: Editorial Manager

Closed to submissions as at December 2018. Aims to re-open in spring 2019. Check website for current status.

Committed to literature and literary publishing. Publishes in all literary areas, from fiction to drama to poetry. Also publishes nonfiction of Irish interest, especially social affairs and biographies. No children's books. Not currently accepting drama and poetry. Seeking submissions of literary fiction, general fiction, crime fiction, short stories, history, biography, memoir, autobiography, and food and drink. Accepts submissions by email only. Send query with one-page synopsis and full manuscript or poetry collection as Word .doc or .docx attachments. Include details of any previous publications. No submissions by post. See website for full details.

The O'Brien Press

12 Terenure Road East
Rathgar
Dublin 6
D06 HD27
Tel: +353-1-4923333
Fax: +353-1-4922777
Email: books@obrien.ie
Website: http://www.obrien.ie

Publishes: Fiction; Nonfiction; Reference; *Areas:* Architecture; Arts; Autobiography; Biography; Business; Cookery; Crafts;

Crime; Drama; Historical; Humour;
Lifestyle; Literature; Music; Nature;
Photography; Politics; Religious; Sport;
Travel; *Markets:* Adult; Children's; Youth

Mainly publishes children's fiction,
children's nonfiction and adult nonfiction.
Generally doesn't publish poetry, academic
works or adult fiction. Send synopsis and
two or three sample chapters. If fewer than
1,000 words, send complete ms. See website
for full guidelines.

Poolbeg

123 Grange Hill
Baldoyle Industrial Estate
Baldoyle
Dublin 13
Tel: +353 1 806 3825
Email: info@poolbeg.com
Website: http://www.poolbeg.com

Publishes: Fiction; Nonfiction; *Areas:*
Cookery; Gardening; Travel; Women's
Interests; *Markets:* Adult; Children's

Contact: Paula Campbell, publisher

Publishes mainly women's and children's
fiction, but also some nonfiction. Send query
with synopsis, bio, and three chapters, both
in hard copy and on a USB stick. If no
response after three months assume
rejection. See website for full guidelines.

Somerville Press

Dromore
Bantry
Co. Cork
Tel: 353 (0) 28 32873
Fax: 353 (0) 28 328
Email: somervillepress@eircom.net
Website: http://www.somervillepress.com

Publishes: Fiction; Nonfiction; *Markets:*
Adult

Publishes fiction and nonfiction, mainly of
Irish interest.

Thomson Reuters Round Hall

13 Exchange Place
International Financial Services Centre
Dublin 1
Tel: 01 602 4832
Email: pamela.moran@thomsonreuters.com
Website: http://www.roundhall.ie

Publishes: Nonfiction; Reference; *Areas:*
Legal; *Markets:* Academic; Professional

Contact: Pamela Moran

Publishes information on Irish law in the
form of books, journals, periodicals,
looseleaf services, CD-ROMs and online
services. See website for submission
guidelines.

University College Dublin (UCD) Press

UCD Humanities Institute Room H103
Belfield
Dublin 4

Tel: + 353 1 4716 4680
Email: ucdpress@ucd.ie
Website: http://www.ucdpress.ie

Publishes: Nonfiction; *Areas:* Criticism;
Drama; Historical; Literature; Military;
Music; Nature; Politics; Religious; Science;
Sociology; *Markets:* Academic

Contact: Noelle Moran, Executive Editor

Peer-reviewed publisher of contemporary
scholarship with a reputation for publications
relating to historic and contemporary Ireland.
Send synopsis with market description, a
paragraph about the career and publications
of the author(s), and two specimen chapters
in hard copy (not email attachments). Will
accept proposals up to 8 pages by email, but
unlikely to consider a proposal without
specimen material. See website for full
guidelines.

Australian Publishers

For the most up-to-date listings of these and hundreds of other publishers, visit https://www.firstwriter.com/publishers

*To claim your **free** access to the site, please see the back of this book.*

Allen & Unwin

SYDNEY:
83 Alexander St
Crows Nest, NSW 2065

MELBOURNE:
406 Albert Street
East Melbourne, Vic 3002
Tel: +61 (0) 2 8425 0100
Fax: +61 (0) 2 9906 2218
Email: fridaypitch@allenandunwin.com
Website: https://www.allenandunwin.com

Publishes: Fiction; Nonfiction; Poetry;
Scripts; *Areas:* Arts; Autobiography;
Biography; Business; Crime; Culture;
Current Affairs; Fantasy; Finance; Health;
Historical; Humour; Lifestyle; Literature;
Media; Military; Music; Mystery; Nature;
Philosophy; Politics; Psychology; Religious;
Science; Self-Help; Sociology; Sport;
Travel; *Markets:* Academic; Children's;
Professional; Youth; *Treatments:*
Commercial; Literary; Popular

Publisher with offices in Australia, New
Zealand, and the UK. Accepts queries by
email. See website for detailed instructions.

Melbourne University Publishing Ltd

Level 1, 715 Swanston Street
Carlton
Victoria
3053

Tel: +61 (0) 3 9035 3333
Fax: +61 (0) 3 9342 0399
Email: mup-submissions@unimelb.edu.au
Website: https://www.mup.com.au

Publishes: Nonfiction; *Areas:* Arts;
Autobiography; Biography; Crime; Design;
Historical; Lifestyle; Literature; Politics;
Science; Sociology; Sport; *Markets:*
Academic; Adult

Publishes nonfiction only. No fiction,
children's literature, or poetry. Send
submissions by email only. See website for
full submission guidelines.

SisterShip Press Pty Ltd

Email: sistershippress@gmail.com
Website: https://sistershippress.com

Publishes: Fiction; Nonfiction; Poetry;
Reference; *Areas:* Adventure;
Autobiography; Biography; Business;
Cookery; Crafts; Crime; Entertainment;
Fantasy; Film; Health; Hobbies; How-to;
Humour; Leisure; Lifestyle; Mystery;
Nature; Psychology; Romance; Science;
Self-Help; Short Stories; Technology;
Thrillers; Women's Interests; *Markets:*
Academic; Adult; Children's; Family;
Professional; Youth; *Treatments:*
Contemporary; In-depth; Light; Literary;
Mainstream; Niche; Popular; Positive;
Progressive; Satirical; Traditional

Contact: Jackie Parry and Shelley Wright

We are passionate about writing. We are excited about books.

We (initially) are here for women; women with finished manuscripts. A nautical theme is our favourite but we are keen to read any adventure/travel/inspirational story – fiction or nonfiction. Technical books are also invited. We have a team with vast experience in all aspects of boating – professionally and recreationally.

Read our FAQ on our website.

Publishers Subject Index

This section lists publishers by their subject matter, with directions to the section of the book where the full listing can be found.

You can create your own customised lists of publishers using different combinations of these subject areas, plus over a dozen other criteria, instantly online at https://www.firstwriter.com.

To claim your **free** access to the site, please see the back of this book.

Adventure
Birlinn Ltd (*UK*)
Black Coffey Publishing (*UK*)
Blue Trident Books (*UK*)
Caitlin Press Inc. (*Can*)
Cynren Press (*US*)
4RV Publishing (*US*)
HarperCollins (*US*)
Hellgate Press (*US*)
Heritage House (*Can*)
IDW Publishing (*US*)
JourneyForth (*US*)
Lost Tower Publications (*UK*)
Marvel Comics (*US*)
Mountaineers Books (*US*)
The Orion Publishing Group Limited (*UK*)
Pan Macmillan (*UK*)
The Salariya Book Company (*UK*)
SisterShip Press Pty Ltd (*Aus*)
Sunstone Press (*US*)
Tumblehome Learning, Inc. (*US*)
W.W. Norton & Company Ltd (*UK*)
WaterBrook & Multnomah (*US*)
We Are One Body Audio Theatre (*US*)
Anthropology
Abdo Publishing Co (*US*)
Algora Publishing (*US*)
Cornell University Press (*US*)
Dunedin Academic Press Ltd (*UK*)
Elm Books (*US*)
Fernwood Publishing (*Can*)
Garnet Publishing (*UK*)
Heritage House (*Can*)
Oneworld Publications (*UK*)

Sage Publications (*UK*)
Seren Books (*UK*)
Syracuse University Press (*US*)
Temple University Press (*US*)
Truman State University Press (*US*)
The University of Michigan Press (*US*)
University of Washington Press (*US*)
Verso (*UK*)
W.W. Norton & Company Ltd (*UK*)
Antiques
Krause Publications (*US*)
Pen & Sword Books Ltd (*UK*)
Archaeology
Algora Publishing (*US*)
Council for British Archaeology (CBA) Publishing (*UK*)
Edinburgh University Press (*UK*)
Fernwood Publishing (*Can*)
Four Courts Press (*Ire*)
Garnet Publishing (*UK*)
The History Press (*UK*)
National Museum Wales (*UK*)
The Orion Publishing Group Limited (*UK*)
Pen & Sword Books Ltd (*UK*)
Saffron Books (*UK*)
Sage Publications (*UK*)
Sunstone Press (*US*)
Thames & Hudson Inc. (*US*)
Thames and Hudson Ltd (*UK*)
The British Museum Press (*UK*)
Truman State University Press (*US*)
University of Exeter Press (*UK*)
The University of Michigan Press (*US*)
W.W. Norton & Company Ltd (*UK*)

Architecture
Birlinn Ltd (*UK*)
Black Dome Press (*US*)
Carlton Publishing Group (*UK*)
Chronicle Books LLC (*US*)
Cork University Press (*Ire*)
Countryside Books (*UK*)
Dovecote Press (*UK*)
Edinburgh University Press (*UK*)
Floris Books (*UK*)
Four Courts Press (*Ire*)
Garnet Publishing (*UK*)
George Braziller, Inc. (*US*)
Gibbs Smith, Publisher (*US*)
Gingko Library (*UK*)
Laurence King Publishing Ltd (*UK*)
The Lilliput Press (*Ire*)
Lund Humphries Limited (*UK*)
Metro Publications Ltd (*UK*)
The O'Brien Press (*Ire*)
Phaidon Press Limited (*UK*)
Princeton Architectural Press (*US*)
Santa Monica Press (*US*)
Saqi Books (*UK*)
Sheldrake Press (*UK*)
Sunstone Press (*US*)
I.B. Tauris & Co. Ltd (*UK*)
Thames & Hudson Inc. (*US*)
Thames and Hudson Ltd (*UK*)
Truman State University Press (*US*)
University of Pittsburgh Press (*US*)
Verso (*UK*)
W.W. Norton & Company Ltd (*UK*)
WIT Press (*UK*)
Yale University Press (London) (*UK*)
Arts
ABC-CLIO / Greenwood (*US*)
Abdo Publishing Co (*US*)
Allen & Unwin (*Aus*)
Alma Classics (*UK*)
Anness Publishing Ltd (*UK*)
Arsenal Pulp Press (*Can*)
Aurora Metro Press (*UK*)
Birlinn Ltd (*UK*)
Black Dome Press (*US*)
Bodleian Library Publishing (*UK*)
Caitlin Press Inc. (*Can*)
Carlton Publishing Group (*UK*)
Chronicle Books LLC (*US*)
Clarkson Potter (*US*)
Co & Bear Productions (*UK*)
Cork University Press (*Ire*)
The Crown Publishing Group (*US*)
Da Capo Press (*US*)
Duckworth Publishers (*UK*)
Enitharmon Press (*UK*)
Fairleigh Dickinson University (FDU) Press (*Can*)
Floris Books (*UK*)
Four Courts Press (*Ire*)
Garnet Publishing (*UK*)
George Braziller, Inc. (*US*)
Gibbs Smith, Publisher (*US*)

Gibson Square Books Ltd (*UK*)
Gingko Library (*UK*)
Gomer Press (*UK*)
Greystones Press (*UK*)
Hal Leonard Performing Arts Publishing Group (*US*)
Hendrick-Long Publishing Co. (*US*)
Heritage House (*Can*)
Italica Press (*US*)
Jacaranda Books Art Music Ltd (*UK*)
Kaya Press (*US*)
Kent State University Press (*US*)
Laurence King Publishing Ltd (*UK*)
The Lilliput Press (*Ire*)
Luath Press Ltd (*UK*)
Lund Humphries Limited (*UK*)
Mandrake of Oxford (*UK*)
McGraw-Hill Education (*US*)
McSweeney's Publishing (*US*)
Melbourne University Publishing Ltd (*Aus*)
Metro Publications Ltd (*UK*)
National Museum Wales (*UK*)
New Holland Publishers (UK) Ltd (*UK*)
The O'Brien Press (*Ire*)
Oneworld Publications (*UK*)
The Orion Publishing Group Limited (*UK*)
Peter Owen Publishers (*UK*)
Pavilion Books Group Limited (*UK*)
Penguin Random House (*US*)
Phaidon Press Limited (*UK*)
Pimpernel Press (*UK*)
Quarto Publishing Group UK (*UK*)
Quarto Publishing Group USA (*US*)
Repeater Books (*UK*)
Robert Hale Publishers (*UK*)
Saffron Books (*UK*)
Sage Publications (*UK*)
Santa Monica Press (*US*)
Saqi Books (*UK*)
September Publishing (*UK*)
Seren Books (*UK*)
Southern Illinois University Press (*US*)
Sterling Publishing Co. Inc. (*US*)
Stone Bridge Press (*US*)
Sunstone Press (*US*)
Tate Publishing (*UK*)
I.B. Tauris & Co. Ltd (*UK*)
Temple University Press (*US*)
Thames & Hudson Inc. (*US*)
Thames and Hudson Ltd (*UK*)
The British Museum Press (*UK*)
TouchWood Editions (*Can*)
Truman State University Press (*US*)
Unicorn Publishing Group (*UK*)
The University of Michigan Press (*US*)
University of Washington Press (*US*)
Verso (*UK*)
Walch Education (*US*)
Wide-Eyed Editions (*UK*)
Yale University Press (London) (*UK*)
ZigZag Education (*UK*)
Autobiography
Academy Chicago (*US*)

Allen & Unwin (*Aus*)
Allison & Busby Ltd (*UK*)
Alma Classics (*UK*)
Asabi Publishing (*US*)
Bancroft Press (*US*)
BearManor Media (*US*)
Birlinn Ltd (*UK*)
Black & White Publishing Ltd (*UK*)
John Blake Publishing (*UK*)
Blink Publishing (*UK*)
Caitlin Press Inc. (*Can*)
Canongate Books (*UK*)
Chicago Review Press (*US*)
Coteau Books (*Can*)
The Crown Publishing Group (*US*)
Cynren Press (*US*)
Dalkey Archive Press (*US*)
DB Publishing (*UK*)
Dream of Things (*US*)
Dref Wen (*UK*)
Duckworth Publishers (*UK*)
Encounter Books (*US*)
Garnet Publishing (*UK*)
Gomer Press (*UK*)
Granta Books (*UK*)
Halban Publishers (*UK*)
Half Mystic Press (*US*)
HarperCollins (*US*)
HarperCollins Publishers Ltd (*UK*)
Headline Publishing Group (*UK*)
Hellgate Press (*US*)
Hesperus Press Limited (*UK*)
High Plains Press (*US*)
Hodder & Stoughton Ltd (*UK*)
Honno Welsh Women's Press (*UK*)
Houghton Mifflin Harcourt (*US*)
Imbrifex Books (*US*)
Infinite Ideas (*UK*)
Jacaranda Books Art Music Ltd (*UK*)
Kensington Publishing Corp. (*US*)
The Lilliput Press (*Ire*)
Little, Brown Book Group (*UK*)
Lost Tower Publications (*UK*)
Melbourne University Publishing Ltd (*Aus*)
Merlin Unwin Books (*UK*)
Michael Joseph (*UK*)
MIrror Books (*UK*)
Myriad Editions (*UK*)
Native Ink Press (*US*)
New Island (*Ire*)
The O'Brien Press (*Ire*)
The Orion Publishing Group Limited (*UK*)
PaperBooks (*UK*)
Pen & Sword Books Ltd (*UK*)
Penguin Random House (*US*)
Periscope (*UK*)
Portobello Books Ltd (*UK*)
Pushkin Press (*UK*)
Robert D. Reed Publishers (*US*)
Route Publishing (*UK*)
Saddle Road Press (*US*)
September Publishing (*UK*)
Serpent's Tail (*UK*)

Seven Stories Press (*US*)
Shearsman Books (*UK*)
Shipwreckt Books Publishing Company (*US*)
Simon & Schuster UK Limited (*UK*)
SisterShip Press Pty Ltd (*Aus*)
Sunstone Press (*US*)
TouchWood Editions (*Can*)
Triangle Square (*US*)
Truman State University Press (*US*)
Two Sylvias Press (*US*)
University of Alaska Press (*US*)
The University of Michigan Press (*US*)
Verso (*UK*)
W.W. Norton & Company Ltd (*UK*)
Yale University Press (London) (*UK*)
Zumaya Publications (*US*)
Beauty and Fashion
Carlton Publishing Group (*UK*)
Chronicle Books LLC (*US*)
Co & Bear Productions (*UK*)
Grand Central Publishing (*US*)
Jacaranda Books Art Music Ltd (*UK*)
Laurence King Publishing Ltd (*UK*)
Luath Press Ltd (*UK*)
The Orion Publishing Group Limited (*UK*)
Pavilion Books Group Limited (*UK*)
Phaidon Press Limited (*UK*)
Quadrille Publishing Ltd (*UK*)
Quarto Publishing Group UK (*UK*)
Thames & Hudson Inc. (*US*)
Thames and Hudson Ltd (*UK*)
Yale University Press (London) (*UK*)
Biography
ABC-CLIO / Greenwood (*US*)
Abdo Publishing Co (*US*)
Allen & Unwin (*Aus*)
Allison & Busby Ltd (*UK*)
Alma Classics (*UK*)
Asabi Publishing (*US*)
Aureus Publishing Limited (*UK*)
Aurora Metro Press (*UK*)
Bancroft Press (*US*)
BearManor Media (*US*)
Birlinn Ltd (*UK*)
Black & White Publishing Ltd (*UK*)
Black Ace Books (*UK*)
Black Dome Press (*US*)
John Blake Publishing (*UK*)
Caitlin Press Inc. (*Can*)
Candy Jar Books (*UK*)
Canongate Books (*UK*)
Carcanet Press Ltd (*UK*)
Carlton Publishing Group (*UK*)
Chicago Review Press (*US*)
Colin Smythe Ltd (*UK*)
College Press Publishing (*US*)
Cornell University Press (*US*)
The Crown Publishing Group (*US*)
Cynren Press (*US*)
Dalkey Archive Press (*US*)
DB Publishing (*UK*)
Dovecote Press (*UK*)
Duckworth Publishers (*UK*)

Dunedin Academic Press Ltd (*UK*)
Encounter Books (*US*)
Faber & Faber Ltd (*UK*)
Fairleigh Dickinson University (FDU) Press (*Can*)
Fleming Publications (*UK*)
Floris Books (*UK*)
Formac Publishing Company Limited (*Can*)
Forward Movement Publications (*US*)
Garnet Publishing (*UK*)
George Braziller, Inc. (*US*)
Gibson Square Books Ltd (*UK*)
Gill Books (*Ire*)
Gingko Library (*UK*)
Gomer Press (*UK*)
Granta Books (*UK*)
Halban Publishers (*UK*)
HarperCollins (*US*)
HarperCollins Publishers Ltd (*UK*)
Hay House Publishers (*UK*)
Head of Zeus (*UK*)
Headline Publishing Group (*UK*)
Hendrick-Long Publishing Co. (*US*)
Heritage House (*Can*)
Hesperus Press Limited (*UK*)
The History Press (*UK*)
Hodder & Stoughton Ltd (*UK*)
Houghton Mifflin Harcourt (*US*)
House of Lochar (*UK*)
Impress Books Limited (*UK*)
Infinite Ideas (*UK*)
Jacaranda Books Art Music Ltd (*UK*)
JourneyForth (*US*)
Kensington Publishing Corp. (*US*)
Kent State University Press (*US*)
The Lilliput Press (*Ire*)
Little, Brown Book Group (*UK*)
Luath Press Ltd (*UK*)
Manor House Publishing (*Can*)
Melbourne University Publishing Ltd (*Aus*)
Native Ink Press (*US*)
New Holland Publishers (UK) Ltd (*UK*)
New Island (*Ire*)
The O'Brien Press (*Ire*)
Michael O'Mara Books Ltd (*UK*)
Oleander Press (*UK*)
Omnibus Press (*UK*)
Oneworld Publications (*UK*)
The Orion Publishing Group Limited (*UK*)
Peter Owen Publishers (*UK*)
Pan Macmillan (*UK*)
Pen & Sword Books Ltd (*UK*)
Penguin Random House (*US*)
Periscope (*UK*)
Profile Books (*UK*)
Red Moon Press (*US*)
Robert Hale Publishers (*UK*)
Route Publishing (*UK*)
Salt Publishing Ltd (*UK*)
Santa Monica Press (*US*)
SelfMadeHero (*UK*)
September Publishing (*UK*)
Seren Books (*UK*)

Serpent's Tail (*UK*)
Shepheard-Walwyn (Publishers) Ltd (*UK*)
Simon & Schuster UK Limited (*UK*)
SisterShip Press Pty Ltd (*Aus*)
Southern Illinois University Press (*US*)
SportsBooks Limited (*UK*)
St Pauls (*US*)
Sunstone Press (*US*)
Syracuse University Press (*US*)
I.B. Tauris & Co. Ltd (*UK*)
Temple University Press (*US*)
Thames & Hudson Inc. (*US*)
Thames and Hudson Ltd (*UK*)
TouchWood Editions (*Can*)
Triangle Square (*US*)
Truman State University Press (*US*)
Unicorn Publishing Group (*UK*)
University of Alaska Press (*US*)
The University of Michigan Press (*US*)
University of Washington Press (*US*)
Verso (*UK*)
W.W. Norton & Company Ltd (*UK*)
Yale University Press (London) (*UK*)

Business
ABC-CLIO / Greenwood (*US*)
Allen & Unwin (*Aus*)
The Authority Guides (*UK*)
John Blake Publishing (*UK*)
Nicholas Brealey Publishing (*UK*)
Bristol University Press (*UK*)
Career Press (*US*)
Colourpoint Educational (*UK*)
Crown House Publishing (*UK*)
The Crown Publishing Group (*US*)
Diversion Books (*US*)
Entrepreneur Press (*US*)
Fernwood Publishing (*Can*)
Harper Business (*UK*)
Harper Business (*US*)
HarperCollins (*US*)
Hay House Publishers (*UK*)
Heritage House (*Can*)
Infinite Ideas (*UK*)
Insomniac Press (*Can*)
Kensington Publishing Corp. (*US*)
Kogan Page Ltd (*UK*)
LexisNexis Canada (*Can*)
The Lilliput Press (*Ire*)
Manor House Publishing (*Can*)
McGraw-Hill Education (*US*)
The O'Brien Press (*Ire*)
Oneworld Publications (*UK*)
PassKey Publications (*US*)
Profile Books (*UK*)
Robert D. Reed Publishers (*US*)
Saffron Books (*UK*)
Sage Publications (*UK*)
Silver Lake Publishing, LLC (*US*)
Simon & Schuster UK Limited (*UK*)
SisterShip Press Pty Ltd (*Aus*)
Stone Bridge Press (*US*)
Sunstone Press (*US*)
Temple University Press (*US*)

TSO (The Stationery Office) (*UK*)
The University of Michigan Press (*US*)
W.W. Norton & Company Ltd (*UK*)
Yale University Press (London) (*UK*)
ZigZag Education (*UK*)
Cookery
Abdo Publishing Co (*US*)
Andrews McMeel Publishing (*US*)
Anness Publishing Ltd (*UK*)
Arsenal Pulp Press (*Can*)
Aurora Metro Press (*UK*)
Black & White Publishing Ltd (*UK*)
John Blake Publishing (*UK*)
Blink Publishing (*UK*)
Bull Publishing Company (*US*)
Caitlin Press Inc. (*Can*)
Chronicle Books LLC (*US*)
Clarkson Potter (*US*)
Cork University Press (*Ire*)
The Crown Publishing Group (*US*)
Farcountry Press (*US*)
Flame Tree Publishing (*UK*)
Formac Publishing Company Limited (*Can*)
Garnet Publishing (*UK*)
Geddes & Grosset (*UK*)
Gibbs Smith, Publisher (*US*)
Gill Books (*Ire*)
Grub Street Publishing (*UK*)
HarperCollins (*US*)
HarperCollins Publishers Ltd (*UK*)
The Harvard Common Press (*US*)
Harvest House Publishers (*US*)
Headline Publishing Group (*UK*)
Hendrick-Long Publishing Co. (*US*)
Hippocrene Books, Inc. (*US*)
Hodder & Stoughton Ltd (*UK*)
Igloo Books Limited (*UK*)
Infinite Ideas (*UK*)
The Lilliput Press (*Ire*)
Mabecron Books Ltd (*UK*)
McSweeney's Publishing (*US*)
Merlin Unwin Books (*UK*)
Michael Joseph (*UK*)
Native Ink Press (*US*)
New Holland Publishers (UK) Ltd (*UK*)
New Island (*Ire*)
Nourish Books (*UK*)
The O'Brien Press (*Ire*)
The Orion Publishing Group Limited (*UK*)
PaperBooks (*UK*)
Pavilion Books Group Limited (*UK*)
Penguin Random House (*US*)
Phaidon Press Limited (*UK*)
Poolbeg (*Ire*)
Quadrille Publishing Ltd (*UK*)
Quarto Publishing Group UK (*UK*)
Quarto Publishing Group USA (*US*)
Quintet Publishing (*UK*)
Saqi Books (*UK*)
Sheldrake Press (*UK*)
Simon & Schuster UK Limited (*UK*)
SisterShip Press Pty Ltd (*Aus*)
Sunstone Press (*US*)

TouchWood Editions (*Can*)
The University of Michigan Press (*US*)
Willow Creek Press, Inc. (*US*)
Crafts
Abdo Publishing Co (*US*)
Anness Publishing Ltd (*UK*)
Arsenal Pulp Press (*Can*)
Beercott Books (*UK*)
C&T Publishing (*US*)
Chicago Review Press (*US*)
Chronicle Books LLC (*US*)
Craftsman Book Co. (*US*)
Floris Books (*UK*)
Gibbs Smith, Publisher (*US*)
Gill Books (*Ire*)
Haldane Mason Ltd (*UK*)
HarperCollins Publishers Ltd (*UK*)
Hobar Publications (*US*)
Interweave Press (*US*)
Native Ink Press (*US*)
New Holland Publishers (UK) Ltd (*UK*)
The O'Brien Press (*Ire*)
Pavilion Books Group Limited (*UK*)
Quadrille Publishing Ltd (*UK*)
Quarto Publishing Group UK (*UK*)
Quarto Publishing Group USA (*US*)
Quintet Publishing (*UK*)
SisterShip Press Pty Ltd (*Aus*)
Snowbooks (*UK*)
Sterling Publishing Co. Inc. (*US*)
Stone Bridge Press (*US*)
Sunstone Press (*US*)
Thames and Hudson Ltd (*UK*)
W.W. Norton & Company Ltd (*UK*)
Crime
ABC-CLIO / Greenwood (*US*)
Allen & Unwin (*Aus*)
Allison & Busby Ltd (*UK*)
Asabi Publishing (*US*)
BakerSteele Publishing (*UK*)
Black & White Publishing Ltd (*UK*)
Black Coffey Publishing (*UK*)
John Blake Publishing (*UK*)
Blink Publishing (*UK*)
bookouture (*UK*)
Cynren Press (*US*)
DB Publishing (*UK*)
Diversion Books (*US*)
Duckworth Publishers (*UK*)
Fahrenheit Press (*US*)
Gill Books (*Ire*)
HarperCollins Publishers Ltd (*UK*)
Head of Zeus (*UK*)
Heritage House (*Can*)
Hesperus Press Limited (*UK*)
The History Press (*UK*)
Honno Welsh Women's Press (*UK*)
Impress Books Limited (*UK*)
Insomniac Press (*Can*)
Jacaranda Books Art Music Ltd (*UK*)
Jewish Lights Publishing (*US*)
Joffe Books Ltd (*UK*)
Kensington Publishing Corp. (*US*)

Legend Press (*UK*)
Little, Brown Book Group (*UK*)
Lost Tower Publications (*UK*)
Luath Press Ltd (*UK*)
Mandrake of Oxford (*UK*)
Mango Books (*UK*)
Melbourne University Publishing Ltd (*Aus*)
Michael Joseph (*UK*)
MIrror Books (*UK*)
Myriad Editions (*UK*)
New Island (*Ire*)
The O'Brien Press (*Ire*)
Orenda Books (*UK*)
Pan Macmillan (*UK*)
Pen & Sword Books Ltd (*UK*)
Periscope (*UK*)
Quercus Books (*UK*)
Red Rattle Books (*UK*)
Robert Hale Publishers (*UK*)
Sage Publications (*UK*)
Salt Publishing Ltd (*UK*)
Sandstone Press Ltd (*UK*)
SelfMadeHero (*UK*)
Serpent's Tail (*UK*)
Severn House Publishers (*UK*)
SisterShip Press Pty Ltd (*Aus*)
Snowbooks (*UK*)
Southern Illinois University Press (*US*)
Sterling Publishing Co. Inc. (*US*)
Sunstone Press (*US*)
Temple University Press (*US*)
The Charles Press, Publishers (*US*)
Three Hares Publishing (*UK*)
Twenty First Century Publishers Ltd (*UK*)
W.W. Norton & Company Ltd (*UK*)
We Are One Body Audio Theatre (*US*)
Zumaya Publications (*US*)
Criticism
Colin Smythe Ltd (*UK*)
Cornell University Press (*US*)
Dalkey Archive Press (*US*)
Duckworth Publishers (*UK*)
Enitharmon Press (*UK*)
Fence Books (*US*)
Fernwood Publishing (*Can*)
Four Courts Press (*Ire*)
Gibson Square Books Ltd (*UK*)
Granta Books (*UK*)
Halban Publishers (*UK*)
Insomniac Press (*Can*)
Kaya Press (*US*)
Kent State University Press (*US*)
The Lilliput Press (*Ire*)
New Island (*Ire*)
Northcote House Publishers Ltd (*UK*)
Peter Owen Publishers (*UK*)
Portobello Books Ltd (*UK*)
Red Moon Press (*US*)
Salt Publishing Ltd (*UK*)
Seren Books (*UK*)
Shearsman Books (*UK*)
Truman State University Press (*US*)
University College Dublin (UCD) Press (*Ire*)

Yale University Press (London) (*UK*)
Culture
ABC-CLIO / Greenwood (*US*)
Abdo Publishing Co (*US*)
Allen & Unwin (*Aus*)
Allison & Busby Ltd (*UK*)
Arsenal Pulp Press (*Can*)
Asabi Publishing (*US*)
Augsburg Fortress (*US*)
Aurora Metro Press (*UK*)
Bess Press (*US*)
Birlinn Ltd (*UK*)
Black Dome Press (*US*)
Blink Publishing (*UK*)
Blue Guides Limited (*UK*)
Nicholas Brealey Publishing (*UK*)
Canongate Books (*UK*)
Carlton Publishing Group (*UK*)
Charlesbridge Publishing (*US*)
Chicago Review Press (*US*)
Cork University Press (*Ire*)
Coteau Books (*Can*)
Cynren Press (*US*)
Da Capo Press (*US*)
Diversion Books (*US*)
DK Publishing (*US*)
Edinburgh University Press (*UK*)
Elm Books (*US*)
Encounter Books (*US*)
Fernwood Publishing (*Can*)
Flame Tree Publishing (*UK*)
Garnet Publishing (*UK*)
Gibson Square Books Ltd (*UK*)
Gomer Press (*UK*)
Grand Central Publishing (*US*)
Granta Books (*UK*)
Hendrick-Long Publishing Co. (*US*)
Heritage House (*Can*)
Hesperus Press Limited (*UK*)
Infinite Ideas (*UK*)
Insomniac Press (*Can*)
Kaya Press (*US*)
Lantana Publishing (*UK*)
Lawrence & Wishart (*UK*)
The Lilliput Press (*Ire*)
Mandrake of Oxford (*UK*)
The Orion Publishing Group Limited (*UK*)
Paulist Press (*US*)
Pavilion Books Group Limited (*UK*)
Phaidon Press Limited (*UK*)
Policy Studies Institute (PSI) (*UK*)
Portobello Books Ltd (*UK*)
Profile Books (*UK*)
Quintet Publishing (*UK*)
Repeater Books (*UK*)
Rivers Oram Press (*UK*)
Route Publishing (*UK*)
Saffron Books (*UK*)
Santa Monica Press (*US*)
Serpent's Tail (*UK*)
Shipwreckt Books Publishing Company (*US*)
Stone Bridge Press (*US*)
Syracuse University Press (*US*)

I.B. Tauris & Co. Ltd (*UK*)
Temple University Press (*US*)
Thames & Hudson Inc. (*US*)
Thames and Hudson Ltd (*UK*)
The British Museum Press (*UK*)
Torrey House Press, LLC (*US*)
TouchWood Editions (*Can*)
Unicorn Publishing Group (*UK*)
University of Alaska Press (*US*)
University of Exeter Press (*UK*)
The University of Michigan Press (*US*)
University of Wales Press (*UK*)
University of Washington Press (*US*)
Vallentine Mitchell & Co., Limited (*UK*)
Verso (*UK*)
Wayne State University Press (*US*)
Wesleyan University Press (*US*)

Current Affairs
ABC-CLIO / Greenwood (*US*)
Abdo Publishing Co (*US*)
Allen & Unwin (*Aus*)
Birlinn Ltd (*UK*)
Bloomberg Press (*US*)
Bristol University Press (*UK*)
Clarity Press, Inc. (*US*)
Cork University Press (*Ire*)
Duckworth Publishers (*UK*)
Dunedin Academic Press Ltd (*UK*)
Encounter Books (*US*)
Fernwood Publishing (*Can*)
Garnet Publishing (*UK*)
Gibson Square Books Ltd (*UK*)
Gill Books (*Ire*)
Hay House Publishers (*UK*)
Infinite Ideas (*UK*)
Lawrence & Wishart (*UK*)
The Lilliput Press (*Ire*)
Luath Press Ltd (*UK*)
New Island (*Ire*)
Oneworld Publications (*UK*)
The Orion Publishing Group Limited (*UK*)
Periscope (*UK*)
Portobello Books Ltd (*UK*)
Profile Books (*UK*)
Quarto Publishing Group USA (*US*)
Repeater Books (*UK*)
Rivers Oram Press (*UK*)
Saffron Books (*UK*)
Seren Books (*UK*)
Serpent's Tail (*UK*)
Seven Stories Press (*US*)
Shipwreckt Books Publishing Company (*US*)
Syracuse University Press (*US*)
I.B. Tauris & Co. Ltd (*UK*)
TSO (The Stationery Office) (*UK*)
W.W. Norton & Company Ltd (*UK*)
Yale University Press (London) (*UK*)

Design
Abdo Publishing Co (*US*)
Anness Publishing Ltd (*UK*)
Carlton Publishing Group (*UK*)
Chronicle Books LLC (*US*)
Clarkson Potter (*US*)

Co & Bear Productions (*UK*)
Colourpoint Educational (*UK*)
Duckworth Publishers (*UK*)
Gibbs Smith, Publisher (*US*)
Laurence King Publishing Ltd (*UK*)
Lund Humphries Limited (*UK*)
Melbourne University Publishing Ltd (*Aus*)
New Holland Publishers (UK) Ltd (*UK*)
The Orion Publishing Group Limited (*UK*)
Pavilion Books Group Limited (*UK*)
Phaidon Press Limited (*UK*)
Pimpernel Press (*UK*)
Princeton Architectural Press (*US*)
Quadrille Publishing Ltd (*UK*)
Quarto Publishing Group UK (*UK*)
Quarto Publishing Group USA (*US*)
Robert Hale Publishers (*UK*)
Stone Bridge Press (*US*)
I.B. Tauris & Co. Ltd (*UK*)
Thames & Hudson Inc. (*US*)
Thames and Hudson Ltd (*UK*)
Trentham Books (*UK*)
W.W. Norton & Company Ltd (*UK*)
ZigZag Education (*UK*)

Drama
Aurora Metro Press (*UK*)
Black Coffey Publishing (*UK*)
Blue Trident Books (*UK*)
Chapman Publishing (*UK*)
Colin Smythe Ltd (*UK*)
Cork University Press (*Ire*)
Coteau Books (*Can*)
Cressrelles Publishing Co. Ltd (*UK*)
Duckworth Publishers (*UK*)
Faber & Faber Ltd (*UK*)
Gomer Press (*UK*)
Italica Press (*US*)
The Lilliput Press (*Ire*)
Luath Press Ltd (*UK*)
MIrror Books (*UK*)
New Island (*Ire*)
New Playwrights' Network (NPN) (*UK*)
The O'Brien Press (*Ire*)
Oberon Books (*UK*)
Samuel French Ltd (*UK*)
Seren Books (*UK*)
Temple University Press (*US*)
University College Dublin (UCD) Press (*Ire*)
W.W. Norton & Company Ltd (*UK*)
We Are One Body Audio Theatre (*US*)
ZigZag Education (*UK*)

Entertainment
Abdo Publishing Co (*US*)
Ascend Books, LLC (*US*)
John Blake Publishing (*UK*)
Carlton Publishing Group (*UK*)
HarperCollins Publishers Ltd (*UK*)
Infinite Ideas (*UK*)
Little, Brown Book Group (*UK*)
Penguin Random House (*US*)
Quarto Publishing Group UK (*UK*)
Santa Monica Press (*US*)
SisterShip Press Pty Ltd (*Aus*)

Syracuse University Press (*US*)

Erotic
Abuzz Press (*US*)
Asabi Publishing (*US*)
Aurelia Leo (*US*)
Hesperus Press Limited (*UK*)
Mandrake of Oxford (*UK*)
NBM Publishing (*US*)

Fantasy
Allen & Unwin (*Aus*)
Allison & Busby Ltd (*UK*)
Aurelia Leo (*US*)
Baen Books (*US*)
Black Coffey Publishing (*UK*)
Blue Trident Books (*UK*)
Candlemark & Gleam (*US*)
Candy Jar Books (*UK*)
Colin Smythe Ltd (*UK*)
Coteau Books (*Can*)
Cuil Press (*US*)
Diversion Books (*US*)
EDGE Science Fiction and Fantasy Publishing (*Can*)
Entangled Teen (*US*)
4RV Publishing (*US*)
HarperCollins (*US*)
HarperCollins Publishers Ltd (*UK*)
Head of Zeus (*UK*)
Hesperus Press Limited (*UK*)
Honno Welsh Women's Press (*UK*)
Kensington Publishing Corp. (*US*)
Less Than Three Press (*US*)
Little, Brown Book Group (*UK*)
Lost Tower Publications (*UK*)
Luna Press Publishing (*UK*)
Manor House Publishing (*Can*)
Martin Sisters Publishing (*US*)
Marvel Comics (*US*)
NBM Publishing (*US*)
The Orion Publishing Group Limited (*UK*)
Pace Press (*US*)
Pan Macmillan (*UK*)
Penguin Random House (*US*)
Pure Indigo Limited (*UK*)
Quercus Books (*UK*)
The Salariya Book Company (*UK*)
Shipwreckt Books Publishing Company (*US*)
SisterShip Press Pty Ltd (*Aus*)
Snowbooks (*UK*)
Sunstone Press (*US*)
Tor/Forge (*US*)
We Are One Body Audio Theatre (*US*)
World Weaver Press (*US*)
Zumaya Publications (*US*)

Fiction
a...p press (*US*)
Abdo Publishing Co (*US*)
Abuzz Press (*US*)
Academy Chicago (*US*)
Albert Whitman & Company (*US*)
Allen & Unwin (*Aus*)
Allison & Busby Ltd (*UK*)
Alma Books Ltd (*UK*)

Alma Classics (*UK*)
Andersen Press Ltd (*UK*)
Andrews McMeel Publishing (*US*)
April Gloaming (*US*)
Arsenal Pulp Press (*Can*)
Asabi Publishing (*US*)
Augsburg Fortress (*US*)
Aurelia Leo (*US*)
Aurora Metro Press (*UK*)
Avatar Press (*US*)
Award Publications Limited (*UK*)
Baen Books (*US*)
BakerSteele Publishing (*UK*)
Bancroft Press (*US*)
Baobab Press (*US*)
Barrington Stoke (*UK*)
Be About It Press (*US*)
Beacon Publishing Group (*US*)
BearManor Media (*US*)
Belle Lutte Press (*US*)
Beyond Words Publishing (*US*)
Birlinn Ltd (*UK*)
BkMk Press (*US*)
Black & White Publishing Ltd (*UK*)
Black Ace Books (*UK*)
Black Coffey Publishing (*UK*)
John Blake Publishing (*UK*)
Bloomsbury Spark (*UK*)
Blue Trident Books (*UK*)
bookouture (*UK*)
Caitlin Press Inc. (*Can*)
Candlemark & Gleam (*US*)
Candy Jar Books (*UK*)
Canongate Books (*UK*)
Cedar Fort (*US*)
Chapman Publishing (*UK*)
Charlesbridge Publishing (*US*)
Chicago Review Press (*US*)
Chronicle Books LLC (*US*)
Classical Comics Limited (*UK*)
Colin Smythe Ltd (*UK*)
Comma Press (*UK*)
Coteau Books (*Can*)
The Crown Publishing Group (*US*)
Crux Publishing (*UK*)
Cuil Press (*US*)
Dalkey Archive Press (*US*)
David Fickling Books (*UK*)
DB Publishing (*UK*)
De Montfort Literature (*UK*)
Dedalus Ltd (*UK*)
Diversion Books (*US*)
Dodo Ink (*UK*)
Down The Shore Publishing (*US*)
Dref Wen (*UK*)
Duckworth Publishers (*UK*)
EDGE Science Fiction and Fantasy Publishing (*Can*)
Educe Press (*US*)
Elektra Press (*US*)
Elm Books (*US*)
The Emma Press Ltd (*UK*)
Enitharmon Press (*UK*)

Red Rattle Books (*UK*)
Repeater Books (*UK*)
Robert Hale Publishers (*UK*)
Route Publishing (*UK*)
Saddle Road Press (*US*)
Saffron Books (*UK*)
Saguaro Books, LLC (*US*)
The Salariya Book Company (*UK*)
Salt Publishing Ltd (*UK*)
Salvo Press (*US*)
Sandstone Press Ltd (*UK*)
Saqi Books (*UK*)
Scholastic (*UK*)
Scholastic Library Publishing (*US*)
Scribner (*US*)
SelfMadeHero (*UK*)
Seren Books (*UK*)
Serpent's Tail (*UK*)
Seven Stories Press (*US*)
Severn House Publishers (*UK*)
Shipwreckt Books Publishing Company (*US*)
Silvertail Books (*UK*)
Simon & Schuster UK Limited (*UK*)
SisterShip Press Pty Ltd (*Aus*)
Sky Pony Press (*US*)
Snowbooks (*UK*)
Somerville Press (*Ire*)
Southern Illinois University Press (*US*)
Star Bright Books (*US*)
Sterling Publishing Co. Inc. (*US*)
Stone Bridge Press (*US*)
Stonewood Press (*UK*)
Sunstone Press (*US*)
Sweet Cherry Publishing (*UK*)
Tailwinds Press (*US*)
Tango Books Ltd (*UK*)
The Templar Company Limited (*UK*)
Thomas Dunne Books (*US*)
Three Hares Publishing (*UK*)
ThunderStone Books (*US*)
Tiny Owl (*UK*)
Tor/Forge (*US*)
Torrey House Press, LLC (*US*)
TouchWood Editions (*Can*)
Triangle Square (*US*)
Tumblehome Learning, Inc. (*US*)
Twenty First Century Publishers Ltd (*UK*)
University of Alaska Press (*US*)
The University of Michigan Press (*US*)
Vegetarian Alcoholic Press (*US*)
Vehicule Press (*Can*)
Verso (*UK*)
W.W. Norton & Company Ltd (*UK*)
WaterBrook & Multnomah (*US*)
We Are One Body Audio Theatre (*US*)
World Weaver Press (*US*)
WorthyKids / Ideals (*US*)
Zumaya Publications (*US*)
Film
Aurora Metro Press (*UK*)
BearManor Media (*US*)
John Blake Publishing (*UK*)
Carlton Publishing Group (*UK*)

Chicago Review Press (*US*)
Chronicle Books LLC (*US*)
Cork University Press (*Ire*)
Duckworth Publishers (*UK*)
Edinburgh University Press (*UK*)
Faber & Faber Ltd (*UK*)
Fairleigh Dickinson University (FDU) Press (*Can*)
Focal Press (*US*)
HarperCollins Publishers Ltd (*UK*)
Laurence King Publishing Ltd (*UK*)
McGraw-Hill Education (*US*)
Nick Hern Books Ltd (*UK*)
Phaidon Press Limited (*UK*)
Route Publishing (*UK*)
Santa Monica Press (*US*)
SisterShip Press Pty Ltd (*Aus*)
Southern Illinois University Press (*US*)
Stone Bridge Press (*US*)
I.B. Tauris & Co. Ltd (*UK*)
Temple University Press (*US*)
University of Exeter Press (*UK*)
Verso (*UK*)
W.W. Norton & Company Ltd (*UK*)
Wesleyan University Press (*US*)
Finance
ABC-CLIO / Greenwood (*US*)
Algora Publishing (*US*)
Allen & Unwin (*Aus*)
Bancroft Press (*US*)
Birlinn Ltd (*UK*)
Bloomberg Press (*US*)
Nicholas Brealey Publishing (*UK*)
Bristol University Press (*UK*)
Career Press (*US*)
Clarity Press, Inc. (*US*)
Duckworth Publishers (*UK*)
Dunedin Academic Press Ltd (*UK*)
Entrepreneur Press (*US*)
Fernwood Publishing (*Can*)
Gingko Library (*UK*)
HarperCollins (*US*)
Hay House Publishers (*UK*)
Insomniac Press (*Can*)
Kogan Page Ltd (*UK*)
LexisNexis Canada (*Can*)
PassKey Publications (*US*)
Policy Studies Institute (PSI) (*UK*)
Profile Books (*UK*)
Robert D. Reed Publishers (*US*)
Saffron Books (*UK*)
Sage Publications (*UK*)
Shepheard-Walwyn (Publishers) Ltd (*UK*)
Silver Lake Publishing, LLC (*US*)
Sterling Publishing Co. Inc. (*US*)
Temple University Press (*US*)
Twenty First Century Publishers Ltd (*UK*)
The University of Michigan Press (*US*)
Verso (*UK*)
W.W. Norton & Company Ltd (*UK*)
Yale University Press (London) (*UK*)
ZigZag Education (*UK*)

Gardening
Anness Publishing Ltd (*UK*)
Chicago Review Press (*US*)
HarperCollins Publishers Ltd (*UK*)
Headline Publishing Group (*UK*)
Hobar Publications (*US*)
Infinite Ideas (*UK*)
Insomniac Press (*Can*)
Native Ink Press (*US*)
New Holland Publishers (UK) Ltd (*UK*)
The Orion Publishing Group Limited (*UK*)
Pavilion Books Group Limited (*UK*)
Pen & Sword Books Ltd (*UK*)
Pimpernel Press (*UK*)
Poolbeg (*Ire*)
Quadrille Publishing Ltd (*UK*)
Quarto Publishing Group UK (*UK*)
Shipwreckt Books Publishing Company (*US*)
Sterling Publishing Co. Inc. (*US*)
Sunstone Press (*US*)
Thames & Hudson Inc. (*US*)
Thames and Hudson Ltd (*UK*)
TouchWood Editions (*Can*)
Willow Creek Press, Inc. (*US*)

Gothic
Aurelia Leo (*US*)
HarperCollins (*US*)
Lost Tower Publications (*UK*)
Salt Publishing Ltd (*UK*)
We Are One Body Audio Theatre (*US*)
Zumaya Publications (*US*)

Health
ABC-CLIO / Greenwood (*US*)
Allen & Unwin (*Aus*)
American Psychiatric Association Publishing (*US*)
American Psychiatric Association Publishing (*US*)
Anness Publishing Ltd (*UK*)
Arsenal Pulp Press (*Can*)
Bancroft Press (*US*)
Beyond Words Publishing (*US*)
John Blake Publishing (*UK*)
Bull Publishing Company (*US*)
Chronicle Books LLC (*US*)
Colourpoint Educational (*UK*)
Crown House Publishing (*UK*)
DB Publishing (*UK*)
Dunedin Academic Press Ltd (*UK*)
Eastland Press (*US*)
Fernwood Publishing (*Can*)
Findhorn Press Ltd (*UK*)
Floris Books (*UK*)
Geddes & Grosset (*UK*)
Haldane Mason Ltd (*UK*)
Hampton Roads Publishing (*US*)
HarperCollins Publishers Ltd (*UK*)
Harvest House Publishers (*US*)
Hay House Publishers (*UK*)
Health Professions Press (*US*)
Human Kinetics (*US*)
Idyll Arbor (*US*)
Insomniac Press (*Can*)

Kensington Publishing Corp. (*US*)
Mandrake of Oxford (*UK*)
McGraw-Hill Education (*US*)
New Holland Publishers (UK) Ltd (*UK*)
The Orion Publishing Group Limited (*UK*)
Pavilion Publishing (*UK*)
Pen & Sword Books Ltd (*UK*)
Quadrille Publishing Ltd (*UK*)
Quarto Publishing Group UK (*UK*)
Quarto Publishing Group USA (*US*)
Robert D. Reed Publishers (*US*)
Robert Hale Publishers (*UK*)
Sage Publications (*UK*)
Seven Stories Press (*US*)
Shipwreckt Books Publishing Company (*US*)
Simon & Schuster UK Limited (*UK*)
Singing Dragon (*UK*)
SisterShip Press Pty Ltd (*Aus*)
Southern Illinois University Press (*US*)
Sterling Publishing Co. Inc. (*US*)
Sunrise River Press (*US*)
Sunstone Press (*US*)
Temple University Press (*US*)
The Charles Press, Publishers (*US*)
Triangle Square (*US*)
W.W. Norton & Company Ltd (*UK*)
Wild Goose Publications (*UK*)
Yale University Press (London) (*UK*)
YMAA Publication Center, Inc. (*US*)
ZigZag Education (*UK*)

Historical
ABC-CLIO / Greenwood (*US*)
Abdo Publishing Co (*US*)
Algora Publishing (*US*)
Ian Allan Publishing Ltd (*UK*)
Allen & Unwin (*Aus*)
Allison & Busby Ltd (*UK*)
Alma Books Ltd (*UK*)
Amber Books Ltd (*UK*)
Anness Publishing Ltd (*UK*)
Asabi Publishing (*US*)
Augsburg Fortress (*US*)
BakerSteele Publishing (*UK*)
Bancroft Press (*US*)
Birlinn Ltd (*UK*)
Black & White Publishing Ltd (*UK*)
Black Ace Books (*UK*)
Black Dome Press (*US*)
John Blake Publishing (*UK*)
Blink Publishing (*UK*)
Bloomsbury Spark (*UK*)
Blue Trident Books (*UK*)
Bodleian Library Publishing (*UK*)
bookouture (*UK*)
Caitlin Press Inc. (*Can*)
Candy Jar Books (*UK*)
Canongate Books (*UK*)
Carlton Publishing Group (*UK*)
The Catholic University of America Press (*US*)
Cedar Fort (*US*)
Charlesbridge Publishing (*US*)
Chicago Review Press (*US*)
Clarity Press, Inc. (*US*)

Colin Smythe Ltd (*UK*)
College Press Publishing (*US*)
Colourpoint Educational (*UK*)
Cork University Press (*Ire*)
Cornell University Press (*US*)
Coteau Books (*Can*)
Countryside Books (*UK*)
Crabtree Publishing (*US*)
The Crown Publishing Group (*US*)
Cynren Press (*US*)
Da Capo Press (*US*)
DB Publishing (*UK*)
Diversion Books (*US*)
DK Publishing (*US*)
Dovecote Press (*UK*)
Down The Shore Publishing (*US*)
Duckworth Publishers (*UK*)
Dunedin Academic Press Ltd (*UK*)
Edinburgh University Press (*UK*)
Elm Books (*US*)
Encounter Books (*US*)
Entangled Teen (*US*)
Enthusiast Books (*US*)
Fairleigh Dickinson University (FDU) Press (*Can*)
Farcountry Press (*US*)
Fernwood Publishing (*Can*)
Fleming Publications (*UK*)
Florida Academic Press (*US*)
Floris Books (*UK*)
Formac Publishing Company Limited (*Can*)
Four Courts Press (*Ire*)
Garnet Publishing (*UK*)
Geddes & Grosset (*UK*)
Genealogical Publishing Company (*US*)
Gibson Square Books Ltd (*UK*)
Gill Books (*Ire*)
Gingko Library (*UK*)
Gomer Press (*UK*)
Granta Books (*UK*)
Greystones Press (*UK*)
Grub Street Publishing (*UK*)
Halban Publishers (*UK*)
Haldane Mason Ltd (*UK*)
HarperCollins (*US*)
HarperCollins Publishers Ltd (*UK*)
Harvest House Publishers (*US*)
Head of Zeus (*UK*)
Headline Publishing Group (*UK*)
Hellgate Press (*US*)
Hendrick-Long Publishing Co. (*US*)
Heritage House (*Can*)
Hesperus Press Limited (*UK*)
High Plains Press (*US*)
Hippocrene Books, Inc. (*US*)
The History Press (*UK*)
Hodder & Stoughton Ltd (*UK*)
Hopscotch (*UK*)
Houghton Mifflin Harcourt (*US*)
House of Lochar (*UK*)
Impress Books Limited (*UK*)
Indiana Historical Society Press (*US*)
Italica Press (*US*)

Jewish Lights Publishing (*US*)
JourneyForth (*US*)
Kensington Publishing Corp. (*US*)
Kent State University Press (*US*)
Kettillonia (*UK*)
Laurence King Publishing Ltd (*UK*)
Lawrence & Wishart (*UK*)
Legend Press (*UK*)
Less Than Three Press (*US*)
The Lilliput Press (*Ire*)
Little, Brown Book Group (*UK*)
Luath Press Ltd (*UK*)
Lund Humphries Limited (*UK*)
Mango Books (*UK*)
McGraw-Hill Education (*US*)
Melbourne University Publishing Ltd (*Aus*)
Myriad Editions (*UK*)
National Museum Wales (*UK*)
New Holland Publishers (UK) Ltd (*UK*)
New Island (*Ire*)
The O'Brien Press (*Ire*)
Michael O'Mara Books Ltd (*UK*)
Oleander Press (*UK*)
Oneworld Publications (*UK*)
The Orion Publishing Group Limited (*UK*)
Osprey Publishing Ltd (*UK*)
Peter Owen Publishers (*UK*)
Pace Press (*US*)
Pan Macmillan (*UK*)
Pavilion Books Group Limited (*UK*)
Pen & Sword Books Ltd (*UK*)
Penguin Random House (*US*)
Periscope (*UK*)
Phaidon Press Limited (*UK*)
Portobello Books Ltd (*UK*)
Profile Books (*UK*)
Quarto Publishing Group UK (*UK*)
Quarto Publishing Group USA (*US*)
Rivers Oram Press (*UK*)
Robert D. Reed Publishers (*US*)
Robert Hale Publishers (*UK*)
Saffron Books (*UK*)
Sage Publications (*UK*)
The Salariya Book Company (*UK*)
Santa Monica Press (*US*)
Saqi Books (*UK*)
Scribner (*US*)
Seren Books (*UK*)
Seven Stories Press (*US*)
Severn House Publishers (*UK*)
Sheldrake Press (*UK*)
Shepheard-Walwyn (Publishers) Ltd (*UK*)
Shipwreckt Books Publishing Company (*US*)
Simon & Schuster UK Limited (*UK*)
Snowbooks (*UK*)
Southern Illinois University Press (*US*)
Sunstone Press (*US*)
Syracuse University Press (*US*)
Tate Publishing (*UK*)
I.B. Tauris & Co. Ltd (*UK*)
Temple University Press (*US*)
Thames & Hudson Inc. (*US*)
Thames and Hudson Ltd (*UK*)

Hodder & Stoughton Ltd (*UK*)
Insomniac Press (*Can*)
Kettillonia (*UK*)
Leaping Dog Press (*US*)
Little, Brown Book Group (*UK*)
Marvel Comics (*US*)
McSweeney's Publishing (*US*)
Merlin Unwin Books (*UK*)
NBM Publishing (*US*)
New Holland Publishers (UK) Ltd (*UK*)
New Island (*Ire*)
The O'Brien Press (*Ire*)
Michael O'Mara Books Ltd (*UK*)
Pavilion Books Group Limited (*UK*)
Penguin Random House (*US*)
Piccadilly Press (*UK*)
Profile Books (*UK*)
Quadrille Publishing Ltd (*UK*)
Robert D. Reed Publishers (*US*)
Santa Monica Press (*US*)
September Publishing (*UK*)
Sheldrake Press (*UK*)
Shipwreckt Books Publishing Company (*US*)
Simon & Schuster UK Limited (*UK*)
SisterShip Press Pty Ltd (*Aus*)
Sterling Publishing Co. Inc. (*US*)
Sunstone Press (*US*)
W.W. Norton & Company Ltd (*UK*)
We Are One Body Audio Theatre (*US*)

Legal
ABC-CLIO / Greenwood (*US*)
Birlinn Ltd (*UK*)
John Blake Publishing (*UK*)
Bloomberg BNA Books (*US*)
Bristol University Press (*UK*)
Clarity Press, Inc. (*US*)
Colourpoint Educational (*UK*)
Cork University Press (*Ire*)
Dunedin Academic Press Ltd (*UK*)
Edinburgh University Press (*UK*)
Four Courts Press (*Ire*)
Hart Publishing Ltd (*UK*)
ICSA Publishing (*UK*)
Insomniac Press (*Can*)
Jordan Publishing (*UK*)
LexisNexis (*UK*)
LexisNexis Canada (*Can*)
McGraw-Hill Education (*US*)
Shipwreckt Books Publishing Company (*US*)
Silver Lake Publishing, LLC (*US*)
Southern Illinois University Press (*US*)
Sunstone Press (*US*)
Temple University Press (*US*)
Thomson Reuters Round Hall (*Ire*)
The University of Michigan Press (*US*)
University Press of Kansas (*US*)
W.W. Norton & Company Ltd (*UK*)
Yale University Press (London) (*UK*)
ZigZag Education (*UK*)

Leisure
Anness Publishing Ltd (*UK*)
Appalachian Mountain Club Books (*US*)
Career Press (*US*)

Cicerone Press (*UK*)
Countryside Books (*UK*)
Cynren Press (*US*)
Gill Books (*Ire*)
Gomer Press (*UK*)
HarperCollins Publishers Ltd (*UK*)
Human Kinetics (*US*)
Idyll Arbor (*US*)
Lost Tower Publications (*UK*)
Luath Press Ltd (*UK*)
Merlin Unwin Books (*UK*)
Metro Publications Ltd (*UK*)
Mountaineers Books (*US*)
Robert Hale Publishers (*UK*)
Seaworthy Publications (*US*)
Shipwreckt Books Publishing Company (*US*)
Singing Dragon (*UK*)
SisterShip Press Pty Ltd (*Aus*)
Snowbooks (*UK*)
Sunflower Books (*UK*)
Temple University Press (*US*)
Venture Publishing, Inc. (*US*)
W.W. Norton & Company Ltd (*UK*)
Willow Creek Press, Inc. (*US*)
ZigZag Education (*UK*)

Lifestyle
Allen & Unwin (*Aus*)
Andrews McMeel Publishing (*US*)
Anness Publishing Ltd (*UK*)
Arsenal Pulp Press (*Can*)
Augsburg Fortress (*US*)
Bancroft Press (*US*)
Bess Press (*US*)
Beyond Words Publishing (*US*)
Black & White Publishing Ltd (*UK*)
Black Dome Press (*US*)
Blink Publishing (*UK*)
Blue Mountain Arts, Inc. (*US*)
Career Press (*US*)
Chicago Review Press (*US*)
Chronicle Books LLC (*US*)
Clarkson Potter (*US*)
Co & Bear Productions (*UK*)
Countryside Books (*UK*)
Cynren Press (*US*)
Flame Tree Publishing (*UK*)
Free Spirit Publishing (*US*)
Gill Books (*Ire*)
Grand Central Publishing (*US*)
Haldane Mason Ltd (*UK*)
HarperCollins Publishers Ltd (*UK*)
The Harvard Common Press (*US*)
Harvest House Publishers (*US*)
Hawthorn Press (*UK*)
Hay House Publishers (*UK*)
Hodder & Stoughton Ltd (*UK*)
Igloo Books Limited (*UK*)
Infinite Ideas (*UK*)
Insomniac Press (*Can*)
Kensington Publishing Corp. (*US*)
Lost Tower Publications (*UK*)
Luath Press Ltd (*UK*)
Mandrake of Oxford (*UK*)

Melbourne University Publishing Ltd (*Aus*)
Michael Joseph (*UK*)
New Holland Publishers (UK) Ltd (*UK*)
The O'Brien Press (*Ire*)
The Orion Publishing Group Limited (*UK*)
Pavilion Books Group Limited (*UK*)
Pen & Sword Books Ltd (*UK*)
Quarto Publishing Group UK (*UK*)
Quintet Publishing (*UK*)
Robert D. Reed Publishers (*US*)
Robert Hale Publishers (*UK*)
Shipwreckt Books Publishing Company (*US*)
Silver Lake Publishing, LLC (*US*)
SisterShip Press Pty Ltd (*Aus*)
Sterling Publishing Co. Inc. (*US*)
Stone Bridge Press (*US*)
Temple University Press (*US*)
Thames and Hudson Ltd (*UK*)
The Charles Press, Publishers (*US*)
Torah Aura Productions (*US*)
TouchWood Editions (*Can*)
W.W. Norton & Company Ltd (*UK*)
Watkins Publishing (*UK*)
WorthyKids / Ideals (*US*)
Literature
Algora Publishing (*US*)
Allen & Unwin (*Aus*)
Alma Books Ltd (*UK*)
Alma Classics (*UK*)
Aurora Metro Press (*UK*)
Bodleian Library Publishing (*UK*)
Broadview Press (*Can*)
Carcanet Press Ltd (*UK*)
The Catholic University of America Press (*US*)
Classical Comics Limited (*UK*)
Colin Smythe Ltd (*UK*)
Cork University Press (*Ire*)
Cornell University Press (*US*)
Coteau Books (*Can*)
Dalkey Archive Press (*US*)
Dedalus Ltd (*UK*)
Duckworth Publishers (*UK*)
Edinburgh University Press (*UK*)
Fairleigh Dickinson University (FDU) Press
(*Can*)
Fence Books (*US*)
Fernwood Publishing (*Can*)
Floris Books (*UK*)
Four Courts Press (*Ire*)
Garnet Publishing (*UK*)
George Braziller, Inc. (*US*)
Gingko Library (*UK*)
Gomer Press (*UK*)
Greystones Press (*UK*)
Halban Publishers (*UK*)
Hesperus Press Limited (*UK*)
Houghton Mifflin Harcourt (*US*)
House of Lochar (*UK*)
Insomniac Press (*Can*)
Kaya Press (*US*)
Kent State University Press (*US*)
Kettillonia (*UK*)
The Lilliput Press (*Ire*)

Little, Brown Book Group (*UK*)
Melbourne University Publishing Ltd (*Aus*)
New Island (*Ire*)
Northcote House Publishers Ltd (*UK*)
The O'Brien Press (*Ire*)
Oleander Press (*UK*)
Oneworld Publications (*UK*)
The Orion Publishing Group Limited (*UK*)
Peter Owen Publishers (*UK*)
Red Moon Press (*US*)
Repeater Books (*UK*)
Salt Publishing Ltd (*UK*)
Santa Monica Press (*US*)
Shearsman Books (*UK*)
Sterling Publishing Co. Inc. (*US*)
Stone Bridge Press (*US*)
Syracuse University Press (*US*)
Temple University Press (*US*)
Thames and Hudson Ltd (*UK*)
Truman State University Press (*US*)
University College Dublin (UCD) Press (*Ire*)
University of Exeter Press (*UK*)
The University of Michigan Press (*US*)
University of Wales Press (*UK*)
W.W. Norton & Company Ltd (*UK*)
We Are One Body Audio Theatre (*US*)
Wesleyan University Press (*US*)
Yale University Press (London) (*UK*)
Media
Allen & Unwin (*Aus*)
Coteau Books (*Can*)
Edinburgh University Press (*UK*)
Focal Press (*US*)
Garnet Publishing (*UK*)
HarperCollins Publishers Ltd (*UK*)
Infinite Ideas (*UK*)
Sage Publications (*UK*)
I.B. Tauris & Co. Ltd (*UK*)
Temple University Press (*US*)
The University of Michigan Press (*US*)
University of Wales Press (*UK*)
Verso (*UK*)
Wayne State University Press (*US*)
ZigZag Education (*UK*)
Medicine
Abdo Publishing Co (*US*)
Birlinn Ltd (*UK*)
Bull Publishing Company (*US*)
Dunedin Academic Press Ltd (*UK*)
Eastland Press (*US*)
Fernwood Publishing (*Can*)
Hay House Publishers (*UK*)
Health Professions Press (*US*)
Human Kinetics (*US*)
Idyll Arbor (*US*)
Insomniac Press (*Can*)
Myriad Editions (*UK*)
Sage Publications (*UK*)
Shipwreckt Books Publishing Company (*US*)
Silver Lake Publishing, LLC (*US*)
Singing Dragon (*UK*)
Springer-Verlag London Ltd (*UK*)
Sunrise River Press (*US*)

The Charles Press, Publishers (*US*)
TSO (The Stationery Office) (*UK*)
W.W. Norton & Company Ltd (*UK*)
Yale University Press (London) (*UK*)
YMAA Publication Center, Inc. (*US*)
Men's Interests
Cynren Press (*US*)
Harvest House Publishers (*US*)
Hay House Publishers (*UK*)
Jewish Lights Publishing (*US*)
Military
ABC-CLIO / Greenwood (*US*)
Abdo Publishing Co (*US*)
Algora Publishing (*US*)
Ian Allan Publishing Ltd (*UK*)
Allen & Unwin (*Aus*)
Allison & Busby Ltd (*UK*)
Amber Books Ltd (*UK*)
Anness Publishing Ltd (*UK*)
BakerSteele Publishing (*UK*)
Birlinn Ltd (*UK*)
John Blake Publishing (*UK*)
Blink Publishing (*UK*)
Candy Jar Books (*UK*)
Clarity Press, Inc. (*US*)
Countryside Books (*UK*)
Enthusiast Books (*US*)
Grub Street Publishing (*UK*)
HarperCollins Publishers Ltd (*UK*)
Hellgate Press (*US*)
Hendrick-Long Publishing Co. (*US*)
Heritage House (*Can*)
The History Press (*UK*)
Jane's Information Group (*UK*)
Kensington Publishing Corp. (*US*)
The Orion Publishing Group Limited (*UK*)
Osprey Publishing Ltd (*UK*)
Pen & Sword Books Ltd (*UK*)
Quarto Publishing Group USA (*US*)
Shipwreckt Books Publishing Company (*US*)
Sunstone Press (*US*)
Unicorn Publishing Group (*UK*)
University College Dublin (UCD) Press (*Ire*)
University Press of Kansas (*US*)
Music
Algora Publishing (*US*)
Allen & Unwin (*Aus*)
Anness Publishing Ltd (*UK*)
Arc Publications (*UK*)
Aureus Publishing Limited (*UK*)
Aurora Metro Press (*UK*)
John Blake Publishing (*UK*)
Blink Publishing (*UK*)
Carlton Publishing Group (*UK*)
Chicago Review Press (*US*)
Chronicle Books LLC (*US*)
Cork University Press (*Ire*)
Da Capo Press (*US*)
Duckworth Publishers (*UK*)
Dunedin Academic Press Ltd (*UK*)
Faber & Faber Ltd (*UK*)
Fairleigh Dickinson University (FDU) Press
(*Can*)

Flame Tree Publishing (*UK*)
Focal Press (*US*)
Gingko Library (*UK*)
Gomer Press (*UK*)
Greystones Press (*UK*)
Hal Leonard Performing Arts Publishing Group
(*US*)
Half Mystic Press (*US*)
Insomniac Press (*Can*)
The Lilliput Press (*Ire*)
Kevin Mayhew Publishers (*UK*)
McGraw-Hill Education (*US*)
The O'Brien Press (*Ire*)
Omnibus Press (*UK*)
Phaidon Press Limited (*UK*)
Quarto Publishing Group USA (*US*)
Repeater Books (*UK*)
Route Publishing (*UK*)
Seren Books (*UK*)
Serpent's Tail (*UK*)
Sheldrake Press (*UK*)
Sterling Publishing Co. Inc. (*US*)
Sunstone Press (*US*)
Triangle Square (*US*)
University College Dublin (UCD) Press (*Ire*)
The University of Michigan Press (*US*)
Vehicule Press (*Can*)
W.W. Norton & Company Ltd (*UK*)
Wesleyan University Press (*US*)
Yale University Press (London) (*UK*)
ZigZag Education (*UK*)
Mystery
Academy Chicago (*US*)
Allen & Unwin (*Aus*)
Allison & Busby Ltd (*UK*)
Asabi Publishing (*US*)
Bancroft Press (*US*)
Black Coffey Publishing (*UK*)
Bloomsbury Spark (*UK*)
Blue Trident Books (*UK*)
Coteau Books (*Can*)
Cynren Press (*US*)
Diversion Books (*US*)
Elm Books (*US*)
4RV Publishing (*US*)
Grand Central Publishing (*US*)
HarperCollins (*US*)
Harvest House Publishers (*US*)
Head of Zeus (*UK*)
Insomniac Press (*Can*)
Jewish Lights Publishing (*US*)
Joffe Books Ltd (*UK*)
JourneyForth (*US*)
Kensington Publishing Corp. (*US*)
Lost Tower Publications (*UK*)
Mandrake of Oxford (*UK*)
NBM Publishing (*US*)
Pace Press (*US*)
Penguin Random House (*US*)
Salt Publishing Ltd (*UK*)
Salvo Press (*US*)
Scribner (*US*)
Severn House Publishers (*UK*)

Shipwreckt Books Publishing Company (*US*)
SisterShip Press Pty Ltd (*Aus*)
Sterling Publishing Co. Inc. (*US*)
Sunstone Press (*US*)
Thomas Dunne Books (*US*)
Tor/Forge (*US*)
WaterBrook & Multnomah (*US*)
We Are One Body Audio Theatre (*US*)
Zumaya Publications (*US*)
Nature
ABC-CLIO / Greenwood (*US*)
Algora Publishing (*US*)
Allen & Unwin (*Aus*)
Anness Publishing Ltd (*UK*)
Appalachian Mountain Club Books (*US*)
Birlinn Ltd (*UK*)
Black Dome Press (*US*)
John Blake Publishing (*UK*)
Bristol University Press (*UK*)
Caitlin Press Inc. (*Can*)
Charlesbridge Publishing (*US*)
Co & Bear Productions (*UK*)
Cornell University Press (*US*)
Dawn Publications (*US*)
DK Publishing (*US*)
Dovecote Press (*UK*)
Down The Shore Publishing (*US*)
Duckworth Publishers (*UK*)
Dunedin Academic Press Ltd (*UK*)
Encante Press, LLC (*US*)
Farcountry Press (*US*)
Fernwood Publishing (*Can*)
Formac Publishing Company Limited (*Can*)
Gill Books (*Ire*)
Gomer Press (*UK*)
Granta Books (*UK*)
Hay House Publishers (*UK*)
Heritage House (*Can*)
High Plains Press (*US*)
Hobar Publications (*US*)
JourneyForth (*US*)
The Lilliput Press (*Ire*)
Luath Press Ltd (*UK*)
Merlin Unwin Books (*UK*)
Mountaineers Books (*US*)
National Museum Wales (*UK*)
Native Ink Press (*US*)
New Holland Publishers (UK) Ltd (*UK*)
The O'Brien Press (*Ire*)
Oneworld Publications (*UK*)
The Orion Publishing Group Limited (*UK*)
Pan Macmillan (*UK*)
Pen & Sword Books Ltd (*UK*)
Policy Studies Institute (PSI) (*UK*)
Robert Hale Publishers (*UK*)
Ruby Tuesday Books (*UK*)
The Salariya Book Company (*UK*)
Sawday's (*UK*)
Shipwreckt Books Publishing Company (*US*)
SisterShip Press Pty Ltd (*Aus*)
Sterling Publishing Co. Inc. (*US*)
Sunstone Press (*US*)
Temple University Press (*US*)

Thames and Hudson Ltd (*UK*)
Torrey House Press, LLC (*US*)
TouchWood Editions (*Can*)
Triangle Square (*US*)
Truman State University Press (*US*)
University College Dublin (UCD) Press (*Ire*)
University of Alaska Press (*US*)
The University of Michigan Press (*US*)
University of Wales Press (*UK*)
University of Washington Press (*US*)
University Press of Kansas (*US*)
Venture Publishing, Inc. (*US*)
W.W. Norton & Company Ltd (*UK*)
Wide-Eyed Editions (*UK*)
Willow Creek Press, Inc. (*US*)
WIT Press (*UK*)
New Age
Abuzz Press (*US*)
Anness Publishing Ltd (*UK*)
Findhorn Press Ltd (*UK*)
Manor House Publishing (*Can*)
Sterling Publishing Co. Inc. (*US*)
Nonfiction
ABC-CLIO / Greenwood (*US*)
Abdo Publishing Co (*US*)
Abuzz Press (*US*)
Academy Chicago (*US*)
Albert Whitman & Company (*US*)
Algora Publishing (*US*)
Ian Allan Publishing Ltd (*UK*)
Allen & Unwin (*Aus*)
Allison & Busby Ltd (*UK*)
Allyn and Bacon / Merrill Education (*US*)
Alma Books Ltd (*UK*)
Amber Books Ltd (*UK*)
American Psychiatric Association Publishing
(*US*)
American Psychiatric Association Publishing
(*US*)
Andrews McMeel Publishing (*US*)
Anness Publishing Ltd (*UK*)
Appalachian Mountain Club Books (*US*)
Appletree Press Ltd (*UK*)
April Gloaming (*US*)
Arsenal Pulp Press (*Can*)
Asabi Publishing (*US*)
Ascend Books, LLC (*US*)
Association for Supervision and Curriculum
Development (ASCD) (*US*)
Augsburg Fortress (*US*)
Aureus Publishing Limited (*UK*)
Aurora Metro Press (*UK*)
The Authority Guides (*UK*)
Award Publications Limited (*UK*)
Bancroft Press (*US*)
Baobab Press (*US*)
Barrington Stoke (*UK*)
Beacon Hill Press of Kansas City (*US*)
Beacon Publishing Group (*US*)
BearManor Media (*US*)
becker&mayer! (*US*)
Bernard Babani (publishing) Ltd (*UK*)
Bess Press (*US*)

Beyond Words Publishing (*US*)
Birlinn Ltd (*UK*)
BkMk Press (*US*)
Black & White Publishing Ltd (*UK*)
Black Ace Books (*UK*)
Black Dome Press (*US*)
John Blake Publishing (*UK*)
Blink Publishing (*UK*)
Bloomberg Press (*US*)
Blue Guides Limited (*UK*)
Blue Mountain Arts, Inc. (*US*)
Bodleian Library Publishing (*UK*)
bookouture (*UK*)
Nicholas Brealey Publishing (*UK*)
Brewers Publications (*US*)
Bristol University Press (*UK*)
Broadview Press (*Can*)
Bull Publishing Company (*US*)
C&T Publishing (*US*)
Caitlin Press Inc. (*Can*)
Candy Jar Books (*UK*)
Canongate Books (*UK*)
Canopus Publishing Ltd (*UK*)
Carcanet Press Ltd (*UK*)
Career Press (*US*)
Carlton Publishing Group (*UK*)
Carson-Dellosa Publishing Company, Inc. (*US*)
The Catholic University of America Press (*US*)
Cedar Fort (*US*)
Cengage Learning (*UK*)
Charlesbridge Publishing (*US*)
Chicago Review Press (*US*)
Chronicle Books LLC (*US*)
Cicerone Press (*UK*)
Clarity Press, Inc. (*US*)
James Clarke & Co. (*UK*)
Clarkson Potter (*US*)
Co & Bear Productions (*UK*)
Coaches Choice (*US*)
Colin Smythe Ltd (*UK*)
College Press Publishing (*US*)
Colourpoint Educational (*UK*)
Cork University Press (*Ire*)
Cornell University Press (*US*)
Coteau Books (*Can*)
Council for British Archaeology (CBA) Publishing (*UK*)
Countryside Books (*UK*)
Crabtree Publishing (*US*)
Craftsman Book Co. (*US*)
Cressrelles Publishing Co. Ltd (*UK*)
The Crossroad Publishing Company (*US*)
Crossway (*US*)
Crown House Publishing (*UK*)
The Crown Publishing Group (*US*)
Crux Publishing (*UK*)
CSLI Publications (*US*)
Cynren Press (*US*)
Da Capo Press (*US*)
Dalkey Archive Press (*US*)
Dawn Publications (*US*)
DB Publishing (*UK*)
Discovery Walking Guides Ltd (*UK*)

Diversion Books (*US*)
DK Publishing (*US*)
Dovecote Press (*UK*)
Down The Shore Publishing (*US*)
Dream of Things (*US*)
Dref Wen (*UK*)
Duckworth Publishers (*UK*)
Dunedin Academic Press Ltd (*UK*)
Eastland Press (*US*)
Edinburgh University Press (*UK*)
The Educational Company of Ireland (*Ire*)
Educe Press (*US*)
Elektra Press (*US*)
Elm Books (*US*)
Encante Press, LLC (*US*)
Encounter Books (*US*)
Encyclopedia Britannica (UK) Ltd (*UK*)
Enthusiast Books (*US*)
Entrepreneur Press (*US*)
Exley Publications (*UK*)
Faber & Faber Ltd (*UK*)
Faculty of 1000 Ltd (*UK*)
Fairleigh Dickinson University (FDU) Press (*Can*)
Farcountry Press (*US*)
Farrar, Straus & Giroux, Inc. (*US*)
Farrar, Straus and Giroux Books for Younger Readers (*US*)
Fence Books (*US*)
Fernwood Publishing (*Can*)
Findhorn Press Ltd (*UK*)
Fitzrovia Press Limited (*UK*)
Flame Tree Publishing (*UK*)
Fleming Publications (*UK*)
Florida Academic Press (*US*)
Floris Books (*UK*)
Focal Press (*US*)
Footprint Handbooks (*UK*)
Formac Publishing Company Limited (*Can*)
Forward Movement Publications (*US*)
The Foundry Publishing Company (*US*)
Four Courts Press (*Ire*)
4RV Publishing (*US*)
Fox and Hound Books (*US*)
Franciscan Media Books (*US*)
Free Spirit Publishing (*US*)
George Ronald Publisher (*UK*)
The Gallery Press (*Ire*)
Galley Beggar Press (*UK*)
Garnet Publishing (*UK*)
Geddes & Grosset (*UK*)
Gemstone Publishing (*US*)
Genealogical Publishing Company (*US*)
George Braziller, Inc. (*US*)
Gertrude Press (*US*)
Gibbs Smith, Publisher (*US*)
Gibson Square Books Ltd (*UK*)
Gill Books (*Ire*)
Gingko Library (*UK*)
GL Assessment (*UK*)
Gold Wake Press (*US*)
Gomer Press (*UK*)
Grand Central Publishing (*US*)

Parthian Books (*UK*)
PassKey Publications (*US*)
Patrician Press (*UK*)
Paulist Press (*US*)
Pavilion Books Group Limited (*UK*)
Pavilion Publishing (*UK*)
Pearson UK (*UK*)
Pen & Sword Books Ltd (*UK*)
Penguin Random House (*US*)
Penguin Random House UK (*UK*)
Periscope (*UK*)
Phaidon Press Limited (*UK*)
Philosophy Documentation Center (*US*)
Phoenix Yard Books (*UK*)
Piccadilly Press (*UK*)
Pimpernel Press (*UK*)
Pocol Press (*US*)
Policy Studies Institute (PSI) (*UK*)
Poolbeg (*Ire*)
Portobello Books Ltd (*UK*)
Princeton Architectural Press (*US*)
Profile Books (*UK*)
Pure Indigo Limited (*UK*)
Pushkin Press (*UK*)
Quadrille Publishing Ltd (*UK*)
Quarto Publishing Group UK (*UK*)
Quarto Publishing Group USA (*US*)
Quercus Books (*UK*)
Quintet Publishing (*UK*)
Ransom Publishing Ltd (*UK*)
Red Moon Press (*US*)
Red Rattle Books (*UK*)
Repeater Books (*UK*)
Rivers Oram Press (*UK*)
Robert D. Reed Publishers (*US*)
Robert Hale Publishers (*UK*)
Route Publishing (*UK*)
Ruby Tuesday Books (*UK*)
Saffron Books (*UK*)
Sage Publications (*UK*)
The Salariya Book Company (*UK*)
Salt Publishing Ltd (*UK*)
Sandstone Press Ltd (*UK*)
Santa Monica Press (*US*)
Saqi Books (*UK*)
Sawday's (*UK*)
Scholastic (*UK*)
Scholastic Library Publishing (*US*)
Science Museum Group (*UK*)
Scribner (*US*)
Seaworthy Publications (*US*)
SelfMadeHero (*UK*)
September Publishing (*UK*)
Seren Books (*UK*)
Serpent's Tail (*UK*)
Seven Stories Press (*US*)
Shearsman Books (*UK*)
Sheldrake Press (*UK*)
Shepheard-Walwyn (Publishers) Ltd (*UK*)
Shipwreckt Books Publishing Company (*US*)
Silver Lake Publishing, LLC (*US*)
Silvertail Books (*UK*)
Simon & Schuster UK Limited (*UK*)

Singing Dragon (*UK*)
SisterShip Press Pty Ltd (*Aus*)
Sky Pony Press (*US*)
Snowbooks (*UK*)
Somerville Press (*Ire*)
Southern Illinois University Press (*US*)
SportsBooks Limited (*UK*)
Springer-Verlag London Ltd (*UK*)
St Pauls (*US*)
St Pauls Publishing (*UK*)
Star Bright Books (*US*)
Sterling Publishing Co. Inc. (*US*)
Stone Bridge Press (*US*)
Sunflower Books (*UK*)
Sunrise River Press (*US*)
Sunstone Press (*US*)
Syracuse University Press (*US*)
Tailwinds Press (*US*)
Tango Books Ltd (*UK*)
Tate Publishing (*UK*)
I.B. Tauris & Co. Ltd (*UK*)
The Templar Company Limited (*UK*)
Temple University Press (*US*)
Thames & Hudson Inc. (*US*)
Thames and Hudson Ltd (*UK*)
The British Museum Press (*UK*)
The Charles Press, Publishers (*US*)
Thomas Dunne Books (*US*)
Thomson Reuters Round Hall (*Ire*)
Three Hares Publishing (*UK*)
ThunderStone Books (*US*)
Tor/Forge (*US*)
Torah Aura Productions (*US*)
Torrey House Press, LLC (*US*)
TouchWood Editions (*Can*)
Trentham Books (*UK*)
Triangle Square (*US*)
Trotman & Co. Ltd (*UK*)
Truman State University Press (*US*)
TSO (The Stationery Office) (*UK*)
Two Sylvias Press (*US*)
UCL Press (*UK*)
Ugly Duckling Presse (*US*)
Unicorn Publishing Group (*UK*)
University College Dublin (UCD) Press (*Ire*)
University of Alaska Press (*US*)
University of Exeter Press (*UK*)
The University of Michigan Press (*US*)
University of Pittsburgh Press (*US*)
University of Wales Press (*UK*)
University of Washington Press (*US*)
University Press of Kansas (*US*)
Vallentine Mitchell & Co., Limited (*UK*)
Vehicule Press (*Can*)
Venture Publishing, Inc. (*US*)
Verso (*UK*)
W.W. Norton & Company Ltd (*UK*)
Walch Education (*US*)
WaterBrook & Multnomah (*US*)
Watkins Publishing (*UK*)
Wayne State University Press (*US*)
Welsh Academic Press (*UK*)
Wesleyan University Press (*US*)

Half Mystic Press (*US*)
Hesperus Press Limited (*UK*)
High Plains Press (*US*)
Honno Welsh Women's Press (*UK*)
Ibbetson Street Press (*US*)
Indigo Dreams Publishing (*UK*)
Insomniac Press (*Can*)
Italica Press (*US*)
Jacar Press (*US*)
Kaya Press (*US*)
Kettillonia (*UK*)
Leapfrog Press (*US*)
Leaping Dog Press (*US*)
Les Figues Press (*US*)
The Lilliput Press (*Ire*)
Lost Horse Press (*US*)
Lost Tower Publications (*UK*)
Luath Press Ltd (*UK*)
Luna Bisonte Prods (*US*)
Mad Gleam Press (*US*)
Manor House Publishing (*Can*)
McSweeney's Publishing (*US*)
New Island (*Ire*)
Oberon Press (*Can*)
Oleander Press (*UK*)
Oversteps Books (*UK*)
Pan Macmillan (*UK*)
Parthian Books (*UK*)
Patrician Press (*UK*)
Penguin Random House (*US*)
Penguin Random House UK (*UK*)
Phoenix Yard Books (*UK*)
Quattro Books (*Can*)
Red Moon Press (*US*)
Repeater Books (*UK*)
Saddle Road Press (*US*)
Salt Publishing Ltd (*UK*)
Seren Books (*UK*)
Shearsman Books (*UK*)
Shepheard-Walwyn (Publishers) Ltd (*UK*)
Shipwreckt Books Publishing Company (*US*)
Sibling Rivalry Press, LLC (*US*)
SisterShip Press Pty Ltd (*Aus*)
Southern Illinois University Press (*US*)
Stone Bridge Press (*US*)
Stonewood Press (*UK*)
Sunstone Press (*US*)
Two Sylvias Press (*US*)
Ugly Duckling Presse (*US*)
University of Alaska Press (*US*)
University of Pittsburgh Press (*US*)
Vegetarian Alcoholic Press (*US*)
Vehicule Press (*Can*)
W.W. Norton & Company Ltd (*UK*)
Wave Books (*US*)
We Are One Body Audio Theatre (*US*)
Wesleyan University Press (*US*)
Wild Goose Publications (*UK*)
Yellow Flag Press (*US*)
ZED Press (*Can*)
Politics
ABC-CLIO / Greenwood (*US*)
Abdo Publishing Co (*US*)

Algora Publishing (*US*)
Allen & Unwin (*Aus*)
Arsenal Pulp Press (*Can*)
Birlinn Ltd (*UK*)
John Blake Publishing (*UK*)
Bristol University Press (*UK*)
Caitlin Press Inc. (*Can*)
Canongate Books (*UK*)
The Catholic University of America Press (*US*)
Chicago Review Press (*US*)
Clarity Press, Inc. (*US*)
Colourpoint Educational (*UK*)
Cork University Press (*Ire*)
Cornell University Press (*US*)
The Crown Publishing Group (*US*)
Duckworth Publishers (*UK*)
Edinburgh University Press (*UK*)
Encante Press, LLC (*US*)
Encounter Books (*US*)
Faber & Faber Ltd (*UK*)
Fernwood Publishing (*Can*)
Florida Academic Press (*US*)
Formac Publishing Company Limited (*Can*)
Garnet Publishing (*UK*)
Gibson Square Books Ltd (*UK*)
Gingko Library (*UK*)
Granta Books (*UK*)
Halban Publishers (*UK*)
Heritage House (*Can*)
Infinite Ideas (*UK*)
Insomniac Press (*Can*)
Lawrence & Wishart (*UK*)
Lawrence Hill Books (*US*)
The Lilliput Press (*Ire*)
Luath Press Ltd (*UK*)
Manor House Publishing (*Can*)
McGraw-Hill Education (*US*)
Melbourne University Publishing Ltd (*Aus*)
Myriad Editions (*UK*)
New Island (*Ire*)
The O'Brien Press (*Ire*)
Oneworld Publications (*UK*)
Pan Macmillan (*UK*)
PaperBooks (*UK*)
Penguin Random House (*US*)
Periscope (*UK*)
Policy Studies Institute (PSI) (*UK*)
Profile Books (*UK*)
Quarto Publishing Group USA (*US*)
Repeater Books (*UK*)
Rivers Oram Press (*UK*)
Sage Publications (*UK*)
Saqi Books (*UK*)
September Publishing (*UK*)
Seren Books (*UK*)
Serpent's Tail (*UK*)
Seven Stories Press (*US*)
Shepheard-Walwyn (Publishers) Ltd (*UK*)
Shipwreckt Books Publishing Company (*US*)
Silver Lake Publishing, LLC (*US*)
Simon & Schuster UK Limited (*UK*)
Southern Illinois University Press (*US*)
Sunstone Press (*US*)

Syracuse University Press (*US*)
I.B. Tauris & Co. Ltd (*UK*)
Temple University Press (*US*)
Thames & Hudson Inc. (*US*)
Thomas Dunne Books (*US*)
Triangle Square (*US*)
University College Dublin (UCD) Press (*Ire*)
University of Alaska Press (*US*)
The University of Michigan Press (*US*)
University of Wales Press (*UK*)
University Press of Kansas (*US*)
Verso (*UK*)
W.W. Norton & Company Ltd (*UK*)
Welsh Academic Press (*UK*)
Wild Goose Publications (*UK*)
Yale University Press (London) (*UK*)
ZigZag Education (*UK*)
Psychology
ABC-CLIO / Greenwood (*US*)
Algora Publishing (*US*)
Allen & Unwin (*Aus*)
American Psychiatric Association Publishing (*US*)
American Psychiatric Association Publishing (*US*)
Black & White Publishing Ltd (*UK*)
Black Ace Books (*UK*)
bookouture (*UK*)
Nicholas Brealey Publishing (*UK*)
Bull Publishing Company (*US*)
Crown House Publishing (*UK*)
Encounter Books (*US*)
Gibson Square Books Ltd (*UK*)
Hay House Publishers (*UK*)
Health Professions Press (*US*)
Human Kinetics (*US*)
Idyll Arbor (*US*)
McGraw-Hill Education (*US*)
Oneworld Publications (*UK*)
Profile Books (*UK*)
Robert D. Reed Publishers (*US*)
Sage Publications (*UK*)
Scribner (*US*)
SisterShip Press Pty Ltd (*Aus*)
Temple University Press (*US*)
The Charles Press, Publishers (*US*)
Three Hares Publishing (*UK*)
Twenty First Century Publishers Ltd (*UK*)
The University of Michigan Press (*US*)
W.W. Norton & Company Ltd (*UK*)
ZigZag Education (*UK*)
Radio
BearManor Media (*US*)
Reference
ABC-CLIO / Greenwood (*US*)
Ian Allan Publishing Ltd (*UK*)
Amber Books Ltd (*UK*)
Anness Publishing Ltd (*UK*)
Award Publications Limited (*UK*)
Barrington Stoke (*UK*)
Beercott Books (*UK*)
Birlinn Ltd (*UK*)
Bloomberg BNA Books (*US*)

Bloomberg Press (*US*)
Career Press (*US*)
Carlton Publishing Group (*UK*)
Cicerone Press (*UK*)
James Clarke & Co. (*UK*)
Edinburgh University Press (*UK*)
Encyclopedia Britannica (UK) Ltd (*UK*)
Fernwood Publishing (*Can*)
Footprint Handbooks (*UK*)
Geddes & Grosset (*UK*)
Gemstone Publishing (*US*)
Gill Books (*Ire*)
Gomer Press (*UK*)
Grub Street Publishing (*UK*)
HarperCollins (*US*)
HarperCollins Publishers Ltd (*UK*)
Health Professions Press (*US*)
Hesperus Press Limited (*UK*)
Hippocrene Books, Inc. (*US*)
Houghton Mifflin Harcourt (*US*)
ICSA Publishing (*UK*)
Igloo Books Limited (*UK*)
Insomniac Press (*Can*)
Jane's Information Group (*UK*)
Kirkbride Bible Company (*US*)
Kogan Page Ltd (*UK*)
Krause Publications (*US*)
LexisNexis (*UK*)
LexisNexis Canada (*Can*)
The Lilliput Press (*Ire*)
New Holland Publishers (UK) Ltd (*UK*)
The O'Brien Press (*Ire*)
Oleander Press (*UK*)
The Orion Publishing Group Limited (*UK*)
Pavilion Publishing (*UK*)
Penguin Random House (*US*)
Penguin Random House UK (*UK*)
Philosophy Documentation Center (*US*)
Quarto Publishing Group USA (*US*)
Robert Hale Publishers (*UK*)
Santa Monica Press (*US*)
Scholastic Library Publishing (*US*)
Silver Lake Publishing, LLC (*US*)
SisterShip Press Pty Ltd (*Aus*)
Sterling Publishing Co. Inc. (*US*)
Stone Bridge Press (*US*)
Sunstone Press (*US*)
Thames and Hudson Ltd (*UK*)
Thomson Reuters Round Hall (*Ire*)
Trotman & Co. Ltd (*UK*)
TSO (The Stationery Office) (*UK*)
Unicorn Publishing Group (*UK*)
University of Exeter Press (*UK*)
The University of Michigan Press (*US*)
Willow Creek Press, Inc. (*US*)
Yale University Press (London) (*UK*)
Religious
ABC-CLIO / Greenwood (*US*)
Abdo Publishing Co (*US*)
Algora Publishing (*US*)
Allen & Unwin (*Aus*)
Anness Publishing Ltd (*UK*)
Augsburg Fortress (*US*)

Beacon Hill Press of Kansas City (*US*)
The Catholic University of America Press (*US*)
Cedar Fort (*US*)
James Clarke & Co. (*UK*)
College Press Publishing (*US*)
Colourpoint Educational (*UK*)
The Crossroad Publishing Company (*US*)
Crossway (*US*)
Duckworth Publishers (*UK*)
Dunedin Academic Press Ltd (*UK*)
Edinburgh University Press (*UK*)
Encounter Books (*US*)
Fairleigh Dickinson University (FDU) Press
(*Can*)
Floris Books (*UK*)
Forward Movement Publications (*US*)
The Foundry Publishing Company (*US*)
Four Courts Press (*Ire*)
4RV Publishing (*US*)
Franciscan Media Books (*US*)
George Ronald Publisher (*UK*)
Garnet Publishing (*UK*)
Gingko Library (*UK*)
Gomer Press (*UK*)
Gresham Books Ltd (*UK*)
Halban Publishers (*UK*)
HarperCollins (*US*)
Harvest House Publishers (*US*)
Hay House Publishers (*UK*)
Hodder Faith (*UK*)
Impress Books Limited (*UK*)
Insomniac Press (*Can*)
InterVarsity Press (IVP) (*UK*)
Jewish Lights Publishing (*US*)
JourneyForth (*US*)
Judson Press (*US*)
Kirkbride Bible Company (*US*)
Lillenas Drama Resources (*US*)
Loyola Press (*US*)
Martin Sisters Publishing (*US*)
Kevin Mayhew Publishers (*UK*)
Messianic Jewish Publishers (*US*)
Mud Pie Books (*UK*)
The O'Brien Press (*Ire*)
Oneworld Publications (*UK*)
Paulist Press (*US*)
Sage Publications (*UK*)
Scribner (*US*)
St Pauls (*US*)
St Pauls Publishing (*UK*)
Sunstone Press (*US*)
Syracuse University Press (*US*)
I.B. Tauris & Co. Ltd (*UK*)
Temple University Press (*US*)
Thames & Hudson Inc. (*US*)
Thames and Hudson Ltd (*UK*)
The Charles Press, Publishers (*US*)
Torah Aura Productions (*US*)
Triangle Square (*US*)
Truman State University Press (*US*)
University College Dublin (UCD) Press (*Ire*)
University of Exeter Press (*UK*)
The University of Michigan Press (*US*)

University of Wales Press (*UK*)
Vallentine Mitchell & Co., Limited (*UK*)
Vehicule Press (*Can*)
W.W. Norton & Company Ltd (*UK*)
WaterBrook & Multnomah (*US*)
Watkins Publishing (*UK*)
Wayne State University Press (*US*)
We Are One Body Audio Theatre (*US*)
Wild Goose Publications (*UK*)
WorthyKids / Ideals (*US*)
Yale University Press (London) (*UK*)
ZigZag Education (*UK*)
Romance
Abuzz Press (*US*)
Aurelia Leo (*US*)
Black & White Publishing Ltd (*UK*)
Bloomsbury Spark (*UK*)
Blue Trident Books (*UK*)
bookouture (*UK*)
Cuil Press (*US*)
Elm Books (*US*)
Entangled Teen (*US*)
4RV Publishing (*US*)
Grand Central Publishing (*US*)
Harlequin Dare (*Can*)
Harlequin Desire (*US*)
Harlequin Heartwarming (*Can*)
HarperCollins (*US*)
Harvest House Publishers (*US*)
Head of Zeus (*UK*)
Hesperus Press Limited (*UK*)
Jacaranda Books Art Music Ltd (*UK*)
Kensington Publishing Corp. (*US*)
Less Than Three Press (*US*)
Pace Press (*US*)
Pan Macmillan (*UK*)
Penguin Random House (*US*)
Robert Hale Publishers (*UK*)
Severn House Publishers (*UK*)
SisterShip Press Pty Ltd (*Aus*)
Sunstone Press (*US*)
WaterBrook & Multnomah (*US*)
We Are One Body Audio Theatre (*US*)
World Weaver Press (*US*)
Zumaya Publications (*US*)
Science
ABC-CLIO / Greenwood (*US*)
Abdo Publishing Co (*US*)
Algora Publishing (*US*)
Allen & Unwin (*Aus*)
American Psychiatric Association Publishing
(*US*)
American Psychiatric Association Publishing
(*US*)
Anness Publishing Ltd (*UK*)
Black Dome Press (*US*)
John Blake Publishing (*UK*)
Canongate Books (*UK*)
Canopus Publishing Ltd (*UK*)
Charlesbridge Publishing (*US*)
Chicago Review Press (*US*)
Colourpoint Educational (*UK*)
Cornell University Press (*US*)

Crabtree Publishing (*US*)
Dawn Publications (*US*)
DK Publishing (*US*)
Duckworth Publishers (*UK*)
Dunedin Academic Press Ltd (*UK*)
Edinburgh University Press (*UK*)
Encante Press, LLC (*US*)
Encounter Books (*US*)
Faculty of 1000 Ltd (*UK*)
Floris Books (*UK*)
Gingko Library (*UK*)
Haldane Mason Ltd (*UK*)
HarperCollins Publishers Ltd (*UK*)
Headline Publishing Group (*UK*)
Hendrick-Long Publishing Co. (*US*)
Hobar Publications (*US*)
Hopscotch (*UK*)
Human Kinetics (*US*)
McGraw-Hill Education (*US*)
Melbourne University Publishing Ltd (*Aus*)
Oneworld Publications (*UK*)
Pan Macmillan (*UK*)
Penguin Random House (*US*)
Periscope (*UK*)
Profile Books (*UK*)
Quarto Publishing Group USA (*US*)
Ruby Tuesday Books (*UK*)
Sage Publications (*UK*)
The Salariya Book Company (*UK*)
Science Museum Group (*UK*)
Scribner (*US*)
Simon & Schuster UK Limited (*UK*)
SisterShip Press Pty Ltd (*Aus*)
Springer-Verlag London Ltd (*UK*)
Sterling Publishing Co. Inc. (*US*)
Temple University Press (*US*)
Thames and Hudson Ltd (*UK*)
Trentham Books (*UK*)
Tumblehome Learning, Inc. (*US*)
University College Dublin (UCD) Press (*Ire*)
University of Alaska Press (*US*)
University of Pittsburgh Press (*US*)
W.W. Norton & Company Ltd (*UK*)
Walch Education (*US*)
WIT Press (*UK*)
Yale University Press (London) (*UK*)
ZigZag Education (*UK*)
Sci-Fi
Allison & Busby Ltd (*UK*)
Aurelia Leo (*US*)
Baen Books (*US*)
Black Coffey Publishing (*UK*)
Bloomsbury Spark (*UK*)
Blue Trident Books (*UK*)
Candlemark & Gleam (*US*)
Candy Jar Books (*UK*)
Colin Smythe Ltd (*UK*)
Cuil Press (*US*)
Diversion Books (*US*)
Duckworth Publishers (*UK*)
EDGE Science Fiction and Fantasy Publishing (*Can*)
Elm Books (*US*)

Entangled Teen (*US*)
4RV Publishing (*US*)
HarperCollins (*US*)
HarperCollins Publishers Ltd (*UK*)
Head of Zeus (*UK*)
Hesperus Press Limited (*UK*)
Honno Welsh Women's Press (*UK*)
IDW Publishing (*US*)
Jewish Lights Publishing (*US*)
Kensington Publishing Corp. (*US*)
Less Than Three Press (*US*)
Little, Brown Book Group (*UK*)
Lost Tower Publications (*UK*)
Luna Press Publishing (*UK*)
Mandrake of Oxford (*UK*)
Martin Sisters Publishing (*US*)
Marvel Comics (*US*)
NBM Publishing (*US*)
The Orion Publishing Group Limited (*UK*)
Pace Press (*US*)
Pan Macmillan (*UK*)
Penguin Random House (*US*)
Pure Indigo Limited (*UK*)
Quercus Books (*UK*)
SelfMadeHero (*UK*)
Severn House Publishers (*UK*)
Shipwreckt Books Publishing Company (*US*)
Snowbooks (*UK*)
Sunstone Press (*US*)
Tor/Forge (*US*)
WaterBrook & Multnomah (*US*)
We Are One Body Audio Theatre (*US*)
World Weaver Press (*US*)
Zumaya Publications (*US*)
Scripts
Allen & Unwin (*Aus*)
Alma Classics (*UK*)
Aurora Metro Press (*UK*)
Beercott Books (*UK*)
Chapman Publishing (*UK*)
Colin Smythe Ltd (*UK*)
Coteau Books (*Can*)
Cressrelles Publishing Co. Ltd (*UK*)
Dalkey Archive Press (*US*)
Faber & Faber Ltd (*UK*)
The Gallery Press (*Ire*)
Gomer Press (*UK*)
Half Mystic Press (*US*)
Italica Press (*US*)
Lillenas Drama Resources (*US*)
The Lilliput Press (*Ire*)
New Island (*Ire*)
New Playwrights' Network (NPN) (*UK*)
Nick Hern Books Ltd (*UK*)
Oberon Books (*UK*)
Samuel French Ltd (*UK*)
We Are One Body Audio Theatre (*US*)
Self-Help
Allen & Unwin (*Aus*)
Allison & Busby Ltd (*UK*)
John Blake Publishing (*UK*)
Blue Mountain Arts, Inc. (*US*)
Nicholas Brealey Publishing (*UK*)

Bull Publishing Company (*US*)
Career Press (*US*)
Cedar Fort (*US*)
Cork University Press (*Ire*)
Crown House Publishing (*UK*)
Fleming Publications (*UK*)
Floris Books (*UK*)
Free Spirit Publishing (*US*)
Geddes & Grosset (*UK*)
HarperCollins (*US*)
Hawthorn Press (*UK*)
Hay House Publishers (*UK*)
Health Professions Press (*US*)
Infinite Ideas (*UK*)
Insomniac Press (*Can*)
Kensington Publishing Corp. (*US*)
Mandrake of Oxford (*UK*)
Martin Sisters Publishing (*US*)
Native Ink Press (*US*)
New Holland Publishers (UK) Ltd (*UK*)
Oneworld Publications (*UK*)
Pan Macmillan (*UK*)
Paulist Press (*US*)
Quarto Publishing Group USA (*US*)
Robert D. Reed Publishers (*US*)
Singing Dragon (*UK*)
SisterShip Press Pty Ltd (*Aus*)
St Pauls (*US*)
Sunrise River Press (*US*)
W.W. Norton & Company Ltd (*UK*)
Watkins Publishing (*UK*)

Short Stories
a...p press (*US*)
Allison & Busby Ltd (*UK*)
Aurelia Leo (*US*)
Aurora Metro Press (*UK*)
Baobab Press (*US*)
Be About It Press (*US*)
BkMk Press (*US*)
Black Ace Books (*UK*)
Black Coffey Publishing (*UK*)
Caitlin Press Inc. (*Can*)
Cedar Fort (*US*)
Chapman Publishing (*UK*)
Comma Press (*UK*)
Coteau Books (*Can*)
Down The Shore Publishing (*US*)
Educe Press (*US*)
Elm Books (*US*)
The Emma Press Ltd (*UK*)
Fence Books (*US*)
Four Way Books (*US*)
Galley Beggar Press (*UK*)
George Braziller, Inc. (*US*)
Gertrude Press (*US*)
Half Mystic Press (*US*)
Head of Zeus (*UK*)
Honno Welsh Women's Press (*UK*)
Insomniac Press (*Can*)
Kettillonia (*UK*)
Leapfrog Press (*US*)
Les Figues Press (*US*)
Less Than Three Press (*US*)

Lost Horse Press (*US*)
Luna Press Publishing (*UK*)
Manor House Publishing (*Can*)
Martin Sisters Publishing (*US*)
New Island (*Ire*)
Parthian Books (*UK*)
Patrician Press (*UK*)
Pocol Press (*US*)
Saddle Road Press (*US*)
Salt Publishing Ltd (*UK*)
SisterShip Press Pty Ltd (*Aus*)
Stonewood Press (*UK*)
Sunstone Press (*US*)
Vegetarian Alcoholic Press (*US*)
We Are One Body Audio Theatre (*US*)
World Weaver Press (*US*)
Zumaya Publications (*US*)

Sociology
ABC-CLIO / Greenwood (*US*)
Abdo Publishing Co (*US*)
Algora Publishing (*US*)
Allen & Unwin (*Aus*)
Alma Classics (*UK*)
Arsenal Pulp Press (*Can*)
Birlinn Ltd (*UK*)
Bristol University Press (*UK*)
The Catholic University of America Press (*US*)
Clarity Press, Inc. (*US*)
Cork University Press (*Ire*)
Crabtree Publishing (*US*)
DB Publishing (*UK*)
Duckworth Publishers (*UK*)
Dunedin Academic Press Ltd (*UK*)
Edinburgh University Press (*UK*)
Encounter Books (*US*)
Fairleigh Dickinson University (FDU) Press (*Can*)
Fernwood Publishing (*Can*)
Florida Academic Press (*US*)
Floris Books (*UK*)
Free Spirit Publishing (*US*)
Garnet Publishing (*UK*)
Granta Books (*UK*)
Hay House Publishers (*UK*)
Head of Zeus (*UK*)
The Lilliput Press (*Ire*)
Luath Press Ltd (*UK*)
McGraw-Hill Education (*US*)
Melbourne University Publishing Ltd (*Aus*)
National Museum Wales (*UK*)
New Island (*Ire*)
PaperBooks (*UK*)
Pavilion Publishing (*UK*)
Pen & Sword Books Ltd (*UK*)
Periscope (*UK*)
Policy Studies Institute (PSI) (*UK*)
Rivers Oram Press (*UK*)
Saffron Books (*UK*)
Sage Publications (*UK*)
Syracuse University Press (*US*)
Temple University Press (*US*)
The Charles Press, Publishers (*US*)
Trentham Books (*UK*)

University College Dublin (UCD) Press (*Ire*)
University of Exeter Press (*UK*)
The University of Michigan Press (*US*)
University of Wales Press (*UK*)
Vehicule Press (*Can*)
Venture Publishing, Inc. (*US*)
Verso (*UK*)
W.W. Norton & Company Ltd (*UK*)
Walch Education (*US*)
Wild Goose Publications (*UK*)
Yale University Press (London) (*UK*)
ZigZag Education (*UK*)

Spiritual
Anness Publishing Ltd (*UK*)
Beyond Words Publishing (*US*)
Career Press (*US*)
Cedar Fort (*US*)
Coteau Books (*Can*)
The Crossroad Publishing Company (*US*)
Crown House Publishing (*UK*)
Cynren Press (*US*)
Findhorn Press Ltd (*UK*)
Fitzrovia Press Limited (*UK*)
Floris Books (*UK*)
Forward Movement Publications (*US*)
Geddes & Grosset (*UK*)
Gill Books (*Ire*)
Hampton Roads Publishing (*US*)
Hay House Publishers (*UK*)
Hodder & Stoughton Ltd (*UK*)
Insomniac Press (*Can*)
Jewish Lights Publishing (*US*)
Lost Tower Publications (*UK*)
Loyola Press (*US*)
Mandrake of Oxford (*UK*)
Kevin Mayhew Publishers (*UK*)
New Holland Publishers (UK) Ltd (*UK*)
Robert D. Reed Publishers (*US*)
Robert Hale Publishers (*UK*)
Shipwreckt Books Publishing Company (*US*)
Simon & Schuster UK Limited (*UK*)
Singing Dragon (*UK*)
St Pauls (*US*)
Sterling Publishing Co. Inc. (*US*)
Stone Bridge Press (*US*)
Sunstone Press (*US*)
WaterBrook & Multnomah (*US*)
Watkins Publishing (*UK*)
We Are One Body Audio Theatre (*US*)
Wild Goose Publications (*UK*)
YMAA Publication Center, Inc. (*US*)

Sport
Abdo Publishing Co (*US*)
Allen & Unwin (*Aus*)
Anness Publishing Ltd (*UK*)
Ascend Books, LLC (*US*)
Aureus Publishing Limited (*UK*)
Bancroft Press (*US*)
Birlinn Ltd (*UK*)
Black & White Publishing Ltd (*UK*)
John Blake Publishing (*UK*)
Blink Publishing (*UK*)
Bull Publishing Company (*US*)

Caitlin Press Inc. (*Can*)
Carlton Publishing Group (*UK*)
Chicago Review Press (*US*)
Coaches Choice (*US*)
Cork University Press (*Ire*)
Coteau Books (*Can*)
Da Capo Press (*US*)
DB Publishing (*UK*)
Diversion Books (*US*)
Duckworth Publishers (*UK*)
Fernwood Publishing (*Can*)
Gill Books (*Ire*)
Gomer Press (*UK*)
HarperCollins Publishers Ltd (*UK*)
Head of Zeus (*UK*)
Headline Publishing Group (*UK*)
Heritage House (*Can*)
The History Press (*UK*)
Human Kinetics (*US*)
Insomniac Press (*Can*)
JourneyForth (*US*)
Krause Publications (*US*)
The Lilliput Press (*Ire*)
Luath Press Ltd (*UK*)
Melbourne University Publishing Ltd (*Aus*)
Merlin Unwin Books (*UK*)
New Holland Publishers (UK) Ltd (*UK*)
The O'Brien Press (*Ire*)
The Orion Publishing Group Limited (*UK*)
Pen & Sword Books Ltd (*UK*)
Quarto Publishing Group UK (*UK*)
Quarto Publishing Group USA (*US*)
Robert Hale Publishers (*UK*)
Santa Monica Press (*US*)
Seren Books (*UK*)
Shipwreckt Books Publishing Company (*US*)
Simon & Schuster UK Limited (*UK*)
Snowbooks (*UK*)
SportsBooks Limited (*UK*)
Sterling Publishing Co. Inc. (*US*)
Sunstone Press (*US*)
Syracuse University Press (*US*)
Temple University Press (*US*)
Thomas Dunne Books (*US*)
University of Alaska Press (*US*)
The University of Michigan Press (*US*)
W.W. Norton & Company Ltd (*UK*)
Willow Creek Press, Inc. (*US*)
YMAA Publication Center, Inc. (*US*)
ZigZag Education (*UK*)

Suspense
Black Coffey Publishing (*UK*)
Blue Trident Books (*UK*)
bookouture (*UK*)
4RV Publishing (*US*)
HarperCollins (*US*)
Harvest House Publishers (*US*)
Head of Zeus (*UK*)
Insomniac Press (*Can*)
Joffe Books Ltd (*UK*)
Kensington Publishing Corp. (*US*)
Lost Tower Publications (*UK*)
Penguin Random House (*US*)

Scribner (*US*)
Shipwreckt Books Publishing Company (*US*)
Thomas Dunne Books (*US*)
Tor/Forge (*US*)
TouchWood Editions (*Can*)
WaterBrook & Multnomah (*US*)
We Are One Body Audio Theatre (*US*)

Technology

ABC-CLIO / Greenwood (*US*)
Abdo Publishing Co (*US*)
Bernard Babani (publishing) Ltd (*UK*)
Canopus Publishing Ltd (*UK*)
Colourpoint Educational (*UK*)
Focal Press (*US*)
Gingko Library (*UK*)
Hopscotch (*UK*)
Information Today, Inc. (*US*)
Kogan Page Ltd (*UK*)
MC Press (*US*)
McGraw-Hill Education (*US*)
No Starch Press, Inc. (*US*)
P8tech (*UK*)
Quarto Publishing Group USA (*US*)
Ruby Tuesday Books (*UK*)
Sage Publications (*UK*)
Science Museum Group (*UK*)
SisterShip Press Pty Ltd (*Aus*)
Springer-Verlag London Ltd (*UK*)
Temple University Press (*US*)
Trentham Books (*UK*)
W.W. Norton & Company Ltd (*UK*)
WIT Press (*UK*)
Yale University Press (London) (*UK*)
ZigZag Education (*UK*)

Theatre

Aurora Metro Press (*UK*)
Beercott Books (*UK*)
Colin Smythe Ltd (*UK*)
Duckworth Publishers (*UK*)
Faber & Faber Ltd (*UK*)
Fairleigh Dickinson University (FDU) Press (*Can*)
Focal Press (*US*)
The Gallery Press (*Ire*)
Gomer Press (*UK*)
McGraw-Hill Education (*US*)
New Playwrights' Network (NPN) (*UK*)
Nick Hern Books Ltd (*UK*)
Oberon Books (*UK*)
Southern Illinois University Press (*US*)
Sunstone Press (*US*)
The University of Michigan Press (*US*)
We Are One Body Audio Theatre (*US*)

Thrillers

Allison & Busby Ltd (*UK*)
Asabi Publishing (*US*)
Bancroft Press (*US*)
Black & White Publishing Ltd (*UK*)
Black Coffey Publishing (*UK*)
Bloomsbury Spark (*UK*)
Blue Trident Books (*UK*)
bookouture (*UK*)
Diversion Books (*US*)

Duckworth Publishers (*UK*)
Entangled Teen (*US*)
Fahrenheit Press (*US*)
4RV Publishing (*US*)
Grand Central Publishing (*US*)
HarperCollins Publishers Ltd (*UK*)
Head of Zeus (*UK*)
Hesperus Press Limited (*UK*)
Honno Welsh Women's Press (*UK*)
Joffe Books Ltd (*UK*)
Kensington Publishing Corp. (*US*)
Little, Brown Book Group (*UK*)
Lost Tower Publications (*UK*)
Luath Press Ltd (*UK*)
Michael Joseph (*UK*)
Myriad Editions (*UK*)
Orenda Books (*UK*)
Pace Press (*US*)
Pan Macmillan (*UK*)
Salt Publishing Ltd (*UK*)
Salvo Press (*US*)
Sandstone Press Ltd (*UK*)
Severn House Publishers (*UK*)
SisterShip Press Pty Ltd (*Aus*)
Snowbooks (*UK*)
Thomas Dunne Books (*US*)
Three Hares Publishing (*UK*)
Twenty First Century Publishers Ltd (*UK*)
We Are One Body Audio Theatre (*US*)
Zumaya Publications (*US*)

Translations

Algora Publishing (*US*)
Alma Classics (*UK*)
Arc Publications (*UK*)
Aurora Metro Press (*UK*)
Canongate Books (*UK*)
Carcanet Press Ltd (*UK*)
Dedalus Ltd (*UK*)
Duckworth Publishers (*UK*)
Fernwood Publishing (*Can*)
Garnet Publishing (*UK*)
George Braziller, Inc. (*US*)
Greystones Press (*UK*)
Hesperus Press Limited (*UK*)
Italica Press (*US*)
Leaping Dog Press (*US*)
Mantra Lingua Ltd (*UK*)
Oneworld Publications (*UK*)
Peter Owen Publishers (*UK*)
Periscope (*UK*)
Portobello Books Ltd (*UK*)
Red Moon Press (*US*)
Seren Books (*UK*)
Seven Stories Press (*US*)
Shearsman Books (*UK*)
Stone Bridge Press (*US*)
Syracuse University Press (*US*)
Truman State University Press (*US*)
Ugly Duckling Presse (*US*)
University of Alaska Press (*US*)
Vehicule Press (*Can*)
Yale University Press (London) (*UK*)

Travel
Abdo Publishing Co (*US*)
Ian Allan Publishing Ltd (*UK*)
Allen & Unwin (*Aus*)
Allison & Busby Ltd (*UK*)
Anness Publishing Ltd (*UK*)
Appalachian Mountain Club Books (*US*)
Bess Press (*US*)
Birlinn Ltd (*UK*)
John Blake Publishing (*UK*)
Blink Publishing (*UK*)
Blue Guides Limited (*UK*)
Nicholas Brealey Publishing (*UK*)
Caitlin Press Inc. (*Can*)
Canongate Books (*UK*)
Chicago Review Press (*US*)
Chronicle Books LLC (*US*)
Cicerone Press (*UK*)
Cork University Press (*Ire*)
Coteau Books (*Can*)
Countryside Books (*UK*)
Cynren Press (*US*)
DB Publishing (*UK*)
Discovery Walking Guides Ltd (*UK*)
DK Publishing (*US*)
Dref Wen (*UK*)
Duckworth Publishers (*UK*)
Encante Press, LLC (*US*)
Enthusiast Books (*US*)
Footprint Handbooks (*UK*)
Formac Publishing Company Limited (*Can*)
Garnet Publishing (*UK*)
George Braziller, Inc. (*US*)
Gibson Square Books Ltd (*UK*)
Gomer Press (*UK*)
Granta Books (*UK*)
HarperCollins (*US*)
Hellgate Press (*US*)
Hesperus Press Limited (*UK*)
Hodder & Stoughton Ltd (*UK*)
House of Lochar (*UK*)
Imbrifex Books (*US*)
Infinite Ideas (*UK*)
Insomniac Press (*Can*)
Italica Press (*US*)
The Lilliput Press (*Ire*)
Lonely Planet (*UK*)
Luath Press Ltd (*UK*)
Metro Publications Ltd (*UK*)
Mountaineers Books (*US*)
New Holland Publishers (UK) Ltd (*UK*)
New Island (*Ire*)
The O'Brien Press (*Ire*)
Oleander Press (*UK*)
The Orion Publishing Group Limited (*UK*)
PaperBooks (*UK*)
Penguin Random House (*US*)
Phaidon Press Limited (*UK*)
Poolbeg (*Ire*)
Portobello Books Ltd (*UK*)
Quarto Publishing Group USA (*US*)
Santa Monica Press (*US*)
Sawday's (*UK*)

Seaworthy Publications (*US*)
September Publishing (*UK*)
Seren Books (*UK*)
Sheldrake Press (*UK*)
Simon & Schuster UK Limited (*UK*)
Sterling Publishing Co. Inc. (*US*)
Stone Bridge Press (*US*)
Sunflower Books (*UK*)
Sunstone Press (*US*)
I.B. Tauris & Co. Ltd (*UK*)
Thames & Hudson Inc. (*US*)
Thames and Hudson Ltd (*UK*)
TouchWood Editions (*Can*)
Truman State University Press (*US*)
The University of Michigan Press (*US*)
W.W. Norton & Company Ltd (*UK*)
Wide-Eyed Editions (*UK*)
ZigZag Education (*UK*)
TV
BearManor Media (*US*)
John Blake Publishing (*UK*)
Candy Jar Books (*UK*)
Chronicle Books LLC (*US*)
Headline Publishing Group (*UK*)
Syracuse University Press (*US*)
Westerns
Black Coffey Publishing (*UK*)
HarperCollins (*US*)
Harvest House Publishers (*US*)
Hendrick-Long Publishing Co. (*US*)
JourneyForth (*US*)
Pace Press (*US*)
Robert Hale Publishers (*UK*)
Sunstone Press (*US*)
We Are One Body Audio Theatre (*US*)
Zumaya Publications (*US*)
Women's Interests
ABC-CLIO / Greenwood (*US*)
Algora Publishing (*US*)
Allison & Busby Ltd (*UK*)
Aurora Metro Press (*UK*)
Beyond Words Publishing (*US*)
Black & White Publishing Ltd (*UK*)
bookouture (*UK*)
Bull Publishing Company (*US*)
Caitlin Press Inc. (*Can*)
Chicago Review Press (*US*)
Cork University Press (*Ire*)
Cornell University Press (*US*)
Coteau Books (*Can*)
The Crossroad Publishing Company (*US*)
Cynren Press (*US*)
Fairleigh Dickinson University (FDU) Press (*Can*)
Fernwood Publishing (*Can*)
Gibson Square Books Ltd (*UK*)
Harlequin Dare (*Can*)
Harvest House Publishers (*US*)
Hay House Publishers (*UK*)
Heritage House (*Can*)
Honno Welsh Women's Press (*UK*)
Jewish Lights Publishing (*US*)
Kensington Publishing Corp. (*US*)

Lawrence Hill Books (*US*)
Lost Tower Publications (*UK*)
Michael Joseph (*UK*)
New Island (*Ire*)
Poolbeg (*Ire*)
Rivers Oram Press (*UK*)
Shipwreckt Books Publishing Company (*US*)
SisterShip Press Pty Ltd (*Aus*)
Southern Illinois University Press (*US*)

Sunstone Press (*US*)
Syracuse University Press (*US*)
Temple University Press (*US*)
Thomas Dunne Books (*US*)
Tor/Forge (*US*)
Trentham Books (*UK*)
The University of Michigan Press (*US*)
W.W. Norton & Company Ltd (*UK*)

Get Free Access to the firstwriter.com Website

To claim your free access to the firstwriter.com website simply go to the website at https://www.firstwriter.com/subscribe and begin the subscription process as normal. On the second page, enter the required details (such as your name and address, etc.) then for "Voucher / coupon number" enter the following promotional code:

- **XM91-Q7ZP**

This will reduce the cost of creating a subscription by up to $15 / £10 / €15, making it free to create a monthly, quarterly, or combination subscription. Alternatively, you can use the discount to take out an annual or life subscription at a reduced rate.

Continue the process until your account is created. Please note that you will need to provide your payment details, even if there is no up-front payment. This is in case you choose to leave your subscription running after the free initial period, but there is no obligation for you to do so.

When you use this code to take out a free subscription you are under no obligation to make any payments whatsoever and you are free to cancel your account before you make any payments if you wish.

If you need any assistance, please email support@firstwriter.com.

If you have found this book useful, please consider leaving a review on the website where you bought it.

What you get

Once you have set up access to the site you will be able to benefit from all the following features:

Databases

All our databases are updated almost every day, and include powerful search facilities to help you find exactly what you need. Searches that used to take you hours or even days in print books or on search engines can now be done in seconds, and produce more accurate and up-to-date information. Our agents database also includes independent reports from at least three separate sources, showing you which are the top agencies and helping you avoid the scams that are all over the internet. You can try out any of our databases before you subscribe:

Search dozens of **current competitions**

Search **over 2,400 magazines**

Search **over 2,500 literary agents and agencies**

Search **over 2,000 book publishers** that **don't** charge fees

PLUS advanced features to help you with your search:

- Save searches and save time – set multiple search parameters specific to your work, save them, and then access the search results with a single click whenever you log in. You can even save multiple different searches if you have different types of work you are looking to place.
- Add personal notes to listings, visible only to you and fully searchable – helping you to organise your actions.
- Set reminders on listings to notify you when to submit your work, when to follow up, when to expect a reply, or any other custom action.
- Track which listings you've viewed and when, to help you organise your search – any listings which have changed since you last viewed them will be highlighted for your attention!

Daily email updates

As a subscriber you will be able to take advantage of our email alert service, meaning you can specify your particular interests and we'll send you automatic email updates when we change or add a listing that matches them. So if you're interested in agents dealing in romantic fiction in the United States you can have us send you emails with the latest updates about them – keeping you up to date without even having to log in.

User feedback

Our agent, publisher, and magazine databases all include a user feedback feature that allows our subscribers to leave feedback on each listing – giving you not only the chance to have your say about the markets you contact, but giving a unique authors' perspective on the listings.

Save on copyright protection fees

If you're sending your work away to publishers, competitions, or literary agents, it's vital that you first protect your copyright. As a subscriber to firstwriter.com you can do this through our site and save 10% on the copyright registration fees normally payable for protecting your work internationally through the Intellectual Property Rights Office.

Monthly newsletter

When you subscribe to firstwriter.com you also receive our monthly email newsletter – described by one publishing company as "the best in the business" – including articles, news, and interviews for writers. And the best part is that you can continue to receive the newsletter even after you stop your paid subscription – at no cost!

Terms and conditions

The promotional code contained in this publication may be used by the owner of the book only to create one subscription to firstwriter.com at a reduced cost, or for free. It may not be used by or disseminated to third parties. Should the code be misused then the owner of the book will be liable for any costs incurred, including but not limited to payment in full at the standard rate for the subscription in question. The code may be used at any time until the end of the calendar year named in the title of the publication, after which time it will become invalid. The code may be redeemed against the creation of a new account only – it cannot be redeemed against the ongoing costs of keeping a subscription open. In order to create a subscription a method of payment must be provided, but there is no obligation to make any payment. Subscriptions may be cancelled at any time, and if an account is cancelled before any payment becomes due then no payment will be made. Once a subscription has been created, the normal schedule of payments will begin on a monthly, quarterly, or annual basis, unless a life Subscription is selected, or the subscription is cancelled prior to the first payment becoming due. Subscriptions may be cancelled at any time, but if they are left open beyond the date at which the first payment becomes due and is processed then payments will not be refundable.